D1259354

TEXT AND CONTEXT

Series Editor: Frank Coulson

CLASSROOM COMMENTARIES

Teaching the *Poetria nova* across Medieval and Renaissance Europe

MARJORIE CURRY WOODS

THE OHIO STATE UNIVERSITY PRESS
Columbus

Copyright © 2010 by The Ohio State University.
All rights reserved

Library of Congress Cataloging-in-Publication Data
Woods, Marjorie Curry, 1947–
  Classroom commentaries : teaching the Poetria nova across medieval and Renaissance Europe /
Marjorie Curry Woods.
    p. cm. — (Text and context)
  Includes bibliographical references and index.
  ISBN-13: 978-0-8142-1109-0 (cloth : alk. paper)
  ISBN-10: 0-8142-1109-7 (cloth : alk. paper)
  ISBN-13: 978-0-8142-9206-8 (cd-rom)
  1. Geoffrey, of Vinsauf, fl. 1200. Poetria nova. 2. Rhetoric, Medieval. 3. Didactic literature, Latin
(Medieval and modern) 4. Latin poetry, Medieval and modern—History and criticism. I. Title.
II. Series: Text and context (Columbus, Ohio)
  PA8442.V5P638 2009
  808.1—dc22
                              2009012875

This book is available in the following editions:
Cloth (ISBN 978-0-8142-1109-0)
CD-ROM (ISBN 978-0-8142-9206-8)

Cover design by Janna Thompson Chordas
Text design by Jennifer Shoffey Forsythe
Type set in Adobe Garamond
Printed by Thomson-Shore, Inc.

 ∞ The paper used in this publication meets the minimum requirements of the American National
Standard for Information Sciences—Permanence of Paper for Printed Library Materials. ANSI
Z39.48-1992.

9 8 7 6 5 4 3 2 1

TO THE MEMORY

of my parents

Marjorie Williams Woods

Mark William Woods

and of my Doktormütter

Sister Frances Nims

Virginia Brown

CONTENTS

chapter 3

chapter 4

chapter 5

afterword

ABBREVIATIONS[1]

add.	added
BAV	Biblioteca Apostolica Vaticana
BL	British Library
BnF	Bibliothèque nationale de France
cent.	century
corr.	corrected
esp.	especially
ff.	and following
fol(s).	folio(s)
in marg.	in the margin
in ras.	erased
l(l).	line(s)
lit.	literally
MS(S)	manuscript(s)
mm	millimeters
n.d.	no date
n.p.	no publisher
no.	number
om.	omitted
p(p).	page(s)
vol(s).	volume(s)

---

1. Full bibliographical information for works not cited here is in the Bibliography; shortened versions of citations are used throughout the notes.

Auct. Aris.   *Les Auctoritates Aristotelis. Un florilège médiéval. Étude historique et édition critique.* Ed. Jacqueline Hamesse. Louvain 1974.

Black, *Humanism*   Robert Black, *Humanism and Education in Medieval and Renaissance Italy: Tradition and Innovation in Latin Schools from the Twelfth to the Fifteenth Century.* Cambridge, UK, 2001.

Camargo, "Models"   Martin Camargo. "Beyond the *Libri catoniani:* Models of Latin Prose Style at Oxford University ca. 1400." *Mediaeval Studies* 56 (1994): 165–87.

Camargo, "*Tria sunt*"   Martin Camargo. "*Tria sunt:* The Long and the Short of Geoffrey of Vinsauf's *Documentum de modo et arte dictandi et versificandi.*" *Speculum* 74 (1999): 935–55.

CIMAGL   *Cahiers de l'Institut du Moyen-Âge Grec et Latin.*

CTC   *Catalogus Translationum et Commentariorum: Medieval and Renaissance Latin Translations and Commentaries.* Ed. Edward Cranz, Virginia Brown, and Paul Oskar Kristeller. Washington, DC, 1960–.

CWE   *Collected Works of Erasmus.* Toronto, 1974–.

DBI   *Dizionario biografico degli italiani.* 69 vols. Rome, 1960–2007.

DBL   *Dansk Biografisk Leksikon.* 27 vols. Copenhagen, 1933–34.

EC   *An Early Commentary on the* Poetria nova *of Geoffrey of Vinsauf.* Ed. [and trans.] Marjorie Curry Woods. New York, 1985.

Far.   Edmond Faral. *Les arts poétiques du xiiᵉ et du xiiiᵉ siècle. Recherches et documents sur la technique littéraire du moyen âge.* Paris, 1924; rpt. Paris, 1962.

IRHT   Institut de Recherche et d'Histoire des Textes, Paris.

Iter ital.   P. O. Kristeller. *Iter italicum: A Finding List of Uncatalogued or Incompletely Catalogued Humanistic Manuscripts of the Renaissance in Italian and Other Libraries.* 8 vols. London-Leiden, 1963–2003.

Jaffe, *Declaracio* Samuel P. Jaffe. *Nicolaus Dybinus' Declaracio Oracionis de beata Dorothea: Studies and Documents in the History of Late Medieval Rhetoric.* Wiesbaden, 1974.

Kelly, *Arts*   Douglas Kelly. *The Arts of Poetry and Prose.* Turnhout, 1991.

MBDS   *Mittelalterliche Bibliothekskataloge Deutschlands und der Schweiz.* Vol. I. Munich, 1990.

Munari, *Catalogue*   Franco Munari. *Catalogue of the Mss of Ovid's* Metamorphoses. London, 1965.

Munari, *Catalogo*   Franco Munari. *Mathei Vindocinensis opera.* Vol. 1, *Catalogo dei manoscritti.* Rome, 1977.

Nims   Margaret F. Nims, trans. *Poetria nova of Geoffrey of Vinsauf.* Toronto, 1967.

PN   *Poetria nova*

Polak, *Eastern Europe*   Emil J. Polak. *Medieval and Renaissance Letter Treatises and Form Letters; A Census of Manuscripts Found in Eastern Europe and the Former U.S.S.R.* Leiden, 1993.

Polak, *Western Europe*   Emil J. Polak. *Medieval and Renaissance Letter Treatises and Form Letters; A Census of Manuscripts Found in Part of Western Europe, Japan, and the United States of America; The Works on Letter-Writing from the Eleventh through the Seventeenth Century Found in Belgium, Denmark, Finland, Greece, Ireland, Liechtenstein, Luxembourg, Netherlands, Norway, Portugal, Spain, Sweden, Switzerland, United Kingdom of Great Britain and Northern Ireland, Japan, and the United States of America.* Leiden, 1994.

Szklenar, *Magister Nicholaus*   Hans Szklenar. *Magister Nicolaus de Dybin. Vorstudien zu einer Edition seiner Schriften. Ein Beitrag zur Geschichte der literarischen Rhetorik im späteren Mittelalter.* Munich, 1981.

Walther   Hans Walther. *Initia carminum ac versuum medii aevi posterioris latinorum. Alphabetisches Verzeichnis der Versanfänge mittellateinischer Dichtungen.* Göttingen, 1959.

Witt, *Footsteps*   Ronald G. Witt. *"In the Footsteps of the Ancients": The Origins of Humanism from Lovato to Bruni.* Leiden, 2000.

Verfasserlexikon   *Die deutsche Literatur des Mittelalters: Verfasserlexikon.* Berlin, 1977–.

PLATES DESCRIBED

1. Short *accessus* or introduction to the *Poetria nova,* describing its double structure as both a work on rhetoric and a rhetorical treatise. Brescia, Biblioteca Civica Queriniana, A.IV.10, fol. 93r.[1]

2. First page of a glossed French copy of the *Poetria nova.* Angers, Bibliothèque municipale, 523, fol. 1r.

3. The short *accessus* or introduction to the *Poetria nova* by the Dominican schoolteacher Reiner von Cappel in the upper right-hand corner. Wolfenbüttel, Herzog August Bibliothek, Cod. Guelf. 286 Gud. lat., fol. 1r.

4. Glosses in several hands added to a thirteenth-century copy of the *Poetria nova* owned by the Dominicans at Leicester. Cambridge, Trinity College, R.14.22, fol. 13v.

5. Bartholomew of Pisa's introduction to Geoffrey of Vinsauf's example of digression. Rome, Biblioteca Casanatense, 311, fol. 23v.

6. First page of the commentary by Pace of Ferrara, copied separately (without the text) in 1395. Seville, Biblioteca Capitular y Colombina, Col. 5-4-30, fol. 2r (5r).

7. Guizzardo of Bologna on Geoffrey's examples of description. A later reader has identified in the margin Jove's lovers (Alcmena, Callisto, Io, Europa) whose stories are summarized in the commentary. Vatican City, Biblioteca Apostolica Vaticana, Ottob. lat. 3291, fol. 6r.

8. A comparison of the *Poetria nova* with the *Rhetorica ad Herennium*—to the advantage of the medieval text. Naples, Biblioteca Nazionale "Vittorio Emanuele III," Vind. lat. 53, fol. 1r (upper right-hand corner).

9. *Dicta* (dictated) version of the commentary by Dybinus of Prague

---

1. The form of the manuscript signature on each plate is that preferred by each library, although a standardized format has been followed in the rest of the volume.

recorded at the University of Prague on August 10, 1375. Prague, Národní Knihovna České Republiky, XII.B.12, fol. 1r.

10. *Scripta* or written version of the same commentary copied in 1389. Prague, Národní Knihovna České Republiky, VIII.H.22, fol. 27r (bis).

11a–b. Numbers added over words in the *Poetria nova* to indicate prose order as well as copious commentary. Vienna, Österreichische Nationalbibliothek, 4959, fols. 102v–103r.

12. First page of the *Poetria nova* and glosses copied at Leipzig in 1462 in a manuscript owned by Hartmann Schedel. Munich, Bayerische Staatsbibliothek, Clm 237, fol. 15r.

13a–b. *Accessus* and glosses on the first lines of the *Poetria nova* copied by Johannes Tegernpeck, future abbot of St. Emmerau, when he was a student at Leipzig in 1465–66. Munich, Bayerische Staatsbibliothek, Clm 14529, fols. 3v–4r.

14. Anonymous *accessus* added at the end of a fifteenth-century manuscript of the *Poetria nova* used at the University of Oxford. London, British Library, Royal 12.E.XI, fol. 52r.

15a–b. Geoffrey of Vinsauf (*Ganfredus*) as Quintilian's good orator. St. Gall, Stiftsbibliothek, 856, pp. 296–297.

Incipit poetria nouella magistri Gualfredi.

Papa stupor mundi si dixero papa nocenti.
Acephalum nomen tribuam t. si caput addam.
Hostis est metri. nomen t uult sociari.
Nec nomen metro. si uult tua max uita
Claudit mesura. nichil e q̃ metiar illa.
Transit mesuras hoium. si diuidas nomen.
Diuidas sic nomen. in prefer. et adde nocenti.
Efficiat q̃ comes metri. sic et tua uirtus
Pluribus equatur diuisa. si integra nulli.
Egregius sanguis te confert Bartolomeo.
Ante cor Andree. preciosa iuuenta Iohani.
Firma fides Petro. perfecta sciencia Paulo.
Ista simul nulli. superest de dotibus una
Quam nulli fas e pertingere. gratia lingue.
Augustine tace. Leo papa quiesce. Iohes
desine. Gregori sibsiste. quid elaquar omnes!
Esto q̃ in uerbis aut hic aut ille sit ore
Aureus. et totus resplendeat. os tñ eius
Impar est. oris q̃ tu preiudicat aurum.
Tras hoiem es totus. ubi corpus ista uinet
Tam grandis seny! ul' cordis tanti senectus
Insita tam iuuenem! q̃ mira rebellio rex.
Ecce senex iuuenis. fiat sub tempore prime
Cum dominus petro psferret amore iohem.
Papatu petrū noluit preferre Iohani.
In te papa modo noua res huc accidit anis.
Papa senex petrus. et papa iuuenta iohes.

Papa stupes? Opus ist q̃ diuini si pte rethice. rsm simone rethoica. huc diuidui i pter. V. bm q̃ s.
pter rethoie. si iunctio. diuisio. eloquio. memoia. pnuitatis. De inectio ptinuat illic sig'l't hidio. de
diue illic Non shl'igret. De clenitē i. si hius au long. De memoia i. Cellulaq̃. De pnuita t. Jn uiuutes
sic at m diuidutur i pter. hi. bm q̃ sxij. pter simonis rethoia. si exordium. narratio. diuisio. confmatio. co
futatio. q̃ clusio. De exordio agis illic Papa stupes. De narratie sig'l't hidiare De diuisione. Otro bñl
out is. De cofmatiue. si bñ ta notes. De cofutatiē. Jn pmus q̃ De conclusione. Jam marc Cociduri.

PLATE 1
Brescia, Biblioteca Civica Queriniana, A.IV.10, fol. 93r

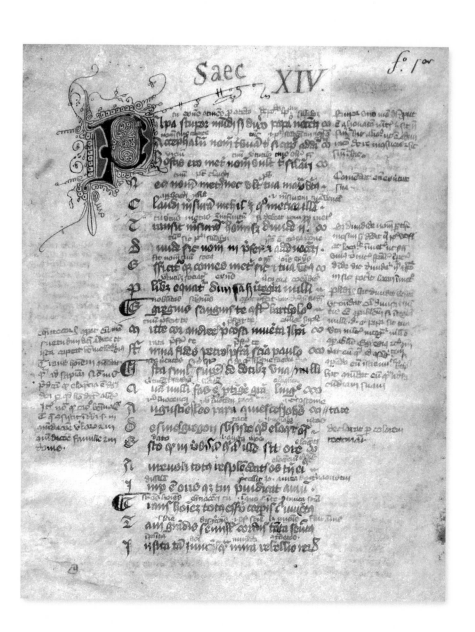

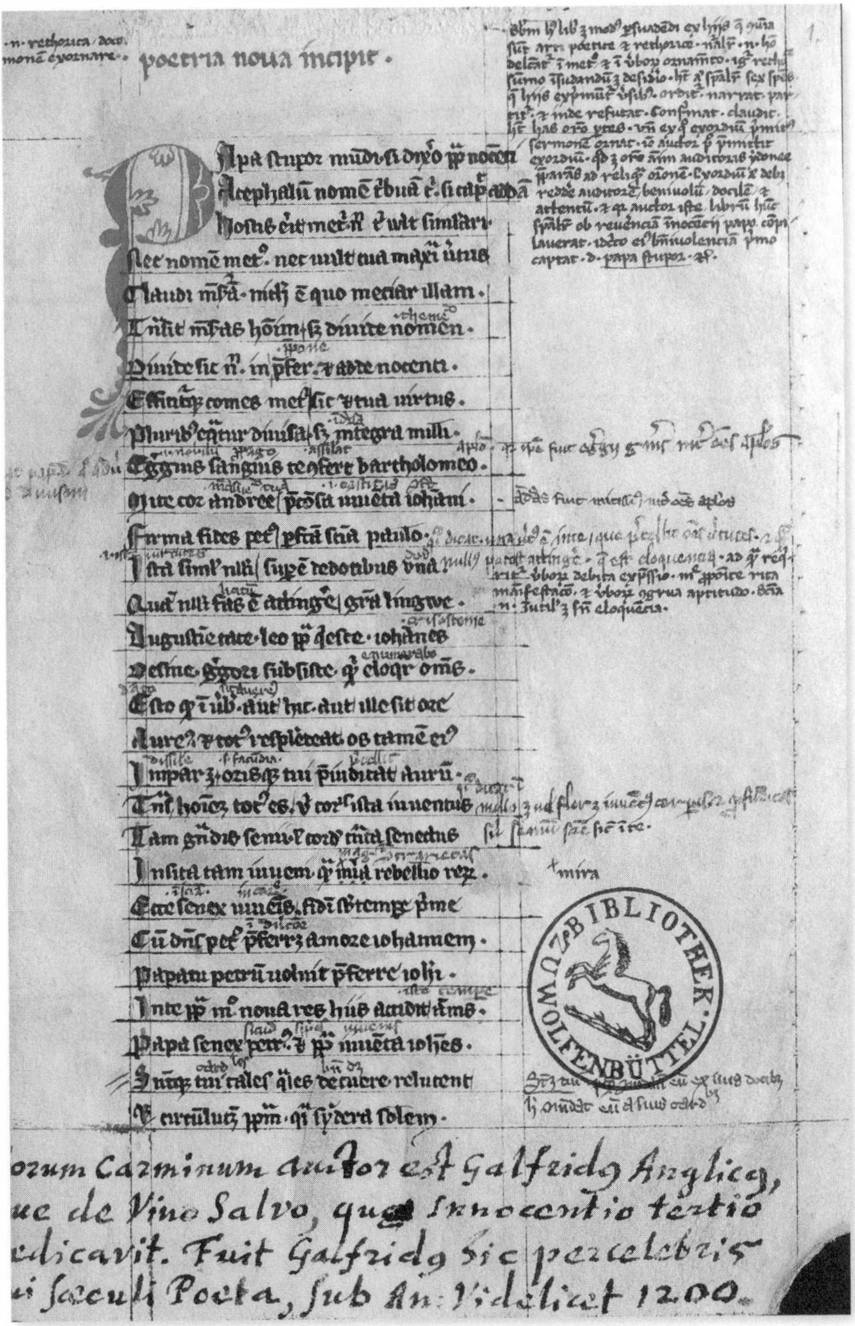

PLATE 3

Herzog August Bibliothek Wolfenbüttel: Cod. Guelf. 286 Gud. lat., fol. 1r

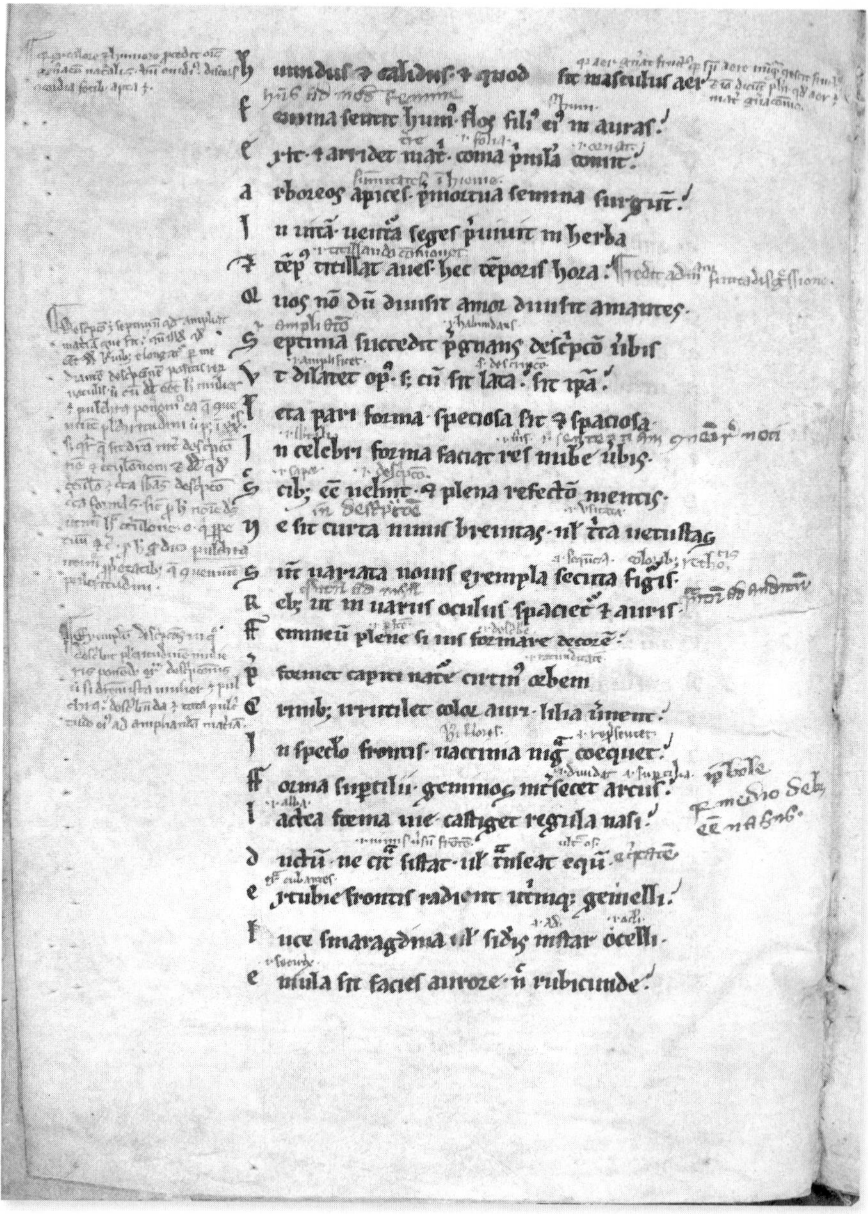

PLATE 4
Trinity College Cambridge, R.14.22, fol. 13v

Vnicus astringit. hic exsicat de utroque predictorum modorum. et
primo de secundo tanquam de leuiori. s. Cum que prius omissa sunt postea reassumuntur. sic. Vnicus astringit. z cetera. idest duo
se diligebat. etc. Vna. Secundo. dimisso medio uadit ad
tertium. sic. Corpora disiungit noua causa. idest ab inuicem
discesserunt. Deinde redit ad medium quod dimiserat. dicens
Sz an recessus. oscula prefigit. z cetera. Sz iste modus non
uidetur apliare magis. Vnde potest dici quod auctor non posuit
ipsos qui aplicaret. sz ne forte credetur esse unus solus modus
digressionis. s. qui apliat. posuit z istum qui prius. Vel
dic quod hic modus intantum apliat. inquantum ea que potuerunt
quiescere prius resumuntur z explicatur.
Exemplum de utroque modo digressionis

    Ricus astringit duo pectora nodus amoris

    Corpora disiungit noua causa. sz an recessus

Oscula prefigit os ori. cingit utrumque

Agitur z stringit apex? fons oculorum

In faciem lacrimas deriuat. z ultra uerba

Singultus medios intersecat. estque doloris

Calcar amor. uires que dolor testatur amoris.

Secundo ibi Vere redit hyems. postea exsicat de primo modo digressionis
Vnde addendo ad predicta disgreditur ad describendum tempus. dicens
quod erat tempus quando hyemps redit uel. i. recedente hyeme
z ueniente uere. quando aer diffibulat. i. aperit. z depellit nebulas. celum lasciuit. i. iocundatur in terra. et
quod aer humidus z calidus sit masculus. i. uirtute grandi
hyeat. femina humus sentit. ita quod flos filius exit. et
arridet terre. quia tunc pratum ridet. et coma primula frondium comit siue ornat apices. i. summitates arborum. et
tunc titillat aues. i. ad amorem promouet. hec tempus hora
diuisit amantes. etc. quo redit ad oppositum.

PLATE 5
Rome, Biblioteca Casanatense ms. 311, fol. 23v

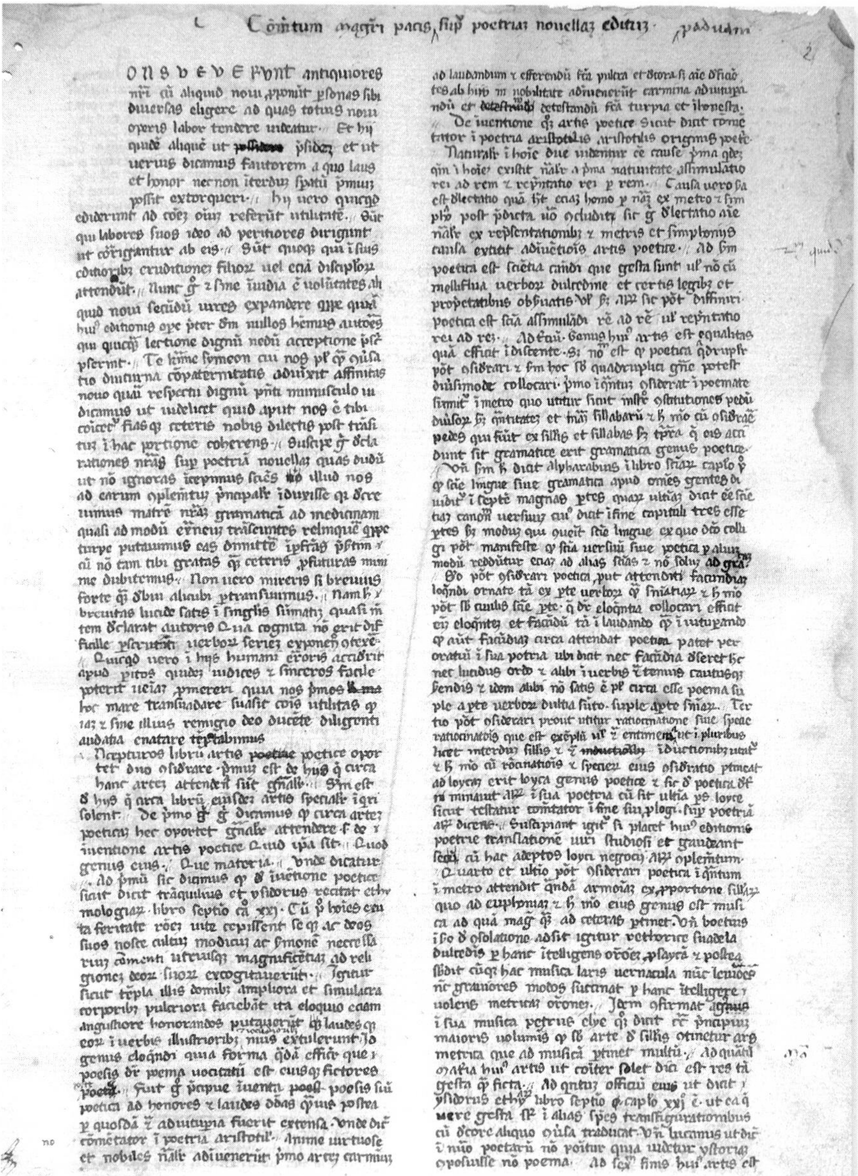

PLATE 6

Cabildo Catedral de Seville, Biblioteca Colombina MS 5–4–30, fol. 2r

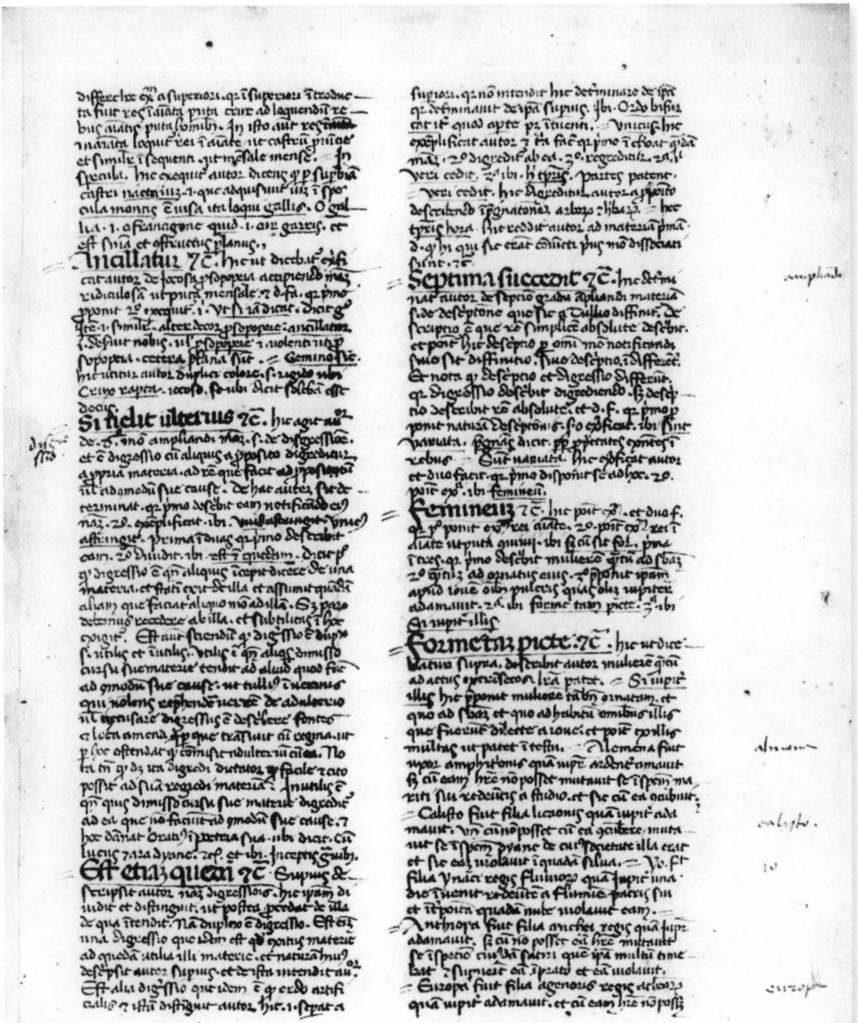

amphia[us]

alcumen

calypho

io

europa

PLATE 7
Vatican City, Biblioteca Apostolica Vaticana, Ottob. lat. 3291, fol. 6r

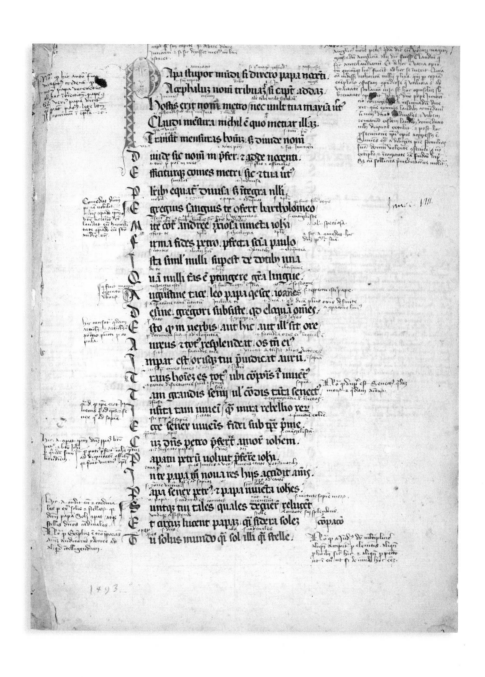

PLATE 8

Naples, Biblioteca Nazionale "Vittorio Emanuele III," Ms. ex Vind. Lat. 53, fol. 14, su
concessione del Ministero per i Beni e le Attività Culturali

PLATE 9
Prague, Národní Knihovna České Republiky, XII.B.12, fol. 1r

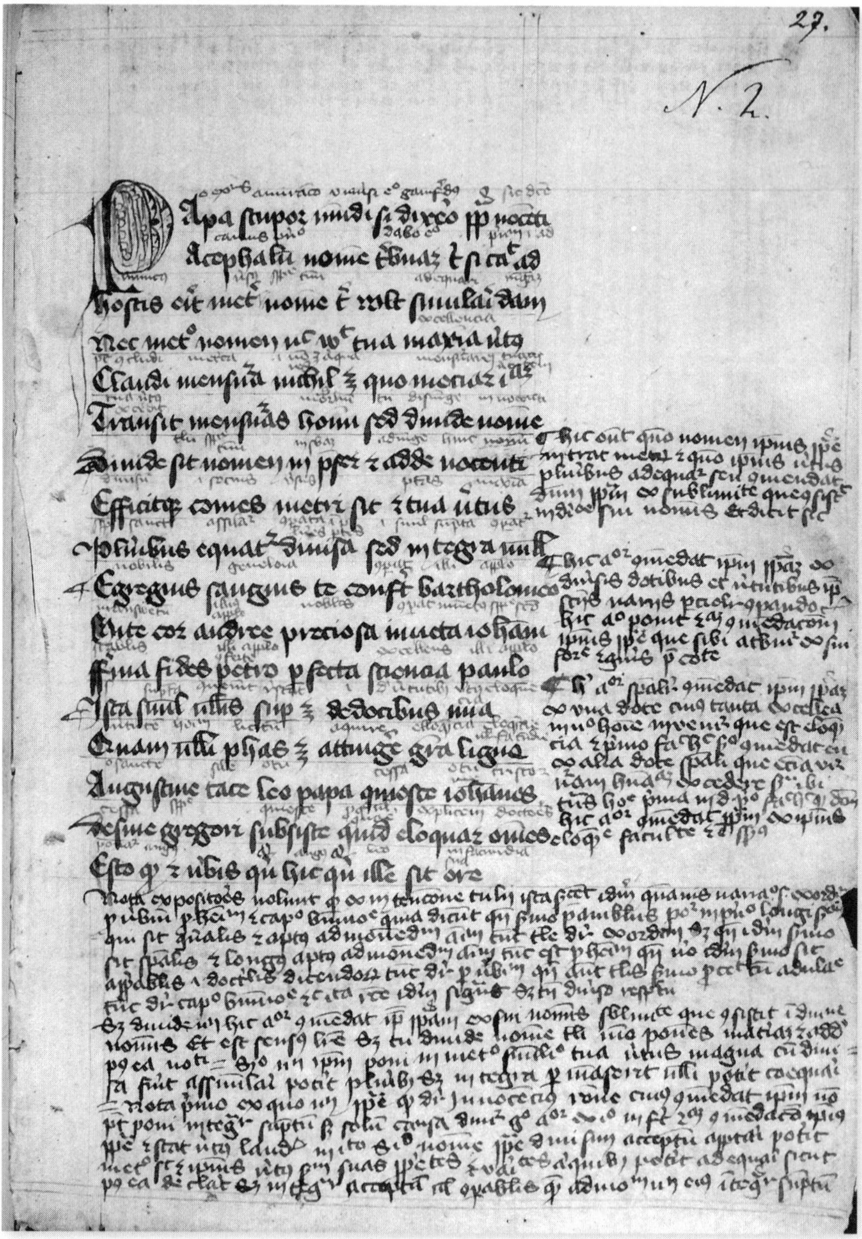

PLATE 10

Prague, Národní Knihovna České Republiky, VIII.H.22, fol. 27r (bis)

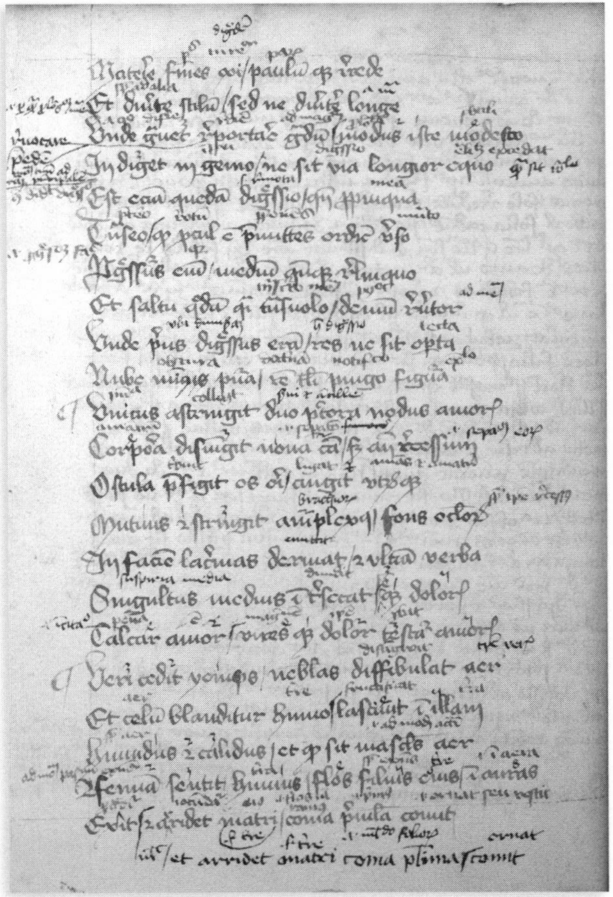

PLATE 11a

ÖNB/Vienna, Picture Archive, Cod. 4959, fol. 102v

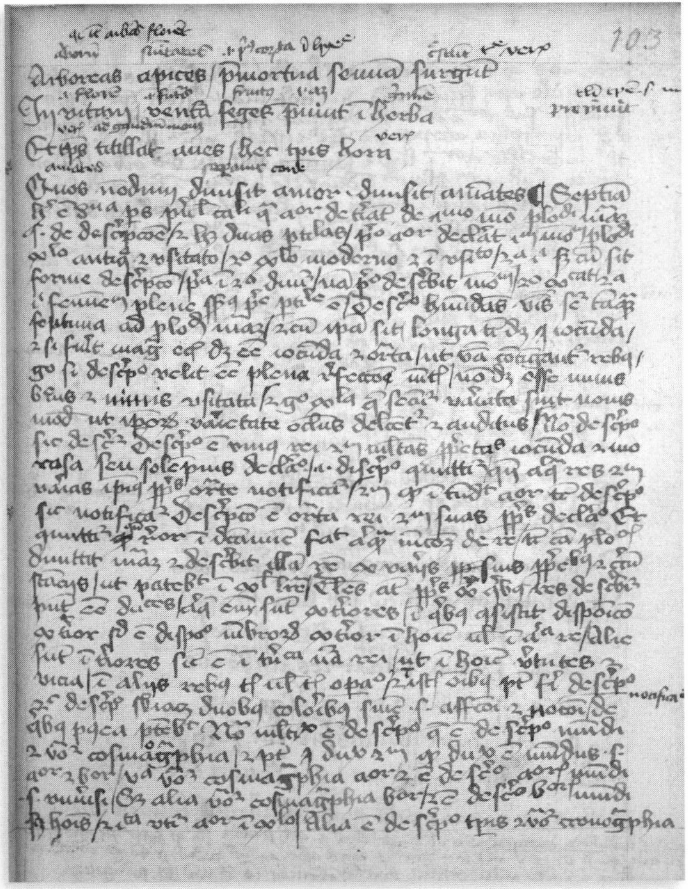

PLATE 11b

ÖNB/Vienna, Picture Archive, Cod. 4959, fol. 103r

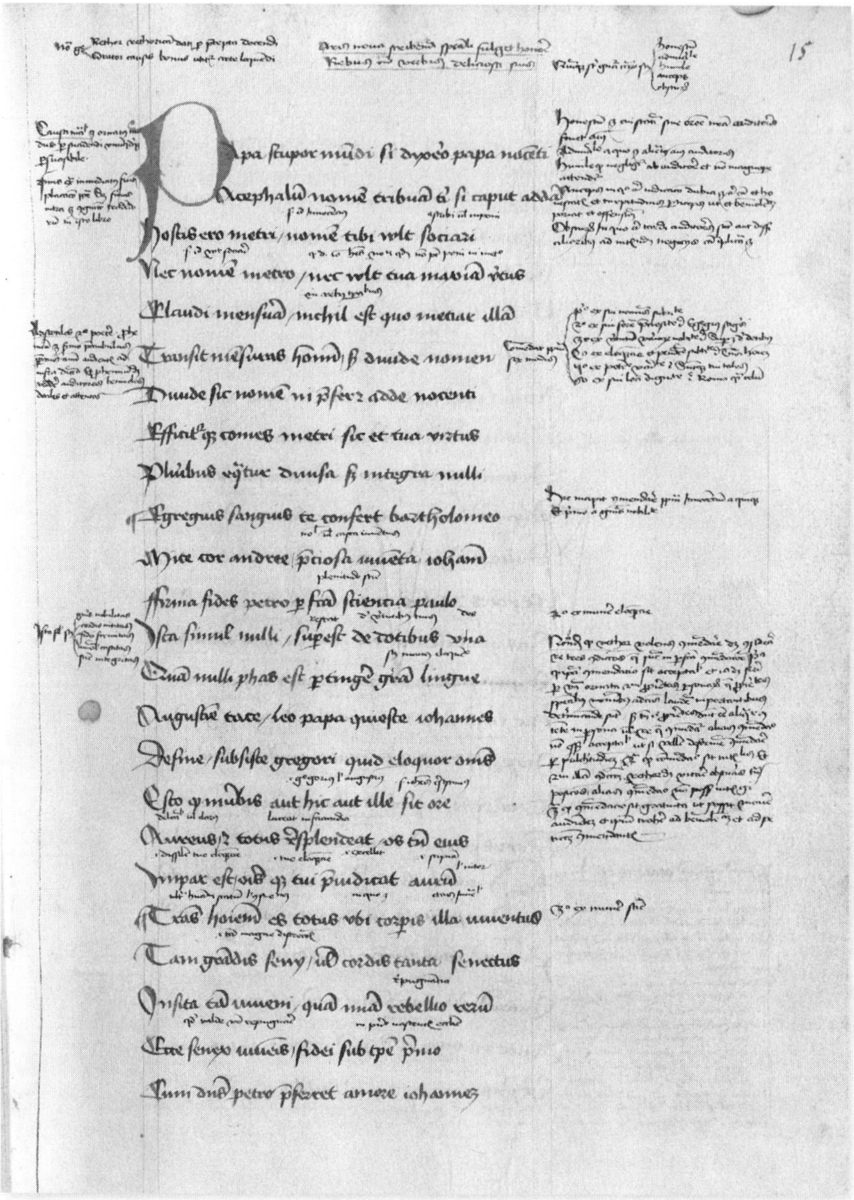

PLATE 12

Munich, Bayerische Staatsbibliothek, Clm 237, fol. 15r

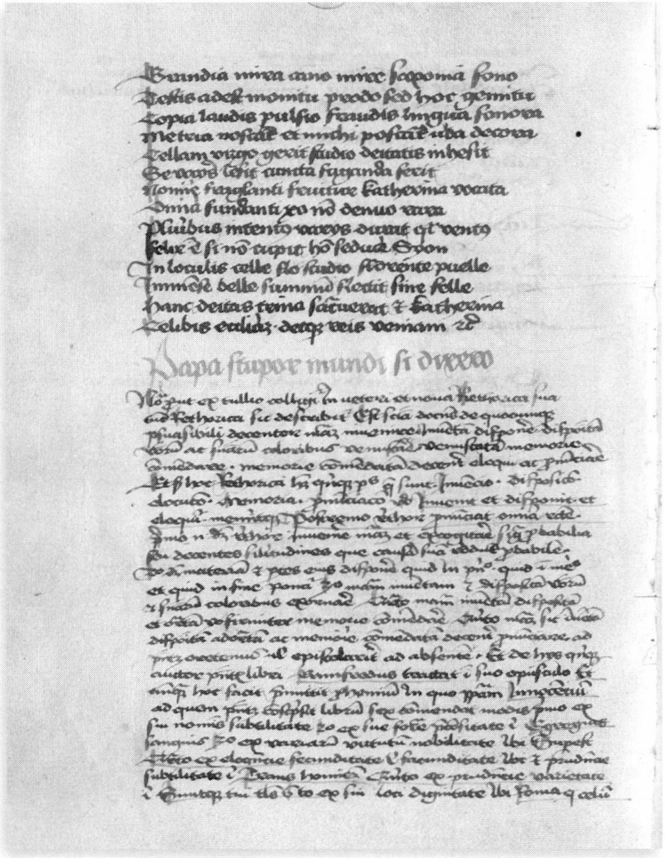

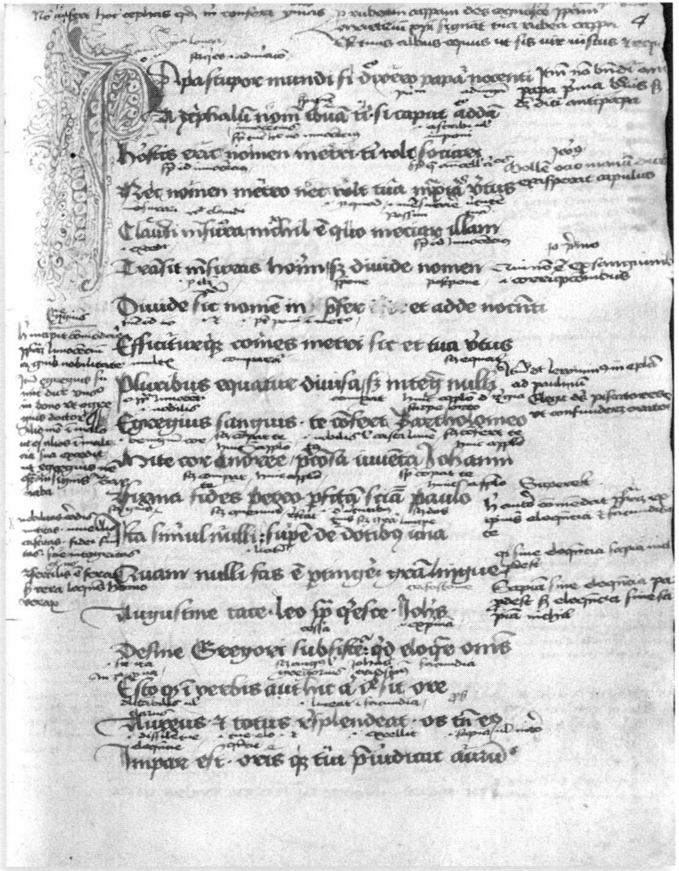

PLATE 13b

Munich, Bayerische Staatsbibliothek, Clm 14529, fol. 4r

PLATE 13a

Munich, Bayerische Staatsbibliothek, Clm 14529, fol. 3v

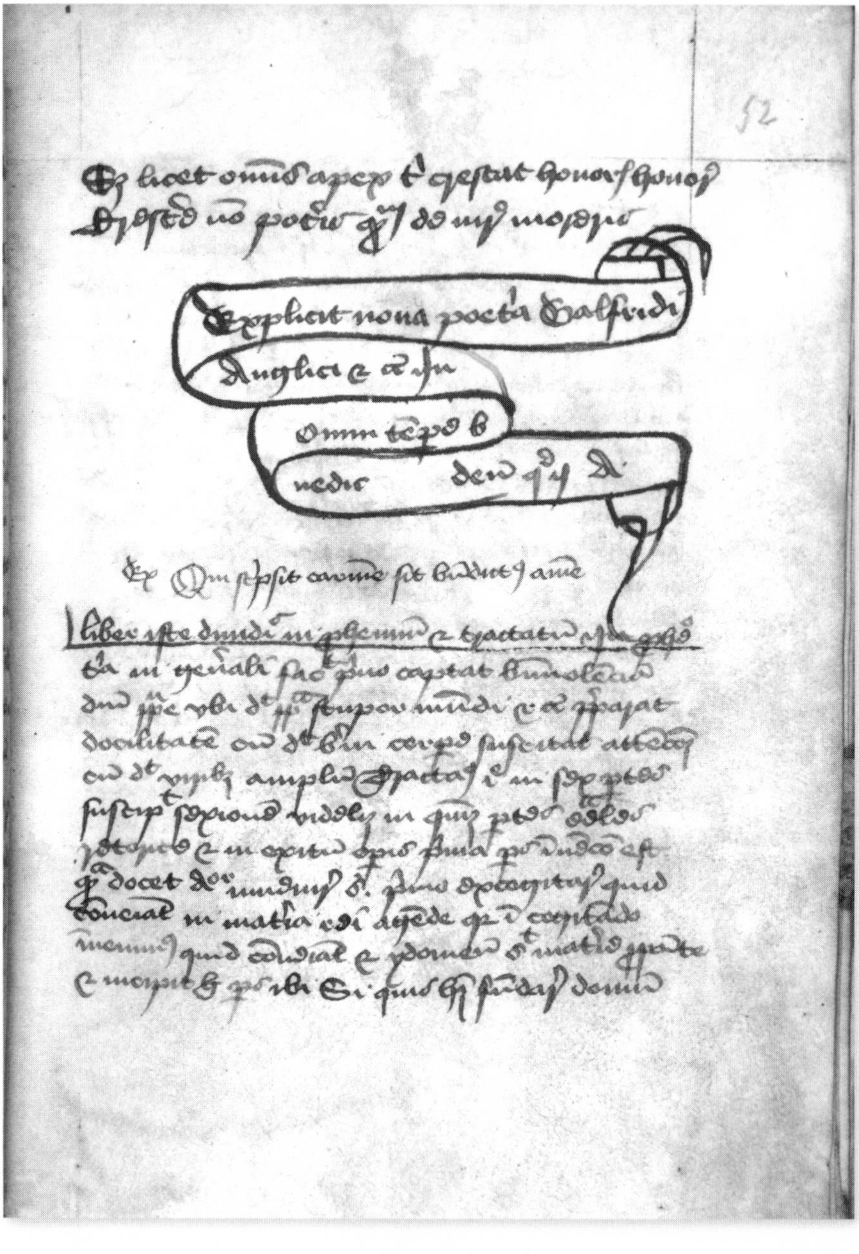

PLATE 14
London, The British Library, MS Royal 12.E.XI, fol. 52r

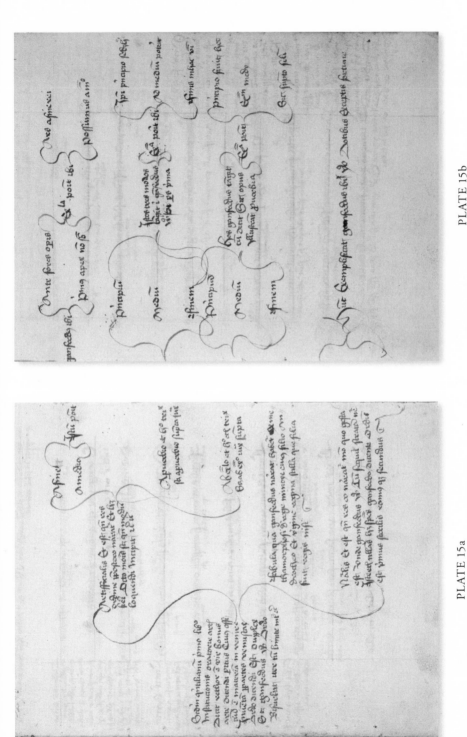

PLATE 15a
Stiftsbibliothek St. Gallen, Cod. Sang. 856, page 296

PLATE 15b
Stiftsbibliothek St. Gallen, Cod. Sang. 856, page 297

PREFACE
AND ACKNOWLEDGMENTS

Many years ago at the Bayerische Staatsbibliothek in Munich, when I was first working on manuscripts of the *Poetria nova*, I glanced up and saw open on another desk a beautiful, three-foot-high illuminated parchment codex, with tiers of gorgeously colored narrative. The person working on it I recognized from graduate school. With a sigh I looked down at the school and university manuscripts in front of me: no pictures, written on smelly parchment or rough-cut paper, and full of illegible writing that I was supposed to be able to read. [Yet the worn condition and even the poor materials of glossed copies of the *Poetria nova* suggest how widely and avidly the text was used.] The manuscripts reproduced in the plates in this volume reflect the much lower status of those for whom the commentaries on the *Poetria nova* were written: teachers and students.

The *Poetria nova* is a two-thousand line poem written at the beginning of the thirteenth century that teaches Latin verse composition according to rhetorical principles. It vividly demonstrates the craft that it describes, and generations of students across Europe learned how to write by studying Geoffrey's virtuoso examples and savoring his aphorisms and sly wit. That he was a gifted poet was recognized immediately, and the assessment of his ability and achievement has been part of the academic tradition of interpreting the *Poetria nova* from the beginning. Yet, although incredibly popular during the late Middle Ages and the early Renaissance, today the *Poetria nova* can fall through scholarly cracks, or at least be pushed to the edges of our disciplines; modern scholars often come across it when they are pursuing something else. Here I have tried to create a sense of how it appeared to those for whom it was a work of special satisfaction and appreciation. The attention to student capacities and interests on the part of the scribes and commentators indicates a sophisticated pedagogy focused on providing students with an acquired linguistic culture. This culture of *latinitas* was trans-European, and what it lacked in gender participation it made up for in international inclusiveness.

As you can see from the Manuscript List near the end of the volume, more than two hundred and twenty manuscripts or fragments of the *Poetria nova* have survived (and others will probably turn up). This number is five times that of any other medieval *ars poetriae,* or art of poetry and prose. Less than a quarter of these have no glossing whatsoever; more than a quarter contain only sporadic glosses, or at least rubrics and notes that help guide the reader to various parts of the text; and about half that number contain sufficient interpretive material—sometimes in several hands—to suggest what teachers thought was important and how they imparted such information to their students. Short, discrete glosses that stayed close to one section of text at a time were favored by those teaching younger or less prepared students; students at a more intermediate level were taught ways of connecting parts of the text together and making comparisons with other works; and sophisticated, continuous-text commentaries incorporated new interpretive approaches for the most advanced students.

A book about centuries-old teachers' notes on a school text that relatively few modern scholars or teachers have actually read would not normally reach an audience beyond a few specialists, so I have tried to make the material described here as appealing as possible while keeping access to it relatively straightforward. The chapters are broken into small units with many cross-references to make it possible to devise one's own path through them. And, because the *Poetria nova* is itself a witty book, full of allusions and echoes intended to instruct and delight, in the subtitles to the chapters I have tried to create a modern analogue of the premodern experience of studying it. The casual reader browsing the table of contents might be attracted enough by "The Female Body in the Classroom" or "The Importance of Being Aristotelian" to turn to one of these sections first. But for those already interested in medieval rhetoric, poetics, or pedagogy, the chapters are arranged to expose readers to the teaching of the *Poetria nova* in stages that roughly follow a medieval student's pedagogical development.

The first chapter—"Why Was the *Poetria nova* So Popular?"—places Geoffrey's work in a general context, much as a medieval *accessus* or academic introduction introduces the genre to which a text belongs and answers traditional questions about it. This chapter approaches the *Poetria nova* from a variety of perspectives: descriptions of the author and the work, including comparisons with classical treatises; the rhetorical force of the dedication to Pope Innocent III; the student audience; the contents and self-referential structure of the text; and the pedagogical uses to which it could be put in teaching both rhetoric and poetics.

The second, third, and fourth chapters concentrate on large groups of commentaries; each represents a significant mass of the material remains of the text, and each provides a different kind of insight into the medieval classroom. Chapter 2 provides a horizontal view of lower school commentaries across Europe; chapter 3 looks at several levels of commentaries written in one geographical area; and chapter 4 looks at university-level texts in one particular region. These chapters suggest that the institutional level for which commentaries were intended and the competence in Latin that students had attained were as important in determining the approaches to the text as where or when the commentaries were composed. Most of the evidence for establishing the level of student for which a specific commentary is intended is relational (how it compares or contrasts with other commentaries, especially those for which we have a known pedagogical setting) or contextual (who owned it—if this is known—and what other works are copied with it). Such data are open to interpretation, and I have tried to be as clear as possible about the criteria on which a conclusion about the level of teaching is based.

The second chapter, "The *Poetria nova* as School Text," looks at the most basic commentaries on the text from across Europe, those that concentrate on very small portions of the text. This chapter moves sequentially through major sections of the *Poetria nova* as the teachers did; it introduces the passages whose interpretations these teachers considered important and that will be examined in the other chapters as well for comparison. It provides at least partial answers to the following questions: on what did medieval teachers of younger or less prepared students focus? What did those teachers think that their students needed help with, or would catch their attention? What might their comments imply about classroom exercises based on the rhetorical techniques that Geoffrey describes and exemplifies? School commentaries engage students in the creative process at a minute level. For those of us who teach premodern literature, this chapter demonstrates the kind of analytical techniques learned and compositional training undergone by almost all late medieval and early Renaissance writers, in Latin or the vernacular. As James J. Murphy has remarked, "The most frequently overlooked influences on medieval literature are the fundamental processes by which authors learned how to write (and to speak)."[1]

The next two chapters of *Classroom Commentaries* follow the *Poetria nova*

---

1. Murphy, "The Discourse of the Future," 368.

through time, across space, and up the educational ladder. Chapter 3, "The *Poetria nova* as Early Humanist Text," examines the commentaries on the *Poetria nova* written by the early humanists and later teachers in Italy who shared their special interest in the work. That a majority of the surviving manuscripts of these commentaries date from the fifteenth century indicates the continuing relevance and longevity of their approaches to the text. These men used the *Poetria nova* as part of their campaign to raise the textual and stylistic analysis of Latin texts to an advanced discipline. One of the contentions of this chapter is that specific characteristics of the *Poetria nova* were well fitted to the approaches to texts that these teachers were developing. The context provided by the other works with which their commentaries on the *Poetria nova* were copied places the poem squarely within a literary as well as a rhetorical tradition. Most of the commentaries discussed in this chapter were aimed at intermediate or advanced students. Their teachers continued the focus on minutiae of the text while expanding the application of rhetorical and aesthetic principles to larger structural units, interpretive issues, and other works in the curriculum.

The fourth chapter, "The *Poetria nova* as University Text in Central Europe," draws on statutory as well as manuscript evidence to show that the work occupied an important transitional position in the faculties of arts in this region. While ensuring that students gained sufficient training in prose rhetoric, especially the art of letter writing, the commentaries on the *Poetria nova* examined in this chapter also introduced students to the elements of basic logical analysis drawn from the elementary works of Aristotle. This chapter includes a discussion of the English manuscripts of the *Poetria nova* that can be associated with the universities at Oxford and Cambridge. Because students in northern Europe entered universities at an earlier age and sometimes were less advanced in their study of Latin, the teachers whose work is recorded in these manuscripts often worked through the *Poetria nova* word by word while also introducing students to theoretical analytical discourse at the same time.

The structures of these three chapters intentionally mirror the pedagogy that they describe. In each I have quoted from one commentary in more detail than the rest in a such a way as to convey the experience of the textual education of the student. In chapter 2, for example, short extracts from the basic commentary by Reiner von Cappel, which concentrate on the interpretation of specific words and phrases, are interspersed throughout. Chapter 3 compares intermediate-level commentaries by known teachers like Bartholomew of Pisa and Guizzardo of Bologna with the sophisticated commentary by Pace of Ferrara, which was almost always copied as a separate text. Pace's approach to the *Poetria nova* combines a focus on poetics with a scholastic division into analytic subsets and was very popular. And chapter 4 provides an extensive comparison of the *accessus* and first glosses on the *Poetria nova* in two different versions of the influential commentary by Dybinus of Prague, one of which was taken down on the spot from dictation.

Chapter 5, "Seventeenth-Century Commentaries on the *Poetria nova*," examines the work of two contemporary later scholars, one of whom assessed the *Poetria nova* for the current pope and was somewhat critical of it, while the other gathered an almost 400-page compendium of excerpts from the best Greek and Latin writers to illustrate it. Although both were teachers, neither looked at the *Poetria nova* as a pedagogical tool; it had become an historical artifact of medieval literary culture instead. The Afterword suggests some of the reasons why the *Poetria nova* disappeared from the classroom. It examines the evaluations of Geoffrey and the *Poetria nova* by two late-fifteenth-century commentators, one Italian and one central European, written after the rediscovery of important classical rhetorical treatises. The penultimate section of the Afterword considers Erasmus's early reference to Geoffrey, the relationship of his *De copia* to the *Poetria nova,* and what our knowledge of the commentaries on the *Poetria nova* may reveal about how he was taught as a boy. At the end I suggest how we might look at the *Poetria nova* not just as scholars, but as teachers ourselves.

Unless there is evidence to the contrary, I have assumed that a commentary reflects classroom practice. Techniques and phrases that as late as the twelfth century could suggest that a commentary was written for other purposes have, by the time that most of the commentaries on the *Poetria nova* were composed, been assimilated into approaches clearly intended for schools or universities.[2] Because I have already edited and translated one complete commentary on the *Poetria nova* (with variants of a second version),[3] selections from as wide a variety of commentaries as possible are presented here. I have endeavored to pick representative as well as intriguing examples, and I have sought evidence that both helps us describe medieval and early Renaissance[4] teaching methods in general and suggests patterns that may be potentially applicable to other large bodies of commentary material as well.

---

2. Lodi Nauta cautions against "taking glosses as direct and unambiguous reflections of the actual teaching in the class," in his edition of William of Conches's commentary on Boethius's *Consolation of Philosophy,* xxix. For a careful examination of general principles that can help us distinguish between pedagogical and non-pedagogical contexts of glossing practices, see the work of Gernot Wieland, particularly "The Glossed Manuscript."

3. *An Early Commentary on the* Poetria nova *of Geoffrey of Vinsauf* (New York, 1985); hereafter *EC.* The version of the commentary for older students is edited and translated in its entirety; differences in the version for younger students are reproduced (untranslated) in the extensive two-part textual apparatus at the back.

4. I have deliberately not used the term "early modern" because of the concentration of early-fifteenth-century texts and the almost complete disappearance of the *Poetria nova* for nearly two centuries afterwards.

TERMINOLOGY AND LAYOUT

Although some medieval commentators on other texts, most famously William of Conches, made careful distinctions among terms that they used to refer to commentaries or parts thereof, I have not found consistent terminology in the manuscripts that I have studied. When a commentator uses a specific term (e.g., *glossa, declaracio,* etc.), I have tried to render it in English as closely as possible, although I have allowed myself some latitude when otherwise I would repeat the same word over and over. The phrase "interlinear gloss" refers to a word or short phrase written above a line of text (as in plates 2, 3, 4, 8, 10, 11a, 12, 13b). "Gloss" and "comment" are used interchangeably to refer to individual notes on a section of text; often these are introduced in the manuscripts with paragraph marks (plates 1, 4, 5). I use the term "commentary" loosely to refer to any connected or coherent sequence of glosses and/or comments; some of these are rather spare (e.g., plate 3), while others are very dense (plates 6 and 11b); most are somewhere in between (plates 2, 8, and 12). In a few important cases a commentary is copied by itself without the text of the *Poetria nova* (plates 6, 7, and 9).

An *accessus* (plural also *accessus*) is a standard academic introduction, often organized as a conventional series of questions and answers. It can be short (plates 1, 3, 8, and 14) or long (plates 6 and 9). A *lemma* (plural *lemmata*) is a word or phrase from the beginning of a section of the text being commented on; it is often underlined or sometimes written in a different script in order to distinguish it from commentary (plates 1, 2, 5, and 7). Commentators also used *lemmata* rather than line numbers in cross references; the first few words would have been enough to generate the rest of the passage, or at least the rest of the sentence, in the students' heads (as with most modern students' ability to continue, at least for a phrase or two, "To be or not to be"). Because of the mnemonic advantages of this technique and the effect that it has had on my knowledge of the *Poetria nova* after spending so many years reading commentaries, I have adopted a similar method with the cross-references in this volume and identify them by section title.

The term "incipit" refers to the first words of a text (or commentary), "explicit" to the last words. The latin word *incipit* ("here begins") is often part of the official title of a work in a given manuscript: *"Titulus talis est 'Incipit liber magistri Galfidi de Uino Salvo'. . ."* ("The title is as follows: 'Here begins the book of *magister* Geoffrey of Vinsauf . . .'" [Cambridge, Trinity College, R.14.22, fol. 2r]). A colophon is a statement added at the end by the scribes; sometimes it includes the word *explicit* ("here ends"): *"Explicit liber Poetrie. Amen."* ("Here ends the book of the *Poetria*. Amen" [London, British Library, Harley 2586, fol. 45v]).

Quotations are translated into English in the body of the text. The Latin of unpublished commentaries (and works printed before 1800) is provided in the footnotes.[5] Manuscript orthography is retained, while capitalization, punctuation, and emphasis such as bolding are editorial unless otherwise noted.[6] Alterations to the manuscript readings follow traditional usage in editing English for the translations (square brackets [ ] for all alterations and additions) and those in Latin for the transcriptions (pointed brackets < > enclose additions or alterations to manuscript readings, while square brackets [ ] indicate otiose material to be deleted and also rejected manuscript readings). Curved brackets { } identify the sources of quotations. Three asterisks *** indicate an illegible reading. Emendations have been kept to a minimum, and translations aim for accuracy and clarity rather than elegance. When using Latin terms I have (reluctantly) altered them to classical spelling for greater ease of recognition. The titles of medieval Latin texts have not been classicized. In referring to commentators' names I have translated them into English or kept the Latin, except when they are so well known that such usage would be confusing. Titles of works familiar to an English-speaking audience have been translated (e.g., *The Consolation of Philosophy*, but *De disciplina scolarium*).

Lemmata identifying a gloss are printed in block capitals; sometimes these have been expanded in the translation if the shorter form employed by the commentator would not make sense in English or could be misunderstood. Although premodern teachers identified lines of text by *lemmata* alone, the seventeenth-century commentator Zacharias Lund cites verse numbers. All other line numbers are editorial and refer to Edmond Faral's edition and Margaret F. Nims's translation; the latter is also the source for quotations from the text of the *Poetria nova*, sometimes altered without comment to clarify a gloss or problem.

THE TASK of adequately expressing my gratitude to those who helped with this book is almost as daunting as writing it was. But such a debt is also a pleasure and a reflection of the supportive, inclusive nature of the disciplines of the history of rhetoric and related fields. I could not have been more fortunate in my choice of research.

Working with Margaret (Sister Frances) Nims before her untimely death and with her wonderful translation of the *Poetria nova* throughout this project was a delight. Manuscript training first with Leonard Boyle and then more extensively with Virginia Brown provided me with research tools of the highest caliber and sage, practical advice. Virginia continued to be an inspiration, and she passed awway while I was writing these acknowledgments. I feel especially

---

5. The Latin text of the edited *Early Commentary* normally has not been included.

6. The capitalization and punctuation of works published before 1800 and manuscripts copied after 1600 are retained.

fortunate that I was able to spend time with her in Rome during the year that this study was brought to final completion. John Conley's generosity with his microfilms both at the beginning of my work on the commentaries and near the end provided a different kind of foundation.

In preparing the book manuscript itself—the final step in a long process of working with the commentaries on the *Poetria nova* that began in graduate school—I was fortunate to have a spectrum of readers willing to offer suggestions and corrections as well as encouragement: Linda Ferreira-Buckley suffered through an early, unreadable draft. Samuel Baker, Daniel Birkholz, and I formed a writing group in which all of us finished our manuscripts. Peter Mack gave me a deadline and the courage to pull out of other commitments to meet it. Rita Copeland, Greti Dinkova-Bruun, Mitchell Harris, Peter Jelavich, Manfred Kraus, Alastair Minnis, James Simpson, Vessela Valiavitcharska, Gernot R. Wieland, and an anonymous reader helped to refine and correct the book manuscript, and Laurie Frick gave me an artist's perspective. I owe most, however, to Martin Camargo, who, besides reading the whole manuscript more than once, has unstintingly shared with me his unparalleled knowledge of rhetoric in late medieval England and of dictaminal materials throughout Europe; and to Frank Coulson, who chose this book for his new series and watched over its revisions and production with an attentive and benevolent eye. Any inaccuracies and errors that remain must be laid at my door.

For answering questions and making suggestions pertaining to specific sections I would like to thank Harald Anderson, Christopher Baswell, Robert Black, James Carley, Mary Carruthers, Peter Clarke, John Dillion, Christoph Egger, Paul Gehl, Lawrence Green, Elizabeth Harris, Louis Holtz, Samuel Jaffe, Minna Skafte Jensen, Craig Kallendorf, Ernest Kaulbach, Lodi Nauta, Marco Petoletti, G. W. Pigman III, Emil Polak, Bert Roest, Hans Szklenar, Loris Sturlese, and Ronald Witt. Even when I have not followed their advice, I have benefited from it.

Among the many friends and colleagues who have provided special support I am especially grateful to Tomás Albaladejo, Rebecca Beal, Vicki Behm, Brenda Bolton, Sandy Camargo, Penelope Reed Doob, Susan Einbinder, Betty Sue Flowers, Carmela Franklin, Alison Frazier, Florence Eliza Glaze, Joan Holladay, Douglas Kelly, Monika Linder, Elizabeth Moose, Charlotte Morse, James J. Murphy, Patricia Osmond, Carolina Ponce, Elizabeth Scala, Lindsey Schell, Susan Schultz, Eva Struhal, Esme Thompson, John Ward, Jeffrey Walker, James Wimsatt, Patrick Zutshi—and the Austin Soup Peddler.

The English Department at University of Texas at Austin has been a supportive home base for someone whose research ranges far outside the boundaries of English and England. I have been particularly fortunate in the Chairs of the department, Joseph Kruppa, James Garrison, and Elizabeth Cullingford, and my medievalist colleagues. Students at all levels have been willing to try out medieval school exercises themselves and to discuss that experience and this project with me, and my research assistants Mark Mitchell, Donna Hobbs, Brad Irish, Jennifer Lehman, Jason Leubner, Mary MacCarthy, Ninamarie Ochoa, Sarah Stanford, and Joey Taylor organized my manuscript materials and kept up my spirits and enthusiasm. The librarians and staff at the University of Rochester and The University of Texas at Austin made possible the extensive use of secondary sources that put the manuscripts in context.

I am grateful, too, for institutional support at every stage of the project. The University of Rochester purchased microfilms from the Hill Monastic Manuscript Library and other collections, and the American Council of Learned Societies, the American Philosophical Society, and the National Endowment for the Humanities provided funds for travel. The University of Texas at Austin generously provided three Faculty Research Assignments and a Dean's Fellowship, as well as several Special Research Grants for research materials. Especially fruitful were two senior fellowships from the National Endowment for the Humanities, residencies at the National Humanities Center and the Centro Studi Ligure in Bogliasco, and a Virginia Brown Fellowship at the Center for Epigraphical and Palaeographical Studies at The Ohio State University. The Paul W. Mellon Rome Prize in Renaissance and Early Modern Studies at the American Academy in Rome during 2007–2008 for my next project allowed me to work out last-minute details on this one as well.

But it is the manuscripts of the *Poetria nova* that generated this book. The staff at the many libraries that provided microfilms or answered questions, and especially those that I was fortunate enough to visit over the years, generously shared with me their collective knowledge and insights in addition to their archives, and while I cannot thank them individually here, I hope that the short descriptions that I have been able to provide in the Manuscript List will help to convey my appreciation. Special mention should be made of those libraries that granted permission to reproduce pages from their codices as illustrations of the range of glosses on the *Poetria nova*.[7] These include, in the order in which their manuscripts are reproduced, the Biblioteca Civica Queriniana in Brescia, Bibliothèque municipale d'Angers, Herzog August Bibliothek Wolfenbüttel, Trinity College Cambridge, Biblioteca Cansanatense, Biblioteca Capitular y Colombina, Biblioteca Apostolica Vaticana, Biblioteca Nazionale "Vittorio Emanuele III," Národní Knihovna České Republiky, Österreichische Nationalbibliothek, Bayerische Staatsbibliothek, British Library, and Stiftsbibliothek St. Gallen. Dr. Paolo Vian, Director of the Department of Manuscripts at the Vatican Library; Nuria Casquete de Prado Sagrera, Managing Director of the Institución Colombina in Seville; Gianmaria Porini of the Biblioteca Querini-

---

7. The form of the manuscript signature on each plate is that preferred by each libary, although a standardized format has been followed in the rest of the volume.

ana; and Tomáš Klimek of the National Library of the Czech Republic were especially helpful. The richness of surviving collections of premodern material, in many of which there are manuscripts that have not been studied since they were first deposited centuries ago, is beyond description and belief. The allure of lost or forgotten manuscripts pales for me in comparison with the unused resources that we already know about. I hope that this book will encourage more scholars to work on them.

The most recent phase of this project has been one of the most pleasant: working with The Ohio State University Press on the production of the volume itself was an enlightening exercise in cooperation. I want to thank general editor Malcom Litchfield, managing editor Eugene O'Connor, and production manager Jennifer Shoffey Forsythe, who made seemingly difficult tasks easy and even enjoyable.

Finally, my siblings, Shauna Colton Woods, Rondi Woods Pike, Pace Woods Wilson, Robert Black Woods, and Mark Williams Woods, their families, and my uncle, F. Pace Woods, have always enjoyed my weird interests and celebrated my accomplishments. To them and to all those who have brought love into my life I am more grateful than I can express.

Marjorie Curry Woods
The University of Texas at Austin

I

why was the *poetria nova* so popular?

"THE EFFICIENT CAUSE OF THIS BOOK"

[T]he efficient cause of this book was Geoffrey, the notary of King Richard of England.[1]
— Leipzig, Universitätsbibliothek, MS 1084

The author of this book is Master William the Englishman, but some do not know [his] name.[2]
— Erfurt, Wissenschaftliche Allgemeinbibliothek der Stadt, Amplon. Q.75

Sometime during the late twelfth century, Galfridus (or Galfredus or Gamfredus or Ganfredus or Gualterus) de Vino Salvo, an Englishman who had studied rhetoric at Paris,[3] returned to his homeland, where he began teaching. This Geoffrey of Vinsauf, as his name is translated into English, was also called Galfridus (with all variants thereof) Anglicus: Geoffrey the Englishman. According to a short complaint poem found in one of the most famous of all medieval rhetorical manuscripts, a certain Geoffrey who was probably ours began lecturing at Northhampton.[4] Here he fell afoul of another teacher named Robert,

---

1. "causa efficiens presentis libri fuit Ganfredus notarius regis Rigardi [*sic*] Anglie . . . " (Leipzig, Universitätsbibliothek, MS 1084, fol. 232r). The use of the Aristotelian four causes to introduce a text is discussed in "The *Accessus* and Frame" later in this chapter.

2. "Auctor istius libri est magister Willelmus Anglicus, sed quidam ignorant *** <nomen> [nomine *MS*] (Erfurt, Wissenschaftliche Allgemeinbibliothek der Stadt, Amplon. Q.75, fol. 83r).

3. "He received much of his rhetorical training in Paris, where he may possibly have encountered Matthew [of Vendôme] and Alan [of Lille]; it is certain that he knew the works of both men" (Nims, "*Translatio*," 222).

4. It is referred to as the "Causa Magistri Gualfredi" or by its incipit, "Si liceat michi

1

who tried to take Geoffrey's students and even attacked him physically. Geoffrey's short poem is a presentation of the case to the Archbishop of Canterbury. There is no archival record of such a case, but the dozen or so early English manuscripts of the *Poetria nova* and the English manuscript traditions of two related works support the hypothesis that he taught for many years in England.[5] In the dedication of the *Poetria nova,* Geoffrey states, "England sent me to Rome" (31). No archival evidence supports this statement either, although there is no reason to doubt its veracity,[6] and Geoffrey also was rumored to have taught at the University of Bologna.[7] Other than these few snippets we know nothing about him; some medieval commentators knew much less: at most that he was English, sometimes not even his own name. Whoever wrote the popular *Early Commentary* on the *Poetria nova* simply calls him "the author."[8] Everything that we do know points to a career spent in the schools—both the more sophisticated international university centers on the continent as well as regional schools in his native country. His own background in various pedagogical settings may be one of the reasons that his work was useful to so many kinds of teachers over such a long period of time.

Off with his head!

The word "acephalous" comes from *a* which means "without" and *cepha* which means "head," [like] a monk who has left the cloister without the permission of his abbot.[9]

—from a manuscript that belonged to the monastery of St. Georgensberg

Geoffrey begins his *Poetria nova* with an arresting image: the decapitation of the pope, or at least of his name. He dedicated the work to the current pontiff,

---

pauca loqui," in Glasgow, University Library, Hunter 511 (V.8.14), fol. 101r–v. On this manuscript see Faral, "Le manuscrit 511"; Harbert, *A Thirteenth-Century Anthology;* and Rigg, *History of Anglo-Latin Literature,* III. On Geoffrey's teaching career see Richardson, "Schools of Northampton"; Southern, "From Schools to University," 11–12; and Rigg, *History of Anglo-Latin Literature,* 68. On the relationship of this poem to other works by Geoffrey, see Rigg, *History of Anglo-Latin Literature,* 108–109.

5. Geoffrey's early work, the *Documentum de modo et arte dictandi et versificandi,* has survived in five manuscripts of English origin. The influence of another work that draws on Geoffrey's *Documentum* and has been called the longer version of the *Documentum* (now called the *Tria sunt*) is also confined to England, where it inspired much of the teaching of rhetoric in late medieval Oxford. See Camargo, "*Tria sunt.*" These and the other *artes poetriae* are discussed in "The Arts of Poetry and Prose" later in this chapter.

6. An otherwise unidentified clerk "W(alter?)" is listed as one of the envoys of archbishop of Canterbury in Pope Innocent III's calendar of 1214; Cheney and Cheney, *Letters of Pope Innocent III,* 162 (976). There is no other evidence to identify this person with Geoffrey, however. For Walter as a variant of Geoffrey's name, see "The English Encyclopedists" in chapter 5.

7. See "Our Englishman in Italy" in chapter 3.

8. *EC accessus,* passim.

9. "Acephalus dicitur ab 'a' quod est sine et 'cepha' quod est caput, quasi sine capite, idest monachus qui sine licentia abatis exit de claustro" (London, BL Add. 18153, fol. 4r); cf. Balbus, *Catholicon,* "acephali"; and Eberhard of Béthune, *Grecismus,* 8.86.

Innocent III (1198–1216), whose name, *In-no-cens,* composed of one short sylla-ble between two long ones, does not fit into dactylic hexameter, the traditional metrical form for didactic verse. Geoffrey's solution to this metrical problem is ingenious; he turns an insurmountable compositional problem with the name of his dedicatee into praise of that dedicatee. Making a strength out of a poten-tial problem is an excellent lesson for students to learn at the beginning of a text on how to write:

> Holy Father, wonder of the world, if I say Pope Nocent I shall give you an acephalous name; but if I add the head, your name will be at odds with the metre. That name seeks to resemble you: it will no more be confined by metre than your great virtue by the shackles of measure. There is no standard by which I may measure your virtue; it transcends the measures of men. But divide the name—divide the name thus: set down first "In," then add "nocent" and it will be in friendly accord with the metre. In the same way your excellence, if it is divided up, is equalled by many, but taken in its wholeness it is equalled by none. . . . (*PN* 1–9)

The playful audaciousness that was one of the attractions of Geoffrey's work is evident in this very first image: Innocent's name can be cited only in an acepha-lated or headless state. That the potential dangers of such a headless condition were recognized is clear from the gloss on "acephalous" quoted at the beginning of this section.

But this version of the name, *Nocens,* is a present participle that means "causing injury." Thus, there is something not just playful but even subversive in removing the first syllable or head of the word. Another passage addressed to the pope, a plea for clemency for the ruler of England, occurs at the end of the work in a number of manuscripts. Here the verb *nocere* ("to harm, to injure") appears three times in two lines (2086–2087):

> Quando *nocere* potes, noli: satis est *nocuisse*
> Posse *nocere*. . . .
> (Although you can **inflict injury,** do not wish to; the power to **injure** is already **injury** enough. . . .)

Here again the verb is couched in praise, but it is hard to imagine anyone liter-ate in Latin not reacting with a little gasp to this echo of the pope's acephalated name in the beginning of the poem.

Nor is this the only such example: the first words of the text are *Papa stupor mundi,* "Holy Father, wonder of the world." The phrase *stupor mundi* is echoed later in the longest set piece in the *Poetria nova* comprising all the figures of thought (patterns of repetition and variation in meaning or content). While nominally focusing on the responsibilities of the pope, this section of the *Poetria nova* is, like all of Geoffrey's set pieces, a virtuoso display with surprising twists and turns. Although at first it appears to be a general address about the potential abuse of power by any pope, the phrase that Geoffrey puts into the mouth of the pope in this section, "sole wonder of the sphere" (*stupor unicus orbis* [1315]), echoes the phrase "wonder of the world" (*stupor mundi*) in the first line, suggesting that Innocent himself has the potential to abuse power. This echo is apparently so obvious that many commentators do not bother to point it out. When they do, however, it is more like a reminder than a discovery, as when one notes, "THAT I AM THE SOLE WONDER OF THE SPHERE as in the beginning, 'Holy Father, wonder of the world.'"[10] There is a potentially negative meaning of *stupor,* of course: its original one of "bewilderment," as in the modern English meaning of "stupor." Given that Geoffrey plays with the negative meaning of *nocens* in his Dedication, it is conceivable that he also wants us to think of both connotations of *stupor,* but the double meaning is rarely discussed in glosses.[11] One commentator in a late-fourteenth-century French school manuscript that is described in the next chapter does mention the negative connotation, but dismisses it: "*STUPOR* In one way it means a mental state, but it is not used like that here; in another way it means admiration of something out of the ordinary, and that is how it is used here."[12]

After the introductory lines quoted above, Geoffrey connects Innocent's incomparable name to his incomparable rhetorical talents, his *gratia linguae* (14). Geoffrey's praise of Innocent's rhetoric is more than merely conventional, although it could have been based on reputation rather than personal knowledge. According to an anonymous but knowledgeable contemporary, Innocent was "as fluent in the vernacular as in Latin."[13] An account of the consecration ceremony of Santa Maria in Trastevere, which took place in 1215, the year before Innocent's death, says that "the Lord conferred on him [Innocent] such grace in preaching that not only his friends but also his enemies listened to his preaching gladly."[14] It was said of Innocent's voice that it "was so sonorous that every-

---

10. "1315 UT SIM STUPOR Unde in principio, 'Papa stupor mundi.'" A note added in one of the manuscripts of the *Early Commentary* (*EC* 1315 in "Omissions and Variants," p. 400).

11. Matthew Paris used the phrase to refer to Pope Innocent III in 1217 in his *Historia Anglorum seu chronica minor* ("Eodem anno papa Innocentius, qui vere stupor mundi erat"), though he had described Frederick II with the same phrase in an earlier work (*Chronica maior*). Since Matthew was not fond of Innocent, it is quite possible that he is using the phrase ironically. See Egger, "Papst Innocenz III.," 1–4; also Sommerlechner, *Stupor mundi?*, 226. I am grateful to Christoph Egger for fruitful discussions regarding this phrase and for references to Innocent's rhetorical ability.

12. "STUPOR Vno modo dicitur prout est asicnacio mentis et sic non sumitur hic; alio modo ut est admiracio de re inconsueta et sic sumitur hic" (Angers, Bibliothèque municipale, 523, fol. 1r; plate 2). For more on this manuscript see "Back to Basics" in chapter 2. Pace of Ferrara's negative interpretation of "stupor" is quoted in "Divide and Elevate" in chapter 3.

13. "sermone tam vulgari quam litterali disertus" (*Liber pontificialis,* quoted in Gress-Wright, ed., "Gesta Innocentii III," p. 1.7–8).

14. "Tantam itaque ei dominus gratiam in predicatione contulit, quod non solum amici sed etiam

one could hear and understand it even though he spoke softly."[15] While there is surely an element of hyperbole in these statements, there was also enough truth in them not to render Geoffrey's praise absurd.

THE OTHER AUDIENCE

. . . this work that I undertake for the benefit of your sons on the *Poetria novella* of Geoffrey, which I lecture on every year so that they may be instructed in the fruits and meters of rhetoric.[16]

—Giovanni Travesi

[T]he subject of comedy is light; to such a subject the sportive period of youth readily devotes itself.[17]

—Geoffrey of Vinsauf

Geoffrey dedicated the *Poetria nova* to Innocent, but he wrote it for students. While the range of verbal attractions of the *Poetria nova* eventually made it useful at all levels, it was probably originally intended for intermediate students, that is, those with some knowledge of Latin who were able to comprehend larger sections of text at a time, rather than just line-by-line analysis. Most early-thirteenth-century English manuscripts of the *Poetria nova* were originally unglossed, and the works with which it is copied in them are Latin verse texts considerably longer and more complex than those in the manuscripts produced for more basic instruction that are discussed in the next chapter.[18] For example, Cambridge, Corpus Christi College, 406, once owned by Matthew Parker, contains what might be the earliest English manuscript of Seneca's tragedies, the *Architrenius* of John of Hautville, Bernardus Silvestris's *Cosmographia,* the Troy poem of Dares Phrygius (thought during the Middle Ages to be an eyewitness account), Alan of Lille's *Anticlaudianus,* and Walter of Châtillon's *Alexandreis.*[19] These are all literary texts highly regarded and widely taught during the Middle

---

inimici eius predicationem libenter audiebant" (transcription of Vatican City, BAV Vat. lat. 10999, fol. 152a by Christoph Egger). The text has been published in an incomplete and in some places unreliable version in Morettus, *Ritus dandi presbyterium papae.* For more information about the source see Schimmelpfennig, "'Mitbestimmung,'" 455–470.

15. Petrocchi, "L'ultimo destino perugino," cited in Paravicini-Bagliani (*The Pope's Body,* 194), who continues, "Moreover, Innocent is described as handsome (*pulcher*), though the author also emphasizes that the pope's countenance (*aspectus*) was 'much respected and feared by all.'"

16. "hoc opus . . . quod in uestrorum filiorum utilitatem facio super *Poetria novella* Gualfredi quam annuatim lego ut fructibus et rethorice metricis imbuantur" (Seville, Biblioteca Capitular y Colombina, Cap. 56–2–27, fol. 2r).

17. *PN* 1912–1914.

18. These are among the manuscripts whose texts of the *Poetria nova* Margaret Nims deemed most important for a revised edition of the text.

19. On Cambridge, Corpus Christi College, 406, see James, *A Descriptive Catalogue,* II, 2, 288–91; Ludwig Gompf, *Joseph Iscanus,* 27–29; and Schmidt, *Architrenius,* 94 (B).

Ages for their rhetorical style as well as exciting content. Another Cambridge manuscript dating from the first half of the thirteenth century, Trinity College R.3.29, contains an important collection of school texts: Horace's *Epistles* and *Satires,* the *Satires* of Persius, Alexander de Villa Dei's *Doctrinale,* Ovid's *Remedia amoris* (Cures for Love), and John of Garland's *Equivoca* (Homonyms).[20] Several of the texts have interlinear glosses (including some in the vernacular), and an *accessus* added to the *Poetria nova* is discussed later in this chapter.

Perhaps the most important early English copy of the *Poetria nova* is the Glasgow manuscript that Edmond Faral made famous in the early part of the last century as Hunterian 511, now also known by a second signature of V.8.14.[21] A small volume (168 x 101 mm), it contains all the works now attributed to Geoffrey of Vinsauf, Matthew of Vendôme's *Ars versificatoria* (attributed to Geoffrey in the manuscript), Gervase of Melkley's *Ars versificaria* (which quotes Geoffrey), and forty-nine short poems.[22] Some of these are anthology pieces on themes like the Trojan War also found in other school collections. Others are thought to be student composition exercises on mythological subjects probably drawn from Ovid's *Metamorphoses:* three each on Phaethon and on Apollo and the Python; two each on Pyramus and Thisbe (more on this couple in the second chapter), Deucalion and Pyrrha, Lycaon, and Niobe.[23] Those on Niobe appear to be a matched pair, one an exercise in condensation and abbreviation, the other a showpiece using almost all the figures of words in order,[24] techniques described in sections of the *Poetria nova* to which commentators pay special attention. Although the *Poetria nova* is unglossed, there are a few marginal comments on other works in the manuscript, such as a reference to Thisbe in Ovid's *Ars amatoria* (*Tybie, ut in Ovidius de arte amandi,* although it is in the *Metamorphoses* that she and Pyramus appear) in a gloss on Geoffrey's *Summa de coloribus rhetoricis.*[25] Such references to other works are characteristic of intermediate rather than elementary commentaries (levels that will be examined in full in the later chapters).

Another clue to the level of student for which the work was written may lie in an alternate title found in some manuscripts and book inventories, mostly in Italy[26]: *Poetria novella. Novella* is a diminutive form of the adjective *nova* ("new"); hence *Poetria novella* means "New Little Poetics." But the masculine

20. On Cambridge, Trinity College, R.3.29, see James, *Western Manuscripts,* 2.104–106; and Hunt, *Teaching and Learning Latin,* 1.89–91.

21. On this manuscript see above, note 4.

22. One of these short pieces is the autobiographical complaint by a Geoffrey cited in "The Efficient Cause of This Book" earlier in this chapter.

23. Harbert, *Thirteenth-Century Anthology,* 4 and passim.

24. On the Niobe poems see Faral, "Le manuscript 511," 34–35; and Woods, "Teaching of Poetic Composition."

25. Glasgow, University Library, Hunter 511 (V. 8. 14), fol. 36v.

26. E.g., the popular commentary by Pace of Ferrara that is a focus of chapter 3. The title by which the work was usually known, *Poetria nova,* is explained in "Better than the Ancients."

form *novellus* can also mean "intermediate," as in the first line of Alexander de Villa Dei's *Doctrinale:* "I prepare to write the *Doctrinale* for the intermediate little academics (*clericulis novellis*)."[27] As one commentator on the *Doctrinale* notes on this passage: "he adds *novellis,* for with that word he designates writing for those at the middle level. . . . "[28] During the later Middle Ages such students would have ranged in age from about eleven to eighteen years, although many entered university at around fourteen.[29]

The *Poetria nova* shares important characteristics with other works that were written for students in what we would call the teenage years.[30] That young men of the age group that we refer to as adolescents were the intended audience for many medieval works is a fact.[31] That adolescence in the modern sense was in any way a medieval concept is less well established, although research in this area is increasing.[32] Texts widely read in medieval schools during the late Middle Ages contain stories, images, and techniques that were thought to have a particular, even transgressive appeal to boys at this liminal stage of life.[33] Perspicacious writers like Geoffrey took advantage of what were considered to be student interests and incorporated these in their teaching, while earlier works that were chosen for basic readers may have been picked for content as well as increasing length and hence difficulty.[34] Works from outside the Latin curriculum also show an attempt to appeal to adolescent males by using similar techniques. Specific verbal patterns and themes in some twelfth- and thirteenth-century Hebrew lament poems, for example, suggest that they were written for "a core of adolescent and young adult men" to help them resist the allure of Christian conversion tactics directed against those of this gender and age group. These

---

27. Suggestion of Robert Black, e-mail correspondence, May 2001.

28. "cum dicit novellis. Nam isto vocabulo mediocribus scribere designat" (Thurot [1868], 120, n.3, on v. 1; Alexander de Villa Dei, *Doctrinale,* 7).

29. Moran, *Growth of English Schooling,* 65. Some manuscripts and commentaries intended for younger students are discussed in chapter 2.

30. Cf. Kelly, *Arts,* 91–92.

31. The Latin adjective "adolescens" could refer to anyone who had not yet reached full manhood. Augustine used it to refer to himself at twenty-nine, just before his conversion, and see the discussion of different ages associated with the term in Chojnacki's chapter on "Measuring Adulthood: Adolescence and Gender," *Women and Men in Renaissance Venice,* 185–205. Kline, drawing on Seymour's edition of Trevisa's translation of *On the Properties of Things,* notes that "'children' has been taken to mean the age cohorts from infancy (*infancia*) to childhood (*puericia*) through adolescence (*adholencia*) and does not exclude a mixed child-adult audience" (*Medieval Literature for Children,* 5). See also the collection of essays edited by Classen, *Childhood in the Middle Ages,* especially the resources outlined in Carlsmith, "The Child in the Classroom."

32. E.g., Jordan, "Adolescence and Conversion in the Middle Ages"; Eisenbichler, ed., *The Premodern Teenager*; Einbinder, *Beautiful Death*; also the works cited in the previous note.

33. As Einbinder notes with regard to the Hebrew martyrdom poems, "The crude vulgarity of some of the polemical segments complements the sophisticated reinforcement of scholarly authority in ways that might appeal especially to privileged and intelligent young men" (*Beautiful Death,* 181); also see Wheatley, *Mastering Aesop,* 91–96. On the tastes of modern male pre-adolescents, see Blos, *Adolescent Passage,* 120. For techniques considered effective with adolescent women during the Middle Ages, see Millett and Wogan-Browne, *Medieval English Prose,* xvii–xviii.

34. Woods, "Teaching of Poetic Composition"; and Woods and Copeland, "Classroom and Confession."

poems emphasize "the bold and heroic ideal" and "the conjunction of refined and vulgar elements,"[35] characteristics also found in the *Poetria nova* and other Latin school texts. The *Ilias latina,* which was sometimes included in the *Liber Catonianus* (a Latin school reader), was a verse summary of Homer's narrative that emphasizes a simplistic version of the heroic ideal, with "the battle fray [as] the most significant action in the poem; in the body of the poem Baebius presents us with an almost interminable series of clashes between individual Greek and Trojan heroes."[36]

Fraught but funny wordplay of the kind that Geoffrey uses in his opening address to Innocent is also typical.[37] Images of inverted power, such as the aforementioned pontiff without a head, church luminaries silenced, and the lecture to the pope on potential abuses of papal power were intended to amuse students as well as adults. In addition, the *Poetria nova* contains examples of God chastised (412), a boy made master (438–443), and an anecdote of three poor friends, perhaps students (the work when copied separately goes by the title of *De tribus sociis*), who get the best of an irascible if righteously indignant shopkeeper (1888–1909).[38] When Geoffrey provides more than one example of a rhetorical technique, his practice is to end with a light or funny example, such as when the lament of the cross is followed by a lament of a worn-out tablecloth. Putting the comic example in the stronger position is another indication of his intended audience, since "comedy is an immature form, attractive to green years" (1911–1912). Geoffrey's association of humor with youth is one of the reasons that there are so many humorous examples in his teaching.[39]

SHAPING THE STUDENT

> Transfer the iron of the material, refined in the fire of the understanding, to the anvil of the study.[40]
> —Geoffrey of Vinsauf

Medieval schools, whether monastic or urban, sought to inculcate students with habits of mind and thought that formed new bonds among them while separating them from the environments in which they had grown up. Bourdieu's *Language and Symbolic Power* has offered medievalists several terms with which

---

35. Einbinder, "The Voice from the Fire"; also *Beautiful Death,* 181, and note 33 above.

36. McKinley, "The Medieval Homer," 5.

37. Wheatley notes the ludic aspects of medieval school texts (*Mastering Aesop,* 91).

38. Several of these examples are discussed in the next chapter.

39. On medieval theory of satire and comedy, including Geoffrey's "iocosa materia," see Gillespie, "From the Twelfth Century," 223–233. For more on this subject see "Comedy and the *Commedia*" in chapter 3.

40. *PN* 723–24.

to analyze aspects of this process,[41] and Freud notes that "Society must defend itself against the danger that the interests which it needs for the establishment of higher social units may be swallowed up by the family; and for this reason, in the case of every individual, *but in particular of adolescent boys,* it seeks by all possible means to loosen their connection with their family—a connection which, in their childhood, is the only important one" (emphasis mine).[42] Many of the rhetorical examples in the *Poetria nova* may have helped to foster a sense of solidarity among boys and young men while introducing them to the hierarchies of the church and academic life. Satirical sketches such as the "boy-made-master" mentioned earlier could serve to reinforce traditional roles, especially since Geoffrey's description exemplifies one who is ridiculous. He introduces it by saying, "A lively theme is under discussion: 'Boys are raised up and made masters.' Let their 'masterly status' evoke laughter" (437–438). Then comes the example: "Now he sits, loftily graced with the title of master, who up to now was fit for the rod. For laymen, the cap on his head guarantees him authentic; as do the cut of his robes, the gold on his fingers, his seat at the head, and the crowd in his study" (439–443). Geoffrey assumes that this exercise will be delivered orally to an audience ("have recourse to gestures, but let these be consistently fitting" [435]). Other evidence that we have of how students wrote rhetorical exercises in medieval classrooms, while sketchy, does suggest that such work was presented in a group context and at times composed extemporaneously.[43] Sometimes a student had the last word, however. The formulaic, positive ownership statement in a fifteenth-century Italian copy of the *Poetria nova* in the university library in Turin is implicitly contradicted by an amateurish sketch beneath it. The former states, in words probably dictated if not written by the teacher, "This book belongs to me, Johanotus de Georgis; I go to the school of *dominus* Euxobus of Vercelli, who is a good grammar teacher."[44]

---

41. E.g., Wheatley on Bourdieu's concept of *habitus* (*Mastering Aesop*, 52–54) and Copeland on his "rites of institution" (*Pedagogy*, 84–85).

42. "Transformations of Puberty," 225. See also Blos, *The Adolescent Passage*, 118. I am grateful to Debra Roth for these references. Cf. Münster-Swendsen, "Model of Scholastic Mastery . . . *c.* 970," 317.

43. A medieval source on group exercises is John of Salisbury's oft-quoted description of Bernard of Chartres in the *Metalogicon* (1.24). While some composition theorists have decried the competitive nature of such practice (an assessment with which St. Augustine would have agreed), others have suggested possible positive results in the modern classroom; see "Looking Ahead" in the Afterword. Wenger notes differences between shared and individual learning throughout *Communities of Practice*. On extemporaneous composition in the medieval classroom see "Conversion: The Origin of Style" in chapter 2.

44. "Iste liber est mei Iohanoti de Georgis qui vado ad scolas domini Euxobi de Uercellis, qui est bonus magister in sua gram<ma>tica" (Turin, Biblioteca Nazionale Universitaria, F.IV.11, fol. 41v). This is a composite manuscript in which the *Poetria nova* is bound with works on speculative grammar including Martin of Dacia's *De modis significandi* and legal *consilia* by Bartolus de Saxoferrato and Baldus de Perusio, both entitled *De duobus fratribus simul habitantibus;* see Mazzatinti and Sorbelli, *Inventari dei manoscritti* 28.92; *Iter ital.* 2.180; Paradisi, "La diffusione europea," 1.438; and Ascheri, "*Consilia* collection," 195. Compare the wording of ownership notes in New Haven, Yale University, Beinecke Rare Book Room and Manuscript Library, 597: "uado ad scolas uenerabilium magistrorum et <sapientium> [sapientiam *MS*] magistri Gaspari ac Simonini praeceptoris gramatice loyce [= logice] rethorice" (fol. 46v; information supplied by Robert G. Babcock and Eric Knibbs, private communication); in Milan, Biblioteca Ambrosiana, E 129 sup.: "Iste liber

Drawn below, however, is a sketch of someone wearing what looks like the soft academic cap of those with a university degree. His hand is raised and he is pointing his finger in the air. The figure could be a pontificating professor—or an unprepared one, as in Geoffrey's rhetorical example. Whoever he is meant to be, he is being hit, possibly even stabbed, from behind.[45]

Educational theorist Etienne Wenger contends that, for a pedagogy to be successful, "Information . . . must capture our identities and expand them. . . . A learning community must become self-conscious about appropriating the styles and discourses of the constellations in which it expects to have effects."[46] Medieval pedagogy drew on the rhetorical tradition for some of its most basic concepts. One of these was the *captatio benevolentiae,* or capturing of the good will of the audience, outlined in the *Rhetorica ad Herennium* (1.9). There the author explains in some detail the methods of making the hearer "receptive (*docilem*), well-disposed (*benivolum*), and attentive (*adtentum*)."[47]

The pseudo-Boethian *De disciplina scolarium* (On the Learning/Disciplining of Students), written at the University of Paris during the thirteenth century, uses this terminology to describe how a student should make himself receptive to the teacher's influence: "through *attencio* (the student must listen), *benevolentia* (the student must show good will towards his master), and *docilitas* (the student must let himself be formed without showing resistance to the master's teaching or person)."[48] Students were familiar with these terms, either from the *Rhetorica ad Herennium* itself or from the commentaries on the *Poetria nova* where they are used to describe how Geoffrey approaches Pope Innocent III in his dedication, e.g., "Note here the first part of the discourse, namely the Introduction, where the good will (*beneuolentia*) and receptiveness (*docilitas*) and attention (*attentio*) of the listener are secured. . . ."[49]

Image clusters in the text of the *Poetria nova* that describe the molding of

---

45. The two parts of the drawing may have been made by different students. See also the beginning of a colophon quoted in Gehl, *Moral Art,* 48: "Finito libro frangamus ossa magistro" ("This book's done, now let's break teacher's bones!").

46. Wenger, *Communities of Practice,* 273 and 274. A more nefarious interpretation based on Foucault's elaboration of power relationships could be made here, beginning with the resonance between the titles of *Discipline and Punish* and *De disciplina scolarium.*

47. *Ad Her.* 1.7; the advice on how to accomplish this shaping of the audience occupies several paragraphs (1.7–8). For the medieval and early Renaissance tradition of the *Rhetorica ad Herennium,* see Ward, *Ciceronian Rhetoric*; also Camargo, "Latin Composition Textbooks."

48. Münster-Swendsen, "Making of the Masters," 94–95, paraphrasing *De disciplina scolarium* 2.1: "Debet autem discipuli subieccio in tribus consistere: in attencione, benivolencia et docilitate. Docilis ingenio, attentus exercisio, benivolus animo. Attentus, inquam, ad audiendum, docilis ad intelligendum, benivolus ad retinendum." The text has been edited by Olga Weijers, and see also Lewry, "Grammar, Logic and Rhetoric," 408–409.

49. *EC* 1. Compare the description of Guarino's approach in his commentaries (Grafton and Jardine, *From Humanism,* 22–23).

rhetorical discourse have also been interpreted as analogous to the molding of students. Mia Münster-Swendsen draws on the *Poetria nova* in her study of power relationships in medieval universities; as she suggests, "The majority of [the metaphors] derive from the world of artisans—of craftsmen, thus stressing that education meant formation—shaping—fashioning."[50] The violence of some of these metaphors does give one pause; here is how Geoffrey evokes the full effort of the mind needed to condense material effectively: "Let the hammer of the intellect make it pliable; let repeated blows of that hammer fashion from the unformed mass the most suitable words" (725–727). From such a perspective the student's struggle to subdue words becomes the passing on of physical abuse.[51] But Geoffrey's examples are for the most part positive and generative: they emphasize the endless possibilities of rhetorical composition and how the student can control at least that aspect of his world. It is also possible to see the association of shaping students with shaping matter (by the students) as a holistic version of the pedagogy of creation, with rhetoric as the foundation.[52]

Commentators vary the degree of technical explanation that they provide according to the level of their students. For example, in the version of the *Early Commentary* on the *Poetria nova* intended for younger students, the gloss on the necessity of dividing Innocent's name is very short ("through a figure, namely tmesis") and omits any mention of the metrical problem. In the version intended for older students, more explanation is added but still without discussion of the metrical problem: "He says that this name can be put into the line [of verse] through a figure, namely tmesis (through which a word is completed after the insertion of a word or phrase) in between the parts."[53] Teachers of more advanced students go into more technical detail. Benedict of Aquileia, who taught at a notarial school in Ravenna, describes a point of contention among various commentators about this same passage:

> Note that some criticize the author here, saying that since *Innocens* is a proper name, and a proper name can be put into the meter at the author's discretion, they want to put *Innocens* in the verse as it stands. To this criticism others say that it is only the first syllable of a proper name that can be put into the meter at the author's discretion.[54]

50. Münster-Swendsen,"The Model of Scholastic Mastery, c. 1000," unpublished paper quoted with the author's permission. (The published version does not contain this reference to the *Poetria nova*.) See also Karras, *From Boys to Men*, 67–108.

51. On physical abuse in medieval schools (a practice that did not end, of course, with the end of the Middle Ages), see Enders, "Rhetoric, Coercion, and the Memory of Violence"; and Münster-Swendsen, "Making of the Masters," 54–56, and "Model of Scholastic Mastery . . . c. 970," 313–316.

52. Compare the description of the (re)creating of the physical world in rhetorical terms at the beginning of Bernardus Silvestris's *Cosmographia* (Wetherbee, 68; Dronke, I.60–64), a work discussed at the end of this chapter in "The Masterpiece."

53. *EC* 6.1 (translation revised) and p. 177 in "Omissions and Variants."

54. "Nota quod quidam reprehendunt hic autorem dicentes quod cum Innocentius sit proprium nomen

I have not (so far) discovered evidence of this controversy in other commentaries, and the dispute may have been invented by Benedict in order to explain this aspect of metrics to his students.

Such a gradation makes sense.[55] It is important to remember that a commentary is affected by both academic context and the background of the students. For example, the degree of abstraction in marginal commentary is determined more by whether the students are studying the *Poetria nova* in a university setting than by how much Latin they already know. But the density of interlinear glossing may be affected by both the degree of Latin literacy that the students have attained (especially if found in a student-owned manuscript) and what a teacher might feel would be helpful in order to construe at sight in class. That some commentators were so attuned to the needs of students may help to explain their preference for the *Poetria nova* over classical texts that covered some of the same material.

BETTER THAN THE ANCIENTS

The reason for undertaking the project . . . was so that he might expound perfectly the art of poetry, which Horace had taught in too condensed and confused a way.[56]

—Pace of Ferrara

When he saw that Tully's *Rhetoric* [*Rhetorica ad Herennium*] was somwhat prolix because of the overabundance of examples, succinctly gathering together what seemed most useful for pupils, he composed this abbreviated little work.[57]

—Franciscellus Mancinus

Many medieval and early Renaissance teachers recognized the unparalleled efficacy of the *Poetria nova* in the classroom. Horace's *Art of Poetry* was too short,

---

et proprium nomen ponatur ad libitum petunt ponere Innocentius in metro. Ad quod dixerunt aliqui quod sola prima sillaba proprii nominis erat ad libitum ordinanda." (Naples, Biblioteca Nazionale "Vittorio Emanuele III," V.D.6, fol. 2r) Benedict's commentary is described in chapter 3.

55. Compare Grendler, *Schooling,* 244: "By the time of the Renaissance, the paraphrase-commentary served the student from his first serious reading of the text through university studies. The teacher might offer a simple paraphrase to 12 year olds, to be followed by more comprehensive treatment in the secondary school. The university professor commented at length on the basis of his own research, while the degree candidate wrote down as complete a set of notes as possible to serve his future needs." The kinds of commentaries on the *Poetria nova* described in the following chapters suggest that it was taught at various levels.

56. "Causa suscepti operis fuit . . . ut perfecte artem poeticam posset determinare quam Oratius nimis confuse et compendiose docuerat" (Seville, Biblioteca Capitular y Colombina, Col. 5-4-30, fol. 2va [5va], plate 6). See "Pace of Ferrara" in chapter 3.

57. "Quia cum uidisset *Rethoricam* Tullii prolixam <ali>quantum propter copiam exemplorum confusam, <colligens> compendiose que vtiliora sibi ad vtilitatem scolarium uisa sint, hoc opusculum sub breuitate composuit" (Naples, Biblioteca Nazionale "Vittorio Emanuele III," Vind. lat. 53, fol. 1r [plate 8]). See "Franciscellus Mancinus, Benedictine Humanist," in chapter 3.

the *Rhetorica ad Herennium* was too long, but the *Poetria nova* was just right. The clarity of the *Poetria nova* praised by the early humanist commentators quoted above is in contrast to both the later Renaissance emphasis on elegance and classical style as well as the modern equation of clarity with simplicity. The *Poetria nova* is constructed according to medieval pedagogical values: it is clear in that it is definite (what is being taught is overstated for pedagogical effect) and self-explanatory (the author does what he says while he is saying it). Yet these values are not medieval only: while to modern scholars the *Poetria nova* can appear indirect, difficult, and needlessly complex, modern students often find the work useful not just for understanding how writers in earlier periods composed but also for honing the rhetorical focus of their own writing.

When an innovative book like the *Poetria nova* breaks into syllabuses (as it clearly did), it may be because it presents in a more efficient fashion trends that are developing in the interpretation and use in the classroom of earlier texts that have long been available. The combination of rhetorical and poetic doctrine in the *Poetria nova,* for example, was anticipated in the commentaries on Horace.[58] The success of the *Poetria nova* came in no small part from the author's seamless dovetailing of compositional techniques with rhetorical strategies in a work that exemplifed as well as taught them. As a Dominican teacher of the late fourteenth century put it, "The subject of this book is a method of persuading taken from what is common to the art of poetry and rhetoric."[59] The commentators saw Geoffrey's *Poetria* as a new version of Horace's *Ars poetica,* called the *Poetria* during the Middle Ages. Geoffrey took from Horace not only the verse form but also much of the same doctrine and advice, such as a consideration of audience and the methods of describing character and action according to conventional modes. The *Poetria nova* amplifies this doctrine in an exaggerated way meant to make it clear to those students for whom the sophistication and allusiveness of Horace's work could present problems, as Pace of Ferrara notes above. For medieval students still struggling with basic compositional principles, the old *Poetria* was not so practical as the new one, even though (or perhaps because) Horace's is a more pleasurable text for adults, especially mod-

---

58. Gillespie, drawing on Friis-Jensen, notes, "The blending of rhetoric and poetic, the reapplication of Cicero's oratorical dicta to poetry and the creative synthesis of different strands of theoretical discourse . . . was already there in embryo in the earlier tradition of commentary on and imitation of Horace's *Ars poetica*" ("From the Twelfth Century," 177).

59. "Subiectum huius libri est modus persuadendi ex hiis que communia sunt arti poetice et rethorice" (Wolfenbüttel, Herzog August Bibliothek, Cod. Guelf. 286 Gud. lat., fol. 1r). See chapter 2 for more on this commentary by Reiner von Cappel. Murphy notes the "high correlation between the ideas of Horace and the rhetorical precepts of Cicero" (*Three Medieval Rhetorical Arts*, xi), and Fredborg reminds us that the "conflation of rhetorical and Horatian doctrine was to have far-reaching consequences for literary studies. . . . It meant that purely inventional matters, topics for arguments used in a wider context as the basis for character delineation and plot, became tied up with categories of elocutional and stylistic concerns . . . " ("Ciceronian Rhetoric and the Schools," 32).

ern scholars, to read.[60] Yet Geoffrey did not replace but rather complemented Horace. These two *Poetriae* are found together in more than ten percent of the manuscripts of the *Poetria nova,* where they reinforced each other and helped to maintain an emphasis on poetics as well as rhetoric in the medieval teaching of composition.[61]

The *nova* of *Poetria nova* (a title that may have been created by the commentators[62]) was interpreted as an echo of the medieval name for the *Rhetorica ad Herennium.* This work was thought to be by Cicero and called the *Rhetorica nova* to distinguish it from his earlier work, the *De inventione,* also known as the *Rhetorica vetus.* Geoffrey's tropes and figures and other general rhetorical principles are drawn from the fourth book of the *Rhetorica ad Herennium,* but Geoffrey's work is much more condensed, and he gives examples of the figures in set pieces of connected discourse, rather than separately. This condensing was considered a pedagogical improvement, as the quotation from Franciscellus Mancinus above makes clear.[63] The passages on the figures are often among the most densely glossed parts of the *Poetria nova,* and there is evidence that students were assigned exercises based on one group of them.[64] Sometimes teachers choose a more innovative book but focus on the parts that are most traditional.[65] They like to show consistencies and reinforcements between set texts. There is evidence that the prose *Rhetorica ad Herennium* was used to teach verse composition,[66] just as the verse *Poetria nova* was used to teach the composition of prose. Yet these two works are copied together in only three extant manuscripts.[67] They did not become a pedagogical matched set like the *Poetriae.*

---

60. According to Friis-Jensen, " . . . Horace was too difficult to read without the help of introductory texts and glosses, and, in the *Art of Poetry,* insufficiently explicit in terms of prescriptive doctrine" ("Horace and the Early Writers," 362).

61. Aristotle's *Poetics* was also called the *Poetria,* so some commentators, such as Pace of Ferrara, refer to three different works entitled *Poetria.* Neither Aristotle's *Poetics* nor his *Rhetoric* appears to have been taught with the *Poetria nova,* but the *Rhetoric* is sometimes quoted in the commentaries.

62. According to Martin Camargo, "During the thirteenth century, the most popular title for Geoffrey's work appears to have been the 'Book about skill in speaking' ('Liber de artificio loquendi'). Variants of this title appear in more of the earliest manuscripts than either 'Poetria nova' or 'Poetria novella.'" ("What's in a Name?," unpublished paper). The earlier title is used by several commentators quoted later in this chapter, while most of those in the following chapters use "Poetria nova" or "Poetria novella." In the *Early Commentary* it is referred to throughout simply as "this book" ("hic liber," "huius libri," etc.).

63. Commentators on the *Poetria nova* and on the *Rhetorica ad Herennium* at times cite the examples or definitions of the figures from the other work; see, for example, *EC* 1098 ff. and Camargo, "Latin Composition Textbooks," 268 and 276–277.

64. See "The Display of Figures" in the next chapter.

65. Camargo suggests that the title *Poetria nova* "prevailed simply because it aligned Geoffrey's treatise with a major curricular text already being used to teach some of the same subjects, the *Ars poetica* . . . " ("What's in a Name?").

66. Camargo, "Latin Composition Textbooks," 276.

67. Assisi, Biblioteca Storico-Francescana della Chiesa Nuova, 309; Erlangen, Universitätsbibliothek, 635; and Munich, Universitätsbibliothek, 4° 814.

THE ARTS OF POETRY AND PROSE

> Its purpose is to teach the reader what he should know of speaking rhetorically, whether in verse or in prose. . . . [68]
>
> —*Early Commentary* on the *Poetria nova*

> The subject of this section is held to be poetry or the art of letter-writing. . . . [69]
>
> —introduction to excerpts from the *Poetria nova*, Oxford, Bodleian Library, Rawlinson C 552

One reason that both "Tully" and Horace were appropriate classical models for Geoffrey was that the so-called *artes poetriae* (arts of poetry) were used to teach prose as well as verse composition. A number of commentaries, including the one cited earlier praising Geoffrey's improvement of the *Rhetorica ad Herennium*, apply Geoffrey's techniques explicitly to the composition of letters. Later in the same manuscript, for example, Franciscellus Mancinus introduces Geoffrey's treatment of digression (527 ff.) by saying, "In this section he presents another method of amplifying a letter. . . ." [70] Thus, Douglas Kelly argues cogently that the medieval Latin term *ars poetriae* should more correctly if less literally be translated as "art of poetry and prose." [71]

This genre arose in France in the last third of the twelfth century, during or just after the great flowering of medieval Latin verse epic and during the same period that Geoffrey of Vinsauf himself was a student at Paris. The first of the medieval *artes poetriae* was Matthew of Vendôme's *Ars versificatoria,* which appeared before 1175, followed in the last quarter of the twelfth century by an early work of Geoffrey, the *Documentum de modo et arte dictandi et versificandi,* a prose treatise with verse examples. The *Poetria nova* was written ca. 1202 (with some parts revised 1208–1213); Gervase of Melkley's *Ars versificaria* sometime between 1208–1216; John of Garland's *Parisiana poetria* ca. 1220, revised 1231–1235; and Eberhard the German's *Laborintus* (The Labyrinth) sometime between 1213 and 1280. [72] The anonymous *Tria sunt,* as it is called after the incipit or first words of the text, is based on Geoffrey's *Documentum* and was at one time thought to be Geoffrey's own later revision, sometimes referred to as the longer version of the *Documentum.* According to Martin Camargo, however, the *Tria sunt* was written much later: between 1256 and 1400. [73] The only example of the genre to incorporate Aristotelian principles,

---

68. *EC accessus,* 56.

69. "Huius materia perpenditur esse poesis, aut ars dictandi . . . ." (Oxford, Bodleian Library, Rawlinson C 552, fol. 14v).

70. "In parte ista componit alium modum ampliandi materiam epistole . . ." (Naples, Biblioteca Nazionale "Vittorio Emanuele III," Vind. lat. 53, fol. 10r).

71. Kelly, *Arts,* 39–40.

72. Several of these works have gone by various names (Camargo, "What's in a Name?").

73. Camargo, "*Tria sunt*" and "Latin Composition Textbooks."

the *Poetria* of Matthias of Linköping, who was confessor to St. Bridget of Sweden, dates from the fourteenth century.[74]

The various arts of poetry and prose cover different aspects of composition, presumably because they were originally intended for students at different levels, as Gervase of Melkley points out in the introduction to his treatise. According to the taxonomy outlined by Kelly, based on Gervase's analysis, the most elementary kind of composition treatise, such as Gervase's *Ars versificaria,* "emphasizes the rudiments the masters deemed necessary for those as yet untrained in verse and prose composition, usually the tropes and figures and versification." A mid-level or grammatical treatise, like Matthew's *Ars versificatoria* or Eberhard's *Laborintus,* covers "sentence composition and topical elaboration in short verse and prose exercises that emphasize topical description, ornamentation, choice of words and versification." The third level, or rhetorical treatise, such as the *Documentum, Poetria nova, Parisiana poetria,* or *Tria sunt,* "includes instruction on all phases of verse and prose composition, notably invention and/or disposition as well as memory and delivery along with material style, amplification/abbreviation, and ornamentation."[75] Despite such distinctions, however, there are significant areas of overlapping content among the various examples of the genre. All of them discuss the tropes and figures, provide examples that "constitute a small *florilegium* of ornamental devices and narrative techniques,"[76] and emphasize very short units of composition suitable for classroom use and imitation.[77] And, as we shall see in the following chapters, commentators could take a text like the *Poetria nova* and teach it at a variety of levels.

"THE USEFULNESS OF THE WORK"

A threefold usefulness can be attributed [to the *Poetria nova*]: first is complete knowledge of the poetic art in general; second, crafted eloquence; third and last, the delight that comes as much from the ornamentation and harmony of the words as from the beauty of the content.[78]

—Pace of Ferrara

---

74. Matthias of Linköping, *Poetria,* 9–10.

75. Kelly, *Arts,* 63. Kelly also describes a fourth category of "masterpiece," discussed at the end of this chapter.

76. Kelly, *Arts,* 41.

77. Franz Quadlbauer's "Tendenz zur kleinen Einheit" (*Die antike Theorie,* 71), discussed in Kelly, *Arts,* 39. For more information about what kinds of material are covered in different rhetorical treatises, see Camargo, "Latin Composition Textbooks." On the short units of composition, see "Separating the Men from the Boys" in chapter 2.

78. "Vtilitas uero assignari potest triplex: prima plena cognitio artis poetice in communi, secunda artificiosa elloquentia, tertia et ultima est <delectatio> [declaratio *MS*] que habetur tam ex uerborum ornatu et simphonia quam ex sententiarum pulcritudine" (Seville, Biblioteca Capitular y Colombina, Col. 5-4-30, fol. 2vb [5vb]).

[For a sense of the scope and comprehensiveness of the *Poetria nova* as a classroom text we turn to a fifteenth-century list of its contents as they could be used by a teacher](or writer). It is appended to the end of a copy of the *Poetria nova* in which sections of the commentary by Bartolomew of Pisa (fl. 1300) introduce and alternate with sections of text.[79] The list shows us how the *Poetria nova* was divided into lessons, and it also provides a guide to this manuscript of the text, since each item in the list is followed by a folio number where we find that section of text (see Appendix I). We can see how Bartholomew or someone using his commentary organized his lectures, and this guide would also have made it easy to consult a specific part of the *Poetria nova* during the composition process.[80] The copy of the *Poetria nova* in the manuscript is preceded by an *accessus,* or academic introduction, and then a short passage of the text is glossed phrase by phrase *before* the lines themselves are quoted, a pattern that is repeated throughout the text. Each item in the list summarizes a section of this commentary-cum-text and replicates a rubric written in between the commentary and the lines it has introduced. For example, the first two, "That rhetoric makes a man honorable" and "Praise of Pope Innocent in Five Ways," are the themes of Bartholomew's introduction to the whole text and his analysis of Geoffrey's first lines respectively.[81]

The items in bold below are those that the scribe has marked with two vertical slashes in the margin, probably so that they could be located quickly. Some of the marked items, like personification and apostrophe, might have been particularly useful in the composition of sermons (Bartholomew and presumably also his scribe were Dominicans). Geoffrey's treatment of personification includes a mini-sermon spoken in the persona of the cross calling for a new crusade,[82] and the objects of Geoffrey's examples of apostrophe are identified in terms of what we might call personality types: "those overly happy in good times," "the presumptuous," "the fearful," "those who are confident in their elevated position," etc. While some of these passages were mentioned earlier in terms of their potential appeal in the classroom, the study of generic types was also useful preparation for the composition of sermons. Each of the ways of beginning a text, the methods of amplification, the various tropes, and the kinds of determination, is listed separately. In contrast, the methods of abbreviation, the figures of words and of thought, and the kinds of conversion are not itemized, a distinction that

---

79. Rome, Biblioteca Casanatense, 311, fols. 69v–70v. For bibliography on this manuscript, see chapter 3, note 18. There is also a list of the contents of the *Poetria nova* (without a copy of the text) in Vatican City, BAV Vat. lat. 14415, fols. 82r–86v. For a summary of the rubrics in another manuscript, Florence, Biblioteca Medicea Laurenziana, Strozzi 137, see Black, *Humanism,* 346–349.

80. Cf. Rouse and Rouse on the development of the chapter list (preceding the text) as a tool a couple of centuries earlier: "we may safely assume that chapter lists are intended not only as an overview or summary of the contents but also as a device to facilitate searching" (*Authentic Witnesses,* 197).

81. These passages are quoted in "The Subject is Rhetoric" in chapter 3.

82. See "Sermons?" in chapter 2.

may indicate that these groups of techniques were considered single exercises or less important for the composition of sermons. Explanatory comments and the relevant line numbers are added in square brackets.

CONTENTS OF THE *POETRIA NOVA* AND COMMENTARY BY
BARTHOLOMEW OF PISA IN ROME, BIBLIOTECA CASANATENSE, 311[83]

That rhetoric makes a man honorable [a theme in Bartholomew's *accessus* or introduction]

Praise of Pope Innocent in five ways [name, family, age, eloquence, companions] [1]

On thinking about the subject before the act of writing [43]

That the subject ought to be ornamented in words [60]

What the rhetorician ought to consider [77]

The difference between natural and artificial order [87]

That there are eight ways of beginning artificially [101]

On beginning from the end [112]

On beginning from the middle [118]

On beginning with a proverb [126]

On beginning with an exemplum [143]

A composition (*thema*) showing all the ways of beginning[84] [155]

On beginning according to natural order [158]

Example of beginning from the end [167]

On a beginning taken from the middle [173]

On a proverb related to (*iuxta*) the beginning [180]

On a proverb related to the middle [185]

On a proverb related to the end [190]

On an exemplum related to the beginning [193]

On an exemplum related to the middle [197]

On an exemplum related to the end [200]

On amplifying or abbreviating [203]

First method of lengthening: through repetition [219]

Second method of lengthening: through circumlocution [226]

Third method of lengthening: through comparison [241]

Fourth method: through apostrophe [264]

Apostrophe to those overly happy in good times [277]

Apostrophe against the presumptuous [292]

Apostrophe against the fearful [304]

Apostrophe against those who are confident in their lofty position [324]

---

83. For the Latin of this list of contents see Appendix I.
84. See "Shaping the Narrative" in chapter 2.

Apostrophe in time of grief [367]

Apostrophe against the ridiculous [431]

Fifth method of lengthening: through personification [461]

Example of a new personification [an English fortress] [515[85]]

Another example of a new personification [the cross] [467]

Example of a funny personification [a tablecloth] [508]

Sixth method of amplifying: through digression [527]

Example of two kinds of digression[86] [538]

Seventh method of amplifying: through description [554]

Example of a description examining (*circa*) the female form[87] [562]

Example of a description of [female] adornments [600]

Example of a description of those feasting [622]

Eighth method of amplifying: through a double sentence [the technique of opposites] [668]

On ways of abbreviating [690; Geoffrey lists eight]

The method of greatest abbreviation[88] [twin renderings of the story of the snow child] [718]

He teaches the ornamenting of thoughts and words in general [737]

General remarks on the rhetorical color of transference (*transumptionis*)[89] [figurative language, or tropes] [756]

He teaches [metaphoric] transference from the non-human to the human [765]

[Metaphoric] transference from the human to the non-human [778]

Another example of the same technique: on the subject of winter [800]

Yet another example of the same: on the weather for navigating [807]

Yet another example: on the works of a metal smith [813]

Praise of transference [830]

On adding adjectives to transferred [metaphoric] words [844]

On combining [surface] opposition in sound and [underlying] agreement in sense [872]

When the same word is used literally and metaphorically [886]

On transference of a verb [metaphor] [893]

On transference of an adjective [908]

On transference of a noun [*nominatio:* onomatopoeia, and *pronominatio:* antonomasia] [919]

On transference of several expressions [*permutatio:* allegory] [937]

That transference should be kept within bounds [945]

---

85. In this manuscript the example of the angry fortress has been moved.
86. See "Better than Sex" in chapter 2.
87. See "The Female Body in the Classroom" in chapter 2.
88. See "Shortest is Not Best" in chapter 2.
89. See "Transference and Transformation" in chapter 2.

---

90. The second and third kinds of metonymy (cause for effect and container for contents) are not included in the list of contents.

91. A kind of synecdoche in most commentaries; see *EC* 1022 but *Ad Her.* 4.43–44.

92. See below, note 160, as well as "The Display of Figures" in chapter 2.

93. According to most commentators, understatement (like hyperbole) is a kind of emphasis rather than a separate category.

94. See "Separating the Men from the Boys" and "Conversion: The Origin of Figures" in chapter 2.

95. See "Student Determination" in chapter 2.

On observing the attributes of the subject[96] [1842]

On comparing prose and poetry[97] [1853]

That sometimes rhetorical colors are to be avoided [1888]

What and how many are the faults of speech [1920]

On spending a long time checking for faults [1946]

On memory [1969]

On delivery [2031]

The conclusion of the book and a short address (*sermocinatio*) **to the pope** [2066]

How he sends this book to Lord William[98] [the second dedication, 2099]

Some items in this list are techniques, others are specific examples, and still others refer to general lessons about the craft of writing; they are listed in order, but not systematically. What is identified is what the commentator, Bartholomew, focuses on in his introduction to each section. Although as modern readers we might be more comfortable with outlines that stick to one kind of information or another (see the list of examples in "Purple Patches" below, for example), ⌈Geoffrey's combination of instruction, description, and example was what made the *Poetria nova* such a goldmine and so attractive to medieval teachers.⌉

THE SUCCESS OF THE *POETRIA NOVA*

[H]e does what he teaches, which is the custom of a good teacher.[99]
    —*Early Commentary*

Geoffrey's combination of theory and practice meant that medieval teachers got several texts in one with the *Poetria nova.* Yet because there is so much similar doctrine shared among the arts of poetry and prose, the number of manuscripts of the *Poetria nova* is still startling. Matthias of Linköping's *Poetria* has survived in only one manuscript; Gervase's *Ars versificaria* has survived in four; John of Garland's *Parisiana poetria* and Geoffrey's *Documentum* in five each; Matthew's *Ars versificatoria* in nine copies; and the *Tria sunt* in eleven with two additional fragments. Eberhard's *Laborintus,* however, which was, like the *Poetria nova,* a required text in some central European universities, is extant in at least forty-three manuscripts.[100] But the *Poetria nova* has survived in more than two hundred, including a number of fragments (see the Manuscript List); these

---

96. See "Geoffrey after Quintilian" in the Afterword.

97. See "Comedy and the *Commedia*" in chapter 3.

98. This William has been variously identified; see Nims, p. 110.

99. *EC accessus,* 54.

100. Camargo, "Latin Composition Textboooks"; see also "*Tria sunt,*" 939, updating Kelly, *Arts,* 97–98.

range in date from the thirteenth to the seventeenth centuries, although the number of post-fifteenth-century manuscripts is extremely small. To modern readers the popularity of the *Poetria nova* may seem surprising, since the format of prose instruction combined with verse examples found in most of the other *artes poetriae* (those by Matthew, Gervase, and John of Garland, as well as Geoffrey's own *Documentum* and the *Tria sunt*) might seem more appropriate for the classroom.

That the *Poetria nova* is written completely in verse can make it appear to be a more difficult text, since, like Innocent's name, definitions and rhetorical techniques often must be expressed obliquely. Yet the *Laborintus,* which has survived in the second highest number of manuscripts, is also in verse, as was the *Doctrinale* of Alexander de Villa Dei, a grammar treatise that continued to be used well into the fifteenth century—despite extremely critical assessments by humanists—because of the pedagogical utility of its mnemonic tags.[101] When we remember that medieval students often had to memorize the texts that they studied, the greater popularity of verse treatises becomes more understandable. As a fifteenth-century gloss on the *Poetria nova* explains, "For Aristotle says in book three of the *Rhetoric* that things in verse are more easily committed to memory . . . , on account of which all things in verse are remembered better than those not joined together."[102] Since many textbooks were learned by heart, verse was a positive advantage.

Just as significantly, the verse form of the *Poetria nova* allows Geoffrey to practice what he preaches, as the Early Commentator notes above. By writing in verse about verse composition and by writing rhetorically about rhetoric, Geoffrey has created a text that simultaneously teaches and demonstrates.[103] This complementarity was noticed and commented on almost immediately. The *Early Commentary* provides the most elaborate statement of the reflexivity of Geoffrey's work:

> Note, therefore, that in this book the author is both a rhetorician and an orator. There is a difference between a rhetorician and an orator; a rhetorician is one who teaches the art of beautiful expression; an orator is one who acts in accordance with the art that Cicero teaches. It is one thing to speak about rhetoric, another to speak rhetorically. A rhetorician speaks about rhetoric, an

---

101. On the popularity and criticism of the *Doctrinale*, see Reichling's introduction, lxxxiii ff.; and Black, *Humanism,* esp. 74–83 and 87–91. On the phenomenon of turning teaching material into verse, see Haye, *Das lateinische Lehrgedicht.*

102. "Dicit etiam Aristotelis 3° *Rhetoricorum* quod metra facilius memorie commendantur his verbis propter quod et metra omnes memorantur magis quam non ligata" (Florence, Biblioteca Medicea Laurenziana, Strozzi 137, fol. 32r, quoted in Black, *Humanism,* 291, also 52 ff. and 190–192; and Black and Pomaro, *Boethius's* Consolation of Philosophy, 11–12, also 35 and 39). David Thompson "notes a 'strong preference for verse authors in the reading texts' found in fourteenth-century Oxford grammar-school manuscripts" ("Grammar Masters Revisited," quoted in Camargo, "Models," 183).

103. Alexandre Leupin has analyzed Geoffrey's metaphors for the creative act in "Absolute Reflexivity."

orator rhetorically. This author does both; he speaks about rhetoric and does so rhetorically. Similarly, it is one thing to write about verse, another to write in verse. Virgil wrote in verse, but not about verse; Donatus wrote about verse,[104] but not in verse. This author does both. Similarly, it is one thing to speak about an art (*de arte*), another to speak artfully (*ex arte*). To speak about an art is to give the precepts of the art. To speak artfully is to imitate the precepts, which is more difficult, just as it is more difficult to write verse than to give the precepts of verse. This author does both: he says about his art what he demonstrates from it; he writes verse while giving the precepts of verse.[105]

The all-encompassing nature of this text made it an especially useful and efficient classroom textbook.

Geoffrey's description of a rhetorical technique is often encoded with the very technique he is explaining: his treatment of amplification is amplified, while his treatment of abbreviation is short; his discussion of circumlocution walks around and around the subject, and his introduction to the ornaments of style is highly ornamented. The effect is of an almost gleeful—and completely unforgettable—virtuosity. The glosses added to several thirteenth-century manuscripts of the *Poetria nova* consist entirely of statements distinguishing between where the author "offers" (*ponit*) or "teaches" (*docet*) a topic on the one hand, and where he "exemplifies" (*exemplificat*) it on the other.[106]

An impression of inexhaustible generativeness is typified by one of the most popular and well-known sections of the *Poetria nova*. This passage was copied separately as a text on its own and was rumored, incorrectly, to be the first part of the *Poetria nova* to have been printed.[107] It is the extraordinary series of apostrophes lamenting the demise of Richard I of England (April 6, 1199). In the list of contents quoted earlier, this section is called "Apostrophe in time of grief." Apostrophe is one of Geoffrey's eight methods of amplifying a topic, and what he offers his students is a tour de force, a seemingly endless series of apostrophes which are addressed to England, the day of the week on which Richard was wounded (Friday), the soldier who killed him, Nature herself, and, finally, God: the addressees are in bold type for a reason that will be clear later. I quote this passage in full and suggest that it be read aloud for full effect.

---

104. On this description of Donatus, see Woods, "Classical Examples," 6.

105. *EC accessus*, 42–53. It is curious that the *EC* does not refer to Horace's parallel accomplishment, especially since in one of the most important manuscripts of this commentary, Munich, Bayerische Staatsbibliothek, Clm 4603, it is followed immediately by a commentary on Horace's *Ars poetica*.

106. E.g., London, BL Harley 3775, fols. 150r–178r, of English provenance. See also the many such glosses in Paris, BnF lat. 15150, fols. 88r–123v, a late-thirteenth- or early-fourteenth-century manuscript from the Abbey of St. Victor in Paris (as is Paris, BnF lat. 15135, a thirteenth-century manuscript containing a copy of the *Poetria nova* with commentary on fols. 163r–189r).

107. The passage was excerpted as early as the thirteenth century: Oxford, Bodleian Library, Add. A. 44, fol. 7v; and Oxford, Bodleian Library, Bodley 656, fol. 145r–v. On the printing history of the *Poetria nova*, see "An End and a Beginning" in chapter 5.

APOSTROPHES ON THE DEATH OF KING RICHARD

Once defended by King Richard's shield, now undefended, **O England,** bear witness to your woe in the gestures of sorrow. Let your eyes flood with tears, and pale grief waste your features. Let writhing anguish twist your fingers, and woe make your heart within bleed. Let your cry strike the heavens. Your whole being dies in his death; the death was not his but yours. Death's rise was not in one place only but general.

O tearful day of Venus [Friday]! O bitter star! That day was your night; and that Venus your venom. That day inflicted the wound; but the worst of all days was that other——the day after the eleventh[108]—which, cruel stepfather to life, destroyed life. Either day, with strange tyranny, was a murderer.

The besieged one pierced the besieger; the sheltered one, him without cover; the cautious one pierced the incautious; the well-equipped soldier pierced an unarmed man—his own kind! **O soldier,** why, treacherous soldier, soldier of treachery, shame of the world and sole dishonour of warfare; O soldier, his own army's creature, why did you dare this against him? Why did you dare this crime, this hideous crime?

O sorrow! O greater than sorrow! O death! O truculent death! Would you were dead, **O death!** Bold agent of a deed so vile, how dare you recall it? You were pleased to remove our sun, and condemn day to darkness. Do you realize whom you snatched from us? To our eyes he was light; to our ears melody; to our minds an amazement. Do you realize, impious death, whom you snatched from us? He was the lord of warriors, the glory of kings, the delight of the world. Nature knew not how to add any further perfection; he was the utmost she could achieve. But that was the reason you snatched him away: you seize precious things, and vile things you leave as if in disdain.

And **Nature,** of you I complain; for were you not, when the world was still young, when you lay new-born in your cradle, giving zealous attention to him? And that zeal did not flag before your old age. Why did such strenuous effort bring this wonder into the world, if so short an hour stole the pride of that effort away? You were pleased to extend your hand to the world and then to withdraw it; to give thus, and then to recall your gift. Why have you vexed the world? Either give back to us him who is buried, or give us one like him in excellence. But you have not resources for that; whatever you had that was wondrous or precious was expended on him. On him were exhausted your stores of delight. You were made most wealthy by this creature you made; you see yourself, in his fall, most impoverished. If you were made happy before, in proportion to happiness then is your misery now.

If heaven allow it (*Si fas est*), I chide even God. **O God,** most excellent

---

108. Richard died twelve days after he was wounded.

of beings, why do you fail in your nature here? Why, as an enemy would, do you strike down a friend? If you recall, your own Joppa gives evidence for the king—alone he defended it, opposed by so many thousands. Acre, too, gives evidence—his power restored it to you. The enemies of the cross add their witness—all of them Richard, in life, inspired with such terror that he is still feared now he is dead. He was a man under whom your interests were safe.

If, **O God,** you are, as befits your nature to be, faithful and free of malice, just and true, why then did you shorten his days? You could have shown mercy to the world; the world was in need of him. But you choose to have him with you, and not with the world; you would rather favour heaven than the world.

O Lord, if it is permissible to say it, let me say—with your leave—you could have done this more graciously, and with less haste, if he had bridled the foe at least (and there would have been no delay to that end; he was on the verge of success). He could have departed more worthily than to remain with you. But by this lesson you have made us know how brief is the laughter of earth, how long are its tears. (*PN* 368–430; paragraphing and emphasis mine)

It is hard to read this amplified example of amplification aloud now without smiling, despite or even perhaps because of its dead seriousness. It is also hard not to be moved.[109] Geoffrey may be appealing here to schoolboy patriotism as he does later in another popular rhetorical example in the *Poetria nova* (not present in all copies, however) that also was excerpted: the speech of a proud English fortress on a hill addressing the massed French army below.[110] In any case, once read, the passage is not easily forgotten.

How readily a teacher could assume that his students would remember this virtuoso demonstration is indicated by the fact that Chaucer's well-known parody of the passage in the *Nun's Priest's Tale* plays on the themes, author, subject, seriousness, and seriality of the original.[111] Chaucer's narrator laments his inability to memorialize the threatened (but later avoided) death of his own protagonist, a barnyard rooster named Chauntecleer, with the same facility and power with which Geoffrey of Vinsauf ("Gaufred") lamented the death of Richard. In the quotation below I have divided the paragraphs to show structural similarities with the *Poetria nova* and put in bold type the objects of apostrophe and

---

109. This passage was considered a model lament well into the seventeenth century, and not just in England; see "The English Encyclopedists" in chapter 5, as well as Woods, "A Medieval Rhetorical Manual in the 17th Century." During the Middle Ages it was, as Young points out, considered a "literary gem" ("Chaucer and Geoffrey," 172).

110. This example is excerpted in an important poetic anthology, London, BL Cotton Titus A.XX, fols. 97v–98r, copied in England, perhaps St. Albans, ca. 1375; see Rigg, *History of Anglo-Latin Literature*, passim, esp. 308. For a list of rhetorical examples in the *Poetria nova*, see "Purple Patches" later in this chapter.

111. Whether Chaucer and the ex-schoolboy members of his audience knew the whole *Poetria nova* or just excerpts is immaterial (although I believe the former to be true). On the two laments by the two Geoffrey's see also Young, "Chaucer and Geoffrey"; and Richmond, *Laments for the Dead*, 17–20. As Richmond points out, "Only a well established tradition is characteristically signaled out for travesty . . . " (20).

the references to the same themes in the *Poetria nova:*

> O destinee, that mayst nat been eschewed!
> Allas, that Chauntecleer fleigh fro the bemes!
> Allas, his wyf ne roghte nat of dremes
> And on a **Friday** fil al this meschaunce.
>   **O Venus,** that art goddesse of plesaunce,
> Syn that thy servant was this Chauntecleer,
> And in thy servyce dide al his poweer,
> Moore for delit than world to multiplye,
> Why woldestow suffre hym on thy day to dye?
>   **O Gaufred,** deere maister soverayn,
> That whan thy worthy **kyng Richard** was slayn
> With shot, compleynedest his deeth so soore,
> Why ne hadde I now thy sentence and thy loore
> The **Friday** for to chide, as diden ye?
> For on a **Friday,** soothly, slayn was he.
> Thanne wolde I shewe yow how that I koude pleyne
> For Chauntecleres drede and for his peyne. (*NPT* 3337–3354)

By recalling for the schooled in his audience a section of text that seemed to go on forever, Chaucer makes his own apostrophes appear longer and even more self-indulgent than they are. And he adds another layer of mockery to the parody by adding an apostrophe to the author of the original apostrophe, with whom, of course, he shares his own first name.[112]

THE *ACCESSUS* AND FRAME

> In the beginning of this book, we should see what is treated in this work and why and how.[113]
>
> —*Early Commentary*
>
> In the beginning of this book, as in the beginning of others, three things are to be asked in sequence: first, what and how many are its causes? second, what is the title of the book? third, what part of philosophy does it belong under?[114]
>
> —Venice, Biblioteca Nazionale Marciana, Marc. lat. XII.244 (10531)

---

112. The whole of the *Nun's Priest's Tale* can be read as one long exercise in amplification (Woods, "*Verba and sententia*," 31). On other kinds of schoolroom echoes in the *NPT*, see Travis, "*The Nun's Priest's Tale*."

113. *EC accessus*, 1.

114. "In principio huius libri sicut in principiis aliorum tria sunt per ordinem inquirenda: prima que et quot sint cause, secundo quis sit libri titulus, tercio cui parti philosophie supponat<ur>" (Venice, Biblioteca Nazionale Marciana, Marc. lat. XII.244 [10531], p. 32). I am grateful to Dott. Gian Albino Ravalli Modoni and to Craig Kallendorf for additional information about this manuscript.

Medieval manuscripts produced in all but the most elementary academic settings often contain a formal prologue or introduction, called in Latin an *accessus,* which shows how medieval teachers approached a text. It presents a series of topics to be discussed before turning to the text itself, the latter called by some commentators the analysis *ad litteram.* The topics discussed in an *accessus* were highly conventional and predictable, especially in certain periods and for certain kinds of texts.[115] In general, the more advanced the text, the longer and more sophisticated the *accessus.* For students at a basic level, the introductory comments were short and simple, but even these were condensed versions of those used at more advanced levels. The status conferred on a text by the mere existence of an *accessus* to it was as important as what was actually said.[116] Usually an *accessus* is copied before the beginning of the text, often on the preceding folio. Because the first leaves of manuscripts become worn and sometimes fall off, the lack of an *accessus* preceding a text may simply mean that it has disappeared. *Accessus* were considered little texts in themselves, and some circulated separately, even attaching themselves to other commentaries.

The *accessus* is the intellectual grid through which a work is presented to students. The twelfth century, important for many developments in medieval literature, pedagogy, and epistemology, saw the evolution of the "Type C" *accessus,* so called from the nomenclature based on R. W. Hunt's classic study.[117] The extensive *accessus* to the version of *Early Commentary* intended for older students is of this type. Following is the list of topics addressed in a Type C *accessus* (slightly altered from that in Minnis and Scott) and how each is treated in that commentary.

TOPICS ADDRESSED IN A TYPE C *ACCESSUS:*

1. *titulus:* the **title** of the book
   The *Early Commentary* states simply that "A title can be put to it in accordance with the tenor of the material."[118] Other commentaries are more specific, e.g., "The title is as follows: 'Here begins the book of Master Geoffrey

---

115. E.g., Quain, "Medieval *Accessus ad auctores*"; R. W. Hunt, "Introductions to the 'Artes'"; Huygens, *Accessus ad auctores;* Allen, "Commentary as Criticism"; Minnis, *Theory of Authorship;* Coulson, "Hitherto Unedited (I)"; Kelly, "Accessus ad auctores"; Meyer, "*Intentio auctoris, utilitas libri*"; and Minnis and Scott, *Medieval Literary Theory,* 12–36. See also the recent collection of essays on *Les prologues médiévaux* edited by Jacqueline Hamesse and the various *accessus* quoted in the ongoing volumes of the *CTC* series.

116. "The very presence of an *accessus* seems as likely an influence on a reader's attitude as the definitions given in it. In a broader context, these *accessus* are simply part of the metalanguage that validates the study of the text they introduce." (Wheatley, *Mastering Aesop,* 75). See also Suerbaum, "*Accessus ad auctores.*"

117. Hunt, "Introductions to the 'Artes.'" The most accessible outline of this format for students of literature is Minnis and Scott, *Medieval Literary Theory,* 2, a short summary based on Minnis, *Medieval Theory of Authorship,* 9–39 and 219–34. Minnis and Scott provide translations of numerous examples of *accessus* (15–36), as does Elliott, "*Accessus ad auctores.*"

118. *EC accessus,* 60.

of Vinsauf *On Skill in Speaking*.'"[119] This or a variant thereof may have been the original title of the *Poetria nova*.[120]

2. *materia:* the **subject**

   "The subject of this book is artful eloquence, namely rhetoric, according to which art the book teaches poets to speak metrically."[121]

3. *intentio auctoris:* the **purpose,** or **aim,** of the author

   "Its purpose is to teach the reader what he should know of speaking rhetorically, whether in verse or in prose, seeing that what is noted there [in this book] serves prose as well as verse."[122]

4. *modus agendi,* also called *modus tractandi:* the stylistic or didactic **method of proceeding**

   In the *Early Commentary* this topic is called "how the work is handled" (*qualiter hoc opus tractetur*): "Next is seeing how the work is handled. Note, therefore, that in this book the author is both a rhetorician and an orator."[123]

5. *ordo:* the **arrangement** or ordering of the parts

   The *Early Commentary* discusses this topic under (2), the *materia* or subject, which is rhetoric, because the book is divided according to the parts of the art of rhetoric and the parts of a rhetorical discourse, a double structure discussed in the next section. "The book principally consists of the five parts of rhetoric. . . . And the book consists, in a secondary way, of these six parts of a discourse."[124]

6. *utilitas:* the **usefulness** of the work

   "The usefulness of the work is the knowledge of this art [of rhetoric]."[125]

7. *cui parti philosophie supponatur:* the **branch of philosophy** or the area of general knowledge to which it belongs

   This last category is not addressed in the *Early Commentary.* Literary texts were usually classified under ethics (as in the *accessus* quoted below), because they taught *mores*.[126] Other categories were also possible, as we see from an

---

119. "Titulus talis est 'Incipit liber magistri Galfridi de Uino Salvo *De artificio loquendi*'" (Cambridge, Trinity College, R.14.22, fol. 2r). The complete *accessus* is quoted below.

120. See above, note 65.

121. *EC accessus,* 3.

122. *EC accessus,* 56.

123. *EC accessus,* 41–42.

124. *EC accessus,* 4 and 25.

125. *EC accessus,* 59.

126. This term is often translated into English as "morals," but some of the examples of what kind of *mores* are taught indicates that a broader and less judgemental term is meant. An *accessus* to *Pamphilus,* for example, says that "the usefulness is that, after this book has been read thoroughly, anyone should know how to get beautiful girls for himself . . . " (Woods, "Rape," 64). On "ethics" in medieval schools as kinds of behaviour, see also Jaeger, *Envy of Angels,* 140.

accessus to the *Poetria nova* in a manuscript in Florence: "[I]t was asked in what part of philosophy it should be classified; we say that it is classified as poetry itself, which is philosophy veiled."[127]

Below is a complete transcription of a Type C *accessus* added as a single long paragraph to a thirteenth-century English manuscript of the *Poetria nova* that belonged to the Dominicans at Leicester in the fifteenth century.[128] The works in this composite manuscript, Cambridge, Trinity College, R.14.22 (including a popular epitome of the Troy story, the only surviving copy of Matthew of Vendôme's "Pyramus and Thisbe," and a copy of the *Tria sunt*), are typical of English anthologies from this period: short pieces of verse based on classical subjects along with rhetorical treatises.[129] The *accessus* in MS R.14.22 quoted next (one of two added to the text at the beginning) includes an additional category, the *causa suscepti operis,* the reason for undertaking the work, but it lacks the *modus agendi/tractandi,* and the discussion of the title is at the very end, preceded by the treatment of *ordo* or arrangement. The commentator begins by listing the questions that will be answered concerning the work, or, as he frames it, the author. The statement that Geoffrey wrote the work to cover the low and middle styles is unusual, although praise of him in comparison with Horace is not unknown.[130] Note his conflation of rhetoric with poetics and the assumption that what one learns from the *Poetria nova* is the art of both prose and verse. The end of the *accessus* focuses on words etymologically related to *poetria.* Note the generally positive attitude toward the *Poetria nova* and the emphasis on connection rather than distinction, and also the equating of "studying thoroughly" with "memorization." Finally, this commentator like many others reinforces the learning of terms by using etymologically related words in the definitions, a pedagogical technique that I have tried to reproduce in the translations, even though it has resulted in tautological explanations like those of the aim (*intentio*).

---

127. Florence, Biblioteca Medicea Laurenziana, Strozzi 137, fol. 1r, quoted in Allen, *Ethical Poetic*, 54.

128. Cambridge, Trinity College, R.14.22, *PN* on fols. 3r–44r; the *accessus* quoted next is on fol. 2r. Interlinear glosses and marginal comments in various hands as well as another *accessus* (on fol. 1v) were also added. On this manuscript see Munari, *Catalogo*, 38–39 (23); Camargo, "*Tria sunt*," 937; Polak, *Western Europe*, 273; James, *Western Manuscripts*, 2.304–6; and other sources listed in their bibliographies. Another folio of this manuscript is reproduced as plate 3.

129. On the Troy poem, "Pergama flere volo" (Walther 13985), often anthologized in English manuscripts, see Rigg, *History of Anglo-Latin Literature*, passim.

130. See "Better than the Ancients" earlier in this chapter.

A TYPE C *ACCESSUS*

1 O HOLY FATHER, WONDER OF THE WORLD At the beginning [of our study] of this author,[131] as with any other, these questions occur to the inquiring mind: what was the reason for undertaking the work? what is its aim? its usefulness? to what part of philosophy does it belong? what is the arrangement [of parts]? and what is its title? Therefore, since cause precedes effect, the first question is the **reason for undertaking the work.** And the answer is because Master Geoffrey of Vinsauf the Englishman, seeing that many students were unskilled (*rudes*[132]) and lazy in the art of writing prose and verse, conceived in his mind a specific treatise, *On Skill in Speaking*,[133] for their instruction. The reason for initiating the work can be explained as follows: because Horace did not treat the three levels of style comprehensively except for the grand style, this author, aiming to make up for Horace's defect, aims to treat thoroughly the low and middle styles. Its **subject** is poetry made for the purpose of usefulness. Every poem (*carmen*) that is perfected by a poet for [its] usefulness or for enjoyment ought to be studied carefully, to which Horace attests, saying, "Poets wish either to instruct or to delight" {*Ars* 333}. The **aim** concerns the subject he aims at primarily. The **usefulness** is twofold, both general and specific. The general usefulness ascribed to every work is that when it has been read and examined, the useful things taught in it are committed to memory. The specific usefulness is that when this book has been studied thoroughly and its eloquence appreciated, we end up instructed in the art of prose and verse. It belongs under **ethics,** because authors of a rhetorical discourse (*oracionis*) often put their books under ethics, that is, under moral philosophy. There are three branches of philosophy, namely [1] ethics, that is moral knowledge, and the word comes from [the Greek] *ethis* (morals) and *ycos* (knowledge) that is, knowledge of *mores;* [2] logic, that is, rational knowledge, and it comes from *logos* (reason) and *ycos* (knowledge); [3] physics, that is, natural knowledge, and it comes from *phisis* (nature) and *ycos* (knowledge). The book follows **a natural order:** first, he teaches one to consider the subject matter and to generate (lit.: devise) it there at "If one [has a house to build]." Second, to arrange the material generated in a specific order there at "In the hidden chamber of the mind" (60). Third, to amplify the subject matter, saying that there are "eight" ways to amplify a subject (103). Fourth, to abbreviate the subject matter there at "If [you wish] to be brief" (690). Fifth, to give the subject matter rhetorical color there at "Whether it be brief or long" (737).

---

131. The more common and less awkward phrase is "At the beginning of this book," but in this *accessus* the first two categories are phrased in terms of the author.

132. On this word as a descriptor for students of the *Poetria nova*, see "Reading between the Lines" in chapter 2.

133. The phrase could be simply descriptive, e.g., "a treatise on artistic expression," but it is cited as the title at the end of the *accessus*; see also note 65 above.

Sixth, to commit the subject to the memory there at "If you wish to remember all that reason invents" (1969). Seventh and last, to say the subject matter aloud there at "You wish to know the whole thing" (1990).[134] The **title** is as follows: "Here begins the book of Master Geoffrey of Vinsauf *On Skill in Speaking.*" And the word "title" comes from *titan, -nis,* which is the sun, since just as the sun illuminates the world, so the title illuminates the whole work to come. [The title] could be the *Poetria. Poetria* (poetics) is the art of devising a theme, arranging what has been devised, adorning what has been arranged, memorizing what has been adorned, delivering aloud what has been memorized. Poesis is the art devoted to this subject, as the author attests in the text of his poem where he says "To clothe the subject with words let [*poesis*] come forward" (61). A poem is defined by Tully as follows: a poem is something made for the enjoyment or the use of individuals and explaining the backgrounds of actions. . . . A poet is one who puts the poems into meter. Now let us go to the text itself (*ad litteram*): "Holy Father" (1), etc.[135]

A newer kind of *accessus* arose after Latin translations of Arabic translations of Aristotle's works made most of them available in western Europe. The influ-

---

134. An error for the beginning of the section on delivery, "In reciting aloud, let three tongues speak" (2031). The manuscript has "cupis" for "sitis"; cf. "velis," a variant reading in Faral.

135. "I PAPA STUPOR MUNDI, etc. In principio istius auctoris sicut cuiuslibet alterius ista occiderunt inquisitioni, scilicet que causa suscepti operis? que intencio? que utilitas? cui parti philosophie supponatur? quis ordo? quis titulus? Cum ergo causa precedat effectum, inde est primo querenda **causa suscepti operis.** Et talis est quod magister Galfridus de Uino Saluo anglicus plures uidens rudes et ignares in arte dictatoris et uersificatoris constituit in animo suo ad eorum instructionem tractatum quemdam *De artificio loquendi.* Quia uero causa prohemii sic potest <expla>nari quia Oracius de triplici stilo non plene tractauit nisi de grandiloco, quare auctor iste defectum illius suplere intendens humili et mediocri in hoc libro intendit pertractare. **Materia** uero ipsius est poesis causa utilitatis facta. Omne enim carmen quod <ab> aliquo poeta perficitur causa utilitatis uel delectacionis pertractari debet, quod testatur Oracius dicens 'Aut prodesse uolunt aut delectare poete' {*Ars* 333}. **Intencio** autem uersatur circa materiam de qua principaliter intendit. **Vtilitas** autem est duplex, scilicet generalis et specialis, generalis que assignatur in quolibet libro ut perlecto libro utilia que in eo docentur memoria commendentur; specialis ut perlecto libro isto et uiso eiusdem elocucione instructi simus in arte dictatoria et uersificatoria. **Etice** supponitur quia oracionis sepe auctores libros suos etice supponunt, idest morali sciencie. Et sunt partes philosophie tres, scilicet ethica, idest moralis sciencia, et dicitur ab *ethis,* mos, et *ycos,* sciencia: quasi moralis sciencia; logica, idest ratiocinalis sciencia et dicitur a *logos,* sermo, et *ycos,* sciencia; phisica, idest naturalis sciencia et dicitur a *phisis,* natura, et *ycos,* sciencia. **Ordo** huius libri naturalis(?) est: primitus docet materiam [gi]cogitare et inuenire ibi, 'Si quis,' etc. (43). Secundo materiam ordinare inuentam ibi, 'Mentis in archano,' etc. (60). Tercio materiam ampliare, dicens quod 'octo' sunt que ampliant materiam (103), quarto materiam abreuiare ibi, 'Si breuis esse,' etc. (690). Quinto materiam colorare ibi, 'Si breuis aut longus' (737). Sexto materiam memorie commendare ibi, 'Omnia que recipit ratio,' etc. (1969). Septimo et ultimo materiam pronunciare ibi, 'Scire cupis hanc rem' (1990). **Titulus** talis est 'Incipit liber magistri Galfridi de Uino Saluo *De artificio loquendi.*' Et dicitur titulus a *titan, -nis,* quod est sol quia sicut sol illuminat mundum, sic titulus totum opus subsequens. *** autem sit *Poetria. Poetria* est ars thema inueniendi, inuentum disponendi, dispositum exornandi, ornatum memorandi, memoratum pronunciandi. Poesis est ars circa materiam ut testatur auctor in textu poematis, ubi dicit, 'Materiam uerbis ueniat,' etc. (61). Poema sic describitur a Tullio: poema est factum causa delectationis uel utilitatis siue utriusque personarum et negociorum proprietates exprimens. Poeta est ille qui carmina fingit ad metra. Modo ad litteram accedamus: 'Papa' etc. (1)" (Cambridge, Trinity College, R.14.22, fol. 2r). When the manuscript was rebound, some of the inside edges were cut off and there is a bad discoloration at the top, making some words nearly illegible.

ence of the *Physics* and *Metaphysics* led to an *accessus* based on the four Aristotelian causes.[136] Following are excerpts gathered from various commentaries that show how the four causes were applied to the *Poetria nova:*

THE ARISTOTELIAN FOUR CAUSES

causa efficiens: the **efficient cause** or "motivating agent of the text," that is, the author. "The efficient cause was *magister* Geoffrey of Vinsauf. . . . [137]

causa materialis: the **material cause,** that is, the subject matter (the same as number 2 above). "The material cause of this book is the craft of the prose writer (*dictatoris facultatis*)."[138]

causa formalis: the **formal cause** or formal principles, often overlapping with number 4 above, *modus agendi* (method of proceeding), e.g., "The formal [cause] is the aspect of the work consisting of the method of proceeding in its organization: the method of proceeding [in this book] is twofold: metrical and by division into chapters."[139] Often the formal cause is subdivided into the *forma tractandi* (the form of the treatment, "the way in which a book treats its subject matter"), and the *forma tractatus* (the form of the treatise, "the separation into books and chapters, and their order"),[140] as in the *accessus* of another English manuscript translated below.

causa finalis: the **final cause,** the author's "ultimate end or objective in writing,"[141] sometimes the same as either the *intentio,* the author's aim or purpose (3) above, or the *utilitas,* the usefulness of the book (6): "The final cause, or usefulness, is that through this book we can devote [ourselves] to the poetic art."[142]

Thus, the topics of Type C *accessus* and the Aristotelian or four-causes *accessus* overlap and reinforce each other. Indeed, two of the examples above come from a second *accessus* added to Cambridge, Trinity College, R.14.22, the same manuscript whose Type C *accessus* was translated above.

We can see how the Type C categories could be restructured as the Aristote-

---

136. Minnis and Scott, *Medieval Literary Criticism,* 2–3.

137. "Causa efficiens fuit magister Galfridus Vinesauf . . ." (Cambridge, Trinity College, R.14.22, fol. 1v). See also the epigraphs in the first section of this chapter.

138. "causa materialis est ars dictatoris facultatis" (Pistoia, Archivo Capitolare del Duomo, C. 143, fol. 1r).

139. "Et formalis est qualitas operis constans in modo agendi in ordine; modus agendi est duplex, metricus et per capitula distinctus" (Cambridge, Trinity College, R.14.22, fol. 1v).

140. These definitions of "forma tractandi" and "forma tractatus" are by Jordanus of Saxony, quoted in Rouse and Rouse (following Grabmann and Pinborg), *Authentic Witnesses,* 218.

141. Minnis and Scott, *Medieval Literary Criticism,* 3.

142. "Causa finalis siue vtilitas est, vt per hunc librum <possumus> [possumus *MS*] addicere artem poeticam" (Uppsala, Universitetsbibliotheket, C 40, fol. 20v). On "vtilitas" as a literary category, see Glendinning, "Pyramus and Thisbe," 68; and "Shorter is Better" in chapter 2.

lian causes in an *accessus* in Oxford, Corpus Christi College, 144.[143] This manuscript was put together by the English Benedictine John Bamburgh between 1420–1432 and contains texts of divergent levels, from an "abc" (a pen trial?) to astronomical texts.[144] Bamburgh wrote the signed *accessus* to the *Poetria nova* in space left at the end of Alan of Lille's *De planctu Nature,* right before the text of the *Poetria nova.* It provides a condensed version of some of the material found in the *Early Commentary* (a continental treatment of the *Poetria nova*) and standard in many earlier *accessus,* but here adapted to Aristotelian terminology.

At the beginning of this book, we should examine the four causes: The **material cause** is crafted eloquence, that is rhetoric, according to which he teaches poets to speak in prose and in verse. Note following this that the book principally consists of the five parts of rhetoric, so that if one is missing, it cannot be called rhetoric, just as a house is whole if its parts, namely foundation, roof, and walls, are there. These are the parts of rhetoric: Invention, Arrangement, Style, Memory, and Delivery. "Invention is the devising of true things or things that seem to be true. Arrangement is the order and distribution of parts, which shows what ought to be put in which positions. Style is the adaptation of suitable words and thoughts. Memory is the firm retention of thoughts and words in the mind. Delivery is the graceful moderation of voice, expression, and gesture"[145] {*Ad Her.* 1.3}. Such is the order of these parts. For when an orator wishes to persuade the judge of something, first he deliberates by what reasons he can render his cause probable; this is Invention. Next he arranges what is to be gathered in the beginning, middle, and end; this is Arrangement. Next he devises by what ornamentation of words and thoughts to express the individual parts; this is Style. Next he puts the individual parts in the memory so that they can be recalled; this is Memory. Afterwards he examines how to moderate the voice, expression, and gesture; this is Delivery. And since the discourse is the instrument of a rhetor, note that it has six parts: the Introduction, Narration, Division, Confirmation, Refutation, Peroration or Conclusion. And this book consists secondarily of these parts, of which one may find examples in Tully [*Rhetorica ad Herennium*].[146] The **formal cause** is divided into the form of the treatment and the form of the treatise. The **form of the treatise** consists in the division of the work.[147] The **form of the treatment** is the method of proceeding, and it is rhetorical [that is, divided into the parts of an oration]. It should be noted that the author is both a rhetorician and an orator. There is this distinction between them: the rhetorician is one who passes on the

---

143. On Oxford, Corpus Christi College, 144, see Coxe, *Catalogus Codicum manuscriptorum,* 2.56–57; and Krochalis, "Alain de Lille," 149–154.

144. On Bamburgh and this manuscript, see also Clark, *Monastic Renaissance,* 145–146, with a plate of the "abc" and *accessus* to the *Poetria nova;* also "Excursus on the English Orbit" in chapter 4.

145. *EC accessus,* 6–10.

146. Cf. *EC accessus,* 17–25.

147. The division into parts was discussed earlier under the "Material Cause" of the art of rhetoric.

art of speaking, the orator is one who performs according to this art. This author does both, for he passes on rhetoric rhetorically. In the same way it is something different to treat the subject of verse and to treat that subject in verse while writing about the art.[148] The **efficient cause** is Master Geoffrey the Englishman. The final cause is both general and specific. The general final cause: to instruct the reader / teacher (*lectorem*)[149] in rhetoric. The specific final cause: the problem of Richard King of England, who offended the pope by means of some sin unknown to us.[150] The title refers to the "New Poetics" to differentiate it from the "Old Poetics" that Horace wrote, which begins, "If a painter chose to join a horse to a human head" {*Ars* 1}. BAMBURGH[151]

By this point the four causes had been around for a long time. Bamburgh's *accessus* lacks the integrated analysis of the Type C introduction to the *Early Commentary* or the detailed, multilayered Aristotelian approaches to the *Poetria nova* common in universities in central Europe. But it provides the necessary framework: the double structure of the text (analyzed in the next section of this chapter), the author's dual role as rhetorician and orator, the historical background and the practical value of the text, and the position of the *Poetria nova* in the historical tradition—not a bad introduction after all, and one that would have been useful in almost any context.[152] The *Poetria nova* was a service text,

---

148. Cf. *EC accessus,* 42–52.

149. On *lector* see Teeuwen, *Vocabulary of Intellectual Life,* 85–87.

150. On this "unknown sin" of King Richard's, see "A Double Structure" next.

151. "In principio huius libri videndum est de quattuor eius causis. **Causa materialis** est artificiosa eloquencia. Hec est rethorica, secundum quam docet poetas et prosaice loqui et metrice. Unde nota quod ex quinque partibus rethorice principaliter constat liber iste, quarum si vna desit rethorica dici non potest, sicut domus est integra si sint partes, scilicet fundamentum tectum et paries. Sunt autem iste partes: Invencio, dispositio, eloqutio, memoria et <pronunciatio> [permutacio *MS*]. 'Invencio autem est rerum verarum uel verisimilium excogitacio. Dispositio est ordo et distribucio rerum que demonstrat quid quibus locis sit ponendum. Elocutio est idoneorum uerborum et sententiarum accommodacio. Memoria est firma rerum in animo conceptio. <Pronunciatio> [permutacio *MS*] est vocis, vultus et gestus cum venustate moderacio.' {*Ad Her.* 1.3} Istarum partium talis est ordo. Orator enim cum vult aliquid persuadere iudici primo aput se cogitat quibus racionibus causam probabilem reddat, ecce inuencio. Deinde disponit que in principio, medio, vel fine sint collocanda, ecce disposicio. Postea inuenit quo ornatu verborum et sententiarum singula proferat, ecce elocucio. Deinde singula in memoria reponit ut recapitulet. Ecce memoria. Post hec qualiter moderetur vocem vultum et gestum inspicit. Ecce <pronunciatio> [permutatio *MS*]. Et quia oracio est instrumentum rethoris, nota quod sex sunt species rethorice. Exordium. Narracio. Particio. Confirmacio. Confutacio. Peroracio siue conclusio, et ex istis partibus secundario constat liber iste quarum exempla habentur in Tullio. **Causa formalis** diuiditur in formam tractatus et formam tractandi. **Forma tractatus** consistit in diuisione libri. **Forma tractandi** est modus agendi et ille est rhetoricus. Et notandum quod auctor in hoc libro est rethor et orator. Inter quos talis est differentia, quod rethor est qui tradit artem loquendi, orator est qui agit secundum illam artem. Iste autor facit utrumque, tradit enim rethoricam rethorice sicut aliud est agere de versibus et agere versifice artem et de arte. **Causa efficiens** est magister Galfridus Anglicus. **Causa finalis** communis et privata. Communis instruere lectorem in rethorica. Privata negotium Ricardi regis Anglie qui culpa nobis ignota papam offenderat. **Titulus** est de *Nova poetria* ad differentiam veteris quam composuit Oracius que sic incipit, 'Humano capiti equum pictor' {*Ars* 1}. BAMBWRGH" (Oxford, Corpus Christi College, 144, fol. 18v)

152. See Clark, *Monastic Renaissance,* 145–146 and 233–234 on the background of this manuscript; also "Excursus on the English Orbit" in chapter 4.

not an avant garde one; for such works, changes in academic fashion trickled down (or up) slowly. Commentators were more practical and eclectic than doctrinaire, and they used whatever helped make sense of the text. Almost every variation of the introductory categories is extant in the commentary tradition of the *Poetria nova.*

A DOUBLE STRUCTURE

This work can be divided according to the part of rhetoric and according to a rhetorical utterance.[153]

—Brescia, Biblioteca Civica Queriniana, A.IV.10

Geoffrey rhetorically shaped (*edidit*) the *Poetria nova* for writers and so that he might reconcile the King of England with the pope through his book.[154]

—Hugh of Trimburg

The shorter the *accessus,* the greater the focus on a single aspect of the *Poetria nova.* The brief introductory note at the bottom of the first folio of the *Poetria nova* in a fourteenth-century manuscript of school texts in Brescia, for example, provides a stark outline of the *Poetria nova*'s double structure according to the parts of rhetoric and the parts of a rhetorical discourse (plate 1)[155]:

HOLY FATHER etc. This work can be divided according to the part of rhetoric and according to a rhetorical composition (*sermonem*).[156] In the first way it is divided into five sections according to the five parts of rhetoric, namely Invention, Arrangement, Style, Memory, and Delivery.[157] He treats Invention there at "If one has a house to build, etc." (43), Arrangement there at "In order that the pen may know" (78),[158] Style at "Whether brief or long" (737), Memorization at "The little cell" (1972), Delivery at "In reciting aloud" (2031). In the second way it is divided into six sections according to the six parts of a rhetori-

---

153. "Opus istud potest <diuidi> [didiui *MS*] secundum partem rethorice et secundum sermonem rethoricum" (Brescia, Biblioteca Civica Queriniana, A.IV.10, fol. 93r).

154. "Ganifredus rethorice novam poetriam / Edidit scribentibus et ut conciliaret / Pape regem Anglie per librumque placaret" (Hugh of Trimburg, *Registrum multorum auctorum*, 300–302).

155. This manuscript also contains Horace's *Ars poetica* and Boethius's *Consolation of Philosophy;* see Beltrami, "Index codicum classicorum latinorum," 42–43; and Passalacqua and Smith, *Codices Boethiani* 3.56 (28).

156. Cf. "Sermons?" in chapter 2.

157. Fredborg, "Ciceronian Rhetoric and the Schools," argues that while "the medieval *Artes Poeticae* also pay their respect to Ciceronian rhetoric by treating all five duties of the orator: invention, disposition, style, and a little on memory and delivery, in practice, however, this rhetorical framework meant little compared with their concern for Horatian decorum and their preoccupation with style and the topics" (33–34).

158. This is not where most commentators and modern editors make the break, but Geoffrey does say here what he is going to do next, which is to discuss order.

cal composition, namely the Introduction, Narration, Division, Confirmation, Refutation, and Conclusion. The Introduction is treated there at "O Holy Father, wonder" (1), the Narration at "If one has a house to build" (43), the Division at "The material's order may follow two possible courses" (88), the Confirmation at "If you heed the directives carefully" (1842), the Refutation at "It is, however, of primary importance" (1920), the Conclusion at "Now I have crossed the sea" (2066).[159]

The congruence of the two structures is clearer in some places than others. Let us look at Margaret Nims's division of the structure of the *Poetria nova* in her translation of the work, where she draws on Edmond Faral's outline of the *Poetria nova* in his edition. Both of these scholars were familiar with many manuscripts of the text. Drawing on the commentators' identification of the parts of the work with the parts of rhetoric, Nims divides the *Poetria nova* as follows:

STRUCTURE OF THE *POETRIA NOVA*

Dedication [to Pope Innocent III] (lines 1–42).
I. General Remarks on Poetry; Divisions of the Present Treatise (43–86).
II. Ordering the Treatise (87–202).
III. Amplification and Abbreviation (203–689).
    A. Amplification.
    B. Abbreviation.
IV. Ornaments of Style (737–1968).
    1. Difficult Ornament [Tropes].
    2. Easy Ornament [Figures of Words and Figures of Thoughts].[160]
    3. Theory of Conversions [the effect of changing the expression of a concept from one part of speech to another].

---

159. "PAPA STUPOR etc. Opus istud potest <diuidi> [didiui *MS*] secundum partem rethorice et secundum sermonem rethoricum. Primo modo diuiditur in partes quinque secundum quod sunt quinque partes rethorice, scilicet inuentio, dispositio, eloqutio, memoria, et pronuntiatio. De inuentione determinatur illic, 'Si quis habet fundare,' etc. (43). De dispositione illic, 'Neu stilus ignoret' (78). De elocutione ibi, 'Si breuis aut longus' (737). De memoria ibi, 'Cellula que' (1972). De pronuntiatione ibi, 'In recitante' (2031). Secundo autem modo diuiditur in partes sex, secundum quod sunt sex partes sermonis rethorici, scilicet exordium, narratio, diuisio, confirmatio, confutatio, et conclusio. De exordio agitur illic, 'Papa stupor' (1). De narratione, 'Si quis habet fundare' (43). De diuisione, 'Ordo bifurcat iter' (88). De confirmatione, 'Si bene dicta notes' (1842). De confutatione, 'In primis igitur' (1920). De conclusione, 'Iam mare transcurri' (2066)" (Brescia, Biblioteca Civica Queriniana, A.IV.10, fol. 93r).

160. Faral and Nims use the terms "Difficult Ornament" and "Easy Ornament" from the *Documentum* (Far. p. 284) for what Geoffrey in the *Poetria nova* calls "transsumptio" (metaphoric language) and "flores verborum et sententiarum" (the flowers [figures] of words and of thoughts) respectively. The figures were considered comparatively easy or "levis" (light) because, although at times complex, they do not involve transferred or figural meaning as do the tropes, which were also called "gravis" (weighty, or serious—hence, difficult). See "The Usefulness of the *Poetria nova*" earlier in this chapter and "Comedy and the *Commedia*" in chapter 3.

4. Theory of Determinations [qualifying a word by means of modifiers[161]].

5. Various Prescriptions.

    Choice of Words.

    Comic Style.

    Faults to Avoid.

V. Memory (1969–2030).

VI. Delivery (2031–2065).

Epilogue (2066–2115).

The medieval commentators' division of the text into the five parts of rhetoric (invention, arrangement, style, memory, and delivery) ignores the frame of the Dedication and Epilogue and collapses numbers III and IV, but otherwise it divides the text the same way: Invention, or finding the material, corresponds with part of Nims's section I, General Remarks on Poetry, where Geoffrey talks about developing the ideas in the mind before putting them into a particular form; arrangement, or the ordering of the material, corresponds with section II; style, or putting the content into ornamented discourse, with both III and IV (amplification and abbreviation as well as the tropes and figures); and memory and delivery correspond with sections of V and VI of the same names. The commentators' secondary division of the text into the parts of a rhetorical composition (introduction, narration, division, proof, rebuttal or refutation, and conclusion) foregrounds those parts ignored by the first: the Dedication (called the introduction) and Epilogue (called the conclusion).

According to this double organization of the text, Geoffrey's work is not just about the art of rhetoric (the first structure), but is itself a rhetorical argument directed at Pope Innocent III (the second structure).[162] What Geoffrey is arguing for does not become clear until the Epilogue, where, in a section mentioned earlier that is not found in all manuscripts, Geoffrey again addresses Innocent, here asking help for "our prince" (*principe nostro,* 2089 and 2096), also referred to in the passage as "king" (*regemque,* 2094). Here is the part of the Epilogue in which Geoffrey pleads with the Pope:

> Do you not see, if you regard the true qualities of our prince, that he has become the soldier of the cross and of Christ and sword of the entire church? Devotion so great calls for love, not for hatred; for praise, not reproach; for rewards and not penalties. Therefore, you who conquer all else, allow yourself to be conquered here. Be pleased to turn, and desire the king to return. . . . I plead for our prince. (*PN* 2089–2097)

---

161. See "Student Determination" in chapter 2.

162. There is a second dedication at the very end of the poem (to a William, noted in the Table of Contents quoted above) not treated in either structure.

This passage is interpreted by modern scholars as a reference either to Innocent's Interdict of England under King John from 1208–1214[163] or to John's political impasse with the English nobles after Magna Carta and his later attempt to gain Innocent's support in 1215 by taking up "the crusader's cross."[164]

But most medieval commentators assume that Geoffrey is referring to John's much more popular brother and predecessor, and that the passage is a plea for Innocent's help in freeing Richard I of England from imprisonment. The king had been captured by Duke Leopold of Austria, "who handed him over to the Emperor Henry VI, who held him for ransom."[165] Sometimes, however, the English king is not identified or is identified differently, as, for example, in the gloss on this part of the Epilogue by Bartholomew of Pisa: "He supplicates for Henry the King of England, who is a soldier of Christ and the third sword of the Church."[166] Or the king is identified as Richard I but for the wrong reason: Guizzardo of Bologna states that Geoffrey was sent to Rome to plead indulgence for "Richard of England, who had killed Thomas of Canterbury [à Becket] to obtain the treasures of the church,"[167] whereas it was Henry II who had trouble with Becket.

The interpretation of the *Poetria nova* as a rhetorical argument begins with the Dedication, about which the Early Commentator states, "As we learn from the text of this book, [the author] served as the emissary of King Richard of England; the king's cause was so bad that it had alienated the mind of the listener [that is, Innocent]. Whence it seems that the whole book is a Subtle Approach to the cause which is to be treated at the end."[168] Richard's misdeed may refer to the rumor that Richard had helped in the assassination of Conrad of Montferrat in 1189 in Palestine[169] or perhaps to his reputed homosexuality.[170] At the end of the work the Early Commentator states,

2066 NOW I HAVE CROSSED THE SEA Note here the Conclusion, which is the last

---

163. Cf. Far., p. 26; Gallo, *Poetria nova*, 127; and Nims, pp. 109–110 (for the various ways that this passage could refer to John).

164. Turner, *King John*, 233, quoting Cheney, "The Eve of Magna Carta," 313. An earlier version of this discussion appeared in Woods, "Innocent III."

165. Rigg, *History of Anglo-Latin Literature*, 107.

166. "Supplicat pro Henrico rege anglie qui est Christi miles et tertius ensis ecclesie" (Rome, Biblioteca Casanatense, 311, fol. 68v).

167. "Hic autem propter ueniam impet<r>andam a summo pontifice ad curiam Romanam pro Richardo rege Anglie qui beatum Thomam de Conturbia interfecerat ob thesauros ecclesie habendos" (Vatican City, BAV Ottob. lat. 3291, fol. 1r). The interpretation of this section of the *PN* as an attempt to placate the pope for the killing of Thomas à Becket probably comes from Hugh of Trimburg's *Registrum multorum auctorum*, 304–306, cited in Far., p. 31.

168. *EC accessus*, 32–33.

169. Gillingham, *Richard the Lionheart*, 206. See also Nicholson, *Chronicle of the Third Crusade*, 384. For a summary of Anglo-Latin verse both for and against Richard, see Rigg, *History of Anglo-Latin Literature*, 105–108.

170. Gillingham analyses the evidence but dismisses it as a modern misunderstanding (7, 107, 130, 161, 162, 283, and [with a survey of the scholarship, including that with which he is in disagreement] 298).

of the six parts of the discourse, for he concludes artfully what he had proposed. With praise of the pope this work began, with praise of him it ends; he praises him here for his power and his strength, which are necessary for powerful men. And at this point he also reveals the cause for which he wrote this book to the pope. He put the cause not in the beginning, but in the end, for this reason: because the King of England's cause was so shameful on account of his serious crime that the crime had alienated the mind of the hearer from the cause. For this reason, if he had revealed his cause in the beginning, the rest of the book would not have been accepted.[171]

There is, of course, a problem with interpreting the whole work as a plea for King Richard: he is already dead in the most famous passage in the work, the series of apostrophes quoted above.[172] But since this inconsistency was discussed by a few commentators only, I address it later.[173]

The division of the text into the five parts of a rhetorical argument fits particularly well with the frame passages that address Innocent, and at a more abstract level other parts of Geoffrey's teachings accord well with the function assigned to them. Geoffrey's opening remarks on how to start a poem become the narration or statement of events of a case; the discussion of natural and artificial order felicitously becomes the division of the argument; the confirmation includes Geoffrey's discussion of word choice and comic style; and the "refutation" section of a discourse includes Geoffrey's list of "Faults to Avoid." The ingenuity that went into this series of correspondences may have been one of the attractions of the *Poetria nova* for medieval teachers: the more one looked at this text, the more one found.

While various commentators sometimes locate the divisions between the parts of either structure at slightly different places in the text, the sequence and the interweaving of the two structures are consistent. Following is a summary showing both based on the description of the double structure in the *Early Commentary.* The five parts of rhetoric (**Invention, Arrangement, Style, Memory, and Delivery**) and the six parts of a discourse (*Introduction, Narration, Division, Confirmation, Rebuttal, and Conclusion*) are identified below in bold (the latter in Italics).

THE DOUBLE RHETORICAL STRUCTURE OF THE *POETRIA NOVA*

The Dedication is the *Introduction* to the work (1–42). The first section of the text proper, about planning a work before beginning to write it down, both covers **Invention** and constitutes the *Narration* portion of the discourse (43–86).

---

171. *EC* 2066, 1–4.
172. See "The Success of the *Poetria nova*" above.
173. "Stand and Counterstand" in chapter 3.

The discussion of natural and artificial order both concerns **Arrangement** and is the *Division* section of the discourse (87–202). **Style** (203–1842) encompasses Amplification and Abbreviation as well as the Tropes and Figures and the Theories of Conversion and Determination. The *Confirmation* portion of the discourse (1842–1919) comes at what Nims calls "Choice of Words," the first section under her "Various Prescriptions." The *Rebuttal* is at "Faults to Avoid" (1920–1968). **Memory** (1969–2030) and **Delivery** (2031–2065) are treated next. At the end comes the *Conclusion* (2066 ff.).[174]

Commentators were careful to point out where each part of each structure began and especially where the two structures coincided. For example, the first gloss after the *accessus* in the Brescia manuscript occurs at the beginning of the famous house metaphor used by Geoffrey of Vinsauf to describe the careful planning and preparation needed in writing: "If a man has a house to build, his impetuous hand does not run into action . . . (43 ff.). According to medieval commentators, Narration and Invention coincide here: "IF A MAN HAS A HOUSE TO BUILD This can be called Narration according to one method of dividing the text and Invention according to the other, as was made clear above."[175] Vinsauf's description was used by that other famous English Geoffrey, Chaucer, in his narrative of the relationship of *Troilus and Criseyde,* in which context it describes the importance of careful planning as Pandarus devises a scenario to generate the seduction of Criseyde by Troilus:

> For everi wight that hath an hous to founde
> Ne renneth naught the werk for to bygynne
> With rakel hond; but he wol bide a stounde,
> And sende his hertes line out from withinne.[176]

This passage comes at both an important turning point in Chaucer's larger structure (Narration, the second part of a rhetorical discourse, where the important events are outlined) as well as at the inception (Invention, the first part of rhetoric, the "devising of matter true or plausible, that would make the case convincing"[177]) of Pandarus's machinations leading to the climax of what he thinks will be the whole story. This double function of the passage

---

174. Adapted from Woods, "Teaching the Tropes." For a different interpretation of Geoffrey's structure, see Friis-Jensen, "Horace and the Early Writers," 381–382.

175. "43 SI QUIS HABET Hic potest dici narratio et inuentio, secundum alium et alium modum diuidendi, ut supra patuit" (Brescia, Biblioteca Civica Queriniana, A. IV. 10, fol. 93v). Here, as with other manuscripts, I have silently expanded the *lemma,* or initial quotation from the text, to render it comprehensible in English.

176. Chaucer, *Troilus and Criseyde,* I.1065–68. I borrowed the idea of using Chaucer's translation from Rigg, *History of Anglo-Latin Literature,* 109.

177. *Ad Her.* 1.3.

in Chaucer's work could be described in more abstract medieval terms in the same way that the same passage functions in the *Poetria nova* itself: it can be called Narration according to one method of looking at the text and Invention according to another.

PURPLE PATCHES

The *forma tractandi* is the same as the *modus agendi,* which is small units with transitions and the insertion of examples.[178]

—Guizzardo of Bologna

Works with noble beginnings and grand promises often have one or two purple patches so stitched on as to glitter far and wide . . . .[179]

—Horace

One way to look at the *Poetria nova,* according to Guizzardo of Bologna's description above, is as a series of techniques interspersed with examples. Later, echoing Horace, Guizzardo refers to "purple speech" (*sermone purpureo*) in paraphrasing the continuation of Geoffrey's house metaphor.[180] Geoffrey's rhetorical examples encompass a wide range of topics, and they vary in length from a few lines to almost a fifth of the text. Commentators note his command of tone and his ability to switch between serious and comic subjects (the latter an aspect of the *Poetria nova* suppressed in the excerpted proverbs discussed in the next section).

RHETORICAL EXAMPLES IN THE *POETRIA NOVA*

1. General remarks on the composition process as an architect's planning of a building, the grooming of a woman by her servant, and the responsibilities to guests of an attendant, host, and herald (43–87).
2. The forking branches of natural and artificial order and the techniques of beginning based on the story of King Minos, the murder of his son, Androgeos, and the betrayal of Scylla, the daughter of his enemy (87–158).
3. Apostrophes to the exultant, the presumptuous, the timid, and the overconfident (277–324).
4. Apostrophes on the death of King Richard (368–430).

---

178. "forma tractandi idem est quod modus agendi, qui est diuisiuus continuatiuus et exemplorum positurus" (Vatican City, BAV Ottob. lat. 3291, 1r). This is a very free translation; for a more exact rendering see "Meanwhile Back in Padua: Guizzardo of Bologna" in chapter 3.

179. *Ars* 14–16.

180. On "Certus preliminet" (56): "Dicit primo quod premittendum est in materia describenda uel sermone purpureo reserando sicut in edificiis" (Vatican City, BAV Ottob. lat. 3291, fol. 2ra).

5. The Boy Made Master (439–454).

6. Personifications: the lament of the cross (a short sermon with a call to arms), the lament of a worn-out tablecloth, and the boasting of a famous English Fortress (469–527).

7. Digression on love and springtime (538–553).

8. Descriptions of a beautiful naked woman, a beautiful dressed woman (with a list of Jove's lovers whose beauty she is said to surpass), a well-dressed table, and the feast for which it has been prepared (563–665).

9. Several versions of the story of the snow child, his adulterous mother, and his vindictive father (713–717 and 733–736).

10. Four passages exemplifying the power of metaphor as two seasons (spring and winter), the north wind, and a metal forge (792–829).

11. Adam's sin and Christ's redemption using the thirty-five figures of words (1098–1218).

12. Warnings to a pope: set pieces using the nineteen figures of thought with fourteen sub-categories, including a description of a lazy person, a dialogue between Pontius Pilate and the Jews, the thoughts and motives of Lucifer, and an anecdote about Alexander the Great (1280–1527).

13. Conversions: another beautiful woman (1668) and a plea for time to compose (1745).

14. Determinations: a badly set table (1768), Nero at table (1788), a well-set table (1798), someone dying (1804), and a gambler (1820).

13. The Three Friends: exemplification of comic style (1888–1909).

The appeal of Geoffrey's examples to both audiences—pope and pupils—is clear from the recurrence of certain themes, notably bodies, behavior, and tables of food. The marginal glosses in some manuscripts consist almost entirely of statements beginning "Here he exemplifies" (*Hic exemplificat*).

While all Geoffrey's display pieces are, like the apostrophes on the death of Richard quoted earlier, deliberately exaggerated, they are also distinctive, thematically tight, and above all memorable and imitable.[181] Several of these set pieces circulated independently, including the long passage on the death of the king and the speech of an English fortress already discussed, as well as the lament of the cross,[182] the anecdote of the three friends,[183] and the description of a lazy man. This last was a special favorite in the fifteenth century.[184] Two late-

---

181. In the discussion of these apostrophes in his full-length study of the *Poetria nova*, Jean-Yves Tilliette shows how an appreciative modern critic can help us to perceive Geoffrey's aesthetic accomplishments in such passages (*Des mots*, 107–111).

182. See "Sermons?" in chapter 2.

183. E.g., one of three excerpts in Oxford, Bodleian Library, Bodley 496, at fol. 241v; another is the description of the lazy man discussed next.

184. In addition to the two manuscripts discussed in the text and Oxford, Bodleian Library, Bodley 496, the excerpt (with others) is also found in Paris, BnF lat. 16708, fols. 37v–39r.

fifteenth-century humanist miscellanies[185] in Prague, Knihovna Metropolitní Kapituli, L 93 and Národní Knihovna České Republiky, III.E.27, suggest how it might have resonated in Renaissance classrooms. The passage is an example of *notatio* or character delineation, part of the mightily extended rhetorical display of all the figures of thought in which the potential pitfalls of being a pontiff are elaborated.[186] When read on its own in a pedagogical setting, however, the excerpt has an obvious and humorous relevance to students, and it contains an allusion to a work widely taught in schools:

> Do you know the procrastination of the lazy so-and-so? If he is called in the morning he refuses to hear. If he is summoned repeatedly, with insistent voice, he snores loudly through his nose, although he is awake. Forced at length by the shouts, but sluggish of speech, he gets his tongue moving and "What do you want with me?" he says.—"Get up! Come on!"—"It's night, let me sleep." "No, it's daytime; get up!"—"Ye gods! Look—I am getting up. Go ahead; I'll be there." But he doesn't follow the man he's fooling; and then: "Aren't you coming?" "I'd have been there by now, but I'm looking for my clothes and can't find them."—"It's no use—I know you, Birria. Get up at once!"—"Sir, I'm right with you." But he isn't; rather he turns his head to this side and that, or scratches his arms, or stretches his limbs. So he looks for any excuse for delay. With his lips, he is always coming—but not with his feet. So, coming, he never arrives—not he. Driven to it, perhaps, he drags his steps as he moves, matching a turtle's pace. (*PN* 1366–1380)

Geoffrey's little dialogue strikingly echoes a dialogue involving the lazy servant Birria in the Latin comedy *Geta* (61–68) by Vitalis of Blois.[187] In Prague MS L 93, the excerpt from the *Poetria nova* is specifically entitled "*Ganfredus de pigro servo*" ("Geoffrey on the Lazy Servant"), whereas in Prague III.E.27 it is simply called "*Ganfredus de pigro*" ("Geoffrey on the Lazy So-and-So").

---

185. Emil Polak categorizes Prague, Národní Knihovna České Republiky, III.E.27, copied in the late fifteenth or early sixteenth century, as a "humanist miscellany" (*Eastern Europe*, 68; 68–69 for description of manuscript); the excerpt is on fol. 121a and has interlinear glosses. On this manuscript see also Truhlár, *Catalogus* no. 502, 199, and *Iter ital.* 3.162. The same excerpt was also copied, glossed, and annotated on fol. 4r–v in Prague, Knihovna Metropolitní Kapituli, L 93 in 1499–1500 (e.g., see fol. 11a). On this manuscript see Podlaha, *Soupis Rukopisů*, 253–256.

186. Other aspects of this long passage are discussed in several sections of this study: "Sermons?" in chapter 2, "A Teacher of Notaries in Ravenna" in chapter 3, and "Jesuit Polymath Athanasius Kircher" in chapter 5.

187. *Geta* has been edited by Etienne Guilhou in Gustave Cohen, *La "comédie" latine*, 1.1–57, and by Ferruccio Bertini in *Commedie latine*, 3.139–242; it is translated along with other school dramas in Elliott, *Seven Medieval Latin Comedies*, 26–49. This short play is found with the *PN* in Chicago, University of Chicago Library, 476; Salamanca, Biblioteca Universitaria, 72; and in Vatican City, BAV Ottob. lat. 1961. There is also an excerpt from *Geta* in Novacella, Convento dei Canonici Regolari, 327. For an echo of this play in Guizzardo of Bologna's commentary on the *PN*, see "Women in the Margin" in chapter 3.

This passage would lend itself particularly well to in-class performance, where the association of *piger* with student could be heightened.[188] The humor and popularity of this passage and others like it may reflect the developing interest in Latin classroom comedies and colloquies in the Renaissance. Many of the rhetorical examples in the *Poetria nova* are all or partially in dialogue form, exercises in swift characterization via well-chosen narrative detail and dialogue. Texts like the *Poetria nova,* parts of which cry out for spirited rendition, demonstrate the aural and visual component of learning and may have facilitated the apprehension of dramatic detail as well.

PROVERBIAL WISDOM

> If your strength is but moderate, love what is moderate.[189]
>
> —excerpt from the *Poetria nova* in a proverb collection

Proverbs and exempla were almost as popular with medieval teachers as with their Renaissance counterparts, but the cost of writing materials earlier made it difficult for students to compile individual collections. The *Poetria nova* was mined almost immediately for statements about human experience that could be re-used in other compositions, a practice suggested by a thirteenth-century proverb collection in an English manuscript at the Bodleian Library, Rawlinson C.552. That the *Poetria nova* was a *florilegium* item in England so early is significant.[190] Tony Hunt remarks that this manuscript, along with another containing an index of the authors of which it was originally a part, "form a most instructive picture of the poets studied in the schools in the thirteenth century."[191] The excerpts are identified by author, title, or both and come from Virgil, Lucan, Walter of Châtillon (not identified), Juvenal, Horace, Persius, Ovid, Claudian, Alan of Lille (*Anticlaudianus,* and also later his *Parabolarum* with no identification), Prudentius, the *Poetria nova* (author not identified), Matthew of Vendôme, Maximian, "Homer,"[192] Arator, and Avianus. The sections are divided by author and work, and most of the headings identify the excerpts as proverbs, e.g., "Proverbs of Prudentius from the *Psychomachia.*" Each grouping is introduced by a sentence describing the subject of the work as

---

188. For another passage interpreted with students in mind (1745–1748), see "Conversion: The Origin of Style" in chapter 2.

189. *PN* 297 quoted in Oxford, Bodleian Library, Rawlinson C.552, fol. 14v.

190. Noted in Margaret Nims's unpublished notebooks.

191. Hunt, *Teaching and Learning Latin*, 1.28–29.

192. During the Middle Ages, the story of the Trojan War was known primarily through two Latin texts, the verse summary-paraphrase known as *Ilias latina* (McKinley, "Medieval Homer"), and *De excidio Troiae historia*, which purports to be an eyewitness account by Dares Phrygius.

a whole; on the excerpts from the *Poetria nova* the scribe says, "The subject of this section is held to be poetry or the art of letter-writing. . . . "[193] Ninety-five lines are quoted in all, presented in the text as thirty-eight separate examples; some taken together comprise single sections of the *Poetria nova*. These excerpts range from one to six lines, and they have been copied in order, as if by someone culling them directly from the text.

Following are those excerpts drawn from just the first 300 lines of the *Poetria nova* (a few out of order), about one-sixth of the text. Each proverb is formatted separately in the manuscript and in the translation below, although several groups comprise continuous passages in the text, as noted above. Only the first, on the problem of Innocent's name (discussed in "Off with His Head!" at the beginning of this chapter), is not a proverb. Its inclusion shows how memorable Geoffrey's acephalous pontiff was.

PROVERBS OF THE *POETRIA NOVA*

Holy Father, wonder of the world, if I say Pope Nocent I shall give you a name without a head, but if I add the head, your name will be at odds with the metre (1–3).

A touch of gall makes all the honey bitter; a single blemish disfigures the entire face (68–69).

If a man has a house to build, let his impetuous hand not push into action (43–44).[194]

The next five examples are drawn from Geoffrey's proverbs and exempla demonstrating how to begin the story of Minos at various points in the narrative.[195]

What is more desirable is more evanescent. All things augur decline, and prosperity is prompter to ruin. Ever blandly, fierce chance lays its snares, and happier fortunes wiftly anticipates flight (181–184).

Envy, vilest of things, wholly a mortal poison, good only for evil, malign only toward good, silently plots all malign counsel, and spreads abroad to the world whatever bitter thing it conceives (186–189).

Just is the law that strikes guile with grief; that turns grief back on the hand whence it issued (191–192).

Suddenly the grim gale rages under a joyous sky; the murky air pours rain after a sun serene (194–195).

---

193. "Huius materia perpenditur esse poesis, aut ars dictandi . . . " (Oxford, Bodleian Library, Rawlinson C.552, fol. 14v; the excerpts are on fols. 14v–15v).

194. Reading "currat" for "currit."

195. On this story see "Shaping the Narrative" in chapter 2.

Often the arrow learns to rebound on the archer, and the stroke, turned aside,
> to recoil on the striker (201–202).

The next five are a single continuous passage in the *Poetria nova* (282–289), part of the first example of apostrophe:

> If your venture has prospered, regard not beginnings but issues.
> From the setting sun, appraise the day, not from its rising.
> When you think that you have done all, the serpent lurks in the grass.
> Keep in mind, as example, the sirens; learn from them in a happier time ever
> to beware an unhappy.
> There is nothing stable in things of this world: after honey comes poison; dark
> night brings the day to a close, and clouds end calm weather.

And the next four are also a single unit (292–303):

> If vaulting presumption impudently puffs up a man, pour the oil of mild words
> on his swelling pride.
> Let your eyes go ahead of your footsteps; take stock of your mind and measure
> your strength. If you are strong, dare great things. If you are weak, lay
> lighter burdens on your shoulders.
> If your strength is but moderate, love what is moderate. Assume nothing which
> you are presumptuous in assuming. In all things virtue is one: to heed your
> true measure. Firmly imprint on your mind; although you are greater than
> others, feign yourself less, and deceive yourself in your own regard. Do not
> thus hurl others down to the depths, nor rate yourself above the heavens.
> Let deeds surpass words; boasting diminishes fame.[196]

The cumulative impression of these quotations is of a much more somber book than the *Poetria nova* itself; there are no excerpts from Geoffrey's treatment of digression, for example, although several of his general statements in it, e.g., "Love is a spur to grief," could have been included. This disjuncture of affect between a work and excerpts drawn from it is a common effect of proverbial *florilegia,* and such lugubriousness is even more striking in collections of proverbs from works of more salacious content like the popular medieval Latin drama *Pamphilus.*[197] Aphoristic expressions reinforced the pedagogical focus on small

---

196. These are followed by one copied out of order: "Though happily all man's affairs are subject to change, misfortune is wont to return with greater alacrity" (290–291). The other excerpts from the *Poetria nova* copied here are lines 309–12, 357–58, 337–39 (out of order), 365, 437–40, 489–91, 493, 640, 749–50, 876–78, 880–81, 1078–84, 1707–08, 1403–06 (also out of order), 1955–56, 1977–82, 1986–87, 2041–42.

197. Woods, "Rape," 71–72. A similar effect was accomplished by the early excerpting of Margery Kemp, by means of which published passages she was known as a devout anchoress for centuries until a manuscript of her complete text surfaced in 1934 (Summit, *Lost Property,* 126–138).

units of composition, but proverbs also provided fertile material for amplification and variation exercises of the kind at which Geoffrey of Vinsauf excels.

THE MASTERPIECE

The [*Poetria nova*] is resplendent with special beauty, equally charming in substance and words.[198]
—Eberhard the German, *Laborintus*

Although poetry did not have the elevated status during the Middle Ages that it has occupied in the post-romantic era, medieval teachers did associate specific qualities with successful poetry.[199] We have read premodern commentators' praise of Geoffrey's conciseness and clarity (what we might call instead his efficiency and memorableness), his agreement of words and thoughts, his useful content, and its appropriate presentation; these characteristics made it particularly useful to teachers. But to determine what other qualities were associated with poetical composition, it will be helpful to compare further the *Poetria nova* with other works singled out for particular admiration. In *The Arts of Poetry and Prose*, Douglas Kelly makes the case for a specific medieval category of "masterpiece" with which he designates those medieval Latin works that achieved a special, elevated status in the schools. He draws his argument from a statement made by Gervase of Melkley in the "Dedicatory Epistle" to the *Ars versificaria:* "Matthew of Vendôme wrote fully about this art; Geoffrey of Vinsauf more fully; most fully, of course, Bernardus Silvestris—in prose a parrot; in meter, a nightingale."[200] Gervase is referring here first to Matthew of Vendôme's *Ars versificatoria* and then to Geoffrey of Vinsauf's *Poetria nova*. Kelly convincingly identifies (partly because of Gervase's constant quoting of it) the otherwise unknown *ars poetriae* by Bernardus as none other than the *Cosmographia,* a famous work about the (re)creation of man and his acquisition of knowledge, written in passages of alternating prose (Bernard as parrot) and verse (Bernard as nightingale).

As we saw earlier, Kelly outlines for modern readers a graded series of medieval rhetorical treatises based on Gervase's categories: the elementary treatise emphasizing rudiments; the grammatical treatise or "full" treatment and the rhetorical treatise or "fuller" treatment.[201] He concludes with an additional cat-

---

198. Carlson, "*Laborintus*," 50–51.

199. Although the focus of this study is on the *Poetria nova* and pedagogy, the reader is directed also to the interpretation of the work as a poem by Yves Tilliette, *Des mots*.

200. Giles, "Gervais," 1; Gräbener, *Ars poetica*, 1.9–12. I have emended Giles's "Bernard Silvester" to the Latinate form of his name used elsewhere in this study.

201. See "The Arts of Poetry and Prose" earlier in this chapter.

egory, "[t]he masterpiece, or the fullest and most complete presentation of the art of poetry and prose, . . . illustrated by Bernardus Silvestris' *Cosmographia* and Jean of Hauville's *Architrenius*."[202] I would suggest that for many medieval teachers the category of masterpiece included Geoffrey's *Poetria nova* as well as two works by Alan of Lille, the *Anticlaudianus* (included by Gervase) and *The Complaint of Nature*. Both of Alan's works are extant in more known manuscripts than either the *Cosmographia* or *Architrenius*, although in barely more than half as many as the *Poetria nova*.[203] And, like the *Poetria nova*, these two works by Alan were taught at both school and university levels during the latter centuries of the Middle Ages.[204] What these works by Geoffrey and Alan (and to a lesser extent those by Bernardus Silvestris, John of Hautville, and others mentioned by Gervase) have in common is a particularly teachable aesthetic that is very foreign to modern tastes; it emphasizes repetition and variation, the tiniest units of composition, a "set piece" aestheticism, extreme examples, and a penchant for self-reflexive (sometimes grotesque) metaphors that talk about and imitate pedagogical techniques at the same time.[205]

The "new poetics" as well as the "new rhetoric" of the *Poetria nova* gave medieval teachers a text of great flexibility and applicability, as witnessed by the attention given to it by the early humanists in Italy and its adaptability to scholastic codes of university discourse in central Europe—even while it continued to be used in more elementary schoolrooms. Yet this flexibility and applicability came from the very rigid and programmatic aspects of the text itself. While the *Poetria nova* may not have been a "masterpiece" in Gervase's eyes (he quotes it much less often than the *Cosmographia* or the *Architrenius*, both works more in line with modern aesthetics as well), Gervase himself seems to have been a far more individually gifted pedagogue than the run-of-the-mill medieval teacher[206]—or modern one, for that matter. But most medieval teachers needed a text that would work under any circumstances and with almost all students, and for this purpose Geoffrey's may have been better suited. The great literary masterpieces of the twelfth century, such as the *Cosmographia* so highly praised by Gervase, changed the stakes for medieval teachers in the centuries that followed. Educators then as now chose texts that enabled them to say what they

---

202. Kelly, *Arts*, 63.

203. The *Cosmographia* has survived in 46 manuscripts (Dronke, 64); the *Architrenius* in 27 (Schmidt, *Architrenius*, 93–103); *Anticlaudianus* in 111 (Sheridan, *Plaint of Nature* 34); and *De planctu Nature* in 138 (Krochalis, "Alain de Lille," 2; for English manuscripts see now Gibson et al., "Manuscripts of Alan of Lille"). These statistics may increase as manuscript studies become more comprehensive. Most classical texts taught in the medieval schools have survived in hundreds more copies.

204. Krochalis, "Alain de Lille," passim. Other authors' works were taught at various levels, of course; see, for example, Baswell, *Virgil in Medieval England*, 61; and Nauta, "William of Conches" (on Boethius), 389–391.

205. Most of the works of earlier authors also cited by Gervase in the same context (Claudian, Dares Phrygius, Lucan, Statius, and Virgil [Giles, "Treatise," 4; Gräbener, *Ars poetica*, 3.26–4.3]) can also be described—*si fas est*—the same way.

206. On a fifteenth-century comparison of Gervase and Geoffrey favoring the former, see Clark, *Monastic Renaissance*, 225.

wanted to say, and the new genre of the arts of poetry and prose, of which the *Poetria nova* became the favorite example, allowed them to talk about poetry in terms of rhetoric, and to speak about rhetoric in terms of all kinds of compositions. The *Poetria nova* generated by the commentators—for no medieval work, like no modern one, existed out of context—was a highly successful poem that still has much to teach.

2

the *poetria nova* as school text

READING BETWEEN THE LINES

This should be omitted or interpreted carefully on account of the *rudes,* who could be confused.[1]

—*Early Commentary*

I have corrected the text as much as possible; it wearied me to erase the puerile glosses that the scribe put in.[2]

—Padua, Biblioteca Universitaria, 505

The first quotation above comes from the version of the *Early Commentary* intended for teachers of younger students.[3] It refers to one of the series of apostrophes on the death of King Richard; the problematic section is Geoffrey's criticism of God ("If heaven allow it, I chide even God" [412]). The commentator suggests that the teacher be attentive to its possible negative effect on *rudes:* the young, ignorant, or uncultivated. Marbode of Rennes uses the same term to describe the intended audience for his introductory work on rhetorical fig-

---

1. "Istud omittatur uel sane legatur propter rudes qui possent confundi" (*EC* 412 in "Additions and Changes," 272).

2. "Correxi textum ut potui; glosas pueriles quas scriptor apposuit teduit me abradere" (Padua, Biblioteca Universitaria, 505, fol ii'). On this manuscript see the unpublished "Catalogo dei manoscritti della Biblioteca Universitaria" I, fols. 162v–163r.

3. The glosses in this version are simpler in syntax but include more examples illustrating a given technique. The version for older students includes more analysis of the structure and organization of the *Poetria nova* and approaches it from a more abstract point of view. The differences between the versions are described more fully in *EC* xxix–xxx, also Woods, "Classical References" and "Verba and Sententia," as well as "Questioning Authority" in chapter 4.

ures, and Gervase of Melkley uses it to describe the audience for his own art of poetry—in contrast to that of more advanced works like the *Poetria nova*.[4] Yet this version of the *Early Commentary* tells us that some students of the *Poetria nova*, too, were *rudes* and that teachers might have to be careful what such students were taught. (By referring to them in the third person this commentator underscores that he is writing for other teachers rather than to students directly.) The commentaries discussed in this chapter show us that medieval teachers had a very different idea of what should be censored for their younger, less experienced students—or not. Modern scholars had thought that rhetorical texts like the *Poetria nova* were "rarely glossed since they would be primarily used by students with a good knowledge of Latin" and that a manuscript of the *Poetria nova* with interlinear glosses to help with basic comprehension or in-class translation would be "[a]n exception."[5] Such a situation probably was true originally: few early English manuscripts of the *Poetria nova* are accompanied by contemporary glossing of any kind, and the works with which it is copied in most English manuscripts indicate an intermediate level of teaching.[6] Gradually, however, the *Poetria nova* moved both up and down the pedagogical ladder.[7]

Some school manuscripts of the *Poetria nova* were owned by students themselves. According to Robert Black, Italian students "bought or wrote their own copies [of school texts],"[8] a conclusion supported by a number of Italian manuscripts. He describes eleven fourteenth- and fifteenth-century Italian manuscripts of the *Poetria nova* now in Florence, "all of them probable or certain schoolbooks," and notes the type of glosses on each.[9] As he concludes, "among Italian manuscript schoolbook collections it would be difficult to overlook the powerful presence of Geoffrey of Vinsauf's *Poetria nova*. . . . "[10] Earlier Paul Gehl described a group of Italian school manuscripts of grammatical and rhetorical texts, including some of the *Poetria nova*,

---

4. Camargo describes Marbode's audience as "elementary students of Latin versification" ("Latin Composition Textbooks," 301, on "rudis" in *De ornamentis verborum* 9). Giles characterizes Gervase's students as "those who are in the early stages of language study" ("Treatise," ix). I translated it above (in "The *Accessus* and Frame" in chapter 1) as "unskilled" in an *accessus* where it is used to describe the students Geoffrey wrote for, and the term also occurs in a different context in a commentary discussed in "Comedy and the *Commedia*" in chapter 3.

5. Hunt, *Teaching and Learning Latin*, 1.35.

6. See "The Arts of Poetry and Prose" in chapter 1. The interlinear glosses in thirteenth-century central European manuscripts of the *Poetria nova* were often added later, and none of the thirteenth-century manuscripts of the *Early Commentary* contains interlinear glosses. Gernot Wieland suggests that glosses written above the line in teachers' (as opposed to students') copies were to help with the pressure of translating on the spot ("Glossed Manuscript," 166). See also "The *Poetria nova* at Vienna, Krakow, and Erfurt" in chapter 4.

7. More advanced commentaries are discussed in chapters 3 and 4.

8. Black, *Humanism*, 85. See the ownership notes discussed in chapter 1, note 44.

9. Black, *Humanism*, 342–349.

10. Black, *Humanism*, 342; see also Black, *Education and Society*, 160.

which, although "for the most part larger in overall format," were "very similar in design to Tuscan elementary readers . . . ": relatively portable, made of inexpensive materials, and containing only a single work.[11] In these manuscripts the text is written with few abbreviations, and room is left for interlinear glossing; sometimes there are schoolboy scribbles and drawings, but the text is usually not defaced.[12]

Additional Italian school manuscripts of the *Poetria nova* elsewhere in Italy support Black and Gehl's research. In his study of fragments of school texts from Udine, for example, Cesare Scalon examines several remnants of manuscripts of the *Poetria nova* that may have been owned by students and are discussed later in this chapter.[13] The Biblioteca Civica "Angelo Mai" in Bergamo, a small city that had a tradition of education during the later Middle Ages and the Renaissance,[14] owns two school manuscripts of the *Poetria nova* (and a third with Pace of Ferrara's advanced commentary discussed in the next chapter). One of these, MA 7, is enclosed in crude wooden covers with sixteenth-century ownership marks and a partial student drawing of a house.[15] The other, MA 259, a more deluxe manuscript with an illustrated initial, contains numerous interlinear and short marginal notes.[16]

Outside Italy, however, codices owned by students at the lower levels are an exception. Most manuscripts of the *Poetria nova* intended for the schoolroom (rather than the university lecture hall) were owned by teachers. Any commentary in such manuscripts concentrates on small sections of the text at a time. If the text is introduced with an *accessus,* it is very short and limited to the most basic questions: who wrote this book? what is its subject? The glosses in the school manuscripts explain the most basic issues: why the *Poetria nova* begins as it does, what the author is teaching in each section, how the examples illustrate the techniques, and what should be remembered.

---

11. Gehl, *Moral Art,* 277; he discusses or lists eight copies of the *Poetria nova* (278–279 [II.4, II.6, II.9, II.10, II.12, II.13], 282, 284–85). My study considerably expands the number and types of Italian manuscripts of the *Poetria nova* under discussion, but it builds, of course, on the pioneering work of Gehl and Black.

12. Gehl, *Moral Art,* 252, 262; among the drawings that he records in manuscripts of Tuscan school texts are a "roughly drawn armored knight," "inexpert but charmingly drawn" illustrations for Aesop's *Fables,* "(male genitalia?)," a "roughly sketched duck," and "a clumsily drawn picture of a student and teacher" (256, 261, 262, 265). Black notes the "puerile drawing of a crenellated tower" in a Florentine manuscript of the *Poetria nova* (*Education and Society,* 63).

13. Scalon, *Libri, scuole e cultura.* For more on the Udine fragments see "The Female Body in the Classroom."

14. On education in Bergamo, see Carlsmith, "Le *scholae* e la scuola," esp. 235–236.

15. Bergamo, Biblioteca Civica "Angelo Mai," MA 7, fols. 1r–30v. On this manuscript see *Iter ital.* 5. 484.

16. On Bergamo, Biblioteca Civica "Angelo Mai," MA 259, fols. 1r–40v, see *Iter ital.* 5.480; and Gatti Perer, *Codici e incunaboli miniati,* 35–36 and plate.

BACK TO BASICS

> He compares him in gentleness to the Andrew mentioned, and that [comparison] captures his goodwill.[17]
>
> —Angers, Bibliothèque municipale, 523

Most of the manuscripts discussed in this chapter have discrete marginal glosses that focus on simple concepts but show that there is more to the *Poetria nova* than will fit between the lines. Typical is Angers, Bibliothèque municipale, 523, whose gloss on *stupor* was quoted earlier.[18] This very legible fourteenth-century manuscript has a pleasing appearance (plate 2), although the large initials are sometimes incorrect, indicating possible inattention on the part of the scribe who added the decoration. There is no *accessus*. The interlinear glosses add phrases or referents that help one to construe the Latin. For example, *tu* (you) over the first word of the text, *Papa* (Holy Father), explains that it is in the vocative case, indicating direct address to a single person.[19] The interlinear gloss on the third word, *mundi* (of the world), is *continens pro contento* (the container [the world] for the content [those who live in it]).[20] Where Geoffrey of Vinsauf praises Innocent's eloquence in "Silence, Augustine!" (15), the interlinear gloss above the phrase explains that this command means "with respect to Innocent."[21] The longer comments in the margins paraphrase the *Poetria nova* in simpler words and explain the rhetorical technique at work, as in the gloss used as the epigraph above. There the commentator introduces the important rhetorical concept and terminology of the *captatio benevolentiae* (capturing of goodwill) of the person to whom the work is dedicated, taken from the first book of the *Rhetorica ad Herennium* (1.6).[22] Later, at the closing of the dedication where Geoffrey officially presents his work to the pope ("Receive, great man, this little work, brief in form, vast in power," 41–42), the commentator reinforces Geoffrey's strategy: "RECEIVE, GREAT MAN Here he captures the goodwill of the pope in that he makes him receptive (*docilem*)," going on to cite the doctrine "according to Tully."[23]

---

17. "Comparat eum mansuetudini dicti Andree et ista captat beneuolenciam eius" (Angers, Bibliothèque municipale, 523, fol. 1r).

18. See "Off with His Head!" in chapter 1. The copy of the *PN* in Angers, Bibliothèque municipale, 523, fols. 1r–48v, was originally a separate manuscript; see LeMarchand, *Catalogue des manuscrits . . . d'Angers,* 156 (old no. 503); and *Catalogue général* (Octavo Series), 31.359. According to the unpublished IRHT description it is from western France.

19. The vocative is more usually indicated by a little "o" over the first word; see plates 8 and 10; also Coulson, *"Vulgate" Commentary,* 8.

20. Angers, Bibliothèque municipale, 523, fol. 1r.

21. "respectv Innocencii" (Angers, Bibliothèque municipale, 523, fol. 1r).

22. See the application of this terminology in "Shaping the Student" in chapter 1. For the medieval and early Renaissance tradition of the *Rhetorica ad Herennium,* see Ward, *Ciceronian Rhetoric.*

23. "ACCIPE MAGNE etc. Hic captat beniuolenciam pape in eo quod reddit eum docilem. Nam secundum Tullium . . . " (Angers, Bibliothèque municipale, 523, fol. 1v)

As plate 2 shows, the text of the *Poetria nova* is the dominant focus of the *mise-en-page*. Commentary is ancillary and fragmentary. Some scholars would not call such collections of discrete glosses "commentaries" at all, reserving that appellation for continuous-text interpretations of the work, the *catena* or "chain" commentaries extant as independent texts.[24] Yet the marginal glosses in school manuscripts contain coherent approaches to and consistent interpretations of the *Poetria nova,* and they have much to teach us about both the insights of individual teachers and the shared experience of the *Poetria nova* on the part of generations of students. In them we find evidence that Geoffrey's own examples were based on well-known school texts and themes, and that passages which could be interpreted as reflections of student life were targeted for explanation, perhaps even in-class performance.[25] The focus in school commentaries is on similarity and connection.[26] These commentators are, literally, less discriminating than those described in the following chapters. They teach by association, analogy, and reinforcement, using simple pedagogical techniques like etymology and repetition. The overwhelming impression gained from reading through a great many school commentaries is of how much of the same kind of material is passed on to the student no matter where or when the text is being taught.[27]

DOMINICAN REINER VON CAPPEL

> The subject of this book is a method of persuading taken from what is common to the art of poetry and rhetoric.[28]
>
> —Reiner von Cappel

While we have no idea who wrote the *Early Commentary* or the glosses in the Angers manuscript, other commentaries on the *Poetria nova* can be placed

---

24. Ward, *Ciceronian Rhetoric,* 59; also "From Marginal Gloss to *Catena*" and "The *Catena* Commentaries." The manuscript of the *EC* used as the base manuscript for the edition and translation is in *catena* form, as are the manuscripts of the commentary by Pace of Ferrara and several of those of the commentary by Dybinus of Prague.

25. See Tilliette on Geoffrey's use of known literary genres (*Des mots,* e.g., 137). The possibilities of in-class dramatic readings of the *Poetria nova* were evoked by Martin Camargo's inspired performance, with gestures, of Geoffrey's example of the boy made master (*PN* 445 ff.) at the session on "Medieval Composition Exercises for the Modern Classroom" at the biennial conference of the International Society for the History of Rhetoric at Calahorra in 2003. This passage includes the following instructions: "Mock him with the ciconia's sign of derision; or pull a wry mouth, or draw in your nostrils . . . " (452–53). Cf. Camargo, "Medieval Rhetoric Delivers," 51–53.

26. See "Transference and Transformation" later in this chapter.

27. Cf. Nauta, "William of Conches," 357.

28. "Subiectum huius libri est modus persuadendi ex hiis que communia sunt arti poetice et rethorice" (Wolfenbüttel, Herzog August Bibliothek, Cod. Guelf. 286 Gud. lat., fol. 1r).

in a specific pedagogical environment. For example, there is a straightforward, nuts-and-bolts school commentary by the Dominican teacher Reiner von Cappel in the Herzog August Bibliothek in Wolfenbüttel.[29] Reiner, who died in 1384, taught in Saxony. The short *accessus* and series of notes on the *Poetria nova* in Cod. Guelf. 286 Gud. lat. (plate 3) comprise his teaching on the text.[30] He owned another manuscript that suggests the context in which Reiner taught the *Poetria nova*. Now divided and dispersed, this codex originally contained a large collection of school texts, some with commentaries. Although not all of it has survived, Reiner made a complete list of the contents, which included the *Distichs of Cato,* a version of the *Facetus* (a conduct manual), *Phagifacetus,*[31] *De contemptu mundi* (On Contempt for the World), Ovid's *Ars amatoria,* the fables of Avianus and Aesop, and the *Ecloga Theodoli* (Eclogue of Theodolus), with commentaries on the last three.[32] Four of these works were part of a late medieval core school anthology sometimes called the *Auctores octo* or "Eight Authors" that in various forms replaced the *Liber Catonianus* (Cato book) as an introductory reader during the later Middle Ages, and the rest were also widely taught.[33] Given the relatively easy Latin of these works and their position in the curriculum, it should come as no surprise that Reiner's commentary on the *Poetria nova*

---

29. I am grateful to Loris Sturlese for identifying the hand of the commentary as Reiner's.

30. There are no other contents in the manuscript. On Wolfenbüttel, Herzog August Bibliothek, Cod. Guelf. 286 Gud. lat., see Köhler and Milchsack, *Die Gudischen Handschriften,* 230 (4591). It came to the library as part of the collection of Marquard Gude. I have not found another version of this commentary, and I assume that Reiner composed rather than merely copied the glosses.

31. On this still obscure school text, see Henkel, *Deutsche Übersetzungen,* 297–99, also 28.

32. On Reiner and his other manuscripts see Sturlese, "Der Söster Lektor" esp. 186–188, and the bibliography in the notes therein; a transcription of Reiner's list of contents is provided on 187. Sturlese expressed there the hope of publishing on Reiner's glosses on Aesop and Geoffrey (188), but the direction of his research changed thereafter. See also Shailor, *Medieval Book,* 68–69, on "Reynerus de Capella."

33. The standard contents of the *Auctores octo* (much honored in the breach) included the *Disticha Catonis* (one- and two-line classical proverbs), *Theodoli Ecloga* (a debate poem composed of quatrains telling anecdotes from the Hebrew Bible and classical literature), a version of *Facetus, Chartula* (also called *De contemptu mundi*), *Tobias* (a reworking by Matthew of Vendôme of a biblical tale), *Alani Parabolae* (parables by Alan of Lille), the *Aesopi Fabellae* (Fables of Aesop), and *Floretus* ("a versified manual of Christian dogma," Pepin, *Auctores octo,* 213; on *Floretus* see also "Erasmus and Geoffrey" in the Afterword). For an English translation of the *Auctores octo* and some bibliography see Pepin. Much work remains to be done on the evolution, versions, and influence of the *Auctores octo,* which lasted well into the age of printing; Donna Hobbs is currently working on the use and influence of some of these texts in England. The earlier *Liber Catonianus* contained only classical or pseudo-classical works, including the same first two works (e.g., Clogan, *Medieval Achilleid,* 3; Woods, "Teaching of Poetic Composition," 125–126; the classic study is Boas, "De librorum Catonianorum historia"). Thomson and Perraud's *Ten Medieval Latin Schooltexts* contains translations of several texts in the earlier group. On both collections see Orme, *English Schools,* 102–106; Gillespie, "Literary Form," 55–85; Hunt, *Teaching and Learning Latin,* 1.59–79; Woods and Copeland, "Classroom and Confession," 380–385. See also Avesani's argument against using the terms "Liber Catonianus" and "Auctores octo" in favor of the more general phrase used by some medieval authors, "minores auctores" ("Il primo ritmo," 475–488); this term, while useful and perhaps more historically accurate, obscures the later shift in focus and subject matter.

is a basic one.[34] As M. Michèle Mulchahey points out, "In the early decades of the fourteenth century, when vocations generally became fewer, the pressures for new membership meant that Dominican—and Franciscan—grammar schools were energetically promoted in many cities, ever more so after the ravages of the Black Death made falling numbers and failing recruitment an acute problem indeed." By the mid-fourteenth century, restrictions limiting entrance to the orders to those aged eighteen and over were loosened and even abandoned, with oblates (those under the age of fifteen) now formally accepted. Thus, more basic schooling had to be provided than had been part of the organized program before.[35]

Reiner's commentary is introduced by an abbreviated *accessus* written in the upper right corner of the first folio (plate 3).[36] Although his focus is on persuading, which may reflect a Dominican perspective,[37] he demonstrates the typical school commentator's emphasis on the overlapping of rhetoric and poetics.[38] Note Reiner's short, simple sentences and use of mnemonic verses to make retention easier. He divides the *Poetria nova* into the six parts of a rhetorical discourse according to the *Rhetorica ad Herennium,* from which he introduces the classical concept of *captatio benevolentiae* also outlined in the Angers commentary. Reiner signals the end of the *accessus* in conventional fashion by citing the first words of the text.

The subject of this book is a method of persuading taken from what is common to the art of poetry and [art] of rhetoric. Man naturally delights in meter and verbal ornament; therefore, rhetoric is to be struggled over [lit.: sweated] with great desire. It [rhetoric] has precisely six parts, which are expressed in these verses[39]:

It introduces; it narrates; it divides by subject.

and then,

It refutes, it confirms, it concludes.

A rhetorical discourse has these parts.[40] Whence an introduction decorates a

---

34. Fragments of several other manuscripts associated with Reiner have survived, indicating that some of his students may have been working at a more advanced level (Sturlese, "Der Söster Lektor," 190 ff.).

35. Mulchahey, *First the Bow,* 94, also 95–97. See also Roest, *History,* 214 and 240–243 (on the Franciscans); and "The *Poetria nova* and the Preaching Orders" in chapter 3.

36. The four-line description at the bottom is much later.

37. For a more sophisticated emphasis on persuasion see the sections on his fellow Dominican, Bartholomew of Pisa, in chapter 3.

38. One of the manuscripts quoted below, Paris, BnF lat. 8171, glosses "poesis" in line 61 as "ars rethorica" (fol. 2v).

39. These verses are cited by Dybinus of Prague's commentary, see "*Scripta* vs. *Dicta* in Practice," where they are translated differently.

40. The verbs in the little poem refer to the introduction, narration, division, refutation, confirmation, and conclusion; see *Ad Her.* 1.4.

composition / sermon (*sermonem*) at the beginning,[41] for which reason the author puts the introduction first; it is the [part of the] discourse that prepares the mind of the hearer appropriately for the remaining discourse. The introduction ought to "render the listener well disposed, receptive, and attentive" {*Ad Her.* 1.6}. And, since the author composed this book specifically to honor Pope Innocent, he first captures Innocent's goodwill, saying, "O Holy Father, wonder," etc. (1).[42]

Not until later, in his comments on individual sections of the text, does Reiner introduce the second element of the double structure of the *Poetria nova*, which was based on the five parts of rhetoric as well as the six parts of a rhetorical discourse. His introductory comment on the passage where Geoffrey compares building a house to constructing a poem (43 ff.) resembles the Brescia manuscript, whose *accessus* was one of those quoted in the first chapter.[43] Reiner says, "Here he carries out his intention by determining first the narration [the second part of a discourse] as well as invention [the first part of the art of rhetoric] . . ."[44] In the marginal comments that follow, Reiner takes his students through the *Poetria nova* in an orderly fashion: identifying, paraphrasing, summarizing, and explaining. He carefully points out where Geoffrey makes a specific point or gives an example; many of his glosses begin with "Here he teaches" or the similar "Here he shows," even "Here he recapitulates what has been said."[45] Sometimes Reiner merely notes that such-and-such a technique "is clear here in the text."[46]

---

41. On the translation of "sermo" see "Sermons?" later in this chapter.

42. "Subiectum huius libri est modus persuadendi ex hiis que communia sunt arti poetice et rethorice. Naturaliter enim homo delectatur in metro et in verborum ornamento. Igitur rethorica summo <insudanda> [*corr.*: insudandum *MS*] est desiderio. Habet autem specialiter sex species, que hiis exprimuntur versibus: 'orditur, narrat, partitur,' et inde 'refutat, confirmat, claudit.' Habet has oratio partes. Vnde ex quo exordium primitus sermonem ornat, ideo auctor primo premittit exordium, quod est oratio animum auditoris ydonee preparans ad reliquam orationem. Exordium autem debet reddere auditorem beniuolum, docilem, et attentum. Et quia auctor iste librum hunc specialiter ob reuerenciam Innocencii pape compilauerat, idcirco eius beneuolenciam primo captat, dicens 'Papa stupor,' etc. (1)." (Wolfenbüttel, Herzog August Bibliothek, Cod. Guelf. 286 Gud. lat., fol. 1r)

43. See "The Double Structure" in chapter 1.

44. "Hic exequitur intentum, determinando primo de narracione et materie inuencione . . ." (Wolfenbüttel, Herzog August Bibliothek, Cod. Guelf. 286 Gud. lat., fol. 1v). That the double structure of the *Poetria nova* is articulated in basic commentaries like Reiner's and that in the Brescia manuscript indicates how fundamental a concept it was in the apprehension of the work in medieval schools. The structure of the book was analyzed very differently in some of the very advanced and university commentaries.

45. E.g., "Hic ostendit," "Hic docet," "Hic recapitulat ea que dicta sunt" (Wolfenbüttel, Herzog August Bibliothek, Cod. Guelf. 286 Gud. lat., fol. 3r).

46. E.g., "et patet in littera" (Wolfenbüttel, Herzog August Bibliothek, Cod. Guelf. 286 Gud. lat., fols. 12v, 14v, 15v, 17r, 33v).

SHAPING THE NARRATIVE

And note the story.[47]
—Reiner von Cappel=

Reiner pays particular attention to the myth that Geoffrey uses as the basis for demonstrating the ways to begin a narrative: the story of King Minos of Crete, his murdered son Prince Androgeos, and Princess Scylla, daughter of Minos's sworn enemy, King Nisus of Athens, who betrays her father after falling in love with Minos. Geoffrey introduces the narrative as follows: "That your eyes may see as witness what we have said to your ears, consider the brief story that has as its first part Minos, as its second the death of his son, as its conclusion the thwarting of Scylla" (156–157).[48] Reiner fills in the story for his students and explains what Geoffrey is doing with it:

155 THAT YOUR EYES MAY SEE. Using natural order,[49] he demonstrates here through examples what he described earlier. And note the story: Minos, the rich and powerful King of Crete, had a son named Androgeus whom he sent to Athens to study. This is the first part of the story. The second part is that this Androgeus, as is natural with one of superior intelligence, quickly surpassed all of his companions; for this reason they hated him and killed him. The third part is that Minos, on account of the murder of Androgeos, collected an army and besieged the city of Athens, where King Nisus, who had a daughter by the name of Scylla, reigned.[50] Attracted by the beauty of Minos, Scylla begged him to marry her, saying that she would cut off her father's fatal lock of hair, and in this way Minos could capture the city.[51] Minos promised Scylla that it [the marriage] would happen. But when victory was at hand he deceived her, and thus it is said here, "as its conclusion the thwarting of Scylla" (157).[52]

---

47. "Et nota fabulam" (Wolfenbüttel, Herzog August Bibliothek, Cod. Guelf. 286 Gud. lat., fol. 3v).

48. Nims notes that the story of Minos and his family "may have had special status in the schools as a type of poetic invention" (p. 100, note on lines 155 ff., citing the so-called Bernardus Silvestris commentary on *Aen.* 6.20).

49. For Geoffrey's doctrine of natural and artificial order, see Quadlbauer, "Zur Theorie der Komposition," and Friis-Jensen, "Horace and the Early Writers," 368–371.

50. According to Ovid, *Met.* 8.7, Nisus is King of Megara, and the action takes place there.

51. As Ovid explains in *Met.* 8.8–10, "This venerable white-haired king had one bright purple tress right in the middle of his head. On its safety depended the safety of his kingdom."

52. "155 VT VIDEANT Hic de ordine naturali prius dicta declarat per exempla, et nota fabulam. Mynos rex Cretensis diues et potens filium habuit Androgeum, quem misit Athenis ad studium; hec est prima pars fabule. Secunda pars est quod iste Androgeus utpote miri ingenii prosecit(?) in breui supra omnes coetaneos suos propter quod eum odientes interfecerunt ipsum. Tercia pars est quod ob hanc causam Mynos, collecto exercitu, obsedit ciuitatem Atheniensem, vbi regnabat Nisus rex habens filiam nomine Cillam. Hec Mynois pulchritudine illecta demandauit sibi, quod si eam duceret in vxorem, ipsa patri suo crinem fatalem abscideret, et sic Mynos ciuitatem caperet. Ille vero hoc se facturum promisit. Set adepta victoria eam decepit, et ideo dicitur hic, 'Finis confusio Cille' (157)." (Wolfenbüttel, Herzog August Bibliothek, Cod. Guelf. 286 Gud. lat., fol. 3v)

This story, even in Reiner's bland summary, contains a number of elements common to narratives widely used in the schools.[53] Using artificial order and starting from the end of the narrative, we have a young princess dangerously in love with the king who has come to defeat her father; she is willing to betray her father in order to satisfy sexual desire, but she is herself betrayed (was there any doubt?). Earlier another king's child, this time a prince and the son of that beautiful and desired enemy, is sent away to school in this exotic land; his possible emotions might be fear, anticipation, alienation, even (he does have superior intelligence after all) a desire for knowledge. But the only ones who could assuage his loneliness are jealous of this newcomer who has been foisted upon them, and instead they turn on him. He is killed far from home. His father—and most of these stories revolve around a father[54]—sets forth to avenge the death of his child and to destroy the happiness of the child of his enemy. Reiner's approach to this lurid material is straightforward and unflinching, typical of school treatments. The Angers commentator, while providing a shorter summary, includes two other details about the son Androgeos: his looks and how he was killed: "Note that the author touches on the story in natural order, in that Minos, king of the Cretans, had a beautiful son by the name of Androgeos, whom he sent to Athens, who in a short time surpassed the others in knowledge, and through envy he was thrown from a certain tower. . . ."[55] Schoolboy emotions are at the heart of the story.

Geoffrey presumably chose this narrative for its focus on conflicts in age, sex, status, accomplishments, and familial relationships. These "attributes of persons" or "circumstances" were the building blocks of rhetorical characterization, and Geoffrey gives a truncated list of them much later (1844 and 1846–1847).[56] Students were taught to consider the actions and speeches appropriate to various kinds of characters, and a combination of paradoxical qualities was particularly desirable for rhetorical elaboration. Niobe, the subject of two student poems in the Hunterian manuscript, and Dido, an enduring focus of schoolboy obsession, were both royal (= powerful) and female (= emotional).[57] Examples often involved a conflict of motives (such as Scylla's love for both her father and her father's enemy) or transgressing of boundaries (that *puer-senex*

---

53. On the themes that were thought to appeal to adolescents, see "The Other Audience" and "Purple Patches" in chapter 1.

54. See Woods, "Rape," 68. Some of the early humanist commentaries examined in the next chapter adapt Geoffrey's teaching on natural and artificial order and on beginning with proverbs and exempla to a biblical narrative instead, one also involving a father and son ("Bible Stories in Composition Class" in chapter 3).

55. "Nota quod actor tangit fabulam de ordine naturali quantum Minos rex Cretensum habuit filium pulchrum nomine Androcheum quem misit Athenas qui in sciencia in breui tempore ceteros superauit et per inuidiam fuit a quadam turre precipitatus . . ." (Angers, Bibliothèque municipale, 523, fol. 4r).

56. Too truncated a version according to some; see "Geoffrey after Quintilian" in the Afterword. They are treated in detail in Cicero's *De inventione*.

57. See Woods, "Weeping for Dido" and "Boys Will Be Women."

himself, Pope Innocent III).[58] The nexus of events in the narrative that Geoffrey chose was ideally suited to the classroom, where immediacy of emotional effect was more important than plausibility.

BETTER THAN SEX

Note the sophistication (*curialitatem*) and restraint of the author.[59]

—Biblioteca Apostolica Vaticana, Ottob. lat. 1472

Like the story of Androgeos and his family and the passages that challenge authority discussed in the first chapter, other set pieces of the *Poetria nova* were probably designed to interest adolescent males: lovers embracing and the springtime seduction of the earth by the air (538–553), the parts of a woman's body (563–597), Jupiter's female conquests (613–621), and several versions of a joke about adultery leading to pregnancy (713–717 and 733–736).[60] Medieval teachers did feel some topics to be unsuitable for the young, as we saw at the beginning of this chapter. But sex scenes, explicit physical detail, and acts of violence were considered especially effective aids to the memory,[61] and school texts were saturated with such material.[62] That medieval teachers taught younger students more explicitly sexual material than was considered appropriate for older ones is one of the most significant differences with their modern counterparts.[63]

The rhetorical examples in the *Poetria nova* are remarkably tasteful and circumspect in comparison with those in treatises that, according to Gervase of Melkley, were written for students less advanced than Geoffrey's: his own and that of Matthew of Vendôme.[64] Gervase routinely quotes textual examples that

58. Curtius points out that "All 'harmonies of opposites' (*puer senex,* and the like) are emotive formulas and as such have especial vitality" (*European Literature,* 202, and also 381, 424, 427; on some of Geoffrey's examples, 98–101). The "puer-senex," literally a boy with the mind of an old man, was a particularly appropriate image for Innocent because of his youth, and Geoffrey uses it several times in the *Poetria nova,* e.g., 20–23, 1309–1312.

59. "Nota curialitatem et verecundiam actoris" (Vatican City, BAV Ottob. lat. 1472, fol. 8v).

60. The issue of sexual preference is not necessarily signaled by the focus on women in such examples. Power relationships of all kinds are coded in terms of gender in medieval schooltexts; see Woods, "Rape." For a more complete list of Geoffrey's examples, see "Purple Patches" in chapter 1.

61. Mary Carruthers notes in an art of memory attributed to Thomas Bradwardine an "emphasis on violence and sexuality which runs through all the interaction of the figures . . . " (*The Book of Memory,* 168).

62. Elliott, *Seven Medieval Latin Comedies,* xliii–xlix, esp. xliv and xlix; Woods, "Rape"; and the references cited in "The Other Audience" in chapter 1. Other works aimed at male adolescents also contain "images of pollution and vulgar polemic, with their own range of associations (many sexual)" (Einbinder, *Beautiful Death,* 37). On the often complementary emphasis on restraint, see Bowers, "Augustine as Addict," 426.

63. See also Hexter, *Ovid and Medieval Schooling,* 25.

64. See "The Arts of Poetry and Prose" in chapter 1. This restraint may be evidence in itself that Geoffrey's own intended level of student was intermediate.

demand a knowledge of sexual facts. One such image that he uses more than once comes from Suetonius and was also cited by Rudolf Agricola[65]:

Who denies that Nero [descends] from the great stock of Aeneas?
He lay under his mother as Aeneas held up his father.
[*Quis negat Enee magna de stirpe Neronem:*
   Sustulit hic matrem, sustulit ille patrem.][66]

Gervase later reshapes it as, "Aeneas bore the weight of his father, Nero his mother" (*Eneas patrem, Nero matrem sustulit*).[67] He also employs extended double entendres[68] and cites additional rhetorical examples with themes of seduction, castration, and more incest.[69] Matthew of Vendôme's coarse imagery was also popular, with "a certain flair for what appealed to the younger adolescent."[70] His description of Davus's erection as a dactylic foot (‾ⅎⅎ) was meant to fix itself in the student imagination[71]:

He turns to lewdness as a foul passion suffuses his genitals,
Causing love's orbs to bulge and Venus's lance to stiffen.
Yet before the lengthy member of this dactyl can pierce home,
The short syllables shake and destroy the enterprise. (*Ars versificatoria* 53.77–80)

In stark contrast is the following passage from the *Poetria nova*, which also employs sexual imagery but of a very different kind. Geoffrey offers it as an example of the amplification technique of digression (paragraph breaks inserted):

The bond of a single love bound together two hearts; a strange cause divided them one from the other. But before they were parted, lips pressed kisses on lips; a mutual embrace holds and enfolds them both. From the fount of their eyes, tears flow down their cheeks, and sobs alternate with farewells. Love is a spur to grief, and grief a witness to the strength of love.

Winter yields to spring. The air unclasps its robe of cloud, and heaven caresses the earth. Moist and warm, air sports with earth, and feminine earth feels the masculine power of the air. A flower, earth's child, bursts forth into the breeze and smiles at its mother. Their first foliage adorns the tops of the trees;

---

65. See Suetonius, *Nero,* 39.2; and Agricola, *De inventione dialectica,* 119.

66. Giles, "Gervais," 75, n. 18; and Gräbener, *Ars poetica,* 21.8–9.

67. My translation; see Giles, "Gervais," 78, n. 48; Gräbener, *Ars poetica,* 31.4.

68. Giles, "Gervais," 84, n. 140 (explained on 46), and 151, n. 137 (explained on 128); Gräbener, *Ars poetica,* 56.10–15 and 135.5–9.

69. Giles, "Gervais," 175, n. 13, 177, n. 43; 174 n. 8; Gräbener, *Ars poetica,* 160.2, 167.8–9, 158.11.

70. Elliott, "The *Facetus,*" 27; see also the excerpt from his *Ars versificatoria* (1.58) quoted in Woods, "Teaching of Poetic Composition," 130–34.

71. Alan of Lille uses the same image for this metrical foot in *De planctu Nature* 1, m. 1.

seeds that were dead spring up into life; the promise of harvest to come lives first in the tender blade. Now is the season in which birds delight.

This hour of time found the lovers apart, who yet through their love were not parted. (*PN* 538–553)

Geoffrey's anecdote is short, charming, and suggestive. Although another section of the *Poetria nova* is the subject of the epigraph quoted at the beginning of the section, this passage perfectly embodies the "sophistication and restraint" admired by the commentator.[72] Geoffrey's less explicit approach gave teachers great latitude for interpretation, as we shall see in the following chapters. His subtlety reminds us that the *Poetria nova* was admired not just as a treatise in verse but also as an exemplary poetic composition: Yves Tilliette calls this example "une belle et triste scène d'amour."[73]

The digression itself is admirably integrated into the "main" or frame narrative: it conveys the passing of time while describing the sexual act in a way that keeps the lovers' longing before us (and, if one were to pursue the analogy, probably echoes their own thoughts). Reiner focuses on Geoffrey's transitions:

> 532 THERE IS [A KIND OF DIGRESSION] Here he shows that there are two parts to a digression. One is the initial (*propinqua*) part, when the subject of the digression is a continuation of the story at the beginning, as if one were to say that the "love" of those two (544) is connected to when "Winter yields to spring" (543), etc. The other is the final (*remota*) part when the subject of the digression is continued in the story at the end, that is to say that "This hour of time" (553), etc. [is what] separated those lovers.[74]

Here Reiner understands as the two parts of one digression (the transitions away from and back to the original story) what other commentators see as two different kinds of digression: the first is digressing to something that is obviously connected or close (*propinqua*) to the original subject; and the second, bringing in something seemingly far away (*remota*) from the subject at hand and then integrating it.[75]

The general approbation with which commentators react to this passage does not mean, however, that all were satisfied with Geoffrey's discretion. One

---

72. The comment there is made about the line in Geoffrey's description of a naked woman where he is "silent" about "the other parts" below the waist (594–595).

73. Tilliette, *Des mots*, 95.

74. "532 EST ECIAM. Hic ostendit quod duplex est digressio, vna est propinqua, quando id per quod fit digressio continuatur materie in principio, ut si dicatur amor istorum contigebat quando 'Veri cedit hyemps' (543), etc. Alia est remota, quando id per quod fit digressio continuatur materie in fine, vt si dicatur istos amantes disiungit 'hec temporis hora' (553), etc." (Wolfenbüttel, Herzog August Bibliothek, Cod. Guelf. 286 Gud. lat., fol. 9v).

75. See Woods, "Poetic Digression"; also "A Preacher and a Teacher" in chapter 3.

commentator, whose manuscript (now in Barcelona) was formerly the property of the Benedictine monastery in Ripoll, keeps insisting that Geoffrey's lovers engage in an explicitly sexual relationship.[76] At the first line, "The bond of a single love bound together two hearts" (538), the commentator adds in the margin, "and understanding this: that it was in bed or in a place where there was sexual intercourse (*choitus*) between them."[77] Over "two hearts" he writes a sequence of elaborations: "that is, of the boyfriend, that is of the girlfriend (*idest amici, idest amice*), at sexual intercourse in one bed (*ad choitum in vno lecto*)."[78] When Geoffrey continues, "a mutual embrace holds and enfolds them both" (541), the commentator adds "in the act of sex (*acto choitu*)," and over the clauses "tears flow down their cheeks, and sobs alternate with farewells" (542–543) he has written, "namely in the act of sex" (*scilicet acto choitu*)."[79] All the references to love in this passage of the *Poetria nova* are glossed as sex acts.

PYRAMUS AND THISBE IN THE *POETRIA NOVA*

> In this example he implies the story of Pyramus and Thisbe in a few words
> (*breviter*). . . . [80]
> —Paris, Bibliothèque nationale de France, lat. 8171

Geoffrey's language is deliberately abstract and generic when he refers to the couple in the narrative framing the digression. They are not named or physically described, or even identified separately. Some commentators refer to them together, as Geoffrey does, using masculine plural forms of pronouns and adjectives that can be interpreted as either specifically masculine or of indefinite gender. Other commentators identify their gender generically, as when the Barcelona commentator glosses them as "boyfriend" and "girlfriend" in one of the glosses quoted above, and also later over the last word in the passage: "lovers (that is, girlfriend and boyfriend)."[81] The commentator of the Angers manuscript, however, explicitly states that the two are "a man and a

---

76. Barcelona, Archivo de la Corona de Aragón, Ripoll 103, fols. 1r–46r; it also contains a section of Lucan and Ovid's *Epistulae ex Ponto*. See Beer, *Los manuscrits de Monastir*, 137–170, 230–277, 299–320, 329–365, and 492–520; also Woods, "Some Techniques." In this manuscript the commentator has gone through the text numerous times, sometimes stating the same thing over and over both in the margins and between the lines, especially at the beginning.

77. "et hoc intelligens quod fuit in lecto uel in loco ubi fuit choitus inter eos . . . " (Barcelona, Archivo de la Corona de Aragón, Ripoll 103, fol. 12v).

78. Is the single ("vno") bed perhaps an echo of the single ("Vnicus" in this manuscript) love introduced in the first word of the passage?

79. Barcelona, Archivio de la Corona de Aragón, Ripoll, fol. 12v. There are many other interlinear and marginal glosses on these lines that I have not quoted.

80. "In hoc exemplo breuiter insinuat fabulam de Piramo et Tisbe . . . " (Paris, BnF lat. 8171, fol. 10v).

81. "amantes (idest amicam et amicum)" (Barcelona, Archivo de la Corona de Aragón, Ripoll 103, fol. 13r). Above on line 541 "utrumque" (both) is also glossed "idest amicum et amicam" (fol. 12v).

woman," writing "*virum et feminam*" over "both" (*utrumque*) at line 540.[82] Yet other than identifying their genders here, he reinforces Geoffrey's emphasis on the mutuality of their feelings and actions and their near indistinguishability. Here is a literal translation of the second sentence of the passage with the interlinear glosses in the Angers manuscript added in parentheses: "Before the parting (of the one from the other), the mouth (of the one) presses (gives) kisses on the mouth (of the other); and a mutual (reciprocal) embrace constricts each of them (a man and a woman)."[83] These glosses highlight two aspects of the lovers: they are a single unit, equal and almost identical; yet they are also a man and a woman.

Another commentator identifies them twice as Pyramus and Thisbe. These identifications are among the marginal glosses added to a thirteenth-century copy of the *Poetria nova* in the Bibliothèque nationale de France in Paris, lat. 8171.[84] The commentator introduces the passage saying, "In this example he implies the story of Pyramus and Thisbe in a few words, insinuating [the story] subtly. . . . "[85] Over the very last word, *amantes* (lovers), he again writes "Pyramus and Thisbe."[86] This identification may seem farfetched, but it is not unreasonable. The clause that Geoffrey uses to introduce the lovers, "A single knot of love bound together two hearts," is remarkably resonant with the opening image of several medieval "Pyramus and Thisbe" poems that were probably school compositions.[87] For example, Matthew of Vendôme's poem on Pyramus and Thisbe, which has survived in a single late copy bound with the *Poetria nova*,[88] was probably a product of his own schooldays. Here are several sentences from Matthew: "Pyramus and Thisbe are two, and yet not two. One love joins them both, and does not allow their being two. They are two and yet not two, because they are one in mind, one in trust, one in spirit, one in love. . . . So they are two in body but one in mind, and so does a single love unite the two."[89]

---

82. Angers, Bibliothèque municipale, 523, fol. 12v.

83. The interlinear glosses are "vnius ab alio," "vnius alterius," "alternus" (emended from "alterus"), and "virum et feminam" (Angers, Bibliothèque municipale, 523, fol. 12v).

84. Paris, BnF lat. 8171, fols. 1r–33v (to line 1835). The only other work in this manuscript is a fifteenth-century note on three aspects of prudence. On this manuscript see Gallick, "Medieval Rhetorical Arts in England," 67–69; and Glorieux, *Faculté des arts*, 141. It shares some glosses with the version of the *EC* intended for younger students, but not this reference. The first folio is so worn that the incipit and glosses there are illegible.

85. "In hoc exemplo breuiter insinuat fabulam de Piramo et Tisbe, inferens subtiliter . . . " (Paris, BnF lat. 8171, fol. 10v).

86. "Piramum et Tisbem" (Paris, BnF lat. 8171, fol. 11r).

87. See Raby, "*Amor* and *Amicitia*," 601; Glendinning, "Pyramus and Thisbe"; and Thomson and Perraud, *Ten Latin Schooltexts*, 217–226.

88. Cambridge, Trinity College, R.14.22. An *accessus* and some glosses in this manuscript are quoted in "The *Accessus* and Frame" in chapter 1.

89. Translated by Thomson and Perraud, *Ten Latin Schooltexts*, 227; edited by Franco Munari in "Il 'Piramus et Tisbe'" and in vol. 2 of *Mathei Vindocinensis opera*. Matthew reused proverbial statements from his "Pyramus and Thisbe" in the *Ars versificatoria;* cf. "Proverbial Wisdom" in chapter 1.

Other Pyramus and Thisbe poems in what Robert Glendinning refers to as "the Anglo-French group" also employ this image, so it appears to have been one of the conventions of telling the story of this heterosexual couple in the schools of England and France.[90] Matthew emphasizes the equality of Pyramus and Thisbe, their status as a matched pair even though man and woman, which is also an aspect of both Geoffrey and the Angers commentator's treatments of them. Matthew continues: "Equals in intelligence, they are blessed by an equal beauty, an equal grace of manner, an equal claim to high birth, and equal reputation for piety. Their outward forms are similar; only their sex dares by its difference to make them unequal, equal as they are otherwise in all other ways." Like the story of Minos and his family, that of Pyramus and Thisbe was well suited to what were perceived to be adolescent tastes, with the lovers' escape from home, blurring of gender-specific personal traits, and romantic double suicide.[91] That in most versions of the story they did not have sex would have been particularly appealing to some sensibilities: Glendinning notes that the medieval Pyramus and Thisbe poems, like the *Poetria nova*, are noticeably free of the kind of "vulgarity" displayed elsewhere by Matthew and Gervase.[92]

Geoffrey's story describes the separation of lovers who sound a lot like Pyramus and Thisbe.[93] Both Matthew and Gervase re-used their own classroom versions of Pyramus and Thisbe in their *artes poetriae*,[94] and Geoffrey may have as well. If the identification in the Paris manuscript is correct, Geoffrey is teasing students (and teachers) by evoking a text that they know in a different form, yet with some explicit thematic clues. That this allusion was lost to later generations illustrates one of the dangers of brevity, the topic to which we now turn our attention.

---

90. Glendinning, "Pyramus and Thisbe," 54 and 62; also Brassel, "Composition of Medieval Love." The image of one heart in two bodies comes from ancient male friendship literature, which makes an interpretation of the pair as two men, possibly implied in some of the later commentaries, also one rooted in literary tradition; see "In Season" in chapter 3.

91. See the more elaborate version in Ovid, *Met.* 4.87 ff.

92. "Eros, Agape and Rhetoric," 900.

93. He gives us none of the later elements of the narrative, however, and there is some evidence that the composition topic of Pyramus and Thisbe assigned in the schools may have focussed on the beginning of the story; see Glendinning, "Pyramus and Thisbe," 60, and Brassel, "Composition of Medieval Love," 40 and 46, on the use of just part of the story in another version. The *Poetria nova* is found in manuscripts of five of the six known Pyramus and Thisbe poems based on Ovid (Cambridge, Trinity College R. 14. 22 [PT I cited as 895 by Glendinning]; Glasgow, University Library, Hunter 511 (V. 8. 14) [PT II and III]; Krakow, Biblioteka Jagiellońska, 2141 [PT IV]; Munich, Bayerische Staatsbibliothek, Clm 237 [PT VI, both copies of which were owned by Hartmann Schedel]); Glendinning, "Pyramus and Thisbe," 51–52.

94. Glendinning, "Pyramus and Thisbe," 58–62.

SHORTER IS BETTER

> A useful digression is when we digress . . . and then quickly (*breviter*) return to
> those earlier things. . . . [95]
>
> —Paris, Bibliothèque nationale de France, lat. 8171

Later in the same gloss in which he first identifies the lovers as Pyramus and
Thisbe, the commentator of Paris, BnF lat. 8171 makes a connection between
the brevity and the usefulness of a digression: "In this example he implies the
story of Pyramus and Thisbe in a few words (*breviter*), insinuating subtly, creating a useful digression. . . . "[96] That Geoffrey sketches the story with a swift
stroke (as he will do with a less savory story of lovers in his example of abbreviation[97]) is repeated in this commentator's gloss on the first line of the digression
proper:

> 545 [WINTER YIELDS] TO SPRING Having introduced the subject, the author
> fashions a digression by describing springtime. At the end of the digression he
> takes up the part [of the story] that he set aside earlier. Note that there are two
> kinds of digression. A useful digression is when we digress from the abandoned
> subject to the other things to be said and then quickly (*breviter*) return to the
> earlier material; he talks about this here. The other kind is when, after a long
> digression, one does not know how to return [to the original subject].[98]

The commentator creates the analogy that useful is to brief as useless is to
long, an important point, since the amplified treatment of amplification and
abbreviated treatment of abbreviation in the *Poetria nova* sometimes have mis-
led modern scholars about their relative importance in medieval composition
theory.[99] The prodigious length of many adult medieval literary compositions
has obscured the obvious practicality of abbreviation exercises in the medieval
classroom, when most students did not own permanent writing materials and
usually presented their compositions orally.[100] Almost all of the (unfortunately

---

95. "utilis quando relicta materia digredimur ad alia dicenda et breuiter redimus ad priora . . . ." (Paris,
BnF lat. 8171, fol. 10v).

96. "In hoc exemplo breuiter insinuat fabulam de Piramo et Tisbe, inferens subtiliter faciens digressionem
utilem . . . " (Paris, BnF lat. 8171, fol. 10v).

97. See "Shortest Is not Best" later in this chapter.

98. 545 VERI Posita materia digressionem facit autor amodo describendo tempore veris. In fine
digressionis arripit illam partem quam prius omisit. Et nota quod duplex est digressio: utilis quando relicta
materia digredimur ad alia dicenda et breuiter redimus ad priora; de hac hic dicit. Alia est quando post
digressionem longam nescit quibus redire" (Paris, BnF lat. 8171, fol. 10v). The concept of the "other kind,"
or "digressio inutilis" as it is sometimes called, may have come from Horace commentaries; see Friis-Jensen,
"Horace and the Early Writers," 364–65.

99. But see Curtius, *European Literature,* 487–494; also Friis-Jensen, "Horace and the Early Writers,"
374–375.

100. For example, the famous description by John of Salisbury of the classroom procedure of Bernard

very few) examples of medieval student compositions that have come down to us are of abbreviation,[101] a technique that Geoffrey's own example of Pyramus and Thisbe—for I do take the Paris commentator's point—shows can be difficult to detect unless we are looking for it. This difficulty is particularly significant when we consider that brevity *within* amplification is what is at issue here: Geoffrey's abbreviation of the Pyramus and Thisbe story is part of his example of an amplification technique. Thus, in a single composition a writer can both simultaneously condense and expand the material he is working on.[102] The difficulty of detecting abbreviation means that we may be getting only half the story when we perceive amplification alone.[103]

THE FEMALE BODY IN THE CLASSROOM

Here he praises the swelling of the breasts, and note that he says "virginal," that is, hard and small.[104]
—Vatican City, Biblioteca Apostolica Vaticana, Ottob. lat. 1472

Geoffrey's treatment of description, which is the next technique of amplification after digression, includes an example of how to describe a beautiful woman's body (563–597). School commentators pay a great deal of attention to this passage, apparently presuming the students' willingness to examine the phrasing very carefully.[105] The set piece of head-to-toe description was a common school exercise (see the numerous examples in Matthew of Vendôme's *Ars versificatoria*) and became a staple of medieval literature. Perhaps because of its established conventions and predictability, a notable characteristic of the passage is a high concentration of polysyllabic words and metaphoric expressions. Here is Geoffrey's description of the breasts: *Pectus, imago nivis, quasi quasdam collaterales / Gemmas virgineas producat utrimque papillas* ("Let her breast, the image of snow, show side by side its twin virginal gems" [591–592]). In the section immediately following the description of the breasts, Geoffrey describes

---

of Chartres makes no mention of students writing down their compositions, which were presented every evening in contests (*Metalogicon* 1.24).

101. See Harbert, *A Thirteenth-Century Anthology,* 3–4; and Woods, "Boys Will Be Women," 147–51; also "Shortest Is Not Best" later in this chapter.

102. Chaucer's *Monk's Tale,* for example, is an amplified series of abbreviations; see Woods, "In a Nutshell," 31–32.

103. See Lafferty, *Walter of Châtillon's* Alexandreis, 120–121, on ekphrasis and abbreviation and their dependency on shared knowledge of school texts.

104. "Hic commendat tumorem mammarum, et nota quod dicit 'uirgineas,' idest duras et modicas" (Vatican City, BAV Ottob. lat. 1472, fol. 8v).

105. One is reminded of the modern academic rumors of teachers using *Playboy* centerfolds to teach anatomy. On Dante's possible use of one (unsalacious) detail in Geoffrey's description, see Bertolucci Pizzorusso, "Gli smeraldi di Beatrice" (12) with references to two commentaries.

the smallness of the woman's waist in an elegant circumlocution ("Let her midsection be close girt, able to be encircled in the narrowness of a fist" [593–594]). Yet he deliberately varies the difficulty of his lines; his allusion to her genitals, while indirect and evocative, is simple: "For the lower parts I am silent, here the mind's speech is more apt than the tongue's" (594–595); this is the statement that was singled out for its "sophistication and restraint" by the commentator quoted above in the epigraph to "Better than Sex." The comment in the epigraph to the present section, that the adjective *virgineas* (virginal) means that the breasts are "small" and "hard," comes from the same late-thirteenth- or fourteenth-century French manuscript in the Vatican Library.[106]

Indeed, school commentators expend most of their energy on this passage explaining complex words.[107] With regard to these same breasts, Reiner von Cappel explains that *collaterales* (side by side) means "hanging there on the chest, . . . where in the ancient world women were accustomed to bind themselves up."[108] He carefully annotates the fancy words in Geoffrey's description of the waist, glossing *astrictus* (close girt) with "that is, by a belt," and at *brevitate pugilli / circumscriptibilis* (lit.: able to be encircled in the narrowness of a fist) he uses the vernacular to make sure that his students understand the point: "that is, not as if it were big (*grosse*), but rather as if a man's hand were able to enclose it."[109] He ignores the reference to "the lower parts."

Perhaps the simplest but most memorable reaction to Geoffrey's description of a naked woman is recorded in the margins of another copy in the Vatican Library.[110] This Tuscan manuscript, Chig. I.IV.145, which contains the *Poetria nova* only, dates from the late fourteenth or early fifteenth century; the glosses, both interlinear and marginal, were added later.[111] In the margin, the identification of each body part is put next to where Geoffrey describes it. Since these

---

106. On Vatican City, BAV Ottob. lat. 1472, fols. 2r–28r, see Pellegrin et al., *Les manuscrits classiques latins*, 1.711, and the unpublished description by the IRHT. This manuscript was owned by Queen Christina of Sweden; she also owned another copy of the *Poetria nova* (Leiden, Bibliotheek der Rijksuniversiteit, Voss. lat. O.69, fols. 90r–123v), but it contains no commentary or glosses.

107. For a rare exception, see Besançon, Bibliothèque municipale, 534, a late-thirteenth-century French composite manuscript of school texts and some commenatries; the *PN* (to 2077) is on fols. 147r–178r. It is heavily glossed in the margins and interlinearly, glossing that stops abruptly at the top of fol. 156r, at line 573 (where Geoffrey has descended to the woman's teeth) and only resumes at the beginning of the next section (600). On this manuscript see also Jeudy and Riou, *Les manuscrits classiques latins* 2.257–261; Sanford, "The Use of Classical Authors," 239 (no. 395); Osternacher, "Die Überlieferung," 358 (16); Gallick, "Medieval Rhetorical Arts," 83; Quinn, "ps. Theodolus," *CTC* 2.390a and 400a; and Wheatley, *Mastering Aesop*, 237.

108. "idest de latere pendentes in loco . . . vbi antiquitus mulieres se cingere consueuerunt" (Wolfenbüttel, Herzog August Bibliothek, Cod. Guelf. 286 Gud. lat., fol. 10v).

109. "idest non sicut grosse, sed sicut virilis manus potest capere" (Wolfenbüttel, Herzog August Bibliothek, Cod. Guelf. 286 Gud. lat., fol. 10v).

110. Vatican City, BAV Chig. I.IV.145, fols. 1r–49r. The first gloss is illegible. Gehl describes it as "a grammar course book taken on to a University-level course" in "Latin Readers," 439, and *Moral Art*, 279, although its glosses are much simpler than those of the most advanced Italian commentaries (see chapter 3, especially the sections on Pace of Ferrara).

111. Most of these annotations are in one hand, but an even later one can be detected in places, e.g., "poma mamillarum modico suspense tumore" at the bottom of fol. 14v.

glosses are rather hard to decipher and some guesswork has been involved, I provide the Latin next to the translations:

On the eyebrows	*De supercilliis*
On the nose	*De naso*
On the eyes	*De oculis*
On the [cheeks]	*De <genis>*[112]
On the mouth	*De ore*
On the lips	*De labris*
On the teeth	*De dentibus*
On the breath	*De flatu*
On the chin	*De mento*
On the neck	*De collo*
On the throat	*De gula*
On the shoulders	*De humeris*
On the upper arm	*De lacertis*
On the hands	*De manibus*
On the chest	*De pectore*
On the breasts	*De mamillis*[113]
Against the tongue	*Contra linguam*[114]
[On the] leg	*<De> tibia*
[On the] foot	*<De p>ede*[115]

This is a guide to the female body. It functions as a string of cues for producing a (voyeuristic?) mental picture while reinforcing the vertical orientation and downward movement of the model school exercise.

Part of the description of a woman's body is among the fragments of the *Poetria nova* preserved in the Archivio di Stato di Udine mentioned above.[116] Many of the interlinear and short marginal glosses added in several hands to MS 68, a late-thirteenth-century fragment of eight folios from the Friuli region,[117] are illegible (including a rather longish note on the breasts), but

---

112. The manuscript has "de genibus" (on the knees), a visual error indicating that the commentator may have been copying the list instead of composing it.

113. The breasts are described by Geoffrey as part of the chest; this gloss is written next to the line where Geoffrey describes the waist, another sign that the list was copied from another manuscript.

114. These last three glosses are on a new folio and partly hidden in the binding; there may be something preceding "Contra linguam." This rather disconcerting gloss next to Geoffrey's avowal of silence with regard to "the lower parts" refers to Geoffrey's advice about (not) describing them: "the mind's speech is more apt than the tongue's" (595). I am grateful to Ronald Witt for his deciphering of this gloss.

115. Vatican City, BAV Chig. I.IV.145, fols. 14r–15r.

116. See "Reading between the Lines."

117. Udine, Archivio di Stato di Udine, 68. On this manuscript see Scalon, *Libri, scuole e cultura*, 146–147, with reproduction of fol. 4v in figure xxvi. It was owned by a notary, Andrea Pittiani of San Daniele del Friuli, in the early sixteenth century.

those that can be read consist primarily of simple paraphrasing or restatement of Geoffrey's words in prose. For example, "let her arms be pleasing" (586) is glossed "he describes the upper arms, saying that [they] should be pleasing."[118] Geoffrey's comment that "For the other parts I am silent—here the mind's speech is more apt than the tongue's" (594–595) is glossed, "Here he says that for those parts hidden below the navel, the mind knows more (*est doctior*) than the tongue."[119]

This section ends here with one-word glosses on scraps of parchment[120]: the dregs of the school tradition of the *Poetria nova*. But read against the commentaries examined earlier, even a word or two can tell us what kind of approach to the text the whole manuscript might have shown us. Geoffrey presents a version of a standard rhetorical exercise, here head-to-toe description, in a manner meant to arouse interest via the content and to teach sophisticated vocabulary in the rendering of it. The teacher's job at this level is to make sure that the students understand both the words and the technique. What teachers at advanced levels do with Geoffrey's *other* examples of description, which in general they find more interesting than the female body, is discussed in the next two chapters.

DESCRIPTION AND CIRCUMLOCUTION

> And description differs from circumlocution, since circumlocution relates to the underlying idea or content, whereas description relates to the outer form.[121]
> —Paris, Bibliothèque nationale de France, lat. 8171

An important function of school commentaries is to distinguish among related rhetorical techniques that students might find confusing. Although earlier I used the term "circumlocution" when describing Geoffrey's example of description, commentators are careful to distinguish between the two techniques, relating circumlocution to content and description to form. The distinction is common, found for example in the Paris manuscript quoted above as well as in the work of one of the commentators who added glosses to the thirteenth-century English copy of the *Poetria nova* owned by the Dominicans in Leicester, now Cambridge, Trinity College, R.14.22 (plate 4). As part

---

118. "describit lacertos dicens quod placea<n>t" (Udine, Archivio di Stato di Udine, 68, fol. 4v).

119. "Hic dicit quod <de> partibus sub umbilico latentibus animus est doctior quam lingua" (Udine, Archivio di Stato di Udine, 68, fol. 4v).

120. The Udine fragments survived because the manuscripts were cut up and used as file folders in the municipal archives; see Scalon, *Libri, scuole e cultura.*

121. "Et differt a circumlocutione, quia circumlocutio fit circa substantiam, siue materiam, descriptio circa formam" (Paris, BnF lat. 8171, fol. 11r).

of his introductory gloss on description, the Cambriege commentator says, "But, it is asked, what is the difference between description and circumlocution? And it should be said that circumlocution concerns substance [while] description concerns outer forms, such as when instead of the noun 'God' we use this circumlocution: 'O you who in perpetual [order govern the universe].'"[122] He is quoting the first words of the famous Hymn to the Creator at the center of the *Consolation of Philosophy*. Boethius's sonorous abstractions convey the power of circumlocution in a compelling way: the circularity of the heavens is mirrored in the circumlocution and repetition of the expressions in Boethius's introduction.

> O you who in perpetual order govern the universe,
> Creator of heaven and earth, who bid time ever move,
> And resting still, grant motion to all else;
> Whom no external causes drove to make
> Your work of flowing matter, but the form
> Within yourself of the highest good, ungrudging; from a heavenly pattern
> You draw out all things, and being yourself most fair,
> A fair world in your mind you bear, and forming it
> In the same likeness, bid it being perfect to complete itself
> In perfect parts. (III, m. 9.1–9)[123]

Geoffrey's own description of circumlocution earlier, expressed periphrastically of course, instructs in part as follows: "Do not let your words move straight onward through the subject, but, circling it, take a long and winding path around what you were going to say briefly" (231–233). Boethius's justly famous passage is a perfect example of this technique.

---

122. "Sed queritur que sit differencia inter descripcionem et circumlocutionem. Et dicendum quod circumlocucio est circa substancias, descripcio circa formas, sicut pro hoc nomine 'deus' utimur hac circumlocutione: 'O qui perpetua,' etc." (Cambridge, Trinity College, R.14.22, fol. 13v; the Type C *accessus* added to this manuscript is translated in "The *Accessus* and Frame" in chapter 1). A similar distinction is made in other commentaries, e.g., Paris, BnF lat. 15135, fol. 170r.

123. O qui perpetua mundum ratione gubernas,
   terrarum caelique sator, qui tempus ab aeuo
   ire iubes stabilisque manens das cuncta moueri,
   quem non externae pepulerunt fingere causae
   materiae fluitantis opus uerum insita summi
   forma boni liuore carens, tu cuncta superno
   ducis ab exemplo, pulchrum pulcherrimus ipse
   mundum mente gerens similique in imagine formans;
   perfectasque iubens perfectum absoluere partes. . . .
   (*Philos. cons.* III, m. 9.1–9)

SHORTEST IS NOT BEST

> An example of a shorter composition exercise in which the five basic elements are touched on, namely man, woman, boy, snow, sun.[124]
> —Cambridge, Trinity College, R.14.22

In his abbreviated treatment of abbreviation, which comes right after his ampli-fied treatment of amplification, Geoffrey summarizes eight techniques (empha-sis, staccato speech, participles [ablative absolutes], avoidance of repetition, implication, asyndeton, and fusion of clauses) and uses them in ever shorter versions of the story of the snow child, a theme already famous for more ampli-fied treatments: a commentator who devotes a lot of attention to it in a more advanced commentary refers to it as "that long story."[125] First is an elegant ren-dition in five lines that often receives special recognition in the manuscripts; a quatrain version of this narrative may have been a common school assign-ment.[126] In the Angers manuscript, it is signaled by a two-line decorated capi-tal.[127]

> Her husband abroad improving his fortunes, an adulterous wife bears a child. On his return after a long delay, she pretends it begotten of snow. Deceit is mutual. Slyly he waits. He whisks off, sells, and—reporting to the mother a like ridiculous tale—pretends the child melted by sun. (713–717)

Reiner says about this example simply, "He exemplifies the seven aforemen-tioned ways of abbreviating material."[128] Other commentators point out individ-ual techniques, e.g., "when he says ADULTEROUS WIFE he implies the meaning of several statements in one."[129]

Geoffrey's next instructions go against the modern conventional emphasis on verbs as the strongest part of a statement: "Do not be concerned about verbs;

---

124. "Exemplum breuioris tematis in quo tanguntur illa quinque principalia, scilicet vir, femina, puer, nix, sol" (Cambridge, Trinity College R.14.22, fol. 17r).

125. "istam longam fabulam" (Munich, Universitätsbibliothek, 4° 814, fol. 86v). See the version in the Cambridge Songs (no. 14) edited by Ziolkowski, who provides the most extensive current discussion of the theme (62–69 and 209–215). French analogues have survived (Montaiglon, *Recueil des fabliaux*, 1.162–167; Bédier, *Les Fabliaux*, 460–461; Harrison, *Gallic Salt*, 380–89), and the story was well known enough to have been cited ironically in the trial of Joseph and Mary in English N-Town plays; Specter, ed., *The N-Town Play*, 1.148 (play 14, lines 306–313); see also Woolf, *The English Mystery Plays*, 176; and Lipton, "Language on Trial," 121–125. I am grateful to Emma Lipton for her help with these references.

126. Dain, "De mercatore," 263–64, 278; Ziolkowski, *Cambridge Songs*, 211.

127. Angers, Bibliothèque municipale, 523, fol. 16v.

128. Technically, this comment is a gloss on Geoffrey's introduction to the example, "Here is a model of abbreviation; the whole technique is reflected in it" (712): "ECCE Exemplificat de septem predictis modis abbreuiandi materiam" (Wolfenbüttel, Herzog August Bibliothek, Cod. Guelf. 286 Gud. lat., fol. 12v).

129. "VXOR MECHA tangit sensum multarum clausularum in vno" (Berlin, Staatsbibliothek zu Berlin—Preussischer Kulturbesitz, lat. qu. 515, fol. 45v). On this manuscript see Camargo, "*Tria sunt*," esp. 937; also Ker, *Medieval Libraries*, 141; Gallick, "Medieval Rhetorical Arts," 82; and *Iter ital.* 3.478.

rather, write down with the pen of the mind only the nouns; the whole force of a theme resides in the nouns" (719–722). The popularity of verbal nouns and adjectives (also considered nouns) in Latin is one explanation for this advice, but there are, in fact, modern circumstances where similar advice has been given. Tim McCarver, who makes his living summarizing live action on television as a sports announcer, recounts, "I learned, with prompting from Al Michaels, to eliminate the verb when doing play-by-play on television . . . you say 'Ground ball to Vizquel . . . over to Thome . . . one out.'"[130]

Geoffrey concludes his treatment of abbreviation by retelling the story of the snow child *twice* in four lines (733–736), extreme exercises in compression that are almost as awkward in the Latin as in translation. Here is the first: "A husband, selling him whom the adulterous mother feigns begotten of snow, in turn feigns him melted by sun." School commentators apparently considered this kind of treatment extreme and not to be recommended. In contrast to the earlier example, these two couplets are rarely commented on.[131] A gloss in the manuscript owned by the Leicester Dominicans describes the couplet version, as we saw in the epigraph, as "an example of a shorter composition exercise (*brevioris tematis*) in which the five basic elements are touched on, namely man, woman, boy, snow, sun."[132] These five nouns remind the writer to make sure to get all the important points in, and that this is possible in even the most circumscribed of forms. It is the shortest version of all.

TRANSFERENCE AND TRANSFORMATION

through a resemblance (*per similitudinem*)
—Berlin, Staatsbibliothek zu Berlin—Preussischer Kulturbesitz, Haus II, lat. qu. 515, fol. 46v

where the single word and the single concept come together in a union that is at the same time a conflict[133]
—Margaret F. Nims

Geoffrey places his long discussion of the ten tropes (738–1093), the part of style also called "difficult" or "weighty" ornament, after the methods of amplification and abbreviation and before "easy" or "light" ornament (the figures of

---

130. McCarver, *Tim McCarver's Baseball for Brain Surgeons,* xv (last two ellipses in original).

131. The first of the two couplets (that beginning "De nive conceptum"), however, is written on the flyleaf of London, BL Royal 12.E.XXV. For a more recuperative interpretation of the final couplets, see Woods, "Boys Will Be Women," 149–150.

132. "Exemplum breuioris tematis in quo tanguntur illa quinque principalia, scilicet vir, femina, puer, nix, sol" (Cambridge, Trinity College, R.14.22, fol. 17r).

133. Nims, "*Translatio,*" 215.

words and thoughts). The basic teaching for this complex topic is simple: look for a resemblance between two entities in different realms (preferably human and nonhuman) and bring, or transfer, a word from one over to illuminate the other: hence *trans(s)umptio*.[134] Both the initial perception and the result function *per similitudinem:* through a perceived similarity and a resulting metaphor or analogy. For example, when Geoffrey talks about using nonhuman characteristics to make metaphors describing parts of the human body, such as "*snowy* teeth, *flaming* lips, *honied* taste, *rosy* countenance" (773–74), three of the six marginal glosses on the passage in a fourteenth-century English manuscript use a variation of a phrase with the word "*similitudo*" (similarity, resemblance): "*aliquam similitudinem*," "*per aliquam similitudinem*," "*per similitudinem*."[135] Yet the most sophisticated kind of metaphor, according to Geoffrey, is one in which the words "clash on the surface, but beneath there is friendly and harmonious accord" (873–875), or, as Margaret Nims paraphrased him in her seminal article on medieval metaphor quoted above, "where the single word and the single concept come together in a union that is at the same time a conflict."[136] Geoffrey's famous example, much marked in manuscripts, is "Before the face of God, devout silence cries out" (878).

Geoffrey's instructions on creating metaphoric language are themselves sophisticated metaphorical renderings that teach *per similitudinem* and sometimes draw, as was his custom, on other known texts. He evokes Horace when he says, "Adorning [only] the face of a word is painting a worthless picture; it is a false thing, its beauty fictitious" (742–744). The commentator of the St. Georgensberg manuscript, an intermediate-level commentary, provides the source: "Horace: 'A poem is like a picture: one strikes our fancy more the nearer you stand; another, the farther away. This [one] courts the shade, that [one] will wish to be seen in the light'" (*Ars* 361–363).[137]

Geoffrey uses metaphors while describing them. His introduction to composing metaphors employs a sequence of them brought over from the human realms of medicine, gardening, and hospitality:

> In order that meaning may wear a precious garment, if a word is old, be its physician and give to the old a new vigour. Do not let the word invariably reside on its native soil—such residence dishonors it. Let it avoid its natural location, travel about elsewhere, and take up a pleasant abode on the estate of another. There let

134. See the discussion of "likening" (*assimilationis*) as the basis of figurative language in Averroes's commentary on Aristotle's *Poetics* (Minnis and Scott, *Medieval Literary Theory,* 289–91). On Geoffrey's treatment of metaphoric language, see Nims, "*Translatio*"; Allen, *Ethical Poetic,* 198–201; Purcell, "Transsumptio: A Rhetorical Doctrine"; Woods, "Teaching the Tropes"; and Tilliette, *Des mots,* 122–125.

135. Berlin, Staatsbibliothek zu Berlin—Preussischer Kulturbesitz, lat. qu. 515, fol. 46v.

136. Nims, "*Translatio*," 215.

137. "Oracius: 'Vt pictvra poesis; erit que, si propius stes, / te capiat magis, et quedam, si longius abstes; / hec amat obscurum, illa uolet sub luce uideri' {Ars 361–363}" (London, BL Add. 18153, fol. 18v).

it stay as a novel guest, and give pleasure by its very strangeness. (*PN* 756–763)

Reiner introduces the passage as a rhetorical example:

> 756 IN ORDER THAT MEANING Here he demonstrates his method of adding
> rhetorical color to a subject through words taken metaphorically. And this color
> is called transference, which is the adapting of a foreign word to the proposed
> subject through some resemblance (*per aliquam similitudinem*), as in saying "the
> meadow smiles" (1765–1766) instead of "the meadow is in flower."[138]

Others make sure that students understand the instructions at the literal level.
Where Geoffrey says, "let it travel about elsewhere," an interlinear gloss in the
St. Georgensburg manuscript specifies "through a metaphor."[139]

THE DISPLAY OF FIGURES

> [I]n that he is both a rhetorician and the author of a treatise on the art [of rhetoric],
> he uses his own examples.[140]
> —*Early Commentary*

While "difficult" or "weighty" ornament refers to expressions "transferred" from
their literal meaning, "easy" or "light" ornament encompasses two kinds of figures fixed in place, both in terms of the order in which they occur and because
they are based on fixed patterns that can best be conveyed in almost visual terms
(e.g., repetition at a particular place in the sentence, or a specific sequence of
question and answer). Students listening to rather than reading the examples
perceive the shapes created by the figures almost automatically, whereas when
reading we have to consciously look for the patterns. Thus Geoffrey's "easy"
ornament often appears more difficult, or at least contrived, to modern readers.

The first group, the figures of words, are highly artificial: crafted in an
obvious, artistic way that draws attention to and fixes them in the memory.
They were considered recognizable from examples alone, and Geoffrey does
not define them. But nearly all commentators provide definitions, often gen-
erating here the most heavily glossed sections of the text. Geoffrey presents his
examples of the figures of words in a highly concentrated form: all thirty-five
in the standard order taken from the *Rhetorica ad Herennium* in just over two

---

138. "756 VT RES Hic ostendit modum colorandi materiam respectv verborum prout sumuntur
inproprie. Et iste color dicitur transsumpcio, que est ad rem propositam per aliquam similitudinem aliene
vocis accomodacio, vt dicendo 'pratum ridet' (1765–66) pro 'pratum floret'" (Wolfenbüttel, Herzog August
Bibliothek, Cod. Guelf. 286 Gud. lat., fol. 131r).

139. "per metaphoram aliquam" (London, BL Add. 18153, fol. 191r).

140. *EC* 1098.1–12.

hundred lines (1098–1215). Such a Display of Figures may have been a conventional show-off exercise (analogous to the ancient defense of Helen of Troy) for teachers and advanced students.[141] Furthermore, like other examples of rhetorical techniques in the *Poetria nova,* it retells a familiar story: the fall and redemption of man, an abbreviation of the Christian bible. He begins with Adam and the apple, then moves to a discussion of what aids can help those fallen; next comes the gift of the Incarnation, an interrogation of the serpent as to why he later sought the death of Christ, an elaboration of Jesus as the source of holiness and his coming to "recover the sheep he had lost," and the conquering of death by the death of God-made-man. Such extreme condensation paradoxically creates the same effect as Geoffrey's amplified apostrophes on the death of Richard I: virtuosity and a kind of over-the-top emotionalism. Intensity of effect is the pedagogical principle at work in both techniques, and they are more closely related than is sometimes recognized.

Reiner numbers the first eight figures, an indication that he may have assigned this initial group as a composition exercise. The gloss for each is written in the margin next to the line where it occurs, and was probably read immediately before the example, which I have added below so that they are together as students would have heard them.

REINER VON CAPPEL ON THE FIRST EIGHT FIGURES OF WORDS

1098 DEED SO EVIL! Here he puts the **first** color, which is called *repeticio* (epanaphora), which occurs when several statements following one right after the other begin with the same word.[142] *Deed so evil! Deed more evil than others! Deed most evil of all deeds!*

1099 O APPLE! Here he puts the **second** color, which is called *conversio* (antistrophe), which occurs when the same thing is repeated at the end of different phrases.[143] *O apple! Wretched apple! Miserable apple!*

1100 WHY DID IT AFFECT YOU? Here he puts the **third** color which is called

141. See Woods, "Teaching of Poetic Composition," for other examples, including one presumably by a student. According to Martin Camargo, full or partial copies of a version he calls *Colores rethorice seriatim,* perhaps by Matthew of Vendôme, are extant in nine English manuscripts, including two in which the *Poetria nova* is also found: London, BL Cotton Cleopatra B.VI (a composite manuscript bound by Cotton); and Douai, Bibliothèque municipale, 764 (fragment) ("Latin Composition Textbooks," 272–273). Gallo rightly calls Geoffrey's Display of Figures a "tour de force" (*Poetria nova,* 207), and Tilliette seconds this opinion (*Des mots,* 138).

142. "1098 RES MALA! Hic ponit primum colorem qui dicitur repeticio, que est cum plures orationes continue subsequentes ab eadem dicione incipiunt" (Wolfenbüttel, Herzog August Bibliothek, Cod. Guelf. Gud. lat. 286, fol. 19r).

143. "1099 O MALUM! Hic ponit secundum colorem qui dicitur conuersio, que est cum idem repetitur in fine diuersarum clausularum" (Wolfenbüttel, Herzog August Bibliothek, Cod. Guelf. Gud. lat. 286, fol. 19r).

complexio, which occurs when different phrases have one beginning and one ending.[144] *Why did it affect you, that tasting of Adam? Why do we all weep for the fault of that one man, Adam?*

1101 THIS <TASTE OF THE APPLE> WAS Here he puts the **fourth** color which is called *traductio,* which is when the same word is repeated frequently with various meanings.[145] *This taste of the apple (māli) was the general cause of evil (māli). The father (pater), to us so cruel a foe, showed himself not to be father (patrem).*

1103 HE WHO WAS RICH[146] Here he puts the **fifth** color, which is called *contentio* (antithesis), which is the assigning of opposite words to opposing things, yet not by proving one of the opposites through the other.[147] *He who was rich became poor; he who was happy, wretched; he who enjoyed such radiance was thrust back into darkness.*

1105 WHERE NOW? Here he puts the **sixth** color, which is called *exclamatio* (apostrophe), which is a close-packed outcry expressing indignation, grief, or happiness.[148] *Where now is paradise, and that joy of which you were lord? I ask you, most powerful of creatures, whence sprang your great crime?*

1107 YOU SIN BY APPROVING IN SPIRIT Here he puts the **seventh** color, which is called *interrogatio,* which, after several statements that tell against an adversary, confirms the superior argument.[149] *You sin by approving in spirit the deed of your wife, by tasting forbidden fruit, by defending your actions in speech. Approving, tasting, defending, do you not then merit your fall?*

1110 TELL ME, WHY DID YOU Here he puts the **eighth** color, which is called

---

144. "1100 CUR TETIGIT Hic ponit tercium colorem qui dicitur complexio, que est cum diuerse clausule vnum habent principium et vnum finem" (Wolfenbüttel, Herzog August Bibliothek, Cod. Guelf. Gud. lat. 286, fol. 19r).

145. "1101 FUIT HEC Hic ponit quartum colorem qui dicitur traductio, que est quando dicio eadem sub diuersa significatione frequenter repetitur" (Wolfenbüttel, Herzog August Bibliothek, Cod. Guelf. Gud. lat. 286, fol. 19r). Nims distinguishes two kinds of *traductio,* both used by Geoffrey: "(a) use of words with the same sound, but different meaning or function; or (b) repetition of a single word, preferably in different cases" (p. 103).

146. The translated *lemma* sometimes differs from the Latin; Nims's translation is used unless a literal translation is needed.

147. "1103 DE DIVITE Hic ponit quintum colorem qui dicitur contencio, que est contrariorum ad contraria assignacio, non tamen probando vnum contrariorum per reliquum" (Wolfenbüttel, Herzog August Bibliothek, Cod. Guelf. Gud. lat. 286, fol. 19r). Nims explains this technique more simply: "a statement built on contraries" (p. 103). Reiner's qualification at the end shows him distinguishing for his students between this technique based on words with contrary meanings and the technique of amplification by opposites in which a statement is made and then repeated as a denial of its opposite, e.g., he is poor; he is not rich.

148. "1105 VBI NUNC Hic ponit sextum colorem qui dicitur exclamacio, que est causa indignacionis, doloris, uel leticie crebra vociferacio" (Wolfenbüttel, Herzog August Bibliothek, Cod. Guelf. 286 Gud. lat., fol. 19r).

149. "1107 ERRAS Hic ponit septimum colorem qui dicitur interrogacio, que est ex pluribus enumeratis que obsunt aduersario, superiorem confirmat orationem" (Wolfenbüttel, Herzog August Bibliothek, Cod. Guelf. 286 Gud. lat., fol. 19r). There seems to be some disagreement about where the seventh, *interrogatio,* begins, perhaps because the sixth, seventh, and eighth all involve a question. I have numbered them as Reiner does.

ratiocinatio, in which we answer our own questions.[150] *Tell me, why did you touch fruit so harmful? My wife offered it to me. But why did you taste it? She was persuasive. Knowing the deed to be pernicious, why did you approve? I was afraid of making her angry. After the deed, why were you slow to repent your guilt by petitioning God for pardon? Say, in this deed of death, what reason was found? There was only delusion for reason.*

The first three (repetition of the first word, repetition of the last word, and repetition of the first and last word of successive clauses) are immediately recognizable and highly memorable; they are familiar to us today from slogans and commercials ("Eat it for breakfast, eat it for lunch, eat it for dinner!"). The next three (use of the same word or sound with different meanings, a statement built on contraries, and apostrophe) are also used today in popular musical genres such as country music (e.g., "If I said you had a beautiful body / Would you hold it against me?" by the Bellamy Brothers). The translations of the last two (summing up, and question and answer) do not reflect the tight patterning of those preceding. But in Latin the staccato effect of short sentences echoing or commenting on each other is clearer; the seventh ends, "*Favens igitur, gustansque tuensque, / Nonne ruis merito?*" (1110). And, like other examples of short dialogues in the *Poetria nova,* these last two would have been particularly effective read aloud (and performed) in class.

While Reiner provides simple, clear explanations—in some cases clearer than those of modern scholars—other commentators go into more detail. (Keep in mind that Geoffrey gives no definitions of these figures, only examples of them in a set order.) For example, among the twenty-seven remaining figures there are two, *occupatio* and *praecisio,* in which a sentence is interrupted for rhetorical effect. Reiner simply defines them:

> 1159 WHENCE Here he puts another color, which is called *occupatio,* which is the color in which we say forcefully that we want to pass over or do not know something that nevertheless we set forth very fully.[151] *Whence the demands of justice decreed—but I pass this by as well known—that as the enemy brought death to mankind through treacherous means, so man by subtle maneuver should bring death to the enemy, taken captive in the toils of divinity* (1159–1161).

---

150. "1110 DIC ERGO Hic ponit octavum colorem qui dicitur ratiocinacio, que est a nobis ad interrogacionem per nos factam responsio" (Wolfenbüttel, Herzog August Bibliothek, Cod. Guelf. 286 Gud. lat., fol. 19r).

151. "1159 VNDE Hic ponit alium colorem qui dicitur occupatio, que est color quo dicimus aliquid velle preterire uel nescire, quod tamen maxime enarramus" (Wolfenbüttel, Herzog August Bibliothek, Cod. Guelf. 286 Gud. lat., fol. 20r).

1213 HOW GREAT AN EVENT Here he puts another color which is called *praecisio,* which is the color when what he begins to say is cut off. Or *praecisio* is when what has been started is about to be said but is set aside as if it corresponds to the judgment of the listeners.[152] *How great an event was this! And what . . . but I let the word pass, for no word can be found adequate to so great a marvel* (1213–1214).

A gloss found in both the manuscript that identifies Geoffrey's lovers as Pyramus and Thisbe (Paris, BnF lat. 8171) and the related version of the *Early Commentary* intended for younger students helps the student to distinguish between them, here from the Paris manuscript: "And it (*precisio*) differs from *occupatio* because in *occupatio* we say that we are passing by while we are, in fact, expressing very fully. In *precisio* what is begun is put aside and left unfinished in such a way that a great deal of suspicion is created."[153]

Quintilian describes a figure as "a change analogous to the different positions our bodies assume when we sit down, lie down, or look back."[154] Minute changes in position make a difference, and medieval teachers wanted their students to watch for them. Anticipating the traditional sequence of the Display of Figures is part of the pleasure, analogous to knowing the story of a traditional ballet when watching a new production, or perhaps more exactly, given the strictness of the structure, watching known choreography danced by a new performer. Even today when students compose and read aloud a Display of Figures, they anticipate with much pleasure the more difficult ones.[155]

SERMONS?

For the rhetorical art teaches one to ornament a *sermo.*[156]
　　—Reiner von Cappel

---

152. "1213 RES HEC Hic ponit alium colorem qui dicitur prescisio, que est color dum quod dici incipitur, sub[r]iectitur. Vel prescisio est quando id quod conceptum est ad loquendum, relinquitur tamquam congruit[ur] iudicio audiencium" (Wolfenbüttel, Herzog August Bibliothek, Cod. Guelf. 286 Gud. lat., fol. 21r).

153. "Et differt ab occupatione quia in occupatione dicimus nos preterire quod maxime dicimus; in precisione quod inceptum est relinquitur et non perficitur ut inde maior nascitur suspicio" (Paris, BnF lat. 8171, fol. 22v). The distinction is also made in the version of the *Early Commentary* for older students (*EC* 1213.2), but the form of the gloss in the version for younger students is closer to that in the Paris manuscript (see *EC,* "Omissions and Variants," 377). Gallo summarizes Geoffrey's fuller treatment of *praecisio* in the *Documentum* (*Poetria nova,* p. 218).

154. Quintilian, *Inst. orat.* 9.1.2.

155. Intense figuration works best in emotional or humorous scenarios, and the possibilities for student variations are almost limitless.

156. "Ars enim rhetorica docet sermonem exornare" (Wolfenbüttel, Herzog August Bibliothek, Cod. Guelf. 286 Gud. lat., fol. 1r).

... when we return often to the same [theme], as if I were to say, "Blessed are they that mourn," etc. {Matt. 5.4}, and afterwards this is repeated often, as preachers do in sermonizing.[157]

—Vatican City, Biblioteca Apostolica Vaticana, Ottob. lat. 1472

The figures of thoughts are harder to describe than the figures of words because they are structures of content rather than verbal form, although there are areas of overlap. (Are question-and-answer sequences patterns of words or of content? The answer is, of course, both.) Perhaps for this reason Geoffrey does provide definitions of the second group, nineteen in all, some with multiple parts. The examples of the figures of thoughts, as with those of the figures of words, are presented as continuous discourse, an exercise that occupies an eighth of the text (1280–1528). The theme here is a warning to a pope, or rather, *the* Pope, Innocent III, Geoffrey's dedicatee, as we find out in the passage. The order of the figures of thought, like those of words, is determined by their order in the *Rhetorica ad Herennium*. Thus, Geoffrey must begin with *distributio,* which, he says, "assigns specific roles to various things or among various persons" (1233–1234), and *licentia,* which "chides masters or friends, offending no one with its words" (1234–1236), exemplified thus: "To proclaim sacred laws is the pope's prerogative; to observe the form of law prescribed is the part of lesser men. But very many go astray, and that straying judges you, holy father" (1280–1282).[158]

Certain features of the whole passage resemble a sermon, but it is not the only one in the *Poetria nova.* An earlier example deliberately mimics a sermon while exemplifying a method of amplification that Reiner introduces as follows: "Here he teaches the fifth method of prolonging material, namely through prosopopeia, which is a kind of speaking attributed to something not possessing the ability to speak, provoking the listener to either laughter or pity."[159] The appeal to pity comes first, in the form of a mini-sermon of the type known as a "Sermon of the Cross" (469–507). Geoffrey's begins "I the ravished cross," and the "speaker" goes on to describe how it has been "seized by violent and brutish hands and defiled by the touch of curs" (469–470). The last third of the passage is a call to arms beginning, "Awake! If the holy cross has redeemed you, redeem the cross by the sword" (490–491), and continuing in a series of figures of words: "'Let my cause be martial for you, even though it is mortal. If

---

157. "cum . . . sepius ad eandem reuertimur, ut si dicam, 'Beati qui lugent' et cetera {Matt. 5:4}, et hoc sepius postea repetatur sicut faciunt predicatores sermocinando" (Vatican City, BAV Ottob. lat. 1472, fol. 17r).

158. For a detailed seventeenth-century summary of this passage, see "Athanasius Kircher, Jesuit Polymath" in chapter 5.

159. "Hic docet quinto modo prolongare materiam scilicet per prosopopeiam, que est quidam modus loquendi rei non potenti loqui attributus ad loquendum, prouocans auditorem uel ad iocum uel ad compassionem" (Wolfenbüttel, Herzog August Bibliothek, Cod. Guelf. 286 Gud. lat., fol. 8v).

you are vanquished, by that very defeat you are victor . . . " (501–503). The last lines include the exhortation, "let the ready hand be swift to take arms . . . " (506–507). The crusade sermons were developed in Paris, although much of this development took place after Geoffrey's departure from France.[160] In a manual on composing Sermons on the Cross, Humbert of Romans, master vicar-general of the Dominicans, notes that "preachers divided their sermons up into relatively short passages and . . . after each division they addressed their audience with a formal 'invitatio' to take the cross."[161] Geoffrey follows this pattern in his example, which would have appealed to his dedicatee, who was obsessed with crusades, and also to the preachers who in the following centuries were the papacy's major propaganda arm in this battle.[162] Geoffrey's crusade sermon was a popular part of his text, receiving extra attention from some commentators.[163] The mood changes immediately, however, with the second example of prosopopeia, the one to provoke the listener to laughter.[164] It is the lament of a worn-out tablecloth: "I was once the pride of the table, while my youth was in its first flower and my face knew no blemish. But since I am old, and my visage is marred, I do not wish to appear. I withdraw from you, table; farewell!" (509–513). The later, much longer sermon-like passage of the *Poetria nova* exemplifying all the figures of thoughts also employs changes of tone, but within the extended example itself. The description of the "Lazy So-and-So" quoted in the first chapter comes from this passage, where it exemplifies the figure of thought called *notatio* (character delineation). This character sketch is introduced as symptomatic of human apathy in the face of "the second Adam, who opened for us the gates of life with the key of his death. Called as we are to those joys, what are we to do? We are apathetic, in the image of the lazy man" (1363–1365), and then the *notatio* begins.

The whole passage on the figures of thoughts is a call to action on the part of the pope to root out corruption (and apathy) in the church. The identification of the addressee as Innocent III, Geoffrey's dedicatee, comes in an echo ("I am sole wonder of the sphere" [1315]) of the first line of the poem ("Holy Father, wonder of the world"). It occurs near the beginning, in Geoffrey's version of *expolitio* (refining). The figure of *expolitio* requires a specific sequence of tactics: verbal changes, dialogue, arousal, theme stated with reason added, theme restated with reason, theme restated without reasons, argument from the contrary, exemplum, and closing of the argument. The most complex of the figures of words, the multi-part example of *expolitio* takes up almost

---

160. Maier, *Preaching the Crusades,* 112.

161. Humbert of Romans, *De predicatione S. Crucis,* paraphrased in Maier, *Preaching the Crusades,* 115.

162. See Maier, *Preaching the Crusades,* especially the Introduction and chapter 5.

163. For example, the longest continuous gloss in the voyeuristic manuscript in the Vatican, BAV Chig. I.IV.145, is on this passage (fol. 12r).

164. On Geoffrey's practice of following a serious example with a comic one, see "The Other Audience" in chapter 1.

forty lines in the *Poetria nova* (1305–1344). Half of these are devoted to the "dialogue," or, as Geoffrey models it, an interior monologue, where the pope ponders as follows:

> Not much time has passed since my heart was a novice in knowledge; my speech was unpolished, my power slight. Now he has so raised up my heart and my lips and my power, and so placed them in this office above others, that I am **the sole wonder of the sphere**. . . . Hence I am bound more firmly, and more strictly obliged to him to put down what he wills to put down, to raise up what he wills to raise, to wish what he wishes, to hate what he hates. (*PN* 1305–1324)

The other parts of the *expolitio* continue the same theme, as in "the arousal" and "the theme stated with reason added" (1325–1331): "Who is so void of wit, so destitute of soul, so distracted, that he would not praise this work, that he would not judge it to be the work of a prudent nature? So a prudent pope bases all his efforts on this, and because of this, that such great power has accrued to him for this end: to take away the sins of the world, to make the world clean, in order to lead it by the straight path to heaven." After several intervening sections comes the "closing of the argument": "Suppress wickedness, then, holy Father, successor of Peter; and with his Simon let simony be brought to destruction" (1343–1344).

Throughout this example of *expolitio* Geoffrey says the same thing over and over. He has defined the figure earlier as follows: "By turning a subject over repeatedly and varying the figure, I seem to be saying a number of things whereas I am actually dwelling on one thing, in order to give it a finer polish . . . " (1244–1246). The subsequent figure is actually called *commoratio,* or "Dwelling on a Point" as Harry Caplan terms it in his translation of the *Rhetorica ad Herennium;* Geoffrey does not give an example of it, following, as Nims points out, "the precedent set by the *Ad Herennium,* IV, xlv, 58, which states that *commoratio* is not separable from the composition as a whole, but flows through it as blood flows through the body."[165] One of the commentators identifies it as a type of rhetorical coloring often used by preachers: "Dwelling on a Point is when . . . we often return to the same [theme], as if I were to say, 'Blessed are they that mourn,' etc. {Matt. 5.4}, and afterwards this is repeated often, as preachers do in sermonizing."[166] This description comes from the French manuscript that was quoted earlier with regard to Geoffrey's "sophistication and restraint." It refers to a different type of sermon, the thematic or

---

165. Nims, p. 106.

166. "Commoratio est cum . . . sepius ad eandem reuertimur, ut si dicam, 'Beati qui lugent' et cetera {Matt. 5:4}, et hoc sepius postea repetatur sicut faciunt predicatores sermocinando" (Vatican City, BAV Ottob. lat. 1472, fol. 17r).

university sermon, that also arose at and was associated with the University of Paris.[167] Such dwelling on a theme, or repetition with variation, is thus central to both basic rhetorical pedagogy and the composition of sermons at all levels.

How, then, is *sermo* in the commentaries on the *Poetria nova* to be translated? As its original meaning of "speech," or generically as "discourse," or perhaps as "sermon"? The question is especially intriguing with regard to Reiner's commentary, where the word is used often and variously, since he was a member of a preaching order that, at the time he was teaching, was officially allowing into the order those who might still have needed basic training in rhetoric. Sometimes, of course, he appears to mean simply "speech."[168] More intriguing are the occasions when the term refers to what he is teaching his students to compose: e.g., "the art of rhetoric teaches one to ornament a *sermo*," and "an introduction decorates a *sermo* at the beginning."[169] On Geoffrey's treatment of amplification and abbreviation (203 ff.), Reiner says, "For a *sermo* that is too short obscures the purpose, while one that is too prolix generates tedium."[170] When he paraphrases Geoffrey's advice to "Bring together flowers of diction and thought, so that the field of discourse may blossom with both sorts of flowers, for a mingled fragrance, blending adornment of both kinds, rises and spreads its sweetness" (1584–1587), Reiner becomes grandiloquent himself: "Here he provides specific instruction on using the preceding colors, saying that we ought to combine them in our *sermo* and not use just one color, since out of a confluence of the preceding colors bursts an appropriateness of wondrous ornamentation."[171] At

167. See D'Avray, *Preaching of the Friars*, 193–97; and Maier, *Preaching the Crusades*, 111–115. This technique of organizing discourse around a biblical citation also influenced university lectures later, as in the *accessus* to the commentary on the *Poetria nova* by Dybinus of Prague translated in chapter 4. On the close connection between the Paris sermon and teaching techniques from the very beginning, see Rouse and Rouse, *Preachers, Florilegia and Sermons*, 67.

168. He says, for example, that the second part of *expolitio* "is created through dialogue (*sermocinationem*), namely when we attribute speech (*sermonem*) to someone according to his status" ("Hic ponit exemplum secundi modi expolicionis eiusdem, qui fit per sermocinacionem, scilicet cum sermonem alicui attribuimus secundum suam dignitatem" [Wolfenbüttel, Herzog August Bibliothek, Cod. Guelf. 286 Gud. lat., fol. 22v]). Reiner is drawing here on the *Rhetorica ad Herennium* (4.55), but substituting "sermo" for "oratio," a change that may have been dictated by his predilection for defining technical terms by using etymologically related ones.

169. "Ars enim rhetorica docet sermonem exornare" and "exordium primitus sermonem ornat" (Wolfenbüttel, Herzog August Bibliothek, Cod. Guelf. 286 Gud. lat., fol. 1r). With regard to the second quotation, which is from the *accessus*, Reiner has used "oratio" as a generic term for a rhetorical discourse in the preceding sentence ("an *oratio* has six parts"), so the use of "sermo"in the sentence following may indeed connote a specific genre.

170. "Sermo enim nimium breuis intentionem obscurat, prolixus tedium generat" (Wolfenbüttel, Herzog August Bibliothek, Cod. Guelf. 286 Gud. lat., fol. 4r). That he may be paraphrasing Horace, "in laboring to be brief I become obscure" (*Ars* 25–26), undercuts my point, however.

171. "Hic ponit quoddam documentum circa vsum predictorum colorum, dicens quod ipsis in sermone permixtim vti debeamus, et non tantum vnius coloris vsum habere, quia ex predictorum colorum concursu consurgit miri ornatus decencia" (Wolfenbüttel, Herzog August Bibliothek, Cod. Guelf. 286 Gud. lat., fol. 27r). See also Reiner's use of "sermo" in the example of conversion quoted in the previous section. There I translate it as "sermon," but it could also mean simply "composition."

the very end of the text (2066) Reiner again uses the term: "Here he treats the sixth and last part of rhetoric, namely the Conclusion, which is the artistic end of the discourse (*orationis*) comprising the beginning, middle, and end of a sermon (*sermonis*) . . . "[172]

If I am correct in inferring that *sermo* may mean "sermon" in these instances,[173] they suggest that the *Poetria nova* could have been used as an entry-level *ars pr(a)edicandi*—perhaps one of the reasons that it was popular among Dominicans.[174] We know that the members of the mendicant orders received rhetorical training, although most of the evidence about older students points to practical experience in listening to preachers and classes in which sermons were analyzed. What they were taught when they entered the order younger, or at least less well educated, has been less well documented, and the commentaries on the *Poetria nova* may help fill in the gap. Reiner was teaching students for many of whom the sermon would be the most common rhetorical composition as well as the most common rhetorical experience. To do so he used a work whose strength was its wide applicability, a recognized factor of the *Poetria nova*'s success. In such a setting the resonance between the general and specific meanings of *sermo* could have been an effective pedagogical tool. In the manuscripts that I have looked at, the teaching of grammar (that is, literary texts in verse) and rhetoric by those in the religious orders appears to have resembled more than differed from that in other kinds of schools.[175] There is nothing specifically "Dominican" about Reiner's commentary. Most of the research on education in the religious orders has focused on what was specific to them and/or (often the same thing) what was taught to more advanced students. But equally significant may be what was not distinct, what was shared with students outside the order as well, although more definite conclusions are hampered by our not knowing the origin of many of the surviving commentaries on the *Poetria nova*.

172. "Hic determinat de sexta et vltima parte rethorice, scilicet de conclusione, que est artificialis terminus oracionis, principium, medium, et finem sermonis consummans . . ." (Wolfenbüttel, Herzog August Bibliothek, Cod. Guelf. 286 Gud. lat., fol. 35v).

173. Cf. Karen Margareta Fredborg's hesitation between the two translations of "sermo" in a quotation from Bene of Florence in "Ciceronian Rhetoric," 28; and Camargo, "Pedagogy," 82. For an example of a commentator's using the term both ways, see Minnis and Scott, *Medieval Literary Theory*, 34, in an *accessus* to Horace: "The discourse (*sermo*) is so called because it is distributed between the writer and at least two other persons, and is tailored to suit the character speaking. For this reason too, the preaching of bishops is rightly called 'a sermon' (*sermo*)."

174. Especially in Italy; see Manacorda, *Storia della scuola*, 1.2.238, and "Fra Bartolomeo," 148.

175. Cf. Hasebrink, "Latinität als Bildungsfundament," 76; and Ward, "Rhetoric in the Faculty," 202–203. See also "A Preacher and a Teacher" and "The *Poetria nova* and the Preaching Orders" in chapter 3.

SEPARATING THE MEN FROM THE BOYS

This teaching is like milky food for the nourishment of boys; the one above is like the solid food of those who are grown and independent.[176]
　　—Paris, Bibliothèque nationale de France, lat. 8171

After the figures of words and of thoughts come two very technical (and to modern readers, unfamiliar and uncongenial[177]) writing techniques to which the commentators pay a lot of attention. The first is conversion, in which a concept is expressed in the form of a noun that is declined through the various cases, from which the most felicitous form of expression for the specific purpose is chosen (1588–1761). The second is determination, in which the effect of a word is modified and often made figurative by joining it to or juxtaposing it with an additional word or words (1762–1842). As was mentioned in the first chapter, these techniques embody one of the most important aspects of medieval composition as it was practiced in the schools: a focus on very small units of composition, here single words and short phrases.[178] Thus, if one assumes that teachers assigned exercises in composition according to the order of the techniques as they are treated in the *Poetria nova,* students were assigned longer, complicated, sustained exercises in metaphoric language and patterned discourse before tiny, precise exercises in word variation and elaboration.

This surprising sequence did not go unnoticed. The food analogy in the epigraph, cited above from Paris, BnF lat. 8171, is also found in the *Early Commentary.* Here is how the analogy is introduced in the version of the *Early Commentary* for younger students:

> 1588 YOU KNOW WHAT IS FITTING After the author finished versifying about those aspects [of composition] that pertain to adornment [i.e., the tropes and figures], he treats those that concern the basics. For here he teaches about the conversion of words and the suitable joining of one part to another. And since many possess this knowledge from usage alone, here he teaches how it may be accomplished according to art. This teaching is like the milky food and nourish-

---

176. "Itaque hec doctrina est quasi lacteus cibus ad nutrimentum puerorum; superior quasi solidus cibus perfectorum et discretorum" (Paris, BnF lat. 8171, fol. 29v), almost exactly the same gloss as in *EC* 1588.3. On other examples of milk as an image of what boys learn, see Glendinning, "Pyramus and Thisbe," 65–66. Geoffrey himself employs the image earlier when he says that "Orleans . . . rears tender youth on the milk of the authors" (*PN* 1011–12).

177. Tilliette declines to discuss conversion and determination in his reading of the *Poetria nova* as poem; he calls the passage on conversion "vrai fort ennuyeux" and says that both techniques are "très méchanique" (*Des mots,* 159).

178. See "The Arts of Poetry and Prose" in chapter 1.

ment of boys while the one above is like the solid food of those who are grown and independent.[179]

The Paris manuscript and the version of the *Early Commentary* for younger students conclude by repeating why this teaching is important, rather than examining the issue of the order of parts in the *Poetria nova:* "Therefore, although some write beautiful words from usage alone and put them in any old case, the author persuades us to proceed according to the art that makes [us] certain."[180]

The version for older students, however, omits this conclusion and analyzes the order of parts in the *Poetria nova* in aesthetic terms[181]:

> Accordingly it seems that this teaching [on conversion and determination] ought to be put first since one who is instructed ought to be instructed first in the lesser subjects and afterwards in the greater ones. . . .
>
> In answer to this objection, it should be said that the author of this book is not only a poet but also a teacher of poets in this book. There are two kinds of order, namely the natural and the artificial. . . . Note that in this book he subtly combines both orders although he gives no instruction about this, through which he hints that such a technique is not to be recommended, just praised. He uses natural order since he follows the parts of rhetoric and the six parts of a speech that were discussed above according to their own order, which could not be changed.[182] He uses artificial order since he puts afterward the doctrine that ought to have been put first according to natural order, as is proven above.[183]

That Geoffrey's combination of natural and artificial orders is described as a "technique not to be recommended, just praised" suggests that other techniques not so dismissed, like those we shall be looking at next, *were* to be recommended and perhaps assigned as classroom exercises. That this more complex approach to Geoffrey's text is found only in the version of the commentary for older students is a reminder that the teachers of younger students did not stray so far from the portion of the text at hand or discuss compositional issues

---

179. "1588 QUID DECEAT NOSTI Postquam auctor expediuit ea que circa ornatum sunt uersificature, consequenter agit de hiis que sunt circa utilitatem ipsius. Docet enim hic de commutationibus uerborum et de conuenienti adiunctione unius partis ad alterum. Et quia multi habent hanc scienciam ex solo usu, docet hic quomodo fiat secundum artem. Sic igitur hec doctrina est quasi lacteus cibus et nutrimentum puerorum; illa autem superior doctrina est quasi solidus cibum perfectorum et discretorum" (*EC* 1588.1–2 in "Omissions and Variants," p. 420, quoting Vienna, Österreichische Nationalbibliothek, 2513 [MS P]).

180. "Cum ergo ponant quidam pulcra uerba ex solo usu et casu, et casus sine certitudine sit, suadet auctor ut teneamus artem et discamus procedere secundum artem que certos facit" (*EC* 1588.3 in "Omissions and Variants," p. 420).

181. The format is that of a simplified *quaestio,* an advanced analytical technique discussed in "Questioning Authority" in chapter 4.

182. See "The Double Structure" in chapter 1.

183. *EC* 1588.4, 7, 9, 10–12 (translation slightly altered). A similar argument could be made for his having treated the tropes before the figures.

at such an abstract level. Younger or less prepared students are introduced to Geoffrey's doctrine as something that will give them certainty where heretofore they had been uncertain, while the older students are asked to appreciate aspects of his work beyond what they should incorporate into their own.

CONVERSION: THE ORIGIN OF STYLE

What is style derived from?[184]

—Reiner von Cappel

The preceding discussion of larger structures in the version of the *Early Commentary* for older students would have been beyond the grasp of students working at a more basic level. For the latter students, composition lay in the details of individual words. From this perspective, Geoffrey's focus on increasingly smaller units makes a different kind of pedagogical sense: the theories of conversion and determination demonstrate an increasingly intense focus on the very building blocks of the Latin language. In his introduction to Geoffrey's theory of conversions (1588 ff.), Reiner notes that both conversion and determination relate to the earlier figures of words rather than the figures of thought immediately preceding because of the tight focus on patterns of and within individual words.[185] He exemplifies the technique of conversion by using in as many cases (and meanings) as possible the word *exornatio*, which means an individual figure as well as style or verbal ornamentation in general. In the following passage Reiner plays on these meanings while "converting" *exornatio*, using it in the nominative singular, genitive singular, accusative singular, ablative singular, genitive plural, and accusative plural cases:

> 1588 [YOU KNOW] WHAT IS FITTING Earlier he taught the various figures (*exornaciones*) of words and thoughts. Here he teaches about the locus and origin of the figures (*exornacionum*). That is, what is style / a figure (*exornacio*) derived from? And he is talking about the adornment (*exornacione*) of words, not thoughts. There are two places from which to draw style (*exornacio*); one is in the inflection of words, the other in the addition of words. First he treats the inflection of words in the ornamentation (*exornacionem*) of a sermon/composition (*sermonis*).[186]

---

184. "quid possit esse illud ex quo deducitur exornacio?" (Wolfenbüttel, Herzog August Bibliothek, Cod. Guelf. 286 Gud. lat., fol. 27r).

185. Gallo offers an elegant, detailed analysis of the relationship of the theory of conversions to various aspects of rhetorical word-play (*Poetria nova*, 212).

186. "1588 QUID DECEAT Prius docuit diuersas exornaciones verborum et sentenciarum. Hic docet de exornacionum loco et origine, id est quid possit esse illud ex quo deducitur exornacio? Et loquitur de exornacione verborum, non autem sentenciarum; locus ergo a quo trahitur exornacio est duplex: vnus

Here Reiner agrees with the author of the version of the *Early Commentary* for younger students that, although the theories of conversion and determination come later in the *Poetria nova,* they are the basis of the figures of words treated earlier. Having learned the figures already, the students know what the more basic techniques of conversion and determination are to be used for. Geoffrey's placing of conversion and determination after the figures is depicted as looking deeper into the earlier subject, a simple way to explain Geoffrey's sequence that was appropriate for younger students. Reiner connects conversion (seeing what form of a word is the most effective in a particular situation) and determination (modulating the meaning of a word by adding another one to it) by noting that both involve verbal repositioning, one internal and one external. This association is made easier for students to remember by his parallel constructions in Latin: *in dicionum commutatione:* "in the inflection [lit.: alteration] of words" or conversion; *in dicionum addicione:* "in the addition of words" or determination.

Reiner continues: "The locus of inflection is threefold, as will be clear afterwards,"[187] referring to Geoffrey's summary of the three places one looks for inflection: "first, a word inflected by tense; second, a word inflected by case; finally, a word that remains unchanged" (1599–1600). The trick is to convert all of them—verbs, declinable words like adjectives, and unchangeable words—into nouns, which are in turn declined and used in the various parts of a sentence. As Reiner says at the beginning of the section on the conversion of verbs (1602): "If you want to make a figure out of a verb (the first locus), then you change the verb into a substantive noun. Then, since a given noun has many cases, see in which case it sits most aptly and put the noun in that one, placing it near other words or other verbs appropriate to the proposed topic."[188] His last phrase, "placing it near words or other verbs appropriate to the proposed topic," anticipates the theory of determinations to follow.

Geoffrey's emphasis throughout this section is on the infinite variability of expression, coupled with the work and effort that must be put into finding the best version for the purpose at hand. After his discussion of "converting" a verb he turns his attention to adjectives (take "radiant," convert it to "radiance," and proceed accordingly); how to convert a "raw" statement like "Everyone discusses this deed," where "deed" is in the accusative case (try it

---

consistit in dicionum commutacione, alius in dicionum addicione. Vnde primo agit hic de verborum commutacione, quantum ad exornacionem sermonis faciendam" (Wolfenbüttel, Herzog August Bibliothek, Cod. Guelf. 286 Gud. lat., fol. 27r).

187. Et iste locus commutacionis est triplex, sicut postea patet" (Wolfenbüttel, Herzog August Bibliothek, Cod. Guelf. 286 Gud. lat., fol. 27r). See Kopp's note on "place" as a technical term in Geoffrey's doctrine of conversion (Murphy, *Three Medieval Rhetorical Arts,* 89).

188. "Et primo de loco qui dicitur verbum, ex quo si vis sumere exornacionem, tunc mutes verbum in nomen substantiuum, et cum tale nomen multos habeat casus, vide in quo casu apcius sedet, et in illo ipsum nomen pone, applicando sibi alias diciones, uel alia verba decencia ad propositum" (Wolfenbüttel, Herzog August Bibliothek, Cod. Guelf. 286 Gud. lat., fol. 27v).

in the genitive case: "Common gossip is witness of the deed," etc.); how to convert an indeclinable word (e.g., convert the adverb "then" into the noun phrase "that day," which can then be declined); and how to use pronouns elegantly (do not use two different ones in the same case: not "If that man [nominative case] comes, this one [nominative] will depart" but rather "That man [nominative] will make his arrival the occasion of this one's [genitive] departure" (1730–1732). These are straightforward examples needing little or no glossing according to Reiner.

As an illustration, let us look with some care at Geoffrey's final example of conversion, which medieval teachers do comment on. Nims notes that "the point of Geoffrey's example at 1745 ff. seems to be the reduction of uninflected words to a minimum."[189] The more inflected (declinable or conjugatable) words one has in a sentence, the more possible variations there are at the initial level. Here is Nims's translation of these lines; only the word *instanter* ("on the dot") is uninflected in Latin:

> You are an annoying debt-collector (*oblatrator*); your refrain (*thema*) is: *You are trying to hold out.* [My reply:] *You want things on the dot. I need time: I have to think my way through. You're too persistent a dun. I can't make it today. Be patient. Tomorrow can do what today cannot.* (*PN* 1745–1748)[190]

Medieval commentators interpret this passage differently, with *oblatrator* taken not as "debt-collector" (a technical meaning), but rather more generically as a "fault-finder," and in this pedagogical context as someone who demands extempore composition.[191] The word translated as "refrain" above, *thema,* can also mean a theme, as in an assigned theme or writing exercise, and according to the commentators this little dialogue acknowledges the difficulty of extemporaneous composition assignments (when students might have been tempted to use indeclinable words too often because of their relative ease of use in prose and placement in verse). In this interpretation of the passage, *thema* refers to a composition assignment, and the first-person reply is a plea for more time to compose, as in the following retranslation:

---

189. Nims, p. 107. Declinable words were considered "'more worthy' than indeclinable ones since the former have more ways of indicating the essential and the accidental" (Thurot, *Notices et extraits,* quoted in Gallo, *Poetria nova,* 209).

190. Oblatrator ades, das thema *Resistere temptas:*
—*Rem petis instanter; spatium peto, postulo mentis*
Consilium. Nimis es praeceps exactor: ad horam
Non possum, tolera: poterit mora quod nequit hora. (1745–1748)

191. Gallo translates *oblatrator* (1750 in his numbering) as "railer"; Kopp's translation is the closest to mine, beginning "You want results immediately; I ask for delay"; she interprets it as "a dramatic representation of those struggles of the mind against itself so movingly described by Geoffrey in the concluding paragraph of this section of the *Poetria nova*" (Murphy, *Three Medieval Rhetorical Arts,* 95).

You are too demanding. You present the assignment. [You accuse:] "You are dragging your feet." [My reply:] "You want it on the spot! I need breathing room. I need to think it through. You demand too insistently. I can't do it by then. Be patient. A delay can accomplish what a deadline cannot."

The Early Commentator interprets the example as Geoffrey's response to a possible criticism. The gloss on this passage (in both versions of the commentary) is as follows: "He makes an antipophora and responds to an unspoken objection. For someone could say, 'You teach so much about the art of making verse that you should immediately be able to produce a verse on a given subject.' To this he answers that it is necessary to have time to think."[192] The related commentary in Paris, BnF lat. 8171 phrases this interpretation a little differently: "Through an antipophora he teaches how poets ought to present themselves (*se debent habere*) in a poem and how they ought to resist someone handing out a subject. . . ."[193] Reiner, too, interprets the subject of the dialogue as extempore composition:

> 1745 YOU ARE TOO DEMANDING He answers an unspoken question, for since he said above that art renders us ready, someone could ask, "Cannot one be made ready enough through practice to be able to develop [lit.: find] the conversion of words on the spot?" And he answers, "No, because this kind of conversion is developed through application (*studium*), which demands a lack of pressure and time to compose."[194]

The commentator in the Vatican manuscript (Ottob. lat. 1447), interpreting the need for time in terms of the composition of poetry, renders it as someone "saying to you, 'Compose a verse!' You say, 'Give me the subject,' and he gives it right away and wants to have a verse from you." He continues with phrasing that recalls Paris, BnF lat. 8171: "Here the author teaches how deliberation is sought from those calling out, distributing the topic (*materiam*) and demanding a verse right away."[195]

The passage yields still another scenario in which the accusation is itself the theme or subject of the assignment; the response is, thus, a composition

---

192. "Facit antipophoram et respondet tacite obiectioni. Posset enim aliquis dicere quod, tantum doces de arte uersificandi, sine mora poteris proferre uersum de materia proposita. Ad hoc respondet dicens quod oportet habere tempus ad meditandum" (*EC* 1745.1–3).

193. "Per antipophoram docet qualiter poete se debent habere in carmine et quomodo resistere debent alicui largienti materiam . . . " (Paris, BnF lat. 8171, fol. 32r).

194. "1745 OBLATRATOR Respondet tacite questioni, nam quia supra dixerat ars certos reddit, posset aliquis querere, potestne per usum aliquis tam promptus fieri, ut sine mora et deliberacione dicionum commutacionem ualeat inuenire, et respondet quod non, quia talis commutacio inuenitur per studium, quod indiget mora et tempore" (Wolfenbüttel, Herzog August Bibliothek, Cod. Guelf. 286 Gud. lat., fol. 30r).

195. "dicens tibi, 'Fac uersum!' Tu dicas, 'Da materiam,' et dat statim et uult habere uersum a te. Hic docet actor qualiter petenda est deliberatio a clamatoribus largientibus materiam et instanter uersum petentibus" (Vatican City, BAV Ottob. lat. 1472, fol. 23v). Compare the gloss in another manuscript of the *Poetria nova* (Florence, Biblioteca Nazionale Centrale, Conv. Soppr. I.VI.17) quoted in Black, *Humanism*, 349.

in which the writer says that he cannot do what, in fact, he does: "You are the writing teacher; you assign the theme of 'You try to delay.' [The composition:] 'You want it on the spot! I need breathing room,'" etc. This version, which is implied by Faral's punctuation and italics, falls into a long-standing schoolroom genre of complaining about an assignment while doing it, of which perhaps the most famous modern example is Tom Brown's extemporaneous retort to Dr. Fell (1625–1686), an example of audacity and Latinity of which Geoffrey would have been proud.[196] The final irony of this passage is that its skill and the suggestion of immediate composition on the spot (the first word of the composition follows immediately after the setting of the theme) contradict the content and emphasize what *can* be done while seeming to say what cannot. As is true with so many of the examples in the *Poetria nova,* this example is in dialogue form, and in the commentaries its content was interpreted to reflect humorously on composition practice and classroom experience.

STUDENT DETERMINATION

Here he specifies the second locus [of style], namely the addition of words.[197]

—Reiner von Cappel

The theory of determinations, which follows immediately after the theory of conversions in the *Poetria nova,* teaches students to ornament one word by adding another, creating emphasis and/or altering meaning through the juxtaposition.[198] In his transition from one technique to the other Reiner refers to his earlier linking of conversion and determination in terms of their complementary approaches:

> 1761 ADD [THIS] TO [THE PRECEPTS ABOVE] First he specified the first place to draw a figure from, namely the inflection of words. Here he specifies the second, namely the addition of words. And the latter is twofold: one is when something is added to the word (*dictionem*); the other is when something is added to the composition (*orationem*) [that is, to its meaning].[199]

---

196. Brown was about to be expelled by Fell; offered the chance to stay if he "could translate extempore Martial's lines, 'Non amo te, Sabidi, nec possum dicere quare; / Hoc tantum possum dicere, Non amo te,'" Brown immediately responded, "I do not like thee, Doctor Fell, / The reason why I cannot tell; / But this I know, and know full well, / I do not like thee, Doctor Fell" (*Oxford Dictionary of Nursery Rhymes,* 198–199).

197. "Hic determinat de loco secundo, scilicet de dicionum addicione" (Wolfenbüttel, Herzog August Bibliothek, Cod. Guelf. 286 Gud. lat., fol. 30v).

198. There is a very useful discussion of determination in Roberts, *The Jeweled Style,* 148–55.

199. "1761 ADDICE Primus determinauit de loco primo a quo trahitur exornacio, scilicet de dicionum commutacione. Hic determinat de loco secundo, scilicet de dicionum addicione. Et iste locus est duplex: vnus est quando aliquid additur ad dicionem; secundus est quando aliquid additur ad oracionem" (Wolfenbüttel,

As the Vatican manuscript (Ottob. lat. 1472) explains this concept of two aspects of determination, one of which is metaphorical meaning, "It's logical, for there are two kinds of utterances, simple and complex. A simple utterance (*vox incomplexa*) is just the word itself, while a complex utterance (*vox complexa*) is two connected things that generate meaning through the fact [of being connected]."²⁰⁰ For example, one way to determine a noun is by adding a verb to it, as when Geoffrey determines "meadow" by adding "smiles," resulting in a statement with added meaning as well as an added word: "The meadow smiles" (1765).²⁰¹

Reiner points out that Geoffrey does not proceed systematically: "And note that he does not clarify these methods and types of addition by specific rules; rather, he gives individual examples."²⁰² So Reiner turns the techniques into a numbered list of rules for his students, e.g., rule number six encapsulates the point that a noun in a particular case can determine an adjective (1781–1785). One of Geoffrey's examples is the adjective "full" determined by adding the noun "riches" in the genitive case (rendered in English as a prepositional phrase beginning with "of," as in the phrase "full of riches"). Here is Reiner's rule for making this construction:

> 1781 A NOUN [MAY DETERMINE AN ADJECTIVE] The sixth rule is the following: to an adjective needing a noun in an oblique case, an oblique that satisfies that need is added. For example, if one says "full," this adjective needs a noun in an oblique [i.e., the genitive] case. Therefore such an oblique has to be added to it, by which this need is satisfied, as here, "full of riches" (*plenus opum,* 1785).²⁰³

Where we would say that the adjective *takes* a noun in the oblique case, Reiner teaches his students that the adjective *needs* the noun; it is dependent on it, or leans on it, perhaps visualized as pushing it into an oblique (bent) case.

The point is to be able to generate a sequence of such two-word phrases with a cumulative, reinforcing effect (*plenus opum, vacuus virtutum, avidissima rerum* ["full of riches, empty of virtues, most avid of possessions," 1785]). The Paris commentator notes "another method of making determinations, namely when mul-

---

Herzog August Bibliothek, Cod. Guelf. 286 Gud. lat., fol. 30v).

200. "Hoc est logicale, duplex est enim uox complexa et incomplexa; vox incomplexa est sola dicio, vox uero complexa est duo coniuncta per factum sensum g<e>nerancia" (Vatican City, BAV Ottob. lat. 1472, fol. 23v).

201. A well known conceit, e.g., "Prata jam rident omnia . . . ," Walther, 14450s, with citations from the *Carmina Burana* and Waddell, *Mediaeval Latin Lyrics*. This metaphor and another that Geoffrey quotes ("He plows the shore" [943]), are also used by Averroes in his commentary on Aristotle's *Poetics* (Minnis and Scott, *Medieval Literary Theory,* 290).

202. "Et nota quod istos modos et species addicionis non declarat specialibus regulis, sed singula proponit per exempla" (Wolfenbüttel, Herzog August Bibliothek, Cod. Guelf. 286 Gud. lat., fol. 30v).

203. "1781 MOBILE SUB Sexta regula talis est: ad nomen mobile dependens ad obliquum, competenter obliquus additur per quem ratio sue dependencie diffinitur. Verbi gratia, si dicatur 'plenus,' hoc adiectiuum dependet ad obliquum. Ergo talis obliquus debet sibi addi, quo eius dependencia possit finiri, vt hic: 'plenus opum'" (Wolfenbüttel, Herzog August Bibliothek, Cod. Guelf. Gud. lat. 286, fol. 30v).

tiple verbs are determined according to a pattern (*sigillatim*) by their obliques [nouns in an oblique case],"[204] here the ablative (translated by prepositions in English): "He blazes with anger, terrifies with a look, thunders in speech, threatens with his sword, rages in his gestures" (1810–1812). Note the repetition of sound in the Latin phrases: *Ira / Aestuat, aspectu terret, lingua tonat, ense / Insurgit, gestu furit.* Simple examples are for the novice, as Ernest Gallo points out earlier with regard to conversion.[205] Geoffrey does include more sophisticated examples as well, like a dying body embodying—as it were—the determination of verbs by nouns in the nominative case (1804–1806). But the simple sequence is an important learning tool, as the Paris commentator's attention to it demonstrates.

For medieval students, composition got down to the nitty-gritty: individual words linked to other individual words whose relationship was bound by grammatical rules but—and this is Geoffrey's own emphasis—open to infinite variation. Like his numbering of the first eight figures of words, Reiner's recasting of Geoffrey's teaching as numbered rules suggests that his students were assigned exercises based on such sequences and variations, exercises that would have provided inexperienced writers with an endless supply of phrases and phrasing. The precise rules of grammar could, via these techniques, be turned to artistic use, encouraging exact expression at best—or endlessly varied repetition at worst.[206] The minuteness of detail in these school commentaries on the *Poetria nova* is both impressive and daunting. Simple paraphrasing ensured that students understood all of the imagery and figurative language of the *Poetria nova*, and the constant repetition of "here he teaches" and "here he gives an example" at the beginning of sections of text drilled into students' heads the relationship between theory and practice. Geoffrey's doctrine was meant to be learned and his examples meant to stay in the students' heads, where they could be drawn on in any situation demanding verbal communication. In the next chapter we examine commentaries written at almost exactly the same time as these school commentaries, but we enter a more sophisticated academic world. Yet it is one in which the *Poetria nova* is still prized for the same qualities valued by the commentators examined in this chapter: virtuosity of tone and style, literary resonance, and, above all, memorable teaching.

---

204. "Alius modus determinandi quando scilicet multa uerba sigillatim suis obliquis determinantur" (Paris, BnF lat. 8171, fol. 33v).

205. Gallo, *Poetria nova*, 212.

206. Camargo suggests that one of the statutes of Oxford may have been generated in reaction to the rhetorical excesses that Geoffrey's teachings could have produced ("If You Can't Join Them," 84).

3

the *poetria nova* as early humanist text[1]

OUR ENGLISHMAN IN ITALY

England sent me to Rome. . . . [2]
—Geoffrey of Vinsauf

Just as there is no outside evidence to support Geoffrey of Vinsauf's statement that he had been sent to Rome,[3] no contemporary archival record supports the tradition— often presented as fact—that he taught at the University of Bologna.[4] As early as the sixteenth century literary bibliog-

---

1. A note on the title of this chapter, given recent discussions about what "humanism"—and "early" when paired with it—means. There have been several excellent recent studies of Italian humanism and early versions thereof. The ones that have been most useful to me I have taken into account where they touch on material directly relevant to the manuscripts of the *Poetria nova* or to what I am trying to explain about them. But the patterns that I discern do not always conform to those traced by other scholars, even when I am greatly indebted to their research. Most debates center around the continuity of medieval teaching methods in the Renaissance or lack thereof. In general, I side with those who emphasize the continuity of the pedagogical tradition. And, following in Ronald Witt's footsetps, I have adopted his term "early humanist" to refer to those commentators who are the main focus of this chapter.

2. *PN* 31.

3. See "The Efficient Cause of This Book" in chapter 1.

4. See Siraisi, *Arts and Sciences*, 35, citing Sarti-Fattorini, *De claris*, I.599–602. Giuseppe Manacorda, whose work is always to be given serious consideration, assumes that Geoffrey taught at Bologna (e.g., *Storia della scuola*, I.2.57, 156, 228; he notes a copy of the *Poetria nova* in the possession of a professor at Bologna in 1279 [I.2.232]); and see also Bertoni and Vicini, *Gli studi di grammatica*, 23. A source of confusion was the conflation of Geoffrey of Vinsauf with both another "Galfridus Anglicus" (Far., pp. 15–16) and a Geoffrey of Bologna (*Gaufridus Bononiensis*), author of an *ars dictaminis*, who had flourished in the thirteenth century. This last Geoffrey was extravagantly praised by Simon Friedrich Hahn in 1724–26 (*Collectio monumentorum, veterum et recentium . . .*, quoted in Sarti-Fattorini, *De claris*, 690). Half a century later, Mauri Sarti argued that this Geoffrey was the celebrated "Master Geoffrey of Vinsauf" who had written the *Poetria nova*, and, in the meantime, William Cave argued that

raphers note that he had traveled widely on the continent,[5] and the persistent association of Geoffrey of Vinsauf with Italy, particularly in Italian sources, is a reflection of the importance of the *Poetria nova* in that geographical region. For, whatever Geoffrey's personal experience in Italy, his most famous work arrived there early and stayed late.[6] That there are at least ten thirteenth-century Italian manuscripts of the *Poetria nova* indicates that the work was known and became popular in Italy very quickly, and it continued to be copied in Italy until at least the mid-fifteenth century.

Although there is growing evidence that the *Poetria nova* was used to teach the composition of prose, and especially letters, throughout Europe, it is almost always copied with verse texts, often classical works, in Italian manuscripts,[7] which suggests that it was also used there to teach the interpretation of literary texts. This situation is in distinct contrast with the central European tradition described in the next chapter, where the *Poetria nova* is found almost exclusively with dictaminal texts (treatises on the art of letter-writing, model letter collections, etc.) and quadrivial works. The commentaries in the Italian manuscripts f the *Poetria nova* indicate several levels of teaching, from the elementary glosses discussed in the previous chapter to the more sophisticated treatments of various kinds that are the focus of this one. Again in contrast to the central European tradition, the *Poetria nova* is not named in Italian institutional documents, and the levels of teaching suggested in this chapter are comparative, rather than absolute. They are based on internal evidence, that is, on comparing the approaches and pedagogical techniques found within the commentaries themselves.[8]

Central to the interpretation of the commentaries presented here is that the early Italian humanists were especially—not just vestigially—interested in the *Poetria nova* (which many of them called the *Poetria novella*[9]). Bartholomew of

---

the two works were the same, a conclusion with which Sarti disagreed (Sarti-Fattorini, *De claris,* 1.600). For bibliography of the *ars dictandi* of Bolognese provenance attributed to Geoffrey of Vinsauf, edited by Licitra, see Camargo, "Toward a Comprehensive Art"; also Worstbrock et al., *Repertorium.*

5. See "The English Encyclopedists" in chapter 5.

6. Another reason for the *Poetria nova*'s early appearance in Italy could be that it arrived as part of the train of French school texts and literary practices that came in during the thirteenth century (Witt, *Footsteps,* 78–80, and "The French Cultural Invasion").

7. Milan, Biblioteca Ambrosiana, S 2 sup.; Rome, Biblioteca Casanatense, 311; and Turin, Biblioteca Nazionale Universitaria, F.IV.11 are exceptions.

8. For an example of institutionally defined levels (or "forms"), see Black's studies on Arezzo, "Humanism and Education," esp. 176–177, and *Studio e scuola,* esp. 111; also "Italian Elementary and Grammar Schools." With regard to the broader categories in Black's later study, *Humanism and Education in Medieval and Renaissance Italy,* what I refer to as basic and intermediate commentaries roughly correspond to his "elementary" and "grammar teaching" (as on 30). According to Black, the glosses in Florence, Biblioteca Medicea Laurenziana, Strozzi 137, a composite manuscript containing Horace's *Ars poetica* and the *Poetria nova,* "suggest an academic context near the end of the grammar curriculum, at the point of transition to the study of rhetoric" (246); his analysis of eleven manuscripts of the *Poetria nova* (342–349) places the use of Geoffrey's text at the "new, rhetorical/stylistic level of school education [which] involved kinds of exercises similar to those already encountered at the earlier secondary grammatical stage" (347; see also Black, *Education and Society,* 63).

9. On this title see "The Other Audience" in chapter 1.

Pisa (Bartholomeus de Sancto Concordio), Pace of Ferrara, Guizzardo of Bologna, and Giovanni Travesi left laudatory analyses of the work that remained
current well into the fifteenth century; we have references to commentaries by
Pietro da Muglio and Johannes Bondi; and Gasparino Barzizza admired the
Poetria nova and referred to it in his letters. These commentators have been
singled out by modern scholars for their interest in specific aspects of early
humanism, whether it be experimenting with ancient genres, supporting contemporary writers' efforts in new directions, or teaching classical works of particular interest to the humanists. Why were these commentators so approving
of what seems to us to be such a quintessentially medieval work? I suggest that
Geoffrey's rhetorical skill in both explaining and exemplifying his doctrine, as
well as his focus on the implications of minute changes in rhetorical figures and
grammatical constructions, helped these early humanists make textual analysis
into an advanced discipline. Their interest contributed to a sophisticated appreciation of Geoffrey of Vinsauf in Italy—at least until the increasing focus on
classical writers as the *only* stylists worthy of imitation made Geoffrey's virtuosity less appealing and useful in the classroom.[10]

BARTHOLOMEW OF PISA / BARTHOLOMEUS DE SANCTO CONCORDIO

> Here begins the exposition of the *Poetria nova* according to Brother Bartholomew of
> Pisa of the Order of Preachers.[11]
>
> —Rome, Biblioteca Casanatense, 311

Bartholomew of Pisa's translations of the works of Sallust, which he wrote at
the Convent of S. Maria Novella in Florence, led Ronald Witt to conclude that
"No Italian before Petrarch extolled the importance of studying antiquity as a
guide to life more clearly" and that "Like Latini, he privileged the best Latin
prose."[12] Other surviving works include a commentary on Ovid's *Remedia amoris*[13] and sermons, as well as treatises on grammar and canon law. He also wrote
commentaries, now lost, on Virgil and on the tragedies of Seneca. The attention
to the Latin language and compositional techniques that attracted him to these
classical texts is also clear in his commentary on the *Poetria nova*. Bartholomew

---

10. See "Geoffrey after Quintilian" and "Erasmus and Geoffrey" in the Afterword.

11. "Incipit expositio super *Poetriam nouam* secundum fratrem Bartholomeum Pisanum ordinis
predicatorum" (Rome, Biblioteca Casanatense, 311, fol. 1r; not in Yale manuscript).

12. Witt, *Footsteps,* 187. Cesare Segre notes that he "was part of the work of cultural diffusion [that]
flowed into humanism" (Segre, "Bartolomeo," *DBI* 6. 769; my translation). See also Osmond and Ulery,
"Sallustius," *CTC* 8.201.

13. It is extant only in the manuscript of Bartholomew's commentary on the *Poetria nova* discussed below,
Rome, Biblioteca Casanatense, 311; see Coulson and Roy, *Incipitarium Ovidianum,* no. 17 (but also no. 51).

was born in San Concordio (he is also known as Bartolomeo da San Concordio) in 1262, and he entered the Dominican convent at Pisa at the age of fifteen. He studied law and theology in Bologna and later Paris. After returning to Italy where he taught logic, philosophy, and canon law in Dominican convents and *studia generalia* in Todi, Rome, Florence, Arezzo, and Pistoia. He returned periodically to Pisa, where he became director of the *studium* in 1335; he died in Pisa in 1347.[14] There is no documentary evidence that Bartholomew taught what we call literature (as part of the study of *grammatica*), but his commentaries on Ovid, Virgil, Seneca, and the *Poetria nova* indicate that he did. Thus, Giuseppe Manacorda's suggestion that Bartholomew taught such texts in convent schools in the early years of his career is quite plausible.[15] Fifty years after Bartholomew's death, "The keeper of the conventual chronicle . . . still considered him one of the most learned men of his day and one of the most renowned Dominican preachers in Italy, if not in the whole order."[16]

Bartholomew of Pisa was a prolific writer, and his commentary on the *Poetria nova* is a substantial one.[17] It survives in one fifteenth-century copy, and one partial copy made ca. 1400.[18] This pattern of early humanist commentaries surviving in—and sometimes only in—fifteenth-century manuscripts will occur regularly throughout this chapter. It is one of the most intriguing aspects of the teaching of Geoffrey in late medieval and early Renaissance Italy because it implies that this strand of early humanist pedagogy continued well into the later part of the period. The excerpts from Bartholomew's commentary quoted below come from the only complete copy, Rome, Biblioteca Casanatense, 311, the manuscript to which the list of contents that was translated in the first chapter is a guide.[19] Important points in the commentary and most of the authorities cited by Bartholomew are highlighted in the margins of this manuscript, and the *Poetria nova* together with Bartholomew's commentary comprise the first item in Casanatense 311. This

---

14. Segre, "Bartolomeo," *DBI* 6.768–770; See also Witt, *Footsteps*, 187–189; Guthmüller, "Bartolomeo da San Concordio"; and Mulchahey, *First the Bow*, 454–58.

15. Manacorda, *Storia della scuola*, I.150; see also I.141, 144, and 151.

16. Mulchahey, *First the Bow*, 455; she goes on to quote a long excerpt from Bartholomew's aid for preachers (a collection of quotations organized around themes) taken from the section on "That teaching should be varied" (456–457), a sentiment with which Geoffrey of Vinsauf would have been in perfect agreement; see her reference to Geoffrey's theory of amplification, 408.

17. On his commentary on the *Poetria nova* see Manacorda, "Fra Bartolomeo"; Wilmart, "L'art poétique"; and Gehl, "Preachers," 308. Segre states incorrectly that Manacorda's article is an edition of the commentary on the *Poetria nova*.

18. The complete commentary is in Rome, Biblioteca Casanatense, 311, fols. 2r–70v for *PN*, commentary starting on fol. 1r; on this manuscript see Ceresi, *Catalogo*, 4.21–23; also Manacorda, "Fra Bartolomeo"; Wilmart, "L'art poétique"; Kaepelli, *Scriptores ordinis praedicatorum*, 1.167; and Coulson and Roy, *Incipitarium Ovidianum*, no. 17. The partial copy is in New Haven, Yale University, Beinecke Rare Book Room and Manuscript Library, Osborn fa. 6, fols. 1r–43v. The first part of the *accessus* is missing and marginal glosses are very sparse after the fifth folio. On this manuscript see Faye and Bond, *Supplement*, 97 (no. 8); *Iter ital.* 5.291; and Gallick, "Medieval Rhetorical Work" 83 (8); additional information from Robert G. Babcock and Eric Knildos, private communication.

19. See "The Usefulness of the Work."

codex also contains several other works by Bartholomew (e.g., on metrics and orthography[20]), Ovid's *Remedia amoris,* and texts useful for writers of sermons: a short piece by Bernard of Clairvaux on the crucifix, extracts from Huguccio's book of word derivations, short works on holy communion and the joys of the Virgin, etc. These contents and the rhetorical emphasis of Bartholomew's commentary reinforce the earlier suggestion that the *Poetria nova* may sometimes have served as a basic rhetorical text in the preaching orders.[21]

THE SUBJECT IS RHETORIC

> Therefore let us address the title: "Here begins the *Poetria.*" We could call it, using the same format, "Here begins the *Rhetoric,*" since in this book he instructs rhetors as much as poets, as is clear throughout.[22]
> —Bartholomew of Pisa

Bartholomew is identified as a Dominican in the title of the commentary quoted as the epigraph to the preceding section; that factor may have been a shaping force behind his emphasis on rhetoric (as opposed to poetics) as the subject of the *Poetria nova.* His *accessus* begins with a quotation from Cicero particularly pertinent for students preparing to learn rhetoric: "According to Tully's pronouncement in the second book of *De officiis,* among all the kinds of knowledge (*sciencias*) that render a man honorable, rhetoric obtains the principal part" {cf. 2.66}. Then he continues with a series of quotations that show how the orator persuades. The fifteenth-century scribe has added a rubric to the *accessus* summarizing its message as "Rhetoric renders a man honorable in many ways," and he lists in the margin the prose authorities quoted in it: Tully, Cassiodorus, Ecclesiasticus, and Seneca.[23] Bartholomew defines rhetoric as "the science of appropriate persuasion," which, he goes on to say, "is very sufficiently and fully treated in the book called the *Poetria nova,* which we are going to lecture on (*exponere*)."[24] Throughout the rest of the *accessus* he continues to focus on rhetoric as the subject of the work.

---

20. On this work see Black, *Humanism,* 161 and 164–165.

21. See "Sermons?" in chapter 2.

22. "Igitur ad titulum accedamus. 'Incipit *Poetria.*' Eodem modo potuisset dicere 'Incipit *Rethorica,*' quia tam rethores quam poete in hoc libro instruuntur ut patet per totum" (Rome, Biblioteca Casanatense, 311, fol. 1v). The formula "Here begins" is sometimes treated as part of the title.

23. "<S>Ecundum sententiam Tullii secundo *De officio* inter omnes sciencias que hominem honorabilem reddunt rethorica obtinet principatum," and further down along the margin, "Rethorica reddit hominem honorabilem multipliciter. / Primo Cassiodorus / 2 Tullius / 3 Ecclesiasticus / 4 Seneca / Tullius" (Rome, Biblioteca Casanatense, 311, fol. 1r).

24. "Ex quo etiam capere possumus rethorice diffinitionem, scilicet que est sciencia apte persuadendi. Que quidem sciencia multum sufficienter et plene traditur in libro qui *Poetria noua* dicitur, quem nos in hoc opere intendimus exponere" (Rome, Biblioteca Casanatense, 311, fol. 1r).

Bartholomew glosses the medieval version of the title, "Here begins the *Poetria nova* of Master Geoffrey the Englishman," as if it were the first words of the text, using standard *accessus* categories:

> ¶ Therefore let us address the title: HERE BEGINS THE *POETRIA* We could call it, using the same format, "Here begins the *Rhetoric*," since in this book he instructs rhetors as much as poets, as is clear throughout. NOVA is said on account of the *Poetrie* that were composed before, such as those by Aristotle [the *Poetics*], Horace [the *Ars poetica*, called *Poetria* in the Middle Ages], and others. ¶ OF *MAGISTER* GEOFFREY THE ENGLISHMAN Here the efficient cause of this book is noted, for this man was a magister who was sent in ca. 1200 by King Henry of the English to Pope Innocent III, on the occasion of a certain dispute existing between them. And then the aforementioned *magister* wrote this book for that same pope and obtained complete accord between them.

And so on with the other categories, such as the subject of the work ("speech subjected to the rules of rhetoric") and the final cause or purpose ("so that we can follow rhetoric along a narrow road").[25]

Next he divides the text of the *Poetria nova* into principal parts with subdivisions. This scholastic emphasis on division, which will be discussed in more detail with Pace of Ferrara's commentary, is a way of eliciting complexity from a text, or more correctly conferring it on one. The scholastic approach examines the *Poetria nova* as a text that yields increasing degrees of detail by dividing it into ever smaller parts until one arrives at the very first words. At this point Bartholomew begins commenting on the words of the text itself. His division of the book into parts is very simple and a useful introduction to this important strand of medieval textual pedagogy.

> ¶ 1 HOLY FATHER, WONDER OF THE WORLD This book is principally divided into three parts. In the first the author puts the prohemium, in the second the treatise itself at "If one has a house to build" (43), in the third the conclusion of the work at "Now I have crossed the sea" (2066). ¶ In the prohemium he does three things: first he praises the pope in many ways, second he urges his grace at "General light of the world" (33), third he offers the pope his book at

---

25. "¶ Igitur ad titulum accedamus: INCIPIT *POETRIA* Eodem modo potuisset dicere, "Incipit *Rethorica*," quia tam rethores quam poete in hoc libro instruuntur ut patet per totum. NOVA autem dicitur propter *Poetrias* prius compositas, vt ab Aristotile, Horatio, et aliis. ¶ MAGISTRI GUALFRADI ANGLICI Hic tangitur causa efficiens huius libri. Nam fuit ipse magister qui circa annos domini m.cc missus fuit ab Henrico rege Anglorum ad dominum Innocentium papam tertium occasione cuiusdam discordie existentis inter ipsos. Et tunc dictus magister eidem pape hoc opus scripsit, et plenam inter eos concordiam procurauit. ¶ Materialis uero causa est oratio rethoricis regulis subiecta. . . . ¶ Causa uero finalis est vt uia compendiosa rethoricam assequi ualeamus" (Rome, Biblioteca Casanatense, 311, fol. 1v). For more on Geoffrey's rhetorical argument in the book, the author as efficient cause, and the identity of the king, see chapter 1, "The Double Structure."

"In giving what it has to offer" (40). ¶ In the first part [of the prohemium] he praises the pope in five ways: first in terms of his unbelievable virtue, taking an analogy from his name, saying, O HOLY FATHER, WONDER OF THE WORLD, that is, concerning whom the world is amazed, if in putting in your name I were to say NOCENT, the name would be not whole but ACEPHALOUS (2), that is without a head. BUT IF I ADD THE HEAD by saying "Innocent," (3) IT WILL BE AT ODDS WITH THE METER, that is, it cannot be put into [verse] because the syllable "-no-" is a short one between two long ones. Therefore, just as your name thus cannot be made metrical, so your virtue cannot be measured; indeed, it is vast.[26]

He continues to gloss the rest of the words in the first six lines; then those lines are copied; then he begins to gloss the next eight lines, and then they are copied, and so forth. The sections of commentary precede the portion of text commented on, a sequence implying that the students were introduced to the work phrase by phrase before reading or hearing the passage as a whole.

A PREACHER AND A TEACHER

But this method does not appear to amplify the material.[27]
—Bartholomew of Pisa

In his comments on the latter part of Geoffrey's dedication to Pope Innocent III, it becomes clear that Bartholomew is writing for a Dominican audience. He admires Innocent, who supported the creation of the order (although he did not live to see it come into being). Bartholomew points out to his students that Innocent "was very eloquent, as is clear from the very beautiful books that he composed," and also that Innocent lived at the same time as Saint Dominic, the founder of the order.[28] Bartholomew's reputation as a preacher is significant, especially when combined with Manacorda's suggestion of the impor-

---

26. "¶ <PAPA> STUPOR MUNDI: Iste liber diuiditur principaliter in tres partes. In prima ponit auctor prohemium. In secunda tractatum ibi, 'Si quis habet' (43). In tercia conclusionem operis ibi, "Iam mare transegi" (2066). ¶ In prohemio tria facit. Primo multipliciter commendat papam. Secundo persuadet eius graciam ibi, 'Lux publica mundi' (33). Tertio offert ei hunc librum ibi, 'Inque suis dandis' (40). ¶ Circa primum commendat eum principaliter a quinque. Primo quod uirtute comprehensibili assumendo similitudinem a nomine suo, dicens sic, "O Papa stupor mundi," idest de quo stupet mundus, si ponendo nomen tuum dicerem NOCENTI, non esset nomen integrum sed ACEPHALUM, idest sine capite. SI uero ADDAM CAPUT dicendo Innocenti, ERIT HOSTIS METRI, idest non poterit poni in *** eo quod SILLABA 'no' est breuis inter duas longas. Sicut ergo nomen tuum non capitur metro, sic tua uirtus non capitur mensura sed immensa est" (Rome, Biblioteca Casanatense, 311, fol. 1v).

27. "Sed iste modus non uidetur ampliare materiam" (Rome, Biblioteca Casanatense, 311, fol. 23v).

28. "iste papa eloquentissimus fuit, sicut patet ex pulcerimis libris quos composuit. Et eius temporibus beatus Dominicus vir et eloquentis doctrine et eminentis vite ordinem nostram fundauit" (Rome, Biblioteca Casanatense, 311, fol. 2r–v).

tance of the *Poetria nova* in Dominican libraries in Italy and the influence of Bartholomew's commentary.[29] While the relationship of the religious orders to humanism has been a vexed one, at least in modern scholarship, there is no sign of such conflict in Bartholomew of Pisa. As we have seen, his *accessus* focuses on the rhetorical and "Dominican" aspects of the *Poetria nova* while drawing on Bartholomew's extensive knowledge of classical texts more indicative of humanist interests.

The commentary proper exhibits the characteristics of intermediate-level commentaries: longer and more detailed introductions to individual passages, many references to other authors, cross-referencing among parts of Geoffrey's text, and responding to possible objections to Geoffrey's teaching. It also has some of the characteristics of the more advanced commentaries, but not in full-blown forms: Bartholomew cites Aristotle (but not often), and he does, as we saw in the *accessus,* subdivide the work (but only to a limited degree). In his introduction to Geoffrey's summary of the book (*PN* 78–86), Bartholomew answers three "doubts" (the scribe notes *dubitatio / responsio* three times in the margin) about the *Poetria nova.*[30] In his answers Bartholomew is positive but not unthinkingly so about Geoffrey. For example, Bartholomew brings up here the double structure of the *Poetria nova* according to the parts of rhetoric and the parts of a discourse, but he disagrees with most other commentators who state that Geoffrey has all the parts of each. Bartholomew says that Geoffrey treats neither the confirmation nor confutation parts of a rhetorical discourse since these "pertain more to the arguments of lawyers than to the instruction of writers."[31] With regard to the art of rhetoric, Bartholomew notes that Geoffrey leaves out memory here in this initial summary (though there is a short treatment at the end of the book), so Bartholomew provides a definition from the first book of Aristotle's *Metaphysics* and "the book *On Memory,*" presumably *De memoria et reminiscentia* in the *Parva naturalia,* which was often called *De memoria* for short."[32] He refers to both Virgil and the Book of Proverbs on sirens,[33] and both Boethius and Ovid on apostrophe. These last two examples come at the end of a typical Bartholomew gloss: insightful, helpful, and clear. When Geoffrey describes various modes of apostrophe, such as rebuking error

---

29. Manacorda, "Fra Bartolomeo."

30. Rome, Biblioteca Casanatense, 311, fol. 5r; see also "questio / responsio" in the left margin of folio 23v in plate 5. The term "dubium" or "dubitatio" was used for "simple questions which required straightforward explanations," and "questio" for more intricate questions that required discussion" (Teeuwen, *The Vocabulary of Intellectual Life,* 323); on the *qu(a)estio* see "Questioning Authority" in chapter 4.

31. "De confirmatione autem et confutatione non curauit, quia magis pertinent ad altercationes aduocatorum quam ad instructionem dictatorum" (Rome, Biblioteca Casanatense, 311, fol. 5r).

32. "¶ Queritur tercio quare pretermisit memoriam. ¶ Dic quod memoria est quid naturale nam et alia animalia memoriam habent, vt patet per Philosophum primo *Methaphysice* et in libro *De Memoria*" (Rome, Biblioteca Casanatense, 311, fol. 5r–v). I am grateful to Mary Carruthers for identifying the second work.

33. Rome, Biblioteca Casanatense, 311, fol. 14r–v.

"in the manner of a teacher"[34] or languishing "in tearful complaint" or railing in anger or joking (455–461), Bartholomew summarizes them but adds that there are many others, such as "invoking the deity, as in that passage of Boethius, 'O you who in perpetual order govern the universe' {*Cons.* III, m. 9}, or to express love, as in that passage of Ovid, 'As soon as I wrote this, I said, "Go forth, / happy letter, and before long she / will take you into her graceful hand"'" {*Her.* 18.15–16}.[35]

A good example of his method of close reading comes in his discussion of Geoffrey's treatment of digression, a touchstone in our examination of how commentators approached the *Poetria nova*. Bartholomew is uninterested in the identity or gender of the two lovers, concentrating instead on Geoffrey's two types of digression.[36] He suggests that Geoffrey's example itself contains *two* digressions. Besides the primary one, in which Geofffrey describes the season when the lovers are parted (Bartholomew says, "go outside the bounds of the subject, as in describing times, places, or events coming in between"[37]), there is, according to Bartholomew, another embedded earlier in the outer story. He analyzes the introduction of the story of the two lovers as itself containing an example of a secondary kind of digression: the simple rearranging of the natural order by putting events that happen later earlier.[38] Geoffrey had described this kind but according to most commentators apparently had not given an example of it:

> ¶ 537 THE BOND OF A SINGLE LOVE Here he exemplifies both the aforementioned kinds. And ¶ first the secondary[39] kind, which is the more superficial one, namely when earlier events are omitted and then taken up later, as at "The bond of a single love," that is, two were in love. This is the beginning. ¶ Second, having cut out the middle, he goes to the third part of the story, thus: (539) A STRANGE CAUSE DIVIDED THEM that is, they go away from each other in different directions. Then he goes back to the middle that he had cut out, saying BUT BEFORE THEY WERE

---

34. Nims translates "magistri" here as "magistrate," but commentators interpreted as much of the *Poetria nova* as possible in terms of the schoolroom; see "Conversion: The Origin of Style" in chapter 2.

35. "deum inuocando vt in illo Boetii, 'O qui perpetua mundum ratione gubernas,' vel amorem exprimendo, vt in illo Ouidii, 'Protinus hec scribens et felix litera dixi; / Iam tibi formosam porriget illa manum'" (Rome, Biblioteca Casanatense, 311, fol. 20r). The English version of the quotation from the *Heroides* is taken from Harold Isbell's translation. For more of this passage from Boethius, see "Description and Circumlocution" in chapter 2.

36. The scribe's rubric calls the whole passage "An Example of Both Kinds of Digression" ("Exemplum de utroque modo disgressionis" [Rome, Biblioteca Casanatense, 311, fol. 23v]).

37. "exi de finibus materie, vt describendo tempora, loca, res interuenientes" (Rome, Biblioteca Casanatense, 311, fol. 23r).

38. Black's assertions that Geoffrey's discussion of natural and artificial order introduced at *PN* 87–90 refers to word order rather than narrative order (*Humanism,* 346–348, and *Education and Society,* 50) are not supported by the commentaries; see also Franciscellus Mancinus's comment below (note 282), and the more general discussion in "Shaping the Narrative" in chapter 2.

39. I have translated "secundo" here and "primo" in the following gloss as "secondary" and "primary" respectively, since their relative importance is what has caused Bartholomew to reorder them. Geoffrey himself treats the secondary one first.

PARTED, LIPS PRESSED KISSES etc. ¶ But this method does not appear to amplify the material. ¶ One could reply that the author did not state it as if it amplified. Rather, lest it be thought that there is only one kind of digression, namely the one that amplifies, he put in that one, which changes the order.[40]

That such rearrangement does not amplify the treatment would have been an important consideration for preachers.

Bartholomew pays more attention to the primary example of digression. He restates in prose order Geoffrey's allegorical passage describing the spring season during which the lovers are parted, glossing each phrase. He also introduces a rhetorical example, "The meadow laughs," around which Geoffrey will later build a series of lessons (*PN* 1765 ff.). In contrast to the carefully segmented preceding comment on the division into parts of the example of the human lovers, this gloss on the description of springtime stresses the unity of the passage, and the scribe has added no paragraph marks after the initial one.

¶ Second, at (545) WINTER YIELDS TO SPRING, he puts an example of the primary kind of digression. Whence in adding to the preceding he digresses in order to describe the season, saying that it was the season when "winter yields to spring," that is when winter is receding and spring is coming in, when THE AIR UNCLASPS that is, opens, and drives off THE CLOUDS. 546 THE HEAVEN FLIRTS WITH that is, jokes with, the earth. And because (547) THE MOIST AND WARM AIR IS MASCULINE that is, has the power of procreation, (548) THE FEMININE EARTH RESPONDS in such way that (448–449) A FLOWER, A SON, BURSTS FORTH AND SMILES AT the earth, for then "The meadow laughs" (1765). And THE FIRST TENDRIL of foliage ADORNS or ornaments the (550) THE TIPS that is, the summits, of the trees.[41] And (552) THE SEASON DELIGHTS THE BIRDS that is, moves them to love. (552–553) THIS HOUR OF TIME FOUND THE LOVERS APART Here is how he returns to what came before.[42]

---

40. "¶ VNICUS ASTRINGIT Hic exemplificat de utroque predictorum modorum. Et ¶ primo de secundo tanquam de leuiori, scilicet quando que prius omissa sunt postea reassumuntur sic, 'Vnicus astringit,' etc., idest duo se diligebant. Ecce principium. ¶ Secundo dimisso medio uadit ad tertium, sic: (539) CORPORA DISIUNGIT NOUA CAUSA idest abinuicem discesserunt. Deinde redit ad medium quod dimiserat, dicens (539–40) SED ANTE RECESSUM / OSCULA PREFIGIT etc. ¶ Sed iste modus non uidetur ampliare (=amplificare) materiam. ¶ Vnde potest dici quod auctor non posuit ipsum quasi ampliaret. Sed ne forte crederetur esse unus solus modus digressionis, scilicet qui ampliat, posuit etiam istum qui peruertit" (Rome, Biblioteca Casanatense, 311, fol. 23v).

41. Geoffrey's term is actually the adjective "arboreos" (belonging to trees), for which Bartholomew substitutes the standard genitive plural.

42. "¶ Secundo ibi, (545) VERI CEDIT HYEMS ponit exemplum de primo digressionis. Vnde addendo ad predicta, disgreditur ad describendum tempus, dicens quod erat tempus quando hyemps cedit ueri, idest recedente hyeme et ueniente uere, quando AER DIFFIBULAT idest aperit, et depellit NEBULAS. 546 CELUM LASCIVIT idest iocundatur in terram. Et quod (547) AER HUMIDUS ET CALIDUS SIT MASCULUS idest uirtutem generandi habeat, (548) FEMINA HUMUS SENTIT ita quod (548–549) FLOS FILIUS EXIT ET ARRIDET terre, quia tunc "pratum ridet" (1765). Et (549) COMA PRIMULA frondium COMIT siue ornat (550) APICES idest sumitates arborum. Et (552) TEMPUS TITILLAT AUES idest ad

Bartholomew's observations seem obvious after the fact, yet he notices aspects of the *Poetria nova* that other commentators do not. He cites authorities only where they are relevant and helpful. He adds material where Geoffrey's verse treatment is obscure or incomplete, but he reads the text as if there were a reason for everything that Geoffrey did, and he labors to find it. We see in his attention to detail and knowledge of emotional and verbal resonance what made him a good teacher and a good preacher, and an important early humanist.

THE *POETRIA NOVA* AND THE PREACHING ORDERS

> And at that time St. Dominic, a man of eloquent teaching and exemplary (*eminentis*) life, founded our order.[43]
> —Bartholomew of Pisa

The double emphasis on rhetoric and on the importance of the dedicatee of the *Poetria nova* to the Dominicans in Bartholomew of Pisa's *accessus* introduces the *Poetria nova* to students in terms of the avowed work of his order. His glosses reflect the broad knowledge of the early humanists in general, and his commenting techniques are those of other teachers with students at roughly the same level. In fact, all the commentaries on the *Poetria nova* that we can associate with the preaching orders, by authorship or ownership, reflect the teaching of the *Poetria nova* in general; they would be hard to distinguish as a separate group without external knowledge of the circumstances of their compostion or ownership history. As we saw in the previous chapter, the commentary by the German Dominican Reiner von Cappel has many (if not quite all) the characteristics typical of school commentaries: a very short *accessus*, glosses concentrating on the passage at hand and the specific doctrine expressed within it, more focus on difficult words than abstract concepts, and a positive appreciation of the *Poetria nova* and Geoffrey's accomplishment in it. He introduces the *Poetria nova* to young students as both a general handbook on composition and a rhetorical treatise that could be applied to sermons. What might be specifically "Dominican" aspects of Reiner's commentary—constant use of the word *sermo* for a composition and perhaps also his comparatively restrained discussions of the two lovers and the naked woman—are not particularly pronounced or obvious. Dominicans seem to have used the text as an all-purpose introduction to or review of the principles of composition according to rhetorical models.

---

amorem commouet. 552–553 HEC TEMPORIS HORA . . . DIVISIT AMANTES Ecce quomodo redit ad propositum" (Rome, Biblioteca Casanatense, 311, fol. 23v).

43. "Et eius temporibus beatus Dominicus vir et eloquentis doctrine et eminentis vite ordinem nostram fundauit" (Rome, Biblioteca Casanatense, 311, fol. 2r–v).

Good rhetoricians themselves, some Dominican teachers may have used the context in which their students would be using its teaching—in the composition of sermons—to help students use the *Poetria nova* most effectively.

We have seen passages in the *Poetria nova* itself that could be considered mini-sermons,[44] and the glosses in manuscripts of Dominican origin or provenance do pay attention to these passages, but not so much that one would notice a difference if not looking for it. Bartholomew's commentary on the lament of the cross, for example, is a simple paraphrase, although he does carefully divide the passage into numbered parts. Other manuscripts for which we have no indication of origin do sometimes bring extra attention to this section of text. The commentary in a fourteenth-century northern Italian manuscript in the Academy of Sciences in St. Petersburg quotes the Apostle Paul in a gloss on this passage,[45] and in a homily collection in Paris the lament of the cross has been copied in a blank space left in the manuscript.[46]

The use of the *Poetria nova* by Franciscans is not well documented, but some inferences can be made. I have not found specific references to the composition of sermons in the known Franciscan manuscripts. Nor is special attention paid to the section of the *Poetria nova* in which the cross speaks and calls on listeners to take up another crusade. But the author of a commentary from the Franciscan convent at Landshut analyzes in notable detail Geoffrey's treatment of abbreviation and his successively more abbreviated examples of the Snow Child.[47] Abbreviation may have been a special emphasis in mendicant teaching as well as in school exercises in general. This is, however, too small a thread on which to hang any kind of generalization about Franciscan interests in the commentary.

The manuscripts of the *Poetria nova* and commentaries on it now in the library of the Franciscan mother house in Assisi are a good example of what can be inferred but not proven. All date from the fifteenth century, too late for the inventories of 1381.[48] One of these (Assisi 309) contains the commentary by Pace of Ferrara copied as a separate text.[49] Pace's explicit emphasis on poetics (as opposed to rhetoric) as the subject of the *Poetria nova* shows the difficulty of generalizing about the teaching of rhetoric in the preaching orders on the basis of individual commentaries. This manuscript is one of two included in

44. "Sermons?" in chapter 2.

45. St. Petersburg, Biblioteka Rossiiskoi akademii nauk, Q. 433, fols. 65r–96v for the text, with the commentary starting on 64v; for the Apostle Paul; see fol. 72r. On this manuscript see Kiseleva, *Latinskie Rukopisi*, 123–125 and 286; corrected by Baswell, *Virgil in Medieval England*, 309–310. I am grateful to Christopher Baswell for his help with this manuscript.

46. Paris, BnF lat. 2250, fols. 145v–146r.

47. Munich, Universitätsbibliothek, Cod. 4° 814, fol. 86v.

48. Cenci, *Biblioteca manuscripta*, 34–37.

49. On Assisi, Biblioteca Storico-Francescana della Chiesa Nuova, 309, fols. 1r–74r, see Mazzatinti, *Inventari dei manoscritti*, 4.70; Cenci, *Bibliotheca Manuscripta*, 2.518–519; Sweeney, *Prolegomena*, 35. Judson Allen calls this manuscript, "The fullest commentary on the *Poetria nova* that I know" (*Ethical Poetic*, 168).

the inventory made ca. 1666, while the other two do not show up until the 1844 inventory, but they may have been in Franciscan houses earlier. Three are in similar formats; they are large, thick volumes in which the *Poetria nova* is copied with the work of a classical author: Horace (Assisi 301[50]), Virgil (Assisi 305[51]), or Cicero (Assisi 309), and it is they, not Geoffrey or a commentator, who are listed on the nineteenth-century covers of each codex. The *Poetria nova* is ancillary in the functioning of these manuscripts, although in two of them it is literally primary—the first text, there to be used with all the rest. In the Virgil manuscript, only the first half of the *Poetria nova* is copied; it occupies just five of the ten folios at least that were to be given over to it (the *Poetria nova* stops in mid-line); all the Virgilian texts, some of which are also incomplete or inchoate, are accompanied by similar kinds of glosses. The Horace manuscript has texts copied in similar formats, but none of the works in the manuscript is glossed. The third manuscript is the one that, in addition to selections of Cicero's letters, contains a copy (without attribution) of Pace of Ferrara's extensive commentary on the *Poetria nova*.[52] This copying of the *Poetria nova* or commentaries on it with classical texts is typical of the Italian manuscripts of the *Poetria nova* in general, particularly those containing early humanist commentaries like Pace's.

In contrast, the fourth manuscript, Assisi 561, does not, in fact, contain a copy of the *Poetria nova* or a commentary on it, but only an excerpt occupying four folios.[53] The codex in which it appears is a very late preacher's miscellany from a completely different part of Europe: Bruges, where it was finished on October 22, 1463. Much smaller and more portable than the manuscripts discussed above, it contains, among other works in several hands, selections from the *Postilla litteralis* by Nicholas of Lyra, including several on Jews, as well as the chapter of Robert of Basevorn's *Ars predicandi* on the eight methods of amplifying the theme of a sermon. The excerpt from the *Poetria nova* is Geoffrey's passage on invention in which he cautions that the hand not be too hasty to take up the pen (50 ff.). This Bruges manuscript in Assisi probably was put together for use on the road by someone who had received a more advanced, more specifically "Franciscan" education, as we can see from the selections from Nicholas of Lyra, whose *postilla* could have provided themes for sermons, in particular those on the Jews, an identifiable Franciscan type.[54] The instructions from Rob-

---

50. On Assisi, Biblioteca Storico-Francescana della Chiesa Nuova, 301, fols. 119r–153r, see Mazzatinti et al., *Inventari dei manoscritti*, 4.69; and Cenci, *Bibliotheca Manuscripta*, 2.520 (1725).

51. On Assisi, Biblioteca Storico-Francescana della Chiesa Nuova, 305, fols. 1r–5v, see Mazzatinti et al., *Inventari dei manoscritti*, 4.69; Cenci, *Bibliotheca Manuscripta*, 2.546 (1950).

52. Allen cites several passages from this manuscript of Pace's commentary in *Ethical Poetic*, 8, 52, 130–132, 168–169.

53. On Assisi, Biblioteca Storico-Francescana della Chiesa Nuova, 561, fols. 256r–259v, see Mazzatinti et al., *Inventari dei manoscritti*, 4.108; and Cenci, *Bibliotheca Manuscripta*, 2.550–551.

54. See Roest, *History of Franciscan Education*, 150, 215, and 292; also D'Avray, "Portable *Vademecum* Books."

ert of Basevorn on how to turn a theme into a sermon and the example from the *Poetria nova* on the mental structuring of a composition are copied in the same hand.[55]

Even more than the Dominican manuscripts of the *Poetria nova,* those of the Franciscans are generic and typical of Italian copies from the same period. This fact could indicate a paucity of invention on the part of the Franciscans, a conclusion with which I am loath to agree. It is more likely that the Franciscans, like the Dominicans, recognized the wide applicability of the *Poetria nova* and brought back to their convents methods of rhetorical teaching that were successful elsewhere as well.[56] The most popular Italian commentary on the *Poetria nova* was that of Pace of Ferrara, a copy of which the Franciscans in Assisi owned, and to which we now turn our attention.

PACE OF FERRARA

Item: a parchment book . . . that begins, "It behooves those who are about to begin this book on the art of poetry" and concludes, "Here end the observations on the *Poetria* composed by Master Pace, a most worthy teacher of the schools."[57]
—from the inventory of a fourteenth-century Italian notary

Some of the most important and influential early humanist commentaries on the *Poetria nova* originated in the northeastern region of Italy called the Veneto

---

55. The colophons in another manuscript, that of the Franciscan Jacobus Dam, lector in Bern by 1481 when he completed his copy of the *Poetria nova,* provide a glimpse into one Franciscan's educational path. At the end of his copy of the *PN* he writes, "Finis *Poetrie* Ganfredi Jacobus Dam 1481," and then repeats in an added gloss: "Finis *Rhetorice* seu *Poetrie* Gaufredi per me fratrem Jacobum Dam lectorem Berne anno 1481 anno 2° lectoratus" (Bamberg, Staatsbibliothek, Class. 56, fol. 46r). According to Bert Roest (e-mail correspondence, January 2006), "lectoratus" indicates that Dam had probably gone through the lectorate program and was teaching theology in Bern. Later Dam went to Paris, presumably to read the *Sentences* of Peter Lombard, but what he copied in this manuscript were classical texts: "In arte poetica oracius finit feliciter per fratrem Jacobum Dam lectorem bernensium anno 1485 in Octaua apostolorum petri ac pauli tempore parisionatus sui anno primo" (fol. 56v). "Finitur tocius artis rethorice doctrina sub breuibus concussa per me Jacobum Dam ordinis minorum berne lectorem et parisiensem transscripta 1485 Die secunda Augusti mensis" (fol. 80r). "Auli flacci persii satirarum liber explicit per me Jacobum Dam pro tempore minorum lectorem in berna anno 1484" (fol. 96v). "Explicit Junius Juuenalis per me Jacobum Dam ordinis minorum in berna lectorem et studentem parisiis anno 1485 vigil. petri et pauli" (fol. 162r). And after the *Disticha Catonis:* "Finis 1488 Dam" (fol. 167v). These colophons to the other works are quoted from the transcriptions in Leitschut and Fischer, *Katalog der Handschriften,* 66–67; I have not examined the manuscript *in situ,* and the microfilm that I have of it from John Conley contains only fols. 1r–46r (the *Poetria nova* accompanied by a diagram and a few notes).

56. I am grateful to Bert Roest for suggesting that the *Poetria nova* might have been used this way and for helping me with an early conference paper on this topic.

57. "Item unum librum in membranis . . . qui incipit: Incepturos librum *Artis poetice,* et finit: expliciunt *Rationes supra poetria* composite a magistro Pace scolarum dignissimo professore'" (Battistella, "Un inventario," 147). The incipit given for this manuscript, "Incepturos librum *Artis poetice,*" is that of the second part of the *accessus* to Pace's commentary. "Professor" can mean either a teacher or a professor, just as "schola" can mean "school" in the sense of a schoolroom or a school of advanced studies at a university (Teeuwen, *Vocabulary of Intellectual Life,* 116–117 and 128–130; also "magister," 95–97, and the bibliography for these entries).

and neighboring regions like Friuli, home of the Udine fragments discussed in the preceding chapter.[58] Pace of Ferrara's commentary on the *Poetria nova* is one of the earliest, and it is also the most extensive, the most laudatory, and the most popular of all Italian commentaries on this text. Pace, or Magister Pax Paduanus (Pace of Padua), was teaching logic and grammar in the famous *studium* in Padua by 1300.[59] A poet himself, Pace was associated with the group of early humanists around the poet luminary of Padua, Albertino Mussato. He was probably not, however, a member of Mussato's inner circle, what Dazzi calls "*il cenacolo padovano.*"[60] According to Ronald Witt, Pace was eager "to contribute to the scholarly and literary innovations championed by the Paduans."[61] Both Pace and another important commentator on the *Poetria nova* who spent time in Padua, Guizzardo of Bologna, wrote commentaries on Mussato's influential Senecan tragedy, the *Ecerinis.*[62] The attention that Pace and Guizzardo paid to both the *Ecerinis* and the *Poetria nova* suggests that both works were particularly well suited to the pedagogy of the academic early humanists. Pace was, as Stadter notes, "alive to the new trends in Padua, and was ready to present to his students works which did not fit into the traditional patterns which he had learned, but rather represented the newly won achievements of the Paduan humanists."[63]

In his lengthy *accessus* to the *Poetria nova* Pace says that he has decided to abandon "our mother grammar for medicine, as if crossing into a foreign genre (*modum*)."[64] Such a shift in disciplines would not have been unusual in Padua, where all arts of the trivium were strong during the first half of the fourteenth century; Paduan lawyers and physicians were assumed to have a "knowledge of rhetoric and the *auctores.*"[65] From the colophons appended

58. See "The Female Body in the Classroom" in chapter 2. Scalon has concluded that there was constant interaction among cities in this region where the *Poetria nova* was very popular (*Libri, scuole e cultura,* 50–51); he also argues that grammar and rhetoric schools in Udine achieved a high level of teacher training (47) and notes that classical texts were used more and more frequently in the classroom (49).

59. Witt, *Footsteps,* 114; also Guido Billanovich, "Il preumanesimo padovano," 66; and Gargan, "Il preumanesimo a Vicenza," 152. Stadter notes that Pace was "minister arcium in studio Paduano" where he had Venetian students working with him ("Planudes, Plutarch, and Pace," 144).

60. Dazzi, *Il Mussato preumanista,* 42–43. Stadter, however, argues for Pace's "position in this circle" ("Planudes, Plutarch, and Pace," 156, also 146–147). The assessments of Pace's Latin poetry also vary; e.g., Stadter, 156, and Witt, *Footsteps,* 115–116.

61. Witt, *Footsteps,* 115.

62. According to Gillespie, Guizzardo's co-authored commentary on the *Ecerinis* was "finished in December 1317, perhaps to coincide with that year's performance of the text. Somewhat later came Pace of Ferrara's *Evidentia Ecerinis*" ("From the Twelfth Century," 220). On Pace's introduction to Mussato's work, see "Pace and Mussato," below.

63. "Planudes, Plutarch, and Pace," 146.

64. "matrem nostram grammaticam ad medicinam quasi ad modum extraneum transeuntes" (Seville, Biblioteca Capitular y Colombina, Col. 5–4–30, fol. 2ra [5ra]). Stadter notes that "a passage from logic to medicine" was widespread in the fourteenth century ("Planudes, Plutarch, and Pace," 146). One manuscript has "mundum" for "modum" (Klagenfurt, Bundesstaatliche Studienbibliothek, Pap. 109, fol. 63v).

65. Siraisi, *Arts and Sciences,* 64–65; she notes that "in the second half of the century Petrarch was able to complain that *medici* [in Padua] were expected to be lettered men who had read everything including Cicero, Seneca and Virgil, while, in his somewhat jaundiced view, neglecting medicine" (56). Also, at Padua "studies in arts and medicine were apparently sometimes pursued consecutively and sometimes simultaneously" (30).

to some of the manuscripts of his commentary on the *Poetria nova,* such as the one in the epigraph above, Pace was well known as a teacher. Another states, "Here ends the *expositio* of the *Poetria novella* of [owned by?] Henry of Regensburg that *magister* Pace of Ferrara composed and completed for the use of students."[66] It is thought that Pace was a professor of logic and grammar at Padua,[67] although according to Paul Grendler there is no archival evidence that the *Poetria nova* was ever taught at an Italian university.[68] But the extraordinary length of Pace's commentary,[69] the university-style format of all seven extant copies, and Pace's extended *divisio* method of analysis (examined below) all suggest that Pace and others may have taught it unofficially at the university in Padua and elsewhere, perhaps in the extraordinary lectures on supplemental texts regularly given in the afternoons by university teachers with less seniority,[70] or, as could have been the case with Assisi 309, at the more advanced convent schools or *studia.*[71]

Pace's commentary continued to be copied for more than a century and a half after it was written. Three manuscripts date from the fourteenth century: those now in Rome (Biblioteca Corsiniana, Rossi 22 [36 G15], a shorter version),[72] Klagenfurt (Bundesstaatliche Studienbibliothek, Pap. 109, the only one in a northern script),[73] and Seville (Biblioteca Capitular y Colombina, Col. 5–

---

66. "Explicit expositio *Poetrie nouelle* Henirici [*sic*] de Ratispona, quam magister Pax de Ferraria componuit [*sic*] et conpleuit ad utilitatem scolarium" (Cremona, Biblioteca Statale, Fondo Governativa 88, fol. 87r). The word "sc(h)olaris" can mean "student or pupil" and also "scholar" (Teeuwen, *Vocabulary of Intellectual Life,* 131–132).

67. Gloria, *Monumenti (1222–1318),* 369, and *Monumenti (1318–1405),* 1.487; Stadter, "Planudes, Plutarch, and Pace," 137 and especially 141–142; Guido Billanovich, "Il preumanesimo padovano," 66; Gargan, "Il preumanesimo a Vicenza," 152; Witt, *Footsteps,* 86. Siraisi states that Pace taught logic in Padua from at least 1294–1319, although his interests "align him chiefly with the professors of grammar and rhetoric and with the literary circle outside the schools" (*Arts and Sciences,* 51 and 62). Siraisi and Gloria refer to him as Pace dal Friuli; Stadter sorts out the various persons named Pace or Pax conflated in early sources ("Planudes, Plutarch, and Pace").

68. There is no mention of the *Poetria nova* in Grendler, *Universities of the Italian Renaissance,* a fact that he confirmed for me before its publication. On Pace's "advanced" commentary, see also Fredborg, "Rhetoric and Dialectic," 167–168, n. 15.

69. In Bergamo, Biblioteca Civica "Angelo Mai," MA 484, a sizeable copy (295 x 205 mm) of 65 folios, the scribe must have been dismayed when, after finishing the first ten folios, he looked at how much was left to copy. He increased the number of lines per column from 53 to 68, but he overcompensated: several blank folios remain at the end.

70. Siraisi, *Arts and Sciences,* 30. A lecture was "extraordinary" if "something about the course was not in accordance with the prescribed *ordo:* the course was, for example, taught by a bachelor instead of a master or professor, took place at hours which were not reserved for *lectio ordinaria,* or had a private character, etc." (Teeuven, *Vocabulary of Intellectual Life,* 304–305).

71. On the development of Franciscan schools and *studia generalia* see Roest, *History of Franciscan Education,* 1–117.

72. Rome, Biblioteca Corsiniana, Rossi 22 [36 G 15], fols. 2ra–24va for Pace's commentary, 25r–56v for *PN* and glosses; see Petrucci, *Catalogo,* 12, where the commentary is described as anonymous. This shorter version does not include the final note discussed in "Stand and Counterstand" below.

73. Klagenfurt, Bundesstaatliche Studienbibliothek, Pap. 109, fols. 63v–175va (incomplete); see Menhardt, *Handschriftenverzeichnis,* 144–145.

4–30, in two hands, the second dated 1395).[74] The remaining four are fifteenth-century Italian manuscripts[75]: those now in Bergamo (Biblioteca Civica "Angelo Mai," MA 484, dated 1414),[76] London (BL Add. 10095, dated 1427, copied by a teacher in Friuli),[77] Assisi (Biblioteca Storico-Francesana della Chiesa Nuova, 309),[78] and Cremona (Biblioteca Statale, Fondo Governativa 88).[79] All but the Klagenfurt manuscript are Italian. The Seville manuscript (S) (plate 6) is used as the basis of the transcriptions and translations that follow; corrections in that manuscript (some of which are very faint strokes through individual letters) are not noted. It has been emended with readings from those in Rome (R) and, when necessary, Klagenfurt (K) and Bergamo (B).

Perhaps because of its length, Pace's commentary is the only work in four of the manuscripts: those in Rome (with a separate copy of the *Poetria nova*, however), Seville, Bergamo, and Cremona. In the others, the works with which it is copied or bound suggest a variety of contexts. Klagenfurt Pap. 109, from a Benedictine monastery in Millstatt, Austria, includes the kind of works that we shall see in many other central European manuscripts of the *Poetria nova* in the next chapter: two commentaries on the pseudo-Boethian *De disciplina scolarium*[80] copied in the same hand as Pace's commentary on the *Poetria nova*, bound with sermons, rhetorical works, and theological treatises all indicating advanced training, perhaps specifically for preaching. London, BL Add. 10095, a manuscript compiled for the teaching of poetry, includes Pace's commentary and the *Physiologus* of Theobaldus, bound with Bonacorsa's commentary on Horace and the commentaries by Benvenuto da Imola de Ymola on Virgil's *Eclogues* and *Georgics*.[81] The Franciscan manuscript at Assisi (309) is a collection of school texts in various hands and formats.

---

74. Seville, Biblioteca Capitular y Colombina, Col. 5–4–30, fols. 2ra–102ra (5ra–105ra), Italian, dated 1395 (fol. 102ra [105ra]); the folios in this manuscript have been renumbered recently, and I give the new folio number first, followed by the earlier one in brackets. *PN* commentary only (except for several older folios used as pastedowns), in two hands.

75. There are also in Krakow two fifteenth-century copies of a commentary whose *accessus* (surviving in only one of these manuscripts) draws on Pace's: Biblioteka Muzeum Narodowego w Krakowie, Oddzial Zbiory Czartoryskich, 1464 (with *accessus*), and Biblioteka Jagiellońska, Przyb. 91/52. For more on these manuscripts see chapter 4, note 188.

76. Bergamo, Biblioteca Civica "Angelo Mai," MA 484, fols. 1ra–65rb, commentary only, dated 1414; see Kristeller, *Iter ital.* 1.8. (Stadter corrected this date to 1445, but Kristeller's reading is correct). Pace's commentary only.

77. London, BL Add. 10095, fols. 108r–156r, copied by Iacobus, teacher in Porderone in Friuli. See Watson, *Dated and Datable Manuscripts,* 27 and plate 390.

78. On Assisi, Biblioteca Storico-Francescana della Chiesa Nuova, 309, see above, note 49.

79. Cremona, Biblioteca Statale, Fondo Governativa, 88, fols. 1r–87r. On this manuscript see Mazzatinti et al., *Inventari dei manoscritti,* 70.66.

80. See "The Other Audience" in chapter 1.

81. These last two are copied in the same distinctive two-column format as Pace's commentary. Several of the characteristics of the commentary on Virgil's *Eclogues* by Benvenuto da Imola (born in the 1340s) are also found in Pace's, such as a combination of Aristotelian logical analysis with classical literary references, which may indicate that they were taught at a similar level; see Lord, "Benvenuto da Imola's Literary Approach."

The great length of Pace's commentary and the double-columned, commentary-only format in which it is copied in the Italian manuscripts[82] suggest lectures at an advanced level (plate 6). This format is the same as that of the much shorter lecture notes of Pace's contemporary, Guizzardo of Bologna (plate 7), discussed later in this chapter.[83] (It is also strikingly similar to that of officially dictated lectures in central European university commentaries [plate 9].) There are very few breaks in the columns; in some of the Italian copies, not even the *lemmata* are written in a larger display script. Thus, each folio is dauntingly regular in appearance, creating a difficulty for the scribes.[84] Numerous improperly expanded abbreviations and sections beginning with similar phrasing that were copied twice or omitted, especially in the structurally repetitive *accessus,* are evidence of the visual errors in copying to which such an undifferentiated appearance could lead.[85] In addition, the variety of subjects in Pace's *accessus* caused other problems for individual scribes. For example, the scribe of London, BL Add. 10095 had difficulty with logical terminology but understood a discussion of the interconnection between music and mathematics, while the areas of strength and weakness are reversed with the scribe of the Klagenfurt manuscript.

Pace's commentary opens with an incipit that seems to be about to tell us the level of student for which it was intended: "Our forebears were accustomed, when they proposed something new, to choose various persons to whom the labor of the whole new project seemed to direct itself."[86] But instead of describing the audience, Pace's introduction turns into a dedication to "dearest Simon," probably Simone della Tela, a colleague and *doctor in artibus* at Padua.[87] Just as

---

82. While the scribe of Klagenfurt Bundesstaatliche Studienbibliothek, Pap. 109 began with a single-column format, he later turns to a two-column one (though his columns contain many fewer words per folio side than is the case with the Italian copies).

83. On Guizzardo's teaching in the *studio* in Florence and on this manuscript, Vatican City, BAV Ottob. lat. 3291, as lecture notes, see Witt, *Footsteps,* 130.

84. The scribe of Rome, Biblioteca Corsiniana, Rossi 22, while keeping the traditional two-column format of the commentary, divides it into more visibly separate paragraphs and highlights other internal divisions to a greater degree than that found in the other manuscripts of Pace's commentary. This manuscript looks less impressively uniform, but it is much easier to find one's way through. Only the Corsiniana manuscript, which contains the unique copy of the shorter version of Pace's commentary, also includes the text of the *Poetria nova* as well.

85. Although such errors are usually signs of a written (*scripta*) version, other aspects such as the double columns of most of the manuscripts as well as use of the first and second person, references to hearing the commentary, etc., indicate that it was probably originally, or at least at some point, recorded from lectures delivered orally; see Lord, "Benvenuto da Imola's Literary Approach," 291–292; Hamesse, "La technique" and "Le vocabulaire"; and "*Scripta, Dicta,* and *Reportatio*" and "*Scripta* vs. *Dicta* in Practice" in chapter 4. An anonymous reader cautioned, however, that "Trevet's commentary on Boethius's *Consolation* was often copied in a double-column lemmatic format without the text, but it was never used in university lectures."

86. "<C>onsvevervnt antiquiores nostri cum aliquid noui proponunt personas sibi diuersas eligere ad quas totius noui operis labor tendere uideatur" (Seville, Biblioteca Capitular y Colombina, Col. 5-4-30, fol. 2ra [5ra]).

87. "Te karissime Symeon" (Seville, Biblioteca Capitular y Colombina, Col. 5-4-30, fol. 2ra [5ra]). On Simone see Gloria, *Monumenti (1318–1405),* 1.500 and 2.15–16. Both men owned important codices of classical texts: Pace owned a Greek manuscript of sixty-nine books of Plutarch's *Moralia* annotated and corrected by Maximus Planudes (Stadter, "Planudes, Plutarch, and Pace," 141, 152–52), and Simon was the owner of an

the *Poetria nova* was written to teach students but dedicated to the Pope, Pace's commentary was aimed at students but dedicated to a fellow teacher.

THE SUBJECT IS POETICS

The subject of this book is the art of poetry. . . . They err who say that the subject of this book is eloquence or rhetoric. . . . [88]
—Pace of Ferrara

Pace approaches the *Poetria nova* via a double *accessus* with two canonical sets of questions, one about the art that the book teaches, which for him is the art of poetry, and another about the *Poetria nova* itself: "It behooves those who are about to begin this book on the art of poetry to consider two [sets of considerations]. The first concerns issues which should be dealt with in general terms concerning this art. The second concerns those [questions] that are customarily asked specifically about a given book concerning this same art."[89] His focus on poetics contradicts the approach of his contemporary, Bartholomew of Pisa, whose averred focus is on rhetoric. In his *accessus* Pace poses and answers a long if conventional list of questions (numbered in some manuscripts): "we would say that concerning the art of poetry these issues ought to be addressed in general terms, namely [1] the discovery of the poetic art; [2] what is it? [3] what is its genus? [4] its subject? [5] what is its function? [6] its purpose? [7] what are its parts? [8] what are its aspects? [9] its instrument? [10] what do we call the practitioner of the art?"[90]

Each of these questions receives in order a long, detailed answer with citations.

The **discovery** of the poetic art is illustrated by a series of quotations and definitions from, among others, Isidore of Seville, Aristotle, and Horace. The only part of the discussion that is referred to later, however, is the second para-

---

important manuscript of Aristotle's works in Latin (*Aristoteles latinus: Codices* 2.1040–41, no. 1515; and Stadter, "Planudes, Plutarch, and Pace," 145–146).

88. "Materia huius libri est ars poetica. . . . Errant autem qui dicunt quod materia huius libri est elloquentia siue rethorica. . . . " (Seville, Biblioteca Capitular y Colombina, Col. 5-4-30, fol. 2va [5va])

89. "<I>ncepturos librum artis poetice oportet duo considerare. Primum est de hiis que circa hanc artem attendenda sunt generaliter. Secundum est de hiis que circa librum eiusdem artis specialiter inquiri solent" (Seville, Biblioteca Capitular y Colombina, Col. 5-4-30, fol. 2ra [5ra]).

90. "dicamus quod circa artem poeticam hec oportet generaliter attendere, scilicet de inuentione artis poetice; quid ipsa sit, quod genus eius, que materia, <quod officium, quis finis, que partes, que species, quod instrumentum, quis artifex> [*RK, om. SB*]" (Seville, Biblioteca Capitular y Colombina, Col. 5-4-30, fol. 2ra [5ra]). Although the questions are omitted in several manuscripts, the answers to all of them are provided later in these manuscripts as well. Single minims used as space fillers at the end of lines in the Seville manuscript (and corrections made by the scribe) are not recorded.

graph, which begins with a quotation from Averroes's commentary on "Aristotle's *Poetria*" [= *Poetics*] on how poetry is found naturally in human beings because it is innate and because of "the delight man naturally takes in meter and harmony."[91]

"To the **second** [point]": Pace defines the poetic art as "the knowledge of pleading (*causandi*), with a flowing sweetness of words, what has [actually] happened or not, observing certain rules and properties. Or it can be defined according to Aristotle thus: 'Poetic art is the knowledge of likening (*assimulandi*) one object to another and its exemplification in terms of that object.'"[92]

"To the **third**": the discussion of the genus to which the poetic art belongs is the longest and most learned section of the *accessus*, a fourfold approach elaborated first according to meter and syllabic quantity, for which Pace quotes al-Farabi's *Liber scientiarum* (The Book of the Enumeration of the Sciences) on grammar; second, facility of expression, quoting Horace; third, the process of reasoning, quoting Aristotle (and Averroes) on the relationship of the poetic art to logic; and fourth, the relationship of meter to music, here quoting Boethius, Augustine, and Petrus Helias.[93] The significance of this section is not so much

---

91. "De **inuentione** quoque artis poetice sicut dicit Commentator in *Poetria* Aristotilis. . . . Naturaliter in homine due uidentur esse cause, prima quidem quoniam in homine existit naturaliter a prima natiuitate. . . . Causa uero secunda est delectatio quam habet eciam homo per naturam ex metro et simphonia . . . " (Seville, Biblioteca Capitular y Colombina, Col. 5–4-30, fol. 2rb [5rb]). Cf. Herman the German, "Translation of Averroes' 'Middle Commentary,'" in Minnis and Scott, *Medieval Literary Theory,* 294.

92. "Ad **secundum,** poetica est scientia causandi que gesta sunt uel non cum melliflua uerborum dulcedine et certis legibus et proprietatibus obseruatis. Vel secundum Aristotilem sic potest diffiniri: 'poetica est sciencia assimulandi rem ad rem uel representatio rei ad rem'" (Seville, Biblioteca Capitular y Colombina, Col. 5–4-30, fol. 2rb [5rb]). Cf. Herman the German, "Translation of Averroes' 'Middle Commentary,'" in Minnis and Scott, *Medieval Literary Theory,* 293.

93. "Ad **tercium:** genus huius artis est <qualitas> [*RK:* equalitas *SB*] quam efficit in discente. Sed notandum est quod poetica quadrupliciter potest considerari, et secundum hoc sub quadruplici genere potest diuersimode collocari.

"Primo in quantum considerat in poemate <siue> [*RKB:* sumitur *S*] in metro, quo utitur sicut <instruere> [*corr.:* instrumento *SRK,* in instrumento *B*] constitutiones pedum diuersorum secundum quantitatem et materiam sillabarum, et hoc modo cum considerare pedes qui fiunt ex sillabis et sillabas secundum tempora que eis accidunt sit gramatice, erit gramatica genus poetice. Vnde secundum hoc dicit Alpharabius in *Libro scientiarum* capitulo primo, quod scientie lingue siue gramatica apud omnes gentes diuiditur in septem magnas partes, quarum ultimam dicit esse scientiam canonum uersuum cuius, dicit in fine capituli, tres esse partes secundum modum qui conuenit scientie lingue, ex quo dicto colligi potest manifeste quod scientia uersuum siue poetica per alium modum, redduntur eciam ad alias scientias et non solum ad gramaticam.

"Secundo potest considerari poetica prout attendit[i] facundiam loquendi ornate tam ex parte uerborum quam sententiarum et hoc modo potest sub ciuilis scientie parte que dicitur eloquentia collocari. Efficit enim eloquentem et facundum tam in laudando quam in uituperando. Quod autem facundiam circa attendat poetica patet per Oratium in sua *Poetria* ubi dicit 'Nec facundia deseret hunc, nec lucidus ordo' {*Ars* 41}; et alibi, 'In uerbis etiam tenuis cautusque serendis' {46}; et idem alibi 'Non satis est <pulcra> [*RKB, Hor.:* plus circa *S*] esse <poemata> [*R, Hor:* poetica *K,* poema *SB*]' (suple a parte uerborum) 'dulcia sunto' {*Ars* 99} (suple a parte sententiarum).

"Tertio potest considerari prout utitur ratiocinatione siue specie ratiocinationis que est exemplum uel etiam entimema [= enthymema] ut in pluribus licet interdum sillabis et etiam inductionibus utatvr et hoc modo cum ratiocinationis et specierum eius consideratio pertineat ad loycam; erit loyca genus poetice. Et sic de poetica determinauit Aristotiles in sua *Poetria* cum sit ultima pars loyce sicut testatur Commentator in fine

what Pace says or even what he implies that others say, but the subdivision and impressive assembly of authorities (whether gatherered by himself or from *florilegia,* although the former is more likely). Later Pace will limit the subject of the *Poetria nova* to poetics alone.

"To the **fourth**": In marked stylistic contrast, Pace simply says that there is general agreement that the subject matter of poetry is as much fictional as real events.[94]

"To the **fifth**: the function of the art [of poetry], as Isidore says in Book 7, Chapter 21 of the *Etymologies,* is to change events that really happened into something else by means of elegant transformations with a certain beauty. For this reason Lucan, as he says, 'is not included among the poets since it seems that he composed history, not poetry' {*Etym.* 8.7.10}."[95]

"To the **sixth**": the purpose of the art is "either to delight by trifles and fictions,[96] or to educate in *mores,* or to do both at the same time," which elicits Horace's famous dictum, "Poets aim either to do good or to give pleasure, or to say things that are at the same time both pleasing and useful in life" (*Ars* 333–334), and Averroes on Aristotle that, "Every poem, and all poetic utterance, is either praise or blame."[97] Pace points out, however, that "Aristotle" is talking about the principal purpose, whereas Horace's statement is a corollary.[98]

---

sui prologi super *Poetriam* Aristotilis dicens suscipiant igitur si placet huius editionis poetrie translationem uiri studiosi et gaudeant se cum hac adeptos loyci negocii Aristotilis complementum.

     "Quarto et ultimo potest considerari poetica in quantum in metro attendit quandam armoniam ex proportione sillabarum quo ad euphoniam et hoc modo eius genus est musica ad quam magis quam ad ceteras pertinet. Vnde Boetius in secundo *De consolatione,* 'adsit igitur rethorice suadela dulcedinis' {*Cons.* 2, pr. 1}, per hanc intelligens orationem prosaycam. Et postea subdit 'cumque hac musica laris uernacula nunc leuiores nunc grauiores modos succinat' {*Cons.* 2, pr. 1}, per hanc intelligere uolens metricam orationem. Idem confirmat Agustinus in sua *Musica.* Petrus Elye quoque dicit circa principium maioris uoluminis quod sub arte de sillabis continetur ars metrica que ad musicam pertinet multum" (Seville, Biblioteca Capitular y Colombina, Col. 5–4-30, fol. 2rb [5rb]).

     94. "Ad **quartum**: materia huius artis ut communiter solet dici est res tam gesta quam ficta" (Seville, Biblioteca Capitular y Colombina, Col. 5–4-30, fol. 2rb [5rb]).

     95. "Ad **quintum**: 'officium eius,' ut dicit Ysidorus *Ethymologiarum* libro septimo capitulo 21, 'est ut ea, que uere gesta sunt, in alias species transfigurationibus cum decore aliquo conuersa traducat. Vnde Lucanus, ut dicit, in numero poetarum non ponitur quia uidetur ystoriam composuisse non poema" {*Etym.* 8.7.10} (Seville, Biblioteca Capitular y Colombina, Col. 5–4-30, fol. 2rb [5rb]).

     96. This felicitous translation of Pace's first phrase is Gillespie's, who describes this and several later sections of Pace's *accessus* as the "eclectically subtle handling of critical terminology [that] is characteristic of many humanist treatises on poetics and poetic theory" ("From the Twelfth Century"), but see also "Better Than the Ancients" in chapter 1. The section of text reproduced in plate 6 ends just before the quotation.

     97. Herman the German, "Translation of Averroes' 'Middle Commentary,'" in Minnis and Scott, *Medieval Literary Theory,* 289. Gillespie notes, "The linking of Aristotelian praise and blame with the Horatian ideals of delight and instruction brings out explicitly in a humanist context the potential of poetry for ethical exploration and engagement which had been implicitly present in earlier discussions of some of the most challenging texts to confront medieval commentators and theorists" ("From the Twelfth Century," 178).

     98. "Ad **sextum**: finis huius artis est aut ludicris et fictionibus delectare aut moribus edifficare aut simul utrumque facere. Vnde Oratius in sua *Poetria,* 'Aut prodesse uolunt aut delectare poete / aut symul yocunda et ydonea dicere uite' {*Ars* 333–334}. Secundum Aristotilem uero dici potest quod finis eius est laudare uel uituperare. Vnde Commentator in eius *Poetria* dicit quod omne poema et omnis poetica oratio aut est laudatio aut est uituperatio. Sed nota quod iste finis est principalis, finis uero quem ponit Oratius annexus

"To the **seventh**": the parts of the poetic art are "elegy, comedy, tragedy, and satire, which not only Horace mentions in his *Poetria* but also Aristotle in his."[99]

"To the **eighth**: the aspects of this art are the various kinds of languages in which the art is transmitted. This art is principally transmitted in Greek, Arabic, and Latin."[100]

"To the **ninth**: the instrument of the poetic art is the poem (*poema*), which is the same as a verse or a song. According to Matthew of Vendôme in his *Poetria*, 'Verse is metrical discourse advancing in cadenced periods with the restraint that meter demands and made charming by a graceful marriage of words and by flowers of thought. It contains in itself nothing deficient and nothing redundant. For it is not the accumulation of words, the counting of feet, and knowledge of meter that constitute verse but the elegant combination of words, the vivid presentation of relevant qualities, and the carefully noted epithets of each single thing.' {*Ars* 1.1}."[101]

"To the **tenth**": the practitioner (*artifex*) of this art "is called a poet, who composes a poem according to this art and speaks poetically."[102]

"To the **eleventh** and last: 'poetic' is derived from *poietes,* which comes from the Greek verb *poio, -is,* which is the same as *fingo, -is* (to shape, create), and thus it is a kind of knowledge, as in the knowledge of things made up (*figmentis*)."[103]

Using the rhetorical figure of *transitio,* or summing up what one has just said and outlining what is to follow (a prominent and necessary feature of commentaries that were to be heard, rather than read), Pace concludes, "Having examined these issues concerning poetics generally, now we shall look specifically at those concerning this particular book that we have before us, which is

---

est principali." (Seville, Biblioteca Capitular y Colombina, Col. 5–4-30, fol. 2rb–2va [5rb–5va])

99. "Ad **septimum**: partes sunt quatuor, scilicet elegya, comedia, trayedia, et satyra, de quibus non solum Oratius facit mentionem in sua *Poetria* sed etiam Aristotiles in sua" (Seville, Biblioteca Capitular y Colombina, Col. 5–4-30, fol. 2va [5va]).

100. "Ad **octauum**: species huius artis sunt diuersa genera linguarum in quibus tradita est hec ars. Est autem tradita hec ars precipue in lingua greca, arabica, et latina" (Seville, Biblioteca Capitular y Colombina, Col. 5–4-30, fol. 2va [5va]).

101. "Ad **nonum**: instrumentum artis poetice est poema quod idem est quod metrum siue carmen. 'Versus autem' ut dicit Matheus Vindocinensis in sua *Poetria* 'est oratio metrica succincte et clausatim progrediens uenusto uerborum matrimonio et floribus picturata que nichil diminutum nil in se continet uitiosum. Non enim tantum ut idem dicit dictionum aggregatio, dinumeratio pedum, cognitio temporum facit uersum sed elegans iunctura uerborum expressio proprietatum et uniuscuiusque epiteton expressio' {*Ars* 1.1}" (Seville, Biblioteca Capitular y Colombina, Col. 5–4-30, fol. 2va [5va]). Translation of Matthew from Galyon, *The Art of Versification,* slightly altered to match readings in commentary.

102. "Ad **decimum**: artifex huius artis dicitur poeta, qui scilicet secundum hanc artem poema componit et poetice loquitur" (Seville, Biblioteca Capitular y Colombina, Col. 5–4-30, fol. 2va [5va]).

103. "Ad **undecimum** et ultimum poetica dicitur a *poietes* quod a uerbo greco descendit quod est *poyo, -is,* idem quod "fingo, -gis," et ica [= ita] sciencia quasi sciencia de figmentis [*sic*]" (Seville, Biblioteca Capitular y Colombina, Col. 5–4-30, fol. 2va [5va]). The last phrase is not found in all the manuscripts.

called the *Poetria*. And these are the issues that ought to be taken into consideration: who is the author of this book, the reason for undertaking the work, the subject, the [author's] intention, its usefulness, and the part of philosophy it belongs to; and what is the title of the book?"[104]

In answering this shorter list of questions, Pace continues his focus on poetry to the exclusion of rhetoric.

"The **author** of this book was a certain Galfredus by name, an Englishman, but low in social status, yet exalted in the profession of literature."[105] The phrase "low in social status" is not usually used to describe Geoffrey and was inked out in the Seville manuscript. But Pace builds on this characterization of Geoffrey in the next answer and has used similar phrasing regarding an author in another commentary, so I have supplied it here.[106]

His **reason for undertaking the project** was twofold: First to win the goodwill of the pope so that Innocent might "give him help with food and sustenance because they say he [Geoffrey] was poor, or for the pardon of King Richard of England, which he was attending to in the Roman curia according to some." Pace concludes with the memorable second reason already discussed in the first chapter: "so that he might expound perfectly the art of poetry which Horace had taught in too condensed and confused a way."[107]

"The **subject** of this book is the art of poetry in general, not descending to a particular part of it." And here is where we find the dismissal of rhetoric as the subject of the book:

They err who say that the subject of this book is eloquence or rhetoric. This is not true, since rhetoric and poetics are two different bodies of knowledge according to Aristotle; the evidence of this is that he wrote separate books about them. And the book itself is commonly called the *Poetria* since it determines [=

104. "Hiis uisis circa poeticam generaliter, nunc circa librum quem habemus pre manibus qui dicitur *Poetria* eo quod est de arte poetica specialiter consideranda sunt hec, scilicet, quis sit auctor huius libri, que causa suscepti operis, que materia, que intentio, que vtilitas, cui parti philosophye supponatur, et quis libri titulus?" (Seville, Biblioteca Capitular y Colombina, Col. 5-4-30, fol. 2va [5va]).

105. "**Autor** huius libri fuit quidam Guelfredus [*sic*] nomine, natione Anglicus <sed conditione vilis> [*RK: in ras. S: add. B*], professione <tamen> [*RK: in ras. S: add. B*] litterature sublimis" (Seville, Biblioteca Capitular y Colombina, Col. 5-4-30, fol. 2va [5va]). Geoffrey's name is spelled in a variety of ways in the manuscripts of Pace's commentary; e.g., "Ganfredus" (*K*) and "Galfredus" (Cremona 88), but most have "Gualfredus" (*RB*, also Assisi 309 and London, BL Add. 10095).

106. Cf. Pace's description of Mussato's family background in his *accessus* to Mussato's *Ecerinis:* "Autor iste paduanus fuit, qui, etsi ignobili, non tamen obscuro genere natus patre et matre plebeus" (Megas, *Kuklos Padouas*, 204.59-60).

107. "**Causa suscepti operis** fuit duplex: Vna ut posset Innocentii <tertii> [*RK:* quarti *SB*] pape fauorem et beneuolentiam captare siue in dando auxilium sibi in uictualibus cum pauper esset ut dicunt, siue uenia Ricardi regis Anglie quam ut quidam dicunt in romana curia procurabat. Alia fuit ut perfecte artem poeticam posset determinare quam Oratius nimis compendiose et confuse docuerat" (Seville, Biblioteca Capitular y Colombina, Col. 5-4-30, fol. 2va [5va]).

marks the boundaries of][108] the poetic art; this name would not be given to it if it determined rhetoric or the parts of rhetoric as the principal subject.[109]

If the book were primarily about rhetoric, he goes on to say, it would treat the four types of causes, like Cicero in the first book of *De inventione*, yet "nowhere do you find that the four types of causes are expounded in this book, nor are the other conditions that are considered part of the rhetorical faculty."[110] Pace concludes: "Therefore, I hold in error almost all those saying in the beginning of this book that rhetoric, etc., what we state about poetry."[111] Here Pace is criticizing commentators like Bartholomew of Pisa, who interprets the *Poetria nova* as a book primarily about rhetoric and persuasion. While most commentators give at least lip service to both rhetoric and poetics as the subject of the work, few are evenly divided in their interest in both. It may be significant that Pace's, which places itself so firmly on the side of poetics, is the most popular Italian commentary.

Geoffrey's **intention,** according to Pace, relates to "the aforementioned topic, for he intends to present sufficient teaching concerning the poetic art in general so that he does not descend specifically to some part of it."[112] This rather bland statement allows for the assessment of the *Poetria nova* as an all-purpose composition text not limited to a particular type of discourse.

"A threefold **usefulness** can be attributed to the work: first is complete knowledge of the poetic art in general; second, crafted eloquence; third and last, the delight that comes as much from the ornamentation and harmony of the words as from the beauty of the content."[113]

---

108. On the meanings of *determinatio* see Teeuwen, *Vocabulary of Intellectual Life,* 252; also chapter 4, note 142.

109. "**Materia** huius libri est ars poetica non descendendo ad aliquam eius partem in speciali. Errant autem qui dicunt quod materia huius libri est elloquentia siue rethorica uel quinque partes rethorice facultatis. Hoc enim non est uerum, cum quia [*sic*] rethorica et poetica diuerse sunt scientie secundum Aristotilem in cuius signum diuersos libros de eis composuit. Et liber iste communiter dicitur *Poetria* quia determinat de poetica quod nomen non daretur ei si determinaret de rethorica uel eius partibus ut de principali materia" (Seville, Biblioteca Capitular y Colombina, Col. 5–4-30, fol. 2va [5va]). "Cum quia" appears to be an intensive causal construction, one that Giovanni Travesi retains when he quotes Pace ("Stand and Counterstand" below). Cf. Latham, *Revised Medieval Latin Word-List,* 125a, s.v. "cum quotiens."

110. "Vnde nusquam inuenies quod de generibus causarum determinetur in hoc libro nec de naturis aliis que sunt de consideratione rethorice facultatis" (Seville, Biblioteca Capitular y Colombina, Col. 5–4-30, fol. 2va [5va]).

111. "Hoc ergo errore deceptos audio fere omnes dicentes in principio huius libri quod rethorica etc. que de poetica <diximus> [*RK:* om *SB*]" (Seville, Biblioteca Capitular y Colombina, Col. 5–4-30, fol. 2va–b [5va–b]).

112. "**Intentio autoris** circa predictam materiam uersatur. Intendit sufficienter doctrinam tradere de arte poetica in communi ut scilicet non descendat specialiter ad aliquam eius partem" (Seville, Biblioteca Capitular y Colombina, Col. 5–4-30, fol. 2vb [5vb]).

113. "**Vtilitas** uero assignari potest triplex: prima plena cognitio artis poetice in communi, secunda artificiosa elloquentia, tertia et ultima est <delectatio> [*RK:* dclaratio *S:* declaratio *B*] que habetur tam ex uerborum ornatu et simphonia quam ex sententiarum pulcritudine" (Seville, Biblioteca Capitular y Colombina, Col. 5–4-30, fol. 2vb [5vb]).

"The **part of philosophy to which it belongs** is the rational or the verbal (through grammar or logic or rhetoric). Poetry belongs in these in different ways as is clear from what was said above, but in as much as it pertains to music it falls under [lit.: is placed under] mathematical philosophy, for music is one of the branches of mathematical knowledge."[114] This answer to the question of what part of philosophy it falls under may appear inconclusive, but Pace is trying to show how widely applicable the book is.

"The **title** of the book is the following: 'The *Poetria novella* of Galfredus the Englishman begins.' It is called *Poetria* by reason of the subject matter with which it is concerned, since it is about poetics, as was said above; it is called *novella* [lit.: little new] in comparison with the *Poetria* of Horace and that of Aristotle and with others if any were written earlier."[115]

PACE ON MUSSATO

> This tragedy is first and principally divided into three parts.[116]
> —Pace of Ferrara

Pace's long *accessus* to the *Poetria nova,* which we have not yet finished examining, is in stark contrast to his short introduction to Albertino Mussato's neo-Senecan tragedy, the *Ecerinis.*[117] The much more extensive commentary on the *Ecerinis* co-authored by Pace's colleagues Guizzardo of Bologna and Castellano of Bassano (almost two hundred printed pages as opposed to Pace's three) has received more scholarly attention.[118] Pace's condensed approach, written somewhat later, was part of "[h]is efforts to enhance the use of the *Ecerinis* for teaching purposes. . . ."[119] The *Evidentia Ecerinidis,* as Pace called it (perhaps in imitation of Mussato's study of Senecan tragedy, *Evidentia tragediarum Senece*), has survived in only one copy, yet it must have circulated because according to

---

114. **"Parti quidem phylosophie supponitur** ratiocinali siue sermocinali siue per gramaticam siue per loycam siue per rethoricam quibus poetica diuersimodis supponitur ut patet ex prius dictis in quantum uero ad musicam pertinet, supponitur mathematice phylosophie, musica enim est una de mathemathicis scientiis" (Seville, Biblioteca Capitular y Colombina, Col. 5–4-30, fol. 2vb [5vb]).

115. **"Libri titulus** talis est 'Guelfredi anglici *Poetria nouella* incipit.' Et dicitur *Poetria* ratione materie de qua est quia de poetica ut predictum est. Dicitur autem *nouella* in comparatione ad Po<e>triam Oratii et Aristotilis et ad alias si que prius facte sunt" (Seville, Biblioteca Capitular y Colombina, Col. 5–4-30, fol. 2vb [5vb]).

116. "Tragedia hec primo et principaliter in tres partes diuissa est" (Megas, *Kuklos Padouas,* 205.78).

117. The *Evidentia Ecerinidis* was edited by Megas in 1967 (*Kuklos Padouas,* 203–205). On Mussato see Gillespie, "From the Twelfth Century," 218–220.

118. Guizzardo and Castellano's commentary has been edited by Padrin in his edition of the tragedy; see also Colfi, *Di un antichissimo commento;* Guido Billanovich, "Il preumanesimo padovano," 65–66 and passim; Witt, *Footsteps,* 130; and Gillespie, "From the Twelfth Century," 220. Guizzardo's commentary on the *Poetria nova* is discussed later in this chapter.

119. Witt, *Footsteps,* 115.

Ronald Witt it was instrumental in making Mussato's work the subject of class-room attention and the focus of academic discourse.[120]

Like Pace's *accessus* to the *Poetria nova,* the *Evidentia Ecerinidis* is divided into three parts. We can use the *Evidentia* as a quick review of Pace's prac-tice of approaching a text from these perspectives (generic, authoritative, and structural), the first two of which we have already examined with regard to the *Poetria nova.* Part one of the *Evidentia* focuses on the genre of tragedy and its origins, in the same way that the commentary on the *Poetria nova* begins with a series of questions on the art of poetry. Unfortunately Pace misidenti-fies Sophocles as the author of the *Iliad* and the *Odyssey,* but even this error supports his elevation of Mussato's work by associating it with the person Pace believes to be the author of almost all of the great works of Greek antiquity.[121] Pace presents Senecan tragedy (based on Sophocles) as Mussato's model, just as he places the *Poetria nova* in the company of Horace's *Poetria* and that of Aris-totle. The citation of authorities contextualizes the work while (supposedly) dis-playing the commentator's command of that context. Mussato's work is framed by Sophocles and Seneca, just as the *Poetria nova* is by Horace, Al-farabi, Aris-totle, Isidore, and Matthew of Vendôme.[122] The presence of a series of named authorities, regardless of the works cited—or the correctness of the citations or authorities—has a totemic quality; they generate a scholarly patina for both the commentary and the text being commented upon.

In part two of the *Evidentia Ecerinis,* as in the second part of his *accessus* to the *Poetria nova,* Pace examines the work itself, asking almost identical ques-tions: what is its subject? the author's intention? its usefulness? to what part of philosophy does it belong? and what is its title?[123] Most of the answers are pre-dictable (e.g., "The subject matter is the deeds of Ecerinis"), although the title, "Here begins the tragedy of Ecerinis by the Paduan Albertus Musatus," leads into a short but fulsome and somewhat suspect summary of Mussato's life.[124]

The third part of Pace's *Evidentia* is the subdivision of the work (the cor-responding section in the commentary on the *Poetria nova* will be examined next). As he will do with the *Poetria nova,* Pace divides the tragedy into three

---

120. Witt, *Footsteps,* 115, also 130.

121. "(S)Ophoclem accepimus tragediarum scriptorem. Is Odisseam, Yliadem, Oedippodem, Herculem furentem et alias plures in greco conscripsisse fertur" (Megas, *Kuklos Padouas,* 203.2–3). On this error see Stadter, "Planudes, Plutarch, and Pace," 146; and Guido Billanovich, "Il preumanisimo padovano," 66, where he refers to "la voce ossequiosa di maestro Pace de Ferrara." While it is extremely doubtful that Pace read Greek or knew any of the Greek literary works first hand, he did own a manuscript of Plutarch; see above note 87.

122. The latter group are cited in Pace's commentary on the *Poetria nova* talking about poetry. In contrast, the context in which Bartholomew of Pisa introduced us to Geoffrey was that of Cicero and prose rhetoric.

123. "Hiis prelatis ad operis huius euidentiam solite fiant discutiones dicaturque que materia, que intentio, que utilitas, cui parti philosophye supponatur et quis sit libri titulus" (Megas, *Kuklos Padouas,* 204.40–42).

124. "Libri titulus talis est: *Albertini Musati patauini tragedia Ecerinis incipit*" (Megas, *Kuklos Padouas,* 204.58–59; Mussato's life is summarized from 204.59–77; see also above, note 106).

parts, then subdivides the first and second into two subsections and the third into three, each identified by its first words. Pace's division of Mussato's work takes up only a few sentences (in contrast to his approach to the *Poetria nova*), but the very fact of subdivision, its essentialness as a precondition to further teaching of the text, is significant. Subdivision (like allegory) could be both an analytical approach to a work as well as an inherent aspect of a work uncovered by analysis. Thus, the technique of *divisio* was simultaneously a way of both placing a text within a sophisticated academic context and also demonstrating its worthiness to be so placed (as we saw with Bartholomew's similar degree of division in his analysis of the *Poetria nova*). The revelation and display of divisional complexity helped to elevate a work as an object of study, a feat that Pace accomplished with both Mussato's tragedy and the *Poetria nova*. In this way Pace combines early humanist tastes in contemporary poetry with traditional scholastic academic techniques.[125] His insistence on the *Poetria nova*'s generic identity as a text about poetics, not rhetoric, implies a higher value for the former, part of the humanist metamorphosis of the lowest of the liberal arts, grammar as textual analysis, into a higher study with specifically classical echoes. It was probably Pace's felicitous combination of these approaches that made his own commentary popular for the next century and a half.

DIVIDE AND ELEVATE

> It is clear, therefore, that in the reading before us there are three principal parts, the first of which is divided into two. . . . The second principal part is likewise divided into two. . . . The third principal part of this reading is divided into three. . . . [126]
> —Pace of Ferrara

Pace's much more extensive *divisio* of the *Poetria nova* serves two functions. It is both the conclusion of his *accessus* and the beginning of the commentary proper, as the two different ways that it is indicated in the formats of the manuscripts demonstrate. In most it is treated as a third section of the *accessus* after the questions about the art of poetry and those about the *Poetria nova* as a treatise on poetics, and it is marked simply as a new paragraph. In other manu-

---

125. To describe Pace's efforts as typically scholastic (Allen, *Ethical Poetic,* 8 and 130–32) or typically humanist (Stadter, "Planudes, Plutarch, and Pace," e.g., 137, 136), tells only half the story, as I have argued elsewhere ("A Medieval Rhetoric," 62–65). Dante's "autocomentario" (in the *Vita nuova, Convivio,* and "Letter to Can Grande") is a better known example of such a use of scholastic commentary techniques; see also below, note 132. For the term "autocomentario" see Jenaro-MacLennan, "Autocomentario en Dante"; and "auto-commentary" with the related terms "auto-exegesis" and "self-exegesis" in Ascoli, "Access to Authority."

126. "Patet ergo quod in lectione presenti sunt tres partes principales quarum prima diuiditur in duas. . . . Pars secunda principalis similiter diuiditur in duas. . . . Tertia pars principalis huius lectionis diuiditur in partes tres. . . . " (Seville, Biblioteca Capitular y Colombina, Col. 5-4-30, fols. 3vb–4ra [6vb–7ra])

scripts, however, it is introduced by the first words of the text, a *lemma,* sometimes in display script; this technique conventionally signals the beginning of word-by-word analysis after an *accessus* is finished.[127] The reason for the overlap of function lies in the shift from talking about aspects of the work as a whole (author, title, etc.) to the text itself. What comes in between is a discussion of the subdivisions of the text, which could be seen as either a continuation of the general approach or as the introduction to the individual sections.[128] In his transition from one to the other, Pace begins with the complete text and sloughs away parts until he reaches the first words of the first line, thereby implying, and going on to demonstrate, that almost every word of the text is worth attention.

The transitional sentence (with or without preceding *lemma*) makes it clear that Pace is changing focus: "Having put first thus far the factors pertaining to the **extrinsic** or general knowledge of this book, it remains to us next to descend to an **intrinsic** or specific consideration of the book.[129] This book is divided first into two parts, I) the **prologue** and II) the **treatise,** which begins at 'If one has a house to build' (43)." This first unit is called the prologue (*prologus*) rather than the *prohemium,* Pace remarks, because "as Aristotle says in the third book of the *Rhetoric,* 'The *prohemium* is the beginning of a speech, as a prologue is the beginning of a poem.'"[130] Here Pace reinforces his point that the subject of the *Poetria nova* is poetry rather than rhetoric, but he does go on to acknowledge that *prologus* and *prohemium* can, in fact, mean the same thing.[131]

He continues by subdividing the prologue (lines 1–43) into I.A) the **proposal** (praise of Pope Innocent in order to gain a more favorable reception for the work) and I.B) the **invocation** to Innocent as protector at "General light of the world" (33).[132] At this point Pace concentrates on just the first of these,

---

127. Later in the commentary such *lemmata* signal the first words of the reading for the day's lecture.

128. See the similar variety of treatments with the same section of the commentary by Dybinus of Prague in "*Scripta* vs. *Dicta* in Practice" in chapter 4.

129. On intrinsic and extrinsic analysis, see Minnis, *Medieval Theory of Authorship,* 30–32 and 63–71.

130. The usual division, of poetry as well as prose texts, is into *prohemium* and treatise (*tractatum*), as in Bartholomew of Pisa's division of the text above ("The Subject Is Rhetoric"). See also, for example, Ward, *Ciceronian Rhetoric,* 204, on the early-fourteenth-century commentary on the *Rhetorica ad Herennium* by Bartolinus; Dante, *Vita nuova,* xix; and Lord, "Benvenuto da Imola's Literary Approach" (on Virgil's *Eclogues*), 334.

131. "Ex premissis hucusque habitus que ad cognitionem huius libri generaliter siue extrinsecus concurrebant, restat deinceps ut ad considerationem libri specialiter siue intrinsecus descendamus. Diuiditur ergo liber iste prima diuisione in duas partes, scilicet in prologum et tractatum, qui incipit illic, 'Si quis habet fundare domum' etc. (43). Et nota quod proprie dixi librum istum diuidi in prologum non in proemium et tractatum, quia sicut dicit Aristotiles tercio *Rethoricorum* proemium est principium orationis sicut poesi prologus et in fistulatione preludium. Ex quo patet quod cum autor iste determinet de po<e>si siue de arte poetica et utatur poemate quod istud quod premittit proprie debet dici prologus, quamuis etiam communiter loquendo posset dici prohemium, quia hec sunt idem subiecto et non differunt nisi ratione." (Seville, Biblioteca Capitular y Colombina, Col. 5-4-30, fol. 2vb [5vb]).

132. I have superimposed a modern outline in the summary for later reference. Pace's audience probably would have visualized the degrees of subdivision as a tree diagram with each branch signaled by the *lemma* beginning that section, which he always provides. On manuscripts of the *Poetria nova* with diagrams, see

the proposal (lines 1–32), which is subdivided into two parts, in which I.A.i) he praises the pope in terms of his own person, and I.A.ii) he praises the pope in terms of those around him, the cardinals, starting at "Your retinue" (28). The first of these (lines 1–27) is then subdivided into two, in which I.A.i.a) he commends the pope in terms of the discord between his name and the meter, and I.A.i.b) he commends the pope's singular virtue via an analogy to the metrical properties of his name at "It will no more be confined by meter" (4). Here only the longer second part (lines 4–20) is further divided, into I.A.i.b.I) praise of the pope in general terms and then I.A.I.b.II) praise of the pope's special gifts, beginning at "In illustrious lineage" (10). The first of these (lines 4–9) is subdivided into three, in the first of which I.A.I.b.I.A) he compares the problem of putting Innocent's name into meter to the problem of finding limits to his great virtue; in the second I.A.I.b.I.B) he presents the solution to the problem of Innocent's name, beginning at "But divide the name" (6); and in the third I.A.I.b.I.C) he shows the congruence (literally "harmony") between the solution to the problem and the scope of his virtue, at "In the same way your excellence" (8). Then Pace goes back to the section praising the pope's gifts (I.A.I.b.II, lines 10–20), dividing it into first I.A.I.b.II.A) the [human] gifts of the human spirit and body, and then I.A.I.b.II.B) the ways that Innocent appears to be more than human [his combination of youth and old age], beginning at "You quite transcend the human condition" (20). Here, Pace notes, "this *lectio* ends." That is, everything up to line 20 is the first passage, or subject of the first lecture (*lectio* can mean "reading" as well as "lecture"), which Pace will discuss as a unit afterwards.[133] He continues to subdivide Innocent's human gifts (10–19) into I.A.i.b. II.A.i) "those that can be found individually in others" (e.g., noble blood) and I.A.i.b.II.A.ii) the gift of his eloquence that, although found in others, is greater in him, beginning at "One of your gifts remains to be mentioned" (13).[134]

"Geoffrey after Quintilian" in the Afterword.

133. On "lectio" see Teeuwen, *Vocabulary of Intellectual Life:* "*lectio,* that is, a master reading and simultaneously commenting upon a curricular text . . . " (322). Klagenfurt, Bundesstaatliche Studienbibliothek, Pap. 109 uses elsewhere the term "textus" (e.g., at the transition to line 10 of the *Poetria nova,* "Egregius sanguis te," on fol. 66rb), which could indicate that "reading" (meaning the portion of text under consideration) may be a more correct translation.

134. "Et quia in prologis solent poete preponere et inuocare, in tractatu uero narrare, quod intendunt. Ideo prologus iste diuiditur in duas partes: in prima loco propositionis autor iste multipliciter commendat dominum papam Innocentium <tertium> [*RK:* quartum *SB*] per hoc captare cupiens eius beniuolentiam ut sibi melius faueat in receptione et aprobatione huius operis. In secunda inuocat ipsum tanquam presidem sibi in hoc opere; secunda ibi, 'Lux publica mundi' (33). Prima pars diuiditur in duas: in prima commendat ipsum a suo nomine specialiter tangendo discordiam nominis et metri; in secunda commendat eum a sua uirtute quasi per <sillabam> [*RK:* sillabe *S:* simillem *B*] ostendendo discordiam sue uirtutis cum mensura. Secunda ibi, 'Nec nomen metro' (4). Et hec diuiditur in duas: in prima commendat dominum papam a sua uirtute generaliter, in secunda specialiter et ad eius singulas dotes descendendo. Secunda illic, 'Egregius sanguis' (10). Prima diuiditur in tres partes quia in prima discordiam nominis cum metro adaptat ad discordiam sue uirtutis cum mensura. In secunda ponit remedium circa primam discordiam, scilicet nominis cum metro. In tercia ponit remedium et concordiam circa secundam discordiam, scilicet uirtutis cum

In thus subdividing, Pace has been bringing us closer and closer to the first words of the text; the *divisio* sets the stage for the line-by-line analysis that follows by showing us how complex the work is.[135] As Alastair Minnis points out, the degree of subdivision possible was considered a sign of the sophistication of a work.[136] The Aristotelian privileging of degrees of subordination

> was one result of a desire to conceptualise about the correct techniques of meticulously dividing and subdividing a text for teaching purposes. . . . A master would proceed from a general division by chapters or parts; these components would in their turn be subdivided into smaller sense-units. Thereby, an elaborate framework was provided for precise *explication de texte.*[137]

Minnis's use of a French term more current today in literary (and pedagogical) than philosophical circles helps us understand how division works from a literary perspective. In a famous passage in the *Vita nuova,* Dante says that "to uncover still more meaning in this *canzone* it would be necessary to divide it more minutely."[138] Thus, subdivision is, paradoxically, a generative technique: it produces meaning—or as we might put it, interpretation—and it raises expectations.

After introducing the text through this preliminary division of the content, Pace now takes his audience through a sophisticated and minute elaboration of the words of the text themselves. Unlike the structure of the content of the work, which is based on degrees of subordination, the analysis of the text is based on a partition into equal units. Here Pace is dividing the text into sections, rather than outlining its content as in the first division. While the earlier subdivision fixes the organization of the work in the minds of the students who are listening, this one fixes the words themselves. Pace's term for the two divisions taken together is *constructio.* It is tempting to translate his term as "decon-

---

mensura. Secunda pars incipit illic, 'Sed diuide nomen'; tercia illic, 'Sic et tua uirtus' (8). Illa pars 'Egregius sanguis' diuiditur in duas partes; in prima commendat dominum papam specialiter a dotibus tam animi quam corporis; in secunda commendat ipsum a quodam speciali extrinseco quod est dignitas, in qua ut dicit videtur humanam naturam excedere. Secunda ibi, 'Trans hominem' (6), ubi presens lectio terminatur. Prima pars in duas diuiditur: in prima commendat papam a dotibus pertinentibus uel ad animam uel ad corpus que in aliis hominibus eque possunt reperire. In secunda commendat ipsum a quadam dote pertinente ad utrumque comuniter que licet in aliis quibusdam fuerit, tamen in ipso fuit per excellentiam. Secunda ibi, 'Superest de dotibus una' (13)." (Seville, Biblioteca Capitular y Colombina, Col. 5-4-30, fol. 2vb [5vb])

135. Cf. Ward, *Ciceronian Rhetoric,* on Bartolinus: "The method is to divide the rhetorical structure of each passage into its labelled parts and then to defer all but the first head, which is then divided again, and all parts are deferred except the first, which is in turn divided again, and after one further similar division and deferral, all heads, being this time *lemmata,* are glossed" (204). See also the description below by Guizzardo of Bologna, note 202.

136. Minnis, *Medieval Theory of Authorship,* 145–159, and *Medieval Literary Theory,* 376–77.

137. Minnis, *Medieval Theory of Authorship,* 149.

138. Dante, *Vita nuova,* xix, cited in Minnis, *Medieval Literary Theory,* 377.

struction" because of the detail with which he follows it through, but the more obvious English cognate, "construction," is probably more accurate because of its evocation of Geoffrey's craft as well as the famous architectural metaphor with which the third reading, "If one has a house to build" (43), begins.

The following table shows the correspondences between (or construction of) the division of the content and the partitioning of this first reading. Students listening to the commentary moved down through the first column, then down through the second, with the resonance and correspondences between the two parts of the *constructio* reinforced by the repetitions of the *lemmata,* or introductory phrases.

PACE'S *CONSTRUCTIO* OF THE *POETRIA NOVA*

I. **Prologue,** lines 1–42
   A. **Proposal,** lines 1–32
      i. lines 1–27   **FIRST LECTURE** on lines 1–20
         a. lines 1–3   **Part 1** = lines 1–3
         b. lines 4–27
            I. lines 4–9
               A. lines 4–5   **Part 2** = lines 4–5
               B. lines 6–7   **Part 3** = lines 6–7
               C. lines 8–9   **Part 4** = lines 8–9
            II. lines 10–27
               A. lines 10–19
                  i. lines 10–12   **Part 5** = lines 10–12
                  ii. lines 13–19   **Part 6** = lines 13–19
               B. lines 20–27   SECOND LECTURE (lines 20–43)
      ii. lines 28–32
   B. **Invocation,** lines 33–42
II. **Treatise,** lines 43–2116.[139]   THIRD LECTURE, etc.

After announcing these divisions of the passage for the first lecture, Pace then glosses the lines in each part, thereby both providing and commenting on the text. Here is his treatment of the first three lines of the text:

> There are, therefore, six parts in this *lectio,* in the first of which he commends the pope in terms of his name, saying, (1) O HOLY FATHER you who are the WONDER OF THE WORLD in so much as the whole world admires you, I myself intend to invoke you at the beginning of this my work. And in invoking you

---

139. Pace questions the inclusion of lines 2081–2098, as we shall see below.

I have to say either "O Pope Nocent" or "O Pope Innocent." But which of these should I say? I debate, for IF I SAY, O POPE NOCENT then (2) I SHALL GIVE YOU AN ACEPHALOUS NAME that is, one without a head since without its first syllable, namely "In-." Put in the truncated name, and the meaning does not suit you. BUT IF I ADD THE HEAD that is, the first syllable, by saying "O Pope Innocent," then (3) IT WILL BE AT ODDS WITH THE METER that is, it will be in conflict with the meter. For because it has a short syllable between long ones, it cannot be put into heroic verse. Thus, the complete NAME SEEKS TO RESEMBLE YOU by reason of your supreme virtue, which means that the name suits you. And this is what he says at "Holy Father, wonder," etc.[140]

Here the commentator is both reading aloud and lecturing on the text at the same time—hence the difficulty in translating *lectio*.

Pace then goes through the first three lines a *third* time, adding the equivalent of footnotes.[141] He points out four important aspects of the first three lines that students should remember, each introduced by *Nota* and each citing an authority. He treats the rhetorical aspects first, then the poetic ones.

"But **note first** that the noun *papa* (Holy Father), is derived from the interjection *pape,* which signifies admiration" and has a complex etymological history.[142] (I am condensing quite a bit here.)

"**Second, note** that *stupor* (wonder) can be understood with an implication of vice and evildoing, as in the first book of Boethius's *Consolation of Philosophy.* . . . " The negative connotation occurs, Pace says, when the word is used to mean sluggishness of mind. Here, however, it is a sign of virtue, and Pace cites

140. "Sunt igitur in presenti lectione sex partes in quarum prima commendat dominum papam a suo nomine specialiter dicens (1) O PAPA qui es STUPOR MUNDI quantum ad hoc quod te totus mundus admiratur. Ego te intendo in principio huius mei operis inuocare et ideo te inuocando oportet me dicere uel 'O Papa Nocenti' <uel 'O Papa Innocenti.' Sed quid istorum duorum dicam? Ego dubito, SI enim DIXERO O PAPA NOCENTI> [*RK*: et *SB*] tunc ego (2) TRIBUAM TIBI NOMEN ACEPHALUM, idest sine capite, quia sine prima sillaba eius que s<cilicet> est "in." Cuius (suple:) nominis sic detruncati, significatio tibi non conuenit. SI uero ego ADDAM CAPUT, idest primam sillabam dicendo sic 'O papa Innocenti,' tunc (3) NOMEN ERIT HOSTIS METRI, idest discordabit a metro, quia cum habeat breuem inter longas in heroyco carmine poni non potest. Tale <inde> [enim *RB*, cum *K,* in *S*] NOMEN integrum scilicet UULT SOCIARI TIBI ratione su<preme> [*RK*: su *S, om. B*] uirtutis quam significat que tibi conuenit. Et hoc est quod dicit 'Papa stupor,' etc." (Seville, Biblioteca Capitular y Colombina, Col. 5–4-30, fols. 2vb–3ra [5vb–6ra])

141. A threefold approach appears to be one of the more durable aspects of the commentary tradition. Compare Craig Kallendorf on Jodocus Badius Ascensius's popular early-sixteenth century commentary on the *Aeneid:* "Ascensius's normal procedure is to break Virgil's text into manageable sections, then to construe each section under the rubric *ordo est* ('the order is'), and finally to add a discussion of whatever he feels needs explanation" (*Virgil and the Myth,* 41). See also Blair, "Lectures" and "*Ovidius Methodizatus*" for the same tradition in sixteenth-century France.

142. "Sed **nota primo** quod hoc nomen 'papa' <deriuatur ab hac interiectione 'pape' que> [*RK*: quod *SB*] significat admirationem et ideo papa interpretatur admirabilis in cuius signum addidit 'stupor mundi' etc., potest tamen dici secundum ethimologiam 'papa,' quasi 'pater, patrum.' Vnde aliqui dicunt quod interpretatur custos uniuersalis quia ad omnium animarum custodiam deputatus est" (Seville, Biblioteca Capitular y Colombina, Col. 5–4-30, fol. 3ra [6ra]).

the fourth book of Aristotle's *Topics* to support this interpretation.[143]

"**Note likewise,**" he says, that the phrase "wonder of the world" is an example of metonymy, or the container for contents, "for the world itself cannot be doing the wondering but rather the men living in the world."[144]

Fourth, note that when he says 'If I were to say,' etc., as if doubting what ought to be said, he is using the rhetorical color called *dubitatio*," and Pace quotes the definition in the *Rhetorica ad Herennium:* "when the speaker seems to ask which of two or more words ought better to be used" {4.40} in support of Geoffrey's technique.[145]

Still in the first lesson, Pace then repeats the whole three-part process for each of the other five parts of the first *lectio* of twenty lines: each part is introduced with a summary that echoes the phrasing used in the subdivison of content (repetition is an important part of his pedagogy), then quoted and glossed, then provided with notes.[146] This technique of multiple division and elaboration continues throughout Pace's commentary. How does it work pedagogically? First, although it can seem overly elaborate (and pointless) to a modern reader, it provides a predictable and hence secure sequence of steps through which students can accumulate knowledge about the work. The (con)structural division of the whole work into large units is established early. Then students approach each passage in terms of where it fits into that overall structure of the text. Then they hear the subdivision of the passage that is the subject of each lecture into two or at most three units, and then each of these is subdivided again into two or at most three subsections—a very small number of units, given the memory abilities of medieval students so eloquently evoked by Carruthers. If it is true

---

143. "**Secundo notandum** est quod 'stupor' potest accipi in significatione uicii et malicie sicut est apud Boetium in primo *De consolatione* ubi dicit in persona Philosophye, 'Malem pudore siluisses sed ut uideo te stupor oppressit' {*Cons. Phil.* 1, prose 2.4}. Et est stupor in hac significatione proprie idem quod hebetudo mentis et hoc modo non accipitur hic; potest etiam accipi in significatione uirtutis ut <hic> [*RK:* hac *SB*], ratione enim immense uirtutis et inaudite dicitur hic admirabilis. Vnde dicit Aristotiles in quarto *Topicorum* quod stupor est admiratio superhabundans quia illud proprie admiramur quod nouum est apud nos et inauditum. Et hic papa talis erat quia numquam uidebatur habuisse parem sibi omnibus dotibus consideratis" (Seville, Biblioteca Capitular y Colombina, Col. 5-4-30, fol. 3ra [6ra]). See the discussion of the various meanings of *stupor* in "Off with His Head!" in chapter 1.

144. "**Item nota** quod cum dicitur 'stupor mundi' est methonomia ubi ponitur continens pro contento, non enim mundus admirari potest sed homines in mundo existentes" (Seville, Biblioteca Capitular y Colombina, Col. 5-4-30, fol. 3ra [6ra]).

145. "**Quarto nota** quod cum dicit 'Si dixero,' etc. dubitando quasi quid debeat dicere, vtitur colore rethorico qui dicitur dubitatio. Et est autem secundum Tulium dubitatio cum querere uidetur orator vtrum de duobus sit potius aut quid de pluribus potissimum dicatur" (Seville, Biblioteca Capitular y Colombina, Col. 5-4-30, fol. 3ra [6ra]).

146. Compare Paul Grendler's description of humanist university lectures in Italy during the Renaissance: "What does survive confirms that university humanists employed the paraphrase-commentary format as the basic teaching approach. The professor might begin by reading through the section of the text to be discussed that day, followed by a brief general explanation of the meaning. He would then launch into a word-by-word analysis of the text, explaining grammatical, rhetorical, historical, and interpretive points. The paraphrase-commentary was thorough and comprehensive." (*Universities,* 241; see also Grendler, *Schooling,* 244–250; and "*Scripta* and *Dicta* in Practice" in chapter 4 below)

that the epistemological parameter of easy memorization is 7 plus or minus 2, then the two's and three's of these subdivsions would have caused no anxiety.[147] The subsequent partitioning of the text into (usually) six co-equal units would also have been quite easy, and made even easier still by the small number of notes appended to each of these six parts. What looks to us exceedingly elaborate when reading about it may, in fact, have been intentionally simple in mnemonic terms.

The simplicity of these numerical units is particularly important when we realize that this *explication de texte* may have preceded the reading or hearing of the passage itself.[148] The dividing and partitioning were cued for the medieval students not by outline numerals or by line numbers as I have indicated them for my own audience, but rather by quotations from the text. The words themselves initiated both recognition and expectation, a sense of where the phrase was in relation to both what preceded and what was to follow. Even with the subdivisions, their limitation to three units means that a student was visualizing a very simple relationship; at each point in a subdivision one is aware of only one step: one is going to a unit that is the same as, one step more general, or one step less general than the unit one has just considered. A major subdivision and the division into parts may not correspond (e.g., in the outline of the *constructio* the second reading includes the end of the Proposal as well as the whole Invocation), but the transitions from one part to another (they are called "parts" in both the subdivision and the partition into sections) occur at the same lines, or rather, at the same verbal cues.

To recapitulate: Pace writes a double *accessus* with a set of questions about the art to which the work belongs and a second set concerning the book itself. He provides each passage with a double structure. Initially he goes through the first structure explaining the "descending" sequence of division and subdivision that opens up the text. Then he goes back to the beginning of the passage and elaborates the text by saying how many parts or sections into which it can be partitioned. Then he proceeds through each part (introduced by *Consequenter* 'next in line') in order, commenting phrase by phrase, sometimes word by word. Then he points out what poetic techniques are employed in each section.

In the preceding paragraphs I have restated Pace's method three times (at least). With each repetition, you are perhaps nodding your head in recognition, even in impatience: yes, yes, you know that; I have already told you. Pace's approach has become predictable, although it was probably confusing the first time it was described. So, too, the experience of medieval students: through Pace's systematic, cumulative approach they learned what Geoffrey has to say,

---

147. Carruthers, *Book of Memory*, 104. Cf. the subdivisions of Bartolinus's commentary on the *Rhetorica ad Herennium*, which have been outlined somewhat differently by Ward, *Ciceronian Rhetoric*, 206.

148. Cf. Bartholomew of Pisa's commentary on the *Poetria nova*, for example, in which the commentary precedes the text.

how he says it, and why he says it that particular way.[149] The text, Geoffrey's teaching, and Pace's lectures on them became embedded in the listeners' heads.

IN SEASON

> In the second [part] he creates a digression away from the subject to show the time during which one of the friends is away from the other.[150]
>
> —Pace of Ferrara

> When you transpose a word whose literal meaning is proper to man, it affords greater pleasure, since it comes from what is your own.[151]
>
> —Geoffrey of Vinsauf

Pace considered the *Poetria nova* an improvement over Horace's *Ars poetica* because Geoffrey "was able to explain clearly what Horace had taught in a confused and elliptical way." Pace himself brings clarity and thoroughness to a new extreme in commentaries on the text by his structured, predictable—rigid?—approach, in which he employs Geoffrey's own favorite techniques of repetition and variation. With only slight modifications, the structured division and analysis that Pace introduces at the beginning of his commentary are repeated throughout. This framework must have been reassuring to medieval teachers and students: its predictability made it easy to anticipate and presumably to apply later. As modern readers we can chafe at such a framework; my own interest in specific lines and passages makes me want him to get to the point, and the first several times I read Pace's commentary I kept skipping a lot of the partitioning. But once I took the time to figure it out, I began to enjoy watching a master at work. The expectation of his analysis caused me to begin reading the text according to his approach. How much could he draw out of every line of text?

Medieval teachers and scribes caught on more quickly than I, however, and just where I begin to feel secure with Pace's procedure, they begin to tinker with it. By the time they get to Geoffrey's treatment of Digression, a passage we have viewed from several perspectives in earlier chapters, variations in the numbers of subdivisions, emphases in summaries of content, etc., have cropped

---

149. Charles Singleton's distinction between Dante the poet and Dante the commentator in the *Vita nuova* can serve as an analogy to the student learning and the teacher teaching the *Poetria nova* from such an approach: "the one being he who, though ignorant of the end, moves always toward the end; and the other he who, knowing the end, is constantly retracing the whole line of events with the new awareness and transcendent understanding which such superior knowledge can give" (*An Essay,*" 25).

150. "In secunda facit digressionem ab hac materia ad ostendendum tempus quo vnus amicorum ab alio discessit" (Seville, Biblioteca Capitular y Colombina, Col. 5–4–30, fol. 27ra [30ra]).

151. *PN* 796–797.

up in individual manuscripts of the commentary.[152] Geoffrey's main points in his introduction to digression are 1) an admonishment to the student to "let the pen digress, but not so widely that it will be difficult to find the way back"; 2) a description of digression as "when I turn aside from the material nearby (*propinqua*) bringing in first what is actually remote (*procul*) and altering the natural order . . . "; and 3) another description of digression: "as I advance along the way, I leave the middle of the road, and with a kind of leap I fly off to the side, as it were; then I return to the point whence I had digressed" (527–536). In some manuscripts of Pace's commentary, this passage is subdivided into three (the inital advice and two kinds of digression), in others simply into the two kinds of digression. Some summarize what the two kinds are here as well as later, while others do not. Sometimes the lines that introduce the example ("Lest this matter of digression be veiled in obscurity, I offer the following example" [536–37]) are considered part of the example, sometimes not. For students these variations would not make a difference; it is not which pattern, but the fact of a pattern, that matters for those learning the technique.

The manuscripts of Pace's commentary are in agreement, however, about how to describe the characters in Geoffrey's example. Here is his first description, part of which was quoted as an epigraph to this section:

> And, since the first kind of digression is accomplished by drawing back from the main subject, then adding something suitable to it, and afterwards returning to the first subject, which is the withdrawal and separation of two partners or friends (*duorum sociorum seu amicorum*) from each other, this part is subdivided into three parts. In the first he states the principal subject. In the second he creates a digression away from the subject to show the time during which one of the friends is away from the other. In the third he returns to the principal subject.[153]

The connotation of *sociorum seu amicorum* here is hard to pin down.[154] Geoffrey calls them *amantes* ("lovers," 553) at the end of the passage (one of the places that they were specifically identified as Pyramus and Thisbe in another

152. Of course, some of these differences may have originated as scribal errors rather than conscious decisions on the parts of those who copied the commentaries. Given the amount of Pace's repetition, errors of homoeoteleuton (jumping from a word in one line to the same word further down) were easy for copyists to make, and they all make them.

153. "Et quia digressio secundum primum principalem modum ipsius fit recedendo aliquantulum a materia principali addendo aliquid conueniens ipsi materie et postea cedendo ad materiam principalem que est de recessu et separatione duorum sociorum seu amicorum abinuicem [*sic*]. Et ideo pars ista subdiuiditur in tres partes. In prima ponit materiam principalem. In secunda facit digressionem ab hac materia ad ostendendum tempus quo vnus amicorum ab alio discessit. In tercia reuertitur ad materiam principalem" (Seville, Biblioteca Capitular y Colombina, Col. 5-4-30, fol. 27ra [30ra]).

154. "Utrumque" (540) is glossed "sociori" [*sic*] in Vatican City, BAV Chig. I.IV.145, fol. 13v. In Holkham Hall, Library of the Earl of Leicester, 423, "pectora" is glossed "sociorum" and "amantes" is glossed "illos socios" (fol. 10r–v). See also note 263 below.

manuscript[155]), but *socii* usually connotes something more like "associates" or "colleagues," although it can refer to an established heterosexual couple.[156] Pace's other term, "friend" (*amicus*—more often in the female form *amica*) was a popular term for the beloved in Latin love poetry.[157] It was also employed in intimate but not necessarily physical relationships between those of the same sex, especially in religious orders, where the language of love could express close spiritual bonds both human and divine.[158] In this tradition the trope of one heart in two bodies echoes not Pyramus and Thisbe (as in the "Anglo-French group" mentioned in chapter 2), but the classical world of male friendship.[159] When Augustine describes the importance of his love for a male friend (a relationship that he earlier compared to that of Orestes and Pilates), he says that they share one soul in two bodies.[160] Pace's gloss of *sociorum seu amicorum* emphasizes human emotion and commitment.

Pace is not concerned with the gender of the initial couple, but rather their humanity, an interpretation strengthened by glosses in other manuscripts that identify them as *duos homines*[161] and *duos homines amantes se*.[162] In these glosses "*homines*" probably means "humans" rather than "men," in contrast to the nonhuman couple in the digression: the female earth and male air who copulate and produce a child. As Pace points out later in his interpretation of the passage, Geoffrey teaches elsewhere in the *Poetria nova* how to transfer human qualities metaphorically to something inanimate, which is one of his accomplishments in the digression. It is the nonhuman sex in the digression that interests Pace, or rather the science behind it. He keeps his discussion on an abstract and theoretical plane by invoking Aristotle to explain the content of Geoffrey's digression: "[T]he air itself encouraged the earth, and he shows how, . . . since heat is an active quality and dryness a passive one according to Aristotle in the fourth

---

155. See "Pyramus and Thisbe in the *Poetria nova*" in chapter 2.

156. See the examples from Ovid (one in in the *Metamorphoses,* several in the love poetry) cited in the *Oxford Latin Dictionary.*

157. Ziolkowski, "Twelfth-Century Understandings," 60; and Brassel, "Composition of Medieval Love." One of the most famous of all medieval love poems begins "Iam, dulcis amica, venito." (It was translated by Baudelaire as "L'invitation au voyage," in which the beloved is also called "ma soeur.") "Amicus" and "amica" are translated as "boyfriend" and "girlfriend" in "Better Than Sex" in chapter 2.

158. See, for example, McGuire, *Friendship & Community,* xliii–xliv, 196, 296–298, 315–316, 321–323, etc.

159. It may be significant that none of the six Pyramus and Thisbe school poems that Glendinning describes is from Italy ("Pyramus and Thisbe").

160. *Confessions* 4.6.

161. The "corpora" in line 539 are glossed "duos homines" in Genoa, Biblioteca Durazzo Giustiniani, B II 1, fol. 11v; see "It's Muglio" below on this manuscript.

162. "duos homines amantes se" (London, BL Add. 37495, fol. 10v); added in the margin in a similar hand: "idest duo socii coniuncti nodo dillectionis" (a phrase that is used as a gloss on line 538 in one of the early manuscripts of Pace's commentary [Rome, Biblioteca Corsiniana, Rossi 22 (36 G 15 [R]), fol. 11vb]). On London, BL Add. 37495, an Italian manuscript dated 1382, see *Iter ital.* 4.81; Watson, *Dated and Datable Manuscripts,* 79 (379), with plate of 15r (272); Gallick, "Medieval Rhetorical Arts," 83; and Allen, *Ethical Poetic,* 233.

book of the *Metaphysics*,[163] and, granting that the masculine sex should act and the feminine should submit, [Geoffrey] adds that the earth is like a woman from its passive quality, which is dryness. . . . "[164]

In the next passage Pace refers to a later part of the *Poetria nova*, another sign of teaching at an intermediate or advanced level:

> [N]ote that up to this point he is talking about a kind of metaphoric transference [made] by attributing human qualities to something inanimate. Later, in the chapter on metaphoric transference, he introduces a similar example of the spring (786–90) to show how human qualities are attributed to an inanimate object, such as when one wants to say that the sun adorns the springtime. Since it [the connection between the separation and the season when it occurred] may not be clear here in the Digression, he returns to the original subject, saying [what follows is a paraphrase of 552–553] that it was in this season, namely the spring, when the two friends were separated, whom nevertheless love kept together, since, although separated in body, they are connected and close to each other through love. And 552 NOW IS THE SEASON etc. The meaning of this passage (*lectionis*) is brought to an end in this. Note, therefore, that the description of spring was not irrelevant to what was digressed from. On the contrary, it was very suitable to the material since it was in such a season that the separation was brought about.[165]

Geoffrey and his commentators were intrigued with metaphoric transference from one kind of being to another; it allowed them to play on the root meaning of *transfero* (to carry over) and to speculate about similarities between different kinds of beings. Much of the glossing on the section of text to which Pace refers involves identifying what category is being transferred to what other category.[166]

---

163. That Pace refers to Aristotle's *Metaphysics* indicates an advanced commentary. Cf. Black, *Humanism*, 22: "scholastic subjects were rarely studied before university."

164. "aer ipse blanditur humo et ostendit quomodo, . . . quia caliditas est qualitas actiua et siccitas passiua secundum Aristotilem in quarto <*Methafisicorum*> [*K*: Methaurorum *SB*], ideo cum masculini sexus sit agere, feminini uero pati, addit quod humus est quasi femina a qualitate passiua que est siccitas . . ." (Seville, Biblioteca Capitular y Colombina, Col. 5-4-30, fol. 27va–b [30va–b]). This section of Pace's discussion of digression is not found in the short version of the commentary (MS R).

165. "adhuc nota quod utitur transumptione methaforica attribuendo proprietates hominis rei inanimate. Vnde infra capitulo de transumptione methaforica ponit exemplum simile de descriptione ueris ad ostendendum quomodo proprietates hominis attribuuntur rei inanimate ut si forte uelis hoc dicere 'tempora ueris exornare <solem> [*corr.*: solum *SKB*]' etc. <Cum non patet> [*corr*: Commune ne peccet *SB*: communiter uerum(?) ne peccet *K*] in digressione reuertitur ad principalem materiam, dicens quod tale tempus, scilicet ueris, separati fuerunt amici duo quos tamen nundum amor separauit, quia quamuis corporaliter sint remoti, amore tamen sunt coniuncti et proximi. Et (557) HOC est TEMPUS etc. Et in hoc terminatur sententia presentis lectionis. Nota ergo quod non fuit impertinens descriptio ueris ad quam digreditur, ymo conueniens predicte materie, quia tali tempore factus est recessus" (Seville, Biblioteca Capitular y Colombina, Col. 5-4-30, fol. 27va [30vb]).

166. See the attention given to this kind of transference in the list of contents appended to the *Poetria*

STAND AND COUNTERSTAND

> . . . for this reason we have not undertaken to comment.[167]
>
> —Pace of Ferrara

> The Paduan says that he therefore does not wish to comment on this passage. And for this reason I, Giovanni (*Johannes*), do wish to comment on this passage, stating first that what the Paduan said is simply false.[168]
>
> —Giovanni Travesi

Given Pace's emphasis on analysis and attention to the text, it is startling to read his refusal to comment on a passage—a refusal directly countered later by a better-known commentator. The passage in question is the second appeal to the pope near the end of the *Poetria nova:* [169]

> Crown of the empire, you whom Rome, capital of the world, serves with bent knee . . . with your leave I shall speak, and briefly. . . . Do you not see, if you regard the true qualities of our prince, that he has become the soldier of the cross and of Christ, and sword of the entire church? Devotion so great calls for love, not for hatred; for praise, not reproach; for rewards and not penalties. . . . I plead for our prince. I am least of men, you are greatest; yet be receptive, and let him fare better in his role of suppliant. (2081–2098)

In the commentaries that interpret the *Poetria nova* as a rhetorical argument addressed to Pope Innocent III, this passage asking him to help "our prince"—identified by most medieval commentators as Richard I—is one of the most important parts of the book.[170] But Pace argues that, interpreted this way, the passage is a logical inconsistency because of Geoffrey's famous lament on Richard's death earlier in the text; he concludes his commentary as follows:

> Note that in some manuscripts (*libris*) we find a passage that begins, "Crown of the Empire" (2081). But, as it seems to me, either this part was not put in the book by the author, or, if it was the author's, it should not have been put here, but rather at the beginning; the reason for this is that the author pressures

---

nova in Rome, Biblioteca Casanatense, 311 ("The Usefulness of this Text" in chapter 1). On nonacademic medieval interspecies relationships, see Jeffrey Jo Cohen, *Medieval Identity Machines,* e.g., "Chevalerie," 35–77.

167. "Ideo exponere non curauimus" (Seville, Biblioteca Capitula Colombina, Col. 5–4-30, fol. 102ra [105ra]).

168. "Et ideo dicit paduanus hanc partem exponere noluit. Et ideo ego Johannes hanc partem uolo exponere, primo dicens id quod dicit paduanus esse simpliciter falsum" (Seville, Biblioteca Capitular y Colombina, Cap. 56–2-27, fol. 38v).

169. This note is missing in only one complete manuscript of Pace's commentary, Rome, Biblioteca Corsiniana, Rossi 22, which is much shorter than the others.

170. See "The Double Structure" in chapter 1, and Woods, "Innocent III."

the pope to put his hatred aside and return King Richard, whom some say he excommunicated, to a state of grace. This seems completely absurd: since Richard was dead as is clear from the examples of apostrophe put in earlier, [and] since King Richard was a most Christian man and a warrior for the Church, for these reasons is not possible for hatred to have come between him and the pope. Since, therefore, the passage inserted in some copies should not be there and does not seem to be appropriate to the work, as a consequence we have not undertaken to comment [on it].[171]

Here Pace emphasizes the logical integrity of text rather than the hermeneutic circularity of the interpretation that praises the end for returning to the beginning. His decision to excise a problematic part of the text, rather than to interpolate reasons for its inclusion (as is done, for example, in the *Early Commentary*), suggests a humanist concern with authorial intention and the manuscript tradition.

But this conclusion of Pace's was criticized by Giovanni Travesi(o)—Johannes Travesius—a native of Cremona who was holder of the chair of grammar at Pavia in 1388 when Antonio Loschi and Gasparino Barzizza were students there.[172] Written in blocks of tiny writing in the margins of a copy of the text completed in 1448, Travesi's commentary also contains references to teachings on the *Poetria nova* by his own teacher Johannes Bondi.[173] In the beginning of his commentary Travesi addresses those whose "sons" he is teaching, telling them (in a statement quoted earlier) that he has written his commentary on the work he calls the *Poetria novella* "for the benefit" of those sons and that he "lectures on it every year so that they may imbibe the fruits and meters of rhetoric."[174] He calls the *accessus* categories of the causes, the title, and the part of philosophy "the method of the moderns."[175] With regard to the part of phi-

---

171. "<N>otandum est autem quod in quibusdam libris inuenitur quedam pars que incipit sic, 'Imperalis apex,' etc. (2081). Sed, ut uidetur, pars illa aut non fuit posita ab autore in hoc libro, uel si fuit autoris, non debuit hic poni, sed in principio, cuius ratio est quod autor mouit papam et ei suadet ut, deposito odio, gratia reddatur regi Ricardo quem, ut quidam dicunt, excomunicauerat. Quod uidetur omnino absurdum, cum quia mortuus erat ut patet in exemplis apostrofe superius positis, cum quia christianissimus erat rex Richardus et pugil ecclesie, vnde non erat possibile odium interuenisse inter ipsum et papam. Quia igitur pars posita in pluribus libris non habetur et non apparet esse conueniens huic operi, ideo exponere non curauimus" (Seville, Biblioteca Capitula Colombina, Col. 5–4-30, fol. 102ra [105ra]).

172. Witt, *Footsteps*, 388; see also Federici Vescovini, "Due commenti"; Rossi, "Un grammatico"; Gehl, *Moral Art*, 140–141; and Black, *Humanism*, 20, 28, 31, and 212.

173. On Johannes Bondi de Aquileia, see *Enciclopedia italiana* 7.397; *Lexikon des Mittelalters*, 5.558; *DBI* 55.682–683; and Polak, *Western Europe*, 8–9 (with additional references). I am grateful to Emil Polak for references to Travesi and Bondi.

174. "hoc opus . . . quod in vestrorum filiorum utilitatem facio super *Poetria novella* Gualfredi quam annuatim lego ut fructibus et rethorice metricis imbuantur" (Seville, Biblioteca Capitular y Colombina, Cap 56–2-27, fol. 2r). On this manuscript, copied by "Michelmus de Solerio de Frascarolo," see Faulhaber, "Retóricas clásicas y medievales," 193–194, and *Latin Rhetorical Theory*, 46.

175. "scilicet ad causarum numerum, ad librum titulum, et ad libri supositionem more modernorum" (Seville, Biblioteca Capitular y Colombina, Cap. 56–2-27, fol. 2r).

losophy to which the *Poetria nova* belongs, Travesi says that "it should properly be classified not under philosophy but under rhetoric."[176]

When he gets to the passage that Pace rejects, Travesi presents an exhaustive counterargument. Rather than ignoring the inconsistency, as most medieval commentators did, or wishing to excise part of the text as Pace did, Travesi says that the inconsistency is irrelevant. Indeed, using Pace's own criticism against himself, Travesi twice calls Pace's critique "absurd," arguing that Geoffrey is writing a rhetorical argument, not a description of a real case, and hence it does not matter if the king is already dead or not. Nor does Pace's comment that the passage is not found in all manuscripts count for much with Travesi. Instead, he says, we should take into account the large number of manuscripts in which the passage *is* included. This recognition by both Pace and Travesi of the implications of multiple versions of the text and the necessity of evaluating them is not addressed by earlier, more traditional medieval teachers of the work.[177] Travesi paraphrases and quotes Pace and responds to his points as follows:

> In that part he [Geoffrey] again praises the pope—some say Emperor Frederick—begging him to return King Richard, who had been dismissed in hatred, to a state of grace. Magister Pax of Padua says that the passsage was not originally part of this book since it is not copied in numerous manuscripts. But he is wrong, since, even if it is not copied in numerous manuscripts, it [the decision about whether it is original] ought to be on the basis of those [where it occurs] since he [Geoffrey] specifically reveals his intention here; and, even if the passage is not copied in some [manuscripts], one does not take from this fact that the passage is not the author's, for there are many manuscripts in which it is copied. Doubting that the passage was the author's, the Paduan says, "If this passage were the author's, it should not have been put here but [rather] in the beginning." And Pace states his reason: "since in this passage the author pressures the pope and persuades him to put aside his hatred thus and return King Richard, whom some say he had excommunicated, to a state of grace. This seems completely absurd," the Paduan says, and he gives his reason: "because since King Richard was [already] dead, as is clear in his examples of apostrophe put in earlier; also since King Richard was a good Christian and a fighter for the church." And as a consequence, the Paduan says, he does not wish to comment on this passage.
>
> And as a consequence I, Giovanni (*Iohannes*), do wish to comment on this passage, stating first that what the Paduan said is simply false. He says that it is not true—or rather "totally absurd"—that King Richard was excommunicated, since he was a good man and since he was dead, which are simply two false propositions. One should accept as true that this king had Blessed Thomas

---

176. "Cui parti philosophye supponatur dico quod non supponitur proprie ipsi philosophye sed ipsi rethorice" (Seville, Biblioteca Capitular y Colombina, Cap. 56–2-27, fol. 2v).

177. Many commentators address different readings of a single word or short phrase, however.

murdered at the altar because he [the king] was depraved, and a reconciliation was necessary because the church had been violated; yet it was not violated by the bloodshed therein, but because of [his] depraved spirit, although this is characteristic of one who has ordered murder to be done.

To the argument that "the king was [already] dead as was made clear in the examples of apostrophe" and as a consequence could not be excommunicated, I say that Geoffrey spoke earlier as an example, not that he [Richard] was already dead, but because it could happen that way, and so it came about; or, even if he were dead, he had been excommunicated right after the death of Saint Thomas. I disagree that these verses ought to be put in the beginning, because [the passage] explains his intention, which ought to be explained at the end and not at the beginning. Geoffrey speaks again, therefore, praising the pope so that he can ask more effectively for what he wishes that he did not have to ask for. And it will be clear in the text (*litera*) how much the pope hates King Richard at "O crown of the empire," etc. (2081); the text (*testus*) is clear.[178]

Travesi's detailed response shows the currency of Pace's commentary (and the *Poetria nova* itself) in Italian academic circles both at the end of the fourteenth century, when Travesi wrote it, as well as in the middle of the fifteenth, when this copy of Travesi's commentary was made.

Travesi himself has become a byword for the backward-looking, entrenched commentator who was oblivious of or unable to appreciate the more significant

---

178. "In parte ista iterum commendat dominum papam—aliqui dicunt quod commendat dominum Federicum imperatorem—ei supplicando ut graciam conferat regi Ricardo, odio dimisso. Super quam parte<m> dicit Pax paduanus quod ista pars non est istius libri eo quod in pluribus libris non est scripta. Sed male dicit, quia, dato quod non scripta in pluribus libris, super illis esse debet, quia hic specialiter explicat suum intentum, et, dato quod super illis non sit scripta, non tollit propter hoc quod ista pars non sit <autoris> [nitoris *MS*]; multi autem sunt libri super quibus est scripta. Dicit iterum ille paduanus quasi dubitans utrum ista pars fuerit autoris sic: 'Si hec pars fuit autoris non debuit hic conlocari [colorari *MS*] sed in principio.' Et rationem ponit: 'quia in hac parte autor mouet papam et ei suadet ut deposito sic odio, graciam reddat regi Ricardo quem ut quidam dicunt excomunicauerat. Quod uidetur omnino absurdum,' dicit ille paduanus, et reddit rationem: 'cum quia mortuus erat rex Ricardus ut patet in exemplis supra positis ipsius <apostrophis> [apostrophes *MS*], similiter quia rex Ricardus erat bonus christianus et pugil eclexie.' Et ideo dicit paduanus hanc partem exponere noluit.

"Et ideo ego Iohannes hanc partem uolo exponere, primo dicens id quod dicit paduanus esse simpliciter falsum. Dicit non esse uerum, ymo totaliter absurdum, <scilicet> [sed *MS*] quod rex Richardus fuerit excommunicatus quia bonus erat et quia mortuus, que duo sunt simpliciter falsa. Credendum est quod rex ille [ex quo] fecit interfici [= interfeci] beatum Thomam ad altare<m> quod prauus erat et eclexia ista fuit reconcilianda, quia uiolata fuit; non tamen fuit uiolata ratione sanguinis facti in eclexia [fixi *MS*], sed ratione praui animi, quamuis interficientis est ipsius qui fecit interfici.

"Ad illud quod 'erat mortuus' <rex> [res *MS*] et perconsequens non fuit excommunicatus 'ut patuit in exemplis apostrophis,' dico quod Gualfredus supra fuit locutus gratia exempli non ut esset mortuus sed quia potuit sic accedere et ita euenit; uel, dato quod esset mortuus, fuit excomunicatus subito post mortem beati Thome. Quod autem hec carmina debeant esse in principio nego, quia suam exprimit intencionem que in fine et non in principio debet exprimi. Dicit ergo Gualfredus iterum commendans papam ut melius impetret quod uult quod non impetrauit, et apparebit in litera quomodo papa habuit regem Ricardum in odio, 'O Imperalis apex' etc. (2081), testus [= textus] patet" (Seville, Biblioteca Capitular y Colombina, Cap. 56–2-27, fol. 38v).

aspects of humanism. In an unfortunately memorable phrase, Pierre Courcelle calls Travesi "un pédant prolixe et fastidieux."[179] Lodi Nauta, however, argues that Travesi's approach was appropriate for a work studied "in the grammar schools and in the religious houses before students were sent to the university."[180] If we concede that Travesi's commentary on the *Poetria nova* is, indeed, learned and thorough (another way to say "pedantic and prolix"), these very qualities would have been appropriate for students who are being taught how to talk about texts (and interpretations of them) after they have learned how to read them, but before they learn the theoretical terminology, the jargon, of the more advanced analysis found in Pace's commentary. Nauta suggests that we "equate humanists with the schoolmasters who taught generations of pupils Latin in the fifteenth and sixteenth centuries" rather than relying on "the opinions and the manifestos of . . . famous scholar-philologists" like Valla and Erasmus.[181] Revisionist theories developed later in life may be a less reliable guide to pedagogical history than the stability of commentary traditions on school texts themselves.

GEOFFREY AND BARZIZZA

> Geoffrey the Englishman, a very learned man[182]
> —Gasparino Barzizza

Although there is no evidence that Giovanni Travesi influenced the rhetorical interests of his famous students Loschi and Barzizza,[183] he does refer to public speaking several times in the first part of his *accessus* to the *Poetria nova*.[184] It is quite possible that Gasparino Barzizza (1360–1431) did teach the *Poetria nova*, although a commentary by him has not been identified.[185] As we see in the epigraph above, Barzizza describes Geoffrey as *vir eruditissimus* in his commentary

---

179. He is describing Travesi's commentary on Boethius's *Consolation of Philosophy* (also extant only in a fifteenth-century manuscript), cited in Nauta, "Some Aspects," 770 and 768. Black and Pommaro have demonstrated that Boethius was "the most widely and intensively studied school author in later medieval and early Renaissance Italy," at the same period when the *Poetria nova* was receiving so much attention (and with which it was sometimes copied); Black and Pomaro, *Boethius's* Consolation, cited in Nauta, "Some Aspects," 772.

180. Nauta, "Some Aspects," 770, also 772. The issue of transitional school/university texts is particularly important for the central European manuscripts discussed in the following chapter.

181. Nauta, "Some Aspects," 778 and 770.

182. "Gualfredus, natione anglicus, vir eruditissimus," quoted in Pigman, "Barzizza's Studies of Cicero," 129.

183. Witt, *Footsteps*, 388.

184. E.g., "in arenghis," "arengas," "arengare," "arenget," etc. (Seville, Biblioteca Capitular y Colombina, Cap. 56-2-27, fol. 2r). There are also references to the *ars arengandi* (lit.: art of haranguing) in the commentaries by Guizzardo of Bologna and Benedict of Aquileia; see the sections on them to follow.

185. See Brown, "Gasparino Barzizza and Virgil," for the restraint necessary in evaluating attributions to Barzizza.

on the *Rhetorica ad Herennium,* in his application of the doctrine of the *Rhetorica ad Herennium* to the composition of letters: "Concerning the parts of a letter, it seems clear to many that this ornament [the maxim or *sententia*] is very similar to the introduction (*exordio*), which Geoffrey the Englishman, a very learned man, appears to assert when he discusses artificial order in instructing poets," and Barzizza goes on to talk about Geoffrey's methods of beginning a work from the beginning, the middle, or the end with a proverb.[186] This technique is the first major composition doctrine taught in the *Poetria nova,* where it is elaborated in terms of the story of King Minos.[187] Barzizza encouraged his students to look at other commentaries on the *Rhetorica ad Herennium,* and commentators on that work often cited examples from the *Poetria nova* to illustrate the figures, so it could be argued that he knew the medieval work only from citations of it. But it is more likely that he knew the *Poetria nova* quite well. In fact, I would suggest that Barzizza's imitation exercise based on "changing singular to plural" or "adding or removing" words is based on Geoffrey's long discussions of the theories of conversion, which is finding the best way to express an idea by trying it out in different inflected forms of a word, and determination, in which a word is made more powerful or figurative by juxtaposing it with another word.[188]

The attention to grammatical and rhetorical detail that Geoffrey teaches was, as I have suggested before, consonant with early humanist efforts to make students sensitive to style and nuance. Whether Travesi was responsible for introducing the *Poetria nova* to Barzizza is not so important as the continuity of positive assessment of Geoffrey in the teachings of men who had been exposed to newer material and approaches as well. While scholars tend to put Travesi and Barzizza on opposite sides of the humanist divide,[189] both men were admirers of the *Poetria nova* and appear to have used it regularly in their teaching. The basis for that shared admiration was Geoffrey's ability to teach students to take full advantage of the Latin language.

---

186. "Circa partes epistolae certe nonnullis videtur haec exornatio maxime convenire exordio, quod etiam Gualfredus, natione anglicus, vir eruditissimus, testari videtur cum poetas instruens tractat de ordine artificiali, quem cum in octo species diviserit, tres ex illis attribuit proverbio cum aliquam nobis assumpsimus aut fabulam aut historiam describendam vel initium sumendo a principio rei vel a medio vel a fine per proverbium" (quoted in Pigman, "Barzizza's Studies of Cicero," 129; variants omitted). Pigman assumes that the work of Geoffrey to which Barzizza refers is the shorter prose *Documentum.* Since all the manuscripts of that work are English, however, in contrast to the *Poetria nova* of which so many Italian manuscripts have survived, the *Poetria nova* is the more probable source. I am grateful to Professor Pigman for e-mail discussions about this reference. See also Mercer, *Teaching of Gasparino Barzizza,* 83, 93, and 145.

187. See "Shaping the Narrative" in chapter 2.

188. Barzizza's exercise is described in McLaughlin, *Literary Imitation,* 104–5. On Geoffrey's treatment of these techniques and a teacher's description of them as "the inflection of words" and "the addition of words" see "Conversion: the Origin of Style" and "Student Determination" in chapter 2.

189. E.g., "il Travesi al Barzizza, il metodo vecchio alle idee nuove" (Garin, "La cultura milanese," 573). On this tradition in scholarship see Black, *Humanism,* 20.

MEANWHILE, BACK IN PADUA:
GUIZZARDO OF BOLOGNA

> The efficient cause was Geoffrey (or Walter), a man fecund in literary ability. . . . [190]
>
> —Guizzardo of Bologna

Pace of Ferrara's commentary on the *Poetria nova,* although the longest and most detailed—a text that like several others discussed in this chapter warrants a full edition and monograph of its own—was not unique in remaining current and drawing comment by later humanists. Although Pace remained on the fringes of Paduan humanism, his peripatetic contemporary Guizzardo of Bologna (fl. 1289–1323) was something of an intimate of Mussato in Padua.[191] Guizzardo taught grammar in Florence in the 1290s, in Siena from 1306–1311 and 1314–1315, and then again in Florence in the early 1320s—presumably, according to Ronald Witt, in the short-lived *studio* there.[192] Nancy Siraisi suggests adding him to Andrea Gloria's list of professors of grammar and rhetoric at Bologna as well.[193]

Guizzardo's commentary on the *Poetria nova* survives in a single manuscript in the Vatican Library, Ottob. lat. 3291. It comprises the first seventeen folios of a fifteenth-century commentary collection also containing commentaries on Martianus Capella and on Sallust's *Bellum Catilinae* and *Bellum Iugurthinum.*[194] Witt refers to the whole codex as "notes for some of [Guizzardo's] lectures."[195] Although it is only a fifth the length of Pace's commentary on the *Poetria nova,* Guizzardo's is copied in the same double-columned, commentary-only format (plate 7). Bruno Nardi published Guizzardo's *accessus* to the *Poetria nova* as part of his examination of resemblances between Guizzardo's co-authored commentary on the *Ecerinis* and Dante's "Letter to Can Grande della Scala."[196]

---

190. "Causa quidem efficiens fuit Gualfredus uel Gualterius litteratoria facultate facundus . . . " (Vatican City, BAV Ottob. lat. 3291, fol. 1rb).

191. Guizzardo borrowed a copy of Virgil from Mussato and forgot to return it, as we learn from a 1318 poem, "Ad Magistrum Guizardum grammaticae professorem" (Siraisi, *Arts and Sciences,* 49, citing Hyde, *Padua in the Age of Dante,* 293, and Dazzi, *Il Mussato preumanista,* 52); also Mussato, *Epistolae,* 14, p. 64, cited in Witt, *Footsteps,* 130 and 134, 196, and 224 on Guizzardo.

192. Black, *Education and Society,* 266–267; and Witt, *Footsteps,* 130. There is no mention of Guizzardo in Davies, *Florence and Its University.* On Guizzardo see also Guido Billanovich, "Il prehumanismo padovano," 65, 73, 77, 80, 87, 95, 99; and Foa, "Guizzardo da Bologna," *DBI* 61.555–556, with a short discussion of Guizzardo's commentary on the *PN* on 555.

193. Siraisi, *Arts and Sciences,* 175. As Siraisi notes, "Gloria did not list Guizzardo as a professor at Padua; a grammarian called Guizzardo of Bologna is named in Sarti and Fattorini, *De claris archigymnasii bononiensis professoribus,* II, 245. Can he be identified with the Guizzardo who taught geometry at Bologna in 1304 (*ibid.,* I, 586)?" (49).

194. On Vatican City, BAV Ottob. lat. 3291, see Nardi, "Osservazioni"; Mercati, *Codici latini Pico Grimani Pio,* 251; Livi, *Dante e Bologna,* 71–72 and 109; Sandkühler, *Die frühen Dantekommentare,* 48; and Osmond and Ulery, "Sallustius," *CTC* 8.226b–227a, 285a.

195. Witt, *Footsteps,* 130.

196. Nardi, "Osservazioni," 287.

In the tour-de-force incipit to his *accessus,* meant to impress and tortuous in translation, Guizzardo announces that he is coming to the rescue of those being taught rhetoric by charlatans:

> On account of the false beliefs of those who, for the sake of eloquent speech or in the guise of the dictaminal style, are teaching rhetoric professionally yet "paint a dolphin in the woods, a boar on the waves" {Hor. *Ars* 30}, I, Guizzardo, lowliest servant of *dictatores,* thought that help needed to be brought to those who have already gone astray, by removing the error among them concerning the difference between rhetoric, dialectic, poetry, and ornate speech, which must be outlined clearly (with allowance for correction) before I expound as well as I can on the work before us.[197]

This introduction is a bit of a red herring, however, since the overlap of categories is as important to him as distinguishing among them. He does say that rhetoric and dialectic are two separate things because each is a separate liberal art—a distinction reminiscent in its structure of Pace's triumphant declaration that rhetoric and poetics are two distinct subjects because Aristotle wrote separate books on them. But for Guizzardo poetics, like dictamen, is a part of rhetoric. He notes that "dictaminal speech is composed of sounds," a reflection of the public reading of letters; and, after examining ways of distinguishing rhetoric from other arts, he assures his audience that "in this present work of poetry all such speech is fully discussed."[198]

Because of the similarity of format in the manuscripts of their commentaries, which nevertheless differ so greatly in length, it is tempting to see Guizzardo's commentary as a version of "Pace-made-easy," especially since both were probably written in Padua. The commentaries of these two men do share important characteristics; some years ago I used them as exemplars of the combination of textual and theoretical concerns typical of early humanist commentaries on the *Poetria nova.*[199] But the effect of learning the text from each would have been significantly different. Pace constructs a theory of poetics based on the consistent application of the most distinguished analytical model available

---

197. "<Q>uoniam propter opinantes contrarium ueritati [novitati *Nardi: corr. MS*] qui ob ornatum modum loquendi siue stilo dictaminis subiacentem suspicantes rhetoricam formaliter edocere, 'delfinum siluis appingit, fluctibus aprum' {Hor. *Ars* 30}, ego Guicciardus, minimus dictatorum [donatorum *Nardi*] minister, ipsis deuiantibus fore succurrendum errore sublato de medio propter differentiam inter rethoricam, dyalecticam, poesim, et ornatum sermonem lucide assignandam, cum correptionis [= correctionis] uenia, cogitaui antequam presens opus exponerem sicut possum" (Vatican City, BAV Ottob. lat. 3291, fol. 1ra; Nardi, "Osservazioni," 289–90). This first part of the incipit is quoted in the colophon to Genoa, Biblioteca Durazzo Giustiniani, B II 1, fol. 42v; see below, "It's Muglio."

198. "Sermo autem dictatorius est quiddam compositum uocum. . . . Sed in hoc presenti opere poetrie de tali sermone plenarie determinatur" (Vatican City, BAV Ottob. lat. 3291, fol. 1ra–b; Nardi, "Osservazioni," 290–291).

199. Woods, "A Medieval Rhetoric."

to him: *divisio textus*. Guizzardo, in contrast, is more eclectic; he summarizes and categorizes, using a variety of approaches and whatever means might be at hand to make a point. He is full of interesting insights, even when he is inconsistent, as in the next part of his *accessus* where he addresses the Aristotelian four causes.[200] The formal cause is customarily divided into the "form of the treatise" (*forma tractatus*)—its "separation into books and chapters and their order," such as the parts of a rhetorical discourse—and the "form of treatment" (*forma tractandi*) of the subject matter, such as the parts of rhetoric. But when Guizzardo describes the former, it is the structure of the *Poetria nova* elicited by *divisio textus* or infinite subdivision, like Pace's method, of which Guizzardo's definition is a good short description: "The form of the treatise is the division of the book into its principal parts and the principal parts into more minute parts, until one arrives at the smallest particles containing meaning."[201] "The form of the treatment," Guizzardo says, "is the same as the method of proceeding (*modus agendi*), by means of divisions, transitions, and the insertion of examples (*diuisiuus, continuatiuus, et exemplorum positiuus*)."[202] Note Guizzardo's use of *similiter desinens* (the same case ending for several words in a row) and how he emphasizes aspects of Geoffrey's treatment that made the work particularly suitable for teaching: distinguishing among techniques, showing connections between them, and illustrating them by memorable set pieces. Yet when Guizzardo himself divides the text, it is not into principal parts and subdivisions; rather, we are given the standard twofold division of the work into the parts of rhetoric and the parts of a rhetorical discourse.[203]

Guizzardo's commentary proper continues this combination of traditional and unexpected elements. Like many Italian commentators, he specifically applies the doctrine of the *Poetria nova* to the composition of letters.[204] Yet he also makes more references to public speaking (the *ars arengandi*) than I have found so far in any other commentary.[205] Most intriguing of these is his comment that the examples of hidden comparison "work better for the speech-

---

200. Not that he was incapable of sustained analysis; see Nardi's comparison of Guizzardo and Dante's reasoning in "Osservazioni."

201. "Forma tractatus est distinctio libri per partes principales et partium principalium in partes minutas, quousque deueniatur ad minimas sententiam continentes" (Vatican City, BAV Ottob. lat. 3291, fol. 1rb; Nardi, "Osservazioni," 291).

202. "Forma tractandi idem est quod modus agendi, qui est diuisiuus, continuatiuus et exemplorum positiuus" (Vatican City, BAV Ottob. lat. 3291, fol. 1rb; Nardi, "Osservazioni," 291).

203. If Witt is right that this manuscript comprises notes for lectures rather than the lectures themselves, then both aspects of the *forma tractatus* might have been discussed in class. Guizzardo appears to accept without question the "epilogue of the present work" that Pace wished to excise; see his discussion on "epylogacionem presentis operis" under the material cause in Vatican City, BAV Ottob. lat. 3291, fol. 1rb; Nardi, "Osservazioni," 291.

204. E.g., on Geoffrey's discussion of invention (60 ff.): "cum debeant ipse partes in epistola posite pulchris uocabulis et uariis coloribus insigniri" (Vatican City, BAV Ottob. lat. 3291, fol. 2rb).

205. This art is mentioned by others, however, including Bartholomew of Pisa, Giovanni Travesi, and Benedict of Aquileia.

writer (*aringatorem*) than the letter-writer (*dictatorem*)."[206] His citations are equally eclectic; in the same section he refers to Cicero and Catiline[207] but also later to Palladius's *On Agriculture*.[208]

WOMEN IN THE MARGIN

Alcmena / Calisto / Io / Europa[209]
   —Vatican City, Biblioteca Apostolica Vaticana, Ottob. lat. 3291

An interest that Guizzardo shares with other early humanist commentators on the *Poetria nova* like Bartholomew of Pisa and Pace of Ferrara is a greater emphasis on the mythological references appended to Geoffrey's description of a dressed woman than on that of the naked woman which so occupied teachers in more basic commentaries. The early humanists make the list of Jove's lovers (613–621) a separate example, rather than part of the description of a dressed woman as in modern editions and translations as well as a number of other commentaries. In introducing the section Guizzardo summarizes all the examples of description, including that of the banquet table that follows, but he mentions no details of the woman's body. Notice his emphasis here on the distinction between animate and inanimate subjects:

> 562 A WOMAN'S BEAUTY etc. Here he puts an example, and it is a double one, since first he puts an example of an animate thing [a woman], and second he puts an example of an inanimate thing, as one might think of a banquet there at "But since the description" (622). The first is divided into three, since first he describes a woman with regard to her substance [i.e., naked]; second, with regard to her adornment [i.e., dressed]; third, he puts her with Jove among all the beautiful women whom Jupiter once loved. The second is there at, "The loveliness thus pictured," (600),[210] the third there at, "If Jupiter in those days" (613).[211]

---

206. "Et nota quod ista exempla que posita sunt faciunt pocius ad aringatorem quam ad dictatorem" (Vatican City, BAV Ottob. lat. 3291, fol. 4rb).

207. "Pereque sic, Catalinam rempublicam subuertentem Cicero interfecit" (Vatican City, BAV Ottob. lat. 3291, fol. 4rb).

208. "loquens Palladius in principio sui libri *De agricultura*" (Vatican City, BAV Ottob. lat. 3291, fol. 9vb).

209. Vatican City, BAV Ottob. lat. 3291, fol. 6rb (*in marg*).

210. Medieval commentators, as we have seen, sometimes include the introduction to an example as part of the example; hence the difference in line numbers for where the description of the dressed woman begins in Guizzardo's commentary and in the list of examples in chapter 1, "Purple Patches."

211. "FEMINEUM etc. Hic ponit exemplum, et duo facit quia primo ponit exemplum rei animate, secundo exemplum rei inanimate utputa conuiuii ibi, 'Sed cum sit forme' (622). Prima in tres, quia primo describit mulierem quantum ad substanciam, secundo quantum ad ornatus eius, tercio preponit ipsam apud Iouem omnibus pulcris quas olim Iupiter adamauit; secunda ibi, 'Forme tam picte' (600); tercia ibi, 'Si Iupiter illis' (613)" (Vatican City, BAV Ottob. lat. 3291, fol. 6rb).

This passage is clearly visible in the second column, identified by the first words written in a larger display script, *FEMINEUM etc.* (plate 7). The next *lemma* in the display script, *FORME TAM PICTE etc.* (600), introduces a two-part comment. The first three lines are about the dressed woman: "Here as was said above the author describes a woman with regard to externals; the text is clear."[212] The *lemma* to the third part, "*Si Iupiter illis*" ("If Jupiter in those days," 613), is underlined only. Guizzardo links all the descriptions (body, clothes, lovers) when he says that "her substance and her dress and all those things were delightful to Jove."[213] Then he summarizes the story of each of Jupiter's lovers that Geoffrey mentions, e.g., "Alcmena was the wife of Amphitryon, whom Jupiter ardently loved, but since he could not have her he changed himself into the likeness of her husband coming back from study [or the *studium*], and in this way he went to bed with her."[214] That the husband is a student rather than a warrior indicates that Guizzardo was thinking of the version of the story in the medieval Latin drama *Geta,* which was a staple of the schoolroom and on which Geoffrey's example of the lazy man is based.[215] Guizzardo's notes on Jove's lovers continue through the bottom of this column and halfway down the first column on the back (verso) of the folio. A later hand has identified each woman in the margin of the commentary, the first four of which are visible on the plate (*Alcmena / Calisto / Io / Europa*). These names are among the very few glosses in the margins of the commentary in this manuscript, and similar ones are the only such in several late manuscripts of Pace's commentary as well.

Guizzardo's commentary is roughly a tenth the length of Pace's, and the more condensed form highlights an important characteristic. One of his favorite phrases is a variant of "This is clear in the text."[216] Guizzardo's commentary

---

212. "Hic ut dicebatur supra, describit autor mulierem quantum ad actus extrinsecos; litera patet" (Vatican City, BAV Ottob. lat. 3291, fol. 6rb).

213. "et quo ad substanciam et quo ad habitum omnibus illis que fuerunt dilecte a Ioue. Et ponit ex illis multas ut patet in testu" (Vatican City, BAV Ottob. lat. 3291, fol. 6rb).

214. "Alcmena fuit uxor Amphitrionis quam Iupiter ardenter amauit, sed cum eam habere non posset, mutauit se in speciem mariti sui redeuntis a studio, et sic cum ea concubuit" (Vatican City, BAV Ottob. lat. 3291, fol. 6rb).

215. As Elliott notes about this medieval play by Vitalis of Blois, "Amphitryon himself is demoted from commander-in-chief of the Theban army to impoverished philosophy student, returning laden with books . . . " (*Seven Medieval Latin Comedies,* xxxiv). On *Geta* see also "Purple Patches" in chapter 1.

216. E.g., "littera plana est" (Vatican City, BAV Ottob. lat. 3291, fol. 2ra); "in prima parte sententia est plana" (fol. 2rb); "cetera plana sunt," "littera plana est," "alia littera plana est" (fol. 2va); "littera plana est" (fol. 2vb); "quod totum planum est" (fol. 3rb); "littera plana est" (fol. 3vb); "littera plana est" and "totum est planum" (fol. 4ra); "littera plana est" (fol. 4va); "littera plana est et constructus" and "littera per se patet" (fol. 5ra); "littera et constructus est planus" (fol. 5rb), etc. Toward the end we find slight variations: "littera plana est per totum (fol. 13vb); "littera per se plana est" (fol. 14rb); "in toto isto exempla sunt plana" and "totum etiam est planum" (fol. 14vb); "littera est clara in omnibus" (fol. 16ra). For an interpretation of "plana est littera" as "the literal sense is clear," see Nauta, "William of Conches," 374.

also emphasizes compositional strategies to be drawn from the *Poetria nova*,[217] as we can see when he summarizes Geoffrey's intention in the long series of apostrophes on the death of Richard: "Whence in this part the intention of the author is, as was said, to teach us to expand on our theme; from this we can greatly amplify our composition (*dictamen*) on such a subject, just as the author himself does."[218]

Guizzardo constantly cites Horace—e.g., "And this agrees with Horace"[219]— and "Tully" (the *Rhetorica ad Herennium*),[220] with occasional references to Donatus and later texts such as Boethius's *Consolation of Philosophy* and Alan of Lille's *Anticlaudianus*.[221] He also quotes Terence in a gloss on one of Geoffrey's more endearing bits of advice. In discussing the kind of metaphor where there is surface opposition but underlying agreement (e.g., "Before the face of God, devout silence cries out" [878]), Geoffrey offers an analogy: "Consider other areas of experience and observe that the same thing is true: when lovers quarrel, with mutual recrimination, harmony of spirit grows while tongues are at war; love is built on this estrangement" (879–882). Guizzardo comments, "Here he proves this to be possible through the lovers who outwardly seem to hate and in their hearts love each other exceedingly. As Terence says, 'The quarrels of lovers are the rekindling of love'" {*Andria* 3.555}.[222] This offhand citation of a well-known Terentian tag (which may also have been Geoffrey's inspiration) is typical of Guizzardo's commentary, with its numerous literary allusions and straightforward progress through the text.

Because of the lack of the kind of strict *constructio* that Pace created in his, Guizzardo's commentary on the *Poetria nova* is much easier to read, at least in the possibly condensed form in which it has come down to us. Despite what should be our familiarity with Dante's fervent embrace of scholastic *divisio* in his explication of passages in the *Vita nuova* and attempt in the "Letter to Can Grande" to elevate the *Divine Comedy* to the status of authoritative text, Guizzardo's commentary lacking these techniques may be more congenial to modern readers than Pace's, which incorporates them. With seven extant copies

---

217. One of these, using a bible story as the basis of the exercise in the ways of beginning a narrative, is discussed in the next section.

218. "Vnde in hac parte intentio autoris est ut dictum est docere nos prolongare thema nostrum vnde multum possumus ampliare nostrum dictamen in tali materia sicut autor iste facit" (Vatican City, BAV Ottob. lat. 3291, fol. 4vb).

219. "Et concordat cum Oratio . . . " (Vatican City, BAV Ottob. lat 3291, fol. 15rb); there are references to Lucan and Virgil on fol. 16ra.

220. E.g., Vatican City, BAV Ottob. lat. 3291, fol. 4ra and passim.

221. See, for example, the many citations on Vatican City, BAV Ottob. lat. 3291, fol. 4r–v; for the *Anticlaudianus,* see fol. 14va.

222. "Hic probat hoc esse possibile per amantes qui se uidentur odire extra et in cordibus se diligunt nimium. Vnde Terentius [Ovidi *corr.*] hic, 'amantium <ire> amoris reintegratio est'" {*Andria* 3.555} (Vatican City, BAV Ottob. lat. 3291, fol. 8rb).

to the one of Guizzardo's, however, Pace's appears to have suited medieval and early Renaissance teachers just fine.

BIBLE STORIES IN COMPOSITION CLASS

> You might take the introduction from the story of Abraham.[223]
> —Novacella, Convento dei Canonici Regolari, Cod. 327

References to the bible are rather common in intermediate and advanced Italian commentaries on the *Poetria nova* (and biblical references could be a sign of humanist influence[224]). One of the most interesting from a pedagogical perspective is found in both Guizzardo's commentary and a related one added in the margins of a manuscript of the *Poetria nova* now in the library of the Augustinian canons in Novacella (Neustift).[225] The Novacella manuscript, extremely clear and legible, has no *accessus* and few interlinear glosses (but for an exception see below). Its short, separate marginal glosses contain references to many of the same classical and medieval authors and texts that are noted in Guizzardo's commentary, such as Ovid, Alan of Lille's *Anticlaudianus,* the *Rhetorica ad Herennium* ("Tullius"), Boethius, and even Juvenal—all on the first few folios.[226] Several more occur in the long apostrophe on the death of Richard I of England, where the commentator is attentive to the other rhetorical devices at work in this justly famous passage. Of course, some of these citations may have been taken from *florilegia* of the kind in which the *Poetria nova* itself was sometimes excerpted.[227]

These two commentaries adduce a biblical story where Geoffrey uses a classical one. Geoffrey teaches how to start a composition with a proverb taken from the beginning, the middle, and the end of the narrative, and to illustrate he uses the story of Minos.[228] Guizzardo and the commentator of the Novacella manuscript illustrate this technique with proverbs based on the three parts of the biblical narrative of Abraham and Isaac, and in a manner that assumes that students were familiar with the details and would know why each proverb

---

223. "A principio sumas exordium de hystoria Abrahe . . . " (Novacella, Convento dei Canonici Regolari, 327, fol. 2v).

224. Cf. Witt, *Coluccio Salutati,* 35.

225. Novacella, Convento dei Canonici Regolari, 327, fols. 1r–19v; it also contains part of the medieval Latin drama *Geta,* which may have influenced Guizzardo's commentary (see note 218). On this manuscript see *Iter ital.* 6.122.

226. E.g., Ovid on fol. 1v, twice on 5r, 7r (along with Lucan in a single gloss on the technique of prosopopeia), 8r, etc.; the *Anticlaudianus* on fol. 1v; "Tullius" on 2r; Boethius on 5r; and Juvenal on 7r (Novacella, Convento dei Canonici Regolari, 327).

227. See "Proverbial Wisdom" in chapter 1.

228. See "Shaping the Narrative" in chapter 2.

would be appropriate. Here is how this technique is described in the Novacella manuscript:

> You take the Introduction from the story of Abraham from the beginning: "If you wish to obey God completely in all precepts of the faith, consider here that Abraham sacrificed his son." If from the middle, you say it thus: "A servant is not worthy to see the secrets of the Lord, because of which Abraham sent his servants away at the foot of the mountain," etc. If from the end, thus: "It is appropriate that the servant should deserve to earn rewards from his faithful service."[229]

Though the commentary in the Novacella manuscript is related to Guizzardo's, it is formatted more like and shares certain emphases with commentaries aimed at less advanced students. In contrast to Guizzardo's commentary, for example, the most extensively glossed passage interlinearly in the Novacella commentary is the description of a woman's body, reinforcing the suggestion made in chapter 1 that teachers of less advanced students paid special attention to the exact wording here because of its intrinsic interest and/or the difficulty of Geoffrey's vocabulary. In Novacella 327, as in several commentaries discussed in chapter 2, the interlinear glosses (here in parentheses) provide more familiar terms for Geoffrey's compound or polysyllabic ones; e.g., at lines 563 and 569, "preforms (that is, forms first)," and "radiates (that is, shines)." "Her slender fingers" (588) is glossed "lest she have thick fingers."[230] The scribe of the text first omits and then adds in the margin a line of the description of the woman's breasts, to which the commentator then appends his longest gloss on this section. Here are Geoffrey's line translated literally and the comment somewhat freely: (580) "Let her chest show as virginal gems both nipples" is glossed "that is, on both sides, and the left nipple is that little part of the breast that the boy takes into his mouth."[231] Geoffrey's silence on "the lower parts" is glossed with an apt quotation from the *Heroides*: "Whence Ovid: 'If I could praise the rest, I would be happier' {*Her.* 20.63}."[232]

---

229. "A principio sumas exordium de hystoria Abrahe: 'Si uis fidei preceptis domini totidem in omnibus obedire, hic considerans Abraham filium suum inmolauit.' Si a medio ita dicis: 'Seruus uidere secreta domini non meretur propter quod Abraham seruos dimittens ad radicem montis,' etc. Si a fine sic, 'Dignum est ut seruus de fidelibus seruiciis acipere premia mereatur' (Novacella, Convento dei Canonici Regolari, 327, fol. 2v). Guizzardo's different version is on fol. 3ra of Vatican City, BAV Ottob. lat. 3291.

230. "Preformet: idest prius formet," "radient: idest nitent," "tenues digitos: ne habeat grossos digitos" (Novacella, Convento dei Canonici Regolari, 327, fol. 8r).

231. "idest ex utraque parte scilicet et sinistra papilla, -le, est illa particula mamelle quam accipit puer in os" (Novacella, Convento dei Canonici Regolari, 327, fol. 8r).

232. "Unde Ouidius: 'Cetera si possem laudare beacior essem'" (Novacella, Convento dei Canonici Regolari, 327, fol. 8r). *Heroides,* trans. Isbell, p. 205.

"IT'S MUGLIO"

> Master Guizzardo wrote a treatise on the *Poetria nova,* and Master Pietro da Muglio uses this treatise in what he wrote. . . . [233]
>
> —Genoa, Biblioteca Durazzo Giustiniani, B II 1

The small fourteenth-century manuscript of the *Poetria nova* in the Biblioteca Durazzo Giustiniani in Genoa was purchased in 1801 for three "lire genovesi" by Giacomo Filippo Durazzo (1729–1812) for his vast collection of manuscripts, incunabula, and printed books.[234] He rebound all of his volumes, which are housed together today in a magnificent private library maintained by his descendants.[235] Copied in the last quarter of the fourteenth century, MS B II 1 has the look of a luxurious school book, as can be seen in the plate reproduced by Dino Puncuh in his catalogue.[236] The text is clearly the dominant aspect of the manuscript; the glosses are there in a supporting role. The interlinear glosses indicate an assumed audience of students still needing some help with Latin, and there are several vernacular glosses. For example, when Geoffrey of Vinsauf describes Pope Innocent III's retinue of cardinals rather abstractly: "Yours are fitting to decorate such a man (*Suntque tui quales talem decuere*)" (28),[237] the commentator indicates that this description refers to the pope's entourage by providing the masculine and feminine forms for the word "companion" in both Latin and then Italian: "*Hic comes, -tis, scilicet el compagno; inde, hec comitiua, -ue, idest la compagnia.*"

This manuscript is a more professional and costly product than the Italian school books discussed above.[238] There are important references at the beginning and the end of the manuscript to other commentators. Pietro da Muglio (Moglio), a famous teacher and friend of Petrarch, who lived in Padua between 1362–1368 (roughly the same time that this manuscript was produced), is mentioned twice.[239] The first time is in a note in the left margin of the first folio,

---

233. "Magister Guiccardus fecit scriptum *Poetrie* Gualfredi et hoc habet magister Petrus Muglo in sua" (Genoa, Biblioteca Durazzo Giustiniani, B II 1, fol. 42v).

234. For a description of Genoa, Biblioteca Durazzo Giustiniani, B II 1, fols. 1r–41v, see *Catalogo della biblioteca,* 100; and Puncuh, *Manoscritti,* 189–191.

235. On Durazzo and his collection, see Puncuh, *Manoscritti,* and Petrucciani and Puncuh, *Giacomo Filippo Durazzo.*

236. Puncuh, *Manoscritti,* fig. 82 (fol. 1r).

237. Nims's translation makes the phrase more concrete: "Your retinue—fit men for a man so great."

238. Other glossed Italian manuscripts of the *Poetria nova* share several of these aspects of the formatting and exposition. Bryn Mawr, Bryn Mawr College Library, Gordan MS 97 and Princeton, Princeton University Library, Robert Garrett Library Collection, MS 121 are, like Biblioteca Durazzo Giustiniani B II 1, more elegant versions of the school book.

239. On da Muglio's reputation as a teacher, see Witt, *Footsteps,* 122; on his other commentaries see Frati, *Pietro da Moglio,* as well as Federici Vescovini, "Due commenti"; Giuseppe Billanovich, "Giovanni del Virgilio"; and Billanovich and Monti, "Una nuova fonte," esp. 371–373, 380–389, and 398–399. Note also

est mouglo ("It's Muglio"), presumably identifying the origin of a rather cryptic interlinear gloss on the text to the right: where Geoffrey says, "Let either this one or that be resplendent" (17) the gloss above notes, "He concedes that you might put [either one]."[240] There is a more concrete reference in a colophon on the last folio, after the end of the *Poetria nova*. Here the scribe mentions Pietro's indebtedness to a Guizzardo whom we can identify as our commentator on the *Poetria nova* because the colophon goes on to quote the entire incipit of Guizzardo of Bologna's commentary, only the first portion of which I have translated again below:

> Master Guizzardo wrote a treatise on the Poetria nova, and Master Pietro Muglio uses this treatise in what he wrote. And it begins "On account of the false beliefs of those who, for the sake of eloquent speech or in the guise of the dictaminal style, are teaching rhetoric professionally yet 'paint a dolphin in the woods or a boar on the waves,' I, Guizzardo, lowliest servant of dictatores, . . ."[241]

The individual marginal notes in the manuscript do not appear to be specifically indebted to Guizzardo's commentary as the latter has come down to us, however, and the extant commentaries by Pietro da Muglio are more developed than the notes in this manuscript.

Like the commentary in the Novacella manuscript, most of the glosses in Biblioteca Durazzo, Giustiniani B II 1 appear to be aimed at younger-to-intermediate students, with some interests of the early humanists reflected along with those of earlier medieval teachers. For example, a comment at the beginning of Geoffrey's description of the body of a beautiful woman points out a similar passage in the *Architrenius,* a twelfth-century satirical poem that is found with the *Poetria nova* in some manuscripts[242]: "The *Architrenius* describes a woman's beauty."[243] Later Geoffrey's use of the Greek term *hyle* (1767) for the unformed matter of poetry is identified with the allegorical character Hyle in Alan of Lille's *Anticlaudianus.*[244]

Black and Pomaro, *Boethius's* Consolation of Philosophy, 23–27; and Black, *Humanism,* 28, 30, and 218.

240. "Esto quod in uerbis aut hic aut ille" (*PN* 17) is glossed "Ponas concedat" above, and to the left is written, barely visible in the reproduction in Puncuh, "est mouglo" (*Manoscritti,* fig. 82, page 190, of Genoa, Biblioteca Durazzo Giustiniani, B II 1, fol. 1r).

241. "Magister Guiccardus fecit scriptum *Poetrie* Gualfredi et hoc habet magister Petrus Muglo in sua. Et incipit 'Quoniam propter opinantes contrarium veritati qui ob ornatum modum loquendi sine stilo dictaminis subiacentem suspicantes rhetoricam formaliter edocere 'delfinum silvis appingit fluctibus aprum,' ego Guiccardus, minimus dictatorum minister . . ." (Genoa, Biblioteca Durazzo Giustiniani, B II 1, fol. 42v). On Guizzardo see "Meanwhile Back in Padua: Guizzardo of Bologna" in this chapter.

242. E.g., Cambridge, Corpus Christi College, 406; Munich, Bayerische Staatsbibliothek, Clm 237; Oxford, Balliol College, 276; Oxford, Bodleian Library, Digby 64; and Worcester, Cathedral and Chapter Library, Q. 79.

243. "*Architrenius* describit pulcritudinem mulieris" (Genoa, Biblioteca Durazzo Giustiniani, B II 1, fol. 12r).

244. "1767 YLE Hec *Anticlaudianus*" (Genoa, Biblioteca Durazzo Giustiniani, B II I, fol. 34v).

More specific is a citation of a tragedy by Seneca, an author highly esteemed by the early humanists and especially those in Padua.²⁴⁵ It occurs in a gloss on Geoffrey's dialogue between a student and teacher discussed in the previous chapter, in which the student begs for more time to compose and ends with, "I can't do it by then. Be patient. A delay can accomplish what a deadline cannot" (1748).²⁴⁶ This plea elicits the following citation in the margins of the manuscript in Genoa: "Seneca, in the eighth book of tragedies, namely in the *Agamemnon,* act II: 'What reason can not, delay has ofttimes cured.'"²⁴⁷ The spectacularly different context in Seneca's text—Clytemnestra's nurse is trying to dissuade her from murder—might lead one to suspect (not necessarily correctly) that this proverb was culled from a *florilegium,* rather than a passage recollected from a reading of the drama itself. But the aura of Seneca's name has a certain cachet in either case.

Our last quotation from the Genoa manuscript is a comment on contemporary fashion. In Geoffrey's description of a beautifully dressed woman, where he says that "the girdle conceals the waist" (611), the commentator states that it is "as if he is saying that a woman ought to tie the belt up just under the breasts and not down on the buttocks as is done today."²⁴⁸ This surprising statement is typical of the glosses in the Genoa manuscript: superficially related to others we have seen, but more explicit and memorable. Many of the annotations reveal a wide-ranging intellect with a sense of humor, as befitting the overall elegance of the manuscript.

A TEACHER OF NOTARIES IN RAVENNA

> Here ends the written document (*scriptum*) that Magister Benedict of Aquileia put together on the *Poetria novella* at the urging of the notary students of Ravenna.²⁴⁹
>
> —Naples, Biblioteca Nazionale "Vittorio Emanuele III," V.D.6

The *Poetria nova* was a work known and owned by notaries, as manuscript colophons and surviving book inventories tell us.²⁵⁰ If the colophon above is to be

---

245. Cf. Witt, *Footsteps,* 115 and 122–123.

246. See "Conversion: The Origin of Style" in chapter 2.

247. "Seneca libro tragediarum, viii, scilicet in *Agamenone,* actu ii, 'quod ratio <non quivit> [nequit *MS*] sepe sanauit mora'" {*Ag.* 130} (Genoa, Biblioteca Durazzo Giustiniani, B II 1, fol. 34v).

248. "quasi dicens debet mulier tenere ci<n>gulum parum sub mamis et non super nates ut hodierna die tenet" (Genoa, Biblioteca Durazzo Giustiniani, B II 1, fol. 12r).

249. "Explicit scriptum quod condidit Magister Benedictus Aquieliegiensis [*sic*] super *Poetriam nouellam* ad instantiam scolarium Tabelionum Ravenatum" (Naples, Biblioteca Nazionale "Vittorio Emanuele III," V.D.6., fol. 46v).

250. On the teaching of the *Poetria nova* by notaries, see Gehl, *Moral Art,* 210. Some of the owners of copies of the *Poetria nova* named below in note 305 were notaries, and see also chapter 2, note 117.

believed, the commentary of Benedict of Aquileia was written for his notarial students at their request.[251] The scribe of the Naples manuscript, "Jacobus of Benincasa, a notary of Ravenna," refers to himself as "the least" of Benedict's students and says that his teacher was a "most eloquent professor of grammar, logic and rhetoric."[252] The Naples manuscript contains the commentary of Benedict without a copy of the *Poetria nova;* although not nearly so dense as Pace's commentary and formatted with only one column per page, it still takes up forty-six folios.[253]

In a short prologue Benedict declares his desire to dispel the confusion caused by the torrent of works on eloquence.[254] In his *accessus* proper, in inquiring (rhetorically) whether rhetoric is the subject of Geoffrey's work, he notes that there are three types of rhetoric, demonstrative, deliberative, and judicial, and that Geoffrey does not discuss them. Benedict comments that, "Demonstrative rhetoric is, as Cicero says, what is assigned for the praise or blame of a certain person, and this type of rhetoric is especially valuable in the *ars arengandi* [art of formal speeches]."[255] As if to weaken the case for rhetoric, Benedict notes that, "Some say this book is not about rhetoric but about poetics, and this is what the author himself says: 'Poetic art may see in this analogy [of a man building a house] the instruction to be given to poets'" (48–49).[256] But then he argues that Geoffrey himself is a rhetorician, as is proven by the division of the book into the parts of rhetoric (invention, arrangement, etc.), thereby making rhetoric the subject also. His argument zigzags back and forth, showing that points can be made on behalf of both rhetoric and poetics as the subject. His allegiance, appropriately given his profession, is to the underlying importance

---

251. Another copy of the commentary, Princeton, Princeton University Library, Robert Garrett Library Collection MS 120, pages 3–155, is missing the frame material identifying the author, but the explicit there also says that the commentary was compiled for the students of Ravenna: "Explicit ergo expositio huius libri compillata . . . ad peticionem scolarium Rauennensium" (p. 154). On this manuscript, see Seymour de Ricci, *Supplement,* 1.189; and Gallick, "Medieval Rhetorical Arts," 84.

252. "Reverendo ac metuendo doctori suo domino Benedicto de ciuitate aquiliengense dicte gramatice loyce et rethorice facundissimo profexori [*sic*] suus discipulorum minimus Jacobus Benencase notarius Rauennas ciuis . . . " (Naples, Biblioteca Nazionale "Vittorio Emanuele III," V.D.6, fol. 46v). Benedict is not mentioned in Bernicoli, "Maestri e scuole." The only printed description of this manuscript is in *Iter ital.* i. 415, although there is a five-volume handwritten catalogue.

253. In the Princeton manuscript, the commentary is formatted as glosses around a copy of the text; it is lacking much of the introductory material and the added paragraphs at the end. I quote the Naples manuscript here because of its explicit association with a specific teacher.

254. "Quoniam circa elloquentiam quamplures dispersa uolumina condiderunt quorum alii mare alii riuulos emittentes . . . " (Naples, Biblioteca Nazionale, "Vittorio Emanuele III," V.D.6, fol. 1r).

255. "Demonstratiuus est, ut dicit Tulius, quod attribuitur in alicui<us> certe persone laudem uel uituperacionem et hec species in arenghis maxime ualet" (Naples, Biblioteca Nazionale "Vittorio Emanuele III," V.D.6, fol. 1r). With regard to notaries discussing speeches, Camargo comments that, "Since letters were typically read aloud in public during the Middle Ages, the distinction between them and speeches was never hard and fast in any case" ("Models," 181).

256. "Dicunt quidam hunc librum non fore de rethorica set de poetica doctrina et hec est quod dicit auctor: 'Ipsa poesis spectet in hoc speculo que lex sit danda poetis' (48–49)" (Naples, Biblioteca Nazionale "Vittorio Emanuele III," V.D.6, fol. 1v).

of rhetoric for all writers: "it behooves writers of both verse and prose to use these parts of rhetoric. . . . "[257]

Much of the rest of Benedict's *accessus,* like his explanation of the problem with Innocent's name quoted in the first chapter,[258] consists of explanations couched as further responses to possible objections or criticisms. The analysis of the dedication to Pope Innocent III is quite elaborate; for example, Benedict discusses at some length the vocative (direct address) form. He is also outspoken on the degree of praise that Geoffrey confers on the pope in telling Augustine and others to be quiet:

> 13 ONE OF YOUR GIFTS REMAINS etc., as if he were saying, I compare you with others according to the virtues put forth not together but separately. But you have one special gift (14) WHICH no one is able TO APPROACH whence according to this gift none can compare to you. And this gift is GRACE OF EXPRESSION namely eloquence and wisdom, and he immediately names those who stand out as the most eloquent and established, indeed who are the founders and doctors of the faith. One of these was blessed Augustine, on whom he imposes silence, saying (15) SILENCE, AUGUSTINE as if he were saying, "The loftiness of your wisdom and articulateness is not comparable to the loftiness, even heavenliness, of the knowledge and eloquence of Pope Innocent when he speaks." Next he imposes stillness on Pope Leo, who was powerful, and he says, POPE LEO, BE STILL as if he were saying, "Do not wish to be compared to him, since you are not able to," since both of them composed homilies as well as many other things concerning the foundations of the church.[259]

While this particular elaboration is distinctive if uncontroversial, much of the rest of Benedict's commentary seems familiar after Pace's. There is no evidence of a direct link between the two, but the number of manuscripts of Pace of Ferrara's commentary and other evidence indicate that at least some of his com-

---

257. "poetas et dictatores oportebat uti hiis partibus rethorice . . . " (Naples, Biblioteca Nazionale "Vittorio Emanuele III," V.D.6, fol. 1v).

258. See "Off with his head!" in chapter 1.

259. "13 SUPEREST DE DOTIBUS UNA, etc., quasi dicat secundum uirtutes primissas [*sic*] non simul sed diuidendo comparo te aliquibus sed habens unam specialem dotem ad (14) QUAM nullus potest ATTINGERE, vnde secundum hanc nulli possunt <tibi comparari> [te comparare *MS*]. Et hec dos est GRACIA LINGUE scilicet facundia et sapiencia et statim nominat uiros facundissimos et fundatissimos qui eciam fundatores et doctores fidei extiterunt. Quorum unus fuit beatus Augustinus, cui silentium imponit, dicens (15) AUGUSTINE, TACE quasi dicat sublimitas tue sapiencie et elloquentie non est comparabilis sublimitati etiam excelsitudini sciencie et facundie domini Innocentii pape. Deinde ponit quietem Leoni Pape, qui etiam ualens fuit et dicit LEO PAPA QUIESCE quasi dicat nolite illi comparari, quia non potes quia uterque istorum homelias et multa alia circa fundamenta ecclesie composuerunt" (Naples, Biblioteca Nazionale "Vittorio Emanuele III," V.D.6, fol. 2v; the version in Princeton, Princeton University Library, Robert Garrett Library Collection MS 120, p. 4, is much condensed).

ments were widely known.[260] In discussing Geoffrey's example of digression, for example, Benedict uses the same term for the lovers: he describes them as "two partners (*socii*) delighting in each other from the depths of the heart, but because of something looming they separated in body, the one embracing the other, crying, kissing each other with a mutual kiss."[261] And again like Pace, Benedict points out that the digression is related to the subject because it describes the season in which they were separated. He adds,[262] "Note that the author says that it is the bodies and not the friends [who are separated], since the effect of love is not dissolved but only bodily association."[263]

Yet the most unusual aspect of this manuscript of the *Poetria nova* is not part of the commentary at all, strictly speaking. Near the beginning of Geoffrey's treatment of the figures of thought (lines 1235–1592), one of Petrarch's letters written to Pope Urban V in 1370 has been copied onto an inserted folio.[264] This is the letter that Petrarch wrote when Urban returned the papacy to Rome from Avignon; it was never delivered, put aside in anger and sadness when Urban went back to France. It is entitled in this manuscript "The letter which lord Francis Petrarch, poet laureate, sent to lord Pope Urban V when he [Petrarch] heard that he [Urban] was going to leave Italy, that is, before his departure."[265] Its insertion at this point in the *Poetria nova,* in the middle of Geoffrey's long, outspoken lecture on papal responsibility, is especially appropriate. There is a poignancy to this placement, but also a pointedness: a way of making class material relevant, as we would say now. Although in a different hand from the rest of the manuscript, it suits Benedict's engaged approach to the text.

---

260. See "Stand and Counterstand" earlier in this chapter. No one else adopted Pace's extensive scholastic "divisio" and "constructio" for the work, however.

261. "Erant enim duo socii a medullis cordis dilligentes se causa uero iminente quacumque separauerunt corporaliter ampletendo alterum [alterum] et [et] mutuo osculo osculantes se utroque lacrimante" (Naples, Biblioteca Nazionale "Vittorio Emanuele III," V.D.6, fol. 16r; Princeton, Princeton University Library, Robert Garrett Library Collection MS 120, p. 45). Cf. "In Season" above.

262. The importance of this statement is further emphasized by a "Nota" in the margin of the Naples manuscript here.

263. "Et nota quod auctor significanter dicit corpora et non socios quia effectus dillectionis non dissoluitur sed conuersatio corporalis" (Naples, Biblioteca Nazionale "Vittorio Emanuele III," V.D.6, fol. 16r; Princeton, Princeton University Library, Robert Garrett Library Collection MS 120, p. 45). This excerpt is only the first three-fifths or so of the gloss in the Naples manuscript. The language here of the emotional bond is fervent and emotionally charged, and a similar intensity is present in the paragraph added at the end of the manuscript (partially transcribed in note 252 above). Benedict clearly inspired great devotion in at least one of his students. Perhaps more information about this teacher will be discovered.

264. There are two inserted folios, 37 and 38. Folio 37 is blank. Petrarch's letter begins on the verso side of folio 38 and continues back on the recto side, where it is followed by a letter of Pope Urban to the cardinal of Bologna added in the same hand at the bottom.

265. "Epistola quam misit dominus Franciscius Petrarcha poeta laureatus domino pape Vrban V quando audiuit ipsum de Ytalia recesurum, idest ante ipsius recessum. 1370" (Naples, Biblioteca Nazionale "Vittorio Emanuele III," V.D.6, fol. 38v). On this letter (*Var.* 3), see Wilkins, *Petrarch's Later Years*, 189–190; also Pier Giorgio Ricci, "La cronologia," esp. 53–54.

fRANCISCELLUS MANCINUS,
BENEDICTINE HUMANIST

> And after this [introduction] he commences the rest of the work, taking up the
> example of a diligent paterfamilias wishing to construct a house, who does not
> begin the foundation right away or without reflection, but rather labors with sol-
> licitous forethought.[266]
>
> —Franciscellus Mancinus

The complex relationship between early fifteenth-century humanism and the
traditional teaching of the *Poetria nova* is well conveyed by the other commentary on the *Poetria nova* now in the Biblioteca Nazionale "Vittorio Emanuele
III" in Naples, Vind. lat. 53.[267] It includes the statement quoted in the first
chapter that the *Poetria nova* is pedagogically superior to the *Rhetorica ad Herennium,* valuable evidence that fifteenth-century Italian teachers continued to
find the *Poetria nova* useful. The manuscript is the work of Franciscellus Mancinus, a Benedictine monk. He copied the text in a humanist hand in 1423, and
he is also probably the one who much later added most of the marginal notes in
a different humanist script.[268] Louis Holtz refers to Mancinus as "notre humaniste" because of his knowledge of classical texts as well as his elegant scripts, but
he adds that Mancinus's learned glosses are also deeply exegetical and typical of
a cleric.[269]

Mancinus was a teacher as well as scribe (and probably also librarian) at the
monastery of San Severino in Naples.[270] In him we find the combination of

---

266. "Et post hoc, prosecucionem ipsius operis aggressus est, sumens exemplum a diligenti patre familias
suam domum volente[m] construere qui non extimplo [= extemplo] et incogitate eam fundare incipit, sed cum
sollicita premeditacione molitur" (Naples, Biblioteca Nazionale "Vittorio Emanuele III," Vind. lat. 53, fol. 1r).

267. On Naples, Biblioteca Nazionale "Vittorio Emanuele III," Vind. lat. 53, fols. 1r–38r, see *Iter ital.*
3.60; Martini, "Sui codici Napoletani restituiti," 177–78; Eden, *Theobaldi "Physiologus,"* 17; and most especially
Holtz, "La main de Franciscellus Mancinus," passim. A second fifteenth-century manuscript, Vatican City,
BAV Chig. L.IV.74, fols. 1r–55v, contains the same *accessus* and some similar interlinear glosses, but most of
the marginal notes appear to come from a different source. On this Vatican manuscript see Blume, *Bibliotheca
librorum manuscriptorum,* 175; Pellegrin et al., *Les manuscrits classiques latins,* 1.417; and Buonocore, *Codices
Horatiani,* 74. The general effect of this second manuscript is of a much more intense, possibly hurried
production, an impression supported by numerous errors in transcription. Another copy of the *Poetria nova*
in humanist script is Ferrara, Biblioteca Comunale Ariostea, II. 175, fols. 55r–91v, a fifteenth-century Italian
manuscript with humanist contents; there are only scattered glosses after the first folio.

268. Holtz, "La main," 239 and 241; folios 38r, 78v, and 79r are reproduced in his plates 30, 29, and 28
(a) respectively. Mancinus identifies himself as the scribe on fol. 38r. That he also wrote most of the notes is
"vraisemblable," although the note on the interjection "pape" to the left of the large initial "P" on fol. 1r is
by Giovanni Gioviano Pontano (Louis Holtz, e-mail communication, May 2008). I have benefitted greatly
from discussions with Louis Holtz about this manuscript and the pedagogical nature of the marginal notes.
For another important manuscript copied by Mancinus, see D'Amato, "New Fragment," 488.

269. Holtz, "La main," 224 and 248.

270. Besides the manuscripts that Mancinus copied, he also improved and repaired others in the library's
collection: adding running titles, repairing script that had been worn off, etc. In Holtz's memorable phrase:
"il fait la toilette des manuscrits" ("La main," 246).

scholastic and humanist interests dovetailing in a practical pedagogy for which the *Poetria nova* remained an important classroom vehicle into the fifteenth century. Mancinus was a man of wide reading who examined the effectiveness of texts from a practical yet learned point of view, his "activité à la fois érudite et pédagogique."[271]

Mancinus's copy of the *Poetria nova* is particularly interesting because, while the texts in it (the *Physiologus* as well as the *Poetria nova*) were probably copied during Mancinus's youth, the annotation was added later, from the point of view of a teacher and an adult reader.[272] Mancinus's attentiveness to the needs of students is the basis of his comparison of the *Poetria nova* with the *Rhetorica ad Herennium* so unfavorable to the latter. Here is his full but short *accessus* from the upper-right corner of the folio (plate 8):

> According to some, the author of this book was a certain English clerk named Peter; some say he was called Magister Geoffrey the Englishman; others say that he was the Claudius who wrote the *Anticlaudianus,* and there is a variety of opinion on this. Nevertheless, whichever of those he was, he produced [this book] for the following reason: when he saw that Tully's *Rhetoric* was somewhat prolix because of the overabundance of examples, succinctly gathering together what seemed most useful for pupils, he composed this abbreviated little work.[273] And he offered it to Innocent, whom he praised extravagantly, for correction (*corrigendum*) and to gain favor (*insinuandum*). He described the cardinals and the city of Rome as no less worthy of such praise and commendation than the pope. And after this [introduction] he commenced the rest of the work, taking up the example of a diligent *paterfamilias* wishing to construct a house, who does not begin the foundation right away or without reflection but rather labors with sollicitous forethought.[274]

Mancinus's comparison of the author to a solicitous father refers to one of the most influential passages of the *Poetria nova:* "If a man has a house to build, his impetuous hand does not rush into action" (43). Geoffrey repeats the theme

---

271. Holtz, "La main," 243.

272. Holtz, "La main," 245.

273. Possibly a reference to Geoffrey's description of the work in his dedication as "brief in form, vast in power" ("breve corpore, viribus amplum" [42]).

274. "Auctor huius operis secundum quosdam dicitur fuisse quidam clericus Anglicus nomine Petrus. Quidam dicunt eum vocari magistrum Gaufredum Anglicum. Alii dicunt fuisse Claudium qui fecit *Anteclaudianum.* Et de hoc est varia opinio. Tamen quicumque horum fuerit ad hoc se inuexit. Quia cum uidisset *Rethoricam* Tullii prolixam <ali>quantum propter copiam exemplorum confusam, <colligens> compendiose que vtiliora sibi ad vtilitatem scolarium uisa sint hoc opusculum sub breuitate composuit. Ipsumque domino pape Innocencio corrigen<dum>[***MS] et insinuandum direxit, quem eximiis laudibus commendauit. Nec minus dominos cardinales et vrbem romanam eisdem laudibus et commendationibus dignos extulit. Et post hoc, prosecucionem ipsius operis aggressus est, sumens exemplum a diligenti patre familias suam domum volente[m] construere qui non extimplo [= extemplo] et incogitate eam fundare incipit, sed cum sollicita premeditacione molitur" (Naples, Biblioteca Nazionale "Vittorio Emanuele III," Vind. lat. 53, fol. 1r).

with variations for almost twenty lines (to line 60), yet nowhere in the passage does he talk about a father (though he does mention a workman); the familial context is Mancinus's contribution. It may reflect an almost automatic association of shaping with paternal oversight, a more benign evocation of all those power images discussed in the first chapter.[275] But I am struck more by the resonance of this gloss with that in the St. Georgensburg manuscript on how a monk without his abbot is lost.[276] In these two monastic commentaries we find distinctly positive images of the paternal relationship, whether literal or figural.

In commenting on Geoffrey's images of service and hospitality in the description of the three parts of a work, the beginning, middle, and end (71–76), Mancinus introduces the subject of the composition of letters, which were traditionally divided into three parts.[277] The salutation is the beginning, the narration or petition the middle, and the conclusion the end. And, in a nod to the discussion of natural vs. artificial order still to come, Mancinus explains the structure as follows:

> And note that the letter insofar as it is an art follows the way of nature [in contrast to artificial order], because every natural thing has a beginning since it was made by someone, and it has an end since nothing is made without an end. And because you cannot go from the beginning to the end without the middle, likewise whatever has a beginning and an end has a middle. . . . "[278]

Several shorter glosses assume oral delivery of the letter. Where Geoffrey talks about how "the poem's beginning, like a courteous attendant," should "introduce the subject with grace" (71–72), Mancinus notes, "A letter has to be sophisticated in terms of word choice and meaning, so that when it is read publicly it does not attract criticism."[279] And then at "Let the conclusion, like a herald when the race is over, dismiss it honorably" (73–74), Mancinus adds, "as if saying that you, the letter-writer, ought to deliver[280] your letter in a distinguished manner like a herald who praises his lord; thus, the conclusion praises the content of the letter when it is recited."[281]

---

275. See "Shaping the Student" in chapter 1.

276. See "Off with His Head!" in chapter 1.

277. Mancinus identifies this section as the first of the five parts of rhetoric (Invention) into which the work is divided and lists the others, material that is often presented as part of a (longer) *accessus* (Naples, Biblioteca Nazionale "Vittorio Emanuele III," Vind. lat. 53, fol. 1v).

278. "Et nota quod epistola in quantum ars est sequitur modum nature, quia omne naturatum habet principium cum sit ab aliquo factum, habet finem cum non sit dare aliquid infinitum. Et quare non est transire de principio ad finem sine medio, ideo quodlibet habens principium et finem habet medium . . . " (Naples, Biblioteca Nazionale "Vittorio Emanuele III," Vind. lat. 53, fol. 2r).

279. "Epistola debet esse curialis quo ad vocabula et sentenciam quod quando legatur coram quibus non aliquod capiat vituperium" (Naples, Biblioteca Nazionale "Vittorio Emanuele III," Vind. lat. 53, fol. 2r).

280. Niermeyer, *Mediae latinitatis lexicon minus,* s. v. "definere" for meanings that imply an oral component of the action.

281. "quasi dicens quod tu dictator sub discreto modo debes tuam epistolam definire quem ad modum

Classical texts are mentioned in predictable places. At the beginning of Geoffrey's discussion of artificial order, Mancinus states,

> Note that, according to Horace in his *Poetria,* order is twofold, namely natural and artificial {*Ars* 146–147}. Natural is when what happens first is put first and what happens later is put later. Artificial order is when what happens first is put later and vice versa, and Virgil has this order in the books of the *Aeneid,* as at "Hardly out of sight" etc., {1.34}, and Terence in his comedies.[282]

Bits of information and general cultural lore only tangentially related to the subject at hand are introduced—typical schoolteacher practice that we have seen in other manuscripts, but here drawing on additional sources. When in the lament of the cross, an example of prosopopeia, the cross asks, "Did I not bear sweet fruit for you?" (473), Mancinus inserts an excursus abbreviated from "The Invention of the Holy Cross" in the *Golden Legend* (*Legenda aurea*), which in turn quotes a number of other sources, including the Gospel of Nicodemus and Peter Comestor's *Scholastic History.*[283]

> One reads in the *Scholastic Histories* [*sic*] that Adam, by reason of his good health, was never sick except when he was dying. . . . [H]e sent his son Seth to the angel holding a flaming sword before the gate of the earthy paradise to ask him if Adam was to be cured from that sickness or suffer death. The angel gave him a special branch of the tree whose apple Adam had eaten, and he said, "Go and plant that branch, and from it will be made the tree [by] which, when it shall have born fruit, your father will be freed along with many others." When Seth returned he found Adam dead. Then he planted the branch, which in the passing of time became a mighty tree, and it endured until the time of Solomon, who had it cut down in order to use it for the temple. It was never able to be altered [to fit], so it was laid down as a beam for a bridge on the river beside Jerusalem. When the Queen of Saba [Sheba] went to hear the wisdom of Solomon, having arrived at the bridge she did not want to travel across it. But she was asked why she had done this [i.e., refused to step on it]. She responded that on the wood of the bridge was hanging a man who would destroy the entire population of the Jews. Hearing this, Solomon placed the said wood in a pit next to the temple, and above

---

et preco, qui laudat dominum suum sic finis laudat materiam epistole recitate" (Naples, Biblioteca Nazionale "Vittorio Emanuele III," Vind. lat. 53, fol. 2r).

282. "Nota secundum Oratium in sua *Poetria* quod duplex est ordo, scilicet naturalis et artificialis. Naturalis est quando preponenda preponuntur et postponenda postponuntur. Artificialis est quando preponenda postponuntur et e converso, et hunc ordinem tenet Virgilius *Eneydorum,* vt ibi: 'Vix e conspectu' etc. {1.34}, et Terentius in commediis" (Naples, Biblioteca Nazionale "Vittorio Emanuele III," Vind. lat. 53, fol. 2r).

283. Proper names have been substituted for pronouns without comment and some of the phrasing of the translation of the *Legenda aurea* has been adopted when the paraphrasing is very close; cf. *Golden Legend,* 269–271; *Legenda aurea,* c. 68 (64), 303–305.

it he had a pool constructed, which was called a *probatica*,[284] where the sheep were washed for sacrifice. And on account of the power (*virtutem*) of this wood an Angel came down and stirred the water and whoever first went down in the water was cured of whatever infirmity had limited him before. And when that thunder came at the time of the passion of Christ, the pool was sundered and the wood surfaced. That wood was taken and Christ was crucified on it. Then, indeed, the wood bore that fruit by which men were saved, and on account of this is said, "Did I not bear sweet fruit for you?" (473).[285]

Parabiblical material is rare in Mancinus's commentary, which is infused with references to classical authors. That Mancinus quotes from this source so extensively may indicate that his students would not have been expected to know the story. Note that this gloss, too, evokes the relationship of parent to child, here the son assuming responsibility for the father but needing advice from a new authority figure.[286]

Mancinus has a gift for emotionally inflected commentary. His gloss on the separated lovers describes the effect of their parting:

In saying how love is divided by some cause, he states here the signs of delight. But why do the lovers kiss and embrace in a [sexual] union (*adiunctione*[287])? Because love is in the heart, and, therefore, the heart longs to bring the thing that it delights in close to itself and laments its departure. Thus, the heart cries and emits outbursts to express lamentation; thus, the lamentation is of love interrupted, as a spur to jealousy.[288]

---

284. From "probaticus" (a flock of sheep)?

285. "Legit in *Ystoriis scolasticis* quod Adam ratione bone complexionis numquam infirmus fuit nisi cum mortuus est. . . . Misit Seth filium suum ad angelum habentem flammeum gladium ante portam Paradisi terrestris ut consuleret eum si deberet ipse Adam a tali infirmitate liberari an mortem subire, quod angelus dedit quemdam ramum illius arboris de qua pomum comedit et dixit, 'Vade et planta ramum istum, et ex hoc fiet arbor que cum fecerit fructum pater tuus liberabitur cum multis aliis.' Qui rediens inuenit Adam mortuum; tum ramum plantauit quod in processu temporis facta est arbor magna et durauit arbor illa vsque ad tempus Salomonis qui fecit ipsam decidi ut aptaretur templo. Numquam tamen adaptari potuit set posita est ut trabs pro ponte fluminis quod erat iuxta Ierusalem. Et quando regina Saba iuit audire sapienciam Salomonis cum fuit iuxta pontem noluit equitare per ipsum. Sed interrogatur quare fecisset. Respondet quod in illo ligno quod positum est pro ponte pendebat quidam homo qui destruet omnem populum Iudeorum. Que audiens Salomon dictum lignum positum in quadam fouea iuxta templum et desuper fecit fieri quandam piscinam que dicebatur probatica <aqua?> ubi lauabantur oues sacrificii. Et propter uirtutem istius ligni angelus descendebat et mouebat aquam et quicumque prior descendebat in aqua<m> sanabatur a quacumque detineretur infirmitate. Et tempore paxionis Christi cum tonitruum illud venit, scissa est illa piscina et euacauit lignum et illud lignum acceptum est; in illo crucifixus est Christus. Tunc enim lignum illud fructum pertulit quo saluati sunt homines et propter hoc dicitur 'Nonne tuli fructum?' (473)" (Naples, Biblioteca Nazionale "Vittorio Emanuele III," Vind. lat. 53, fol. 9v). I am grateful to Ernest Kaulbach for help with this passage.

286. Other father-and-son examples are Minos and Androgeos ("Shaping the Narrative" in chapter 2) and Abraham and Isaac ("Bible Stories in the Composition Classroom" in this chapter).

287. Mancinus uses a related term to describe the act by which the wife becomes pregnant in the story of the snow child discussed a few paragraphs below.

288. "Dicendo quomodo amor separatur aliqua causa, dicit hic signa dileccionis, sed quare amantes osculantur et amplectuntur adiunctione. Quia amor est in corde ideo cor appetit sibi approssimari rei quam

Later, at Geoffrey's description of the conceiving and birth of a flower, Mancinus adds, "since just as a man in the womb of his mother first lives the life of a plant, then the life of an animal, and at last the intellectual life, so the crops first live in a seed, then in a sprout, and finally in their own perfect being."[289]

Most revealing of classroom practice is the discussion of Geoffrey's first abbreviation of the story of the Snow Child (713–717). Mancinus begins with a longer version of the story and then produces a prose paraphrase of Geoffrey's first version:

> Here the author puts an example of condensing material by telling the story of a woman who committed adultery with a man, and she had a husband, and from the sexual union (*coniunctione*) with a stranger was born a son. When the man who had been gone a long time [her husband] came back, she said to him, "A son has been born to me, and I conceived him by eating snow." Then the astute husband, wanting to respond by deceit to his having been deceived in a humiliating way, pretended that he believed it. For that reason, after a time the husband of that woman took the boy with him and sold him. And when he arrived back home the wife said to him, "Where is the boy you took with you?" And he said, "We had a heat wave that day, and, since the boy had been made of snow, he melted in the road." But one who wishes to abbreviate this material can say it all briefly by saying "An adulterous woman bears a son whom she pretends begotten of snow on her husband's return after a long delay. He waits. He whisks off, sells, and reports to the woman a like ridiculous tale, saying, 'He was melted by the sun.'"[290]

Mancinus's analyses are characterized by precision and attention to detail, and infused with a sensitivity to personal relationships. When reading his manuscript, one is constantly aware of the small, neat annotating script and the overall elegance and attractiveness of the codex, although it is not a luxurious one. Here matter and form reinforce each other.

---

diligat et dolet de recessu; ideo lacrimatur et emictit singulariter ad expressionem doloris; ideo dolor est cesi amoris et calcar idest emulus" (Naples, Biblioteca Nazionale, "Vittorio Emanuele III," Vind. lat. 53, fol. 10v). The manuscript is very tightly bound, and some of the readings are unclear.

289. "quia sicut homo in vtero matris prius uiuit uita plante, postea uita animalis, deinde vita intellectiua, sic segetes primo uiuunt in semine postea in herba, et deinde pervecte in suo esse" (Naples, Biblioteca Nazionale, "Vittorio Emanuele III," Vind. lat. 53, fol. 10v).

290. "Hic auctor ponit exemplum de modis restringendi materiam, dicens quamdam fabulam, quod fuit quedam mulier que mechata fuit cum quodam viro, et ipsa habebat maritum, et ex tali coniunctione cum extraneo natus est filius quidam. Reuertente viro qui procul abierat, dixit viro, 'Filius natus est mihi et ipsum concepi comedendo niuem.' Tunc astutus maritus simulauit quod istud crederet, volens humiliter fraudi fraude aliqua respondere. Inde post tempus maritus istius mulieris duxit illum puerum secum et vendidit. Et cum veniret ad domum, dixit ei uxor, 'Ubi puer quem duxisti?' Et ille dixit, 'Tali die habebimus magnum calorem et quia puer ille factus fuerat de niue, ideo liquefactus est in uia.' Sed ille qui uult istam materiam breuiare omnia illa potest dicere breuiter dicendo, 'Mulier mecha parit filium, conceptum de niue simulat, post multa reuerso marito. Sustinet ille. Asportat, vendit, et mulieri reportat ridiculum simile dicens, "Liquefactum a sole"'" (Naples, Biblioteca Nazionale "Vittorio Emanuele III," Vind. lat. 53, fol. 13v).

COMEDY AND THE *COMMEDIA*

> And in this kind of comedy one can use an exalted and subtle style and weighty
> colors, as that Florentine poet named Dante did, who wrote his exalted *Comedy* in
> ordinary speech / the vernacular (*uulgariter*).[291]
> —Pistoia, Archivio Capitolare del Duomo, C. 143

Near the end of the *Poetria nova,* after the theories of conversions and determinations but before Geoffrey's treatments of memory and delivery, there are a
series of general dos and don'ts for writers, including the stylistic requirements
of comic and serious subjects (1883–1919). In the analysis of the *Poetria nova* as
a rhetorical argument, this section constitutes both the confirmation (the dos)
and the refutation (the don'ts).[292] Geoffrey confirms the importance of word
choice (1842–1852), the differences between verse and prose composition (1853–
1882), and the stylistic requirements of comic and serious subjects (1883–1919).
In describing the appropriate style for a comic subject, Geoffrey states, "Yet
there are times when adornment consists in avoiding ornaments, except such
as ordinary speech [*sermo . . . vulgaris*] employs and colloquial use allows. A
comic subject rejects diction that has been artfully laboured over; it demands
plain words only" (1883–1887). But a commentary that has survived in two fifteenth-century copies, one in the Vatican, BAV Reg. lat. 1982 (dated 1440),[293]
and one in Pistoia, Archivio Capitolare del Duomo, C. 143,[294] states that there
are not one but two kinds of comedy. It goes on to cite Dante's *Commedia* as an
example of the kind in the high style that uses rhetorical devices, and an altered
version of a classical source to support the argument.

The Vatican manuscript was copied in 1440 by a Blasius Antonius Karulus
of Pisa, who also included the *Doctrinale* of Alexander de Villa Dei.[295] In this

---

291. "Et ista in comedia licet uti alto et subtili stilo et grauibus coloribus, sicut fecit ille poeta florentinus
nomine Dantes, qui uulgariter fecit suam altam *Comediam*" (Pistoia, Archivio Capitolare del Duomo, C. 143,
fol. 47v).

292. What is refuted are the faults to avoid (1920–1942), with a final reminder to revise tirelessly and with
the whole composition in mind (1943–1968). See "The Double Structure" in chapter 1.

293. Vatican City, BAV Reg. lat. 1982, fols. 49r–86v. On this manuscript see Manacorda, "Fra Bartolomeo,"
147 and 148; there is also an unpublished IRHT description. The commentary is copied in the margins next
to the text of the *Poetria nova.*

294. Pistoia, Archivio Capitolare del Duomo, C. 143, fols. 1r–49v (unnumbered). On this manuscript
see Colomb de Batines, *Bibliografia dantesca,* 2.114; Mazzatinti, *Gli archivi della storia,* 3.68; Murano et al.,
Manoscritti medioevali 56, no. 80, with reproductions of folios 11r (*PN* and commentary) and 56r (*Paradiso*).
This manuscript has been in the cathedral library in Pistoia since 1489. The commentary alternates with
sections of text; the original scribe abandoned the text and commentary for an interpolation and his own
conclusion described in "Geoffrey after Quintilian" in the Afterword. After this interpolated section the
Poetria nova and original commentary were then completed by another scribe (or possibly two). It is from
the resumed commentary that the excerpt quoted in this section is taken.

295. The *Doctrinale* of Alexander de Villa Dei, mentioned earlier, was a medieval grammatical treatise
reviled by some humanists, although it continued to be used in the classroom by others because of the
usefulness of its mnemonic verses; see Black, *Humanism,* e.g., 128 and 153–159.

manuscript the Dante comment is formatted as a gloss on the second sentence of the passage: "A comic subject rejects diction that has been artfully labored over" (1885–1886):

> 1885 A COMIC SUBJECT The word "comedy" is taken two ways. One way, comedy means a humble composition, as here. The other way it means when something begins in sadness and ends in joy, and in this way Dante Alighieri, poet of the vulgar tongue (*poeta uulgaris*) and not very illustrious clerk, called his book, *The Inferno*, a comedy. Nevertheless it is sometimes permitted to use exalted words in a humble composition and crude words in an exalted one, which Horace implied there:
>
> > Yet at times even comedy elevates her voice {*Ars* 93},[296]
>
> and
>
> > The tragic man grieves in pedestrian speech {*Ars* 95}.[297]

This version is shorter and probably closer to the original than that in the Pistoia manuscript, where, as we shall see, the criticism of Dante is eliminated awkwardly.[298]

Seventeen cantos of Dante's *Paradiso* have been added at the end of the Pistoia manuscript of this commentary, suggesting a much more positive assessment of the Florentine poet's status than that in the Vatican version. What to do with the description of Dante as "not very illustrious clerk" presumably found in the source manuscript? The changes made in the passage where Dante is named show the degree to which a scribe will revise rather than simply omit material with which he may not agree. First, the comment is moved to the introduction of the whole passage (rather than remaining a gloss on a single line of it), which immediately places the reference to Dante in a more prominent position. Within the comment the scribe begins by paraphrasing Geoffrey's position, giving an historical reason for Geoffrey's restricted advice and expanding on the two different meanings of comedy. In addition, Dante's whole work, rather than just the *Inferno*, is referred to, which makes sense in terms of the subsequent copying of part of the *Paradiso* in this manuscript by this scribe. As for the critical epithet, *clericus non gloriosissimus*, it is removed from Dante and projected onto a separate, unidentified author. The result of all these changes is

---

296. The line coming between these two in Horace changes the meaning; it is omitted in both copies.

297. "1885 RES COMICA Comedia secundum duplicem sumitur. Vno modo comedia dicitur uilis tractatus, et ita hic; alio modo comedia dicitur quando res incipit a tristitia, et finit ad gaudium; et isto modo appellauit Dante Aldigheri poeta uulgaris, et clericus non gloriosissimus. Tamen licet interdum uti altis uerbis in uili tractatu et rudibus in alto, quod Oratius innuit ibi: 'Interdum tamen uocem comedia tollit' {*Ars* 93} et 'tragicus plerumque dolet sermone pedestri {*Ars* 95}. Librum *Inferni* comediam" (Vatican City, BAV Reg. lat. 1982, fol. 82v).

298. Two phrases have been transposed (corrected in the translation), however, so the Vatican manuscript is probably not the original version either.

somewhat clumsy:

> 1883 YET THERE ARE TIMES [WHEN ADORNMENT CONSISTS IN AVOIDING ADORNMENT] Here he notes that we should use the [two kinds of] rhetorical colors differently, for with weighty subjects we should use weighty colors [the tropes], and with light subjects we ought to use light colors [the figures]. And he says about comedy that since in ancient times comedy was created with humble events and characters, back then it was not appropriate to use weighty colors [in comedy]. But note that [the word] "comedy" is taken two ways. One way, comedy means a humble composition about crude actions and humble characters, and that is how it is meant here in the text, because he says there that it is appropriate to use light colors and not exalted or weighty ones. The other way, comedy means a delightful and pleasant poem (*cantu*) that begins in sadness and ends in joy. And in this kind of comedy can use an exalted and subtle style and weighty colors, as that the Florentine poet named Dante did, who wrote his exalted *Comedy* in ordinary speech / the vernacular (*uulgari*). And a not very illustrious cleric did likewise. Thus, sometimes it is permitted to use exalted words and weighty colors in a humble composition and crude colors in an exalted composition, as Horace hinted in his *Poetria* there at
>
> > Yet at times even comedy elevates her voice {*Ars* 93};
> > The tragic man grieves in pedestrian speech {*Ars* 95}.[299]

This reference to Dante is the only naming of a work in the vernacular in a commentary on, and almost the only example of a vernacular work copied with, the *Poetria nova* that I have discovered, although there are other Italian manuscripts of the *Poetria nova* that contain Latin works by authors studied more today for their vernacular texts.[300]

---

299. "1883 ET TAMEN EST QUANDOQUE Hic ponit quod discret<e> debemus uti coloribus rethoricis quia in grauibus sententiis debemus uti grauibus coloribus, et in rebus leuibus uti debemus leuibus coloribus. Et dicit de comedia quia antiquitus comedia fiebat de rebus uilibus et uilanis, in qua tunc non erat congruum uti grauibus coloribus. Set nota quod comedia sumitur dupliciter. Vno modo comedia denominatur uilis tractatus de rebus rusticalibus et de uilibus personis. Et isto modo accipitur hic in testu, quia dicit quod ibi congruit uti leuibus coloribus et non altis et grauibus. Alio modo accipitur comedia pro delectabili cantu et suaui, quando res incipit a tristitia et finit in gaudium. Et ista in comedia licet uti alto et subtili stilo et grauibus coloribus, sicut fecit ille poeta florentinus nomine Dantes, qui uulgari [= vulgari sermone] fecit suam altam *Comediam*. Et similiter fecit clericus non gloriosissimus. Et sic quandoque licet uti altis uerbis et grauibus coloribus in uili tractatu et rudibus in alto. Sicut Oratius innuit in sua *Poetria* ibi: 'Interdum tamen uocem comedia tollit. / Tragicus plerumque dolet sermone pedestri' {*Ars* 93, 95}" (Pistoia, Archivio Capitolare del Duomo, C. 143, fol. 47v).

300. There is a very late (1464), lightly glossed *Poetria nova* copied with Petrarch's *Carmen bucolicum* in another library in Pistoia (Pistoia, Biblioteca Forteguerriana, A. 13) and, in Assisi, a partial copy of Boccaccio's *De genealogia deorum gentilium* bound with the *Poetria nova* and works by Horace (Assisi, Biblioteca Storico-Francescana della Chiesa Nuova, 301).

BACK AND FORTH

> One pair of Senecan tragedies
> Statius's *Achilleid*
> One Horace
> One Lucan
> One *Doctrinale*
> *Poetria nova* of Geoffrey
> Cicero's *Tusculan Disputations*
> One book by Cicero covered in red leather beginning *Admirante brute*
>   [*Paradoxa Stoicorum*]
> *Rhetorica nova* [*Rhetorica ad Herennium*]
> Cicero's *De oratore*
> Some ecclesiastical book without a board cover[301]
>   —inventory of "smaller books" left at the death of Figlio Degli Arditi of Padua in 1440

All the extant Italian commentaries on the *Poetria nova* by known fourteenth-century commentators survive in fifteenth-century copies, and those that were written in the fifteenth century reinforce the approaches developed by earlier commentators: a positive assessment of the *Poetria nova* and its author, attention to both the doctrine and the examples, and the citation of a wide range of Latin authorities, with special emphasis on classical texts taught in the schools and sometimes copied in the same manuscripts. Thus, it is not always possible to determine if anonymous commentaries extant only in fifteenth-century copies (like that with the Dante reference just discussed) were written in the fifteenth century or are later copies of earlier commentaries.[302]

In Italian manuscripts the *Poetria nova* is copied almost exclusively with literary and often (and increasingly) with classical texts.[303] Although in Italian

---

301. Vno paro de traiedie de seneca/
    vno Statio achileydos/
    vno oratio./
    vno Lucan.
    vno doctrinale
    poetria de galfredo/
    Tuscula e de Tulio
    vno libro de Cicerone che comenza Admiranti brute/ couerto de curo rosso./
    vna Rethorica noua
    Tulio de oratore
    Quidam libero Ecclesiastico senza couerta de ase.

Connell, "Books and Their Owners," 171. Connell notes earlier, "The 22 large volumes were legal works, nearly all of civil law—their owner must have been a doctor of law" (169). For additional Italian inventories containing the *Poetria nova* not mentioned earlier, see Bertoni and Vicini, *Gli studi di grammatica,* 164, 172, and 210.

302. See Friis-Jensen on the misdating to the 1340s of a twelfth-century commentary on Horace's *Ars poetica* because of a misattribution in a late manuscript ("Horace and the Early Writers," 363, on Tseng, "Paolo da Perugia").

303. For the study of the classics and other school books in Italy during the centuries that the *Poetria nova* was copied there, see Black, *Humanism* 173–273, esp. here 238–270.

commentaries the *Poetria nova* was often explicitly applied to the composition of prose (speeches and letters), the context in which it was read was literary, poetic, textual. Those who copied it and copied the commentaries on it were primarily interested in the Latin language and how to use it effectively—in whatever way the teacher or student or writer wished or might wish in the future. As long as teachers were interested in Latin generically, the *Poetria nova* remained a potent pedagogical aid. I have not found evidence of a specific rejection of it by the later, more specialized humanists with their more restricted foci, as happened with some other texts. It stands to reason, however, that when teachers wanted to inculcate a specifically classicizing Latin in rhetorical poetry and prose (as opposed to a more generic, flexible concept of the language) a text like the *Poetria nova* with its virtuoso range would become irrelevant.[304]

Yet, while there is some continuity and overlapping of approach and material in all the commentaries examined in this chapter, the attention to the text and the production of commentaries and manuscripts in one region of Italy is hard to ignore. In northeastern Italy, the area around Padua and the Veneto, the work apparently was taught continuously and at all levels. The Friuli region produced both the glossed school manuscripts preserved in the extensive fragment collection in Udine discussed in chapter 2 as well as a number of the manuscripts of the more advanced commentaries like that of Guizzarado, but especially the most advanced, extensive, popular Italian commentary on the text: that of Pace of Ferrara. In some manuscripts he is even called called Pace dal Friuli or Pax of Padua.[305] This part of Italy was also the gateway through which humanist texts reached central Europe, taken by teachers from the south like Peter Luder who introduced them in their classes in the north (there is no evidence that he ever taught the *Poetria nova,* however) or brought home by northern students who went south, often specifically to Padua, to study. Although the *Poetria nova* was already being taught in the lands to the north as early as the thirteenth century, and although the central European university commentaries differ in many ways from the advanced contemporary commentaries of the south, there are surprising currents connecting these two distinctive pedagogical traditions, as we shall see in the following chapter.

---

304. See "Erasmus and Geoffrey" in the Afterword.

305. For "Pace dal Friuli" see above, note 67. As we saw, Giovanni Travesi calls him "Pax paduanus," and the manuscript of his commentary in the British Library was copied by a teacher in Pordenone (in Friuli): "Explicit commentum magistri Pacis super *Poetria novella* magistri Gualfredi scriptum per me Iacobum in Portun. scolas regentem 1427, die vero xiio Iulii indictione v hora vesperarum" (London, BL Add. 10095, fol. 156r). Pace's commentary is also listed among the items bequeathed in the wills of Oliviero Forzetta of Treviso in 1373 and Giovanni del fu Mainardo di Aimaro, who died at Cividale del Friuli in 1429 (Battistella, "Un inventario," 147; and Stadter, "Planudes, Plutarch, and Pace," 150). See also Gargan, "Oliviero Forzetta." I am grateful to Alison Frazier for a number of references cited in this chapter.

4

the *poetria nova* as university text in central europe

The geographical range of this chapter is wide, and, while the titles of some of the subsections below might seem to promise a more precise focus, institutional specificity with regard to individual manuscripts is often impossible to determine. Yet if we accept that limitation, we shall be rewarded with a detailed and coherent picture of one kind of medieval teaching of the *Poetria nova*. Almost all of the manuscripts described in this chapter come from central Europe: the area corresponding to modern-day Germany, Switzerland, the Czech Republic, Austria, and Poland. Central Europe as a whole offers a remarkably stable context in which the *Poetria nova* occupied a specific niche in the university syllabuses. The coherence of this geographical unit with regard to the study of rhetorical texts is notable,[1] although historians of universities often study only a single institution, and scholars working on central Europe rightly emphasize certain differences among the universities located there.[2]

---

1. All the manuscripts of the *Compendium Poetrie nove* by Otto of Lüneberg come from the same area (see below, note 31), as do the manuscripts containing both the *Poetria nova* and the *Laborintus* of Eberhard the German, another work that was required along with or as a substitute for the *PN* in central European university statutes.

2. A very useful comparative study of several of the universities is Lorenz, "*Libri ordinarie legendi.*" For a study that focuses on the differences among these universities, see Spunar, "La Faculté des Arts."

QUESTIONING AUTHORITY

It is asked why . . . [3]

— *quaestio* appended to the *Early Commentary*

The central European universities discussed in this chapter were originally founded in the fourteenth century (and refounded in the fifteenth) as will be outlined below, but earlier manuscripts also show signs of university influence. Most copies of the *Early Commentary* are from this region, for example, and the thirteenth-century manuscripts of the version intended for older students contain much longer "responses to an unspoken question" (*responsiones tacite quaestionis*) that resemble, although they do not reach the technical heights of, the *quaestio* tradition associated with the University of Paris. The *quaestio* was a specific genre of intellectual inquiry in which teachers analysed conflicts between texts.[4] For the *Poetria nova,* these questions revolved around issues of organization and presentation of material, and a very simple *quaestio* added at the end of the *Poetria nova* in Munich, Bayerische Staatsbibliothek, Clm 4603 asks whose sequence of rhetorical figures and faults is correct, Donatus's or that of the *Poetria nova*?[5] Here is the first part, in which the student is asked to consider, in terms of abstract values drawn from Aristotle's *Categories,* the kinds of choices made by an author in structuring a work:

> It is asked why, in contrast to the preceding text [the *Poetria nova*], Donatus defines the faults before the figures. The answer is because, as Boethius said, "An evil is not avoided if it is not recognized."[6] Therefore, since a fault is an evil, it should be discussed earlier, so that after the faults have been excised the figures may be inserted more easily. Against this argument an objection is made: the finite before the infinite. Every virtue is finite, every fault infinite; therefore, the figures before the faults. Also, things are more worthy insofar as they are prior; the figures are more worthy than the faults and therefore prior. Accordingly, if they [the figures] are considered first causally and Donatus began his grammatical art with the faults, it is an error. . . . [7]

Other possible criticisms of Geoffrey's arrangement of material are discussed in

---

3. *EC* Appendix I.B, 1.

4. On the "qu(a)estio" see Teeuwen, *Vocabulary of Intellectual Life,* 322–323; see also Weijers, *Le maniement du savoir,* 61–75. The technique is pre-thirteenth century; see Nauta, ed., *Glosae super Boetium,* xxvii. For a related technique see "A Preacher and a Teacher" in chapter 3.

5. This manuscript was used as the base manuscript for the text and translation in *EC.* For a list of other copies of this commentary, see Munich, Bayerische Staatsbibliothek, Clm 4603 in the Manuscript List.

6. Cf. Thomas de Chobham, *Summa de arte praedicandi,* 4.62, where he attributes the saying to "Boethius in Topicis suis."

7. *EC* Appendix I.B, 1–6.

the body of the commentary. In several important "responses to an unspoken question," different answers are given in the versions for older and younger students, as we saw in chapter 2.[8] The version for younger students is more informal, while the version for older students turns the examination of the issue into a more formal exercise with a different conclusion.[9]

One of these occurs when Geoffrey has just finished treating the figures of words, of which he provided only examples and no definitions. The excerpt below comes in the gloss on the beginning of his treatment of the figures of thought, of which Geoffrey provides definitions as well as examples. Both versions of the commentary begin the comment the same way:

> 1230 After the figures of words the author discusses the figures of thought, but not in the same way. With the figures of words he gave examples without definitions; here he puts definitions first and adds examples afterwards.

The version intended for older students then launches into a double *quaestio*, objecting that Geoffrey's treatment of the two is neither matching nor complementary:

> One might ask the reason for this difference, because it could be argued that since he put only the examples of words in the adornment [figures] of words, in the adornment of thoughts he should have expressed only the definitions without the examples. Or one could argue that just as there he put only examples, so here, too, he should have put just the examples without definitions. To the first objection it should be said that a beautiful thought needs beautiful words, as he said above, "In what has been stated" (751).

Then comes a section found in both versions. The version intended for younger students has *only* this next section, which, since in this version it comes directly after the introductory sentence, simply gives the reason for Geoffrey's decision, rather than framing it as part of a technical query:

> Beautiful words do not always need a beautiful thought. Whence after he has shown the merits of thoughts, which are expressed through definitions, he adds corresponding examples in words lest it seem that thoughts can be written down in just any words. In the figures of words, however, he gives just the bare examples (which are charming and elegant) since any idea at all can be fitted to them.

---

8. E.g., *EC* 1588 (discussed in "Separating the Men from the Boys") and 894.

9. Cf. the discussion of "dubitabilia or traces of the *quaestio* form" in Fredborg, "Rhetoric and Dialectic," 168. For the types of questions asked in the commentaries on the *Rhetorica ad Herennium,* see Ward, *Ciceronian Rhetoric,* 162. Baswell notes one projected into the text of the *Aeneid* in *Virgil in Medieval England,* 72.

The version for younger students ends here.

The version for older students continues the analysis:

> To the second objection it should be said that, although a beautiful thought needs a corresponding setting in words, yet the first consideration is held by the distinction of thoughts. And on account of this, he expressed the thoughts through definitions since they cannot be understood sufficiently through examples alone. In the adornment of words, however, he discusses the various positions of words for adorning an expression; these are understood sufficiently in the examples, and hence it was not necessary to put the definitions.

Here an aesthetic consideration is emphasized in the version for younger students (beautiful words are more important than beautiful thoughts) in contrast to the opposite, more philosophical emphasis in the version for more advanced students (content is more important than form).

Both versions support Geoffrey's answer, but each draws on a different value system.[10] The commentaries discussed in the rest of this chapter come from an environment in which theoretical and analytical values are privileged over textual ones. Although they resemble the most advanced Italian commentary, that of Pace of Ferrara, in analytical terminology and attention to academic and intellectual context, they are almost exclusively concerned with rhetoric, not poetics. In these central European manuscripts the *Poetria nova* is often copied with dictaminal works and/or with grammatical and quadrivial texts taught at the lower levels in the universities (almost never found in Italian manuscripts of the *Poetria nova*).[11]

A UNIVERSITY TEXT

Master Nicolaus de Staw on the *Poetria nova*[12]
—from a list of lecture courses heard for the bachelor's degree at Krakow in 1457

There is much debate about what constituted university teaching during the Middle Ages, particularly in places where other kinds of institutions of higher learning, such as the *studia* of individual religious orders, were also present. Among the questions raised by the material discussed in the last chapter is

---

10. For further analysis of this and a related passage, see Woods, "In a Nutshell."

11. Dictaminal material includes *artes dictaminis,* or arts of letter writing; rhetorical treatises that focus primarily on letters; and model letters—classical, medieval, and, in the later manuscripts, humanist. Quadrivial texts are those related to the works of the *quadrivium* (arithmetic, geometry, music, astronomy).

12. "Maystro Nicolao de Staw Nowam poetriam" (Bodeman, "Cedulae actuum," 455).

whether the commentaries on the *Poetria nova* by Pace of Ferrara and Guizzardo of Bologna were taught at university level; if so, it may have been been
informally, or "extraordinarily." The situation is different in central Europe,[13]
where the *Poetria nova* was the subject of regular, "ordinary" university lectures. Yet it was not just a university text. As was true in Italy, the *Poetria nova*
was taught at different levels in central Europe at the same time. Reiner von
Cappel's basic school commentary on the *Poetria nova,* for example, which was
discussed in the second chapter, is almost exactly contemporaneous with Nicolaus Dybinus's commentary delivered at the University of Prague in 1375, which
is discussed in detail below.

The phenomenon of school texts taught at central European universities
is well documented. Nigel Palmer calls Boethius's *Consolation of Philosophy* a
"school text," but he defines this term as "a book studied in grammar schools
and universities as well as monastery schools."[14] Lodi Nauta has found evidence
that it "was lectured on in the German universities in the later medieval period,
since it is mentioned in records from Erfurt, Prague and Vienna" and "in the
grammar schools and in the religious houses before students were sent to the
university, or in the studia of the religious orders."[15] These descriptions fit the
pattern of the *Poetria nova* manuscripts as well. Such a liminal status emphasizes the foundational nature of the *Poetria nova* and texts like it; they *had* to be
studied before a student could continue in his university career.[16]

Perhaps the most accurate term for works like the *Consolation of Philosophy*
and the *Poetria nova* in central Europe is some hybrid such as "school/uni-
versity" text. Nikolaus Henkel has shown that German translations of Latin
schoolbooks were produced during the late medieval and early modern period,
not to replace but rather to support the study of the Latin works themselves
at both school and university level.[17] Michael Baldzuhn, speaking specifically
about a fable collection, suggests several levels at which such works were taught
in the fifteenth century. The first was "in town schools, probably as part of the
teaching of Latin . . . for more advanced pupils." The other three refer to different aspects of university teaching: in "preparatory elementary courses for new
students, such as the grammar and rhetoric classes taught by baccalaureates; . . .
later, as part of lectures by masters in the area of moral philosophy; and, finally,
after the middle of the [fourteenth] century, in the context of early humanist

---

13. See, for example, Rosłanowski, "Universitäten und Hochschulen in Polen," 166–69; and Spunar,
"The Literary Legacy of Prague Dominicans."

14. Palmer, "Latin and Vernacular," 363.

15. Nauta, "The Study of Boethius's *Consolatio*" (unpublished paper).

16. Nauta suggests that "Boethius's proper place was in the pre-university years" (ibid.), but what I
emphasize about both works is not their "proper place" but rather their importance as background training
to later university study.

17. Henkel's comprehensive monograph also includes an extremely useful alphabetically arranged
introduction to such works (*Deutsche Übersetzungen*, 213–316). See also Palmer, "Latin and Vernacular," 366
and 368, on vernacular translations meant to help with rather than replace Latin texts.

teaching."[18] Histories of universities usually focus on works studied only at the most advanced levels. Yet such works were *ipso facto* read by a smaller number of students than those of a transitional nature like the *Poetria nova* or the *Consolation of Philosophy* or even animal fables. Were lectures on such works seen as remedial? That is, were university lectures on the *Poetria nova* to make up for weaknesses in the students' backgrounds when they arrived at university? Or were they part of the standard curriculum? These questions are not mutually exclusive, and I suggest that the answer to each is "Yes."

This paradox is illustrated by a late fourteenth- or early fifteenth-century manuscript of the *Poetria nova* now in the university library in Leipzig.[19] It was bequeathed to the university in 1490 by a faculty member, *magister* Johannes Kleine, although we do not know where he obtained it.[20] This rather sizeable paper codex (315 x 225 mm) is a typical central European university miscellany. Bound together with the *Poetria nova* are animal fables (which were the subject of extraordinary lectures at Prague, Vienna, and Leipzig[21]), quadrivial texts (a treatise on the sphere with commentary and diagrams illustrating angles), a tree of consanguinity (outlining relationships within which marriage can—and cannot—take place), and philosophical works: the *Parvulus philosophiae* and excerpts from Thomas Aquinas's *Summa* and Aristotle's *Posterior Analytics* and *Metaphysics*.[22] The format of dense commentary overwhelming the text is typical of university texts in central Europe. The extensive interlinear glossing on the text of the *Poetria nova* indicates the need for in-class construing of the Latin, while at the same time the poem is accompanied by an analytical commentary (in the tradition of Dybinus of Prague) that dominates the visual field.

It may be useful to point out here the contrast between the distinct levels of treatment of the *Poetria nova* in Italy described in the previous chapter and the mixing of levels represented by the kind of manuscript typical of this chapter. In Italy, the *Poetria nova* was taught at lower, intermediate, and advanced levels, often indicated by the presence or absence of interlinear glossing and the

---

18. Baldzuhn, "*Quidquid placet,*" 357; my translation. For more on the medieval tradition of Avianus, see Suerbaum, "*Litterae et mores.*" I address the issue of early humanist teaching in Central Europe at the end of this chapter.

19. Leipzig, Universitätsbibliothek, MS 1084, fols. 232r–252v; *PN* to line 1137 only.

20. The item following the *Poetria nova* (in another hand) is a list of statutes from the University of Greifswald from 1478, so the manuscript could have originated there (Helssig, *Katalog der Handschriften* 3.207). On Kleine see Eck, *Symbolae*, III.vi, no. 48 C. The university at Rostock temporarily moved to Greifswald from 1437 to 1443, and then a separate university was established there in 1456. The statutes of Greifswald list the *Laborintus* as a required rhetoric text (Overfield, *Humanism and Scholasticism*, 40, citing Kosegarten, *Geschichte*, 1.309, but the statute is found on this page in the second volume). The *Poetria nova* may also have been used to fulfil the requirement; the two works were taught together or were considered equivalent at several of the other central European universities discussed in this chapter.

21. Henkel, *Deutsche Übersetzungen*, 48–49; Baldzuhn, "*Quidquid placet,*" 338 and 371; see also Wheatley, *Mastering Aesop*, 239 and 250..

22. On this manuscript, which also includes Latin hymns with music, see Helssig, *Katalog,* 205–8; and *Aristoteles latinus: Codices,* 1.694, no. 955.

density and complexity of marginal (or completely separate) commentary. In central Europe, however, where the vernacular would not have been a romance language, there were university students who still needed help understanding the Latin of the text while they were simultaneously learning a more advanced, theoretical approach to the rhetorical doctrine contained in the marginal commentary. Thus, some central European university students, in general "a younger student clientele than was common in southern Europe,"[23] were struggling with Latin and studying Aristotle at the same time.[24]

THE *POETRIA NOVA* AS DICTAMINAL TREATISE

I know that the *Poetria* [*nova*] will provide you with great wisdom and [with what] many are accustomed to treat in an *ars dictandi*. . . .[25]
   —Otto of Lüneberg

As we saw in the preceding chapter, the early humanists' discussion of the composition of letters (and sermons and speeches) in their commentaries on the *Poetria nova* was part of their emphasis on its virtuosity and wide applicability. The commentaries in this chapter, in contrast, focus on the *Poetria nova* almost exclusively as a vehicle for teaching the composition of letters, that is, as an *ars dictaminis,* a context supported by the other contents of many of the manuscripts. In central Europe the *Poetria nova* was often copied or bound with letter-writing manuals and collections of model letters (dictaminal material), but it is almost never found with such works in Italian manuscripts.[26] The widespread interpretation of the *Poetria nova* as a rhetorical argument directed at the pope[27] helped teachers describe the work itself as a long letter: an artistic version of the argument-driven, status-conscious, publicly-performed *epistola* that was the desired product of dictaminal teaching. This association was made very early and was not exclusively central European. In two thirteenth-century manuscripts from western Europe we find the last section of the *Poetria nova*

23. Cobban, *English University Life,* 149. He also states that, "The northern universities, those of England, Scotland, Scandinavia, Germany, Austria, Hungary, Bohemia and Poland, often had large arts faculties as an accompaniment to their superior faculty studies . . . ," perhaps a result of the younger age of the students, although he does not explicitly posit a causal connection. Schwinges notes, "The offer of a university education within the German Empire was surprisingly popular," and, "During the fifteenth century those who attended German universities typically came from small or medium sized towns" ("On Recruitment," 39–40).

24. As Rita Copeland has pointed out (*Rhetoric, Hermeneutics,* 160), "The *artes poetriae* constituted poetry as an academic discipline, and promoted its participation in the methods of logic."

25. "Cerno Poetriam grandem tibi ferre sophiam / Arteque dictandi multis vsus arandi," quoted and translated in Camargo, "Si dictare velis," 270.

26. A summary version of some of the material presented here appears in Woods, "Using the *Poetria nova.*"

27. See "The Double Structure" in chapter 1.

(2099 ff.) moved to the beginning and referred to as a letter, as is the dedication that now follows it in both manuscripts. In Cambridge, Corpus Christi College, 406, an English manuscript, the rubrics identify the last section of the poem as *epistola prima* and the dedication as *epistola secunda* (fol. 101r).[28] In Paris, Bibliothèque nationale de France, lat. 505, a French manuscript, we find the same parts identified as *Epistola Magistri Gaufridi Anglici* and *Epistola eiusdem ad Innocentium papam tertium* (fol. 137r). But central European university commentaries on the *Poetria nova* are the most explicit in making the connection between the doctrine of the text and the composition of letters, as in the *accessus* to the *Poetria nova* by Dybinus of Prague, where rhetoric is described as "preparing letters."[29]

This interpretation of the *Poetria nova* as a dictaminal treatise is highlighted by the existence of another text, the so-called *Compendium Poetrie nove,* whose title implies that it is a "summary" or "companion" to Geoffrey's work.[30] Despite its name, however, it has almost nothing in common with the words of the *Poetria nova* itself. The *Compendium Poetrie nove* is not a summary of material or excerpts from the *Poetria nova,* or what one would find in a much shorter *ars poetriae,* but rather one of the very few examples of an *ars dictaminis* (or art of letter writing) written in verse; most are strictly in prose.[31] Its contents are very different from those of the arts of poetry. The two *artes poetriae* that are named most often in the central European university statutes are the *Poetria nova* and the much shorter *Laborintus* (Labyrinth) of Eberhard the German.[32] These two *artes* share the following contents: the ways of beginning a work, amplification and abbreviation, the tropes, and the figures of words and thoughts (the last without definitions in the *Laborintus* and illustrated by roughly connected statements on religious themes or moral precepts). Eberhard's work also contains a lament on the plight of the teacher, which, along with its shorter length, could have made it especially appealing. It is copied often along with the *Poetria*

---

28. On this manuscript see chapter 1, note 19.

29. "Scienciarum cum regina rethorica cum nobilissima deliciarum epistolas preparans . . . " (Prague, Národní Knihovna České Republiky, XII.B.12, fol. 1v). Other commentaries in this tradition, such as London BL, Add. 15108, (fol. 36r), have similar phrasing, which Dybinus may have borrowed from another of his own works; cf. Jaffe, *Declaracio,* 55.

30. On *compendia* in general see Weijers, *Le maniement du savoir,* 25–35; also Teeuwen, *Vocabulary of Intellectual Life,* 331; and Hamesse, "L'importance de l'étude d'Aristote": "les maîtres tendent toujours à abréger l'explication des textes imposés et cette tendance fait croître le grand nombre de résumés qui se font jour" (57). This tendency became more acute with the invention of printing; see Blair, "Coping Strategies."

31. On this genre see Camargo, "Si dictare velis." Concerning the geographical distribution of the text Camargo remarks, "During the fourteenth and fifteenth centuries the *Compendium* was widely used at universities in the German-speaking region from Bavaria east to Prague, south to Vienna, and including parts of Switzerland—what Worstbrock refers to as the area that provided students for the university at Vienna. In the course of the fifteenth century it also came to be taught at universities in Poland" (269, citing Worstbrock, *Verfasserlexikon,* 7.228). This description almost exactly matches the geographical distribution of *Poetria nova* manuscripts outlined in this chapter.

32. The *Poetria nova* is over two thousand lines long and the *Laborintus* just over one thousand, but the *Compendium Poetrie nove* less than one hundred.

nova, a typical example of redundancy in central European university manuscripts containing rhetorical material.[33] Much of the general rhetorical doctrine in these two works is as applicable to prose as to verse. But the reverse is not true of dictaminal manuals such as the *Compendium.*[34] The contents of the *Compendium* are specifically oriented toward the composition of letters: general introduction; etymology of *dictamen;* five parts of a letter (*salutatio, exordium, narratio, petitio,*[35] *conclusio*); rules for each part; prose rhythm (the *cursus*), clarity; rules for privileges (legal documents); and stylistics (variation, amplification, abbreviation).

So where, then, did the *Compendium Poetrie nove* get its name? Martin Camargo doubts that the title is original, suggesting instead that it may be derived from the statement about the *Poetria nova* quoted in the epigraph to this section: "I know that the *Poetria* [*nova*] will provide you with great wisdom / And [what] many are accustomed to treat in an *ars dictandi.* . . . ."[36] The *Compendium* is so compact (one-twentieth the length of the *Poetria nova*) that very little material extraneous to dictaminal doctrine is expressed therein; thus, the *Poetria nova* reference does stand out. Succinct and specific instruction in verse (easier to memorize) on the composition of letters made the *Compendium* very popular; it has survived "in more copies than most of the best-known prose treatises" on the same subject.[37] Significantly, the *Compendium* is usually accompanied by a commentary almost as long as some of those on the *Poetria nova,* a circumstance virtually unheard of with the prose *artes dictandi,* which almost always stand alone. Also, the commentaries on the *Poetria nova* introduce many of the subjects treated in the *Compendium.* That is, the commentaries on both works teach much the same rhetorical doctrine and the composition of letters.[38] Perhaps part of the popularity of the *Compendium Poetrie nove* came from the fact that it was thought to be a guide to or a digest of the *Poetria nova.* The title makes it sound like a student's aid, perhaps even a way to get out of reading the much longer—and surely increasingly less relevant for some teachers and students—textbook.[39]

---

33. See, for example, the contents of Berlin, Staatsbibliothek zu Berlin—Preussischer Kulturbesitz, lat. qu. 17; Erfurt, Wissenschaftliche Allgemeinbibliothek der Stadt, Amplon. Q.66 and Amplon. Q.286; Gdansk, Biblioteka Gdańska Polskiej Akademii Nauk, Mar. Q.8 and Mar. Q.9; Graz, Universitätsbibliothek, 979; Krakow, Biblioteka Jagiellońska, 1954; Prague, Národní Knihovna České Republiky, VIII.D.19; and Vienna, Schottenkloster, 399.

34. The distinction should not be overstated, however. As Camargo points out, "Linked by common ancestry, shared terminology, subject matter, teaching methods, and often teachers, the *artes dictandi* and the arts of poetry and prose have a special affinity that neither shares with the *ars praedicandi* [art of writing sermons] or the other varieties of text used to teach rhetoric in the middle ages" (Camargo, "Pedagogy," 91).

35. Some of the manuscripts of Dybinus's commentary call the third part of a rhetorical discourse the "petitio" rather than the "divisio," probably because of the close association with letters.

36. Quoted in Camargo, "Si dictare velis," 270.

37. Camargo, "Si dictare velis," 265. See also Worstbrock, "Otto von Lüneburg."

38. Although I have not examined them, I suspect that the commentaries on the *Laborintus* produced in central European university environments contain similar doctrine.

39. Camargo remarks that, "Clearly the *Compendium* was [originally] meant to be taught in conjunction with the *Poetria nova:* it is a supplement to more than a summary of Geoffrey of Vinsauf's work" ("Si dictare

REPETITION, REDUNDANCY, AND
THE LEARNING CURVE

This book . . . is divided in its division into two parts. . . . [T]he form of the treatise is clear in the division of the book as is clear in the little note above.[40]

—Uppsala, Universitetsbiblioteket, C 40

The lengthy commentaries on the *Poetria nova* that were popular in central Europe are extremely repetitive. The lessons that they want students to learn about rhetoric in general and Geoffrey's use of it in particular are stated and restated over and over. Nor is this repetition only within texts: the contents of a number of the manuscripts show that teachers and students who did own copies often amassed collections of similar kinds of works, groupings that are indicative of particular kinds of application and use—even when the manuscripts are written in several hands or are composites of previously separate codices. That repetition is a deliberate pedagogical tool is abundantly clear in the selections from commentaries presented below. Except for the two versions of the *accessus* by Dybinus of Prague, I have not quoted all of the material on any one section of the *Poetria nova* from a given university commentary: it would be too tedious to read.

The central European university commentators characteristically go over and over a passage under comment, bringing up and elaborating on the same point several times and in several ways.[41] (This repetition of doctrine and pointing out of technique is not the same thing as scholastic division and subdivision of the text, which also occurs. The former is a characteristic of all exposition throughout the commentaries; the latter occurs in introductory notes to individual passages, outlining where they fall in the structure of the work as a whole.) The result is a virtual imprinting of rhetorical doctrine onto the mind of the student, and such techniques may have been used as part of a memorization program. As we shall see in Dybinus's commentary on the *Poetria nova,* discussion of a single section of text could demand simple paraphrase, glossing of individual words, summary of doctrine, restatement of doctrine, and introduction of and comparison with doctrine from other rhetoricians or *auctores,* ending with word-by-word glossing of the text. If one reads sections of commentary aloud (or better, listens to someone else reading them), one perceives directly how the repetition reinforces both a concept and its connection to other concepts.

---

velis," 270), and the two are found together in Erfurt, Wissenschaftliche Allgemeinbibliothek der Stadt, Amplon. Q.66; and Gdansk, Biblioteka Gdańska Polskiej Akademii Nauk, Mar. Q.8. For other manuscripts of the *Compendium,* see Camargo, "Si dictare velis," 283–285.

40. "Iste liber . . . sui [*sic*] diuisione diuiditur in duas partes. . . . Forma tractatus patet in diuisione libri sicut patet in superiori notali" (Uppsala, Universitetsbiblioteket, C 40, fol. 20v).

41. Pace of Ferrara's approach in chapter 3 is more systematic, utilizing as much structure and reinforcement but less repetition.

Basic interpretive strategies for teaching the work at an advanced level, some of which we saw in Pace's commentary, include the division into parts and a relentless citing of authorities, especially Aristotle (often simply as *Philosophus*, "The Philosopher"). University teachers in central Europe were interested in rhetorical theory for its own sake and its applicability, rather than as a tool to understand how the *Poetria nova* and other texts function. They concentrate almost exclusively on the application of rhetorical doctrine to prose (even after noting in the *accessus* that the doctrine taught in the *Poetria nova* is applicable to both verse and prose). Implicitly or explicitly they contextualize the *Poetria nova* as a dictaminal treatise, one that teaches the composition of letters. And they sometimes criticize Geoffrey himself.

We can see some of these characteristics in a manuscript now owned by the university library at Uppsala, C 40, part of the collection of the famous Vadstena Monastery, original house of the Brigittine order in Sweden. This was a double monastery of men and women with, like all of the houses in St. Bridget's order, a woman as titular head. Sadly for the women, while their side had many vernacular manuscripts, almost all the Latin manuscripts, including this copy of the *Poetria nova*, were the exclusive possession of the monks.[42] Where it originated is not known, but the approach and content of the commentary indicate an institution of higher learning.[43] In addition to the *Poetria nova* and accompanying commentary, this fourteenth-century composite manuscript contains grammatical treatises on deponent verbs, gerunds, and the composition of verbs.[44] The text of the *Poetria nova* is written on the inner of the two columns, with the outer column devoted to commentary. It is copied in two similar but not identical hands. There are sporadic interlinear glosses; the marginal comments are usually quite lengthy and often bear little resemblance to the text of the *Poetria nova* under discussion, a characteristic of some university commentaries. The main predicate of the incipit of the commentary (quoted in the epigraph) begins the scholastic division into parts. The complete incipit translated below also states that what the poet teaches is the poetic art, seemingly not a university focus, but, as we shall see in what follows, the commentary consistently elaborates the *Poetria nova*'s teaching in terms of how it illustrates Aristotelian doctrine rather than poetic techniques. The *accessus* is divided into two parts, first a summary of the division of the work (what is known as the *divisio textus*), then a more formal introduction to the text via the Aristotelian four causes. It is simple, straightforward, and redundant. Here is how a student might have been introduced to the *Poetria nova* on the first day of lectures:

---

42. See Woods, "Shared Books," 177–178.

43. On university manuscripts in monastic collections, see "Monks at University" later in this chapter.

44. On Uppsala, Universitetsbiblioteket, C 40, see *Iter ital.* 5.25; and Andersson-Schmitt and Hedlund, *Mittelalterliche Handschriften*, 282–283. On the Vadstena collection in general, see Andersson-Schmitt and Hedlund, "Katalogisering," 115–117. Some of the glosses in this manuscript are discussed in Woods, "A Medieval Rhetoric."

UPPSALA, UNIVERSITETSBIBLIOTEKET
C 40, *ACCESSUS*

This book, whose subject according to some is the poetic faculty (*sensus*) or the poetic art, is principally divided according to division into two parts, namely the prologue and the execution [of the text]. The first division is clear and is at "If a man has a house to build" (43). The prologue is [sub]divided into two parts: in the first he praises the pope himself and then his cardinals. The first is at "Holy Father, wonder" (1), the second at "Your retinue" (28). The first [of these is subdivided] into two, in the principal part of which he praises the pope in an absolute sense; in the second he praises him in comparison with others. The first is at "Holy Father, wonder" (1), the second at "In illustrious" etc. (10). The principal part is divided into two: at first he compares the whole of the name of the pope to the whole of his virtues, in the second the division of the name to the division of the virtues. With regard to the first part he proceeds by saying that just as the name of the pope cannot be put into meter, so no one wholly equals the pope. And next, just as the name of the pope when divided can be put into meter, so the virtue of the pope when divided up equals that of many men.

In the beginning of this book we can ask about the name of the authors[45] and the causes and the intention of the authors and to what part of philosophy the book belongs. The author of the book is called Gamfredus, and he was English, as is clear in the text: "England sent me to Rome" (32). The material cause [the subject] is as was stated earlier. The intention of the authors is to versify the subject, and it can be [perceived as] twofold, namely general and specific: specific in terms of Lord Richard, King of England, in whose embassy to the pope he [the author] participated, wishing to reconcile him [Richard] with the pope; general in terms of all of us whom he intends to instruct in the art of poetry. The formal cause is twofold, namely the form of the treatise and the form of the treatment. The form of the treatment is clear, while the form of the treatise is clear in the division of the book as is clear in the little note above. The final cause or usefulness is that through this book we can acquire the art of poetry. This book belongs under grammar, which is established by the fact that this book treats of poetry: the poetic art considers the long and the short accent and the quantity of syllables, which belong to grammar.[46]

---

45. The plural appears to be intentional since it is used twice in this first sentence (and once later), so I have retained it in the translation.

46. "Iste liber cuius subjectum est sensus poeticus secundum quosdam vel ars poetica <principaliter secundum diuisionem> [principalis sui diuisione *MS*] diuiditur in duas partes, scilicet in prohemium et executionem. Prima patet et est ibi 'Si quis habet fundare domum' (43). Prohemium diuiditur in duas: in prima commendat ipsum papam, deinde suos cardinales. Prima ibi, 'Papa stupor' (1); secunda ibi, 'Suntque tui tales' (28); prima in duas, in quarum principio commendat papam absolute; in secunda commendat ipsum in comparatione ad alios; prima ibi, 'Papa stupor'(1), secunda ibi 'Egregius' (10) etc. Pars principalis diuiditur in duas: primo enim comparat integritatem nominis pape integritati virtutum eius, in secunda diuisione nominis diuisioni virtutum. Circa primam partem sic procedit dicens quod sicut pape nomen non est possibile in metro, sic et pape nullus integraliter conuenit. Vel modo et sicut nomen pape diuisum potest poni in metro, sic virtus pape diuisum [*sic*] conuenit multis <personis> [partibus *MS*].

"In principio huius libri possumus querere de nomine actorum [*sic*] et de causis et de intencione actorum et cui parti philosophie supponitur. Actor libri vocatur Gamfredus et fuit anglicus sicut patet in littera illa: 'Me transtulit Anglia' (32). Causa materialis est sicut prius dictum est. Intencio actorum versafica<re> [*sic*]

Thus ends the *accessus*. Then the commentator moves directly into glosses on individual words, beginning with the tenth line of the poem (the first having been treated already in the *accessus*). He refers to the sections of the book as chapters (*capitula*), but he seems to be in some confusion as to their arrangement: the techniques of amplification and abbreviation occur in his "chapter" on style, for example, while most commentators consider them part of the preceding section on arrangement; in addition, this statement comes where other commentators introduce invention.[47]

Except for those on the first lines of Geoffrey's aprostrophes on the death of Richard, there are almost no interlinear glosses until the last kind of amplification: *oppositio,* or saying something twice by stating it and then stating that the opposite is not true, as in, "His is the appearance of youth and not of old age" (*PN 675*). This technique is confusing, and the commentator glosses interlinearly almost every line from here through Geoffrey's treatments of abbreviation and the metaphorical use of verbs and adjectives. The interlinear glosses are straightforward; for example, the "wicked wife" (714) in the example of abbreviation is glossed "adulterous spouse."[48] Perhaps significantly, the last lines glossed interlinearly are, "Discrimination of this sort has imparted a fine polish to the words, removing any trace of obscurity" (870–871). It is not clear why this part of the text was singled out for special attention, especially since it does not correspond with the traditional divisions of the text, but abbreviation and metaphoric language were important parts of medieval composition pedagogy.

THE IMPORTANCE OF BEING ARISTOTELIAN

"You Aristotelize in everything you do"—said of an idiot.[49]
— Nicholas Dybinus (translated by Dilwyn Knox)

In contrast to the school commentators discussed in chapter 2, the early humanist commentator who wrote the most advanced Italian commentary on the

---

materiam et potest esse duplex, scilicet generalis et specialis: specialis quantum ad dominum Richardum regem Anglie cuius legacione fungebatur ad dominum papam volens ipsum reconsiliare pape; generalis quantum ad nos omnes quos intendit instruere artem poeticam. Causa formalis est duplex, scilicet forma tractatus et forma tractandi. Forma tractandi patet sed forma tractatus patet in diuisione libri sicut patet in superiori notali. Causa finalis siue vtilitatis est vt per hunc [i]librum possumus addicere artem poeticam. Grammatice supponitur liber iste quod sic probatur quia iste liber tractat de poesi; ars autem poetica accentum productum et correptum considerat et quantitatem sillibarum, quod est proprium grammatice. . . . " (Uppsala, Universitetsbiblioteket, C 40, fol. 20v) The scribe regularly leaves off abbreviation marks, and I have not indicated places where letters have been supplied unless I might be emending what the scribe had intended.

47. "In capitulo de <eloquencia> [eloquencie *MS*] siue ornatu verborum et sentenciarum est incidens vt de prolongacione et abbreuiacione materie" on line 43 (Uppsala, Universitetsbiblioteket, C 40, fol. 21r).

48. "Vxor metha [= moecha] (coniunx adultera)" (Uppsala, Universitetsbiblioteket, C 40, fol. 34v).

49. Knox, *Ironia*, 14, translating "'tu in omnibus factis tuis aristotelisas,' intelligendo contrarium," from Dybinus's *Declaracio*, 131.

Poetria nova, Pace of Ferrara, took a rather distanced approach to the stories of the human and cosmological pairings in Geoffrey's example of a digression, as we saw in chapter 3. Some central European university commentators take this abstract and theoretical approach to an extreme. Pace introduced Aristotelian doctrine on the qualities of male and female in his gloss on Geoffrey's description of the mating of the feminine earth and male sky to produce a flower, but Pace also connected this theme to the narrative of the lovers from which the digression was made. He thereby reinforced the coherence of Geoffrey's whole passage and portrayed the author as a skilled writer knowledgeable in his craft.[50] In contrast, the commentator whose teaching is recorded in the Uppsala manuscript introduces Aristotelian material for its own sake: he uses Geoffrey as a springboard to a discussion of Aristotelian principles that have no connection to the text of the *Poetria nova.* The commentator's own gloss is an example of the kind of digression that leads away from but not back to the text. Geoffrey says (in Nims's translation), "Moist and warm (*humidus et calidus*), air sports with earth, and the feminine earth feels the masculine power of the air" (546–548). In his notes on Geoffrey's terms, the commentator of the Uppsala manuscript brings in additional Aristotelian categories unrelated to Geoffrey's text ("*humidus*" is translated below as "wet" rather than "moist" as in Nims):

> Note (547) WET AND WARM According to the Philosopher in his book *On Generation and Corruption,* there is a difference between something wet and something soaked {II.2}. He says there that something wet has foreign wetness on its surface, while something soaked has moisture down to its innermost depth. Aristotle says there that something wet is what has its own moisture deep within, while something soaked is what contains foreign moisture there, etc. He states there the difference between something dry and something dried up. Something dry is something that is completely arid [naturally without moisture], but something dried is so because of a lack of its normal moisture, etc. {II.2}
>
> Note that there are four elements, namely fire, air, water, and earth. Fire is warm and dry, air wet and warm, water cold and wet, earth dry and cold. No one ought to say that fire is dry [and warm], but rather warm and dry, or that air is warm and wet, but rather wet and warm, since the Philosopher says in the same book that, indeed, earth belongs more to dry than to cold, water more to cold than to wet, air more to wet than to warm, fire more to warm than to dry.[51]

---

50. See chapter 3, "In Season."

51. "Nota secundum Philosophum in libro *De generacione et corruptione* differenciam inter humidum et infusum {II.2}. Dicit enim ibi quod humidum est quod habet alienigenam humiditacionem superficie tenus, infusum autem humiditacionem in profundo. Aristotiles dicit ibi quod humidum est quod habet propriam humiditatem in profundo, infusum autem quod habet alienam humiditacionem in profundo, etc. Ponit ibi differenciam inter aridum et coagulatum. Aridum enim est quod perfecte siccum est. Coagulatum vero fit propter defectum proprie humiditatis {II.2}.

"Item nota quod quatuor sunt elementa, scilicet ignis, aer, aqua, terra. Ignis est calidus et siccus, aer

These "notes" are the equivalent of footnotes and as such a sign of more advanced treatment of a text. We saw them in Pace's commentary, and we shall encounter them again with Dybinus of Prague. They show us what the teacher thinks that students should be learning: here, Aristotle.[52]

For example, the following sequence of descriptions (naked female body, dressed female body, dressed-up banquet table), celebrated by other commentators, is basically ignored in this manuscript. Instead, the commentator uses the category of description as an excuse to introduce the Aristotelian category of definition: a concept and term that does not come up in the *Poetria nova* at all, but one that is very important in Aristotelian doctrine and in rhetorical theory. It is, of course, a common practice to compare and contrast techniques to make sure that the students understand the differences between them. School commentators, for example, often compare and contrast description with the preceding technique of digression. This commentator, however, contrasts description with definition, a concept that Geoffrey does not treat—but Aristotle does. Our commentator notes that definition treats essential characteristics, while description treats accidental ones; not surprisingly, he goes on to quote Aristotle at length.[53] From a philosophical point of view, substances are much more important than accidents. Since Geoffrey teaches about accidents only here, the commentator is implying the more limited nature of Geoffrey's teaching in contrast to Aristotle's.[54]

This introduction of philosophical categories for their own sake is characteristic of university-level commentaries in central Europe, where scholastic approaches exemplify the pinnacle of intellectual rigor. In contrast, the early humanist commentators to the south were elevating textual (formerly school-level) analysis to a higher discipline, a movement that resulted in the later full-blown humanist focus on language and literature (or philology and poetry) as ends in themselves. When Pace used the elevated terminology of Aristotelian scholasticism it was to help in this project, or, in more modern terminology, to theorize poetic language and raise the textual (as opposed to philosophical) aspect of grammar to the level of adult discourse; think of all the later humanists who became professors of grammar. In central Europe (and France[55]), how-

---

humidus et calidus; aqua frigida et humida, terra sicca et frigida. Nullus enim debet dicere ignem esse siccum <et calidum> sed calidum et siccum, nec aerem calidum et humidum sed humidum et calidum quia Philosophus dicit in eodem libro terra quidem sicci magis quam frigidi, aqua autem frigidi magis quam humidi, aer autem magis humidi quam calidi, ignis autem magis calidi quam sicci" (Uppsala, Universitetsbiblioteket, C 40, fol. 29r–v).

52. Nauta remarks with regard to curricular texts, "The Aristotelian corpus dominated the curriculum in the universities" ("The Study of Boethius's *Consolatio*" [unpublished paper]).

53. "Nota differenciam inter descripcionem et diffinicionem, quia descripcio datur per accidentalia rei extrinsica vel intrinseca, sed diffinicio datur per essencialia vt cum dicitur homo est animal rationale mortale. Dicit enim Aristotiles . . . " (Uppsala, Universitetsbiblioteket, C 40, fol. 29v).

54. See Woods, "A Medieval Rhetoric," 59–60.

55. Lorenz, *Studium generale Erfordense*, 159, on how the university-level study of rhetoric moved from central Europe to Paris. On evidence of the *Poetria nova* at Paris see Ward, "Rhetoric in the Faculty of Arts,"

ever, grammar theorized was the abstract, speculative grammar of the *modiste* (those who studied the *modi significandi* [modes of meaning] of words; the *Poetria nova* was taught at places like Erfurt that were closely associated with this development.[56] Yet although the *Poetria nova* seems on the surface so much less suited for this latter enterprise, it stayed in the advanced curriculum in the north much longer (well into the second half of the fifteenth century), whereas it is hard—but not impossible[57]—to find specific evidence of use in Italy after 1450. Ironically, in the north the *Poetria nova* was considered complementary to later humanist developments in letter-writing imported from Italy, as we shall see in the contents of some of the later manuscripts. But before looking at later developments, we need to go back to the earliest evidence that the *Poetria nova* was taught at a central European university.

THE *POETRIA NOVA* AT PRAGUE

> *Poetria nova*, 2 Groschen for 3 months[58]
> —remuneration for lectures at University of Prague in 1366

The University of Prague was founded in 1348[59] and was an immediate success. As James Overfield remarks, "students from east and central Europe previously deterred by the cost and difficulty of traveling to France or Italy streamed to Prague."[60] Here we find both the earliest and the latest documented teaching of the *Poetria nova* in a university setting. It is listed in the 1366 statutes for the faculty of arts quoted above, where a teacher was paid "two Groschen" for lecturing on the *Poetria nova* for a period of three months. The other rhetorical text listed for that same year, the *Laborintus,* at about half the length of the *Poetria nova,* was lectured on for half the time and half the salary. As a comparison, the *Grecismus* of Eberhard of Béthune, a grammatical treatise, was to be lectured on for six months at a pay of six Groschen, and Boethius's *Consolation of Philosophy* took three months and the lecturer was paid four Groschen. The most lucrative series of lectures was on Aristotle's *Metaphysics:* eight Groschen

---

165 (citing Weijers, *Le travail intellectuel*) and 205.

56. See Pinborg, "Speculative Grammar"; also "The *Poetria nova* at Vienna, Erfurt, and Krakow" below, and "Erasmus and Geoffrey" in the Afterword (on the *modi significandi*). On the complicated relationship between Aristotelianism and the *modiste* [there *Modistae*], see Knudsen, "Intentions and Impositions," 486–87.

57. See "Geoffrey after Quintilian" in the Afterword.

58. "poetria nova 2 gross. per 3 menses" (*Liber decanorum facultatis philosophicae,* 77).

59. Šmahel, "Scholae," 115, who gives 1348 as the date, as do Moraw and others in his volume, "Die Universität Prag im Mittelalter," 15, 22, 26 etc. Rashdall gives the date as 1347–48, *Universities of Europe* 2. vii and 211. The authors of different parts of Ridder-Symoens, *History of the University,* cite variously 1346 (Rüegg, "Themes," 13) and 1347 (Verger, "Patterns," 63; and Nardi, "Relations with Authority," 96).

60. Overfield, *Humanism and Scholasticism,* 6.

for six months.[61] A manuscript in Prague, Národní Knihovna České Republiky (National Library of the Czech Republic), XII.B.12, records a course of lectures on the *Poetria nova* by Dybinus of Prague delivered at Prague within a period of five weeks in the summer of 1375, along with lectures on the *Laborintus*.[62] Josef Tříška includes a commentary on the *Poetria nova* among the rhetoric texts taught in the faculty of arts in Prague during the fifteenth century, along with Guido Faba's *Summa dictaminis,* Dybinus of Prague's *Oracio de beata Dorothea,* the *Summa Jovis,* Alan of Lille's *De planctu Nature,* and Horace's *Poetria,* in addition to a separate *Poetria antiqua,* presumably Aristotle's *Poetics.*[63]

Several late-fourteenth-century manuscripts of the *Poetria nova* are of probable Prague origin. In addition to the 1375 lectures in Prague XII.B.12, a different version of the same commentary was copied fourteen years later in another manuscript now in the same library, Prague VIII.H.22. These two manuscripts form the basis of the analysis of the commentary by Dybinus of Prague discussed in some detail later in this chapter.[64] In addition, at least one of the manuscripts of the *Poetria nova* now in the Amploniana collection in Erfurt, Wissenschaftliche Allgemeinbibliothek der Stadt, Amplon. F.50, probably comes from Prague.[65] It may have been acquired by Amplonius Ratinck de Berka when he was a student in Prague between 1385 and 1387 and brought back to Erfurt when he returned in 1412. In his important study of Dybinus's works, Hans Szklenar conjectures that Amplonius acquired this manuscript before he decided to concentrate on medical texts,[66] but additional copies of the *Poetria nova* in the Amploniana collection suggest that de Berka's taste may have remained eclectic. The author of the commentary is not named in this

---

61. The courses from *Liber decanorum facultatis philosophicae* 1 [*Monumenta Historica Universitatis Carolo-Ferdinandeae* 1.1], 76–77, are simplified and listed in Hautz, *Geschichte der Universität Heidelberg,* 356; see also Lorenz, "*Libri ordinarie legendi,*" 218–219; no literary texts are included. The *Poetria nova* is not in the list of books required at Prague in 1390 according to Lorenz, 229. As early as 1370, however, the university library owned a volume containing "a commentary on the *Poetria nova* and *Anticlaudianus*" and other volumes of literary school texts including Boethius, Sallust, Ovid's *Metamorphoses,* Avianus, etc. (Baldzuhn, "*Quidquid placet,*" 339).

62. Other texts by Dybinus may have been taught in Prague in 1377 or 1386–88; see Szklenar, *Magister Nicolaus,* 59, citing Lemcke, "Die Handschriften und alten Drucke," 1.1–44.

63. "libri, qui in facultate artium saec. xv. legebantur" (Tříška, *Literární Činnost Předhusitké University,* 161). The works included "In rethorica" are "Alanus de planctu nature / Rethorica Gwidonis / Poetria nova / Boecius de disciplina / Oracio Dorothee / Laborintus / Sertum rethorice / Poetria antiqua / Summa Iovis / Copia Latinitatis / Poetria Oracii" (163). Aristotle's *Poetics* is referred to as *a Poetria* in Pace of Ferrara's *accessus* and two manuscripts of a related commentary in Krakow. The catalogue of the university library compiled in the mid-fifteenth century includes two copies of the *Poetria nova* (referred to by the author's name): "10 Gamfreidus . . . 11 Gamfreidus" (Baldzuhn, "*Quidquid placet,*" 343–44).

64. See "*Scripta* vs. *Dicta* in Practice." Both manuscripts formerly "belonged to the so-called Public and University library before 1935" (Tomáš Klimek, e-mail correspondence, May 2008).

65. On Erfurt, Wissenschaftliche Allgemeinbibliothek der Stadt, Amplon. F.50, fols. 1r–59r, see Schum, *Beschreibendes Verzeichniss,* 40–43 (Schum's folio numbers are not always reliable); and Szklenar, *Magister Nicolaus,* 105–106. This manuscript contains a variety of texts, including the papal bulls of Gregory II, Walter Burley's *Auctoritates,* two commentaries on the *Distichs of Cato,* two treatises on the art of love according to the rank and status of the lover, and descriptions of Westphalia. See also Hamesse, *Auct. Aris.,* 26.

66. Szklenar, *Magister Nicolaus,* 105.

Erfurt manuscript, and, although he is identified in Amplonius's own catalogue as Dybinus,[67] he was probably one of Dybinus's followers.[68] Additional manuscripts of the *Poetria nova* now in the National Library at Prague may provide further evidence of how the *Poetria nova* was taught. Prague VIII.D.19, dated 1376, contains the *Poetria nova* and *Laborintus,* both with commentaries.[69] That on the *Poetria nova,* in a typical central-European university format (*accessus,* text with interlinear glosses, and full marginal commentary), has an attractive incipit for those tired of Aristotle: "As Plato says in the *Timaeus,* nothing comes into being which is not preceded by a proper (*legitima*) cause."[70] Prague III. G.22 contains commentaries on a series of transitional texts: the *Poetria nova,* Prosper of Aquitaine's *Epigraphs* on excerpts from Augustine, and the pseudo-Boethian *De disciplina scolarium.*[71]

The cathedral library at Prague contained many manuscripts that were "productions of the medieval schools of law" at the university; most are now part of the Archive of Prague Castle.[72] A manuscript copied by Johannes de Chlumecz in 1403, Prague, Knihovna Metropolitní Kapituli, M 126, contains three glossed texts: the *Poetria nova,* Martianus Capella's *De nuptiis Philologiae et Mercurii* (Marriage of Mercury and Philology) and Horace's *Ars poetica.*[73] A fourteenth-century copy of the *Early Commentary,* MS L 97, is now also part of the collection.[74] Although this manuscript dates from the first half of the fourteenth century, presumably before the founding of the university at Prague, at some point it was owned by a certain Alexius, who had earned a university degree.[75] Introductions have been added to each section of the commentary that provide extensive scholastic divisions and subdivisions of the text.[76] Another manu-

---

67. "Item commentum Tibini super poetriam novam Gaufredi" (Lehmann, *Mittelalterliche Bibliothekskataloge* cited in Szklenar, *Magister Nicolaus,* 105).

68. See Knox, *Ironia,* 191.

69. Prague, Národní Knihovna České Republiky, VIII.D.19, *PN* and commentary on fols. 1r–38v. On this manuscript see Truhlář, *Catalogus codicum manu scriptorum,* 1.557.

70. "Sicut dicit Plato in *Timaeo,* nichil est ortum cuius causa legitima non precesserit" (Prague, Národní Knihovna České Republiky, VIII.D.19, fol. 1r). The interlinear glosses on the *Poetria nova* stop at fol. 7r; there is a hiatus in the marginal glosses from fols. 24v to 26v.

71. On Prague, Národní Knihovna České Republiky, III.G.22, see Truhlář, *Catalogus codicum manu scriptorum,* 1.547. A late-fifteenth- or even early-sixteenth-century manuscript also in the National Library, Prague, Národní Knihovna České Republiky, III.E.27, contains a glossed excerpt from the *Poetria nova* discussed in "Conversion: The Origin of Style" in chapter 2.

72. Kristeller, *Iter ital.* 3.156, and Boháček, "Le opere delle scuole medievali," 307. These statements come from descriptions of the manuscripts from this collection now in Olomouc.

73. The *Poetria nova* (fols. 2r–48v) has interlinear glossing, sporadic after fol. 19r, and scattered marginal notes, some quite long. (There is no *accessus.*) On Prague, Knihovna Metropolitní Kapituli, M 126, see Podlaha, *Soupis Rukopisů,* 2.344.

74. Prague, Knihovna Metropolitní Kapituli, L 97, *PN* on fols. 2r–27r, *accessus* on fol. 1v. On this manuscript, see Podlaha, *Soupis Rukopisů,* 2.257; and Woods, *EC,* xlix. The *PN* and commentary are the only contents.

75. An ownership note on fol. 1r reads "Alexii Baccalarii."

76. We also find a tantalizing bit of information about the shift in focus to prose: a reference at line 527 in all early manuscripts of the *EC* to the kind of examples found in the works of "poetas" has been changed to the more generic "auctores" in this manuscript; see Woods, "Classical Examples and References," 8.

script from the former cathedral library, which contains the *Poetria nova* with interlinear glosses and full marginal commentary copied with a work *On fallacies* (attributed to Thomas Aquinas) with interlinear glosses and a treatise *On grammar,* is now in the Vědecká knihovna v Olomouci, C.O. 575.[77] And in 1449, a schoolteacher made a collection of excerpts of classical and medieval Latin poets, including Geoffrey of Vinsauf, which is now in the State Archive in Třebón.[78]

Prague is not unique in having today so many manuscripts related to the history of the teaching of the *Poetria nova* in the region. Each collection of relevant material examined for this chapter offers almost as much in the way of data for university-level teaching of the text, although much of it cannot be localized to a specific institution.[79] A number of the central European manuscripts of commentaries on the *Poetria nova* were copied by the students themselves. Each constitutes a record of that student's education at an institution of higher education, whether organized university or *studium generale.* The widespread use of paper, a much cheaper writing material than parchment, by this time made it possible for students to make their own copies of primary texts and lectures on them. Since these students were without professional training, it is usually impossible to identify a more specific geographical origin within central Europe on the basis of script alone. Like Amplonius Ratinck de Berka, students often traveled elsewhere within the region to study. Ironically, so much data has survived in the dense commentaries and additional material in the thick central European manuscripts of the *Poetria nova* that it is impossible to convey here all that they could tell us about late medieval pedagogy. This excess of riches is particularly frustrating with the codices that record an individual student's academic experience. In this chapter I have had to limit myself strictly to the commentaries on the *Poetria nova,* and I have tried to reach a compromise between communicating the sheer amount of information preserved and suggesting the details that individual manuscripts may convey about educational experience.

---

77. For Olomouc, Vědecká knihovna v Olomouci, C.O. 575, see *Iter ital.* 3.157; Bistřický et al., *Seznam rukopisů metropolitní kapituly,* 151. The incipit of the commentary is only partially legible: "Cum ornatus modus loquendi ***." It resembles that of the *accessus* in Prague, Knihovna Metropolitní Kapituli, L 97, but the glosses are different.

78. Třebón, Státní Archiv, A 4, fols. 16v–17r. On this manuscript see Weber et al., *Catalogus codicum manu scriptorum,* 29–53; Uebach, *Zwei mittellateinische Pyramus- und Thisbe-Dichtungen,* 56–75; and Munari, *Catalogo,* 105–106 (99). For another collection of excerpts see "Proverbial Wisdom" in chapter 1.

79. A similar situation exists in Munich, not a university site during the period under discussion but where a number of the individual manuscripts described in this chapter are now housed.

DYBINUS OF PRAGUE

> The long-term final cause is so that, when we have taken in and learned what this book [the *Poetria nova*] contains, we can communicate with kings and princes and nobles.[80]
>
> —Dybinus of Prague

The commentary in Uppsala examined earlier is an awkward and ungainly piece of work. Its partitioning of the *Poetria nova* in the *accessus* and introduction of Aristotelian material into the glosses, while staples of university commentaries, are much less well integrated than the same elements in the popular commentary by Dybinus of Prague—one reason, perhaps, that the latter commentary has survived in multiple copies but the former in only one. Yet the very awkwardness and abruptness of the Uppsala commentary make it easy to distinguish the techniques and values at work in it. The commentary by Dybinus or Tibinus of Prague ("Dibinus / Tibinus Pragensis," also known to modern scholars as Nikolaus Dybinus and Magister Nicholas de Dybin[81]) is more complex, elegant, and satisfying. Dybinus lived at the time of the rise of the universities in central Europe (he was rector of a school in Dresden in 1369 and died before 1387[82]), and his rhetorical works, including the commentary on the *Poetria nova,* continued to be taught in this region during the last quarter of the fourteenth and throughout the fifteenth century.

Interest in Dybinus has been growing, and many questions about his life and works have been addressed, if not always definitively answered. For example, how many of the works associated with his name did he actually write, and what are the relationships among them?[83] We know that he taught school at Dresden; did he also teach at Erfurt, and if so at what level?[84] His commentary on the *Poetria nova* was taught at the University of Prague in 1375, but was he the one who taught it?[85] There are at least preliminary answers to these questions, as we shall see below. My focus is not on Dybinus himself, however, or on how he came to write his commentary on the *Poetria nova,* but rather on what the manuscripts of that commentary can tell us about how the *Poetria nova* was

---

80. "Causa finalis remota est ut habito et cognito hoc libro possimus communicare regibus et principalibus et nobilibus" (Prague, Národní Knihovna České Republiky, VIII.H.22, fol. 26v).

81. Szklenar is very definite that the last name should be rendered as "de Dybin" instead to elucidate its geographical origin; see his entry in the *Verfasserlexikon* and the title of his monograph.

82. Szklenar, "Nikolaus von Dybin."

83. For still preliminary arguments that nevertheless give more precise data than was available heretofore, see Jaffe, *Declaracio;* Szklenar, *Magister Nicolaus* and "Nikolaus von Dybin"; and Knox, *Ironia,* 191. Some of the manuscripts listed by Szklenar in his entry in the *Verfasserlexikon,* partially based on information provided by me, may be of a related but different commentary, although there is more than a little overlap of material. I am grateful to Professors Szklenar and Knox for correspondence on this issue.

84. Lorenz, *Studium generale Erfordense,* 278–81.

85. Szklenar, *Magister Nicolaus,* 56–63.

taught. Some of the related questions I am able to answer only provisionally. Did his commentaries become popular because he was a famous teacher, or did he become famous because of the success of his commentaries? I suspect the latter. Was Dybinus's commentary itself a factor in the success of the *Poetria nova* in central Europe? I believe so.

Nicolaus Dybinus wrote commentaries on three of the most popular texts used to teach the trivium (grammar, rhetoric, logic) in central Europe: the *Doctrinale* of Alexander de Villa Dei (a portion of it), the *Laborintus* of Eberhard the German, and the *Poetria nova*. His other rhetorical works, the *Viaticus dictandi* and *Oracio de beata Dorothea,* were also widely taught at central European universities, the latter accompanied by Dybinus's own commentary, or *Declaracio.*[86] One of the paradoxical reasons for the success of Dybinus's rhetorical works at universities may have been his background as a schoolteacher. His commentary could have functioned as either an advanced school commentary or a beginning university one: a fitting introduction to a school/university text. Dybinus's commentary is exceptionally clear and reinforcing and cumulative; he focuses on the construction of the *Poetria nova* as a rhetorical document rather than an aesthetic one (see the epigraph at the beginning of this section). He, too, introduces Aristotelian theory into his discussion of the *Poetria nova,* but not at Geoffrey's expense. That Dybinus became famous and influential so quickly—Vincentius Grüner refers to "Dybinus and his followers" (*Dibinus et sui sequaces*) by 1408[87]—encourages us to take as open and appreciative a look at his commentary as possible.

SCRIPTA, DICTA, AND REPORTATA

> Here end the *dicta* of Dybinus on the *Poetria nova,* completed and recorded (*reportata*) at Prague by Johannes de Montabaur in the year 1375. . . .[88]
> —Prague, Národní Knihovna České Republiky, XII.B.12

Pedagogical popularity wreaks havoc with textual purity.[89] The very messiness of the manuscript traditions of Dybinus's works is evidence of their success with teachers, and most of them, including the commentary on the *Poetria nova,*

---

86. For an edition of two versions of the *Declaracio,* see Jaffe. Knox indicates doubt about Dybinus's authorship of the *Declaracio* (*Ironia,* 191). On the *Viaticus dictandi* see Gueudet, *L'art de la lettre,* passim.

87. On Grüner see Knox, *Ironia,* 195.

88. "EXPLICIUNT DICTA TYBINI *NOUE POETRIE* FINITA ET REPORTATA PRAGE PER MANUS IOHANNIS DE MANTHABUR ANNO DOMINI M°C°C°C°LXX°V^{to} . . . " (Prague, Národní Knihovna České Republiky, XII.B.12, fol. 42rb).

89. The multiple versions of commentaries demonstrate the notorious penchant of medieval teachers for adapting material for their own purposes and hence "corrupting" a textual tradition. See the frequent remarks about pedagogical contamination in L. D. Reynolds, ed., *Texts and Transmission,* passim.

survive in multiple versions. As is the case with his *Declaracio Oracionis de beata Dorothea*,[90] several versions of Dybinus's commentary on the *Poetria nova* are contemporaneous with Dybinus himself. None is an autograph copy, however, and each reflects individual scribal and pedagogical practices. Two of the most interesting and important are a course of lectures recorded at Prague in 1375 via dictation (hereafter the *dicta* version), presumably as a university-sanctioned activity, and an incomplete written copy of the commentary (hereafter the *scripta* version) made fourteen years later, probably at the same university.[91]

Let us look first at the 1375 *dicta* version, which survives in Prague, Národní Knihovna České Republiky, XII.B.12. It is a sizable volume (298 x 220 mm) from the Cistercian monastery of Sancta Corona (Zlatá Koruna) in southern Bohemia (plate 9).[92] The other works in this manuscript are rhetorical: in addition to dictated versions of Dybinus's commentaries on the *Poetria nova, Laborintus,* and *Oracio de beata Dorothea,* it also includes the *Somnium pharaonis* (Dream of the Pharaoh) by John of Limoges and the *Summa* of Henricus de Isernia.[93] This dated copy was made during Dybinus's lifetime, and it may—or may not—be a record of his own delivery of the commentary.[94] As we saw above, the colophon to the manuscript identifies this version as taken down by Johannes de Montabaur.[95] The same scribe also recorded Dybinus's commentary on the *Laborintus* in the manuscript, while a different scribe earlier took down the long fragment of Dybinus's *Declaracio* (Commentary) on his own *Oracio de beata Dorothea*.[96] Each of the commentaries in this manuscript

---

90. The title *Declaracio Oracionis de beata Dorothea* can refer to any of three texts: what Jaffe calls the *Declaracio (minor) Oracionis de beata Dorothea* (also known as the *Colores retoricales*) as well as two versions of what he calls the *Declaracio (maior) Oracionis de beata Dorothea* (Jaffe, *Declaracio*, 29–31, 274, 281–93). See also Szklenar, *Magister Nicolaus*, 40–41 and 119–128. Much of the sorting out of the manuscripts of Dybinus's commentary on the *Poetria nova* has been done by Hans Szklenar (*Magister Nicolaus*, 100–110), with some corrections suggested by Dilwyn Knox (*Ironia*, 191). Several additional manuscripts are included in this study. The knot of relationships among manuscripts is indicated by the various groups of manuscripts that contain the section of the *accessus* with either the primary or the secondary incipit, but not both; see the Manuscript List. Jaffe examines the problem of choosing among four early manuscripts of Dybinus's *Declaracio* and provides separate editions of two of them.

91. Powicke and Emden state about different manuscripts of the same university text, "Some give lectures as written *(scripta)* by the author, others give them as taken down by the hearer *(reportata)*" (Rashdall, *The Universities of Europe,* 1.490 and 496). See Hamesse, "Le vocabulaire de la transmission orale," on the difference between *reportata* and *dicta* versions of lectures taken down by a hearer. Also relevant, but focussing on the earlier and later period respectively, are Ward, "The *Catena* Commentaries," and Schmitt, "*Auctoritates, Repertorium, Dicta*."

92. Jaffe, *Declaracio*, 280; and Tomáš Klimek, e-mail correspondence, May 2008. On Prague, Národní Knihovna České Republiky, XII.B.12, fols. 1r–42r, see Truhlář, *Catalogus codicum manu scriptorum,* 2.177; Jaffe, *Declaracio*, 32–36, 279–281; Szklenar, *Magister Nicolaus*, 94–95, 107–8, 125, 200, 211–214 (on scribe), 247–48, 254–56, and 266; Knox, *Ironia*, 61 and 191; and Woods, "A Medieval Rhetoric."

93. These last two works are often found in university manuscripts; Henricus de Isernia is one of the founders of the rhetorical tradition in Bohemia.

94. As early as 1452, a Czech chronicler who had become a baccalaureate of the university in 1410 stated that Dybinus "had been at one time a member of the faculty at the University of Prague" (Jaffe, *Declaracio,* 50; see also Szklenar, "Hat Nicolaus de Dybin").

95. See note 88.

96. This copy of the *Declaracio* is also a *dicta* version, although unlike the others it is not explicitly

is in the same format; it is copied in two long columns, without the text, a sign of sophisticated attention to the work and often also of university provenance. Most of the manuscripts of Pace of Ferrara's commentary are in a similar format (plate 6), although we have no evidence that those were taken down as dictation (and some have errors caused by misreading).[97]

Although the commentaries in this manuscript appear to have been taken down officially, informally recorded versions called *reportationes* have been treated somewhat dismissively by scholars in general, especially when a written (*scripta*) version of the same commentary is available.[98] Even Jacqueline Hamesse, one of the most sympathetic scholars of medieval university *reportationes,* can sound apologetic about her insistence on their importance.[99] The textual reliability of informal *reportationes* was affected by many factors: professors who read too quickly or who provided only the first word or two of key citations; students who made so much noise that those taking down the lectures could not hear properly; or recorders who were "more interested in the ideas brought up during the lecture than by the exact words used by the professor."[100] Nevertheless, as Hamesse points out, *reportationes*

> are excellent testimonies, not just to the content of a course, but equally to the method of teaching. . . . Only they can give us an idea of the manner in which debates took place: speakers talking at the same time, those objecting interrupting the speech of someone who is talking, interventions on the part of the master to reestablish order or to underline important points.[101]

The rather staid atmosphere generated by the Prague manuscript identified in its colophon as "*dicta . . . reportata*" is in clear contrast to this lively scene. One reason for the more measured impression of Prague XII.B.12 and similar productions is that at central European universities officially dictated (*dicta*) versions of lectures served a more significant and hence regulated function. At Bologna, Padua, Vercelli, Perugia, Treviso, Florence, and Naples in Italy, and

---

identified as such in a colophon. It is one of the versions edited by Jaffe.

97. For the manuscripts of Pace's commentary, see "Pace of Ferrara" in chapter 3; for other manuscripts of Dybinus's commentary see under Prague, Národní Knihovna České Republiky, XII.B.12 in the Manuscript List.

98. An incompetent "reporting" job could have immediately disastrous consequences for a master's academic reputation, particularly in the disciplines of philosophy and theology. In these disciplines, where "the goal . . . was not to remain faithful to the oral performance but to prepare a definitive text, approved by the author and university or religious authority, on which the author's reputation as theologian would rest," the *reportatio* was considered "the author's working draft of his afterthoughts" (Courtenay, "Programs," 344). The grammar and rhetoric courses in which the *Poetria nova* and related texts were studied were a different case, and such works—at least initially—were not a source of controversy.

99. See Hamesse, "La technique de la reportation," and also "L'importance de l'étude d'Aristote."

100. Hamesse, "La technique de la reportation," 408, 410–12, and 404.

101. Hamesse, "La technique de la reportation," 420; my translation. For comparisons of various reportationes of an Italian commentary on Virgil's *Eclogues,* see Lord, "Benvenuto da Imola's Literary Approach."

at Salamanca, Paris, Toulouse, and Oxford, where the *pecia* system of copying official versions of texts was in place, sections (*pecie*) of officially sanctioned versions of required texts were rented out to students to be copied by themselves or by professional scribes.[102] This system was not really put into place in central Europe, perhaps because it had come to an end in western Europe north of the Alps by the time the central European universities were refounded (though it continued longer in Italy).[103] As Mariken Teeuwen points out, "Students were generally required to have their own copies of the curricular texts, but were not always able to afford them. . . . [A]t the universities of central and eastern Europe . . . masters were required to dictate their core texts before the courses started, so that each student could make his own copy."[104] In Prague XII.B.12 (MS D below), however, it is not the text of the *Poetria nova* that has been officially dictated but rather the commentary on it by Dybinus of Prague.[105] The *Poetria nova* is embedded, but only in paraphrase or with glosses. In the 1367 statutes of Prague the *magistri* are authorized to deliver their *dicta* on required books or have them delivered by someone else.[106] (It is possible that students had copies of the text in front of them, onto which they would take down the dictated commentary in a different format.[107]) The most distinctive feature of the *dicta* in Prague XII.B.12 is the double-column, commentary-only format, with large *lemmata* that identify the first words of the section being commented on (plate 9). The incipit of the commentary is the first phrase in large script, while the other phrases in large script are *lemmata* that introduce the passage of the *Poetria nova* that is the subject of that section of commentary. Usually such *lemmata* were filled in later, after the end of the lectures, but sometimes this step was not completed and the spaces for them are blank.

There is a very different and unfortunately incomplete version of Dybinus's commentary written in the margins around the *Poetria nova* in a manuscript copied by Johannes Černý, probably also at Prague, only fourteen years later,

---

102. The most recent treatment of the *pecia* system, and one which includes material from the widest geographical area, is Murano, *Opere diffuse per exemplar*. The standard study is Destrez, *La pecia*; see also Pollard, "The *Pecia* System," and Teeuwen, *Vocabulary of Intellectual Life*, 187–189.

103. Pollard, "The *Pecia* system," 454–455. Pollard's correction of Destrez's suggestion that the system continued until printing began is particularly useful here. Murano does include a list of exemplaria from Olomouc dated approximately 1260 (with no rhetorical texts), 68–70.

104. Teeuwen, *Vocabulary of Intellectual Life*, 253. See also Hamesse, "Approche terminologique," esp. 26. For other evidence of dictation in school/university texts in central Europe, see Bodemann and Kretzschmar, "Textüberlieferung und Handschriftengebrauch," 261.

105. Recall that Třiška lists a commentary on the *Poetria nova* rather than the text itself as the required work in the fifteenth century; see above, "The *Poetria nova* at Prague." Sometimes there may also be a separate copy of the core text copied in the same manuscript.

106. "quivis magistrorum poterit super quolibet libro de facultate artium propria dicta dare per se vel per alium pronuntiare . . ." (*Monumenta historica universitatis Carolo-Ferdinandeae*, cited in Hamesse, "Le vocabulaire de la transmission orale," 184; see also Rashdall, *Universities of Europe*, 2.224).

107. See, however, Saenger, "Silent Reading," 394; and Pollard, "The *Pecia* System," 150.

in 1489: Prague, Národní Knihovna České Republiky, VIII.H.22 (plate 10). This manuscript includes form letters, formularies, *De disciplina scolarium,* and the *Achilleid* of Statius with partial commentary.[108] The Dybinus commentary appears to be a *scripta* version (a written production copied from another manuscript rather than taken down by dictation). The text of the *Poetria nova* was written out completely first. The *accessus* and interlinear and marginal glosses were copied afterwards.[109] The marginal notes, which are written on one side or at the bottom of the text, are at times out of order, perhaps copied from a manuscript in which they were written alternately on either side of the text.[110] The text is complete in almost fifty folios; the interlinear commentary continues for more than twenty folios, the marginal commentary for less than half that. Thus, in contrast to the integrated treatment of the text that we shall see in the *dicta* version, in the *scripta* version the interlinear glosses may have been copied separately from the marginal ones. The text and marginal glosses are not copied in the more hurried cursive script typical of student productions, although some of the interlinear ones are.[111] The *scripta* version has survived in only this one manuscript, whereas the official *dicta* version of the commentary is extant in five, but not all are in the same format.[112]

SCRIPTA VS. DICTA IN PRACTICE

> Friend, ascend higher.[113]
>
> —biblical *thema* {Luke 14:10} used by Dybinus of Prague

Dybinus's *accessus* to the *Poetria nova* is organized around a biblical quotation, called a *thema;* this technique was adopted from university sermons that originated in Paris, and it was carried to central Europe along with other academic

---

108. "Explicit *Nowa poetria* per manus Iohannis dicti niger Finita . . . Sub anno domini M°CCC° octuagesimo viiii°" (Prague, Národní Knihovna České Republiky, VIII.H.22, fol. 93r). On this manuscript see Truhlář, *Catalogus codicum manu scriptorum,* 1.607–8; Doskočil, *Mistr Dybin,* 6; Szklenar, *Magister Nicolaus,* 61, 106–107, and 197–198; Tříška, *Literární Činnost Předhusitké University,* 34 and 38–39; and Polak, *Eastern Europe.* Some of the glosses in this manuscript of the *Achilleid* are quoted in Woods, "Rape and the Pedagogical Rhetoric."

109. Several folios were left blank for the *accessus,* but not all were used.

110. The first and third paragraphs at the bottom of plate 10 refer to the first set of five and a half lines; the one in between and those to the right of the text refer to later lines.

111. See Blair, *"Ovidius Methodizatus,"* on the use of cursive later at the Sorbonne for glosses written in haste (77), and compare the interlinear vs. the marginal notes in the manuscripts of Schedel and Tegernpeck (plates 12 and 13).

112. Also in Gdansk, Biblioteka Gdańska Polskiej Akademii Nauk, Mar. Q.9; Krakow, Biblioteka Jagiellońska, 2141; Vienna, Österreichische Nationalbibliothek, 3251; and Vienna, Schottenkloster, 399.

113. "Amice, ascende superius" (Prague, Národní Knihovna České Republiky, VIII.H.22, fol. 26r; XII. B.12, fol. 1r, et al.).

innovations.[114] For the *Poetria nova* Dybinus chose one tailor-made for students entering an institution of higher education: "Friend, ascend higher" (Luke 14:10).[115] That the phrase alliterates in Latin (*Amice, ascende superius*) doubtless added to its appeal, and I have substituted rhyme to approximate the same effect. Each of the two versions of Dybinus's commentary on the *Poetria nova*, which revolves around this quotation, is valuable for different reasons. The *dicta* version records actual practice in the classroom, complete with additions and also significant *lacunae,* while the *scripta* version would not have been altered by external circumstances, although sections of commentary seem to have been rearranged, perhaps to fit into available space. Yet despite the substantial differences between them—these would be most evident at the beginning[116]—they are versions of the same commentary.

The lecturer whose words are recorded in the *dicta* version (MS D on the right in the columns below) begins by looking at the meaning of the *thema* as a whole in terms of its implications for the study of rhetoric in general. He cites various authorities to show how the *thema* evokes the connections between rhetoric and the highest human endeavors and rewards. This version is fuller in expression and consistently more elaborate, although either the lecturer or the scribe is also prone to lapses. The *dicta* version of a different commentary by Dybinus in the same manuscript has been described by Samuel Jaffee as "prolix" and exhibiting "a kind of verbal 'overkill' in terms of providing alternatives and additional bits of interesting information," especially at the beginning,[117] a description that fits the *dicta* version of the commentary on the *Poetria nova* as well.[118] The position of such additions at the inception may indicate that the lecturer—whether Dybinus or not—is making an effort to catch the attention of his audience during the first days of the course. If so, then more abstract and theoretical contextualizing of the text and additional citations of famous authors were considered especially enticing to students (and perhaps impressive to a professor's colleagues if they also attended).[119]

---

114. Jaffe, *Declaracio,* 44–45. See also "Sermons" in chapter 2.

115. The original context of Luke 14:10 (a parable about seating arrangements and status at table) would also have resonated, somewhat crudely, with Dybinus's emphasis later on social advancement: "But when thou art invited, go, sit down in the lowest place; that when he who invited thee cometh, he may say to thee: Friend, go up higher. Then shalt thou have glory before them that sit at table with thee."

116. The *scripta* version in Prague VIII.H.22 is incomplete. Since Jaffe has noted that the written and dictated versions of Dybinus's *Declaracio* differ most at the beginning, however, presumably we have the section that offers the greatest contrast.

117. Jaffe, *Declaracio,* 34; see also the preceding note.

118. There are also similarities in tone and, if not in exact wording, at least in scholarly register in the *dicta* versions of Dybinus's *Declaratio* on the *Oracio* and his commentary on the *Poetria nova* in Prague XII.B.12. If both were delivered by the same person, he had a standard approach to in-class treatments of rhetorical texts, an aspect of pedagogical efficiency not unknown today.

119. It was recommended that in sermons based on scriptural passages, on which this kind of academic lecture was modeled, "the preacher should confirm every member of a [sub]division with an authority, 'lest it should appear that in dividing he has invented [*finxisse*] the members'" (D'Avray, *Preaching of the Friars,* 194, citing Richard of Thetford's *ars praedicandi* from Oxford, Bodleian Library, Bodley 848, fol. 6va). That

The *accessus* of the *scripta* version (MS S on the left), presumably copied from another manuscript rather than taken down by dictation, joins in afterwards, where both versions of the commentary show how each word of the *thema* is associated with a different use of rhetoric ("Friend" to intimate friendship, "ascend" to ambition, "higher" to honor and renown) and with citations to support the associations. Part of this material is virtually identical in both manuscripts. Finally, classical authorities are then adduced to support this praise of rhetoric. Here again the *dicta* version (MS D on the right) quotes longer citations and identifies them more specifically, although the actual words of quotations tend to be more garbled in this manuscript.[120] The discussion of the art of rhetoric in general ends here.[121]

To recapitulate and anticipate: the *dicta* version of MS D on the right, recorded during actual lectures, is generally longer and fuller. In this recorded live performance, the lecturer adds more citations of authorities and notes on the text. In the *scripta* version in MS S on the left, there is more summary (rather than elaboration), more coherence in general, and a clearer arrangement.[122]

---

is, the act of division is an act of discovery, not of creation, on the part of the commentator.

120. Jaffe notes two additional differences not in the versions of the *PN* commentary: "variation in scriptural motto (*thema*)"—in the *dicta* version of the commentary on the *Poetria nova* the variation is not in the motto but in the way it is first introduced—and a different form of logical proof (*Declaracio,* 34–35).

121. In a fifteenth-century manuscript of the *Poetria nova* with a related commentary, this first part of Dybinus's *accessus* [version on the right] introduces a different rhetorical text; see Vienna, Schottenkloster, 399, fol. 86v ff.

122. MS S, in the column on the left, begins two folios before the portion reproduced in plate 10. The *accessus* in this manuscript (Prague VIII.H.22) was edited by Karel Doskočil in 1948 (*Mistr Dybin,* 89–91). Manuscript D on the right begins at the top of the left-hand column in plate 9. Note what appears to be an error in the numbering of the chapter of Luke in both versions.

ACCESSUS: INTRODUCTION OF THE THEMA
[LATIN TRANSCRIPTION IN APPENDIX I]

[MS S, *scripta* version]

FRIEND, ASCEND HIGHER. THESE
WORDS are written in the fourth *[sic]*
chapter of the evangelist Luke {14:10},

in which words the generosity of rhetoric
and her lofty stature can be praised:

first as the perfect rhetoric of friends, and
this is implied at **Friend**; second as the influential rhetoric of patronage, and this is
implied at **ascend**; third as the redounding

[MS D, *dicta* version, plate 9] FRIEND,
ASCEND HIGHER IS WRITTEN IN THE
FOURTH [sic] CHAPTER OF LUKE. PHIL-
OSOPHICAL ETC.

Friend, ascend higher is written in the
fourth *[sic]* chapter of Luke {14.10}.[123]
Philosophical knowledge elevates anyone
living in accordance with reason, and philosophy, empress of the sciences and mistress
over higher things, is revealed to the worthy
according to Tully {cf. *Inv.* 1.1} and Seneca.[124] It joins man to the God of the heavens and thus renders man an equal (*parem*),
fittingly offering the words of the aforementioned theme to him, saying **Friend, ascend
higher.** When rhetoric, both queen of the
sciences and most noble, [is] then preparing
letters of delights for whoever is her dis-
ciple, he is invited by that greeting of sweet
speech; she recites the words of the aforementioned theme, a shared consolation of
promise, saying, **Friend, ascend higher.** And
these words are written in the fourteenth
chapter of the evangelist Luke.

With these words it is permitted that the
generosity of rhetoric and her lofty stature
be praised from many perspectives, yet right
now she can be praised for her profitability
in three ways:

first as the perfect rhetoric of love, and this
is implied at **Friend**; second as the influential rhetoric of patronage, and this
is implied at **ascend**; third as the redound-

---

123. The *dicta* version on the right states the thema twice (complete with error). The first is the repetition:
the scribe who went through after the dictation in order to put in the lemmata identifying the subject of
each lecture in large script simply recopied the first words of the commentary again into the space left above
them for the introductory rubric and initial, as can be seen at the top of the left-hand column in plate 9.

124. I have been unable to identify a number of the citations in Dybinus's commentary.

rhetoric of prestige, and with this he brings the theme to a close at **higher**. For at first rhetoric is praised for its mellifluous manner of address when **Friend** is said. Second it is approved of for its sweet advancement when **ascend** is added; third it is recommended for the reward of that same most noble knowledge when **higher** is said.

Concerning the **first word** [Friend], Boethius says, "A friend is the most noble, most precious kind of riches" {cf. *Cons.* II. pr. 4}.

Seneca says, therefore, "talk everything over with a friend" {*Ep.* 3.2}. Likewise the Philosopher: "Friendship is mutual goodwill" {*Auct. Aris.* 242 (142)}, which goodwill the most noble Queen Rhetoric gives in abundance to her disciples and friends, teaching them to speak well and with art.

ing rhetoric of prestige, and this is brought to a close at **higher**. For at first rhetoric is praised for its mellifluous manner of address since **Friend** is said. Second, it is approved of for its sweet advancement when **ascend** is added; third it is noted in the reward of that same most noble knowledge when **higher** is said.

Concerning the **first word** [Friend], Boethius says in the second book of the *Consolation of Philosophy*, "A friend is the most precious kind of riches" {cf. II. pr. 4}. And Seneca says in one of his letters, therefore, "talk everything over with a friend" {3.2}, which the Philosopher confirms, saying "Friendship is mutual goodwill not taking refuge in limitations" {*Auct. Aris.* 242 (142)}, which goodwill the most noble Queen Rhetoric gives to her disciples and friends in abundance.

For she teaches man not just to speak but to speak well and artfully, which is widely (*maxime*) considered the preeminent noble characteristic of man and integrally (*maxime*) bound up with friendship. And, therefore, Tully says, "I have found the spirit I have sought, certifying that it teaches [one] to speak" {*Inv.* 1.3}. For as the Philosopher asserts in the fourth book of the *Ethics,* "It is through speech that a man is judged. What kind of person says and does such things?" {cf. 4.7(1127a)}. And, therefore, Seneca says in the book *On morals,* "Have recourse to your ear more frequently than to your tongue," if you wish the friendship of others {*Proverbia Senecae* [=*De moribus*] 104}. Rhetoric knows and dispenses this advice to her friends and disciples. He [Seneca] adds, "One who does not know how to be silent does not know how to speak" {*Proverbia Senecae* 132}.

Concerning the **second word** [ascend] Aristotle says in the ninth book of the *Ethics,* "A friend ought to conduct himself toward a friend as he would toward himself, because a friend is one's other self" {*Auct. Aris.* 245 (177)}, and he adds, "We ought to bestow greater good on friends than on strangers" {*Auct. Aris.* 245 (175)}, which goods most generous Rhetoric indeed favorably bestows on her friends. For "Rhetoric is a persuader of justice, a companion of truth, a fugitive from falsehood and evils" {*Auct. Aris.* 263 (5)}, which [goods] greatly influence advancement, and, therefore, **ascend** is added.

Concerning **the third word** [higher], the Philosopher says in the second book of the *Politics,* "It is impossible for baseness to philosophize" {cf. *Auct. Aris.* 255 (48)}. Therefore, whoever has little ought to cling to this most noble knowledge with burning love and desire. Thus, rhetoric is well described as the amassing of prestige. For Horace says in the *Old Poetria,* "Rhetoric herself expands the most copious faculty of expression and even drives the pauper out of the dust of poverty and directs [him] toward the honors of the most powerful faculty."

Therefore, it is brought to a close with the word **higher,** since thereby this most excellent knowledge, namely rhetoric herself, teaching all men to speak fluently and artfully, raises paupers to higher honors.

The most noble Queen Rhetoric creates abundant eloquence in us, and therefore **ascend** is well said.

Concerning the **second word** [ascend] Aristotle says in the ninth book of the *Ethics,* "A friend ought to conduct himself toward a friend as he would toward himself because a friend is one's other self" {*Auct. Aris.* 245 (117)} and he adds, "We ought to bestow greater good on friends than on strangers" {*Auct. Aris.* 245 (175)}, which goods most generous Rhetoric indeed favorably bestows on her friends. For according to the teaching of Aristotle in the first book of the *Rhetoric,* "Rhetoric itself is a persuader of justice, a recognizer of truth, and a fugitive from evil" {cf. *Auct. Aris.* 263 (5)} which [goods] greatly influence advancement, and, therefore, **ascend** is added.

Concerning the **third word** [higher], the Philosopher says in the second book of the *Politics,* "It is impossible for a needy man[125] to philosophize" {cf. *Auct. Aris.* 255 (48)}. Therefore, whoever has little ought to cling to this most noble knowledge with burning love and burning desire. Thus, rhetoric is well described as the amassing of prestige. For, as Horace says in the *Old Poetria,* "Rhetoric herself expands all kinds of eloquence and the most copious faculty of expression, and she drives the pauper out of the ashes of poverty to higher things and directs [him] toward the honors of the most powerful faculty."

And therefore the theme (*littera*) concludes[126] with **higher.**

---

125. Manuscript D's reading of "indigentem" is an error for "indignitatem" (as in MS S); it contradicts the lesson expounded immediately afterward; see Appendix II.

126. The second column on plate 9 begins here.

Now Dybinus turns to the *Poetria nova* itself. The transition in MS S on the left is generic. The lecturer of the dictated version on the right, in contrast, specifically connects the *thema* to the *Poetria nova*. He also refers to his lectures as a *declaratio* (interpretation), the same term that is used in the title of Dybinus's commentary on his *Oracio de beata Dorothea* and that Pace of Ferrara employed (in the plural) for his commentary on the *Poetria nova*. It implies an extended, thorough treatment.[127]

ACCESSUS, CONT.:

TWO VERSIONS OF THE TRANSITION TO THE *POETRIA NOVA*

[MS S]	[MS D]
Likewise, at the beginning of the commentary, this book on rhetoric is to be approached diligently in terms of what we ask of any book.	Thus, such munificent and noble rhetoric should be sought before all other branches of knowledge effortlessly (*sine opere*) and with the most perfect desire of love.
	Since, therefore, the book of the *Poetria nova* of exalted and subtle rhetoric is the one whose interpretation (*declaracio*)[128] we intend to comment on here because of the worth of its teaching, it must be emphasized that, after the contents of such a fundamental book of rhetoric are acquired, what is written in the theme analyzed earlier can be said to any of us: **Friend, ascend higher,** etc.

Next Dybinus introduces the *causae,* most importantly the four Aristotelian *causae* that were part of the standard late medieval *accessus.* Here for the first time the *scripta* version in MS S on the left is fuller. Before turning to the four Aristotelian causes, MS S begins with a discussion not found in MS D of the general *causa* (reason) for undertaking the work. The lecturer in MS D on the right, while he mentions the four Aristotelian causes, is recorded as treating only the efficient cause, the author (perhaps because the scribe is falling behind).[129] In discussing the fourth and final cause, MS S on the left mentions both the immediate acquisition of a branch of knowledge and the future application of such knowledge: the ability to "communicate with kings and princes and

---

127. See Teeuwen, *Vocabulary of Intellectual Life,* 245; and Hamesse, "Approche terminologique," 11–12 and 14–19.

128. See Hamesse: "*declarare* nécessite une explication, un commentaire" ("Le vocabulaire de la transmission orale," 186).

129. The later manuscripts of this version retain the same omissions, however.

nobles." He is bringing in here the theme of the political usefulness of rhetoric introduced in MS D earlier in the rather mercenary interpretations of the biblical *thema* with which its version of the *accessus* begins. Thus, in both versions the overlapping attractions of ambition and practical knowledge bring the student to the *Poetria nova* with expectations of achieving advancement by following its teachings, a point also addressed in the transitional note at the end of MS D's discussion just above.

ACCESSUS, CONT.: THE CAUSES

[MS S]

First the **reason (***causa***) for undertaking the work** must be understood, next the [Aristotelian] **causes** of the work.

The **reason for undertaking this work** is twofold, the first general and the second specific. The general reason is its usefulness for all wishing to express themselves (*loqui*) artfully, which is why Master Geoffrey, the best rhetorician, wrote this book. But the specific reason was to capture the goodwill of Pope Innocent III in order to obtain grace and absolution for King Richard of England, who incurred excommunication and the anger of the lord pope (*domini pape*). Thus, after his death he [Richard] was denied burial, and his high clerk [Geoffrey] turned to writing this book in order to obtain absolution and favor for his lord. At the beginning of this book he commends the pope in many ways and at the end he petitions on behalf of his lord, saying "I plead for our prince" (2096–97).

But according to some [commentators] the material cause [subject] of the book is poetic art considered as a whole, not focussing on any particular part. According to others, however, the material cause of this book is the artful mode of expression, in itself and in its parts, examined under the very excellent (*melioribus*) colors of rhetoric.

[MS D]

We should see to the **causes** of this book just as with other books.

The **efficient cause** is *magister* Gamfredus in his own voice, who at the urging of King Richard produced this book.

The **final cause** [purpose] is twofold, namely the long-term (*remota*) and the immediate (*propinqua*). The long-term final cause is so that, when we have taken in and learned what this book contains, we can communicate with kings and princes and nobles. The immediate cause is so that, when this book is learned, we possess the rhetorical mode of expression.

But the **formal cause** is twofold, namely the form of the treatise and the form of the treatment. The form of the treatise consists in the division of the book [into parts]. The form of the treatment is the method of proceeding, and that is in verse, as is clear.

The **efficient cause** was Gamfredus, a very eloquent man well taught in the art of rhetoric, and notary of the King of England, which will become clear in the course of things.

The text follows: "O Holy Father, wonder of the world" (1).

A difference in conception of what follows, the *divisio textus* or division and subdivision of the *Poetria nova* into parts, is implied by the formatting of the two manuscripts. MS S on the left treats this next section as a direct continuation of the *accessus,* whose end is signaled by a blank folio before the beginning of the text reproduced in plate 10. The *accessus* of MS D on the right, however, has just concluded with the standard *explicit* introducing the first lines of the *Poetria nova* itself; the division of the text is formatted as a separate lecture signaled by the introductory *lemma* of the first words of the *Poetria nova, PAPA STUPOR MUNDI, SI,* written in the display script near the top of the second column (plate 9).

The *divisio* of the *Poetria nova,* the defining aspect of scholastic treatment of a work, is initiated by a discussion of rhetoric as both an art and a kind of knowledge, corresponding to the double structure of the *Poetria nova* as a kind of knowledge (the five parts of rhetoric) and an instrument of the art (the six parts of a rhetorical discourse), a concept with which we are already familiar. The division of the *Poetria nova* into the parts of the art of rhetoric functions as a secondary *accessus* or introduction.[130] Via different routes and at a different

---

130. In another manuscript of the *dicta* version it constitutes the entire *accessus:* Munich, Bayerische Staatsbibliothek, Clm 18780.

pace, each manuscript will introduce much of the same material. MS S on the left continues its emphasis on doubleness, e.g., rhetoric is a kind of knowledge that stays in the mind as well as an art applied outside the mind to create a discourse. In MS D on the right, in contrast and as before, doctrine is reinforced via repetition. In keeping with his penchant for quoting sources the lecturer of MS D begins with a summary definition of rhetoric that summarizes its five aspects (e.g., "to devise material," "to organize appropriately," etc.), which is then elaborated in what he calls the five "responsibilities" (*officia*) of rhetoric, summarized a third time in a little poem. Then these responsibilities are identified as the subject of the *Poetria nova*, which is divided accordingly into five "chapters or tracts" (*capitula sive tractatus*), in each of which Geoffrey teaches the appropriate skill.

SECONDARY *ACCESSUS:* THE PARTS OF THE ART OF RHETORIC[131]

[MS S, continuation of the above]

But before we divide the book into parts, it should be said that rhetoric can be considered two ways: in one way as an art, in the other as a kind of knowledge. And while it is true that rhetoric can be considered both a kind of knowledge and an art, as if these were the same thing, nevertheless they differ. Rhetoric is a kind of knowledge to the extent that it consists of subordinate principles and effects and stays in the mind (*anima*); rhetoric is an art, however, to the extent that its principles are applied outside the mind to [the creation of] a work. And according to this double approach, rhetoric and the knowledge of this book receive a twofold structure through the medium of a kind of knowledge and the medium of an art.

Rhetoric as a branch of knowledge is divided into **five parts** (*partes*), which are Invention,

[MS D, new section]
1 O HOLY FATHER, WONDER OF THE WORLD, IF, ETC.
Before dealing with the division of the text, first we should see what rhetoric is. For rhetoric is defined as follows according to Tully and Guido [Faba]'s purpose (*intentio*): "Rhetoric is the science that teaches how to develop the topics of anything persuadable, to organize appropriately the particulars of that subject, to adorn the same with appropriate words and thoughts, and afterwards to commit it appropriately to the memory and to present, express, and declaim [it]."

From this description or definition are chosen the **five responsibilities** (*officia*) of

---

131. Szklenar (e.g., *Magister Nicolaus,* 106 and 107) identifies this next section as "Anfang des Kommentars" (beginning of the commentary), while the incipit of the *accessus* he calls "Anfang der Einleitung" (beginning of the introduction).

Disposition second, Style, Memory, and Delivery. Invention, which is the first part, begins at "If one has a house" (42); Disposition is touched on at "Order follows two paths" (87); Style at "For the opening of the poem . . . a variety of paths" (203).[132] Memory, which is the fourth part, is touched on at "All that reason invents" (1969), Delivery at "In reciting aloud" (2031).

rhetoric. The first is the Invention [development] of the subject matter; second the Arrangement of the developed material; third, the ornamented Arrangement of the developed material (or the third can be its ornamented and fitting expression); fourth, committing the material to memory; fifth, the appropriate delivery of the developed, well-organized, ornamented, memorized material. And the five responsibilities are summarized in these verses[133]:

> The rhetor finds and arranges,
> He decorates and memorizes.
> And afterwards he delivers
> Everything correctly.[134]

And the present book, whose subject is the artful method of persuading something, is divided into five chapters or tracts according to these duties. In the first he teaches how the rhetor ought to develop (*invenire*) the subject matter. In the second he teaches how the developed material ought to be organized. In the third, how the developed and arranged material and ornamented material ought to be committed to memory.[135] In the fourth how the developed and arranged material should be ornamented. In the fifth and last, how the developed, organized, and ornamented material should be delivered as required.

The second tract begins at "The material's order may follow two separate paths" (87), the third at "Whether it be brief or long"

---

132. According to Doskočil's outline (and most commentaries), the section on style begins at line 737, but the lemma quoted belongs to the earlier section, normally considered the second part of the book on arrangement (*Mistr Dybin,* 88).

133. The verses are noted in the margin. In another manuscript of this version, Vienna, Österreichische Nationalbibliothek, 3251, fol. 112r, they are outlined so that they stand out very clearly.

134. Not in Walther.

135. The scribe (or the lecturer he is recording) puts the description of the fourth under the third and vice versa. Memory is misnumbered, which leads to various omissions.

> (737),[136] the fourth at "If you wish to
> remember all that reason invents"
> (1969), and the last at "In reciting aloud"
> (2031).

At this point the lecturer in MS D on the right digresses to discuss judicial and epideictic rhetoric. The latter, the rhetoric of praise, is the subject of the *Poetria nova* according to this lecturer. In epideictic rhetoric, the work is "adorned" (rhetorically elaborated) for a specific person, here the pope. Thus, "specific adornments are required," which takes him back to the aforementioned rhetorical *officia*.

DIGRESSION ON JUDICIAL AND EPIDEICTIC RHETORIC [MS D]

Note that according to Aristotle and Tully's formulation, rhetoric is twofold: judicial and epideictic {*Rhet.* 1.3 (1358b); *Ad Her.* 1.2}. Judicial rhetoric is what persuades and teaches what is honest and what is dishonest, what is just and what is unjust, what is permitted or forbidden. Concerning this kind of rhetoric Tully speaks fully in his four-book treatise [*Rhetorica ad Herennium*], and Aristotle treats it in his three-book treatise [the *Rhetoric*]. And he [Aristotle] says in the beginning of the *Ethics,* "This follows logically; one wishes that just as through logic something is demonstrated commendably according to probability, so through demonstrative [i.e., judicial] rhetoric what is just or unjust is demonstrated to someone" {cf. *Eth.* 5.6}. Therefore, Aristotle adds subsequently, "Rhetoric teaches one to accomplish and persuade what is just, to recognize what is true, and to flee the opposite of the good" {cf. *Rhet.* 1.1}. In the book before us there is nothing on judicial rhetoric, only epideictic, which thus focuses on the praise- or blameworthy, since Aristotle says in the first book of his *Rhetoric,* "All poetic rhetoric is either praise or blame" {cf. *Rhet.* 1.3 (1358b)}.[137] Such praise or blame consists in epideictic speech alone. And since it is [the duty] of the rhetorician himself to please men through speech, such speech should be adorned, for which adornment the aforementioned responsibilities of rhetoric, namely Invention, Arrangment, etc., are needed.

Then both versions take up the second structure of the *Poetria nova*: its division according to the six parts of the discourse, the instrument of the art of rhetoric.[138] MS S names them, while MS D on the right describes them in more

---

136. According to the two versions of the commentary, the third section occurs at different places: at the beginning of the discussion of amplification and abbreviation in the version on the left and later at the section on the Tropes and Figures in the version on the right.

137. Cf. Herman the German, "Translation of Averroes' 'Middle Commentary'" (i), in Minnis and Scott, *Medieval Literary Theory,* 289; see also chapter 3, note 98.

138. See "The Double Structure" in chapter 1.

detail, and then both identify where these occur in the *Poetria nova*. Then the *scripta* version in MS S on the left presents a series of subdivisions similar to but less detailed than Pace's in chapter 2. In MS D on the right, however, there is only a single cursory subdivision, which is followed instead by an elaboration of the "five kinds of praise." (These constitute an alternate division rather than a further subdivision.)

DIVISIONS OF THE TEXT

[MS S, continuation of *accessus*]
Rhetoric as an art is rooted in its **instrument.** The instrument of the art of rhetoric is a discourse having **six parts,** which are the (1) Exordium, (2) Narration, (3) Division, (4) Refutation, (5) Confirmation, and (6) Conclusion.

[MS D, beginning of commentary proper]
Note that all such responsibilities (*officia*) are carried out by means of **six instruments.** First in order is the Exhortation, second the Narration, third the Partition or Division, fourth the Refutation, fifth the Confirmation, sixth the Conclusion.

Note, as I have said, that the rhetorician should please others through his expression. It is necessary, therefore, *** that he capture the goodwill of his audience, and this is done through the Exhortation or through the Exordium, which is the first instrument of the rhetorician. Second, when the goodwill of the audience is captured, the rhetorician should present in a specific order what he wants the audience to hear, therefore according to the instrument called the Narration. Third, after the proposed discourse (*sermo*) has been narrated, he should focus his speech (*sermo*) on the reaction of the audience and focus in such a way that he immediately understands in the response given to him whether the response to him is appropriate or not for each part. Therefore, he employs Division: distinguishing the part of the discourse that is not effective for him from those parts that are effective for him. And thus he uses the third instrument which is called the Division. Fourth, when the Division is finished, the rhetorician gets rid of any part that is not effective for him by rejecting and refuting it, and thus he uses the fourth instrument, which is called the Refutation. Fifth, when the refuted and rejected part is no longer effective, he returns to the part that is effective for him by taking it up again and confirming it, and thus he uses the instrument called Confirmation. Sixth, when all these things are done, he concludes the proposition that he has addressed, and thus he uses the sixth instrument which is called the Conclusion. And these instruments are encapsulated in the following verses:[141]

> He embarks, narrates, divides, and then
> He refutes, confirms, closes.

A rhetorical discourse has these parts. And according to its **instruments** this book is divided into **six chapters** (1–6). In the first he wishes to categorize [lit.: determine][142] the Exordium and in the second the Narration, in the third the Division, in the fourth the Refutation, in the fifth the Confirmation, in the sixth the Conclusion. The second chapter begins at "If one has a house to build," etc. (42), the third at "The material's order may follow two possible courses" (87), the fourth at "You know what is fitting" (1588), the fifth at "It is, however, of primary importance" (1920),

The first part, the Exordium, starts at the beginning, namely at "O Holy Father, wonder" (1), but the Narration at "If one has a house to build (43). Division is the part at "Order follows two paths" (87), the Refutation at "You know what is fitting" (1588),[139] the Confirmation at "[It is of primary importance]" (1920),[140] and the Conclusion at "Now I have crossed the sea" (2066).

---

139. The reading in MS S, "est benedicta," is an unidentified tag.

140. This passage is usually interpreted as the beginning of the Refutation.

141. Cf. these verses in "Dominican Reiner von Cappel" in chapter 2, where they are translated differently.

142. See Fletcher, "Some Problems of Collecting Terms," on different meanings of the cognate "determinatio" at Oxford (and in central Europe) and for a general caution regarding too much reliance on statutes for "determining" the meaning of academic vocabulary; and also above, chapter 3, note 108.

the sixth and last at "Now I have crossed the sea" (2066).

According to the earlier division of the responsibilities of the rhetorician, the first tract [Invention] contains two chapters.[144] In the first he captures the goodwill of Pope Innocent, for whose favor he composed it by praising him in many ways. As in the Prologue, so in the Execution; that is, in the second chapter at "If one has a house," (42) etc., the author carries out the first duty of the rhetorician, namely Invention.

Note that the author, wishing to speak of many things, proceeds according to Aristotle's teaching in the third book of the *Rhetoric,* for it is said there, "If someone wishes to say several things, he preambles" {cf. 3.14 (1415a)}. And he says afterwards, "the Preamble is the speech (*sermo*) that goes first, preparing the mind of the hearer for what follows," and he adds, "There should be a Preamble in books like a Prelude in flute-music" {3.14 (1414b)}. Then as a conclusion Aristotle says, "The Preamble ought to render the listeners docile, well disposed, and attentive" {*Ad Her.* I.6; cf. Aris. *Rhet.* 3.14 (1415a)}. The author [of the *PN*] keeps this in mind by placing a Preamble at the beginning of his book according to the teaching of Aristotle, [and] by rendering the listeners first well disposed, second docile, third attentive.

Now a Preamble has **three** parts.

The first of these [the Introduction] is divided into **three** parts, for first [I.A] the author captures the goodwill of the pope, praising him in many ways; second [I.B] he renders his listeners docile; third [I.C] he renders them attentive.[143]

---

143. Doskočil does not include the subdivisions of the *Poetria nova* as a rhetorical discourse in his outline of the contents of the *accessus* of MS S (*Mistr Dybin,* 92).

144. The lecturer in MS D referred to "tractates" (*tractatus*) and "chapters" (*capitula*) above as if they were interchangeable, but we find out here that the five "tractates" are the sections corresponding to the five parts of rhetoric, while the chapters are subdivisions within them.

The second part begins at "Receive, great man" (41), the third at "vast in power" (42).

[Subdivision:]

First [I.A.i] he commends the pope for the magnitude of his virtues, then [I.A.ii] he makes entreaties, and the second part is there at "General light of this world" (33).

The first is [further sub]divided into **three:** first [I.A.i.a.] he commends the pope in terms of his name and the excellence of his person, second [I.A.i.b] in terms of the generosity of his cardinals; third [I.A.i.c] he commends him because of the nobility of his location. The second part is at "Your retinue—fit men" (28), the third at "To Rome as if to heaven" (31).

The second part begins there at "Receive, great man" (41), the third at "vast in power" (42).

Note that the author, wishing through the Preamble to capture the goodwill of the apostolic lord, praises him in many ways and, after [the pope's] goodwill has been captured, presents his petition.

Thus again the Preamble is divided into two. In the first part [I.A.i] he praises the pope, in the second [I.A.ii] he brings in his petition; the second is at "General light of the world" (33).

Note that the author, wishing to be both rhetorician and poet, uses an aspect of poetics called praise (*laudatio*), since according to Aristotle in the first and third books of the *Rhetoric,* "Praise is speech evoking the greatness of virtue" {1.9(1367b); cf. 3.14(1414b)}. From this he concludes that nothing except virtue is to be praised in a man, and, since virtue is manifold in men, therefore one can praise in many ways {cf. 1.9 (1368)}.

Someone can be praised in **five ways** [145]: first, for his good name, second, for the shape and proportion of his body, third for his eloquence, fourth for his power, fifth for his place of residence, and that is clear in these verses:

> Name along with shape, discernment in
>   words, power,
> And location are the pattern by which
>   I may praise. Get to know [this]
>   well! [146]

For any rhetorician can praise someone in terms of these five approaches and primar-

---

145. Bartholomew of Pisa also makes this comment, which is included in the rubrics and also the list of contents of his commentary in Rome, Biblioteca Casanatense, 311; see "The Usefulness of this Text" in chapter 1 and "The Subject Is Rhetoric" in chapter 3. Cf. Bernard of Bologna's *Summa dictaminum* on the five ways of securing the goodwill of the recipient of a letter (Camargo, "Pedagogy of the *Dictatores,*" 76).

146. This translation and the reading on which it is based (See Appendix II) were suggested by Martin Camargo.

ily in terms of his virtues. And the author gives us these in an exemplary way in his Preamble, by praising the pope first in terms of the loftiness of his name, second in terms of his precious body,[147] third in terms of the noble virtues of various men, fourth in terms of the fecundity of his eloquence, fifth in terms of his manifold prudence, sixth in terms of the variety of his powers, seventh in terms of the exaltedness of his place. Accordingly this Preamble serves many particulars, the second there at "In illustrious lineage" (10); the third at "One of your gifts remains" (13). And the other parts will become clear.

Now, at the end of its *accessus,* the *scripta* version in MS S on the left adds several "points to note" (*notabilia*) about the structure and importance of the five parts of rhetoric introduced much earlier.[148] These appear to have been added at this point simply because there were blank folios between the *accessus* and the text here in the manuscript.

ADDENDUM TO *ACCESSUS* [MS S]

Points to note: it very important in terms of this text to note what the **five parts of rhetoric** are, and first what Invention is. According to Tully, Invention is "the devising of true or varied or plausible ideas that render a case convincing" {*Ad Her.* 1.3}. Or thus: Invention is the necessary mental prefiguring of some chosen subject. Or, he invents correctly who devises true or plausible ideas so that his case may be rendered convincing. Thence "Arrangement is the ordering and distribution of parts, through which is shown the places through which each is to be assigned" {*Ad Her.* 1.3}. Whence he arranges correctly who places subjects in a specific order and allots them to places so that each is given a position. As the subject demands, so the rhetorical figure fully realizes. "Style is the thinking through of suitable words and time-honored thoughts [i.e., the figures of words and figures of thoughts]" {*Ad Her.* 1.3}. He also speaks correctly who provides suitable words so that the thought itself is made artful with words.

---

147. Cf. Paravicini-Bagliani, *The Pope's Body,* 194–196.
148. On *notabilia* in commentaries see Hamesse, "La technique de la reportation."

Now we turn to the words of the text itself. The lecturer of MS D introduces the first section of the *Poetria nova,* here five-and-a-half lines, by a prose paraphrase. Such paraphrasing is a very common introduction to *viva voce* treatment of a passage. It is followed first by notes on the passage and then by glosses on individual words. So typical is this pedagogical approach of beginning with a paraphrase that the treatment comprising these three steps is called the paraphrase commentary.[149]

PARAPHRASE OF FIRST SECTION OF TEXT [MS D]

> Therefore he says first, O Holy Father, you who are a wonder, that is, a surprise, if I give you the name of "Nocent," then your name will be acephalous, that is, deprived of a head. But if I were to add the beginning of the name by saying "Innocent," then your name cannot be included in the meter; so in the same way your great virtue is not commensurate (add: with anything in the nature of things) since there is nothing according to which that virtue can be measured, for it transcends the measures of men.

Notes on this passage follow in both manuscripts. MS S records just two, although the second note appears to be the first in a series that was left unfinished.[150] The lecturer in MS D on the right lists eight things to note about the first two lines (a discussion that continues past what is reproduced in plate 9, including etymologies, background information, definitions of rhetorical terms, distinctions among synonyms, and further references. As before, the version in MS D on the right is more prolix.

[MS S, 1st and 3rd note, below text, plate 10]

[MS D continues with list of notes]

Note concerning the text that, according to commentators (*expositores*), the first aspect addressed in the text is the instrument of the rhetorician, which is called the Exordium, which is described by Tully as follows: "The Exordium is a brief, lucid, and sophisticated (*curialis*) introductory speech preparing the mind of the hearer for what is to follow" {cf. *Inv.* 1.20}; that is, the Exordium is the first part of the discourse because it is suitable for directing the mind of the hearer toward what comes later. Hence according to Tully the Exordium has to have three

---

149.   See Grendler, *Universities,* 241, quoted in chapter 3, note 146.

150.   The second note at the bottom of the page on plate 10 refers to a different section.

things. The first is broad applicability in that it has to arise from general statements that contain nothing limited only to what is to be said later. The second is that the Exordium has to have appropriateness, and this appropriateness is nothing other than that the Exordium be formulated so that it suitably and realistically refers to what is to be said later, yet nevertheless fits into the category of general eloquence. Third, there has to be in the Exordium the ability to move [that is, persuade], and this is what makes the Exordium appropriate for what moves the mind of the listener sufficiently in the direction of what is said.

Note: taking Tully's point (*intencione*), the commentators want the following [terms] to mean the same thing although they are variations: Exordium, Proverb, Preamble, Capturing of Goodwill {cf. *Ad Her.* 1.6}, since they say that when a preliminary discourse at the beginning of a long discourse is general and appropriate (*aptus*) for directing the mind, then it is called an Exordium. But when the same discourse is specific and appropriate for directing the mind from further afield, then it is a Preamble. When the same discourse can be appropriated for and applied to teaching the things to be said, then it is called a Proverb. And when such a discourse proceeds via flattery, then it is called the Capturing of Goodwill, etc. Thus, it is correct that each means the same thing but from a different perspective.

Note second: taking Tully's point, the commentators want these terms to mean the same thing expressed in different words: Exordium, Proverb, Preamble, Capturing of Goodwill {cf. *Ad Her.* 1.6}. For when a preliminary discourse at the beginning of a long discourse is brief, general, and appropriate, such a beginning of the discourse is called an Exordium. But when it is a little further afield yet nevertheless still apt, then it is called a Prohemium, from *pros*, which means "first," and *emos*, "discourse," etc. But the same discourse or beginning can be an interpretation or confirmation of what is to be said, and then it is called a Proverb. Yet when such a discourse proceeds via flattery or mollifying, it is called the Capturing of Goodwill. And thus through all of these, although in different ways, the beginning of a discourse is indicated. If someone wishes greater differentiation and clarification among these aforementioned terms, he should look at the chapter on the Exordium in the *Viaticus dictandi* [another work by Dybinus].

Note first from the passage the name of the pope, who is called "Innocent," for which reason he [the author] praises him. Taken whole it cannot be put [in the meter], only when it is divided. Therefore, the author infers praise of the pope from it and the excellence of the praise inheres in it. With the pope having this name, as something divided it can be joined to the meter just as his excellence according to his qualities and diverse talents [when divided] can be equaled to a few others as he will say afterwards. Taken together [his excellence] is incompatible just as is his name taken all together.

Note third: the Preamble of this book, as if coaxing truth from the mind of the author, is better called a Capturing of Goodwill than an Exordium, since the author's Preamble proceeds via mollification or flattery, by means of which he praises the pope in various ways, wishing through this to capture his goodwill.

Note fourth: in terms of the intention of the whole book the efficient cause was Gamfred,[151] the notary of King Richard of England (who had died excommunicated by the pope, and therefore burial in church ground had been denied him). On his account Gamfred addressed himself to petitioning the Apostolic See for sympathy, praising him [the pope] in the beginning in many ways so that he could obtain what he asked for.

Note fifth: the author first praises the pope for the loftiness of his name since he was called "Innocent," and the power of the praise lies in this: just as the name of Innocent cannot be put whole into the meter without creating a defect, so the excellence of that pope taken whole is not measurable. And therefore he says in the text, "If I were to say Papa Nocent," for if he put "Nocent," it would make the name mean the opposite,[152] but if he says "Innocent" then the name cannot be put in the meter, since the first [syllable] is long and the next short and the third long, and such words cannot be put in the meter without defect. Therefore, he says in the text "it will be at odds with the meter" (3).

Note sixth: the text says *PAPA* (Holy Father), and this noun is translated by legal scholars as "protector," but by theologians as

---

151. The Efficient Cause was also discussed above in the *accessus*.
152. See "Off with His Head!" in chapter 1.

"father." It is derived from an exclamation of surprise, namely *pape* since in the beginning when Saint Peter was made pope and the name *papa* was given to him, then men, greatly surprised, created the word *pape* for themselves out of this exclamation of being surprised .

Note seventh: the text says WONDER [*STUPOR*] OF THE WORLD. *Stupor* is a verbal noun from the verb *stupeo, -es, -ere* (to stun), which is the same as *ammiro* (to surprise). Hence *stupor* is the same as surprise and can be interpreted two ways, either as "O Holy Father, you who are the wonder of the world," or as "O Holy Father, if I were to say 'Nocent, ' (add: then he will be) the *stupor,* that is the terror, of the world.

Note eighth: the text says (2) AN ACEPH-ALOUS NAME: *acephalus* is an adjective of the second declension formed from the Greek word *cephas,* which is "head" in Latin, and we call something acephalous which is lacking the beginning, just as a man is called acephalous who is deprived of his head, and from this comes the verb "to acephalate," which means to deprive of a head or a beginning.

Dybinus concludes with glosses on the individual words in these lines, and this glossing is presented very differently in the two manuscripts. In MS S on the left, they are copied interlinearly above the lines of text (plate 10).[153] The lecturer of the *dicta* version in MS D on the right, in contrast, alternates word with gloss, reproducing in linear fashion what is indicated spatially in the manuscript on the left.[154] Yet although the visual format of text and gloss is very different in the two manuscripts, to a student *listening* they would sound very similar, since so many of the glosses are the same in both manuscripts.[155]

---

153. The remaining marginal glosses in MS S reproduced in plate 10 do not refer to the first five and a half lines and are not included here.

154. In MS D the second half of line three is condensed with the first half of line four, and some of the words are rearranged in prose order.

155. On students listening to the Poetria nova, see note 194 below.

At the end MS D indicates that the next passage to be lectured on will begin with the new sentence starting in the second half of line 5: "But divide the name."

DYBINUS: "INTERLINEAR" GLOSSES ON *PN* 1–6

[MS S, text with interlinear glosses, plate 10]

o outstanding surprise   whole I Geoffrey

Holy Father, wonder of the world, If I were

    to say about thus

        to say Pope Nocent,

I shall give   lacking one [syllable]

I attribute to you an acephalous name,

      that is, adjoin the beginning

    but if I add   the head,

(add:) your   unfriendly to the verse

Name will be an enemy to the meter. That

        to be made equal to

      name seeks to resemble you:

              excellence

Neither your name nor your great virtue

    wishes

to be contained in the meter that is, there is

To be shackled by measure. There is

        we might   your

  no such thing   measure   name

    nothing by which I might delimit it.

your virtue   of mortal

  exceeds   beings you

It transcends the measures of men. But

    cut apart   of Innocent

    divide the name . . .

[MS D, text alternating with glosses]

IF I WERE TO SAY The text: O, HOLY FATHER you who are the WONDER OF THE WORLD that is, the surprise of all humanity, I ATTRIBUTE TO YOU AN ACEPHALOUS NAME that is, one without the beginning IF I WERE TO SAY POPE NOCENT. BUT IF I ADD that is, if I put on THE HEAD that is, the beginning, (add: your) NAME WILL BE AN ENEMY that is, something contrary TO THE METER that is, it cannot be put in the meter without an error. (Add: Your) NAME DOES NOT WISH TO RESEMBLE that is, be made equal to THE METER that is, the verse, NOR DOES YOUR GREAT VIRTUE WISH TO BE SHACKLED that is, to be bound BY MEASURE that is, now, since THERE IS NOTHING BY WHICH that is, through which I MIGHT DELIMIT that is, I might measure, THAT namely your virtue, since that virtue TRANSCENDS that is, exceeds THE MEASURES that is, the comprehension OF MEN. Next comes BUT DIVIDE THE NAME.

We leave our two versions of Dybinus here; they continue as they have started, although the version in MS S stops soon hereafter. That in MS D is less fulsome after the *accessus* and first lecture but is still quite extensive: the commentary continues for another forty double-columned folios.

The *dicta* version of Dybinus's commentary in MS D is the one that continued to be copied.[156] Many of the characteristics that appear arbitrary and

---

156. For other manuscripts of this version, see Prague, Národní Knihovna České Republiky, XII.B.12 in the Manuscript List.

individual—the additional citations, the discussion of only one of the four causes, the sequence of "notes"—are retained because this was presumably the official version. In the variety of manuscript formats in which it has survived, the sequence of interpretive approaches to the passage under discussion stays the same: paraphrase, then notes, then word-for-word glossing. This three-part treatment of 1) paraphrase, 2) notes, and 3) glosses was widely used throughout Europe for centuries.[157] The "notes" in the *dicta* version of Dybinus's commentary do follow a rough pattern, although they have the flavor of *ad hoc* comments meant to spice up the presentation of the moment. In contrast, Pace of Ferrara's equally popular commentary discussed in chapter 3 follows a more structured pattern of interpretation (and frames the *Poetria nova* in the context of more literary classical citations). Perhaps because the manuscripts of Dybinus's commentary reflect the teaching of what we would call a required course, a more elastic approach and an emphasis on potential practical applications were deemed more effective.

The value and flexibility of Dybinus's commentary can be seen in imitations and other renderings of his material. One manuscript, Giessen, Universitätsbibliothek, 68, contains many of the same interlinear glosses as the *scripta* version of the "real" Dybinus commentary—I used it to help decipher some of the more illegible ones in MS S above—whereas the rest of the commentary in this manuscript appears to be more closely related to the *dicta* version in MS D. A related *accessus* in an Erfurt manuscript is organized around a different biblical *thema* on power relationships (Psalms 8:8, "Thou hast subjected all things under his feet, all sheep and oxen: moreover, the beasts also of the fields").[158] Several manuscripts of a different commentary containing verbatim elements of Dybinus's have survived.[159] Even much later, when the *thema*-related *accessus* was no longer in fashion, sections of Dybinus's commentary remained useful. A manuscript from southern Germany copied in 1479, Augsburg, Staats- und Stadtbibliothek, 2° 133, contains a one-folio *accessus* summarizing basic Dybinus doctrine. Such overlap and intertwining of traditions is particularly common in central European commentaries; statutory requirements naming the *Poetria nova* may have encouraged informal sharing or collating of manuscripts (especially less expensive paper ones) among both students and faculty.

---

157. For example, Ann M. Blair describes a similar sequence in the lectures on Ovid's *Metamorphoses* in France more than a century and a half later (Blair, "Lectures on Ovid's *Metamorphoses*" and "Ovidius *Methodizatus*"). See also note 141 in chapter 3, and Suerbaum, "*Litterae et mores*," 411–413.

158. Erfurt, Wissenschaftliche Allgemeinbibliothek der Stadt, Amplon. F.50.

159. See under Leipzig, Universitätsbibliothek, MS 1084 in the Manuscript List.

THE *POETRIA NOVA* AT VIENNA, KRAKOW, AND ERFURT

Magister Rudegerus de Rüremunda on the *Poetria nova*[160]
  —from the "ordinary lectures" stipulated in the acta of the University of Vienna, 1394

The *Poetria nova* or a rhetorical handbook[161]
  —a requirement for the baccalaureate degree at Krakow in 1406–09

The *Poetria nova* for two months[162]
  —from the statutes for the University of Erfurt in 1412

These three universities are grouped together not from paucity of material, but rather the opposite: because there is so much evidence of the teaching of the *Poetria nova* at each location and so much overlap in this material. To summarize what follows (almost all of which applies to Prague as well): the *Poetria nova* appears in the statutes for each university soon after its founding, and it reappears sporadically during or at least by the end of the fifteenth century. Manuscript evidence fills in the gaps in the statutory records and strongly suggests continuous teaching of the *Poetria nova* at these universities from the late fourteenth through the fifteenth century. A version of Dybinus's commentary or one drawing on it was taught everywhere, although not exclusively anywhere. It is also probable that the *Poetria nova* was taught in these locations at an advanced level even before the founding of the universities. The manuscripts of commentaries on the *Poetria nova* usually contain additional rhetorical dictaminal material, such as the *Laborintus,* the *Compendium Poetrie nove,* and collections of letters—and the letter collections later in the period often include those of Cicero and Italian humanists. Verse texts in the manuscripts are associated with learning Latin at a beginning or intermediate level (they range from elementary items from the *Liber Catonianus* to intermediate works like the *Consolation of Philosophy* and those of Alan of Lille).

The universities are treated below in the order of the first mention of the *Poetria nova* in the statutes quoted above.

A university at **Vienna** was founded in 1365.[163] It faltered and then (like Erfurt and several other universities) was refounded.[164] Thereafter it "grew vigorously to become the largest institution of its kind in German lands" and has

---

160. "magister Rudegerus de Rüremunda Poetriam novam" (Uiblein, *Acta Facultatis Artium Universitatis,* 106.18).

161. "liber noue poetice, aut exercicium rhetorice" (Muczkowski, *Statuta,* xiii).

162. "poetria per duos menses" (Weissenborn, *Acten der Erfurter Universität,* 2.134).

163. Rashdall, *The Universities of Europe* 2. viii and 234; Overfield, *Humanism and Scholasticism,* 6; and Verger, "Patterns," 63.

164. There was a "near-total departure of German scholars from the University of Paris in the early 1380s as a result of the conflicts growing out of the Great Schism" (Overfield, *Humanism and Scholasticism,* 7). These students went to Heidelberg and Cologne in addition to Vienna and Erfurt.

been called a "typical medieval university."[165] In 1389 the requirement for the bachelor's degree at Vienna was simply "a book on rhetoric."[166] Such a vague description is indicative of the lower prestige of this part of the curriculum, for neither the rhetoric nor the grammar requirement had to be fulfilled at the university itself.[167] Within several years, however, the *Poetria nova* was specified as a subject for "ordinary lectures" to be given by the following *magistri:* Rudegerus de Rüremunda in 1394, Petrus Balse in 1395, Iohannes Trozzinger in 1396, Iohannes Etstaim in 1398, and Zacharias Ridler in 1413.[168] The designation of the lectures as "ordinary" places the text in the standard curriculum, and Joseph Aschbach emphasizes Geoffrey's importance at Vienna.[169]

The *Poetria nova* was not the prize teaching assignment at Vienna. According to the printed statutes, arts professors cast lots to determine the order in which they would choose texts on which to lecture. In keeping with Aristotle's elevated status, one of his works was usually the first choice and the *Poetria nova* about half way down the list. For example, in 1394 the *Posterior Analytics* was chosen first, while Rudegerus de Rüremunda's choice of the *Poetria nova* was eleventh of twenty-five, followed by grammatical texts (among others).[170] The next year, Rudegerus had first choice and picked the *Nichomachean Ethics,* while Balse's choice of the *Poetria nova* was seventh of nineteen; chosen afterwards were logical works, several astronomical texts and, surprisingly, more Aristotle at the very end.[171] In 1396 the *Prior Analytics* was first (Rudegerus again), while

---

165. Kern, "Patterns in Arts Teaching," 321.

166. Lhotsky, *Die Wiener Artistenfakultät,* 236; a rhetoric text was required for the baccalauriat examinations in 1394–96 (73).

167. Parts one and two of Alexander de Villa Dei's *Doctrinale* and part two of Eberhard of Béthune's *Grecismus* were the required grammar texts at Vienna, along with "Vnum librum in Rhetorica." These requirements could be fulfilled "'vbicunque,' i.e. not necessarily 'in scolis publicis alicuius Vniuersitatis'" (Rashdall, *The Universities of Europe,* 2.243, citing Kink, *Geschichte der kaiserlichen Universität*). Overfield describes the situation as follows: "At Vienna rhetoric was classed with grammar as a subject the student could avoid if he had studied it before coming to the university" (*Humanism and Scholasticism,* 41).

168. Uiblein, *Acta Facultatis Artium,* 106, for the meeting to decide courses on September 1, 1394; 121 for September 1, 1395; 137–38 for September 1, 1396; 164–65 for November 10, 1398; and 401 for September 1, 1413. See also Aschbach, *Geschichte der Wiener Universität,* 88; and Lorenz, *"Libri ordinarie legendi,"* 219 and 248. Uiblein published only the first volume; the information in volumes 2 (1416–1447) and 3 (1447–1497) is summarized in Kern, "Patterns in Arts Teaching."

169. "Für das höhere Studium der Rhetorik war Aristoteles zu Grunde gelegt. Sonst waren Führer Boëthius in der Ars dictandi . . . und ganz besonders Godofredus (auch Ganfredus) Anglicus . . . in seiner Poëtria nova . . . " (Aschbach, *Geschichte der Wiener Universität,* 88).

170. "Et sortitum fuit inter magistros et cedidit sors super magistrum Hinricum [sic] de Prucia ad eligendum primo, qui elegit Posteriorum . . . magister Rudegerus de Rüremunda Poetriam novam . . . magister Bartholomeus terciam partem Allexandri, magister Nicolaus Nißel Arsimetricam" (Uiblein, *Acta Facultatis Artium,* 106).

171. "et cecidit sors super magistrum Rutgerum de Rarimunda ad primo eligendum, qui elegit Ethicorum . . . magister Petrus Balse Poetriam novam, magister Leonhardus de Dorfen, Parva loycalia . . . magister Paulus Wyenna Theoricas planetarum, magister Fridricus de Drosendorf De celo et mundo, Magister Iohannes Haroo De generacione et corrupcione, magister Iohannes de Pruscya Elencorum" (Uiblein, *Acta Facultatis Artium,* 121).

Trozzinger's pick of the *Poetria nova* was twenty-third of thirty.[172] In 1398 there was some concern that, should Etstaim not have enough students who wanted to hear (*si non posset habere audientes*) the *Poetria nova,* he was to lecture instead on the third part of Alexander de Villa Dei's *Doctrinale.*[173] If teachers then, as now, associated prestige with teaching at a more advanced level, the *Poetria nova's* status at Vienna is further evidence of the text's transitional function.[174]

For some of the universities discussed in this section, individual *cedulae,* official registration slips or student drafts thereof listing the texts and teachers heard by a particular student for a specific degree, have survived.[175] The *Poetria nova* is sometimes included in those for the baccalaureate.[176] For example, Perchtoldus, Duke of Radawn (Rodaun?), includes "Geoffrey from Master Deckinger" among lectures on Aristotle, Euclid, the *Grecismus,* Peter of Spain, and Donatus in his list for Vienna in 1403.[177]

Several of the seventeen manuscripts of the *Poetria nova* presently in Austrian libraries (including three copies of the *Early Commentary*) date from before the refounding of the university, and other manuscripts with extensive commentaries may have been owned by students who had studied the *Poetria nova* elsewhere at an advanced school of a different kind. Later manuscripts copied elsewhere in Austria may also be the product of such institutions. For example, Prague, Knihovna Metropolitní Kapituli, M 134 contains the *Poetria nova* copied at "Oppavia" (Troppau, Austria) in 1464. It has interlinear notes and a full commentary occupying more than eighty folios (a substantial number of commentary only) and is bound with university grammar texts, one dated 1418.[178] Typical of manuscripts with a probable university origin is

---

172. "Et missa sorte cecidit super magistrum Ruthgerum de Ruremunda, qui eligit librum Priorum, . . . magister Johannes Trozzinger Novam poetriam . . . magister Colomannus de Nova Villa pro tunc rector universitatis Yconomicorum, magister Petrus de Pulka Computum physicum" (Uiblein, *Acta Facultatis Artium,* 137–38).

173. "magister Iohannes Etstaim Gamfredum et si non posset habere audientes, tunc 3ᵃᵐ partem, magister Stheffanus Blůmneg Summam Iovis . . . " (Uiblein, *Actis Facultatis Artium,* 164–165). The *Summa Jovis* listed afterwards was another popular rhetorical text, required at Prague during the fifteenth century. It was also known as *Iupiter Francigena;* see Lorenz, "*Libri ordinarie legendi,*" 219 (who lists them as two separate works), and Camargo, "Si dictare velis." The *Poetria nova* is also listed in the 1413 Vienna statutes (Uiblein, *Actis Facultatis Artium* 401).

174. Claudia Kern, who has studied the choice of texts by senior vs. junior regents masters at Vienna, notes that while all teachers were supposed to be free to choose what text they were going to teach, in fact they made their choices "ranked by age." According to her statistics for the period 1390–1460, "Beginners . . . contributed relatively more to the teaching of [grammar and rhetoric] than their numbers in the regent population would indicate, by a positive difference of fourteen." There seems to have been "tacit agreement that juniors were to give the lectures on grammar and rhetoric, two parts of the ancient *trivium* which were traditionally introductory" ("Patterns in Arts Teaching," 322–324).

175. Bodemann, "Cedulae actuum." The first ones, used as pastedowns in printed books, were discovered by Joseph Förstemann in 1897 ("Meldungen von Baccalaureanden," cited in Bodemann, 437).

176. Those *cedulae* surviving from Prague (Bodermann, "Cedulae actuum," 484–86) are for the Master's degree only, and they do not list the *Poetria nova.*

177. "Item Confredum [*sic*] von maister Dekinger" (Bodmann, "Cedulae actuum," 487). Deckinger had studied at Prague as well as at Vienna. The complete list of Perchtoldus's courses, including "the first part of Alexander" (*primam partem Alexandri,* presumably the *Doctrinale*), is on 486–487.

178. On Prague, Knihovna Metropolitní Kapituli, M 134, fols. 75r–160r, see Podlaha, *Soupis Rukopisů,*

Vienna, Österreichische Nationalbibliothek, 4959, dated 1424. In addition to the *Poetria nova* and an extensive commentary occupying more than a hundred folios, it contains formularies concerning Austria, dictaminal texts including one of Johannes Bondi, and the letters of Petrus de Vinea (Piero della Vigne).[179] After an *accessus* extolling the *Poetria nova* and rhetoric (see the incipit in the Manuscript List), each section of text is commented on first and then glossed interlinearly, often with numbers indicating the prose order of the words.[180] For example, the first words of Geoffrey's digression from the story of the two lovers, *Veri cedit yemps* (546), come six lines up from the bottom on the left-hand side of a folio opening (plate 11a). These words literally mean "To spring yields winter." The scribe has written the numbers "3, 2, 1" over them to indicate that they should be read in reverse order: "Winter yields to spring."[181] Two lines below, he indicates that the first three words in the line, *Humidus et calidus* ("wet and warm" [547]) are already in the normal prose order by numbering them "1, 2, 3." (The phrase before the "1," *scilicet aer* ["namely the air"], identifies what the adjectival phrase describes.) The marginal commentary is very full and takes up almost the entire facing page (plate 11b). The transition to the next technique, description, begins right after the last line of the example of digression in the text, with only a paragraph mark separating them. (This transition occurs in the fourth line of plate 11b, if one does not count the interlinear glosses.) The commentator is expansive in his introduction to the topic of description. He says near the end of the section reproduced in plate 11b, for example, that there are many kinds of description, including "a description of the world, and it is called a *cosmographia*," and "a description of time, and it is called a *chronographia*"— the last word on plate 11b.[182] On the verso side he goes on to say that Geoffrey is giving an example of the latter in his digression (when he describes a passage of time), and that *topographia* describes the "properties of places," an example of

---

2.349–350.

179. On Vienna, Österreichische Nationalbibliothek, 4959, fols. 67r–178r, see especially Schaller and Vogel, *Handschriftenverzeichniss zur Briefsammlung*, 415 (no. 228); also *Tabula codicum* 3.452, and Knox, *Ironia*, 194. The manuscript is dated on fol. 178r: "Explicit textus *Poetrie noue* per manus Johannis filii Organiste de Engetin(?) anno domini m cccco 20 4to." Its contents resemble those in an early manuscript of the *Early Commentary*, Vienna, Österreichische Nationalbibliothek, 526 (MS V), also described in Schaller and Vogel, 389–399; and *EC*, xliii–xlv.

180. Henkel discusses this kind of glossing in some detail (*Deutsche Übersetzungen*, 103–109 and 131–141 [plates 7, 11, 17]). See also Wieland, *Latin Glosses on Arator*, 103, and "The Glossed Manuscript," 165; and Black, *Humanism*, 281–283.

181. Or to prevent a misreading of the first word as the genitive of "verum" (suggestion of Gernot Wieland, e-mail correspondence, September 2006). Longer phrases are also numbered, of course. As Wieland suggests, with regard to much earlier glossed manuscripts (with a different system of construing marks), "There is one situation in which even the initiate would be grateful for these symbols: in the classroom, where a teacher would want to be able to construe a sentence quickly lest he embarrass himself before his students" ("The Glossed Manuscript," 166).

182. "Nota multiplex est descripcio que est descripcio mundi; et vocatur cosmographia [*corr.* cosmagraphia]. . . . Alia est descripcio temporis et vocatur cronographia" (Vienna, Österreichische Nationalbibliothek, 4959, fol. 103r).

which is "tippling England" (1003) from Geoffrey's later passage on metonymy.[183]

The university at **Krakow** was one of the earliest to be founded (originally in 1364); it was then refounded in 1397.[184] The statutory and manuscript evidence taken together document the teaching of the *Poetria nova* at the Jagiellonian University, as it was known after the refounding, throughout the fifteenth century. The 1406–09 statutes include "the *Poetria nova* or a rhetorical handbook" among the required books for the baccalaureate degree,[185] and Geoffrey's work was the subject of lectures there in the last decades of the fifteenth century.[186] The *cedulae* provide valuable information for the middle of the century: two of Johannes de Wratislavia certify the authors on whom he has attended lectures; he includes "*Gammffredum.*"[187] In Poland today there are eight manuscripts of the *Poetria nova* (and three more with excerpts). Three were probably not originally from Krakow, although they appear to be of central European origin. But three of the remaining five were associated with the Jagiellonian University during the fifteenth century, and two others may also have originated there.[188] The high

183. "topographia . . . vtuntur illi qui describunt proprietates locorum, sicut auctor in litera illa 'Anglia potatrix' (1003)" (Vienna, Österreichische Nationalbibliothek, 4959, fol. 103v).

184. Rashdall, *The Universities of Europe,* 3.viii and 289; Verger, "Patterns," 63.

185. "liber noue poetice, aut exercicium rhetorice" is listed under "Qui libri sunt audiendi" (Muczkowski, *Statuta,* xiii and xii).

186. Stanisłaus Stanno lectured on the *Poetria nova* at Krakow in 1487, and others taught it in 1489, 1490, 1491, 1495, 1496, and 1498 (Zabłocki, "Medieval Versified Treatises" [unpublished paper]). On Stanno see Muczkowski, *Statuta* 92 (for 1484) and 97 (for 1487).

187. "Sub . . . magistro Johanne de Glogovia audiui lecturam Veteris artis. / eodem Gammffredum." On first reading, this entry looks as if Johannes studied both Horace and Geoffrey, but the "old art" probably refers to a work of Aristotle's found in a number of the lists (Bodemann, "Cedulae actuum," 455–456). *Lectura* usually was used "in a more abstract sense" than *lectio* ("lesson" or "lecture") to mean "the whole of the lecturing of a master on a certain (curricular) text" (Teeuwen, *Vocabulary of Intellectual Life,* 295). These two *cedulae* from Krakow distinguish between courses taught "Sub maystro / Magistro," including the *Poetria nova,* and "a baccalario," where Donatus is placed, although Johannes lists this work in both categories: "Sub . . . magistro Nicolao de Caschovia audiui exercicium Donati" and "A baccalario Nicolao de Boleslawycze audiui lecturam Donati." More often, the *Poetria nova* is grouped with the texts read at the lower level. Muczkowski also lists it in 1483 (*Statuta,* cxli).

188. One was on loan to the Jagiellonian University from the Royal Library in Berlin when World War II broke out and remained there: Krakow, Biblioteka Jagiellońska, 1891, fols. 156r–209r. It is a central European university manuscript containing mostly quadrivial texts (mathematical and astronomical). The *Poetria nova* has an *accessus* and full marginal commentary with interlinear glossing throughout. On this manuscript (formerly 959) see Rose, *Die Handschriften-Verzeichnisse der Königlichen Bibliothek,* XIII.2.3, 1187–92. There are also two fifteenth-century manuscripts, Biblioteka Jagiellońska, Przyb. 91/52 (beginning missing), and Biblioteka Muzeum Narodowego w Krakowie, Oddzial Zbiory Czartoryskich, 1464, of a commentary copied in a distinctive format. In both, one column of text is accompanied by three very narrow columns of commentary and interlinear glosses. The *accessus* in the complete copy is a pastiche of important points from Pace of Ferrara. The Czartoryskich Library manuscript was owned in the eighteenth century by Tadeusz Czacki (1765–1813), a famous educator and bibliophile who established a renowned lycée for the children of aristocrats; later it became part of the collection made by an even more famous Pole, Prince Adam Czartoryski, who also interested himself in certain aspects of pedagogical reform. Thus, in Poland the impact of the *Poetria nova* in the classroom might have lasted centuries longer than elsewhere. On Krakow, Biblioteka Muzeum Narodowego w Krakowie, Oddzial Zbiory Czartoryskich, 1464, pp. 129–187, see *Iter ital.* 4.408; Kutrzeba, *Catalogus codicum manu scriptorum,* 2.216; Coulson, *Incipitarium Ovidianum,* 41, no. 61; additional information provided by Pawe Prokop. On Krakow, Biblioteka Jagiellońska, Przyb. 91/52, fols. 1r–36v, information provided by Marian Zwiercan. The Jagiellonian Library was closed when I was in Krakow, and I am grateful to Dr. Zwiercan for information provided much earlier.

proportion of localizable codices and similarities in manuscript contents and density of commentary point to a remarkably consistent and intense tradition of rhetorical training in Poland.

Dybinus and his followers were as dominant in Krakow as at Prague, as two important manuscripts from the collection of the Church of St. Mary in Gdansk demonstrate. Both also contain the *Laborintus,* the most likely "other rhetorical handbook" of the Krakow statutes. Biblioteka Gdańska Polskiej Akademii Nauk, Mar. Q.9, from the late fourteenth or early fifteenth century, is one of the manuscripts of the *dicta* version of Dybinus's commentary.[189] In this manuscript the commentary, copied separately in two (shorter) columns, is followed by a few folios of model letters, then the text of the *Poetria nova* with additional marginal and interlinear glossing on the first few folios, the *Laborintus,* and an important elementary textbook, the *Ecloga Theodoli.* The later manuscript, Gdansk, Biblioteka Gdańska Polskiej Akademii Nauk, Mar. Q.8, which was copied in the fifteenth century, contains the *Poetria nova* surrounded—in places overwhelmed—by an extensive commentary based on Dybinus's with interlinear glossing. This manuscript also includes the *Laborintus* with Dybinus's commentary on that text, Vincentius Grüner's *Ars rhetorica* (which refers to Dybinus), Otto of Lüneburg's *Compendium Poetrie nove,* and additional dictaminal material, including several model letters.[190]

One of the Polish manuscripts, Krakow, Biblioteka Jagiellońska, 1934, was part of the university library collection in the fifteenth century; a section of it was copied in Wawel Castle in Krakow in 1420.[191] The first item is the *Poetria nova* with a very full commentary of over a hundred folios, including extensive paraphrases surrounding the text. It also contains a poem on Polish history, grammatical works, and Martin Braga's pseudo-Senecan treatise on the four virtues (with some glosses in Polish). Numbers have been added above the lines of the *Poetria nova* to enable it to be read in prose word order, and there are very long paraphrases of sections of text, often introduced by the phrase, "In this part Geoffrey teaches. . . . "[192] The commentary on the last lines of the dedication reinforces the image of *hearing* the text as the default version of reading it. When Geoffrey offers his work to the pope with "Receive, great man, this little work," the commentator refers to "the hearers of this book."[193]

---

189. On Gdansk, Biblioteka Gdańska Polskiej Akademii Nauk, Mar. Q. 9 commentary on fols. 1r–105r, *PN* on fols. 109r–154r, see Gunther, *Die Handschriften der Kirchenbibliothek,* 473–75; (plate on p. 19); Szklenar, *Magister Nicolaus,* 104–105; *Iter ital.* 4.400.

190. On Gdansk, Biblioteka Gdańska Polskiej Akademii Nauk, Mar. Q.8, fols. 2r–76v (commentary from fol. 1r), see Günther, *Die Handschriften der Kirchenbibliothek,* 471–73; Szklenar, *Magister Nicolaus,* 103–104; *Iter ital.* 4.400; and Polak, *Eastern Europe,* 184–85.

191. Wisłocki *Catalogus codicum manuscriptorum,* 2.465 (with different foliation). Additional information on Krakow, Biblioteka Jagiellońska, 1934, fols. 1r–113v, has been provided by Marian Zwiercan.

192. "In hac parte Ganfredus docet . . . " (Krakow, Biblioteka Jagiellońska, 1934, passim).

193. In hac parte magister Gamfredus reddit auditores huius libri dociles, beniuolos et attentos" (Krakow, Biblioteka Jagiellońska, 1934, fol. 4v). The commentator paraphrases what the author of the *Rhetorica ad*

The three other Polish manuscripts of the *Poetria nova* contain works revealing humanist influence, a topic to which we shall return. An earlier (late-fourteenth- or early-fifteenth-century) manuscript, Krakow, Biblioteka Jagiellońska, 1954, was owned by Andrzeij Grzymała, a famous doctor and book collector who studied and taught at the Jagiellonian University in the 1440s.[194] It contains a combination of classical, medieval, and humanist works, including the satires of Juvenal and Persius and the *Laborintus;* excerpts from Terence; extracts from Seneca's tragedies (with arguments); "Julius Caesar" from Petrarch's *De viris illustribus;* Leonardo Bruni's *Poliscena* with commentary; and various poems, sermons, and orations.[195] It is the only Polish copy of the *Poetria nova* with no commentary of any kind, but space was left for one. Yet another copy of Dybinus's commentary, Krakow, Biblioteka Jagiellońska, 2141, was made in 1450 in Gniezno, the old capital of Poland, by a university graduate.[196] The manuscript includes classical and pseudo-classical authors (Martin Braga again), a "Pyramus and Thisbe" written by a student,[197] medieval dictaminal treatises, Cicero's *Epistulae ad familiares,* letters by Italian humanists (Enea Silvio Piccolomini and Gasparino Barzizza), and Lorenzo Valla's *Elegantiae.* Our last copy of the *Poetria nova* in Poland, made in 1456 and now located in the university library at Wrocław, Biblioteka Uniwersytecka, IV Q 110, is very different in format. Although there is a short *accessus* and marginal glosses throughout, interlinear glosses dominate.[198] It greatly resembles the two copies made at Leipzig about a decade later, and its contents, like theirs, show the shifting nature of teaching by this time.[199] Besides the *Poetria nova* there are predictable classical authors (satires of Persius and Juvenal, and a commentary on Virgil), as well as Guarino's work on diphthongs.

In the geographical region occupied by present-day Germany, the *Poetria nova* is named in the statutes as a required text at **Erfurt** alone. A university originally was founded there in 1379; later, benefitting like the University of Vienna from the migration of students from Paris after the Great Schism, it

---

Herennium says a good Exordium is supposed to do (1.6), which is to "prepare the hearer," but there is no reason to think that the commentator does not mean what he says literally.

194. "Magistri Andree Grizmała pro libreria artistorum" (Krakow, Biblioteka Jagiellońska, 1954, fol. 87r); see Birkenmeyer, "Grzymala, Andrzej z Poznania" and "Andrzej Grzymała."

195. On Krakow, Biblioteka Jagiellońska, 1954, fols. 61r–86r, see Wisłocki, *Catalogus codicum manuscriptorum,* 2.471–72.

196. "Explicit liber Gamfredi, scriptus Gnezne per reverendum baccalaureum in vigilia assumcionis Beate Marie Virginis sub anno nativitatis 1450 etc." (Krakow, Biblioteka Jagiellońska, 2141, fol. 209r). The *PN* is on fols. 104v–209r; commentary begins on 104r. On this manuscript see, with some caution, Wisłocki, *Catalogus codicum manuscriptorum,* 2.516–17; not in Szklenar, *Magister Nicholaus.*

197. This poem and Munich, Bayerische Staatsbibliothek, Clm 237 (note 241 below) constitute two of the three Pyramus and Thisbe poems that Glendinning refers to as "The German Group" ("Pyramus and Thisbe," 52–53 and 63–70); see also note 202.

198. On Wrocław, Biblioteka Uniwersytecka, IV Q 110, fols. 218r–289v, see Aland, *Die Handschriftenbestände der polnischen Bibliotheken,* 43.

199. See "Two Students in Leipzig," below.

was refounded in 1389/92.[200] The *Poetria nova* appears in the Erfurt statutes in 1412, two decades after this refounding, when it was to be lectured on for two months.[201] But some of the most important teaching of the *Poetria nova* in Erfurt may have been done before the founding of the university. The *studium generale* that preceded the university was a sophisticated educational institution. Arguably the most gifted of the speculative grammarians or *modiste* of the fourteenth century was Thomas of Erfurt (fl. 1300–1325), and, although Sönke Lorenz argues that most of Thomas's best work was done while he was still at Paris, Erfurt provided an unmatched environment in which to study the first of the trivial arts at the highest level.[202]

An intense interest in the *Poetria nova* during this period is indicated by two manuscripts now in Erfurt, both of which contain a glossed copy of the *Poetria nova* and a separate commentary as well as another short glossed excerpt. Wissenschaftliche Allgemein-Bibliothek, Amplon. Q.75 is a small, late thirteenth-century quarto volume that, besides the separate commentary and glossed text already mentioned, contains in addition another separate commentary and an extra *accessus* added at the end of the glossed *Poetria nova*. This manuscript also contains excerpts from Herzoni's *Summa Victorini* of Cicero's *Rhetorica*, a *Carmen de moribus* attributed to John of Garland, and miscellaneous excerpts.[203] Amplon. O.17, with a separate commentary and two *accessus* as well as glosses on the text, is an even smaller octavo volume copied in the late thirteenth or early fourteenth century and owned by a certain Nichola (*Iste liber est Nicolae*, fol. 93v).[204] Another manuscript from

---

200. Overfield, *Humanism and Scholasticism*, 7; see also Rashdall, *The Universities of Europe* 2, viii and 245–248; and Verger, "Patterns," 64, with the founding date only. On course material brought back to Erfurt from other universities, see Hamesse, "L'importance de l'étude d'Aristote," 56.

201. "poetria per duos menses" (Weissenborn, *Acten der Erfurter Universität*, 2.134). Overfield argues that "The Greifswald and Erfurt statutes were exceptional in that they specifically mentioned the *Laborintus*" (*Humanism and Scholasticism*, 40), but for Erfurt he cites Weissenborn, where the *Poetria nova* is named in the 1412 list, while the *Laborintus* is bracketed as an addition from 1449 statutes. Peter of Spain was to be lectured on for three months, the pseudo-Boethian *De disciplina scolarium* for one, and Boethius's *Consolation of Philosophy* for four; the *Doctrinale* was divided into three parts and taught for a total of nine months (though it seems to be listed twice and the amounts in the later additions do not match); many other works, mostly quadrivial or grammatical, are also listed.

202. When the university at Prague was founded, scholars from Erfurt were recruited to teach there (Lorenz, *Studium generale Erfordense*, 53; see also Rashdall, *Universities of Europe*, 2.246). On Thomas of Erfurt see Overfield, *Humanism and Scholasticism*, 39. Erfurt may also have been the site of developments in literary narratives; see Glendinning on "Erfurt as a point of origin for the German group of [Pyramus and Thisbe] texts" based on Ovid's *Metamorphoses* ("Pyramus and Thisbe," 64); also note 198 above. On the relationship between the *auctores* and the study of Aristotle at Erfurt, see Denifle, *Entstehung der Universitäten*, 761.

203. On Erfurt, Wissenschaftliche Allgemeinbibliothek der Stadt, Amplon. Q.75, see Schum, *Beschreibendes Verzeichniss*, 343–44; the first *PN* commentary is on fols. 41r–58v, the second much shorter one on fols. 59r–62v, and the *PN* itself on fols. 63r–83v (with added *accessus* on fol. 83v). On the history of the library, see Kadenbach, "Die Bibliothek des Amplonius," and also Hamesse, "L'importance de l'étude d'Aristote."

204. On Erfurt, Wissenschaftliche Allgemeinbibliothek der Stadt, Amplon. O.17 (*PN* on fols. 1r–36r, two *accessus* on fols. 36r–38r and on fol. 38v; and two separate commentaries on fols. 39r–57r and 82r–93r), see Schum, *Beschreibendes Verzeichniss*, 684–85.

the same period, Amplon. O.15, has scattered marginal and interlinear glosses throughout the *Poetria nova,* and the work is copied with other school texts: the Latin school drama *Brunellus,* excerpts from Ovid, an anonymous rhetorical treatise, a commentary on the *Ecloga Theodoli,* and John of Garland's work on synonyms.[205] In Amplon. O.1, a glossed copy of the *Poetria nova* and Statius's *Achilleid* (a widely-used schooltext) are bound together with a separate commentary on the *Poetria nova.*[206]

Two of the manuscripts currently in the Erfurt collection date from the period after the refounding of the university. Amplon. Q.66 is an important late-fourteenth-century collection of university rhetoric texts (e.g., the *Laborintus,* Dybinus's *Declaracio,* a copy of the *Compendium Poetrie nove* dated 1491); the *Poetria nova* has only a few glosses, but there is also a portion of a separate commentary on the digression and description sections.[207] Amplon. Q.286 is a late-fourteenth- or early-fifteenth-century collection of common rhetorical and grammatical university texts made by a certain "Richard."[208] The paper on which the *Poetria nova* is copied in this manuscript is ruled for both text and commentary, and sometimes the text is on only the right-hand page of a folio opening, indicating that an extensive commentary was to have been added later. Two other works in this manuscript are in the typical central-European university format of interlinearly glossed text with heavy, continuous marginal commentary.

Yet in arguing that rhetoric was "virtually abandoned" in the German universities, Overfield states that, except in Vienna, "the rhetoric 'requirement' seems not to have been strictly enforced" and gives Erfurt as an example: "When in 1420 an Erfurt scholar composed a list of the twenty-two books he had studied in preparation for his bachelor's examination, he listed seventeen texts on logic but none on rhetoric."[209] Nor do the Erfurt *cedulae* of 1399 and 1462 transcribed by Bodemann include the *Poetria nova.*[210] But such cases do not mean that the *Poetria nova* was not taught at Erfurt, at least in the fifteenth century. London, British Library, Add. 15108 from a Carthusian monastery near Erfurt suggests otherwise.[211] It is a portable manuscript (quarto size like the "Q" manuscripts in

---

205. On Erfurt, Wissenschaftliche Allgemeinbibliothek der Stadt, Amplon. O.15, fols. 1r–38v, see Schum, *Beschreibendes Verzeichniss,* 682–83; and Quinn, "ps.-Theodolus," *CTC* 2.391b.

206. On Erfurt, Wissenschaftliche Allgemeinbibliothek der Stadt, Amplon. O.1, see Schum, *Beschreibendes Verzeichnis,* 669; Anderson, "Medieval *Accessus,*" 106; *MBDS* 1.1.212; and Polak, *Eastern Europe,* 130.

207. On Erfurt, Wissenschaftliche Allgemeinbibliothek der Stadt, Amplon. Q.66, fols. 74r–119r and 41r–43v (*PN*) and 39r–40v (fragment of commentary), see Schum, *Beschreibendes Verzeichniss,* 338–339; Jaffe, *Declaracio,* 281–285; Szklenar, *Magister Nicolaus,* 122; and Polak, *Eastern Europe,* 126.

208. On Erfurt, Wissenschaftliche Allgemeinbibliothek der Stadt, Amplon. Q.286, fols. 1r–32v, see Schum, *Beschreibendes Verzeichniss,* 526. "Richardus librum <scripsit> suis(?) manibus istum" is written on fol. 32v.

209. Overfield, *Humanism and Scholasticism,* 40 and 41, the latter citing Thorndike, *University Records,* 296 and 297.

210. Bodemann, "Cedulae actuum," 444–445.

211. On London, BL Add. 15108, fols. 236r–303v, see *Catalogue of Additions,* 89; Watson, *Dated and Datable Manuscripts,* 1.141 (18); Polak, *Western Europe,* 301; Lorenz, *Studium generale Erfordense,* 253, 259; and

the Erfurt collection described above), written at Erfurt between 1426 and 1430 by Johannes Paulus di Lortlo (de Lorth). According to Emil Polak, di Lortlo was the author of the *Parvula rhetorica* (Little Rhetoric), which may be the text of the same name that competed with the *Poetria nova* elsewhere.[212] The incomplete copy of the *Poetria nova* in this manuscript (ending at line 1587) is glossed interlinearly and has a full commentary: written around and between sections of the text. Besides the *Poetria nova* this manuscript also contains an impressive collection of grammatical and mathematical works from the list of texts required at Erfurt.[213]

Thus, in the major state and university libraries of central Europe heavily glossed copies of the *Poetria nova* are well represented; a glance at the Manuscript List at the back of this book will show how many more manuscripts have not even been mentioned. While as a rule texts at major collections are more likely to be of diverse origin, this appears to be less true of central than western European collections, at least so far as the *Poetria nova* is concerned. In addition, there are almost as many copies of the *Poetria nova* in smaller cities and regional libraries, where they are even more likely to be situated still in their places of medieval provenance, if not origin. One of the reasons for this regional dispersal of commentaries is examined in the next section.

MONKS AT UNIVERSITY

Rhetoric is defined by Quintilian thus. . . . [214]
—Incipit of *accessus* in a manuscript owned by the Canons Regular of St. Augustine

Many monks in central Europe (and elsewhere) were sent to universities by their monasteries and then returned to those monasteries to teach. Virgil Redlich noted the predominant intellectual influence of the University of Vienna upon the Benedictines in Tegernsee in the fifteenth century.[215] More recently, as Robert G. Babcock has documented, "Close connections between Lambach and the University of Vienna existed in the fifteenth century—Lambach monks and abbots studied and even taught at the university. . . . "[216] This connection is reflected in at least one of the two fifteenth-century Tegernsee manuscripts of the *Poetria nova* in the Bayerische Staatsbibliothek in Munich.[217] A number of

---

MBDS 1.1.22.

212. Polak, *Western Europe*, 301. See also "Two Students at Leipzig" below.

213. Compare Weissenborn, *Acten der Erfurter Universität*, 2.134.

214. "Rhetorica a Quintiliano sic diffinitur . . . ." (St. Florian [Enns], Stiftsbibliothek, XI 108, fol. 34v).

215. Redlich, *Tegernsee*, 8, 29–35.

216. Babcock, *Reconstructing a Medieval Library*, 71; see also Redlich, *Tegernsee*, 13–15.

217. Munich, Bayerische Staatsbibliothek, Clm 18780, dated 1474, contains the commentary by Dybinus of Prague on fols. 72r–177v as well as glossed works by Pseudo-Seneca (Martin of Braga) and Terence, among

other manuscripts of the *Poetria nova* may reflect a similar relationship.[218] One of the glossed Vienna copies of the *Poetria nova*, Österreichische Nationalbibliothek, 5001, with university texts, was owned by the Benedictines at Mondsee, and the *dicta* version of Dybinus's commentary translated earlier, Prague XII. B.12, was the property of the Cistercians at Sancta Corona.[219] The manuscript of the *Poetria nova* from Erfurt now in the British Library was owned by Carthusians, as was the annotated copy of the *Poetria nova* now in the university library at Graz.[220] The latter, from Seitz, contains not only glossed copies of the *Poetria nova* and *Laborintus* and Dybinus's commentary on the *Laborintus* copied separately (dated 1361), but also confessional treatises and university grammatical texts.[221] Other central European manuscripts of the *Poetria nova* still in monastic collections in the region may have come from a university environment as well. A fifteenth-century manuscript in the Benedictine "Scottish Cloister" in Vienna (Schottenkloster 399) is one of the most saturated with Dybinus material of all extant copies of the *Poetria nova*, containing not only a version of Dybinus's commentary on the *Poetria nova* but also his *Oracio de beata Dorothea* with his own commentary on it, his *accessus* to the *Poetria nova* modified to introduce an anonymous rhetorical work, his *accessus* to the *Laborintus*, and his *Viaticus dictandi.*[222]

A fifteenth-century copy of the *Poetria nova* now owned by the Augustinians at St. Florian in Enns, Austria, is an extensive collection (333 folios) in

other works; see Halm et al., *Catalogus codicum latinorum* 2.3.209. The other Tegernsee manuscript of the *Poetria nova*, Clm 18803, is an extensive collection of dictaminal works. The *Poetria nova* (fols. 145r–170v) is accompanied by a few glosses including one that might have been particularly relevant to monks: Alan of Lille's lines on the "Difficult path open to only a few," *Anticlaudianus* 5.57–61 (also quoted in the *EC* 225.5), at line 213. There is extensive bibliography on this manuscript, e.g., Halm et al., *Catalogus codicum latinorum* 2.3.212; Redlich, *Tegernsee* 8, 20–35; *MBDS* 1.2.754; and Jaffe, *Declaracio*, 289; see also Müller, "Die Anfänge der Humanismusrezeption."

218. See also "Two Students at Leipzig" and "Excursus on the Oxford Orbit" later in this chapter. There are almost forty manuscripts of the *Poetria nova* that we know were owned by monasteries (the actual number is probably much higher), but not all of these would have come from universities.

219. On the ownership of the former, see Unterkircher, *Die datierten Handschriften* 1.75; on the latter, Szklenar, *Magister Nicolaus*, 94.

220. London, BL Add. 15108 and Graz, Universitätsbibliothek, 979. There is also an excerpt of the *Poetria nova* in a manuscript previously owned by the Carthusians now in the university library in Basel, A V 23.

221. On Graz, Universitätsbibliothek, 979 (in several hands), fols. 26r–79r, see Anton Kern, *Die Handschriften* 2.172–74; Szklenar, *Magister Nicolaus*, 92–93; and Lorenz, *Studium generale Erfordense*, 279. The manuscript contains three commentaries on works attributed to John of Garland: the *Cornutus* (dated 1373), the *Peniteas cito* (actually by William de Montibus), and the *Synonyma* (dated 1370). Note, however, that Nigel Palmer, in examining a fifteenth-century manuscript of *The Consolation of Philosophy* from the same Carthusian Monastery at Erfurt, distinguishes "typical" Carthusian from school/university treatment: "The diction of these passages suggests a monastic context and excludes the possibility that the translation originated in a school context" ("Latin and Vernacular," 390).

222. On Vienna, Schottenkloster, 399 see Hübl, *Catalogus codicum manu scriptorum*, 56–58; Jaffe, *Declaracio*, 284; and Szklenar, *Magister Nicolaus*, 98–99, 108–110, 125–126, 142–43, 179–180 and 215–17. For the other works by Dybinus in this manuscript, see Szklenar. Jaffe notes about this manuscript that "the influence of Prague models is a distinct possibility" (*Declaracio*, 284).

several hands, reflecting both traditional medieval and more recent humanist interests.[223] It is from this manuscript that the quotation at the beginning of this section was taken. The *Poetria nova* and commentary are in an academic format: full *accessus* and extensive marginal and interlinear glosses (sporadic after first few folios). The manuscript contains other works of academic interest (Dybinus's *Oracio de beata Dorothea,* a commentary on Boethius's *Consolation of Philosophy,* Walter Burley's book on the lives of philosophers), letters including some of Cicero's, and an incomplete copy of Boccaccio's *De genealogia deorum gentilium.* Some of the other letters have a contemporary political focus, such as one on the Hussite conspiracy and another from the bishop of Meißen to the "arms-bearing heretics of Procopium and the noble barons of the king of Bohemia." One is described by Czerny as "from Lucifer to prelates engaged in commerce (*negotiantes*)."[224] Additional contents include notes or short treatises on Pope Innocent III, emperors, and an empress; a list of legal titles; a treatise on blood relationships including consanguinity; and a chronology tracing the Emperor Frederick's descent from Abraham. Taken as a whole, this collection has a definite focus on influential persons and issues of power and responsibility, and the compiler may have found the commentator's standard "reason for undertaking the *Poetria nova*" ("to capture the goodwill of Pope Innocent III") especially relevant.[225] While there is a tendency to think of monks as especially withdrawn from political concerns, such manuscripts suggest a deliberate effort to learn not just the language of the academy but also that of temporal power, rhetoric that could be put to use in practical matters, as well as in the classroom.[226] There were, however, also monks who had more literary interests, especially (if the manuscripts of the *Poetria nova* are typical) in the second half of the fifteenth century. One of these men, Johannes Tegernpeck of the Benedictine monastery of St. Emmeram, is discussed in the next section.

---

223. St. Florian (Enns), Stiftsbibliothek, XI 108, 35r–99r (the commentary starts on 34r), is described in Czerny, *Die Handschriften der Stiftsbibliothek,* 49–51; and Szklenar, *Magister Nicolaus,* 125. The commentary begins, "Rhetorica a Quintiliano sic diffinitur . . . " (fol. 34v). See Jaffe, *Declaracio,* 271–72, on a possible Prague connection.

224. "Epistola ad res Hussiticas," "Epistola episcopi Misnensis ad Procopium haereticorum armiductorum et nobiles barones regni Bohemiae," and "Epistola Luciferi ad praelatos negotiantes" (Czerny, *Die Handschriften der Stiftsbibliothek,* 49–51).

225. "Causa suscepti operis est captatio beneuolentie Innocentii pape . . . ." (St. Florian, Stiftsbibliothek, XI 108, fol. 35r).

226. James Clark has suggested with regard to England that monks had a special interest in *dictamen* (*Monastic Renaissance,* 69 and 144). For the uses of rhetorical and stylistic models outside of an academic setting, see Camargo, "Models" and "Rhetoricians in Black."

TWO STUDENTS AT LEIPZIG

Here ends the *Poetria nova* of Geoffrey the Englishman. . . . In Leipzig on the epiphany of our lord in the year of our lord 1462.[227]
—colophon to Munich, Bayerische Staatsbibliothek, Clm 237

Here ends the *Poetria novella* of Magister Geoffrey the Englishman written by me, Brother Johannes Tegernpeck.[228]
—colophon to Munich, Bayerische Staatsbibliothek, Clm 14529, copied in Leipzig several years later

More than a decade after the invention of printing, two students at the University of Leipzig made their own glossed copies of the *Poetria nova*. Both manuscripts have survived and are located today in the Bayerische Staatsbibliothek in Munich. The earlier one, Clm 237 (plate 12), is in a manuscript owned by Hartmann Schedel, who copied some of the items on later folios.[229] It is not clear whether Schedel himself copied the *Poetria nova* into the codex, but the glosses are similar to those on the texts that he did copy. Something of a prodigy, Schedel arrived at Leipzig in 1456 at the age of sixteen and received the baccalaureate degree a year later and a master's degree in 1460. At the time that the *Poetria nova* was copied he was already teaching in the law faculty; later he became a famous physician, historian, artist, humanist, and bibliophile. The other manuscript, Clm 14529 (plates 13a and 13b), was copied in 1465–66 by Johannes Tegernpeck, a Benedictine who had matriculated in winter semester the year before.[230] Five years after studying the *Poetria nova* Tegernpeck was elected abbot back at his renowned monastery of St. Emmeram.[231]

The 1436–37 statutes of the University of Leipzig, which was founded in 1409, require "some book of rhetoric" (*aliquis liber in rethorica*) for the bachelor's degree.[232] The *Poetria nova* is listed on a *cedula* from Leipzig dated 1440–

---

227. "Explicit *Poetria noua* Gamfredi anglici. . . . In die epiphanie domini in Lipczk anno domini m°cccc° lxii°" (Munich, Bayerische Staatsbibliothek, Clm 237, fol. 60r).

228. "Explicit *Poetria nouella* magistri Gamfredi anglici scripta per me fratrem Johannem Tegernpeck" (Munich, Bayerische Staatsbibliothek, Clm 14529, fol. 69r).

229. On Munich, Bayerische Staatsbibliothek, Clm 237, see Halm et al., *Catalogus codicum latinorum* 1.1.59–61; Henkel, *Deutsche Übersetzungen*, 26; and Schmidt, *Architrenius*, 96 (K). Henkel describes Schedel's manuscript (26–29) and discusses the presence of humanist texts in such manuscripts (22–23). Schedel signed the copies of Avianus and the *Anticlaudianus* in the codex. On Schedel, see *inter alia* Worstbrock, "Hartmann Schedel," *Verfasserlexikon*, 8.609–626; and Hernad, *Die Graphiksammlung des Humanisten Hartmann Schedel*, 13–16. Schedel owned two copies of the *Poetria nova*; the second is Munich, Bayerische Staatsbibliothek, Clm 594, fols. 71r–96v.

230. On Munich, Bayerische Staatsbibliothek, Clm 14529, see Halm et al., *Catalogus codicum latinorum* 2.2.188; Bischoff, "Studien zur Geschichte," 131; Jaffe, *Declaracio*, 272; *MBDS* 1.2.677; and Wheatley, *Mastering Aesop*, 81, 237, 239, and 250. On Tegernpeck's studies at Leipzig, see Bischoff, "Studien zur Geschichte," esp. 130–132.

231. Tegernpeck was abbot from 1471 to 1493. On Tegernpeck as abbot, see Bischoff, "Studien zur Geschichte," 133–134. St. Emmeram had two manuscripts of the *Poetria nova* in its collection; the other is now Munich, Bayerische Staatsbibliothek, Clm 14482.

232. On the founding of the University of Leipzig, see Rashdall, *The Universities of Europe* 2.viii and 258–259; Overfield, *Humanism and Scholasticism*, 9; and Verger, "Patterns," 64. For the requirements see

1442, where an unidentified student declares that he "heard the *Poetria nova* in place of the *Little Rhetoric.*"[233] He includes part of Alexander de Villa Dei's *Doctrinale* and two quadrivial texts in the same grouping as the *Poetria nova,* but most of the works are by Aristotle and Peter of Spain. Two *cedulae* for Schedel have survived. The 1457 list of works that he heard for his bachelor's degree are similar in kind to the earlier student's (though Schedel's list is longer); at this point Schedel heard lectures on the *Little Rhetoric.*[234] It is not surprising that his list for the master's degree in 1460 does not include the *Poetria nova* either, since it was not considered one of the more advanced works.[235] According to Ulrike Bodemann, during the period in which Clm 237 was being copied (1460–1462), Schedel was a member of the law faculty, and he left Leipzig afterwards to study medicine in Padua.[236] But according to Michael Baldzuhn there is another list of lectures that were heard by Schedel at Leipzig for a master's degree in 1465; it includes the entry *Gamfredus—Magister Stephanus Schütz de Nürmberga.*[237] Although these dates are problematic, Schedel's presence in Leipzig during the time when the texts copied in Clm 237 were being lectured on is not in doubt, nor is his eventual ownership of the manuscript.

Typical university texts, usually prose works, continued to be required at Leipzig,[238] but Schedel and Tegernpeck's manuscripts provide evidence of lectures on verse texts.[239] Schedel's also includes classical and pseudo-classical works such as a Pyramus and Thisbe poem,[240] the *Fables* of Avianus, "Walter's" version of Aesop, the *Elegies* of Maximian, the pseudo-Ovidian *De pulice,* and Alan of Lille's *De planctu Nature* and *Anticlaudianus*—there is much overlap with those in the earlier collection of school texts known as the *Liber Catonianus.*[241] Tegernpeck's collection is eclectic and includes a humanist compo-

---

Lorenz, "*Libri ordinarie legendi,*" 219, citing Zarncke, *Statutenbücher,* 326, whose complete list is as follows: "*Libri ad gradum baccalariatus . . . Item libri ad gradum baccalariatus sunt: tractatus Petri Hispani, Priscianus brevior, vetus ars, priorum, posteriorum, elencorum, phisicorum, de anima, spera materialis, Donatus minor vel secunda pars* vel *Florista, algorismus* et computus et aliquis *liber* in *rethorica.*"

233. "*Item audiui Poetriam novam loco Paruuli rethorice . . .*" listed among the works for the baccalaureate (Bodemann, "Cedulae actuum," 457). On the identity of this text see above, p. 219.

234. Bodemann, "Cedulae actuum," 459.

235. Bodemann, "Cedulae actuum," 459–460.

236. Bodemann, "Cedulae actuum," 458.

237. Baldzuhn, "*Quidquid placet,*" 47. Bodemann cites another student's 1466 list on different folios of this manuscript, where the *Poetria nova* does not appear ("Cedulae actuum," 477).

238. Both formal copies and student drafts of these lists have survived from Leipzig; the differences between the two versions are of detail—name and rank of teacher, for example—rather than kind (Bodemann, "Cedulae actuum," 456–484).

239. See Eva Sanford's early article, "Some Literary interests of Fifteenth Century German Students," where she discusses these two manuscripts and others like them, most of which are in the Bayerische Staatsbibliothek.

240. PT VI in Glendenning's list ("Pyramus and Thisbe," 52–53 and 67–71).

241. Henkel notes that more than half of the texts in Schedel's manuscript were part of the school curriculum in central Europe in earlier centuries (*Deutsche Übersetzungen,* 28). On the *Liber Catonianus* see Boas, "De librorum Catonianorum historia," and Pellegrin, "Les *Remedia amoris* d'Ovide," as well as the other works mentioned in chapter 2, note 33.

nent: he recorded school and university texts like Aesop, a version of *Facetus,* mathematical and astronomical works, the *Laborintus* of Eberhard (mentioned so often in this chapter), and model letters for academics, but also works by Boccaccio translated by Leonardo Bruni, the *Ars dicendi* of Augustinus Datus, and Bruni's *Poliscena* with commentary. Two additional manuscripts copied by Tegernpeck that contain humanist works have survived.[242]

Tegernpeck's *accessus,* on the left-hand side of the folio opening before the text of the *Poetria nova* begins, is a simple half-page summary of basic points (plate 13a). Schedel's manuscript does not contain a separate *accessus,* but some of the same information as in Tegernpeck's *accessus* is recorded in bracket diagrams, such as the "six ways" that the author "praises the pope" in the third gloss in the right-hand margin (plate 12).[243] The amount of glossing on the *Poetria nova* in these Leipzig manuscripts looks very different from the dense university commentaries that we have been examining heretofore in this chapter. Yet they are familiar nonetheless, because they resemble the manuscripts with lower- to intermediate-level commentaries discussed in earlier chapters, in which the *Poetria nova* itself, rather than the commentary, dominates the visual space. The glosses in the margins are supporting contributions to the comprehension of the text.

These two Leipzig manuscripts also indicate the same kind of emphasis on the text itself that we have examined in earlier chapters and, in Tegernpeck's copy, the same type of literary analogues that figure so prominently in earlier French and Italian school commentaries. Tegernpeck's gloss on Jupiter's lovers (*PN* 613 ff.) quotes and names Ovid's *Metamorphoses* and the *Ecloga Theodoli,* as well as Seneca on the next folio, while Virgil's *Eclogues* are quoted at the beginning (head) of the description of a woman's body[244]: evidence that the teacher is placing the *Poetria nova* in a literary and textual (rather than dictaminal or quadrivial) context. The marginal glosses on digression are short and conventional (e.g., the commentator says that Geoffrey talks about two kinds of digression and exemplifies both), and the interlinear glosses that I could decipher are simple and unrevealing (the "hour of time" that "found the lovers apart" is glossed

---

242. See Bischoff, "Studien zur Geschichte," 131–132, where there is also a discussion of Tegernpeck's *cedula,* which lists the traditional texts that he heard for master's degree (too advanced for the *Poetria nova*).

243. Compare "sex commendat modis: primo ex sui nominis subtilitate, secundo ex sue forme preciositate ibi 'Egregius sanguis,' tertio ex variarum virtutum nobilitate ibi 'Superest' . . . " (Munich, Bayerische Staatsbibliothek, Clm 14529, fol. 3v) with the diagram of "Commendat papam sex modis: / Primo ex sui nominis subtilitate / Secundo ex sui forme preciositate ibi 'Egregius sanguis' / Tercio ex virtutum variarum nobilitate ibi 'Superest de dotibus'" etc. (Munich, Bayerische Staatsbibliothek, Clm 237, fol. 15r).

244. "SI JUPITER Nota Ouidius in *Metamorphozees* et *Theodolus* . . . " (Munich, Bayerische Staatsbibliothek, Clm 14529, fol. 21r). The commentator calls Amphitryon a merchant, "mercator," later in the same gloss; compare Guizzardo's identification of him as a student in chapter 3 ("Women in the Margin"). One of Seneca's proverbs is quoted in the margin of fol. 22r and "Virgilius in *Bucolicis*" on fol. 19v.

"namely, the hour of spring").[245] Numbers are written over words in the text to put them into prose order, as in lines 1 and 4 on the first folio of text (plate 13b). Two large marginal rubrics identify the places in the long apostrophe on the death of Richard where Geoffrey accuses first Nature and then God.[246] These and other rubrics (such as those naming the numbered branches of artificial order) were added later; they repeat much more legibly other marginal glosses that appear to have been written quickly in a much smaller cursive, presumably during lectures.[247]

While Tegernpeck heard lectures on the *Poetria nova* when he was beginning his university career, Schedel, if he was in fact the scribe of this part of his manuscript, may already have been lecturing in another faculty. There are far fewer interlinear glosses in Schedel's manuscript, and whoever copied it did not add numbers over the words to aid in construing the text. One would assume that Schedel would not have needed interlinear glosses when already a faculty member lecturing in Latin on other subjects, but he could have recorded them automatically during lectures as an aid to absorbing the text. Taken as a whole, the commentary in Schedel's manuscript is sparer and more discerning, often providing in condensed form material expressed in complete sentences and with fuller explanations in Tegernpeck's more numerous and longer marginal comments. There are also differences in the type of allusions adduced. Instead of referring to Virgil in the gloss on description as in Tegernpeck's copy, for example, the comment in Schedel's manuscript quotes a relevant passage from a pseudo-classical text, and Ovid and Theodolus are not named in the glosses on Jupiter's lovers.[248] Tegernpeck's copy of the *Poetria nova* and commentary shows definite signs of having been taken down in the classroom (cramped spacing, later revision, etc.), but Schedel's does not; if he was the scribe, longer experience at the university could explain greater control in taking down lectures. The wording in the two manuscripts is often exceedingly close, however, perhaps reflecting a standard set of Leipzig lectures on the *Poetria nova,* although not necessarily delivered by the same lecturer.[249]

---

245. "Et secundum exposiciones de utroque exemplificat Gamfredus in littera" (Munich, Bayerische Staatsbibliothek, Clm 14529, fol. 18v); "hec temporis hora, scilicet hora vernalis" (fol. 19r).

246. "Hic inuehitur contra naturam" and "Hic inuehitur contra deum" (Munich, Bayerische Staatsbibliothek, Clm 14529, fols. 13v and 14r).

247. E.g., the annotations on fols. 8r–v and 11r–v as well as those cited in the preceding note.

248. "Splendidior stella fuerat mihi visa puella . . . " {Walther, 18532} (Munich, Bayerische Staatsbibliothek, Clm 237, fol. 26r; the glosses on Jupiter's lovers are on fol. 27v).

249. Compare the two versions of the first sentence of the introduction to apostrophe, the fourth method of amplification (*PN* 264 ff.): "Apostropha est quidem modus longandi quando propter aliquem affectum uel causam correccionis sermo de tercia persona dirigitur ad secundam ut, 'Tangere qui gaudes meretricem, qualiter audes . . . '"{Walther, 190013} (Munich, Bayerische Staatsbibliothek, Clm 237, fol. 20r). "Apostropha est quidam modus prolongandi materiam quando propter aliquem affectum uel causam correccionis sermo de tercia persona dirigitur ad secundam; et inde patet per uersum 'Tangere qui gaudes meretricem, qualiter audes . . . '" (Munich, Bayerische Staatsbibliothek, Clm 14529, fol. 10r). Because of such resemblances, I was sometimes able to use Tegernpeck's manuscript to decipher the more attractive but less legible script

The lectures on the *Poetria nova* that these two manuscripts record overlap chronologically with the beginning of Leipzig's prominence as a center of translation of works from Latin into German specifically for use in the university, a period that also coincides with the arrival of Italian humanism into northern Europe in the person of Peter Luder, one of Schedel's mentors.[250] The geographical and chronological specificity of Schedel's and Tegernpeck's glossed copies of the *Poetria nova* is rare; paradoxically it occurs at the institution with the least specific statutory datum about the teaching of the *Poetria nova* (*aliquis liber in rethorica*). The evidence for how books were taught and annotated in Leipzig is very rich, however, and extends well into the era of printed books. Henkel reproduces pages of commentaries on other texts taught at Leipzig at the time that Schedel and Tegernpeck were there, and the catalogue of the Rosenthal collection of early printed books with manuscript notations contains a substantial number from Leipzig (and more from elsewhere in central Europe), many of which are annotated copies of school texts.[251]

In these late university manuscripts of the *Poetria nova* from central Europe we come full circle, to a literary and textual approach and classical context that harken back to earlier school commentaries while perhaps also reflecting new influences from abroad.[252] Henkel emphasizes the conservative aspect of the presence of school texts in Schedel's manuscript,[253] but when these are looked at alongside Tegernpeck's several manuscripts, one can also see them as reflecting the newer emphasis on such texts to the south. The earlier teaching of the *Poetria nova* at central European universities ensured that students received basic rhetorical doctrine while they were being introduced to scholastic theory and methods of logical and grammatical analysis based on the works of Aristotle, Peter of Spain, and John of Garland, among others. In this tradition the *Poetria nova* was further contextualized by studying it along with collections of letters and dictaminal treatises that highlighted how Geoffrey's general rules

---

in Schedel's copy. Schedel's manuscript does not record any comment at all where Geoffrey accuses God in the death of Richard I, and, while the ending of the description of digression in Clm 237 (fol. 25v, middle comment on left) is almost exactly the same as that in Tegernpeck's manuscript, the former does not have an interlinear gloss over the last phrase in line 552 (Clm 237, fol. 26r). With regard to different lecturers giving the same commentary, recall that Dybinus may not have been the one to deliver the officially dictated version of his commentary recorded in Prague, Národní Knihovna České Republiky, XII.B.12 (see "*Scripta* vs. *Dicta* in Practice").

250. Schedel followed Luder to Padua; see Henkel, "Leipzig als Übersetzungszentrum," 559–576; also Baron, "The Beginnings of German Humanism."

251. Henkel, *Deutsche Übersetzungen*, plates 22 and 26; Rosenthal, *The Rosenthal Collection*, e.g., catalogue numbers 33, 100, 118, 119, 126, 151, 152, 153. I am grateful to Robert G. Babcock for bringing Rosenthal's book to my attention and giving me a copy of it.

252. See also Babcock, *Reconstructing a Medieval Library*, 71. On a similar apparently retrograde movement on the part of an English commentator with exposure to the classics, see Clark, *Monastic Renaissance*, 231. On the "*vetus studium* with its emphasis on the *auctores*, a curriculum which was perceived as passing into disregard and neglect before the triumphant advance of dialectic and the 'modern' curriculum," see Glendinning, "Pyramus and Thisbe," 69.

253. Henkel, *Deutsche Übersetzungen*, 11.

could be applied in the practical realm of letter-writing. We find with increasing frequency in the later central European manuscripts of the *Poetria nova* the addition of texts by or dear to the hearts of humanists: letters by Cicero and Enea Silvio Piccolomini, for example, and classical works including school texts that had always been copied with the *Poetria nova* in Italy. The list of central European universities in which the *Poetria nova* was taught the longest is almost identical with the northern universities at which humanism arrived the earliest.[254]

EXCURSUS ON THE ENGLISH ORBIT

> O Gaufred, deere maister soverayn
> —Geoffrey Chaucer

The presence of the *Poetria nova* in university circles in England is not so well attested. We do not have, as in Italy, a continuous stream of commentaries, or, as in central Europe, either university statutes requiring the *Poetria nova* or manuscripts recording official lectures on it. By the later Middle Ages, when a knowledge of French was less widespread, the learning of Latin may have been a longer process for students in England, sometimes extending into the university career, than was the case for those whose native tongue was a romance vernacular.[255] In addition, as was noted earlier in this chapter, students in northern Europe as a whole tended to be younger when they entered university than was the case to the south.[256] Unfortunately, there are few heavily glossed English manuscripts of the *Poetria nova* and no surviving English manuscripts containing commentaries on it copied separately.[257] These facts reveal a weakness in basing a study of the pedagogical tradition of a particular text on commentaries alone, but they do not mean that nothing can be said about the *Poetria nova* as a university text in England.

---

254. Humanists' works and letters were also copied in manuscripts that contain the *Compendium Poetrie nove*. Munich, Bayerische Staatsbibliothek, Clm 4393 and Clm 22403, both from monastic houses, contain among other items the *Compendium Poetrie nove*, Barzizza's *De compositione* and letters of Enea Silvio Piccolomini; see Halm et al., *Catalogus codicum latinorum* 1.2.186–187 and 2.4.47–48; Sottili, "I codici del Petrarca," 281 and 451–456; and Wattenbach, "Peter Luder," 89.

255. Cf. Kristian Jensen, "Text-books in the Universities," 358–359.

256. Cobban, *English University Life*, 149; also "A University Text" above. Riley suggests that in England (but also Paris), they could have been "mere children" (*Registrum Abbatiae Whethamstede*, 2.iiv). On the difficulty of determining the age at which students actually entered university in England, as opposed to being resident in university towns perhaps for preparatory work, see Cobban, *Medieval English Universities*, 351–355.

257. But a copy of the *Poetria nova* with two commentaries on it is listed in the register of books at Syon, c. 1500–c. 1524: "Gaufridus in sua noua poetria scilicet Poetria stupor mundi cum duobus commentis super idem opus" (Gillespie, *Syon Abbey*, 23 [SS1A.68]). There were two other copies of the *Poetria nova* in the collection, 443 (SS2A.49) and 444 (SS2A.19c).

In fact, as Damien Riehl Leader states categorically, "The *Poetria nova* was the most popular of the *artes poeticae* in the English universities."[258] At Cambridge works like the *Poetria nova* were taught under the rubric of grammar, either in a pre-university course preparing students for entry or in the courses of the "semi-autonomous faculties of grammar which were, essentially, medieval teacher-training colleges."[259] Cambridge colleges that owned manuscripts of the *Poetria nova* during the later Middle Ages include Godshouse (one copy) and Peterhouse (with two) in 1424.[260] Corpus Christi College received a copy as part of the bequest of Thomas Markaunt in 1439.[261] At Oxford the *Poetria nova* could have been taught under the rubric of the inception statute of 1431, where, Leader suggests, "rhetoric could also mean poetry." He continues: "Not only Ovid and Virgil, but many other classical and medieval poets were considered worthy of study, as well as poetic theorists like . . . Geoffrey of Vinsauf."[262] Several Oxford colleges owned manuscripts of the *Poetria nova* during the Middle Ages; Canterbury College listed it along with the *Tria sunt* under the heading of *libri poetrie*.[263] Merton College also owned a manuscript of the *Poetria nova,* probably the fifteenth-century unglossed copy now Douai, Bibliothèque municipale, 764, which also contains Gervase of Melkley's *Ars versificatoria,* the *Tria sunt,* Alan of Lille's *De planctu Nature,* and John of Limoges's *Morale Somnium Pharaonis.*[264] Leader identifies three additional university copies of the *Poetria nova* from Oxford.[265] One is an incomplete thirteenth-century copy in

---

258. Leader, *History of the University,* 1.119.

259. Leader, *History of the University,* 1.108.

260. Leader, *History of the University,* 1.119. For the Godshouse/Christ's College manuscript see Peter Clarke, *University and College Libraries,* 110 (UC9.10); for the Peterhouse manuscripts 512 (UC48.278) and 513 (UC48.279a); I am grateful to Peter Clarke for bringing these references to my attention. Jensen cautions against assuming that what college libraries owned were books used by students; he argues instead that they "tended to be owned by masters" ("Text-books in the Universities," 354 and 373–374). Such was not the case, however, with many of the central European manuscripts examined earlier in this chapter.

261. This bequest included "the standard texts, commentaries and reference works of academic study found in many 15th-cent. college library lists . . . " (Clarke, *University and College Libraries,* 185 and 205 [UC19.66f]). There are today four thirteenth-century English manuscripts of the *Poetria nova* in Cambridge colleges (several of which were excerpted in "The *Accessus* and Frame" in chapter 1). One is the important collection of classical texts in Corpus Christi College 406 (apparently not the manuscript of Markaunt's bequest, although both included Seneca's tragedies), and the others are at Trinity College: R.3.29 (with later *accessus*); R.3.51 (from the Benedictine priory of Dover; Ker, *Medieval Libraries,* 58; and Stoneman, *Dover Priory,* 156 [394b]); and R.14.22, with later *accessus* and glosses in several hands (plate 4). Glossing in multiple hands may be a sign of texts that were part of monastic collections; cf. the examples described in Clark, *Monastic Renaissance,* 144.

262. Leader, *History of the University,* 1.118. For the similar situation in central Europe, cf. Baldzuhn, "Quidquid placet." Baswell notes the migration of Virgil manuscripts into university collections in the fifteenth century and also the earlier teaching of Virgil at Oxford as part of the teaching of grammar in the fourteenth century (*Virgil in Medieval England,* 83 and 39, also 143). See also McConica, "Rise of the Undergraduate College," 4–5; Ward, "Rhetoric in the Faculty of Arts," esp. 182 ff.; and Jensen, "Text-books in the Universities," 360.

263. Leader, *History of the University,* 1.118.

264. Camargo, "Models," 178.

265. Leader, *History of the University,* 119; a fourth manuscript, listed as Sidney Sussex MS Delta. 3.11 (56), is a copy of the *Tria sunt* (see below, p. 232), although it is listed as the *Poetria nova* in the catalogue (James,

the Bodleian Library, Digby 104, which contains a large number of both literary and quadrivial texts.[266] The other two are fifteenth-century manuscripts: London, British Library, Royal 12.E.XI, a collection of literary texts including material for teaching Ovid's *Metamorphoses;* and Oxford, Balliol College, 276, a large fragment in two parts, ca. 1442, with classical and medieval Latin literary texts.[267] In none of these is the *Poetria nova* accompanied by a full commentary (although there are a few notes in Digby 104), but in Royal 12.E.XI a short generic *accessus* dividing the book into parts has been copied at the end of the text (plate 14). It begins as follows:

> This book is divided into the preface (*prohemium*) and the treatise. The preface does three things in general. First it captures the goodwill of the pope, where he says, "O Holy Father, wonder of the world," etc. (1). It generates receptiveness when he says "brief in form." It engenders attentiveness when he says "vast in power" (42).[268]

Still another fifteenth-century manuscript from Oxford, Bodleian Library, Laud Misc. 707, contains the *Poetria nova* with a few notes, preceded by a school composition in a much later hand,[269] and followed by proverbs from John of Garland, the *Tragedy of Flavius and Afra,* the *Tria sunt,* Aesop, *Apocalypsis Goliae,* Walter Burley's *Lives of the Philosophers,* a life of Seneca, and a work by pseudo-Seneca (Martin Braga).[270]

In England during the fourteenth and fifteenth centuries, as in central Europe, there were close ties between monasteries, especially those of the Bene-

---

Descriptive Catalogue, 40–41). Leader also includes a manuscript in Oxford, Bodleian Library, Bodley 832; this manuscript dating from the second half of the fifteenth century contains several excerpts (some repeated): fols. 20v–21v, 66v, and 67r–68r (*PN* 1622–1644; 1651–1560; 713–717; 1624–1644; 1651–1665; 1667–1679; line numbers from Martin Camargo, e-mail correspondence, June 2008). There is extensive bibliography on this manuscript, including Clark, *Monastic Renaissance,* 282; and Polak, *Western Europe,* 366–367.

266. *PN* on fols. 21r–33v (ends incomplete at l. 2054). There is much bibliography on Oxford, Bodleian Library, Digby 104; see particularly Ker, *Medieval Libraries,* 204–205; Munari, *Catalogo,* 78–79 (66); and Gibson et al., "Manuscripts of 'Anticlaudianus,'" 980–982 (21).

267. On London, BL Royal 12.E.XI see Warner and Gilson, *Catalogue of Western Manuscripts,* 2.53; Ghisalberti, *Integumenta Ovidii,* 2.31; Krochalis, "Alain de Lille," 110–112; Coulson and Roy, *Incipitarium Ovidianum,* nos. 257 and 333. On Oxford, Balliol College, 276, fols. 2r–14r, see Mynors, *Catalogue of the Manuscripts,* xxvii, 291–293; Watson, *Catalogue of Dated Manuscripts,* 124–125; Munari, *Catalogo,* 72–74 (61); and Krochalis, "Alain de Lille," 145–148.

268. "Liber iste diuiditur in prohemium et tractatum. Isto prohemio tria in generali facit. Primo captat beniuolenciam domini pape vbi dicit 'Papa stupor mundi,' etc. Preparat docilitatem cum dicit 'breui corpore'; suscitat attencionem cum dicit 'viribus amplum' (42)." (London, BL Royal 12.E.XI, fol. 53v) Cf. *Ad Her.* 1.7.

269. A "thema" in the manuscript on the virtue of holding one's tongue (1v–2r) is misidentified as a commentary on the *Poetria nova* by Coxe, *Catalogi codicum . . . Pars secunda,* 505–06. I am grateful to Keith Kitchen for his transcription and translation of this exercise.

270. Oxford, Bodleian Library, Laud Misc. 707, fols. 4r–32v. There is a great deal of bibliography on this manuscript; particularly helpful for my study were Polak, *Western Europe,* 382; Camargo, "*Tria sunt,*" 937; Friis-Jensen, "The Ars poetica," 385–388; and Rigg, "Medieval Latin Poetic Anthologies (IV)," 496. I am grateful to Martin Camargo for conversations about this manuscript and MS Digby 64 discussed below.

dictines, and the universities, especially Oxford.[271] An early-fifteenth-century English copy of the *Poetria nova,* Digby 64 of the Bodleian library, belonged to Hugh Legat, a Benedictine from St. Albans who taught at Oxford in the late fourteenth century. It contains another scholastic *divisio textus* of the *Poetria nova* ("This work is divided into ten parts, of which the first is praise of the pope there at 'O Holy father, wonder of the world,'" etc.[272]). There are interlinear and marginal glosses in several hands around the text of the the *Poetria nova* itself, copied later in the manuscript. Legat had a particular interest in rhetorical and classical texts, and he sought out manuscripts of them. Digby 64 also contains philosophical and rhetorical excerpts, allegorical verses on the Greek myths, and dictaminal material, as well as John of Hautville's *Architrenius* and an incomplete copy of Legat's commentary on it. In 1427 Legat "was dispatched to Tynemouth,[273] where he may have been the teacher of John Bamburgh, who compiled between 1430–1442 a manuscript that includes a partial transcription of the *Poetria nova* with *accessus.*[274] This *accessus,* which was translated in the first chapter, has the same incipit and some of the content of the *Early Commentary.*[275]

Evidence of the indirect influence of the *Poetria nova* on the teaching of rhetoric at Oxford during the late fourteenth and fifteenth centuries comes from Martin Camargo.[276] He makes a compelling case for the extensive use and re-use of material from the *Poetria nova* in a new rhetoric textbook: Thomas Merke's *Formula moderni et usitati dictaminis,* "a deliberate and largely successful effort to incorporate as much as possible of the *Poetria nova* and the *Documentum de modo et arte dictandi et versificandi* (shorter version) into an *ars dictandi.*"[277] Merke, another Benedictine, drew on the *Poetria nova* for the

271. Camargo, "*Tria sunt,*" 957; and "Rhetoricians in Black."

272. "Liber iste diuiditur in decem partes, quarum prima est de commendatione pape ibi, 'Papa stupor mundi'" (Oxford, Bodleian Library, Digby 64, fol. 5r). On this manuscript see Macray, *Catalogi Codicum Manuscriptorum,* 67; Schmidt, *Architrenius,* 98 (P); Polak, *Western Europe,* 370–71; Rigg, *History of Anglo-Latin Literature,* 390; Wetherbee, *Architrenius,* xxxvii; and Clark, *Monastic Renaissance,* 282.

273. Clark, *Monastic Renaissance,* 233–34.

274. Oxford, Corpus Christi College, 144, *accessus* on fol. 18v, *PN* on fols. 19r–43v. The other contents include quadrivial material and part of Alan of Lille's *De planctu Nature;* Ker cites it as "Astronomica varia," *Medieval Libraries,* 191. For the extensive bibliography on this manuscript, see also Coxe, *Catalogus codicum manuscriptorum,* 56–67; Krochalis, "Alain de Lille," 149–155. On Bamburgh see Clark, *Monastic Renaissance,* 145–146, and 233–34.

275. Clark reproduces the *accessus* (*Monastic Renaissance,* 146) and cites Wethamstede's letter, published in Riley's edition of the *Registrum Abbatiae Whethamstede,* 2.312–316 (see Clark, 145). For a translation of the *accessus* see "The *Accessus* and Frame" in chapter 1. Abbot John Whethamstede (possible cause of Legat's earlier banishment) sent Bamburgh a fulsome letter in 1458 praising his learning in spite of its not having been acquired at Oxford or Cambridge. On Whethamstede (Wheathamstead) see also "The English Encyclopedists" in chapter 5.

276. Camargo, *Medieval Rhetorics,* "Toward a Comprehensive Art," "Models," and "If You Can't Join Them."

277. Camargo, "Models," 169; see also Camargo, "If You Can't Join Them," 73–74. Merke's treatise has been edited by Camargo in *Medieval Rhetorics,* 105–147. A similar process may have happened in central Europe with the *Compendium Poetrie nove,* discussed in "The *Poetria nova* as Dictaminal Treatise" earlier in this chapter.

nine methods of beginning a composition, the figures, and the vices to avoid. The contents of the manuscripts in which Merke's work is found connect it with "'undergraduate' studies in the arts curriculum, as well as with 'graduate' studies in the three higher faculties. . . . [T]he codicological evidence consistently indicates the use of the *Formula* at the university level rather than in the grammar schools."[278] As we saw earlier in this chapter, the focus in most central European university commentaries on the *Poetria nova* was on how one could use what Geoffrey of Vinsauf said specifically for the composition of letters (the fast track to career advancement); thus, the limitations of the *Poetria nova* were sometimes pointed out. The reworking of the *Poetria nova* into new texts like Merke's *Formula* and the *Tria sunt* in England may reflect, if not a dissatisfaction with the *Poetria nova,* at least an attempt to put what was considered especially useful about it into greater professional and practical focus.[279]

Manuscripts of works selected from among Alan of Lille's *De planctu Nature,* John of Limoges's *Sompnium Pharaonis,* Guido de Columnis's *Historia destructionis Troie,* Richard of Bury's *Philobiblon,* and Merke's *Formula* may have circulated in England, particularly at Oxford, as collections of models of prose composition (though some of the works also contain verse) for university students.[280] As Camargo points out, "The Latin of these works is simpler than that of the secondary-school authors."[281] Thus, as in central European universities,[282] the teaching of rhetoric at the University of Oxford during the later Middle Ages appears to have focused on prose composition and pre-professional training and often to have taken place at a remedial or transitional stage near the beginning of a student's university career. For example, Benedictines who were sent to Gloucester College, where Merke probably studied, could dispense with the requirement to graduate in arts before proceeding to theology or canon law, but they were expected to have already studied arts for several years. It is probably this practice to which William Courtenay alludes when he observes that "Gloucester College provided remedial work in grammar and the basic courses in philosophy alongside the lectures on the Bible and the *Sentences.*"[283]

---

278. Camargo, "Models," 170.

279. A similar reworking happened to dictaminal works in Italy, where such texts rarely received commentaries. Instead, dictaminal teachers there tended to incorporate earlier material in their own texts rather than reorienting it via commentary. That such reworking did not happen to the *Poetria nova* in Italy, where the text was commented on often, emphasizes the status of the *Poetria nova* there as general text on rhetoric and poetics; see Woods, "Using the *Poetria nova.*"

280. Camargo, "Models," 171. The Douai manuscript includes two of these works and also the *Tria sunt,* so it could have served a similar function (Camargo, "Models," 178).

281. Camargo, "Models," 173.

282. Because of the manuscript patterns of several of these texts, "it is possible that the Oxford masters took over and expanded a text grouping that had originated over a century earlier, in southern Germany and Austria" (Camargo, "Models, 175). The contents of the earlier English manuscripts of the *Poetria nova* place the work in the context of more literary works and verse composition; see "The Other Audience" in chapter 1.

283. Courtenay, *Schools & Scholars,* 80. See also Rouse and Rouse, eds., *Catalogus,* xxxiii.

Like their counterparts in central Europe, when students in Oxford or Cambridge returned to their monasteries after a university sojourn, they often took their books home with them, as was the case with the St. Albans manuscripts.[284] A thirteenth-century Oxford manuscript of the *Poetria nova* mentioned earlier, Digby 104, was given by John Blacman to the Carthusians in Witham, Somerset, sometime between 1463 and 1474; it was one of two copies of the *Poetria nova* that they owned.[285] A fifteenth-century manuscript of the *Tria sunt,* Cambridge, Sidney Sussex College, Delta 3. 11 (56), was carried back and forth between Oxford and Durham,[286] and a similar journey was probably undertaken by the two manuscripts of the *Poetria nova* now in Durham: University Library, Cosin V.V.2, which contains three of the works in Camargo's group, and Cathedral Library, C.IV.23, copied by John Fishborne ("Fyshebone"), who attended Oxford and became librarian of the monastery at Durham in 1416.[287] A late-fifteenth-century catalogue of the Augustinian abbey in Leicester lists a copy that had been given to the library by an "R. Seton," who had been a student at Oxford in 1440.[288] Surviving medieval library catalogues indicate that the *Poetria nova* was no newcomer to British monastic libraries, however.[289]

Even after the copying of its manuscripts stopped, the *Poetria nova* remained a significant text in England, as we shall see in the beginning of the next chapter. The importance of the early manuscripts in which the *Poetria nova* is found, its iconic status as a subject of parody by Chaucer's time, and its continued

---

284. See Clark, *Monastic Renaissance*, 214; and Doyle, *Librarirs of the Carthusians,* 640 and 643.

285. Doyle, *Libraries of the Carthusians*, 640 (C8.13a); see also 643 (C8.21b).

286. Camargo, e-mail correspondence, July 2005.

287. Durham, University Library, Cosin V.V.2, fols. 125r–160 for *PN* (with sporadic notes on the first few leaves), also containing Alan of Lille's *Anticlaudianus* and *De planctu Nature* as well as Richard of Bury's *Philobiblon*; see *Catalogi veteres librorum ecclesiae*, 177–78; Krochalis, "Alain de Lille," 68–71; and Camargo, "Models," 176. Durham, Cathedral Library, C.IV.23, fols. 57r–126r for the *PN* (with marginal paragraph headings only), also contains, among other works, Peter Riga's *Aurora*; see *Catalogi veteres librorum ecclesiae*, 11, 86, 228. For information on Fishborne I am indebted to A. J. Piper.

288. Webber and Watson, *Libraries of the Augustinian Canons*, 302 (A20.1042, "Galfridus Anglicus in noua poetria per R. S<eyton> scolarem in duobus locis"); on Seton see Webber and Watson, 208 (A20.466).

289. The *Poetria nova* occurs in monastic library catalogues as early as 1202 at Rochester (if "Versus Magistri Ge' Vinisalui" refers, as the editors suggest, to the *PN*) and is listed in the 1247 catalogue of the Benedictines at Glastonbury (Sharpe et al., *English Benedictine Libraries*, 512 [124b] and 215 [400]). Peterborough Abbey owned two copies of the *Poetria nova* by the late fourteenth century (Friis-Jensen and Willoughby, *Peterborough Abbey*, 115 [BP21.115f, "Liber qui sic incipit *Papa stupor mundi,*" and BP21.160, "Versus magistri G. Vinesalui de arte loquendi"]). The Premonstratensian abbey at Titchfield owned a copy in 1400 (Bell, *Libraries of the Cistercians*, 221 [P6.144g, "Poetria Galfridi uersificata"]); and Gallick, "Medieval Rhetorical Arts," 92, also lists a copy in the Syon Monastery in Isleworth ("MS A. 68, n.d. Present location unknown"). The Benedictine Henry of Kirkestede (ca. 1314–ca. 1378), monk and prior of Bury St. Edmunds and "founder of English bibliography," includes Geoffrey as "Galfridus Vinesauf" and an excerpt of the *Poetria nova* (368 ff.) as "De eloquentia lib. I" in his *Catalogus de libris autenticis et apocrifis* sometimes attributed to Boston of Bury (*Catalogus*, xxix–xxx and p. 232, no. 227). There is less evidence of the *Poetria nova* in mendicant collections in England, but it was owned by the Austin Friars in York (Humphreys, *The Friars' Libraries*, 126 [A8.503a, "Poetria noua Galfridi"]); this manuscript was donated by John Erghome, who died in 1390 (Tiner, "Evidence," 28 and 37). Gallick lists additional presumably English copies whose present location is not known (82).

presence in late medieval English manuscripts show that it continued to be read and taught, to be part of the standard training of men of letters in the country where it was written. The influence of the *Poetria nova* and that of its author continued in a radically altered form on the continent, but the complete story of the *Poetria nova* in England remains to be discovered.

5

seventeenth-century commentaries on the *poetria nova*

THE ENGLISH ENCYCLOPEDISTS

WALTER of *Vinosalvo, English,* and a man of splendid, polished, glorious eloquence (insofar as his era permitted) . . . [1]
—John Leland

Although the *Poetria nova* continued to be copied until at least the third quarter of the fifteenth century and was lauded later than that as a text that could teach one how to write, it was not printed before 1721, when Polycarp Leyser included it in his important anthology of medieval Latin poetry.[3] Despite this neglect of the *Poetria nova* by printers before the early eighteenth century, Geoffrey of Vinsauf and his works are praised by the authors of the major literary encyclopedias during the same period, particularly those with a special interest in British writers. John Leland, who in the 1530s journeyed through Britain collecting information for Henry VIII about the manuscript holdings of the soon-to-be-disbanded monasteries of the realm, intended to compose "a complete dictionary of British

---

1. "GUALTERUS de *Vinosalvo, Anglicus,* vir, quantum illa permittebant tempora, splendidæ, comptæ, floridæ eloquentiæ . . . " (Leland, *Commentarii de scriptoribus Britannicis,* 1.231).

2. See "Geoffrey after Quintilian" and "Erasmus and Geoffrey" in the Afterword.

3. *Historia poetarum et poematum medii aevi;* see also "An End and a Beginning" at the conclusion of this chapter.

writers—*De viris illustribus.*"[4] His notebooks for this project were edited and published more than a hundred and fifty years later as *Commentarii de scriptoribus Britannicis.* Leland's description of Geoffrey, which was influential long before its publication, is as follows:

WALTER[5] of *Vinosalvo, English,* a man of splendid, polished, glorious eloquence (insofar as his era permitted), focused all the strengths of the keen talent with which he was fully endowed on a literary career alone. Accordingly, not content to attend just the schools in his homeland, he honored those in *France* as well, and, unless I am mistaken, even in *Italy,* for it is known that he was acquainted with Innocent III, the *Roman* pontiff. From this I conjecture that at some time or other he was in *Italy* and lived in *Rome,* where he may have earned *Innocent's* patronage, although in what capacity I have not yet determined. It has long been established that he dedicated to Innocent his book on *The Art of Composition,* a work written in prose and hexameter verse; it was learned, graceful, and richly adorned by the standards of that age. As a result this work rendered his name illustrious both at home and abroad.[6]

After quoting some (as he concedes) unbelievably hyperbolic praise,[7] Leland notes that John Whethamstede, a Benedictine mentioned earlier in this study, "makes honorable mention of *Walter*" in a work called *Granarium.*[8] Near the

---

4. Carley, "John Leland and the Contents," 108; Leland "became insane in 1547 and did not live to produce the books he thought his notes would generate." Anthony Hall published the *Commentarii* in 1709, and that edition is used here. (When citing printed editions and later commentaries, I have kept the original capitalization and italics.) James Carley is preparing a new edition and translation of Leland's work, and I am grateful to him for making the entry on Geoffrey available to me before publication.

5. "Gualterus" is a common variant of "Galfridus" (Geoffrey). By the time he recorded some extracts from the *Poetria nova* in an unpublished notebook (London, BL Cotton Julius C. VI), Leland knew that the name was Geoffrey (Carley, e-mail communication, June 2007).

6. "GUALTERUS de *Vinosalvo, Anglicus,* vir, quantum illa permittebant tempora, splendidæ, comptæ, floridæ eloquentiæ, omnes nervos ingenii sui, quo præditus erat plane acerrimo, in solam fere rem literariam intendebat. Itaque non contentus scholas tantum patrias frequentare, *Gallicas* quoque celebravit, &, nisi male colligo, *Italicas* etiam. nam constat illum *Innocentio* tertio, pontifici *Romano,* notum fuisse. Atque adeo hinc est, quod conjecturam facio, hominem aliquando in *Italia* fuisse, & *Romae* vixisse; ubi forsitan *Innocentium* candidum habere meruit patronum. utcunque sit, non admodum laboro. Illud longe certissimum est, quod *Innocentio* librum, quem prosa & carmine hexametro de *Arte dicendi,* ut illa judicavit ætas, doctum, ornatum, venustum scripsit, dedicaverit. Quo munere cum domi, tum foris gloriam sui nominis reddidit illustriorem. . . ." (Leland, *Commentarii,* 1.231–32)

7. Geoffrey's glory is described as more enduring than that of "the pyramids, ancient columns, triumphal arches, statues, marble tablets," etc. ("quam pyramides, quam columnæ, quam arcus triumphales, quam statuæ, quam tabulæ marmoreæ . . . " [Leland, *Commentarii,* 1.232]).

8. "Sed sit meum leve in hac parte eulogium. non itidem leve erit *Joannis Frumentarii* testimonium, qui in libro suo, cui titulus est *Granarium,* honorificam de *Gualtero* mentionem facit" (Leland, *Commentarii* 1.232). On Whethamstede (Wheathampstead), who was abbot of St. Albans from 1420 to 1440 and 1451–1465, see Léotaud and McHardy, "The Benedictines at Oxford, 1283–1539," 28; Campbell, "Gloucester College," 46; and Clark, *Monastic Renaissance,* 145, 234–238, etc. The title of Whethamstede's book, *Granarium,* is presumably a play on his Latin moniker, Johannes Frumentarius, which itself is a rendering of his English surname (also spelled Wheathamstead). Whethamstede commissioned one of the manuscripts containing the *Poetria nova:* Oxford, Bodleian Library,

end Leland includes the other works of "Walter" that are known to him: "Walter's short poem to the *Roman* emperor, in which he begs the emperor to set free the captured *Richard Lionheart,* King of the *English,* survives.[9] I once came across a not inelegant little book on *Ethics,* which outlines good behavior.[10] *Galfridus Vinesave* is written on its last page."[11]

Here we have the general outline of the sixteenth- and seventeenth-century assessment of the man we know as Geoffrey of Vinsauf and his writings: recognition of a high regard during the Middle Ages for Geoffrey's learning, scholarly travels, and rhetorical ability; knowledge of a book on rhetorical composition as the basis of his reputation; and some uncertainty about other works of his, with an extract from the *Poetria nova* listed as a separate composition. The important rhetorical treatise is described by Leland as half in prose, half in verse, however, indicating a confusion or conflation of the *Poetria nova* (dedicated to Innocent III but written completely in hexameter verse) with either Geoffrey's *Documentum* (a work on the same subject written in prose with verse examples) or the *Tria sunt* (also in verse and prose and until recently erroneously known as the *Longer Documentum*), both of which are extant in English manuscripts only.[12] The "short poem . . . . to the *Roman* emperor" is one of the two dedications at the end of the *Poetria nova* and was the source of some controversy among medieval commentators.[13]

In contrast to the assessments of Geoffrey in medieval commentaries, Leland's is based solely on Geoffrey's accomplishments as a poet, scholar, and rhetorician, with no attention paid to his role as a teacher. To the information provided by Leland, John Bale added the suggestion in *Scriptoru(m) illustrium maioris Brytanni(a)e* (1558) that Geoffrey was of Norman stock.[14] Both John Pits (1560–1616), whose entry on Geoffrey in *De illustribus Angliae scriptoribus* was published posthumously in 1619, and Thomas Tanner in *Bibliotheca Britan-*

Selden Supra 65. See also "Excursus on the English Orbit" in chapter 4; also Camargo, "Rhetoricians in Black," esp. 380–82.

9. This is *PN* 2081–2098, where the passage is addressed to the pope. The excerpt is copied separately in Oxford, Bodleian Library, Add. A. 44, fol. 226v, identified as "Preces imperatori pro liberatione Regis Richardi. . . . "

10. Probably by John of Garland according to Far.,p. 22, but not included in Traugott Lawler's list of John's works (*Parisiana Poetria,* xii), or in Marguin-Hamon, "Tradition me anuscrite."

11. "Extat ejus ad imperatorem *Romanum* breve carmen, quo supplex eum hortatur ut *Richardum Leoninum, Anglorum* regem, interceptum restitueret. Incidi aliquando in libellum non inelegantem de *Rebus Ethicis,* qui bonos informaret mores. Extrema ejus pagella sic inscripta fuit: *Galfridus Vinesave*" (Leland, *Commentarii,* I.232). "Stylus plane Vinosalvum sapiebat" is a comment added by Leland later. (Carley, edition in progress, cited with the author's permission).

12. On the manuscripts and identification of the *Documentum* and *Tria sunt* see Camargo, "*Tria sunt.*"

13. *PN* 2081–2098. Most medieval commentators and modern scholars identify it as another address to Innocent (see "Stand and Counterstand" in chapter 3). For interpretations of this section in the commentaries, including its author and the "prince" for whom a case is being made, see also "A Double Structure" in chapter 3.

14. Bale, *Scriptoru(m) illustrium maioris Brytanni(a)e,* 239.

nico-Hibernica (published in 1748—apparently without knowledge of Leyser's editions) quote much of Leland's description and emphasize that Geoffrey is someone of whom Englishmen can be proud.[15] Pits's chatty, derivative entry on Geoffrey was the most widely known,[16] and both of the scholars examined later in this chapter cite him. Here is how he begins:

> GEOFFREY, called Master Geoffrey Vinsauf, or de Vino Salvo, so named from wine and the cultivation of grapevines—a plausible conjecture, it seems to me. For there is a certain manuscript book whose author is Geoffrey in the library or archives of Gonville and Caius College, Cambridge,[17] on the method of grafting aromatic trees, preserving fruits, recognizing grapevines and wines, reconstituting wines that have turned—in French, *vin mouté*—and restoring wine that is changing into vinegar, and the conditions [necessary for] making any kind of wine or other precious liquids like concoctions for the healthy as well as the sick. Hence, I conjecture, the appellation *De vino salvo*, which I freely offer for comment.
>
> Further, our Geoffrey was born in England, and it is believed that he came from Norman stock. A man of glorious talent with a fluid, succinct, and tightly controlled style, whether you look at his informal or more crafted discourse—in almost exactly these words our John Leland praised him. He [Geoffrey] sought areas of knowledge with an avid and completely insatiable desire, for the acquisition of which nature had formed him most aptly. Not content with the academic institutions of his homeland, in which he had studied for a long and happy time, he betook himself to France and Italy, and in both places he sought out and diligently attended the most celebrated schools; and everywhere, insofar as he was able, he was wont to keep company, share conversation, and discuss literary matters publicly and privately with men famous for their learning. He was known to Pope Innocent III, for he wrote to him partly in prose and partly in heroic verse.[18]

---

15. Tanner, *Bibliotheca Britannico-Hibernica*, 736–737. Pits's entry is quoted below.

16. E.g., Du Boulay, *Historia Universitatis Parisiensis* (1665), 2.520; Fabricius, *Bibliotheca latina mediae et infimae aetatis* (1754), 3.13; Sarti (1769–1772) in Sarti-Fattorini, *De claris*, 601.

17. Pits lists this among the works at the end: "*De vinis, fructibus &c. conseruandis, Librum vnum.* M S. Cantabrigiae in Archiuis Collegij Caij & Gonellij" (*De illustribus Angliae scriptoribus*, 262).

18. "GALFREDVS, dictus Magister Galfredus Vinesalf, vel de Vino saluo, sic cognominatus à vino & vitibus conseruandis, vt mihi non leuis est coniectura. Nam Cantabrigiæ in Bibliotheca vel Archiuis Collegij Caij & Gonellij liber quidam M S. haberi dicitur auctore Galfredo, de modo inserendi arbores Aromaticas, fructus conseruandi, vites & vina cognoscendi, vina inuersa (Gallicè vin mouté) seu deteriorata reformandi & restituendi acetum mutandi, & conditiones cuiuscumque vini, & cæterorum preciosorum liquorum, vt pigmentorum, faciendi, tam pro sanis quàm pro infirmis. Atque huic cognomen ei inditum *De vino saluo*, mea coniectura est, quam libenter veriori censuræ submitto.

"Porrò Galfredus noster in Anglia natus, & stirpe Normannorum oriundus creditur. Vir ingenij florentis, styli compti, tersi, nitidi, siue orationem solutam spectes siue constructam. His enim ferè nominibus eum laudat noster Ioannes Lelandus. Auidè & insatiabili planè desiderio scientias appetebat, ad quas adipiscendas eum natura formauerat aptissimum. Non contentus patrijs Academijs, in quibus diù fœliciterque studuerat, in Galliam & Italiam se contulit, & vtrobique celebriores inuisit & diligenter frequentauit scholas, & vbique

Following Leland, Pits then lists Geoffrey's works and refers to manuscripts that he has seen. First is a composition treatise about which he reports a rumor:

> On the art of composition, or on dialectical and rhetorical precepts, one book. There is a manuscript in the Benedictine College [Gloucester] at Cambridge with this title: On the method and art of prose and verse composition and metaphorical language, one book—unless these are two separate works. The incipit of this book is the following: Once protected by King Richard's shield [PN 368 ff.]. It is said that this work was printed in Vienna, Austria, by Wolfgang Zazius.[19]

But the manuscript to which Pits is probably referring contains instead Geoffrey's Documentum de modo et arte dictandi et versificandi, although the incipit he cites is that of the most famous section of the Poetria nova (the lament on the death of Richard I).[20] Later the printer's name was corrected to that of a known Viennese printer, Wolfgang Lazius (1514–1565), who did, in fact, own a fifteenth-century Italian manuscript of the entire Poetria nova, now Vienna, Österreichische Nationalbibliothek, 2401.[21] There are no signs, however, that this manuscript was used, or was ever intended to be used, as a printer's copy.[22]

Of the eight other books listed as Geoffrey's by Pits, four more are the Poetria nova or parts of it: the Poetria nova itself ("On the Poetria nova; one book. 'O Holy Father, wonder of the world, if I were to say.' A manuscript in Balliol College, Oxford"[23]); the disputed plea to the pope interpreted by Pits (as by Leland) as an address to the emperor ("To the Emperor Henry for his deliberations on King Richard, in verse, one book [PN 2081–2098]"[24]); the dedication at the end to a

---

quantum fieri[t] potuit, cum viris eruditione claris, contubernium habere, sermones conferre, & de rebus litterarijs publicè priuatimque agere solebat, Innocentio Papæ tertio notus erat. Nam ad eum scripsit partim prosa partim versu heroico" (Pits, De illustribus Angliae scriptoribus, 261–262). I am grateful to F. Eliza Glaze for help in translating this passage.

19. "De arte dicendi, seu de præceptis Dialectices & Rhetorices, Librum vnum. M S. Cantabrigiæ in Collegio S. Benedicti sub hoc titulo, de modo & arte dictandi, versificandi, & transferendi, Librum vnum. Nisi fortè duo distincta sint opera. Initium operis sic habet. Neustria sub clipeo Regis defensa Richardi. Dicitur hoc opus excusum typis Viennæ Austriæ apud Vvolfgangum Zazium." (Pits, De illustribus Angliae scriptoribus, 262).

20. Identified as such by, among others, John Selden (Historiae Anglicanae scriptores, col. 1280). The excerpt was published by Selden, but he expresses doubt that it had been printed earlier (ibid.). See also Far., p. 28. The manuscript to which Pits refers (and Faral cites as "372 de Saint-Benoit") may be Cambridge, Corpus Christi College, 217, which contains Geoffrey's Documentum de modo et arte dictandi et versificandi but not the Poetria nova (Camargo, "Tria sunt," 939).

21. He is named as the donor of the manuscript on a flyleaf: "Ex bibliotheca d. Wolfgangi Lazii obsequii ac memoriae ergo donatus 1551" (Vienna, Österreichische Nationalbibliothek, 2401, fol. ir).

22. Some of Pits's misinformation is discussed in Woods, "Unfashionable Rhetoric," 320, along with Leyser's critique of Pits's assertion (860–61) and Leyser's references to what were, in fact, the first parts of the Poetria nova to have been printed (see also note 56 below).

23. "De poëtria noua, Librum vnum. Papa stupor mundi, si dixero. M S. Oxoniæ in Collegio Balliolensi" (Pits, De illustribus Angliae scriptoribus, 262), presumably Oxford, Balliol College, 263 or 276, in each of which the Table of Contents lists the work as Galfridus in Poetria nova (though in MS 276 the beginning of the text is missing). On MS 276 see also "Excursus on the English Orbit" in chapter 4.

24. "Ad Cæsarem Henricum deliberando Richardo Rege, carmine, Librum vnum" (Pits, De illustribus Angliae scriptoribus, 262). Far., p. 18, misidentifies the passage as lines 2099 ff. (the address to William; see

certain William ("*To William, Bishop of Ely and Chancellor, One book.* 'Which I have written for the pope'"[25] [*PN* 2099–2116]); and, for a second time, but here as a separate work identified by title and no incipit, Geoffrey's apostrophes on the death of Richard ("*Lament on the Death of the King, one book*" [*PN* 368 ff.][26]). The remaining four are the book on cultivating wine mentioned earlier and a book called the *Enchiridion* that Pits says are in the same manuscript,[27] *De statu curiae* (the only other item in Lazius's manuscript of the *Poetria nova*[28]), and the work on ethics cited by Leland.[29] This much elaborated picture of Geoffrey and his works is what established Geoffrey's future reputation, especially abroad.[30]

As a significant part of Great Britain's literary and cultural heritage, the *Poetria nova* captured the interest of such famous English collectors as Matthew Parker (1504–1575), Robert Bruce Cotton (1571–1631), William Laud (1573–1645), Kenelm Digby (1603–1665), and Robert Harley (1661–1724).[31] Thus, when commentaries on the *Poetria nova* appear in the seventeenth century, the attitude toward the text is very different from that of the medieval commentaries examined in the preceding chapters. For earlier teachers and students, the *Poetria nova* was a work prized for its combination of instruction and example; even in the university commentaries that have no interest in Geoffrey's command of style and poetic registers, his ability to shape material for a particular purpose is taught as a kind of practical knowledge worthy of study and imitation. In contrast, for the two seventeenth-century scholars whose reactions to the *Poetria nova* are explored in the rest of this chapter, the text has become an artifact from an earlier culture, rather than a work of contemporary usefulness.

---

the next "book"), but he correctly identifies it on page 30. This disputed passage is discussed in "Stand and Counterstand" in chapter 3.

25. The complete sentence in translation: "Accept, O flower of the Kingdom, this special gift of a little book which I have written for the pope" (2098–2100).

26. "*Monodiam in obitum Regis, Librum vnum*" (Pits, *De illustribus Angliae scriptoribus*, 262). See Far., pp. 18–19, on the possible influence of Chaucer's reference to this section. The naming of the passage as a lament is significant, and it was much admired as such in the seventeenth century (Woods, "A Medieval Rhetorical Manual in the 17th Century").

27. Both are uncertain attributions; see Far., pp. 20 and 22. He identifies this manuscript as Gonville and Caius 385, but it does not contain the first text (James, *Descriptive Catalogue*, 2.441–446).

28. Faral discusses this attribution at some length, finally arguing against it (pp. 20–22). He notes that the reputation of the Geoffrey who wrote the *Poetria nova* could have attracted the attribution of works by other Geoffreys (21), as happened with that other famous Geoffrey: Chaucer.

29. For the degrees of certainty of attribution of various works and the sorting out of the attributions by scholars, see Far., pp. 18–33.

30. Fabricius, however, correctly identifies the parts of the *Poetria nova* that Pits lists as separate works (*Bibliotheca latina*, 13).

31. For a general introduction see Ricci, *English Collectors*. These men collected somewhat indiscriminately, however, and the *Poetria nova* may simply have been caught in the wide nets that they cast for as many medieval manuscripts as possible.

ATHANASIUS KIRCHER, JESUIT POLYMATH

> I would judge [the *Poetria nova*] is not unworthy of being printed.[32]
> —Athanasius Kircher

The more famous of the two seventeenth-century scholars who commented on the *Poetria nova* is Athanasius Kircher, a "universal polymath . . . .whose curiosity was matched only by his fantasy."[33] Kircher was a self-proclaimed expert in many fields, from hieroglyphics to music to Oriental studies, and he is included in modern encyclopedias on a myriad of subjects, including science fiction and film.[34] Born near Fulda, he entered Jesuit training at Paderborn in 1618, studied philosophy and theology at the University of Würzburg, and was ordained priest in 1628. In 1635 he went to Rome, where he was appointed to the Chair of Mathematics at the Roman College of the Society of Jesus. He died on 27 November 1680.[35]

In 1662, thirty years after his arrival in Rome, Kircher copied and wrote a short summary and evaluation of the *Poetria nova* for Pope Alexander VII (1655–1667). I have found no record of Kircher's having written on anything else like the *Poetria nova*. More typical of his interests is *Mundus Subterraneus,* published that same year, whose subtitle reads as follows:

> A work in which are exposed the divine workmanship of the underground world, the great gifts of nature there distributed, the form, the wonder, riches and great variety of all things in the Protean region: the cause of all hidden effects are demonstrated and the application of those which are useful to mankind, by means of various experimental apparatus, and new and previously unknown methods, are explained.[36]

Kircher understandably found the *Poetria nova* somewhat uncongenial, and from his reactions as well as other evidence in the manuscript we can assume

---

32. "typo haud indignum iudicem" (Vatican City, BAV Chig. I.VI.229, fol. 87r).

33. IJsewijn, *Companion to Neo-Latin Studies,* 129.

34. In addition to the biographical entries cited in the following notes, Kircher is included in, for example, *Dictionary of Film Makers,* 138; *Encyclopedia of Science Fiction,* 670–671 (and mentioned in five other entries); and *Baker's Biographical Dictionary of Musicians,* 1886. See also the websites on various aspects of Kircher's life and interests listed by Rendel, "Athanasius Kircher on the Web."

35. Sources for Kircher's life and influence include Reilly, *Athanasius Kircher;* Fletcher, *Athanasius Kircher;* Merrill, *Athanasius Kircher* (1602–1680), iii–xxxiii; and Findlen, *Athanasius Kircher.* Useful for comprehending the breadth of Kircher's interests is Godwin, *Athanasius Kircher,* lavishly illustrated with exotic reproductions from Kircher's publications.

36. Quoted in Reilly, *Athanasius Kircher,* 99. See Godwin, *Athanasius Kircher,* 86, for a description of the frontispiece to the 1678 Amsterdam edition of this work, beginning "The hand of God lets down the 'great chain of being.' . . . " For a modern interpretation of the same work, see Smithson's *After Athanasius Kircher* (1971) in Tsai, *Robert Smithson Unearthed,* 193, no. 79.

that the task of analyzing it, like that of copying the text itself, was probably imposed upon him by Pope Alexander VII, to whom Kircher's comments are dedicated. The references to Pope Innocent III and to papal responsibility in the *Poetria nova* to which Kircher devotes special attention would have been especially relevant to this pontiff, given his (and Kircher's) interest in supporting "the orthodox counter-revolution."[37] Pope Alexander VII, born Fabio Chigi,[38] owned five manuscripts of the *Poetria nova* now in the Vatican Library.[39] He commissioned two copies of Chig. I.VI.181, one by the learned Cistercian Giovanni Bona[40] and another, four years later, by Kircher. Their copies were bound together by the pope (with Kircher's original foliation corrected to reflect the new arrangement), resulting in what is now Chig. I.VI.229.[41]

Bona's copy contains no notes, but Kircher appended "A Judgment of the Author and his Work . . . for the BLESSED FATHER ALEXANDER VII, PONTIFEX O.M."[42] As Kircher describes it, "the whole book is in praise of Pope Innocent III, to whom he dedicated this book *On the Poetic Art,* which Pits confirms in a sappy manner (*suculenter*)."[43] Kircher emphasizes the great variety of styles as well as subjects found in the *Poetria nova*—not necessarily a good thing according to Kircher, who finds irritating Geoffrey's combination of high seriousness and what the Jesuit sees as poor taste: exactly those qualities that made it popular in the medieval classroom.[44] He does acknowledge Geoffrey's virtuosity but

---

37. Merrill, *Athanasius Kircher,* iv.

38. There is a colorful biography of Alexander VII by Artaud de Montor (1772–1849) in *Lives and Times of the Popes,* 6.71–106, and a more extensive and measured study by Pastor in *History of the Popes,* 31.1–313; see also Rosa, "Alessandro VII," *DBI* 2.205–215.

39. For short descriptions of Chigi's manuscripts of the *Poetria nova,* see Blume, *Bibliotheca librorum manuscriptorum,* 175. Others include Chig. I.IV.145, fols. 1r–49r (the voyeuristic manuscript described in "The Female Body in the Classroom" in chapter 2); and Chig. L.IV.74, fols. 1r–45v (the second manuscript with a version of Franciscellus Mancinus's *accessus*). A third, Chig. I.VI.230, fols. 5r–36v, is a seventeenth-century manuscript of the *Poetria nova* whose only commentary is Pits's description copied by hand before the text. On Alexander VII as a manuscript collector see Pastor, *History of the Popes,* 31.275.

40. Alexander VII brought Bona to Rome and appointed him co-founder of an academy for the study of church history; on Bona, see Pastor, *History of the Popes,* 328, also 349–350; and Bartòla, "Alessandro VII," 56.

41. At the beginning of each copy the pope noted in his own hand who made it. The best description of Vatican City, BAV Chig. I.VI.229, with two copies of the *Poetria nova* on fols. 1r–49v and 51r–84r, is Bartòla, "Alessandro VII," 55–56.

42. "Athanasii Kircheri / Iudicium de Authore eiusque libello . . . Ad BEATUM PATREM ALEXANDRUM VII PONT. O.M." (Vatican City, BAV Chig. I.VI.229, fol. 85r).

43. "dum totus est in laudibus Innocentij III Pontificis, cui et suum hunc de Arte poetica librum inscripsit, eaque suculenter confirmat Pitseus his verbis in paulo ante allegato libro fol. 262" (Vatican City, BAV Chig. I.VI.229, fol. 85v). Kircher's reference to "fol. 262" is presumably to *page* 262 of the printed edition of *De illustribus Angliae scriptoribus* (the entry on Geoffrey is on 261–262). Thus, we may infer that he was using a copy of Pits's book rather than the excerpt in Vatican City, BAV Chig. I.VI.230, the seventeenth-century manuscript mentioned in note 39. There the name of the printer is corrected to Lazius. Kircher also has the correct name of the printer without comment, so it may have been corrected in the printed version of Pits that he used. Kircher copies almost word for word Pits's list of Geoffrey's works at the end and indicates with his numbering that he agrees with Pits's suggestion that what is described as one text is actually two (Vatican City, BAV Chig. I.VI.229, fol. 85v).

44. "De Stylo Authoris. Stylus Authoris pro rudium temporum conditione in hoc opere omnino varius

concludes that it throws him "from the heights of Parnassus into deep, tortuous paths of gorges, full of obscurity and murkiness."[45] Kircher ultimately excuses and dismisses Geoffrey's style because of the age in which he wrote: "only in a period marked by such rudeness and barbarity would he have been pre-eminent."[46] In examining Pits's claim of publication, Kircher notes correctly that the work that Pits is talking about is actually part of the *Poetria nova* and that there is no evidence of such an edition. Somewhat surprisingly, however, he deems it as "not unworthy of being printed."[47]

At the end of the manuscript he compiles his own list of the contents of the *Poetria nova* (fol. 88r–v), to which I have added line numbers in parentheses:

Index of the Arguments
That the Author Treats in This Volume:

Fol. 1[48] Dedication to Pope Innocent III, whom he extols with wondrous compliments; he admires Rome and proclaims it the sole "light of the world" (33). Next he describes the bases of poetic art, which he expounds at length on folios 3 and 4 under allegorical coverings and by analogy, using a variety of images related to his chosen topics. (43).

Fol. 5 He teaches how the poetic art ought to be adorned through apostrophes and takes an example from the death of Richard, King of England (368); then he puts in an invective against those boastful men who are importunate of honor but not worthy of it (438).

Fol. 8 He teaches how to create personification, and he gives an example of personification in an address of Christ's cross to men (468). Next he inveighs against France in the manner of a propsopopeia (517). He prescribes precepts to be extracted from the shape and adornment of the body and provides instruction through performing what is to be imitated (563). He confirms the precepts of his art through a comparison of youth and old age (675). He plays with verbs deftly displayed in a great variety of metaphors, which are based on the four seasons of the year (792). He ingeniously draws on the blacksmith's art for precepts of his own (814).[49]

Fol. 14 He treats the rhetorical colors introduced by a variegated grafting of

---

est, non dico rerum quas tractat uarietate, sed poeticæ uenæ inæqualitate" (Vatican City, BAV Chig. I.VI.229, fol. 86r).

45. "ex alto Parnassi uertice imas uallium tortuosas semitas obscuritate et caligine plenas . . . " (Vatican City, BAV Chig. I.VI.229, fol. 86v).

46. "tantum in tanta saeculi ruditate et barbarie præstiterit" (Vatican City, BAV Chig. I.VI.229, fol. 86v).

47. "typo haud indignum iudicem" (Vatican City, BAV Chig. I.VI.229, fol. 87r). I am grateful to Gernot Wieland for his suggestion about how to translate this phrase (e-mail correspondence, July 2007).

48. Kircher's folio numbers are of his copy before it was combined with Bona's.

49. See "Shaping the Student" in chapter 1.

metaphors (844).[50]

16 He teaches how to create additional metaphors with a varied display of examples (966).

17 He demonstrates using the [rhetorical] colors of words to describe subjects, and he puts first the theme of the sin of Adam, which he adorns with the beauty of metaphors (1098).[51]

18 He fully describes the fall of Adam and its restoration by Christ, and at the same time he introduces a life of Christ (1132).

20 He begins to treat the figures of thoughts (1230), and he provides an example of the pope's punishing of wicked deeds (1280). [A contemporary hand adds, "But in an incredibly obscure way!"]

22 He continues the same techniques with the Passion of Christ the Lord (1387).

23 He describes at length the fall of Lucifer (1437), his trickery in the eating of the apple (1462), and the restoration of human salvation through the Incarnation of Christ (1489).

25 The topics and techniques in various examples of the art, which he teaches at extraordinary length (1531).[52]

30 How serious and comic topics are introduced in verse (1883).

32 He describes precepts suitable for the rhetor (1920)[53] together with the recommendation of the book to the pope (2066) and the presentation of the book to William, Bishop of the English Chancery, his special friend (2098).

Finished on the fifteenth day of August

In the year 1662.[54]

---

50. This awkward phrasing refers to the portion of the *Poetria nova* where Geoffrey discusses taking a verb that has a metaphoric relationship to its subject, such as "Earth quaffed more of heaven's dew than was right" (862), and making it more emphatic by adding a metaphoric adjective: "The intoxicated earth quaffed . . . " (867).

51. Kircher uses "troporum" although this section of the *Poetria nova* exemplifies the figures, not the tropes. Many of Geoffrey's examples of tropes employ metaphorical language, however.

52. From his emphasis on the length of Geoffrey's treatment ("fusissime") and the lack of an intervening description before the next item, Kircher appears to be grouping together the treatments of signification, conversion, and determination.

53. These are the faults to avoid.

54.   Index argumentorum
                 de quibus Auctor in hoc codice agit
  Fol.
  1 Dedicatoria ad Innocentium III Pontificem, quem miris laudibus
  2 extollit. Romam admiratur, et tanquam unicam lucem
  3 mundi prædicat. Deinde fundamenta poëticae artis describit, quæ
  4 et fol. 3 et 4 deinceps fusè omnia sub allegoricis uerborum in
     uolucris et uarijs assumptarum rerum similitudinibus analogicè
     exponit.
  Fol.
  5 Quomodo per apostrophos adornanda sit ars poetica docet
  6 exemplumque sumit a morte Ricardi Regis Angliæ, deinde

Note the substantial differences in Kircher's table of contents from the one appended to a fifteenth-century manuscript that was translated in the first chapter.[55] The earlier list focuses primarily on techniques that could be used by a teacher or writer as these are framed in the commentary by a noted teacher. Kircher, in contrast, highlights the content of the examples, evidence that the papal subject of many of them was what drew the current pope's attention to the work.[56] With regard to Geoffrey's longest example, the figures of thoughts displayed via an elaboration of the theme of papal responsibility, the summary

7 inuectiuam contra importunos honoris non meriti iactatores ponit.

Fol.

8 Prosopopœiam formare docet, exemplumque in uenerandæ

9 Crucis Christi ad homines prosopopœâ allocutione ponit.

10 deinde in Galli[c]am κατὰ τὴν προσωποποιίαν inuéhitur;

11 à corporis forma et decore sumenda præscribit; rerum

12 per gestus imitandarum documenta præbere confirmat artis

13 præcepta per comparationem iuuentæ et Senectæ: in uerbis
rìtè disponendis magna metaphorarum uarietate ludit,
quas a quatuor anni temporibus, ab arte fabrili ingeniose
ad artis præcepta deducit.

Fol.

14 De coloribus uerbis inducendis uarià metaphorarum insitione

15 agit.

16 Alias metaphoras formare uaria exemplorum exhibitione
docet.

17 Monstrat colores uerborum ad res describendas, et primo
ab Adami peccato paradigma ponit, quod troporum uenustate
adornat.

18 Adami lapsum per Christum restauratum fusè describit,

19 et una Christi uitam introducit.

20 Incipit tractare de coloribus sententiarum exemplumque

21 ponit de Papa uindic<t>e scelerum. [Sed mirum in modum obscurè *in marg.*]

22 Eadem applicat ad Passionem Christi Domini

[23]

23 Casum Luciferi, <suam> [suæ *MS*] in pomi esu deceptionem, humanæ salutis

24 iacturam per Christi Incarnationem restitutam fusè describit.

25 Topica troposque in arte adhibendos uarijs exemplis quam

26 fusissime docet.

27

28

29

30 Quomodo seria et iocosa uersibus introducenda.

31

32 Præcepta Rhetori congrua præscribit, unà cum recommendatione

33 Libri ad Papam, et transmissione operis ad Guilielmum
Episcopum Angliæ Cancellarium Amicum singularem.

Finis die 15 Aug.

Anno 1662

55. See "The Usefulness of This Text" in chapter 1 (and also the much more eccentric list of contents in "Geoffrey after Quintilian" in the Afterword).

56. The first portion of this passage (1280–1324) was the first substantial excerpt from the *Poetria nova* to be published, by Matthias Flacius in 1557 (*Varia doctorum piorum virorum,* 398–399). Shorter quotations of a line or two had appeared earlier with interlinear glosses and comment in Henricus Boort's *Fasciculus Morum* (Antwerp [ca. 1503]), A.VI.a and B.IV.a. See Woods, "An Unfashionable Rhetoric," 320.

in the earlier manuscript merely states, "He exemplifies the aforementioned colors," whereas Kircher (see above on folios 20–23) lists the subheadings of Geoffrey's theme in such a way that his own reader gets a complete picture of Geoffrey's modulation from one part to the next and the inclusiveness and range of his treatment.[57] The earlier list of contents specifies each of the eight ways of beginning while Kircher makes no mention of them, saying only that Geoffrey uses metaphoric language in the early sections of the work (folios 3 and 4). Given Kircher's apparent lack of interest in rhetoric and medieval poetry, it is not surprising that the *Poetria nova* had little appeal for him. Zacharius Lund, to whom we now turn, looked at Geoffrey and the *Poetria nova* completely differently, but, like Kircher, with no recognition of the earlier pedagogical usefulness of the work.

ZACHARIAS LUND: CLASSICAL SCHOLAR AND POET

> Gamfredus [Geoffrey of Vinsauf] . . . is not unsophisticated.[58]
> —Zacharias Lund

The only real commentary on the *Poetria nova* produced during the seventeenth century was that of Zacharias Lund. In approach, method, and attitude, he stands alone among commentators on the text. In level of detail—though a very different kind of detail—his only rivals are Pace of Ferrara and Dybinus of Prague, whose popular commentaries are described in chapters 3 and 4. Lund's handwritten manuscript of more than five hundred pages in the Royal Library in Copenhagen, Gl. kgl. Saml. 2037, has the following parts:

1. An eight-page address "To the Reader" in which Lund, anticipating resistance, recommends the *Poetria nova* and justifies the study of such works on historical grounds. He begins, "Benevolent reader, I offer you this little work, not so much because of its own merits as because of when it was written."[59] As he says later, "Those who show at least a modest degree of erudition should not be ignorant of the literature of any age."[60] His purpose is to "shed some light on Gamfredus."[61]

---

57. For the applicability of the passage to Geoffrey's pope, see "Sermons?" in chapter 2.

58. "Gamfredus . . . rusticus non est" (Copenhagen, Kongelige Bibliotek, Gl. kgl. Saml. 2037, p. ii–iii). Lund's manuscript is numbered in pages.

59. "Ad Lectorem / Benevole Lector, / Opusculum tibi heîc [*sic*] exhibeo, qvod non tam propter se expetas, qvam̃ temporis, qvo scriptum fuit . . . " (Copenhagen, Kongelige Bibliotek, Gl. kgl. Saml. 2037, p. i). This address occupies pp. i–viii.

60. "Qvin interesse, certum est, eorum, qvi in literis eruditionem, saltem mediocrem, affectant, ut nullius seculi literas ignorent" (Copenhagen, Kongelige Bibliotek, Gl. kgl. Saml. 2037, p. ii).

61. "ut et Gamfredo aliqvam lucem adferam . . . " (Copenhagen, Kongelige Bibliotek, Gl. kgl. Saml. 2037, p. vii).

2. A 22-page "INDEX OF THE AUTHORS whose names and writings are either merely quoted or on occasion corrected and indeed clarified in the following NOTES."[62] This is an alphabetical list of the sources of the annotations (item 4) on the *Poetria nova* (item 3).

3. The text: "Gamfredus on the *POETRIA NOVA.*"[63] 84 pages.

4. "The ANNOTATIONS of ZACHARIAS LUND on the *POETRIA* of Gamfredus."[64] A 360-page commentary composed of an introduction (based on a medieval *accessus*), citations, and addenda.

5. An alphabetical "INDEX OF SUBJECTS AND QUOTATIONS" (48 pages) found in both "the *POETRIA* and also the ANNOTATIONS."[65]

6. Four further pages of addenda to the annotations.[66]

Such a prodigious expenditure of scholarly attention was not extraordinary for the period, nor is Lund's annotation by quotation unusual. As Anthony Grafton notes about scholar-philologists of the early seventeenth century, "the immense Latin books that their owners spent their lives writing are more likely to inspire horror than respect. These swollen and prodigious volumes, running to hundreds of pages and studded with interminable quotations in Greek and Hebrew, were around 1600 the staple of Europe's intellectual life."[67] Similarly, Lodi Nauta describes the seventeenth-century commentaries on Boethius's *Consolation of Philosophy* as "concatenations of long quotations from a great number of Greek and Latin authors, which make it difficult to discern their own preferences."[68] Thus, the extent and technique of Lund's commentary on the *Poetria nova* are not unique; what is significant is that this energy was focused on the *Poetria nova*. Lund's attitude toward medieval poetry and poetics, both in his commentary on the *Poetria nova* and elsewhere in his writings, prefigures the antiquarian attention that this subject will receive in the following century from Polycarp Leyser, Johannes Albertus Fabricius, and others.

Zacharius Lund was born on April 5, 1608, in a village in Schleswig-Holstein, and he attended Latin school in Sonderborg.[69] In 1625 he followed his

---

62. "INDEX AUCTORUM qvorum Nomina & Scripta in seqventibus NOTIS vel simpliciter laudantur, vel ex occasione emendantur atque illustrantur" (Copenhagen, Kongelige Bibliotek, Gl. kgl. Saml. 2037, p. x; section on pp. x–xxxi).

63. "Gamfredus de POETRIA NOVA" (Copenhagen, Kongelige Bibliotek, Gl. kgl. Saml. 2037, p. 3; the text continues to p. 87).

64. "ZACH. LUNDII In POETRIAM Gamfredi ANNOTATIONES" (Copenhagen, Kongelige Bibliotek, Gl. kgl. Saml. 2037; title page on p. 89; *accessus* [discussed below] on pp. 91–96; commentary on pp. 91–389; addenda to p. 440).

65. "INDEX RERÜM ET VERBORÜM Qvæ cum in ipsa POETRIA, tum in nostris ANNOTATIONIBUS continentur" (Copenhagen, Kongelige Bibliotek, Gl. kgl. Saml. 2037, p. 441; this index continues to p. 488). The longest entries are those under the headings of "Christ" and "Pope."

66. Copenhagen, Kongelige Bibliotek, Gl. kgl. Saml. 2037, pp. 489–493.

67. Grafton, *Joseph Scaliger,* 1.

68. Nauta, "Magis sit Platonicus," 202.

69. Although not without problems, Moerke, *Anfänge der weltlichen Barocklyrik,* 132–149 (here 136), is

brother to Hamburg, where he studied languages and theology. He spent fifteen months in Wittenberg, returning to his parents' home in 1631 when the political situation deteriorated. From 1632 to 1634 he worked as a tutor in Schleswig-Holstein. In 1634 his *Poemata Juvenilia* were published, with a second edition the next year, and his *Deutsche Gedichte* in 1636.[70] From 1638 to 1640 he lived in Sorø, Denmark, as a tutor for Holger Vind; there he also worked on his commentaries on classical texts.[71] From 1641 to 1645 he toured Europe. First he visited Holland, England, and France, where he worked on his commentaries and his own Latin poetry. Finally Lund arrived in Italy; he lived in Padua from 1643 to 1644 and then ended his journey in Rome.[72] He spent time in the Vatican Library and had some contact with Jesuits (though there is no indication that he knew Kircher).[73]

Lund then returned to Denmark, where he spent the rest of his life, achieving renown as a classical scholar and Latin poet. With regard to his poetry, Minna Skafte Jensen notes that

> the fact that Lund as a young man invested much energy in composing vernacular poetry, while during the rest of his life he concentrated more and more on refining his Latin works, . . . makes him unusual. Both in Denmark and elsewhere, it was normal for poets who composed in Latin as well as vernacular to begin their careers in Latin and end in the vernacular.[74]

In February 1646 Lund took a job lasting eight years as rector of a public school in Herlufsholm, in the meantime receiving a master of arts degree from Copenhagen in 1647. He was not considered a particularly good teacher; it appears that he preferred to spend his time on philological studies.[75] In 1654 he became the librarian for a Danish nobleman, Jørgen Seefeld, at Ringsted, presumably a more congenial occupation since his new employer was a fanatical book collec-

---

the major biographical source for what follows. I have also drawn on Moller, *Cimbria Literata*, 1.369–372; *DBL* 9.179; Lohmeier, *Neue Deutsche Biographie*, 15.520–521; and Svaning and Foss, *Vita Zacharias Lundii*, in Copenhagen, Kongelige Bibliotek, Add. 182 h 4°. For a copy of this source and for additional information and suggestions I am very grateful to Minna Skafte Jensen.

70. The best introduction in English to Lund's poetry is Jensen, "A Latin poem." See also Cysarz, *Deutsche Barockdichtung*, 134–39; Moerke, *Anfänge der weltlichen Barocklyrik*, 133–202; Harper, "Leipzig Poetry after Paul Fleming"; and Jensen, "Dänische Lateindichtung," "En ønskedrøm," "Latindigteren Zacharias Lund," and "Eine humanistische Dichterfreundschaft."

71. The monastery at Sorø had the reputation of being a place where one might find classical texts; for example, "Rumours about a complete Livy in the monastery of Søro in Zealand immediately raised the enthusiasm of Poggio Bracciolini in Rome . . . " (Petersen, "Gudiani Haunienses Galteriani," 140).

72. On Lund's time in Rome see Helk, "Dänische Romreisen," 186.

73. Much later—sometime between 1665 and 1667—he wrote a collection of biblical paraphrases, including a sacred female lament, or heroid, of a kind particularly associated with Jesuit poets. On this genre, see Dörrie, *Der heroische Brief*, 389–403; on Lund's use of it, see Jensen," A Latin poem," 49.

74. Jensen, "A Latin Poem," 34.

75. Moerke, *Anfänge der weltlichen Barocklyrik*, 147. I had hoped that Lund might have used the *Poetria nova* in his teaching but have found no evidence thereof.

tor who owned over 26,000 volumes.[76] Lund died on June 8, 1667, and most of his manuscripts are now in the Royal Library in Copenhagen.[77]

Zacharias Lund drew on one or more medieval commentaries for his own very different treatment of the *Poetria nova*. At the beginning of his annotations (item no. 3 above), in what he calls his "frontispiece" (a reworking of the medieval *accessus*), Lund refers to a specific codex that I have not been able to identify.[78] He describes it as "in a recent hand" and says that it addresses three aspects of the text, which he will do as well; he divides his comments into the typical *accessus* categories of author, subject matter, and form[79]:

"I. The *Author* is called Gamfredus: this name seems to be the same as Godefridus, Goffridus [Gaufridus, Galfridus, Joffredus *in marg.*], Theofredus. He is called Galfridus Vinesaulf, or de Vino salvo by Bale and Pits."[80] Lund disagrees with Bale's assertion that Geoffrey was of Norman stock, however, and he offers his own unique suggestion (which may have been the origin of his interest in the poem[81]): "Among the abbots of the monastery of Sorø in Zealand, I find a certain 'Geoffrey the Englishman' around the date 1200 AD during Innocent III's papacy. I conjecture that he was the author of this poem."[82]

"II. The *Argument* and the *Subject* of the text is clearly Rhetoric, or Oratory."[83] Lund notes that "Oratory and Poetics are distinct categories," but that Geoffrey appropriately entitles the work "*Poetria* rather than *Rhetorica* since the greatest part of it is devoted to Figures and Tropes."[84] When he con-

---

76. On Seefeld, see *DB.L* 21.529 ff.

77. Lohmeier, *Neue Deutsche Biographie*, 15.521.

78. The other copy of the *Poetria nova* in the Royal Library in Copenhagen, Kongelige Bibliotek, Gl. kgl. Saml. 2036, is a fourteenth-century manuscript containing the *EC* without an *accessus*. Lund takes into consideration (and exception to) the division of the text into the parts of rhetoric found in the *EC* and numerous other commentaries, and he may be drawing on a specific later manuscript or adducing information from multiple sources. In his "Address to the reader," Lund mentions that he has received help from Marcus Meibom in deciphering and correcting the text of the *Poetria nova* (Copenhagen, Kongelige Bibliotek, Gl. kgl. Saml. 2037, p. vi). On Meibom (1627–1710), who was a librarian to both Queen Christina in Stockholm and King Frederick in Copenhagen, see *DBL* 15.438–439.

79. "Titulus in nostro Codice, recentiori manu, adpictus erat hujusmodi: Gamfredus de Poetria nova. Tribus verbis, tria dicit [illius iudicis auctor *add. MS*]; totidem etiam notis a nobis heîc [*sic*] in frontispicio expendenda. Innuit 1. *Auctorem* scripti. 2. *Materiam* ejus, sive Subjectum. 3. *Formam,* sive tractandi modum" (Copenhagen, Kongelige Bibliotek, Gl. kgl. Saml. 2037, p. 91). I have not noted Lund's additional corrections.

80. "I. **Auctor** dicitur Gamfredus: qvod nomen videtur idem esse, qvod Godefridus, Goffridus [Gaufridus, Galfridus, Joffredus *in marg.*], Theofredus. Balæo & Pitseo vocatur Galfridus Vinesaulf, seu de Vino salvo" (Copenhagen, Kongelige Bibliotek, Gl. kgl. Saml. 2037, p. 91).

81. Suggestion of Minna Skafte Jensen, e-mail communication, May 2006.

82. "Inter Abbates Monasterii Sorani in Sælandia, Gamfredum aliqvem Anglum reperio, circa annum æræ Christianæ m cc, sedente Innocentio III, Pontifice Romano. Mea conjectura est, hunc ipsum fuisse hujus Poematis auctorem." (Copenhagen, Kongelige Bibliotek, Gl. kgl. Saml. 2037, p. 92)

83. "II. **Argumentum** porro & Subjectum scripti Rhetoricum plane est, seu Oratorium" (Copenhagen, Kongelige Bibliotek, Gl. kgl. Saml. 2037, p. 93).

84. "Nam ut distinctæ facultates sint Oratoria & Poetica. . . . Deinde Poetriam appellat potius ***

tinues that "orations are not the only work of the orator" but also "letters and every kind of writing, and even the sermon," citing Gerhard Vossius and quoting from the *Poetria nova* itself,[85] Lund is reflecting the northern European emphasis on applying the text exclusively to prose composition while acknowledging its roots in verse composition.[86]

"III. The **Form** that he achieves he himself asserts [in the title] to be 'new' (*nova*)."[87] Although he has just acknowledged the appropriateness of "*Poetria*" as the title, in this section Lund takes exception to the addition of "*nova*," objecting that the work cannot possibly be really new. He adds, however, that Geoffrey does contribute examples of description, personification, and amplification, many of which are extremely elegant.[88] Lund ends with a discussion of the medieval division of the text into the five parts of rhetoric (invention, arrangement, style, memory, and delivery).[89]

Lund's "Annotations" that follow consist entirely of citations from the works of other writers that contain the same word or have some other resonance with the given line in Geoffrey's work. Lund's gloss on Geoffrey's description of Pope Innocent III as "golden-tongued" (17–18), for example, contains a short definition of what "golden" (*aureus*) means in this rhetorical context ("held to be delightful, charming, precious, elegant, polished, splendid, appealing—the best and most beautiful"[90]) along with quotations in Greek and Latin that include various forms of the word for "golden" from Pindar, Hesiod, Theocritus, Plato, the Pythagorean *aurea carmina* (on which Lund also left an unpublished commentary), Lucretius, Horace, Virgil, Ovid, Apuleius, and three books of the Bible—among others.

Lund is comparatively restrained here: only one page, and that only partially filled. His practice is to write across two-thirds of the side of a page, leaving the outer third for references discovered or located later. On most pages this outer column is used as well; e.g., the glosses on the traditional

---

Rhetoricam, quod <maxima pars> [maximam partem *MS*] agit de Figuris ac Tropis" (Copenhagen, Kongelige Bibliotek, Gl. kgl. Saml. 2037 p. 94).

85. "Rhetores, solùm propter Orationes, quae qvidem praecipuum, non tamen unicum sunt opus Oratoris, fusè adeo omnis scriptionis, ac sermonis ipsius causa. Uti id rectè monuit Gerh. Vossius, lib. I. *Instit. Orator.* cap. vi. sect. 9. Gamfredus autem ipse ejusmodi qvid innuit, quanto ait vers. 1820 et seqq. [he quotes 1850–52] et postea, vers 1913 [he quotes 1943–44]" (Copenhagen, Kongelige Bibliotek, Gl. kgl. Saml. 2037, p. 94).

86. See chapter 4 for other examples of this interpretation of the work.

87. "III. **Formam** quod attinet, eam ipse novam esse testatur" (Copenhagen, Kongelige Bibliotek, Gl. kgl. Saml. 2037, p. 94).

88. E.g., "Ut nihil nunc dicam de tot elegantibus ac jucundis descriptionibus, Prosopopoeiis, ac dilatandi modis" (Copenhagen, Kongelige Bibliotek, Gl. kgl. Saml. 2037, p. 95).

89. See above, note 78.

90. "amabile, gratum, pretiosum, elegans, politum, splendidum, speciosum, optimum denique ac pulcherrimum habetur" (Copenhagen, Kongelige Bibliotek, Gl. kgl. Saml. 2037, p. 102).

trope of the *puer-senex* (old young man)[91] at line 23, with its many ancient and medieval resonances, fill four pages, and they include cross-references to other uses of the same image in the *Poetria nova,* such as the description of Androgeos (174–176). Sometimes Lund cuts corners, though: when he treats the section of the *Poetria nova* on digression, one of the medieval commentators' favorite places to comment on Geoffrey's skill and deft touch, Lund's glosses on the description of lovers "who through their love were never parted" (553)[92] includes a series of citations on this theme taken, as he acknowledges, from the *Adversaria* of Caspar Barthius (1587–1658). The range of Lund's citations is impressive: the total number of authorial entities in his index exceeds seven hundred. They include Greek authors (Aristophanes, Euripides, Isocrates, Julian the Apostate, Origen, Philo, Xenophon, etc.), Latin authors (e.g., Aldus Manutius, Bede, Jerome, Innocent III, Lorenzo Valla, Matthew of Vendôme, the Apostle Paul, Piero della Vigne, Plautus, Quintilian, Statius, Tacitus, Thomas Walsingham), and collectively authored texts (such as decrees of the Lateran Council and Council of Nicea, and "the Laws of Edward the Confessor").[93]

Lund appears to have had ambivalent feelings about medieval poetics. On the one hand, near the end of his life he included accentual, rhymed Latin poems in a collection of his poetry that he was preparing for publication (with an apologia encouraging the reader to be open-minded about them); on the other, when he further revised the collection, these poems were removed.[94] In his commentary on the *Poetria nova,* which he may have been working on at about the same time, he apologizes to the reader for having written so extensively on a work from a barbarous era. Yet, as he conveys by the title of the manuscript, "GAMFREDUS On the POETRIA NOVA, enlightened (*illustratus*) by Continuous Commentary . . . ,"[95] Lund literally illuminates the work by means of associations, connections, and resemblances between Geoffrey's words and those of the great writers of the western tradition. These do not overshadow the *Poetria nova* but rather raise it to the highest standard.

---

91. "Ecce senex iuvenis," translated by Nims as "a youth of ripe age." Lund's treatment of this phrase occupies pp. 103–107 of Copenhagen, Kongelige Bibliotek, Gl. kgl. Saml. 2037.

92. *PN* 535 in Lund (Copenhagen, Kongelige Bibliotek, Gl. kgl. Saml. 2037, p. 195). Nims, using Faral's "nondum" for "nunqvam," translates the phrase as "who yet through their love were not parted."

93. The greatest number of individual citations are of Virgil (52), Ovid (55), Horace (73), and Cicero (77). The sheer volume of material amassed suggests that it was gathered in the Vatican Library and/or Seefeld's collection.

94. The publication never materialized. I am grateful to Minna Skafte Jensen for this information. Jensen mentions Lund's "medieval pastiches" in "Landigtern Zacharias Lund," 27.

95. "GAMFREDUS De POETRIA NOVA, Perpetuo Commentario illustratus" (Copenhagen, Kongelige Bibliotek, Gl. kgl. Saml. 2037, title page [unnumbered]).

AN END AND A BEGINNING

When he presented Geoffrey's offspring (*foetus*) to the public, it struck the eye of all like a new light.[96]
    —Maurus Sarti, 1770

Zacharias Lund saw the *Poetria nova* as part of a continuum of literary produc-tion in the Latin language. His near-contemporary Athanasius Kircher, whose talents and interests were so different, was assigned the task of evaluating the work because of its subject matter alone. Yet both men were teachers as well as scholars, although they inhabited only the latter role when writing about the *Poetria nova.* The severance of the *Poetria nova* from the classroom was now complete. Polycarp Leyser, professor of poetry at Helmstedt, first printed the *Poetria nova* in 1721 in *History of Poets and Poems of the Middle Ages,* which con-tains a variety of works that its subtitle describes as *Elegant, Ingenious, and Curi-ous.*[97] The *Poetria nova* obviously intrigued Leyser, and he published it again, this time separately, in 1724.[98] Sarti's quotation above, written fifty years later but probably based on an earlier printed excerpt (not the one Pits mentioned), reminds us that Geoffrey's work was a revelation.[99] Thanks to Leyser's editions, the status of the *Poetria nova* as a treasured example of the aesthetic principles of an earlier age was secure. Like many other verse texts originally written to teach, the *Poetria nova* had, in becoming a literary classic, lost its pedagogical purpose. Some of the possible reasons for this transformation are explored in the Afterword.

---

96. "Ac certe cum hic Gaufridi foetus in publicam prodiit, quasi nova luce omnium oculos perstrinxit" (Sarti-Fattorini, *De claris,* 601).

97. *P. Leyseri . . . Historia poetarum et poematum medii aevi decem post annum a nato Christo CCCC, seculorum centum et amplius codicum mstorum* [= *manuscriptorum*] *ope carmina varia elegantia, ingeniosa, curiosa . . . evulgantur, . . . recensentur.* In the table of contents Leyser says that he edited the *Poetria nova* from manuscripts, which are identified later (861) as the Gudiani manuscripts in the Herzog August Bibliothek in Wolfenbüttel. Leyser's discussion of Geoffrey and his works begins on page 855 and concludes on 986; the *PN* is edited on 862–978.

98. *Galfridi de Vinosalvo Ars Poetica ante quingentos annos conscripta. Ex quatuor codicibus manuscriptis et fragmentis impressis, . . . edita et praelectionibus . . . substructa à P. Leyser.*

99. Sarti is referring to Du Boulay's publication of the dedication to Pope Innocent III in 1665 (*Historia Universitatis Parisiensis,* 2.520–521).

AFTERWORD

LOOKING BACK

The efficient cause was *magister* Geoffrey of England, who, although most preeminent in the other arts, yet was most noteworthy in the art of rhetoric, as the depth of this work attests.[1]
— Pistoia, Archivio Capitolare del Duomo, C. 143

The value judgements in the statement above are absolute: Geoffrey of Vinsauf was *gloriosus* at whatever he turned his hand to; in rhetoric there was no one like him; the *Poetria nova* is profound.[2] It has been my intention in this book to explore the pedagogical grounds of such assessments of both this author and his most famous work. At one point or another and in one way or another, the *Poetria nova* came close to being all things to all teachers during the three centuries after it was written. In order to understand how this was possible, I have tried to avoid judgmental language and evolutionary terms in describing the differences

---

1. "Causa efficiens fuit magister Gualfredus de Anglia, qui licet in ceteris artibus gloriosus fuerit, tamen in arte rethorice singularis, quod huius operis profunditas attestatur" (Pistoia, Archivio Capitolare del Duomo, C. 143, fol. 1r).

2. It also reminds us that the boundaries between disciplines during the Middle Ages were very different from our own; cf. Murphy: "Medieval practitioners cared far less than we do whether their ideas came from grammar, rhetoric or dialectic," although some of the comments quoted in this study belie the rest of his sentence: "or whether they had obtained their knowledge from this or that teacher, or from one specific textbook as opposed to some other" ("The Arts," 64).

among commentaries. With each manuscript, even each gloss, I have tried to put myself in the position of someone who taught or heard it. This approach is not the only one that could be taken with the massive amount of surviving commentary material on the *Poetria nova,* only a fraction of which has been discussed here, but it may be the most important one for helping us to understand why so much energy was expended on this text. What interests me is the epistemology of the classroom, how it functions as a site in which the mind is encouraged to work in particular ways. The distinctions that I have emphasized are those that suggest how medieval and early Renaissance students were encouraged to read and think about this work and the sequence of skills that they were taught from it.

What I have found contradicts a number of assumptions that have been made about premodern teaching and the intentions of commentators. It is often assumed, although a number of other scholars have offered evidence to the contrary, that medieval teachers suppressed or censored parts of texts. I have found very few examples.[3] It is also sometimes said, and by scholars whose work I greatly admire, that no interesting (medieval) commentaries were written after 1200, which happens to be when the *Poetria nova* was composed. This whole study obviously challenges that assertion. There is also an assumption that all medieval commentaries are allegorical or scholastic, and that all medieval teachers were pursuing a religious agenda. None of the commentaries on the *Poetria nova* offers an allegorical reading of this admittedly non-narrative work. It is true that some of the commentaries are scholastic, or have elements of scholastic analysis in the introduction of Aristotelian concepts and method; these characteristics are limited to the most advanced commentaries, however. And biblical material is introduced but rarely and usually by Italian commentators equally engaged with teaching the *Poetria nova* in the context of classical writers.

The overwhelming need for efficiency in textbooks, and the consequent attraction for teachers of works that fulfilled several roles at once, declined with the widespread availability of cheaper writing materials and the invention of printing. As we saw in the last chapter, the *Poetria nova* lost its identity as a teaching text. In the next two sections we see glimpses of how gradually and how strangely the *Poetria nova* became just half the text it used to be.

---

3. Yet one of them—the warning against teaching "rudes" those lines in which Geoffrey chides God—is what encouraged me to examine differences among commentaries as possible evidence of various levels of students at whom they might be directed; see "Reading between the Lines" in chapter 2.

GEOFFREY AFTER QUINTILIAN

> We want to adopt from [Geoffrey] the technique of developing admirable determinations, since neither Tully nor Quintilian said anything about them.[4]
>
> —Pistoia, Archivio Capitolare del Duomo, C. 143

Poggio Bracciolini's discovery of a complete text of Quintilian's *Institutio oratoria* in the monastery of St. Gall in 1417 is often heralded as the beginning of Renaissance rhetoric, but this event does not appear to have had a significant impact on the teaching of the *Poetria nova*.[5] Two late commentators on the *Poetria nova* do refer to Quintilian in talking about Geoffrey, but not in a way that disparages the latter.[6] One implies that Geoffrey's work is the fulfilment of Quintilian's famous definition of the orator. It occurs in a late-fifteenth-century manuscript also in St. Gall, Stiftsbibliothek 856. Described as a "humanist miscellany" by Emil Polak, the codex also contains the *Elegantiolae* of Augustinus Datus, Virgil's *Eclogues,* and several comedies by Terence, as well as dictaminal texts including a long excerpt from Dybinus's *Viaticus dictandi*.[7] It reflects the combination of humanist literary preferences and dictaminal interests common in fifteenth-century northern manuscripts of the *Poetria nova*.[8]

The scribe's most attractive contribution is a series of simple, graceful diagrams that precede each section of the *Poetria nova*. In the first of these (plates 15a and 15b), he presents Geoffrey's ways of beginning a narrative as an elaboration of Quintilian's definition. The initial paragraph on the far left states the following:

> In the first book of the *Institutio oratorie artis* Quintilian says that "the orator is a good man well trained in the art of speaking" {*Inst.* 12.1.1}, whose responsibility is to devise the material [and] make it beautiful throughout its parts. The order of expression (*ordo dicendi*) is twofold, i.e., Geoffrey in the verse, "The material's order may follow two possible courses" (88).[9]

---

4. "Sic artificium inueniendi laudabiles determinationes hic uolumus recipere ab eodem, quia nec Tullius, nec Quintillianus [*sic*] aliquid de hiis dixit" (Pistoia, Archivio Capitolare del Duomo, C. 143, fol. 30v).

5. From time to time in earlier commentaries a phrase or statement from Quintilian is cited to add *gravitas* to a discussion of rhetoric in general, usually in the *accessus* to a commentary along with other sources, but not in a way that draws attention to the relationship of the two treatises.

6. Each of the men who produced the manuscripts discussed in this section reconfigures the commentaries that he is drawing on, so I refer to them as both scribes and commentators.

7. St. Gall, Stiftsbibliothek, 856, pp. 283–534 (numbered in pages instead of folios). On this manuscript see Scherrer, *Verzeichniss der Handschriften,* 291; Gallick, "Medieval Rhetorical Arts," 84; Kristeller, *Iter ital.* 5.128; and Polak, *Western Europe,* 242–43 (19 on Augustinus Datus and the *Elegantiolae*). The commentary draws on an older one in the same library, 875, which contains a copy of the *Early Commentary,* for some of its glosses.

8. For more on Valla, Datus, and medieval dictaminal works, see Henderson, "Valla's *Elegantiae.*"

9. "Secundum Quintilianum primo libro *Institucionis oratorie artis,* dicit rethor est 'vir bonus arte dicendi peritus' {*Inst.* 12.1.1} cuius officium est materiam invenire, inuentam per partes venustare.

The scribe designed this folio opening so that from this paragraph flow ribbon brackets outlining Geoffrey's treatment of the two kinds of order and the eight ways of beginning a text. At the top is a branch diagram of the kinds of artificial order. Below is a floating paragraph stating, "The story (*fabula*) that Geoffrey narrates is taken from the metamorphosis of King Minos, his son Androgeos, and the virgin queen Scylla, who was the daughter of King Nisus."[10] The bottom bracket points to a definition of natural order, and another leads to the statement that "Geoffrey exemplifies this there at the verse, 'Aside from the bounty of Fortune'" (159 ff., where Minos's story is told in natural order).[11]

Here is all the information needed to follow Geoffrey's exercise and to recognize the appropriate parts of the text in the passage to follow; the other diagrams that occur at regular intervals throughout the text and commentary are similar. The commentator's divisions of Geoffrey's text and the transitions between doctrine and example are not new, and other manuscripts have diagrams of the content.[12] What is significant in this diagram is the emphasis on authorial names. In an ordinal sense, Quintilian is primary; he establishes the standard for the book. But Geoffrey is the writer who fulfils the standard; he is named in almost all of the complete sentences in this diagram.

Although there was a manuscript of the *Institutio oratoria* in the library at St. Gall, this commentator/scribe may have known Quintilian's definition from a *florilegium*. But an Italian commentator working at roughly the same time knew Quintilian's opus well enough to see what it lacked: the theory of determinations, as we saw in the quotation at the beginning of this section, and also the theory of conversions. At this point in the manuscript the first scribe has already abandoned the commentary he started with, the one citing Dante near the end that was discussed in chapter 3. Just after Geoffrey's discussion of the tropes, however, and long before the reference to Dante's *Commedia*, this first scribe stops copying both the *Poetria nova* and the original commentary. Instead he veers off into a new conclusion with a reassessment and reconfiguration of the *Poetria nova* that continues for a dozen folios.

He omits the figures of words and thoughts altogether and turns to the

---

Ordo dicendi est dupplex, scilicet Ganfredus versv, 'Ordo bifurkat iter tum limite interesse'" (St. Gall, Stiftsbibliothek, 856, p. 296). Quintilian is also quoted in the incipit of the commentary in the manuscript in St. Florian (Enns), Austria.

10. "Et fabula quam Ganfredus narrat habetur ex methamorphosi de rege Minoye, eius filio Androcheo, et virgine regina Scilla, que filia fuit regis Nisi" (St. Gall, Stiftsbibliothek, 856, p. 296).

11. "Hunc exemplificat Ganfredus ibi versv, 'Dotibus exceptis Fortune'" (159) (St. Gall, Stiftsbibliothek, 856, p. 297).

12. Manuscripts with various kinds of diagrams of the content of the *Poetria nova* include London, BL Add., 15108; Munich, Bayerische Staatsbibliothek, Clm 237; Oxford, Bodleian Library, Digby 64; Paris, BnF lat. 8173; and Vienna, Österreichische Nationalbibliothek, 2401. On diagrams, especially in university manuscripts, see Weijers, *Le maniement du savoir*, 187–227; she divides them into two types, first simple tree diagrams discussed under taxonomies of knowledge (187–202), then more complex visual renderings (203–227).

theories of conversion and determination. There he notes, as we saw above, that this part of Geoffrey's doctrine is lacking in the ancient authors. But he finds Geoffrey lacking as well. He treats in some detail the rhetorical attributes, an area of inventional strategy Geoffrey only mentions (lines 1844–1847).[13] This commentator examines them closely, however, drawing on Cicero's extensive treatment in *De inventione* where he divides the attributes into those of persons (name, nature, manner of life, fortune, habit, feeling, interests, purposes, achievements, accidents, and speeches made—used for characterization) and those of actions (place, time, occasion, manner, and facilities—used to construct plot).[14]

The commentator concludes with what he calls an outline of the *Poetria nova*, but it is rather of what he has turned it into.[15] The authority of the *Poetria nova* is maintained here only by radical adaptation. In the summary translated below the commentator ignores what he has omitted from the *Poetria nova* and includes what he himself has brought in from Cicero:

First tractate:

On the invention and arrangement of the material.

On the execution of the material.

On tropes in general.

On fourfold ornamentation [first four tropes].

On six-fold ornamentation [last six tropes].

[*The figures of words and figures of thought are omitted.*]

Second tractate:

On changing parts [of words, i.e., conversion].

On varying determinations.

On the attributes of persons.

On the attributes of actions

[*These two are a very minor part of the* Poetria nova *but an important part of his added commentary.*]

On the summary of diction [word choice and prescriptions].[16]

13. Others criticized Geoffrey on the same grounds; see the section on the attributes in the excerpt from the *Tria sunt* edited by Camargo in Copeland and Sluiter, *Medieval Grammar and Rhetoric*, 670–82.

14. *De inv.* 1.34–36 and 1.37–43. Later Cicero explains how to elaborate and construct convincing scenarios using strategies based on these categories (2.28–37 and 2.38–46). For an analysis of how Cicero's categories may help us understand medieval and Renaissance methods of literary characterization, see Woods, "Chaucer the Rhetorician" and "The Classroom as Courtroom."

15. He notes near the end that the last thing that Geoffrey teaches is "how to make light material serious and serious material light" ("quomodo leuis materia fiat grauis et grauis similiter fiat leuis" [Pistoia, Archivio Capitolare del Duomo, C. 143, fol. 34r]), presumably a reference to Geoffrey's discussion of comedy. The text and commentary (with text preceding at first) are resumed by another scribe at line 957, on fol. 35r; this later portion of the resumed original commentary is discussed in "Comedy and the *Commedia*" in chapter 3.

16. "Primus tractatus [*in marg.*] De inuentione et dispositione materie. / De executione materie. / De transsumptione in generali. / De quadruplici exornatione. / De sexcuplici [*sic*] exornatione. / Secundus tractatus [*in marg.*] / De commutatione partium. / De uariatione determinationum. / De attributis persone.

This reconfiguration is the most ruthless restructuring of the *Poetria nova* that I have seen. Yet by omitting the figures, this commentator places the tropes, which are often based on the juxtaposition of words, right next to conversions and determinations, the latter created by the juxtaposition of words. Thus, he focuses attention on small units of composition and the rhetorical impact of detail, paradoxically an emphasis that Geoffrey himself would have understood. Then with his further reconfiguration these minute variations in words are made to serve the purpose of characterization and plot through the Ciceronian attributes of persons and events listed next. Such an idiosyncratic reworking of rhetorical doctrine shows the potential and flexibility of the *Poetria nova*—however you look at it and whatever you do to it, you come up with something—that helped to keep it in the pedagogical system so long.[17]

ERASMUS AND GEOFFREY

> You know your Cicero, your Quintilian, your Horace, your Geoffrey [of Vinsauf], and you are certainly not unaware of the abundance of excellent advice on the art [of poetry] which they contain; whoever keeps their advice faithfully is bound to fulfil to perfection his function as a poet.[18]
> —Erasmus to Cornelius Gerhard in 1489

Two phrases silently added by the translators to this statement in the *Collected Works of Erasmus* are bracketed above. Here is what Erasmus actually writes to Gerhard: *Nosti Tulium, nosti Quintilianum, nosti Horatium, nosti Gaufredum; quam copiosa, quam praeclara huius artis ediderint praecepta certe non es nescius; quae quisquis recte servaverit, is sane poeticum munus absolute confecit.* For Erasmus and Gerhard (and the commentator of the St. Gall manuscript), the single name of "Geoffrey," like that of the three classical authors, is sufficient for recognition. For a modern audience, however, the translators felt it necessary to add "of Vinsauf." Then, to Erasmus's reference to "the art" *tout court* of which these men are the masters, the translators added "of poetry." But although Erasmus talks about using the advice of these four men to become a perfect poet,

---

/ De attributis negotii. / De epilogatione dictorum." He finishes with a colophon: "Explicit commentum super *Poetriam nouellam* editam <a> Gualtero Anglico" (Pistoia, Archivio Capitolare del Duomo, C. 143, fol. 34r). Geoffrey is called "Gualfredus" in the *accessus* and "Gualtero" here.

17. I admit, however, that this excursus does not feel like a pedagogical experiment, but rather the musings of an idiosyncratic reader. The disconnects in this manuscript are indicated by the fact that it is discussed in two completely different parts of this book; see above, note 15.

18. Erasmus, *CWE* 1, letter 27.44–47. Cf. Henderson, "Valla's *Elegantiae*," 265, on the roughly contemporaneous citation of "Ganfredus in sua nova rethorica" by Paul Lescher in the middle part of his *Rhetorica pro conficiendis epistolis accommodata* (Ingolstadt, 1487).

rhetoric is the art that is being discussed immediately before and it is also the art that encompasses the teaching of "Tully" (as Erasmus actually calls him) and Quintilian in addition to Horace and Geoffrey.[19]

Erasmus notoriously rejected other medieval textbooks from which he was taught Latin, especially the grammatical treatises of John of Garland.[20] Several details of Erasmus's extended criticism in "A Declamation on the Subject of Early Liberal Education for Children" (*De pueris statim ac liberaliter instituendis declamatio*) of how students used to be taught Latin are worth our attention.[21]

> An even more wretched state of affairs prevailed when I was a boy (*puero*); students were cruelly tormented with "modes of meaning" [*modi significandi:* the abstract reasoning of the speculative grammarians[22]] and petty inquiries into the "virtue" of a word. . . .[23] Indeed, the teachers of that time, afraid to teach anything that might seem fit only for boys (*puerilia*), would obscure grammar with the complexities of logic and metaphysics, no doubt for the absurd purpose of making them learn their grammar when they were already advanced, after the more difficult subjects. . . . Good heavens, what a time that was when, with much elaborate ado, the couplets of John of Garland, accompanied with laborious and prolix commentaries, were expounded to young students (*adolescentibus*); when so much time was wasted in dictating, repeating, and closely studying silly verses; and when *Florista* and *Floretus* were learned by heart—Alexander Gallicus [de Villa Dei] I would at least rank among the more tolerable authors.[24] How much time was wasted on sophistry and the futile

19. George Engelhardt, who first brought this quotation (untranslated) to scholarly attention in 1948, called the article where it appeared, "Mediaeval Vestiges in the Rhetoric of Erasmus." Gallo adds "[*scil.* of rhetoric]" when he translates the sentence (*Poetria nova*, 165). Horace's *Art of Poetry* is, of course, rhetorically inflected in its focus on appropriate discourse, and the *Rhetorica ad Herennium* and *De inventione* were also applied to verse composition. On the ancient view of the connections between the two disciplines, see Walker, *Rhetoric and Poetics.*

20. E.g., *CWE* 1, letter 26.96–101; *CWE* 26.345 (quoted below) and 26.389. See Schoeck, *Erasmus of Europe,* 1.46 and 71. Schoeck implies that Erasmus similarly dismissed Geoffrey of Vinsauf (1:71), but I have not been able to find the source of this statement; see also Schoeck 1:210 and 220.

21. One of Margolin's notes on this passage reminds us of how widespread such a view of medieval teaching was when Erasmus was writing: "touts les humanistes contemporains d'Erasme sont d'accord avec lui sur l'abus que le Moyen Age a fait de la dialectique, science obscure et subtile, qui obscurcit tout ce qu'elle touche et notamment la grammaire, dont elle ne se sépare pas à proprement parler . . ." (*Declamatio de pueris,* 591).

22. Overfield, *Humanism and Scholasticism,* 39, on Thomas of Erfurt's *De modis significandi:* "he described how the various properties of being (*modi essendi*) are apprehended by the mind (*modi intelligendi*), which then imposes on vocal sounds (*voces*) modes of signifying (*modi significandi*) through which those sounds become words and parts of speech capable of expressing complex mental concepts." Those who taught the *modi significandi* were called *modiste* (see "The Importance of Being Aristotelian" in chapter 4).

23. The translator's elaboration of "vi" (force) as "of a word" refers to the concept of *virtus sermonis:* "all that belongs to the word in virtue of its *ratio significandi* and *modi significandi*" (Pinborg, "Speculative grammar," 264).

24. Does Erasmus imply in this part of the passage that he memorized not just relatively short works like the *Floretus* but also the *Doctrinale* of Alexander de Villa Dei? Just a part of the *Doctrinale* is sometimes listed

intricacies of logic. Finally, in short, how confused and hateful were the methods of instruction employed for all the subjects, since each teacher, simply for the sake of showing off, would cram his students from the very beginning with the most difficult and often insignificant material.[25]

Though Erasmus—like those advocates of every era intent on reforming education—is probably exaggerating, earlier parts of this study may shed light on the conditions criticized here. If the commentaries on the *Poetria nova* reflect general practice, then when Erasmus talks about "laborious and prolix commentaries" full of "sophistry and the futile intricacies of logic," he is describing the university-level treatments discussed in chapter 4, where texts like the *Poetria nova* were a vehicle for introducing students to Aristotelian logic, not the school commentaries of teachers like Reiner von Cappel.[26] The "modes of meaning" and "virtue of a word" were, as Erasmus's translator Verstraete notes, "concepts introduced by medieval grammarians as part of an attempt to bring Aristotelian logic into the study of grammar."[27] When Erasmus describes "time . . . wasted in dictating, repeating, and closely studying," his objection seems to be primarily to the works on which such attention was expended (and, unlike many humanists, he does not completely dismiss Alexander de Villa Dei's *Doctrinale*).[28] We know that "dictating, repeating, and closely studying"

---

in university statutes, e.g., the "third part" at Vienna in 1394 (see chapter 4, note 170). On Erasmus's attitude to the *Doctrinale* see Margolin, *Declamatio de pueris* 596. The *Floretus* is translated by Pepin in *Auctores Octo*, 213–257; see also "Dominican Reiner von Cappel" in chapter 2.

25. *CWE* 26.345. "Sed infelicior erat aetas, quae me puero modis significandi et quaestiunculis ex qua vi pueros excarnificabat. Nimirum praeceptores illi, ne puerilia docere viderentur, grammaticen, dialectices ac metaphysices difficultatibus obscurabant, nimirum ut praepostere jam provectiores post majores disciplinas grammaticen discerent. Deum immortalem, quale seculum erat hoc, quum magno apparatu disticha Joannis Garlandini adolescentibus, operosis ac prolixis commentariis ennarabantur! Quum ineptis versiculis, dictandis, repetendis et exigendis magna pars temporis absumebatur! Quum edisceretur Florista et Floretus! Nam Alexandrum inter tolerabiles numerandum arbitror. Deinde quantum temporis peribat in sophistica, in supervacaneis dialecticorum labyrinthis? Ac ne sim prolixior, quam perturbate tradebantur omnes disciplinae, quam moleste, dum quisque professor ostentandi sui gratia, statim in initio ea infulciret discipulis, quae sunt difficillima, nonnunquam et frivola" (*Declamatio de pueris*, 461).

26. Dybinus and Reiner are discussed in chapters 4 and 2 respectively.

27. *CWE* 26.579, n. 160 on p. 345. See also Overfield's description of Thomas of Erfurt's *Grammatica speculativa* and Gerhard of Zütphen's *Glossa notabilis* on the *Doctrinale* (this last being the work faintly praised by Erasmus). As Overfield points out about this "logico-philosophical approach" to teaching Latin grammar in the universities, "teaching grammar was not the author's primary goal. Instead he meant to provide an introduction to the basic definitions, concepts and ways of argument that the beginning student could apply to his study of logic and Aristotelian philosophy." (*Humanism and Scholasticism*, 39–40)

28. When John of Garland's grammatical texts are copied with the *Poetria nova*, it is almost always in manuscripts with university-level commentaries, and the *Florista* was one of the required texts at the University of Leipzig; see chapter 4, note 234. Of the titles that Erasmus disparages, the *Florista* is found in only one manuscript of the *Poetria nova* and the *Floretus* in none. Yet the works of "Tully," Virgil, and Horace, whom Erasmus praises along with Geoffrey in his early letter, are copied often with the *Poetria nova*, particularly in manuscripts from Italy; these authors are also quoted constantly in the *Early Commentary* (Woods, "Classical Examples and References"). For a table comparing the geographical impact of Erasmus's editions (and another postclassical source for his instruction on copia), see Mack, *Renaissance Argument*, 275.

could describe the multiple passes through texts found in advanced commentaries like those of Dybinus and Pace of Ferrara.[29] Yet Erasmus says that these commentaries were "expounded to young students."[30] Perhaps lazy or pretentious teachers delivered unrevised university lectures to those under their tutelage "for the sake of showing off."[31] An appalling thought. Erasmus's experience does not reflect what the commentary tradition shows us about how the *Poetria nova* was taught to younger students as outlined in chapter 2, especially during the thirteenth and fourteenth centuries and to some extent still in the fifteenth. Thus, while Erasmus's own reforms do move away from the extremes of late medieval practice, it is in the direction of medieval pedagogy as it was widely practiced earlier.[32]

"On the education of children" was originally composed in 1509 as "an illustrative appendix" to *De duplici copia verborum ac rerum commentarii duo* (*De copia* for short), although it was not printed until 1529 and then separately.[33] *De copia* itself offers a number of the composition techniques from the *Poetria nova* in a form more congenial to contemporary tastes, perhaps one of the reasons

---

29. Dictation was, of course, often a necessity at every level before the age of printing and continued in some areas long afterward because texts copied by the students themselves were cheaper than those purchased, even when mass produced; see, for example, Knox, "Order, Reason, and Oratory." On the "tyrannie" of being made to memorize works like Peter of Spain's *Summulae logicales* (another text found with the *Poetria nova* in copies intended for more advanced students) see Margolin, *Declaratio de pueris*, 591–92. In fact, Erasmus appears to support a similar sequence of tasks but applied only to classical texts and with crucial added steps: "[Sturm] also advocated Erasmus' preferred method of careful exposition of classical texts by the teacher . . . 'to memorize, repeat, analyse, recompose, and imitate . . .'" (Sowards, *CWE* 25.xlviii).

30. The age of the students to which Erasmus refers is vague. He describes himself as "puero" during which time this barbaric custom was still going on, and then to the "adolescentibus" on which these commentaries were forced. But he also says that the students were learning grammar when they were already advanced, which would imply that he was talking about the older students studying philosophically inflected grammar. Such students still might have been relatively young, however, and in his Introduction to volume 3 of *The Literary and Educational Writings* Sowards emphasizes Erasmus's focus on the young and on "pre- and non-university education" (*CWE* 25, xxxviii, also xxvii; he calls *De pueris instituendis* Erasmus's "most complete tract on education," lvi). According to Chomarat, Erasmus does not make a clear distinction among levels of early education (*Grammaire et rhétorique*, 1.163). Allen's evocative picture of "The Young Erasmus," which depicts a man later at pains to emphasize his immaturity at the age when he took holy orders, would appear to place this recollection before the arrival of Alexander Hegius as headmaster in 1483; see Hyma, however, for reasons that Erasmus may have moved the year of his birth earlier as he grew older (*Youth of Erasmus*, 56–57). The date of Erasmus's birth is cited variously by scholars; e.g., 1466 (Allen, 25); 1467 (Schoeck, *Erasmus of Europe*, 1.3 and 259–261); "1469?" (Hyma, *Youth of Erasmus*, 51 and 57; Bainton, *Erasmus of Christendom*, 7; Dorer-Gommermann, "Erasmus," 119). For issues in Erasmus's personal experience that affected his concept of periods of early life, see DeMolen, "Erasmus as Adolescent."

31. Hyma, who was later to write a book on *The Brethren of the Common Life*, acknowledged in *The Youth of Erasmus* that, "The Brethren of the Common Life were very slow to evince much interest in classical scholarship. The printing press of the brethren in Brussels, for example, did not turn out a single classical or humanist production. And when Erasmus was at Deventer, the library of the brethren-house counted only three such works in a total of forty-two titles known to us" (109). Compare *Brethren*, 115–126.

32. For the sometimes confusing similarities between humanist-influenced northern university commentaries and earlier medieval commentaries aimed at younger students, see "Back and Forth" in chapter 3 and "Two Students at Leipzig" in chapter 4. Cf. Jaeger, *Envy of Angels*, 130, on earlier teaching methods and also Glendinning, "Pyramus and Thisbe," 69, on the *vetus studium* and the modern curriculum.

33. On the history of *De pueris instituendis* see Verstraete, *CWE* 26.292–294.

that the medieval work disappeared from the classroom.[34] In 1499 Erasmus was at work on an early version of *De copia* quite different in scope and arrangement from what finally emerged. He begins a letter to Jacob Batt on May 2 of that year with a common metaphor for composition also used by Geoffrey: "The book on letter writing is on the anvil again. . . . "[35] He says that the work will be dedicated to Batt's student, "your Adolph,"[36] and emphasizes that it is "for use in school." Erasmus also mentions "pieces on *copia*, on methods of amplification, on kinds of argumentation, and on the figures."[37] Thus, he was working on separate sections (or even individual works) on letter-writing, *copia*, amplification, logic, and tropes and figures. By dividing the teaching of written composition to younger students into individual instruction for specific genres, Erasmus reverses the medieval tradition of teaching first (and often by means of the *Poetria nova*) a generic rhetoric applicable to any kind of text. The early Italian humanists had raised what had been the focus of schoolboys (textual analysis on aesthetic as well as rhetorical grounds) to an adult discipline, and here Erasmus continues their upending of the medieval tradition by moving the specialized rhetorics taught at an advanced level during the Middle Ages down to a more elementary level of instruction for younger students. In the many printed versions of *De copia* (over 115 by 1550) Erasmus reorganizes amplification and appears to construct it on a foundation of classical Latin, naming Quintilian as his source.[38] Yet *De copia* draws on medieval as well as classical rhetoric, a debt pointed out long ago by Engelhardt, and more recently by Gallo, who presents a strong case for Erasmus's extension of the medieval tradition of *amplificatio*.[39] Other composition techniques in the *Poetria nova* also can be found in *De*

---

34. The suggestion that the *Poetria nova* was replaced by *De copia* comes from a conversation with Lawrence Green, but others like Engelhardt and Gallo have noted Erasmus's debt to the *Poetria nova*. An earlier "avant-garde textbook" that had "a striking resemblance to Geoffrey of Vinsauf's *Poetria nova*" was the *Elegantiolae* of Augustinus Datus (Black, *Humanism,* 360). In his latest book, Black states that "Geoffrey of Vinsauf was displaced by Cicero as the stylistic exemplar in Florentine Schools," although he "was still in use during the later fifteenth century in Florence" (*Education and Society,* 161). On generic characteristics of the rhetoric textbook, see Vickers, "Some Reflections."

35. Letter 95, 2 May 1499, to James Batt, *CWE* 1.187.37–188.4; *Ep.* i.234.33–38. On the anvil and related images see "Shaping the Student" in chapter 1.

36. Jacob's pupil was "Adolph of Burgundy, heer van Veere, son of the rich heiress Anna van Borssele" (Fantazzi, "Introductory Note," *On the Writing of Letters,* 2, in *CWE* 25). A few lines later Erasmus emends this statement to include Batt in a joint dedication. See also Allen on *Ep.* 1.131, regarding letter 35. A little earlier Erasmus had written to Adolph himself in a letter (93) published at the beginning of *Lucubratiunculae* that matches, in the rhetorical strategy of praise by paradoxical unification of seemingly opposite qualities, Geoffrey of Vinsauf's dedication to Pope Innocent III at the beginning of the *PN* (*CWE* 1.181–185).

37. I have modified the translation to reflect the separate but equal status of these works in the Latin: "De Copia, de Amplificationibus, de Argumentationibus, de Schematis adiicietur." Allen suggests that the piece "on amplification" may refer to chapter 4 of the book on letter writing (*CWE* 25.90–93), although this chapter seems too short to have been considered a separate treatise (*Ep.* 1.234). See also Gallo, *Poetria nova,* 167.

38. *CWE* 24.253, 51–52.

39. Engelhardt, "Mediaeval Vestiges"; Gallo, *Poetria nova,* 165–166.

copia.[40] Such unacknowledged, perhaps even unconscious overlapping supports Erasmus's early admiration of Geoffrey and may help to explain the long and complex gestation of the new work.[41]

Medieval teachers, for whom Geoffrey of Vinsauf could provide in one work much of what Erasmus originally thought to cover in several, would have had practical problems with *De copia* as it finally appeared. Some of the aspects that made it so admired in the Renaissance—its range, scope, and depth—would have rendered it unworkable in most medieval pedagogical situations.[42] The first (1512) edition of *De copia* was already much, much longer than the *Poetria nova*, and it grew still longer in later revisions. Yet from a medieval perspective it covered much *less* (though from a Renaissance perspective, of course, it covered much more). Further, while the fact that *De copia* is in prose makes it easier for modern teachers and students to read, this same fact would have made it harder for medieval students to memorize. The widespread use of paper during the later Middle Ages meant that students could produce their own copies of works (and, later, the lists of quotations from other works that were the basis of Erasmus's educational enterprise[43]). What the invention of the printing press made possible was the popularity of school texts that, like *De copia,* are far too long to teach. In England the first book received the most attention, and epitomes of *De copia* for classroom use appeared almost immediately; rare is the modern teacher who assigns the entire text.[44]

For the era before print, then, Geoffrey's work was more appropriate: compact, written in verse, with doctrine and examples that reinforced each other, and divided into short pieces for classroom recitation and performance. Even today seeming eccentricities of Geoffrey's language that can disconcert scholars often make sense when students play with it. The *Poetria nova* was meant to be shared. Its memorable images, innumerable puns, passages of extreme emotion, and abrupt shifts from serious to comic subjects (always in that order) work especially well in that quintessential group context, the classroom.

40. Henderson, "Epistles and *Copia.*"

41. With regard to another aspect of Erasmus's life (his relationship with Luther), Augustijn remarks, "It had taken a long time for him to find himself and know precisely what he wanted," a comment resonant in this context as well (*Erasmus: His Life,* 6).

42. Recall Mancinus's preference for the shorter *Poetria nova* to the *Rhetorica ad Herennium* in the classroom ("Better than the Ancients" in chapter 1).

43. Moss, *Printed Commonplace-Books,* 101–115.

44. See Baldwin, *William Shakspere's Small Latine,* 176–79; and Crane, *Framing Authority,* esp. 79 ff. Rix suggests that there may have been almost as many editions of epitomes and abridgements of *De copia* as there were editions of the complete text: he estimates "some one hundred eighty editions of *De copia*" and "somewhere near the same number of digests of it" ("The Editions," 601, 602). Mack notes that "*De copia* becomes less unwieldy when you concentrate on the 20 methods in book one and the 11 in book two (and when you attend to the long sections on descriptions and examples towards the end of book two)" (e-mail communication, August 2005); compare the observation in the 1570–1576 statutes for the grammar school at Rivington: "Erasm. Copiae verborum et Rerum, et de conscribendis Epistolis, will give a great light, and make the way more easy, if they be not so much tarried in, as laid before them like a pattern to learn by, and to follow" (Baldwin, *William Shakspere's Small Latine,* i.348, 402).

LOOKING AHEAD

What if?[45]

—the title of a modern book of exercises for fiction writers

Medieval teachers, like modern ones, had to take students of various backgrounds and skills and teach them to perform at a high level in an academic discourse of precision and subtlety. Students sometimes arrived at school, even at university, with little exposure to the standard works of the curriculum. Many could not afford copies of textbooks unless they made them themselves or used hand-me-downs. Their knowledge of written texts remained sketchy according to modern standards, although the small percentage who graduated and the even smaller percentage who went on to the most advanced faculties eventually acquired vast stores of other kinds of cultural capital. I would suggest that today, especially with students of varying backgrounds and degrees of preparation, we might be able to use some of the pedagogical techniques that medieval teachers perfected over a long period of time and while working against great odds.

Inspired by the general approach to the *Poetria nova* outlined in chapter 1, we could bring into the classroom multifaceted texts that do (and do more than one thing at a time) as well as say. Like the school commentators of chapter 2 we could teach potentially scurrilous or politically problematic material by sticking to the individual words of the text while demonstrating what is at stake rhetorically with each one.[46] Taking the early humanist teachers of chapter 3 as a model, we could devise methods to provide students with an ever-widening aesthetic experience, integrating more and more complex texts into the conversation while simultaneously uncovering more and more complexity in those already under discussion. Imitating the central European professors of chapter 4 who lectured on the *Poetria nova* to sometimes underprepared university students, we could teach theory on the one hand while going through the texts word for word on the other.[47] Finally, like the teacher-monk at St. Gall, the Dante scribe, Erasmus, and Geoffrey himself, we could combine the old with the new, taking and acknowledging the best of both.

Though Erasmus focused on prose and Geoffrey ostensibly wrote about poetry, for both men the precepts of cogent, effective, and elegant writing were rhetorical. And both knew that the craft of writing and the way to teach it lay

---

45. Bernays and Painter, *What if? Writing Exercises for Fiction Writers.*

46. Susan Reynolds argues that medieval teachers were less aggressive in controlling the implications of texts when they were being taught to younger students still working on acquisition of the language of academic discourse ("Inventing Authority").

47. See Donahue and Quandahl's recounting of teaching a difficult and controversial text, Freud's *Dora,* to "special action or affirmative action" first-year university students. They make a convincing case for "the possibility of a dignified, university-level curriculum, one with strong theoretical underpinnings, for poorly prepared students" ("Freud and the Teaching of Interpretation," 53).

in attention to verbal detail: individual words and phrases that are, in medieval terms, the milky food of the young.[48] The most extreme, seemingly absurd parts of both *Poetria nova* and *De copia*—Geoffrey's exercise of "converting" a word by trying it out as a substantive in every part of a sentence and Erasmus's innumerable ways of saying the same thing—turn out to be invaluable and powerful. After dismissing Geoffrey's theory of conversion for years, I was chagrined to recognize it as a technique that I used and taught for making formulaic compositions like grant proposals, job applications, and letters of recommendation both unique and forceful.[49] As for Erasmus's virtuoso performance, the rewriting of "She done him wrong" or "Please send money" or "The dog ate my homework"—the more banal the starter sentence the better—done as a group exercise in class generates an excitement and intensity that increase, sometimes almost unbearably, the longer it goes on. Artistic versions of the same exercise include the literary creations of the French Oulipo school (*Ou*voir de *li*ttérature *po*tentielle) like Raymond Queneau's *Exercises in Style* (1947) and Georges Perec's *Je me souviens* (1978).[50]

The revival of classical rhetoric in modern pedagogy draws on the part of the tradition embodied in Erasmus and his classical sources, and some teachers are also beginning to draw on a wider, more eclectic historical tradition.[51] Significantly, some of the exercises that are closest to Geoffrey's are found in creative writing manuals. John Gardner's *Art of Fiction* advocates both group and individual exercises for the aspiring writer; some of the latter take students to the very smallest units of composition and their effects: "17. Describe a character in a brief passage [one or two pages] using mostly long vowels and soft consonants; then describe the same character, using mostly short vowels and hard consonants," and even—shades of Boethius, Bernardus Silvestris, and Alan of Lille—"25. Write a short piece of fiction in mixed prose and verse."[52] The titles of the chapters of Ann Bernays and Pamela Painter's *What if? Writing Exercises for Fiction Writers* also resonate with Geoffrey's teaching: "First Sentences:

---

48. On the "milky food of boys" see the discussion of the order of parts in the *Poetria nova* in "Separating the Men from the Boys" in chapter 2.

49. One can look at these particular genres as elaborations on single sentences as well: "So-and-so is a great student" or "Please give me the fellowship."

50. For an introduction in English, see *Oulipo: A Primer* (especially Queneau, "Potential Literature"); the selections translated in the *Oulipo Compendium;* and other items on Paul Taylor's website: http://www.nous.org.uk/oulipo.html. Matt Madden's *99 Ways to Tell a Story: Exercises in Style* is a series of one-page comics telling the same story inspired by Queneau; my favorite is "A Newly Discovered Fragment of the Bayeux Tapestry," 84.

51. For the revival of the classical tradition, see Corbett and Connors, *Classical Rhetoric for the Modern Student;* Connors, Ede, and Lunsford, *Essays on Classical Rhetoric;* Crowley and Hawhee, *Ancient Rhetorics for Contemporary Students;* D'Angelo, *Composition in the Classical Tradition;* also Mack, *Renaissance Argument,* 372–374. Smaller units of composition are also the focus of the so-called sentence-combining school and others, but they have been controversial; see Connors, "The Erasure of the Sentence." As an example of a more eclectic modern historical approach, see Cockcroft and Cockcroft, *Persuading People.*

52. Gardner, *The Art of Fiction;* exercises on 195–206, here 205 and 206.

Beginning in the Middle," "The End Foretold," "Five Different Versions: And Not One is a Lie," and even "Sex is Not All It's Cracked Up To Be: It's More."[53]

The perennially ludic quality of exercises in verbal dexterity[54] is reflected in the popularity of word games like Radio France Culture's "Des papous dans la tête," whose categories for the broadcast of Sunday, June 1, 2003 included "Why make it simple when you can make it complicated?" and "the homophone game."[55] The related online Listener Participation Forum gave instructions for a game in which the participants were to take a sentence of Alfred Jarry's and then, "Choose three substantives in this sentence and replace them with circumlocutions. Then slide the circumlocutions into the original sentence in place of the original terms" (translations mine).[56] The *New Statesman* used to carry a weekly contest with ridiculously restricted rules that put Geoffrey's lists of techniques and variations to shame.[57]

Geoffrey of Vinsauf knew that the playful and the serious were two sides of the same exercise, and his sequences of and transitions between serious and funny anecdotes were much noticed by medieval commentators. The recurring theme in the *Poetria nova* of the constant flux of language and human experience had its origin in the great works of twelfth-century Platonism, and Geoffrey speaks constantly of the generative and creative qualities of language itself. His pedagogical focus on what can be rhetorically altered balances the more pessimistic, philosophically driven cosmic visions of flux in the works of writers like Bernardus Silvestris and Alan of Lille who preceded him.[58] Geoffrey reminds us that all temporal power is temporary, that craft makes something beautiful out of chaos, and that reversing a story can change the world: "Art plays, as it were, the conjurer: causes the last to be first, the future to be present, the oblique to be straight, the remote to be near; what is rustic becomes urbane, what is old becomes new, public things are made private, black things white, and worthless things are made precious" (121–125).

---

53. As Bernays and Painter remark, such exercises work with all ages and levels of student: "In the years since *What if?* was published, we have used it with undergraduate and extension school classes, with graduate writing students in M.F.A. programs, in several four-hour workshops, and with a fourth-grade class. High school teachers use it. People writing at home, alone, use it. Although several exercises may be too advanced for fourth graders, few are too elementary for graduate students" (xiii–xiv). I am grateful to Elizabeth Harris for bringing these works to my attention.

54. See Motte's subtitle, "Scriptor Ludens, Lector Ludens" (*Oulipo: A Primer*, 20 [Introduction]).

55. http://www.radiofrance.fr/chaines/france-culture2/papous/

56. http://www.radiofrance.fr/chaines/franceculture2/papous/forum_participer.php?emission_id=30118.000000&forum_id=35110227

57. *New Statesman Competitions*; also *Salome Dear* and *Never Rub Bottoms*.

58. Bernardus Silvestris concludes the *Cosmographia* with a vision of the futility of human (pro)creation, while Alan of Lille begins the *Plaint of Nature* by describing the sterility of male/male sex and its reversal of grammatical power relationships. The negative or dark passages of the *Poetria nova* are there, of course (e.g., 276 ff. and 326 ff.), but they are confined to the rhetorical examples and are not found in the passages of direct address to writers. Although mutability can be oppressive in a philosophical context, it can occasion optimism in a creative environment. See Woods, "In a Nutshell," on the conflicting values associated with matter and form in philosophical and rhetorical terminology.

Given Geoffrey's emphasis on the transformative as well as the shaping power of the verbal arts, it is no surprise that such exercises work well with students from diverse social and educational backgrounds. In my experience, students who are underprepared academically learn formal discourse more willingly when it is taught rhetorically, as style rather than substance: another version of a language that they already know, but with a different vocabulary, resonance, and effect.[59] Imitation—including parody like Chaucer's—and detailed translation exercises from one mode or genre to another are within the grasp of almost all students, including those who, at times rightfully, balk at a judgmental distinction between one "correct" way to write and all others. Yet the potential for complexity in such exercises attracts and challenges advanced and gifted students as well.[60]

Perhaps, then, the most historically accurate way for us to understand the great popularity of the *Poetria nova* in earlier classrooms may be to use it in our own. For twenty-five years I have taught the *Poetria nova* in rhetoric and literature courses at all levels, from first year to postgraduate.[61] It is intriguing to students as an historical curiosity, but it also becomes a source of insight for those trying to solve their own writing problems. When students find out that they can, like Geoffrey, do the seemingly impossible—rewrite an old story using thirty-five figures of words in order (giving the best lines to reprobate or ignored characters); or, after initially making fun of his name, warn a high-ranking official about possible misconduct via the nineteen figures of thought (with fourteen sub-categories); or, at the other extreme, compress a fraught, disturbing narrative into a two-line ditty—then little remains out of reach. When changing the subject of a sentence to the object of a preposition changes how we think about that subject, the politics of subjection and objectification become transparent. And if altering one word can turn a sentence inside out, what cannot a perfect sequence of sentences accomplish?

<hr>

59. See the success of the Australian non-fiction bestseller *Death Sentences,* by Don Watson, written for non-academics.

60. On the "the paradox of writing under constraint[:] that it possesses a double virtue of liberation," see Bénabou, "Rule and Constraint," 42–43, here 43.

61. For preliminary discussions of some of this material, see Woods, "Teaching of Poetic Composition," and "Weeping for Dido." Modern experimentation with medieval rhetorical exercises is not limited to classrooms in the United States; Carolina Ponce, one of the translators of the *Poetria nova* into Spanish, asks students at the Universidad Nacional de México to write modern versions of Geoffrey's examples of description.

APPENDIX I

Transcription of List of contents of the *poetria nova* in Rome, Biblioteca casanatense, 311

Following is the list of contents of the *Poetria nova* according to Rome, Biblioteca Casanatense, 311, fols. 69v–70v; on the preceeding folios sections of text are copied alternately with the relevant portions of the commentary by Bartholomew of Pisa. This list is translated in "The Usefulness of the Work" in chapter 1. The numbers on the right below refer to the folio openings where the rubrics introducing the relevant section of text appear.[1] The vertical lines at the left may indicate sections of particular interest. Notice the use of Roman as well as Arabic numerals.

‖ Quod rethorica reddat hominem honorabilem	carta	1.
Comendatio Innocentii pape a quinque	c.	2.
De cogitando super materiam ante actum dictaminis	c.	4.
Quod materia sit ornanda uerbis	c.	5.
Que sunt illa que rethoricus habet considerare	c.	6.
Distinctio ordinis in naturalem et artificialem	c.	6.
‖ Quod principium artificiale habet octo modos	c.	7
De principio quod sumitur a fine	c.	7.

---

1. For example, the scribe lists "Exemplum de duobus modis disgressionis, c. 24." The equivalent rubric ("Exemplum de utroque modo disgressionis") is found on the verso or back side of folio 23. That is, it is on the left when one opens the manuscript so that folio 24 is on the right-hand side of the page. You can see the rubric, in a slightly bigger form of the same script, in the middle of plate 5, right after Bartholomew's introduction to the passage (ending "resumuntur et explicantur") and before the portion of the text beginning "Unicus astringit."

---

2. Emended from "59" partially erased.

APPENDIX II

scripta vs. Dicta in practice: Transcriptions

Below are the Latin texts of the *accessus* and glosses on the first six lines of the *Poetria nova* found in the two versions of the commentary by Dybinus of Prague translated in chapter 4. MS D on the right, Prague, Národní Knihovna České Republiky, XII.B.12, was taken down by dictation in 1375 by Johannes de Montabaur from lectures, probably in Prague. MS S on the left, Prague, Národní Knihovna České Republiky, VIII.H.22, whose readings are reproduced in the column on the left, was written in Prague in 1389 by Johannes Niger; the *accessus* in this manuscript was published by Karel Doskočil in 1948.[1]

ACCESSUS: INTRODUCTION OF THE *THEMA*

[MS S, *scripta* format, fol. 27r]

AMICE, ASCENDE SUPERIUS. HEC UERBA SCRIPTA sunt in ewangelio Luce quarto [*sic*] capitulo {14:10},

[MS D, *dicta* format, fol. 1r, plate 9]

AMICE, ASCENDE SUPERIUS SCRIBITUR LUCE CAPITULO QUARTO PHILOSOPHICALIS ETC.

Amice, ascende superius scribitur Luce capitulo quarto {14:10}. Philosophicalis sciencia quemlibet secundum racionem viventem eleuat, philosophiaque scienciarum imperatrix et domina alcioribus est manifestata dignitatibus, secundum Tulium {cf. *Inv.* 1.1} et Senecam. Celorum deo hominem associet et ipsum

---

1. Doskočil, *Mistr Dybin*, 89–91.

in quibus uerbis rethorice generositas excellensque precelsitas potest commendari:

primo ut sit amicorum perfectiua, et hoc
tangitur ibi, **amice;** secundo ut sit fauoris
inpressiua et hoc tangitur ibi, **ascende;** tercio
ut sit honoris collatiua et hoc concluditur
ibi **superius.** Primo enim commendatur
ex ipsius melliflua alocucione cum dicitur
amice; secundo probatur ex ipsius miti promocione cum subiungitur **ascende;** tercio
commendatur ex eiusdem nobilissime sciencie remuneracione, cum dicitur **superius.**

De **primo** dicit Boecius, "**Amicus** est nobilissimum genus diuiciarum preciosissimum"
{cf. *Cons.* II, pr. 4}.
Ergo dicit Seneca: "Cum amico omnia
delibera" {*Ep.* 3.2}. Item Philosophus:
"Amicicia est muttua beniuolencia" {*Auct.
Aris.* 242 (142)}, quam beniuolenciam
copiosiam nobilissima regina rethorica
tribuit suis discipulis et amicis, docens eos
ornate et bene loqui.

sic parem reddat, tribuens digne sibi uerba
thematis quo affando <supradicti> [supradicte *MS*], dicens **Amice, ascende superius.**
Scienciarum cum regina rethorica cum
nobilissima deliciarum epistolas preparans
cuilibet ipsius discipulo, ab ipsa invitatur
mellimanantis affamine sermonis; consolaminem [*sic*] consortem promissionis verba
recitat thematis suprascripti dicens **Amice,
ascende superius.** Et hec sunt verba scripta
in ewangelio Luce capitulo quartodecimo.
In quibus verbis rethorice generositas excellensque preciositas licet multifarie possit
commendari, potest tamen ad presens pro
fructuositate eius tripliciter commendari:
primo ut sit amoris perfectiua et hoc tangitur ibi, **amice;** secundo ut sit fauoris impressiua et hoc tangitur ibi, **ascende;** tercio ut
sit honoris collatiua, et hoc concluditur cum
dicitur **superius.** Primo enim commendatur
ex ipsius melliflua allocucione quia dicitur
amice; secundum probatur ex ipsius miti
promocione cum subiungitur **ascende;**
tercium indicatur in eiusdem nobilissime
sciencie remuneracione et ergo concluditur
superius.

De **primo** dicit Bo<e>cius secundo *De
consolatione Philosophie,* "**Amicus** est preciossimum genus diuiciarum" {cf. II. pr. 4}.
Et ergo dicit Senica [*sic*] in quadam epistola,
"Cum amico omnia delibera" {*Ep.* 3.2},
quod confirmat Philosophus dicens, "Amicicia est beniuolencia mutua in contrapassis
non latens" {*Auct. Aris.* 242 (142)}, quam
beniuolenciam copiosissimam nobilissima
regina rethorica tribuit suis discipulis et
amicis.
Non solum enim <docet>[2] loqui hominem
sed bene et ornate loqui quod maxime
uidetur esse precellens nobilitas in homine et

---

2. docet *Vienna 3251:* decet *D, Gdansk Mar. Q.9.*

maxime amicicie ligamentum. Et ergo dicit Tulius, "Hanc inveni quam quesiui animam certificans eloqui docens" {*Inv.* 1.3}. "Nam per sermonem homo iudicatur," testante Philosopho quarto *Ethicorum.* "Qualis vnusquisque est talia dicit et talia operatur?" {cf. 4.7(1127a)}. Et ergo dicit Senica in libro *De moribus,* "Auribus frequencius vtere quam lingwa" si vis aliorum amiciciam {*Proverbia Senecae* 104}. Illud autem facit rethorica et distribuit suis amicis et discipulis. Et subiungit, "Qui nescit tacere nescit loqui" {*Proverbia Senecae* 132}.

Copiosissimam autem eloquenciam facit nobis nobilissima regina rethorica et ergo bene dicitur **ascende.**

De **secundo** dicit Aristoteles nono *Ethicorum,* "Amicus debet se habere ad amicum sicut ad semet ipsum, quia amicus est alter ipse" {*Auct. Aris.* 245 (177)}, et subdit, "Magis tenemur amicis elargiri bonum quam extraneis" {*Auct. Aris.* 245 (175)}, que quidem bona generosissima rethorica suis inpartitur fauoribiliter amicis. Nam "Ipsa est iusticie perswasiua, ueri comittiua, falsi et malorum fugitiua"[3] {cf. *Auct. Aris.* 263 (5)}, que maxime fauoris inpressiua, et ergo subiungitur **ascende.**

De **tercio** dicit Philosophus secundo *Politicorum:* "Impossibile est indignitatem philosophari" {cf. *Auct. Aris.* 255 (48)}. Ergo quilibet parum habens, huic nobilissime sciencie feruente amore et desiderio debet adherere. Ideo dicitur bene collatiua honoris. Nam dicit Oracius in *Antiqua poetria* quod "Ipsa rethorica elargitur copiosam facundiam loquendi et aut pauperem de

De **secundo** dicit Aristoteles nono *Ethicorum,* "Amicus debet se habere ad amicum sicud ad semet ipsum quia amicus est alter ipse" {*Auct. Aris.* 245 (177)}, et subdit "Magis tenemur amicis elargire bonum quam extraneis" {*Auct. Aris.* 245 (175)}, que quidem bona generosissima rethorica suis impartitur fauorabiliter amicis. Nam secundum doctrinam Aristotelis primo *Rethorice,* "Ipsa rethorica est iusticie perswasiua, veri cognitiua, et mali fugitiua" {cf. *Auct. Aris.* 263 (5)}, que maxime sunt fauoris impressiua, et ergo subiungitur **ascende.**

De **tercio** dicit Philosophus secundo *Politicorum,* "Impossibile est indigentem[4] philosophare" {cf. *Auct. Aris.* 255 (48)}. Ergo quilibet parum habens, huic nobilissime sciencie feruentissimis amore et disiderio debet adhe\<re\>re. Ergo bene dicitur honoris collatiua. Nam ut dicit Oracius in *Antiqua poetria,* quod "Ipsa rethorica omnes elargitur facunditates et copiosissimam facundiam

---

3. fugivita quam *Doskočil.*

4. Manuscript D's reading ("indigentem," also in Vienna 3251 and Gdansk Mar. Q.9) is an error for "indignitatem" (as in MS S).

puluere exigit paupertatis et dirigit ad honores potissime facultatis."

Et ergo bene concluditur **superius** cum
igitur hec excellentissima sciencia videlicet
ipsa rethorica docens omnes facunde et
ornate loqui, erigit pauperes ad alciores
honores.

loquendi et ad alciora pauperem de pulueri-
bus erigit pauperitatis et dirigit ad honores
potissime facultatis."
Et ergo littera[5] concluditur **superius**.

ACCESSUS, CONT.: TWO VERSIONS OF THE TRANSITION TO THE *POETRIA NOVA*

[MS S]
Ideo summo opere iste liber qui tractat de
ipsa rethorica est dilengenti studio attentan-
dus circa quemlibet librum.

[MS D]
Hec itaque largiflua nobilisque rethorica
pre ceteris scienciis sine opere hac
perfectissima amoris desiderio est
appentanda.
Cum igitur liber *Poetrie noue* summe et
subtilis rethorice sit de cuius declaracione
hic intendimus, merito ipsius doctrine est
insistendum ut hiis acquisitis in isto libro
tamquam fundamento rethorice, cuilibet
nostrum potest dici quod scribitur in the-
mathe preassumpto, **Amice, ascende** etc.

ACCESSUS, CONT.: THE CAUSES

[MS S, *accessus* continues]
Primo est uidendum que sit **cause suscepti
operis,** secundo de **causis** libri.
Et **causa suscepti operis** est duplex; <prima>[6]
communis et secunda specialis. Communis
est vtilitas omnium ornate loqui uolen-
cium, ea enim de causa magistri: Gamfridus
<rethor>[7] optimus hunc librum conscripsit.
Sed causa specialis est captacio beneuolencie

[MS D, first *accessus* concludes]
De causis autem huius libri eodem modo
videndum est sicud et in aliis libris.

---

5. The first column in plate 9 ends here.
6. prima *Doskočil:* Roua(?) S.
7. rethor *Doskočil:* rethoi S.

Innocentii pape tercii propter inpetrandam
graciam et absolucionis ueniam Rychardo
regi Anglie, qui inciderat excomunicacionem
et indignacionem domini pape. Ita quod
post mortem suam denegata fuerat sibi sepultura et suu[u]s[8] cancelarius hunc librum
componere procurauit, ut absolucionis
graciam et veniam domino suo inpetraret.
In quo libro primo multipliciter dominum
papam Innocencium commendat. Et in fine
sui libri pro domino suo supplicat, dicens
"Pro principe nostro supplico" (2096–97).
Sed **causa materialis** huius libri secundum
aliquos est ars poetica in communi accepta,
non descendendo ad aliquam sui partem in
speciali. Secundum autem alios causa materialis huius est ornatus modus loquendi in se
et in suis partibus consideratus sub melioribus rethoricis coloribus.

Causa efficiens in propria sua [*sic*] sermone
est magister Gamfredus qui ad instanciam
regis Rychardi hunc edidit librum.

Efficiens autem **causa** fuit Gamfredus
vir eloquentissimus in arte rethorica bene
instructus, et Richardi regis anglice existens
notarius quod patebit in processu.

Causa finalis est duplex, scilicet remota et
propinqua. Causa finalis remota est ut habito
et congnito hoc libro possimus communicare
regibus et principalibus et nobilibus. Causa
autem propinqua est ut hoc libro congnito
habeatur rethoricus modus loquendi.
Sed **causa formalis** est duplex, scilicet
forma tractatus et forma tractandi. Forma
tract<ta>us consistit in diuisione libri. Forma
autem tractandi est modus agendi et ille est
metricus ut patet.

Sequitur littera, "Papa stupor mundi" etc.

---

8. There is an abbreviation line over the word, so it may have been intended to be "summus," in which case it is lacking one minim.

SECONDARY *ACCESSUS:* THE PARTS OF THE ART OF RHETORIC

[MS S, continuation of the above]

Tamen antequam liber diuidatur, dicendum
est quod rethorica consideratur duplicliter.
Vno modo prout est ars, alio modo prout
est sciencia, et licet ut sciencia et ars pro
eodem summitur, tamen in hoc differunt,
quia sciencia est in quantum constat ex suis
principiis subiectis et passionibus, et prout
quiescit in anima. Ars uero dicitur in quantum eadem principia extra animam <appli-
centur>[9] ad opus.

Et <secundum>[10] hanc duplicem consid-
eracionem rethorica et huius libri sciencia
duplicem recipit diuisionem, scilicet per
modum sciencie et per modum artis.

Rethorica per modum sciencie diuiditur in
quinque partes, que sunt inuencio, secunda
disposicio, elocucio, memoria, et pronun-
ciacio. Invencio, que est prima pars, incipit
ibi, "Si quis habet fundare" (42); disposicio
tangitur ibi, "Biffurcat ordo" (87); eloquencia ibi, "Principio variem" (203). Memoria,
que est quarta pars, tangitur ibi, "Omnia
que reperit" (1969); pronunciatio ibi, "In
<recitante>[11] sonent" (2031).

[MS D, new section]

1 PAPA STUPOR MUNDI SI, ETC.
Antequam habeatur diuisio littere prius
videamus quid sit rethorica. Nam secundum
Tulium et intencionem Gwidonis, rethorica sic diffinitur: "Rethorica est sciencia
docens de quocumque perswasibili [docens]
invenire materias, et ipsius materie conueni-
enter ordinare particulas, ipsamque verbis
venustare et sentenciis et postea conueni-
enter memorie commendare uel presentare,
exprimere, et declarare."

Ex qua descripcione seu diffinicione
quinque eliguntur **officia** rethorice: primum
est materie invencio, secundum materie
invente disposicio, tercium materie invente
ornata disposicio, uel tercium potest esse
ipsius ornata et decens locutio; quartum
ipsius materie memorie commendacio, quintum materie invente bene disposite ornate
memorie commendate condecens pronun-
ciacio. Et ista quinque officia conprehendun-
tur hiis versibus[12]:

> Invenit et disponit, eloquitur memo-
> ratque.
> Postremo rethor pronuncciat omnia
> recte.

Et secundum ista officia liber presens cuius
subiectum est ornatus modus perswadendi
de quocumque perswasibili diuiditur in
quinque <capitu>la[13] siue tractatus speciales. In primo docet quomodo rethor debet

---

9. applicentur *Doskočil:* applicere *S.*
10. secundum *Doskočil:* respectu *S.*
11. recitante *Doskočil:* recitata scilicet *S.*
12. versus nota *in marg. D.*
13. capitu- *in ras. D.*

invenire materiam. In secundo docet quomodo materiam inventam debet disponere.
In tercio quomodo materia inventa et disposita et ornata sit memorie commendanda.
In quarto quomodo materia inventa et
disposita sit exornanda. In quinto et vltimo
quomodo materia inventa disposita ornata
et memorata sit debito modo pronuncci-
anda. Secundus tractatus incipit ibi, "Ordo
bifurcat" etc. (87). Tercius ibi, "Sit breuis
aut longus" (737), quartus ibi, "Omnia que
<reperit>"[14] (1969), et vltimus ibi, "In reci-
tante" (2031).

DIGRESSION ON JUDICIAL AND EPIDEICTIC RHETORIC [MS D]

Nota secundum intencionem Aristotelis et Tulii duplex est rethorica, quedam
iudicialis, quedam demonstratiua {*Rhet.* 1.3 (1358b); *Ad Her.* 1.2}. Iudicialis est
que perswadit et docet quid honestum et inhonestum, quid iustum et iniustum,
quid licitum uel illicitum. De tali rethorica Tulius sufficienter loquitur in quattuor
libris suis. Et istam rethoricam pertractat Aristoteles in tribus libris, et de ea dicit in
principio *Ethicorum* quod "ipsa sit assecutiua loyce volens quod sicud per loycam
probabiliter proceditur et demonstratur, sic per rethoricam iudicialem alicui demonstratur quid sit iustum uel iniustum" {cf. *Eth.* 5.6}. Ergo subdit postea Aristoteles,
"Rethorica docet iusta operari et perswadere vera congnoscere et opposita horum
fugere" {cf. *Rhet.* 1.1}. De tali autem iudiciali in presenti libro nichil agitur, sed de
demonstratiua et illa solum dirigit sic aliquod laudabile uel vituperabile, quia dicit
Aristoteles primo sui Rethorice, "Omnis oracio poetica uel est laudacio vel vituperacio" {cf. *Rhet.* 1.3 (1358b)}. Talis aut laudacio uel vituperacio solum consistit in
sermone demonstratiuo. Et cum ipsius rethoris maxime sit hominibus complacere
per sermonem, oportet ergo quod talis sermo sit ornatus, ad quem quidam ornatum
requiruntur officia predicta ipsius rethoris, scilicet invencio, disposicio, etc."

DIVISIONS OF THE TEXT

[MS S, continuation of *accessus*] Rethorica uero prout est ars ipsa radicatur instrvmento. **Instrvmentum** autem artis rethorice est oracio habens **sex partes,** que	[MS D, beginning of commentary proper] **Nota** omnia talia officia perficiuntur **sex** **instrvmentis.** Primum exorditur exortacio, secundum narracio, tercium particio siue

---

14. reperit *Far.:* reperiius *D.*

sunt exordium, narracio, particio,[15] confutacio, confirmacio, et conclusio.

diuisio, quartum refutacio, quintum confirmacio, sextum conclusio.

Nota ut dixi oportet rethorem aliis complacere per sermonem; ergo necessarium est***[16]
captet beniuolenciam audiencium et illud fit
per exhortacionem siue per exordium quod
est primum instrvmentum rethoris. Secundo,
capta beniuolencia audiencium, oportet
quod rethor proponat ordinanda que velit ab
audientibus audire, ergo secundum instrvmentum dicitur narracio. Tercio, proposito
sermone narrato, oportet quod dirigat
sermonem ad responsionem audiencium et
dirigat ita quod statim intelligat in responso
sibi dato an responsum sibi pro omni parte
sit conueniens an non. Ergo vtitur ista diuisione, distingwens partem non sibi valentem
sermonis ab eis que sibi valent, et sic vtitur
tercio instrvmento quod dicitur diuisio.
Quarto diuisione facta rethor partem sibi
non valentem abicit reprobando et refutando
et sic vtitur quarto instrvmento quod dicitur
refutacio. Quinto refutata et reprobata parte
non valente sibi regreditur ad partem valentem sibi ipsam recipiendo et confirmando et
sic vtitur quinto instrumento quod dicitur
confirmacio. Sexto omnibus factis propositum quod intendit concludit et ergo vtitur
sexto instrvmento quod dicitur conclusio.
Et ista instvumenta comprehenduntur hiis
versibus:[17]

Orditur, narrat, partitur
inde
Refutat, confirmat claudit
Habet has oracio partes.

---

15. Doskočil suggests emending "particio" to "peticio" (*Mistr Dybin,* 90). But the *lemma* later and the subject of this section of the *Poetria nova* (the different kinds of order as a branch dividing into eight) make it clear that the manuscript reading is correct.

16. This is the end of the part of the commentary reproduced in plate 9.

17. versus de instrumentis rethoris *in marg. D.*

Exordium, prima pars, incipit ibi a principio, scilicet "Papa stupor," sed narracio ibi, "Si quis habet fundare domum" (43). Particio est pars ibi, "Ordo biffurcat" (87); confutacio ibi, "<Quid deceat nosti>"[18] (1588); confirmacio ibi, "In primis igitur" (1920), conclusio ibi, "Iam mare transiui" (2031).

Et secundum **ista instrvmenta** liber diuiditur in **sex capitula.**

In primo wlt determinare de exordio et secundo de narracione, in tercio de particione, in quarto de refutatione, in quinto de confirmacione, in sexto de conclusione. Secundum capitulum incipit ibi, "Si quis habet fundare" etc. (42); tercium ibi, "Ordo bifurcat" (87); quartum ibi, "<Quid deceat>[19] nosti" (1588); quintum ibi, "In primis ergo" (1920); sextum et vltimum ibi, "Iam mare transcurri" (2031).

Secundum illam diuisionem iam factam de officiis rethoris tunc primus tractatus continet duo capitula; in primo captat beniuolenciam domini pape Inno<cen>cii gracia cuius istum librum composuit ipsum diuersimode commendando. Tanquam in parte prohemiali in secunda parte executiua, scilicet in secundo capitulo, autor exsequitur de primo officio rethoris sicud invencione ibi, "Si quis habet," etc.

Nota autor volens de pluribus loqui facit secundum doctrinam Aristotelis tercio *Rethorice,* nam dicitur ibidem, "Si quis plura velit dicere proemisit [= promisit]" {cf. 3.14(1415a)}. Et subditur "Prohemium est sermo preambulans et preparans animum auditoris ad ea que secuntur," et subditur, "Prohemium debet sic se habere in libris sicud preludium in fistulis" {3.14(1414b)}. Tunc quasi concludendo dicit Aristoteles, "Prohemium debet reddere auditores dociles, beniuolos et attentos" {*Ad Her.* I.6; cf. Aris. *Rhet.* 3.14(1415a)}. Quod considerat autor in principio sui <libri>[20] ponendo prohemium secundum doctrinam Aristotelis primo reddendo auditores beniuolos, secundo dociles,

---

18. Quid decet nosti *Doskočil:* Est benedicta *S.*
19. Quid deceat *Far.:* Quid det *Vienna 3251:* Que otia *D.:* Quid ocia *Gdansk Mar. Q.9*
20. libri *Gdansk Mar. Q.9, Vienna 3251:* libro *D.*

Adhuc prima in **tres**: primo [I.A] enim auctor captat beniuolenciam pape ipsum multipliciter commendans, secundo [I.B] reddit auditores dociles; tercio [I.C] reddit eos attentos.

Secunda ibi, "Accipe magne" (41); tercia ibi, "Viribus amplum" (42).

[Subdivision]

<Primo>[17] [I.A.i] commendat dominum papam ex magnitudine uirtutum, secundo [I.A.ii] porrigit preces, secunda ibi, "Lux publica mundi" (33).

Prima in **tres**: primo [I.A.i.a.] commendat papam quantum ad sui nominis et persone excellenciam, secundo [I.A.i.b.] quantum ad cardinalium suorum generositatem; tercio [I.A.i.c.] commendat ipsum ex sui loci nobilitate. Secunda ibi, "Suntque tui tales"; tercia ibi, "Roma quasi celum."

tertio actentes.

Nam prohemium habet **tres** partes.

Secunda pars incipit ibi, "Accipe magne" (41), tercia ibi, "Viribus amplum" (42).

Nota autor volens per prohemium capere beniuolenciam domini apostolici commendat eum variis modis et capta beniuolencia proponit suam peticionem quam pretendit. Et sic iterum prohemium habet duas partes. In prima parte [I.A.i] commendat papam, in secunda [I.A.ii] infert peticionem; secunda ibi, "Lux publica mundi" (33).

Nota autor volens esse rethor et poeta vtitur vna parte poetice que dicitur laudacio, quia secundum Aristotelem primo et tercio *Rethorice*, "Laus est sermo elucidans magnitudinem virtutis" {1.9(1367b); cf. 3.14(1414b)}. Ex isto concludit quod nichil sit laudandum in homine nisi virtus et quia multiplex est virtus in hominibus, igitur multipliciter aliquis potest commendare {cf. 1.9 (1368)}.

Potest enim aliquis **quinque** modis commendari: primo ex nomine bono, secundo ex forma et disposicione corporis, tercio ex ipsius eloquencia, quarto ex ipsius potencia, quinto ex loci habitacione, et illud patet in hiis versibus[21]:

Nomen cum forma, <verbis>[22] sapiencia, posse

Et loco sunt norma qua laudem. Tu bene nosse!

Quilibet enim rethor ex istis quinque potest aliquem laudare et principaliter ex virtutibus suis. Et ista autor exemplariter dat nobis in

---

21. vnde versus *in marg.* D.

22. verbis *corr. Gdansk Mar. Q.9, Vienna 3251*: varias D.

prohemio primo commendando papam ex sui
nominis sublimitate, secundo ex sue forme
preciositate, tercio ex <virtutum>[23] variorum
nobilitate, quarto ex eloquencie facunditate,
quinto ex prvdencie multiplicitate, sexto ex
sue potencie varietate, septimo ex sui loci
preciositate et secundum hoc prohemium tot
seruat particulas. Secunda ibi, "E<gregius>
sangwis" (10); tercia ibi. "Superest" (13). Et
alie partes patebunt.[24]

ADDENDUM TO *ACCESSUS* [MS S]

Notabilia: circa istam literam est notandum, scilicet quid sint **quinque partes
rethorice,** et primo quid sit inuencio. Et secundum Tulium "Est rerum verarum
[uel veri similium verarum] uel ueri similium excogitatio que causam probabilem
reddunt"[25] {*Ad Her.* 1.3}. Uel sic: Invencio est alicuius materie assumpte debita in
mente prefiguracio. Recte inuenit habere qui res veras ueris similesque cogitat, ut
fiat sua causa probabilis. Inde "Disposicio est ordo uel distribucio per quam osten-
ditur quibus <locis>[26] quelibet res sic collocanda" {*Ad Her.* 1.3}; vnde recte disponit
quisque que res locat ordine certo distribuitque locis ut quidque locatur in illis. "Vt
res poposcit sic plene figura noscit." "Est <e>locucio[27] ydoneorum verborum venusta
sentenciarumque excogitacio" {*Ad Her.* 1.3}. Recte eloquitur quoque qui superaddit
ydonea uerba vt sentencia cum verbis ornata sit ipsa.[28]

PARAPHRASE OF FIRST SECTION OF TEXT [MS D]

"Dicit ergo primo sic, O Papa, qui es stupor, idest ammiracio, mundi si tribuam tibi
hoc nomen Nocenti, tunc nomen tuum erit acephal<um>, idest priuatum capite.
Sed si addi<d>ero principium nominis dicendo Innoce<ns>, tunc nomen tuum non
potest conprehendi in metro; sic similiter tua maxima virtus non est mensurabilis,
(supple: aliqua re in verum natura) quia nichil est quo ipsum metiar, ipsa enim
transcendit omnes mensuras hominum.

---

23. virtutum *Gdansk Mar. Q.9, Vienna 3251:* virtute *D.*
24. The first column of folio 1v ends here in MS D.
25. rerum verarum uel veri similium . . . reddant *Doskočil, Ad Her.*
26. locis *Doskočil:* om. *S.*
27. est locutio *S:* Elocutio est *Ad Her.* MS S's reading is probably a misexpansion of what was originally
"elocutio," with the "est" following then dropped.
28. Doskočil's transcription ends here (*Mistr Dybin,* 91).

NOTES ON FIRST SECTION OF TEXT

[MS S, 1st and 3rd note below text, plate 10]

[MS D continues with list of notes]

Nota circa litteram quod secundum expositores in littera tangitur primum instrvmentum rethoris quod dicitur exhordium quod describitur sic a Tulio: "Exordium est sermo preambulus, breuis lucidus et curialis, preparans animum auditoris ad ea que secuntur" {cf. *Inv.* 1.20}, idest exhordium primo ponitur in sermone quod aptum natum est ad mouendum animum auditoris ad aliam oracionem, idest ad ea que postea recitantur. Vnde secundum Tulium exhordium debet in se habere tria. Primum est generalitas ex eo quod debet procedere ex verbis generalibus, nichil specialiter continens in se de hiis que postea dicenda sunt; secundum est quod debet in se habere exhordium <ydonietatem>,[29] et talis ydonietas non est aliud quam exordium ita formatum sic: quod ydonee et realiter respiciat ea que postea dicenda sunt sed tamen sub eloquio generali. Tercium quod debet esse in exordio dicitur mouendi habilitas et est illud quod exhordium sit aptum ad hoc quod sufficienter moueat animum auditoris ad ea que dicuntur.

Nota: expositores uolunt quod ex intencione Tulii ista significet idem quamuis uariaciones: exordium, prouerbium, prohemium, et captacio beneuolencie, quia dicunt quando sermo preambulans ponitur in principio longi sermonis qui sit generalis et aptus ad mouendum animum tunc tale dicitur exordium. Sed quando idem sermo sit specialis et longus aptus ad mouendum animum tunc est prohemium. Quando uero idem sermo sit appropriabilis et doctrinabilis dicendorum tunc dicitur prouerbium. Quando autem

Nota secundo ex intencione Tulii volunt expositores quod illa significent id sed variomodo, scilicet exhordium, prouerbium, prohemium, captacio benivolencie {cf. *Ad Her.* 1.6}. Nam quando sermo preambulans positus in principio longi sermonis sit breuis et generalis aptus ad mouendum, tale principium sermonis dicitur exhordium. Sed quando sit aliqualitur [= aliqualiter] longus tamen aptus [tamen aptus] ad mouendum, tunc dicitur prohemium a *pros* quod est prius et *emos* sermo quasi, etc. Sed idem

---

29. ydoneitatem *Gdansk Mar. Q.9:* ydoneitas *D., Vienna 3251*

talis sermo procedit cum adulacione, tunc dicitur captatio beniuolencie etc. Ita recte idem significans sed cum diuerso respectu.

[= item] sermo siue principium potest esse declaratiuus seu confirmatiuus dicendorum tunc dicitur prouerbium. Cum vero talis sermo procedit cum quadam adulacione siue mitigacione, talis dicitur captacio beni-uolencie. Et sic per illa omnia significatur principium sermonis quamuis diuersimode. Sed si aliquis voluerit habere sufficientem differenciam et virtutem illorum nominum, iam dictorum respiciat *Viaticum dictandi* capitulo de exhordio.

Tercio nota prout verius elicio ex mente autoris tunc prohemium huius libri pocius dicitur captacio beniuolencie quam exhordium quia prohemium autoris procedit cum aliqua mitigacione uel adulacione ex eo quod diuersimode commendat ipsum papam volens per hoc capere ipsius benuoulenciam.

Quarto nota pro intencione tocius libri causa efficiens fuit Gamfredus notarius Richarde regis anglice qui rex obiit in excommunicacione papali, et ergo prohibita fuit sibi ecclesiastica sepultura, propter quem impetrandum Gamfredus agessit ad apostolicum sibi in complacenciam componens hunc librum, ipsum in prohemio multiplicacione commendans ut posset quod peteret impetrare.

Nota primo ex quo nomen pape quod dicitur Innocencius ratione cuius commendat ipsum. Non potest poni integraliter sumptum sed solum <cum>[30] diuiditur. Ergo auctor ex illo "In-" fert secundam commendacionem ipsius pape et stat uirtus laudis in isto sicud nomine pape diuisim acceptum apptari poterit metro, sic et ipsius uirtus secundum suas proprietates et varietates aliquibus poterit adequari sicut postea declarat, sed

Quinto nota auctor primo commendat papam ex nominis svblimitate quia dictus fuit Innocencius et stat virtus laudis in isto: sicud hoc nomen Innocenti non potest integraliter nisi vicium fuerit poni in metro, sic et virtus ipsius pape si integraliter accipitur non est mensurabilis. Et ergo dicit in littera "dixero Papa Nocenti," quia si poneret Nocenti faceret oppositum sensum nominis, sed si dicit Innocenti tunc nomen non potest poni in metro, quia est prima longa et altera

---

30. cum *corr.:* causa *S.*

ed integra <accepta incomparabilis>[31] quemadmodum nomen eius integraliter sumptum.

breuis et tercia longa et tales dicciones non possunt sine vicio stare in metro, ideo dicit in littera "hostis <erit>[32] metri" (3).

Sexto nota littera dicit PAPA et illud nomen a legistis interpretatur "custos" sed a theologis interpretatur "pater, patrum," et est formatum ab interictione ammirantis, scilicet "pape,"[33] quia cum in principio beatus Petrus constitutus erat in papam et dotauit sibi illud nomen papam, tunc homines ammirati fuerunt formantes sibi ex hoc interictione ammirantis, scilicet "pape."

Septimo nota littera dicit STUPOR MUNDI, vnde stupor est nomen verbale istius verbi "stupeo, -es, -ere," quod est idem quod ammiror. Inde "stupor" est idem quod ammiracio et potest dupliciter exponi, scilicet "O papa qui es stupor mundi," uel sic, "O papa, si dixero Nocenti, (supple: tunc erit) stupor, idest pavor, mundi."

Octauo nota littera dicit ACEPHALUM NOMEN (2), vnde acephalum est nomen adiectiuum secunde declinacionis formatum a greco *cephas* quod est "caput" latine, et dicimus illud acephalum quod est priuatum principio sicud ille dicetur acephalus qui esset priuatus capite, et inde venit "acephalizo," quod est capite uel principio privare.

---

31. accepta incomparabilis *corr.:* acceptam uel comparabilis *S.*
32. erit *Far.:* ero *D. Gdansk Mar Q.9, Vienna 3251.*
33. Folio IV ends here in *D.*

"INTERLINEAR" GLOSSES ON *PN* 1–6

[MS S, text with interlinear glosses, plate 10]

o eximis amiracio vniversi ego Gamfredus sic dicere
Papa stupor mundi   si dixero   Papa Nocenti

carens <uno>[34]   dabo ego   principium i. ad-
Acephalum nomen tribuam tibi; si caput ad-

                                                -iungam
                                                -dam[35]

Inimicus   uersus supple: tuum   adequari
Hostis erit metri. Nomen tibi wlt similari:

                    excellencia
Nec metro nomen, nec wlt tua maxima uirtus

potest concludi metra i. non est aliqua mensuremus tuum
                              res
                                                nomen
Claudi   mensura. Nichil est quo meciar   illam

tua uirtus   mortalium tu   disiunge Innocentii
excedit
Transit mensuras homini. Sed diuide nomen . . .

[MS D, text alternating with glosses]
SI DIXERO littera O PAPA qui es STUPOR
MUNDI idest ammiracio tocius seculi,
EGO TRIBUAM TIBI NOMEN ACEPH-
ALUM idest sine principio SI DIXERO
PAPA NOCENTI. Sed SI ADDAM idest
apponam CAPUT idest principium, TUNC
(supple: nomen tuum) ERIT HOSTIS idest
contrarium METRO idest non potest poni
sine vicio in metro. NEC NOMEN (supple:
tuum) WLT SIMILARI idest adequari
METRO idest versui NEC TUA MAXIMA
VIRTUS WLT CLAUDI idest conprehendi
MENSURA idest modo, quia NICHIL EST
QUO idest per quod MECIOR idest men-
surare possim IPSAM scilicet virtutem, quia
ipsa virtus TRANSIT idest excedit MENSU-
RAS idest comprehensiones HOMINUM.
Sequitur SED DIVIDE NOMEN.

---

34. uno *corr.:* universo *S.*

35. The last syllable of line 2 (and the part of the gloss over it) does not fit at the end of the line in the manuscript and has been added by the scribe at the end of the following line.

MANUSCRIPT LIST OF THE *POETRIA NOVA* AND COMMENTARIES

Included here are manuscripts of the *Poetria nova* and commentaries on it, whether copied separately or in the margins of the text. This list is based on that compiled by Margaret F. Nims in the preparation of her translation of the *Poetria nova,* augmented by manuscripts discovered both by John Conley while gathering information for a proposed edition of the text and by me in my work on the commentaries. My contribution has been much smaller in terms of the number of manuscripts, but final responsibility for the information presented and for all details about commentaries is mine. I have been able to examine a majority of the manuscripts during research trips to more than seventy libraries and have studied microfilms of almost all the rest. In a few cases the information derives solely from printed references or personal communication and is so indicated. Individual manuscripts that include more than one copy of the text or commentary are listed only once, with the folios for the relevant sections identified. Fragments of commentary and/or text are included, but excerpts are not.

Angers, Bibliothèque municipale, 523, 14th cent., French (western France [IRHT]), fols. 1r–48v. Commentary: marginal and interlinear glossing throughout; no *accessus*. Incipit: "STUPOR vno modo dicitur prout est asicnacio mentis. . . ."

Assisi, Biblioteca Storico-Francescana della Chiesa Nuova, 301, 15th cent., Italian, fols. 119r–153r. Commentary: a few scattered glosses.

———, 305, 15th cent., Italian, fragment to line 374, fols. 1r–5v. Commentary: interlinear glosses to top of fol. 3r; marginal notes identifying the ways of beginning with a proverb, etc.

———, 309, 15th cent., Italian, commentary only on fols. 1ra–74r. Commentary by Pace of Ferrara. For other manuscripts see Seville, Biblioteca Capitular y Colombina, Col. 5–4–30. Incipit: "<P>osuerunt antiquiorum [*sic*] nostri cum aliquid noui . . . . "

Augsburg, Staats- und Stadtbibliothek, 2° 133, 15th cent. (*PN* 1479), central European, *accessus* on fol. 61r–v, *PN* on fols. 62r–124v. Commentary: *accessus* with Dybinus material and some marginal glosses; interlinear glosses throughout; related to Leipzig, Universitätsbibliothek, MS 1084. Incipit: "Circa ea que in hoc libro dicenda sunt notandum primo quod secundum intencionem Aristotelis et Tullii triplex est rethorica. . . . " Incipit of secondary *accessus:* "Et secundum illa officia presens liber cuius materia siue subiectum est ornatus modus persuadendi cuiuslibet persuasibilis diuiditur in quinque tractatus."

Bamberg, Staatsbibliothek, Class. 56, 15th cent. (*PN* 1481), central European, fols. 1r–46r. Commentary: *PN* preceded by outline; a few notes on text.

Barcelona, Archivo de la Corona de Aragón, Ripoll 103, 13th–14th cent., Italian?, fols. 1r–46r. Commentary: extensive marginal and layers of interlinear glossing, especially at beginning, becoming more sporadic later. Incipit: "Antequam Gualfredus accedat ad propositum principale premictit prologum. . . . "

Basel, Universitätsbibliothek, F III 35, Italian, fols. 234r–269v. Commentary: interlinear glosses sporadic after beginning; marginal glosses on first few folios only.

———, F IV 27, 13th cent. for *PN,* fols. 52r–82v. Commentary: none (letter of Dr. Martin Steinmann).

Bergamo, Biblioteca Civica "Angelo Mai," MA 7, 14th–15th cent., Italian, fols. 1r–30v. Commentary: some interlinear glosses.

———, MA 259, Italian, 14th–15th cent. (but see Gatti Perer, *Codici e incunaboli,* 35), fols. 1r–40v. Commentary: numerous short marginal glosses and interlinear notes.

———, MA 484, 15th cent. (1414), Italian, commentary only on fols. 1ra–65rb. Commentary by Pace of Ferrara; for other copies see Seville, Biblioteca Capitular y Colombina, Col. 5–4–30. Primary incipit: "Consueuerunt antiquiores nostri cum aliquid noui proponunt." Incipit of secondary *accessus:* "Incepturus librum artis poetice oportet duo considerare."

[Berlin, Deutsche Staatsbibliothek—Staatsbibliothek Preussischer Kulturbesitz, lat. 959; see Krakow, Biblioteka Jagiellońska, 1891.]

Berlin, Staatsbibliothek zu Berlin—Preussischer Kulturbesitz, Hamilton 101, 14th cent. (1394), Italian, fols. 51r–90r. Commentary: marginal glosses to fol. 70v (some very lengthy), interlinear to end, by Nofri di Angelo; no *accessus*. Incipit: "SI QUIS HABET etc. Postquam autor posuit prohemium suum consequenter in hac parte aggreditur partem executiuam."

———, lat. fol. 607, 13th–14th cent., French? (but see Hunt, *Teaching and Learning Latin,* 1.169), fols. 38ra–46vb (beginning missing; begins at 130). Commentary: interlinear and marginal glossing; no *accessus*.

———, lat. qu. 17, 15th cent. (1st half), central European, *PN* (to 368) on fols. 1v–12v, commentary to fols. 1r–4v. Commentary: beginning of very full commentary drawing on Dybinus of Prague. For other MSS see Leipzig, Universitätsbibliothek, MS 1084. Primary incipit: "Circa inicium Ganfreydi siue *Poetrie noue* pro recommendacione rethorice sentencie est notanda illa proposicio, 'Tota pulchra es amica mea.'" Incipit of secondary *accessus:* "PAPA STUPOR MUNDI SI Iste liber cuius subiectum est ornatus modus persuadendi materiam cuiuslibet persuasibilis prima sui [*sic*] diuisione diuiditur in quinque tractatus."

———, lat. qu. 425, 15th cent., Italian, fols. 1r–47r. Commentary: a few glosses.

———, lat. qu. 515, 14th cent., English provenance (Ottery St. Mary [Ker, *Medieval Libraries*, 141]), fols. 37r–68r. Commentary: marginal and interlinear glosses. Incipit: "PAPA STUPOR Hic in principio huius prohemii circumlocutione utitur auctor dicendo 'stupor mundi.'" Similar incipit but different glosses in London, BL Harley 3775 and Vatican City, BAV Ottob. lat. 1472.

Besançon, Bibliothèque municipale, 534, late 13th cent., French, fols. 147r–178r (to 2077). Commentary: both marginal and interlinear glosses; no *accessus* (previous folio cut off). Incipit worn and partly illegible: "Nota quod *** nomina queque(?) sint possunt poni."

[Bologna, Biblioteca Arcivescovile, 47 (Gallick, "Medieval Rhetorical Arts," 83). See Bologna, Libreria Breventani.]

Bologna, Biblioteca Comunale dell'Archiginnasio, A. 2508, late 13th cent.?, Italian, 4 fols. of fragments (some edges cut), about 200 lines. Commentary: some interlinear glosses and marginal comments in various hands; most too worn to read.

Bologna, Biblioteca Universitaria, 2637, late 13th cent., fols. 1r–19v (incomplete; ends at 1145). Commentary: some marginal glosses on first folio, rare thereafter; interlinear glosses throughout.

Bologna, Libreria Breventani, 47, 14th–15th cent., 56 folios. Commentary: marginal and interlinear glosses, some in vernacular. Information from Mazzatinti et al., *Inventari dei manoscritti*, 16.87.

Brescia, Biblioteca Civica Queriniana, A.IV.10, 14th–15th cent., Italian, fols. 93r–134r. Commentary: short *accessus* and some glosses. Incipit: "PAPA STUPOR etc. Opus istius potest diuidi secundum partem rethorice, et secundum sermonem rethoricum."

Breslau. See Wrocław.

Brussels, Bibliothèque Royale Albert 1er, 4988–90, 14th cent., fols. 1r–15v, fragment. Information from *Iter ital.* 3.94; and from Michiel Verweij.

———, 9774, 15th cent. (1450), fols. 2r–74r. Commentary: introductory short note and some interlinear glosses on first folio and only very sporadically thereafter. Incipit: "Incipit *Poetria noua* magistri Gamfredi Anglici; in quinque tractatus diuisa est."

Bryn Mawr, Bryn Mawr College Library, Gordan MS 97, 15th cent. (1417), Italian, fols. 1r–54v (beg. missing). Commentary: some marginal and many interlinear glosses to fol. 30r; incipit missing.

Cambridge, Corpus Christi College, 406, 13th cent. (1st half), English, fols. 101r–112v. Commentary: none.

Cambridge, Trinity College, R.3.29, 13th cent. (first half), English, later *accessus* added on fol. 96v; *PN* on fols. 97r–105r. Commentary: *accessus* only. Incipit: "Cum omnium creaturarum dignissima [= dignissima creatura] sit homo. . . . "

———, R.3.51, 13th cent. (first half), English?, fols. 1r–35r (modern foliation). Commentary: none.

———, R.14.22, 13th cent. for *PN*, English, two *accessus* on fols. 1v and 2r; *PN* on fols. 3r–44r. Commentary: two *accessus* and glosses in several hands added later. Incipit of first *accessus*: "Cum rerum noticiam precedat noticia causarum earum huius operis prius consideremus ut rei sequentis lucidius pateat cognicio." Incipit of second *accessus:* "PAPA STUPOR MUNDI etc. In principio istius auctoris sicut cuiuslibet alterius ista occiderunt inquisitioni, scilicet que causa suscepti operis. . . . " Incipit of glosses on text illegible.

Cambridge, Harvard University, Houghton Library, lat. 154, 14th cent., Italian, fols. 1r–38v. Commentary: marginal identification of figures.

Chicago, University of Chicago Library, 476, 14th–15th cent., Italian (Venice [Ricci, *Census*, 587]), fols. 1r–40r. Commentary: none.

Copenhagen, Kongelige Bibliotek, Gl. kgl. Saml. 2036, 14th cent., central European, fols. 19r–49v. Commentary: *EC, accessus* missing; for other manuscripts see Munich, Bayerische Staatsbibliothek, Clm 4603.

————, Gl. kgl. Saml. 2037, 17th cent., Central European, *PN* on pp. 3–87, commentary on pp. 91–440. Commentary: *accessus* and extensive collection of quotations by Zacharias Lund. Incipit of *accessus:* "Cujusvis statuae cognitio a capite est."

Cracow. See Krakow.

Cremona, Biblioteca Statale, Fondo Governativa 88, 14th cent., Italian, separate commentary only on fols. 1r–87r. Commentary by Pace of Ferrara; for other MSS see Seville, Biblioteca Capitular y Colombina, Col. 5-4-30. Primary incipit: "Consueuerunt antiquiores nostri cum aliquid noui proponunt . . . " Incipit of secondary *accessus:* "<I>ncepimus librum artis poetice oportet duo considerare."

Douai, Bibliothèque municipale, 764, 15th cent. (early [Camargo, "Models," 178]), English, fols. 186r–226v. Commentary: none.

Durham, Cathedral Library, C.IV.23, late 14th cent., English, fols. 56r–126r. Commentary: a few marginal headings or identifications.

Durham, University Library, Cosin V.V.2, 15th cent. (1st half), English, fols. 125r–160r. Commentary: a couple of notes on first seven leaves.

Engelberg, Stiftsbibliothek, 144, 14th cent., central European, *PN* on fols. 1v–43v (ends incomplete at line 2105), *accessus* on fol. 1r. Commentary: *accessus* and marginal glosses. Incipit: "In principio huius libri hec sunt inquirenda, scilicet que materia, que utilitas . . . "

Erfurt, Wissenschaftliche Allgemeinbibliothek der Stadt, Amplon. F.50, 14th cent., central European (probably Prague [Szklenar, *Magister Nicolaus,* 61]), separate commentary only on fols. 1r–59r. Commentary: full and extensive commentary in tradition of Dybinus of Prague. Primary incipit: "'Omnia subiecisti sub pedibus eius oues et boues et uniuersa pecora campi.' Verba proposita scripta sunt per prophetam in Spalmo [*sic*] {8:8}." Incipit of secondary *accessus:* "Tulius primo sue *Rethorice* describit rethoricam, dicens 'Rethorica est sciencia docens de quocumque perswadibili . . .'"

————, Amplon. O.1, central European, 14th cent., *PN* on fols. 20v–57v; separate commentary on fols. 57r–72r. Commentary: both glosses on text and commentary following text. Incipit of glosses on text cut off. Incipit of separate commentary: "Ex quo liber iste supponitur rethorica videndum est quid sit rethorica et ex quibus rebus constituatur . . . "

————, Amplon. O.15, 14th–15th cent., central European, fols. 1r–38v; *accessus* on 38v. Commentary: scattered marginal and interlinear glosses throughout text. Incipit (very worn): "********* hunc librum est docere quedam communia poetice et rethorice . . . " First of notes functioning as *accessus* at end: "Nota causa materialis est ars rethorica . . . "

———, Amplon. O.17, 13th–14th cent., *PN* on fols. 1r–36r, first *accessus* on fols. 36r–38r, second *accessus* on fol. 38v, first commentary on fols. 38v–57r, second commentary on fols. 82r–93r. Commentary: glossing on text; two separate *accessus;* and two separate commentaries. Incipit of glosses around text illegible. Incipit of first *accessus:* "Liber iste per modum sciencie diuiditur in quinque partes . . . " Incipit of second *accessus:* "PAPA STUPOR In printipio videndum quid, qualiter, quare . . . " Incipit of first commentary: "PAPA STUPOR MUNDI In hoc loco premittit actor prologum in quo tria facit . . . " Incipit of second commentary: "PAPA STUPOR etc. Iste liber principaliter in quinque <partes> [per penes *MS*]. . . ."

———, Amplon. Q.66, 14th cent., central European, fragment of commentary on fols. 39r–40v, *PN* on fols. 74r–119r and 41r–43v. Commentary: fragment of separate commentary on digression and description sections of *PN;* a few glosses on text of *PN.*

———, Amplon. Q.75, late 13th cent.?, central European, separate commentary on fols. 41r–58v, second separate commentary on fols. 59r–62v, *PN* on fols. 63r–83r, *accessus* added at fol. 83r. Commentary: two separate commentaries, scattered glosses on text, and separate *accessus.* Incipit of first commentary: "Quemadmodum wlt Aristotelis in libro *Predicamentorum,* 'Omnis sciencia est in anima.'" Incipit of second separate commentary: "CARMINIS Hic ostendit quales debent esse partes . . . " Incipit of *accessus* at end of *PN:* "In principio istius libri sex sunt inquirenda . . . "

———, Amplon. Q.286, 14th–15th cent., fols. 1r–32v. Commentary: introductory note and some interlinear and marginal glossing in last half. Incipit of introductory note: "Ganfredus vir eloquentissimus . . . "

Erlangen, Universitätsbibliothek, 635, 15th cent. (1482–85), central European, fols. 2r–34v. Commentary: marginal and interlinear glosses on first folios. Incipit: "Incipit *Poetria noua* anglici poete Ganfredi Ysagogia. . . ."

Ferrara, Biblioteca Comunale Ariostea, II. 175, 15th cent (first half for *PN*), Italian, fols. 55r–91v. Commentary: full glossing on first folio, very little thereafter. First gloss: "NEC NOMEN Hic captat auctor beneuolenciam dicens 'pape' ab ipsis rebus, idest ab ipsis uirtutibus. . . . "

Florence, Biblioteca Medicea Laurenziana, Acquisti e doni 438, 15th cent. (early [Black, *Humanism,* 342]), Italian, fols. 1r–24v (incomplete; to line 1793). Commentary: marginal glosses (paraphrases) on first two folios, rare thereafter; interlinear glossing very sporadic after fol. 6v. Incipit: "PAPA STUPOR etc. Ego tribuam tibi nomen acephalum."

———, Conv. Soppr. 409, mid-15th cent. (Black, *Humanism,* 342), Italian, fols. 35v–77r. Commentary: interlinear and some marginal glosses (first gloss on line 136).

———, Gadd. 190, 13th–14th cent., Italian?, fols. 14r–47v. Commentary: some marginal and interlinear notes, esp. at beginning, but none on first folio side.

———, Strozzi 137, 14th cent. (early) for *PN,* Italian (Emilia [Black, *Humanism,* 346]), fols. 1r–36v. Commentary: *accessus* and some interlinear and marginal glossing in several hands (very worn). Incipit: "PAPA STUPOR etc. In nomine domini nostri Jesu Christi hic incipiunt diuisiones huius libri premissis primo causis operi cuilibet conuenientibus."

———, Strozzi 139, 15th cent. ("early": Black, *Humanism,* 342; "first half": Black, *Education and Society,* 160), Italian (Florence [Black, *Humanism,* 342, and *Education and Society,* 160]), fols.

1r–41v. Commentary: none.

Florence, Biblioteca Nazionale Centrale, Conv. Soppr. I.VI.17, 14th cent. (1330–1340 [Black, *Humanism,* 342]), Italian, fols. 1r–42v. Commentary: full marginal commentary. Incipit: "Causa efficiens huius operis fuit Gualfredus d'Anglia qui composuit ipsum ad decus domini pape Innocentii tercii a quo optinuit quoddam beneficium. . . . "

———, Panciat. 69, mid-15th cent., Italian (Florence [Black, *Humanism,* 342, and *Education and Society,* 160]), fols. 2r–34v. Commentary: a few scattered marginal and simple interlinear glosses.

Florence, Biblioteca Riccardiana, 682, 15th cent. (first half [Black, *Humanism,* 343, and *Education and Society,* 160]), Italian, fols. 1r–48v. Commentary: interlinear glosses only, stopping on fol. 33r.

———, 874, 14th cent. (1355–1365 [Black, *Humanism,* 343], "third quarter of the fourteenth century" [Black, *Education and Society,* 63]), Italian, fols. 1r–39r. Commentary: a few interlinear and marginal notes, esp. on figures.

———, 1189, 14th cent. (first half), Italian (Tuscany / Angevin Naples [Black, *Humanism,* 343]), fols. 1r–35r. Commentary: marginal and sporadic interlinear glosses stopping abruptly at fol. fol. 24v; incipit illegible.

———, 3600, 15th cent. (early [Black, *Humanism,* 344]), Italian, fols. 49r–71v (ends at 1451). Commentary: glosses on first two folios.

———, 3605, 15th cent. (mid- [Black, *Humanism,* 344]), Italian, fragment at fols. 31r–36v. Commentary: marginal glosses on first and last folios, scattered interlinear glosses throughout; incipit illegible.

Frankfurt am Main, Stadt- und Universitätsbibliothek, Praed. 17, fragment in back binding (lines 1705–08). Information from Powitz, *Die Handschriften des Dominikanersklosters,* 36.

Fulda, Landesbibliothek, C 8 (Kloster Weingarten K 11), 15th cent., central European, fols. 2r–60v. Commentary: *EC.* For other MSS see Munich, Bayerische Staatsbibliothek, Clm 4603. Incipit: "Exordium secundum Tullium in principio *Noue rethorice . . .* "

Gdansk (Danzig), Biblioteka Gdańska Polskiej Akademii Nauk, Mar. Q.8, 15th cent., central European, *PN* on fols. 2r–76v; commentary from fol. 1r. Commentary in tradition of Dybinus of Prague; with *accessus* and extensive, continuous marginal and interlinear glossing (the last sparse after fol. 69r); for related MSS see Leipzig, Universitätsbibliothek, MS 1084. Primary incipit: "'Amice, ascende superius' que quidem verba licet Luce 14° capitulo {14:10} sunt in parabola conscripta. . . . " Incipit of secondary *accessus:* "PAPA STUPOR Iste liber cuius subiectum est ornatus modus perswadendi cuiuslibet perswasibilis prima sui [*sic*] diuisione diuiditur in quinque tractatus."

———, Mar. Q.9, central European, 15th cent., separate comm. on fols. 1r–105r; *PN* with marginal notes on fols. 109r–154r (some passages unglossed; sporadic notes at end; *PN* lacking last two lines). Commentary by Dybinus of Prague copied separately; for other MSS see Prague, Národní Knihovna České Republiky, XII.B.12. Primary Incipit: "'Amice, ascende superius' scribitur Luce capitulo 4°. Philosophicalis sciencia quemlibet secundum racionem viuentem eleuat." Incipit of secondary *accessus:* "PAPA STUPOR MUNDI Antequam habeatur diuisio littere prius videamus quid sit rethorica." Incipit of commentary in margins of *PN* has been cut off.

Genoa, Biblioteca Durazzo Giustiniani, B II 1, 14th cent., Italian (Bologna [Puncuh, *I manoscritti*, 191]), fols. 1r–41v. Commentary: interlinear and marginal glosses naming Pietro da Muglio on fols. 1r and 41v.

Giessen, Universitätsbibliothek, 68, 15th cent. (first half), central European, *PN* (to 1217) on fols. 2r–38v; comm. starts on fol. 1vb. Commentary: marginal and interlinear commentary drawing on Dybinus of Prague (with some interlinear glosses from *scripta* version [Prague, Národní Knihovna České Republiky, VIII. H.22] and marginal glosses more closely related to *dicta* version [see Prague, Národní Knihovna České Republiky, XII.B.12]). Incipit: "PAPA STUPOR MUNDI SI DIXERO Iste liber cuius subiectum est ornatus modus persuadendi cuiuslibet persuasibilis prima <secundum> [sed *MS*] diuisionem diuiditur in quinque tractatus secundum quod quinque sunt officia rethoris." Compare Wolfenbüttel, Herzog August Bibliothek, Cod. Guelf. 37.34 Aug. 2° and Wrocław, Biblioteka Universytecka, IV Q 110; and see also Leipzig, Universitätsbibliothek, MS 1084 and related MSS.

Glasgow, University Library, Hunter 511 (V. 8. 14), 13th cent. (1200–1230), English (East Midlands [Camargo, "*Tria sunt,*" 939]), fols. 72r–97v. Commentary: none.

Gotha, Forschungs- und Landesbibliothek, Membr. II.124, 13th–14th cent., German?, fols. 1r–27v. Commentary: a few later notes.

Graz, Universitätsbibliothek, 979, 14th cent., central European, fols. 26r–79r. Commentary: interlinear and some marginal glosses.

Hamburg, Staats- und Universitätsbibliothek, fragment 3 from MS Petri 9; lines 505–594 and 749–826 on flyleaves, fols. 1 and 242. Commentary: with glosses. Information from Brandis, *Die Handschriften*, 16–18.

Hannover, Niedersächsische Landesbibliothek, IV 518, 14th cent., fols. 1r–49r. Commentary: ". . . dicitur 'stupor mundi' . . . " [much illegible].

Holkham Hall, Library of the Earl of Leicester, 423, 14th cent., Italian, fols. 2r–32v. Commentary: marginal glosses. Incipit: "Nota quod quinque sunt partes rethorice, scilicet inuentio, dispositio, elocutio, memoria, et pronuntiatio."

Keio, Keio University Library, item no. 6, 14th cent. (first half), Italian, 48 folios, *PN* begins on fol. 22. Commentary: "Numerous neat marginal and interlinear notes by various 14th- and 15th-century readers." Information from Matsuda, ed. *Mostly British*, 41–45; and William Snell, e-mail communication, January 2007.

Klagenfurt, Bundesstaatliche Studienbibliothek, Pap. 109, 14th cent., central European, commentary only on fols. 63v–175va (ending missing, from just after line 1600). Commentary by Pace of Ferrara; for other MSS see Seville, Biblioteca Capitular y Colombina, Col. 5–4–30. Primary incipit: "Consueuerunt antiquiores nostri cum aliquid noui proponunt . . . " Incipit of secondary *accessus:* "Inceptoros libri artis poetice debet duo considerare."

Krakow, Biblioteka Jagiellońska, 1891, 14th–15th cent., central European, fols. 156v–209r, commentary from fol. 156r (formerly Berlin, Deutsche Staatsbibliothek lat. 959, earlier believed destroyed). Commentary: *accessus* and interlinear and marginal glosses throughout. Incipit of *accessus:* "Circa principium rethorice sciendum quod rethorica a Tulio sic describitur . . . "

————, 1934, 15th cent., central European, fols. 1r–113v. Commentary: extensive, with *accessus* and marginal and interlinear glossing. Incipit: "<R>ethorica superna gracia facundie red<dit> domina eloquencie et lepide oracionis urbanam fabricatio ex superfund<en>cia sue benignitatis. . . . "

————, 1954, 14th–15th cent., central European, fols. 61r–86r. Commentary: none, but room left for one.

————, 2141, 15th cent. (1450), central European, fols. 104v–209r; comm. from fol. 104r. Commentary by Dybinus of Prague written around and between sections of text, with interlinear glosses. Primary incipit: "Amice, ascende superius et erit tibi gloria coram omnibus simul discumbentibus." Secondary incipit: "Sciendum quod secundum Tulium . . ." For other MSS see Prague, Národní Knihovna České Republiky, XII.B.12.

————, Przyb. 91/52, 15th cent., fols. 1r–36v (text ends at 1837). Commentary: extensive three-columned marginal commentary and interlinear glossing; beginning missing. Same commentary (there with *accessus*) in Krakow, Biblioteka Muzeum Narodowego w Krakowie, Oddzial Zbiory Czartoryskich, 1464.

Krakow, Biblioteka Muzeum Narodowego w Krakowie, Oddzial Zbiory Czartoryskich, 1464, 15th cent. (2nd half), central European, pp. 129–187. Commentary: extensive three-columned commentary as well interlinear glossing; stops abruptly at p. 182, l. 1935. Portions of *accessus* from Pace of Ferrara. Same commentary in Krakow, Biblioteka Jagiellońska, Przyb. 91/52. Incipit: "Pro faciliori invitacione auditorum ad ea instituta que poete nostri . . . "

Leiden, Bibliotheek der Rijksuniversiteit, Voss. lat. O.68, 14th cent., Italian, fols. 1r–50v. Commentary: techniques identified in margin.

————, Voss. lat. O.69, 14th cent. for *PN,* French?, fols. 90r–123v. Commentary: none.

Leipzig, Universitätsbibliothek, MS 1084, 14th–15th cent., central European, fols. 232r–252v (*PN* to line 1137; commentary to fol. 252r). Commentary: extensive marginal and interlinear glosses in Dybinus tradition; versions in Augsburg, Staats- und Stadtbibliothek, 2° 133; Berlin, Staatsbibliothek zu Berlin—Preussischer Kulturbesitz, lat. qu. 17; Gdansk, Biblioteka Gdańska Polskiej Akademii Nauk, Mar. Q.8; and MSS listed under Giessen, Universitätsbibliothek, 68. Incipit: "<P>APA STUPOR Iste liber cuius subiectum videtur esse ornatus modus persvadendi de quocumque persvasibli diuiditur in quinque partes, siue tractatus speciales."

Leningrad. See St. Petersburg.

London, British Library, Add. 10095, 15th cent. (1427), Italian, separate commentary only on fols. 108r–156r. Commentary by Pace of Ferrara; for other MSS see Seville, Biblioteca Capitular y Colombina, Col. 5–4–30. Primary incipit: "Consueuerunt antiquiores nostri cum aliquid noui proponunt . . . " Incipit of secondary *accessus:* "Incepturos librum artis *Poetrie nouelle* oportet duo considerare."

————, Add. 15108, 15th cent. (1426–1430), central European, comm. on fols. 236r –301v, *PN* on fols. 237r–303v (incomplete; ends at 1587). Commentary: extensive marginal commentary and interlinear glosses in Dybinus tradition; commentary stops at line 1490, where hand of text changes. Incipit: "Quia iste liber retoricalis est . . . "

———, Add. 18153, 14th cent., fols. 4r–45r; *accessus* from 2r. Commentary: *accessus* and glosses, some in German. Primary incipit: "In principio huius libri octo sunt uidenda: primo de vita auctoris . . . " Incipit of secondary *accessus:* "In principio istius libri tria sunt precipue inquirenda, scilicet quid in hoc opere tractet, propter quid, et qualiter."

———, Add. 21214, 14th cent., Italian, fols. 3r–33v. Commentary: a few marginal and interlinear glosses.

———, Add. 22159, 15th cent., German?, fols. 61r–102v. Commentary: none.

———, Add. 37495, 14th cent. (1382), Italian, fols. 1r–37v. Commentary: no *accessus;* interlinear and marginal glosses in two similar hands. Incipit: "O PAPA qui es STUPOR MUNDI quantum ad hoc quod te totus mundus admiratur, ego intendo . . . "

[———, Arundel 343, 14th cent.?; burned in 1863.]

———, Cotton Cleopatra B.VI, 14th–15th cent., English (Oxford [Camargo, "*Tria sunt,*" 937]), fols. 4r–33v (new foliation). Commentary: none.

———, Egerton 2261, 13th cent., fragment at fol. 224r (52 of last 73 lines).

———, Harley 2586, 15th cent., fols. 2r–45v. Commentary: marginal notes on first folios that resemble *EC;* no *accessus.*

———, Harley 3582, 13th cent., Italian, fols. 1r–34r. Commentary: a few interlinear glosses, more at beginning.

———, Harley 3775, 13th cent., English provenance for other parts of this composite MS, fols. 150r–178r. Commentary: marginal glosses. No real *accessus;* very faded incipit of first gloss ("PAPA STUPOR Hic in principio *Poetrie* utitur auctor circumlocutione . . .") similar to incipit in Berlin, Staatsbibliothek zu Berlin—Preussischer Kulturbesitz, lat. qu. 515 and Vatican City, BAV Ottob. lat. 1472; commentary that follows is different.

———, Harley 6504, 15th cent., fols. 1r–40r. Commentary: interlinear glosses to fol. 36v; a few scattered marginal glosses.

———, Royal 8.C.VII, 14th cent. (second half [IRHT]), fragment on fols. 3r–4v (lines 204–292). Commentary: none.

[———, Royal 12.B.XVII, fols. 43v–53r (lines 1061–1601). Commentary: marginal and interlinear glossing on most folios. This item is actually a long excerpt of almost one fourth of the *PN* intentionally copied separately and ending in mid-section, included here because of the extent of the glossing.]

———, Royal 12.E.XI, 15th cent., English, *PN* on fols. 3r–52r, *accessus* on fols. 52r–53v. Commentary: some glossing on text *accessus* at end. Incipit of added *accessus:* "Liber iste diuiditur in prohemium et tractatum."

Madrid, Biblioteca Nacional, 3699, 14th–15th cent., Italian. fols. 1r–49r. Commentary: *accessus* added on flyleaf (i^v). Incipit: "Ut huius auctoris intencio et principalis causa . . . "

———, 9589, 15th cent., Italian (w. Aragonese contents), *accessus* on fol. 3r–v, *PN* on fols. 8r–62v. Commentary: extensive prefatory material and consistent glossing. Incipit: "PAPA STUPOR MUNDI etc. In principio huius libri sicut in quolibet opere sunt quattor inquirenda, scilicet que causa efficiens, que materialis, que formalis, et que finalis."

Manchester, Chetham's Library, A.3.130, 14th–15th cent., fols. 1r–25v. Commentary: none.

Melk, Stiftsbibliothek, 883.1, 13th–14th cent., central European, fols. 1v–42r. Commentary: introductory gloss and sporadic marginal comments. Incipit: "PAPA STUPOR Hic magister Gamfredus commendat papam . . . "

[Metz, Bibliothèque municipale, 516, 14th cent. Destroyed.] Commentary: only a few folios, but may have been *EC;* for other MSS of *EC* see Munich, Bayerische Staatsbibliothek, Clm 4603. Incipit: "In principio huius libri videndum est quid tractetur in hoc opere . . . " (*Catalogue général* 5.192–193).

Milan, Biblioteca Ambrosiana, E 129 sup., 14th cent. (second half), Italian (northern), fols. 1r–46r. Commentary: none. Information from Marco Petoletti.

———, G 96 sup., 14th cent., Italian (Veneto [Petoletti]), fols. 1r–43v. Commentary: few marginal but numerous interlinear glosses, some in the vernacular.

———, N 179 sup., 13th cent. (second half [Petoletti]), French, fols. 7v–35v. Commentary: interlinear glosses and some marginal notes.

———, P 9 sup., 14th cent. (end), fols. 1r–50r. Commentary: none. Information from Marco Petoletti.

———, S 2 sup., 14th cent. (1372), fols. 1r–38v. Commentary: none.

———, Trotti 302, 13th cent., (second half or end), Italian (northern: Bologna?), fols. 1r–35v. Commentary: none, but with erased note by Giuseppe Brivio quoting incipit of commentary by Pace of Ferrara, "Consueverunt antiquiores" (see Seville, Biblioteca Capitular y Colombina, Col. 5–4–30). Information from Marco Petoletti.

Milan, Biblioteca Trivulziana, 681, 14th cent. (end [Santoro, *I codici,* 153]), fols. 1r–34v. Commentary: none.

———, 728, 14th cent., Italian, fols. 1r–50v, Commentary: interlinear glossing throughout and some marginal comments starting on fol. 1v.

———, 762, 14th cent., Italian, fols. 1r–46v. Commentary: some short notes in margin. Incipit: "Iste liber principaliter diuiditur in duas partes, scilicet prohemium et tractatum. "

Modena, Biblioteca Estense, Est. lat. 123 (α.T.6.4), 14th–15th cent, Italian?, fols. 45r–75r (beginning at line 68, ending at 2099). Commentary: scattered glosses; incipit missing.

Munich, Bayerische Staatsbibliothek, Clm 237, 15th cent. (1462), German (Leipzig), fols. 15r–60r. Commentary: marginal and interlinear glosses throughout, although sporadic later; shares material with commentary in Munich, Clm. 14529. Incipit: "Causa materialis est ornatus modus persuadendi. . . . "

———, Clm 594, 14th–15th cent., fols. 71r–96v. Commentary: sporadic glossing throughout. Incipit: "Iste liber diuiditur in partes principales in prohemium et in tractatum."

———, Clm 3220, 14th cent. (1306), separate *accessus* on fol. 64r, *PN* with commentary on fols. 57r–96v. Commentary: around text and also separate *accessus* added later. Incipit of commentary around text: "In principio huius libri isti sunt inquirendi[i]: que causa suscepti operis, que materia, . . . " Incipit of added *accessus:* "Incipit *Poetria noua* quam magister Ganfridus componit."

———, Clm 4603, 13th cent., northern, separate commentary only on fols. 130r–136r. Commentary: *EC.* Versions also in Copenhagen, Kongelige Bibliotek, Gl. kgl. Saml. 2036 4°; Fulda, Landesbibliothek, C 8; Prague, Knihovna Metropolitní Kapituli, L 97; St. Gall, Stiftsbibliothek, 875; Vatican City, BAV Vat. lat. 6890; Vienna, Österreichische Nationalbibliothek, 526; Vienna, Österreichische Nationalbibliothek, 1365; Vienna, Österreichische Nationalbibliothek, 2513; Wolfenbüttel, Herzog August Bibliothek, Cod. Guelf. 124 Gud. lat.; Zwickau, Ratsschulbibliothek, LXVI; may have been in Metz, Bibliothèque municipale, 516 (destroyed). Incipit: "In principio huius libri videndum est quid tractetur in hoc opere et quare et qualiter."

———, Clm 14482, 14th cent. for *PN,* fols. 81r–117r. Commentary: scattered glosses, "Burchardus fragment" on fols. 93v–95r (Allen, *Ethical Poetic,* 199–200 and 233).

———, Clm 14529, 15th cent. (1465–66), German (Leipzig), *accessus* on fol. 3v, text on fols. 4r–69r. Commentary: *accessus* and marginal and interlinear glosses; similar to Munich, Clm 237. Incipit of *accessus:* "PAPA STUPOR MUNDI SI DIXERO Nota prout ex Tullio colligi [*sic*] in *Veteri* et *Nova Rhetorica* sua rethorica sic describitur."

———, Clm 18780, 15th cent. (1474), central European, fols. 72r–177v. Commentary by Dybinus of Prague written around and between sections of *PN,* with interlinear glosses; for other MSS see Prague, Národní Knihovna České Republiky, XII.B.12. Incipit of much-abbreviated *accessus:* "<A>ntequam habeatur diuisio littere prius videamus quis sit rethorica."

———, Clm 18803, 15th cent. for *PN,* central European, fols. 145r–170v. Commentary: a few glosses, including "Difficilis ascensus" excerpt (*Anticlaudianus* 5.57–61) at line 213.

Munich, Universitätsbibliothek, 4° 814, 15th cent. (*PN* 1458), German (Nuremburg), fols. 76r–108v (new foliation). Commentary: extensive marginal commentary; no interlinear glosses. Incipit: "Hic autor utitur insinuacione exordio quod est prima pars prime partis rethorice."

Naples, Biblioteca Nazionale "Vittorio Emanuele III," V.D.6, 14th–15th cent., Italian, separate commentary only on fols. 1r–46v. Commentary by Benedict of Aquileia. Incipit of prologue: "Quoniam circa elloquentiam quamplures dispersa uolumina condiderunt quorum alii mare alii riuulos emittentes . . . " Incipit of *accessus:* "In principio huius libri dubitauerunt quidam an de materia sua rethorica diceretur." Also in Princeton, Princeton University Library, Robert Garrett Library Collection MS 120.

———, Vind. lat. 53, 15th cent. (1423 for *PN*), Italian, fols. 1r–38r. Commentary: marginal and interlinear glosses by Franciscellus Mancinus. Similar short *accessus* and some interlinear notes in Vatican City, BAV Chig. L.IV.74. Incipit: "Auctor huius operis secundum quosdam dicitur fuisse quidam clericus . . . "

New Haven, Yale University, Beinecke Rare Book Room and Manuscript Library, 597, 14th–15th cent., Italian, fols. 1r–45r. Commentary: no annotations on first folio; heavy annotations on fols. 24v–26r. Information from Robert G. Babcock and Eric Knibbs.

———, Osborn fa.6 (Box 12, no. 19), 14th–15th cent. (ca. 1400: [Babcock]), Italian, fols. 1r–43v. Commentary by Bartholomew of Pisa (Bartolomeo de Sancto Concordio), incomplete, to fol. 6r; complete copy in Rome, Biblioteca Casanatense, 311. Incipit: "Iste liber diuiditur principaliter in tres partes." Additional information from Robert G. Babcock and Eric Knibbs.

[New York, Phyllis Goodhart Gordan MS 97; now in Bryn Mawr.]

Novacella (Neustift), Convento dei Canonici Regolari (Augustiner-Chorherrenstift), 327, 13th cent., Italian, fols. 1r–19v. Commentary: later marginal and interlinear glosses; no *accessus*. Related to commentary by Guizzardo of Bologna (Vatican City, BAV Ottob. lat. 3291).

Olomouc (Olmütz), Vědecká knihovna v Olomouci, C.O. 575, 15th cent. (1st half), central European, *accessus* on fol. 1r–v, *PN* on fols. 2r–32v. Commentary: full marginal and interlinear glossing. Incipit similar to that of *accessus* in Prague, Knihovna Metropolitní Kapituli, L 97, but glosses different. Incipit (very worn): "Cum ornatus modus loquendi ***."

Osimo, Biblioteca del Collegio Campana, cod. lat. 2, 14th cent., Italian, fols. 1r–40v. Commentary: none.

Oxford, Balliol College, 263, 14th–15th cent., English, fols. 32v–44v. Commentary: none.

———, 276, 15th cent. (ca. 1442), English, large fragment in two parts, fols. 2r–14v. Commentary: none.

Oxford, Bodleian Library, Auct. F.1.17, 14th cent., English, fols. 109r–121v. Commentary: none.

———, Digby 64, 15th cent. (1st half), English, *accessus* on fols. 5r–8r, *PN* on fols. 25v–45v (ends incomplete at 1859). Commentary: separate *accessus* (actually a "divisio textus"). Incipit: "Liber iste diuiditur in decem partes, quarum prima est de commendacione pape ibi, 'Papa stupor mundi.'"

———, Digby 104, 13th cent. (1st half for *PN*), English, fols. 21r–33v (ends incomplete at line 2054). Commentary: a few notes on first folios.

———, lat. misc. a.3, 13th cent., one of a group of unrelated fragments bound together, *PN* lines 1311–1181 at fol. 56r–v. Commentary: a few interlinear glosses and marginal notes.

———, Laud Misc. 515, 13th cent. (early [Hunt, *Teaching and Learning Latin*, 1.36]), English, fols. 141v–181r. Commentary: examples identified.

———, Laud Misc. 707, 15th cent., English (Oxford), fols. 4r–32v. Commentary: a few marginal notes.

———, Selden Supra 65, 15th cent. (early [Camargo, "*Tria sunt*," 937]), English, fols. 85r–111r and 140r–145v (two omitted passages added at end of MS). Commentary: a few marginal notes and identifications.

Oxford, Corpus Christi College, 132, 15th cent., English, fols. 108r–116r (incomplete; *PN* ends after 600 lines). Commentary: none.

———, 144, 15th cent. (1430–1442, [Clark, *Monastic Renaissance*, 282]), English, *accessus* on fol. 18v; *PN* on fols. 19r–43v. Commentary: *accessus* by John Bamburgh and some marginal notes, manicula, etc. Incipit: "In principio huius libri videndum est de quattuor eius causis."

Padua, Biblioteca Antoniana, Scaff. II. n. 50, 14th cent.?, Italian, fols. 1r–40v. Commentary: scattered marginal and interlinear glosses.

Padua, Biblioteca Universitaria, 505 (III. 2), 15th cent., fols. 1r–50v. Commentary: very sporadic marginal notes to fol. 23v; interlinear glosses to fol. 26r.

Paris, Bibliothèque nationale de France, lat. 505, 13th cent., French (Notre-Dame de Foucarmont [Samaran and Marichal, *Catalogue des manuscrits*, 2.17]), fols. 137r–142v (to 1852). Commentary: none.

———, lat. 8171, 13th cent., northern (French?), fols. 1v–33v (to 1835). Commentary: interlinear and marginal glosses, some same as *EC* (see Munich, Bayerische Staatsbibliothek, Clm 4603); no *accessus*. Incipit illegible (very worn).

———, lat. 8172, 14th cent., Italian, fols. 1r–36v (ending at 2098). Commentary: some glosses, mostly interlinear.

———, lat. 8173, 15th cent., central European, *PN* on fols. 12v–71r ; *accessus* on fol. 71r–v; separate commentary on fols. 73r–126r. Commentary: glosses around text (with some amateur drawings and diagrams of content), also an *accessus* at end as well as commentary copied separately. Incipit of glosses around text: "Incipit prologus *Poetrie nouelle* in quo Gaufredus Anglicus hunc librum commendat pontifici. . . . " Incipit of *accessus:* "Ars ista supponitur rethorice sciencie quia tendit ad suum finem per eundem methodum sicut rethorica. . . . " Secondary incipit: "In principio huius operis sicut cuiuslibet artificis ista concurrunt inquisicioni, scilicet que causa suscepti operis, que intencio, que vtilitas, cui parti philosophie supponatur, quis ordo, quis titulus." Incipit of separate commentary: "PAPA STUPOR MUNDI etc. Cum intentionis proposite sit quedam pauca de istius libri exposicione componere . . . "

———, lat. 8174, 15th cent., fols. 1r–37v (ending at 2080). Commentary: sporadic glosses starting at 1v, dense in some sections.

———, lat. 8246, 13th cent., French, fols. 107r–129v. Commentary: scattered glosses.

———, lat. 15135, 13th cent., French, fols. 163r–189r. Commentary: *accessus* a shortened version of *EC* (see Munich, Bayerische Staatsbibliothek, Clm 4603) but different glosses; followed by diagrams of rhetorical terms (fols. 189v–190r). Incipit: "In principio huius libri uidendum est quit [*sic*] tractetur in hoc opere et quare et qualiter."

———, lat. 15150, 13th–14th cent., French, fols. 88r–123v. Commentary: scattered marginal and interlinear glosses in several hands.

———, nouv. acq. lat. 647, 13th cent., fragment (fols. 3, 5–7). Commentary: none.

———, nouv. acq. lat. 699, 15th cent. (first half), English (Beverly? [Camargo, "*Tria sunt,*" 939]), fols. 60r–91r (to 2085). Commentary: none.

Perugia, Biblioteca Comunale Augusta, I.123, fols. 103r–159v. Commentary: interlinear notes on first two folios.

[Perugia, Museo dell'Opera (Biblioteca Dominicani), 653. Destroyed.]

Pistoia, Archivio Capitolare del Duomo, C. 143, 15th cent., Italian, fols. 1r–49v. Commentary: same as Vatican City, BAV Reg. lat. 1982; breaks off in middle with new added ending; resumes in another hand. Incipit: "PAPA STUPOR MUNDI Auctor in hoc opere intendit tractat [*sic*] de quinque partibus rethorice."

Pistoia, Biblioteca Comunale Forteguerriana, A. 13, 15th cent. (1464), Italian, fols. 74r–94v. Commentary: a few marginal notes.

Prague, Knihovna Metropolitní Kapituli, L 97, 14th cent. (1st half), central European?, fols. 2r–27r, *accessus* on fol. 1v. Commentary: interlinear glossing throughout; marginal glosses are *EC* with added scholastic divisions and subdivisions; for other MSS of *EC* see Munich, Bayerische Staatsbibliothek, Clm 4603. *Accessus* similar to that in Olomouc, Zemský Archiv, C.O. 575, however: "Cum ornatus modus loquendi non solum in prosa rerum eciam in metrica modulacione consistat" (very faded).

———, M 126, 15th cent. (1403), central European?, fols. 2r–48v. Commentary: interlinear glosses sporadic after fol. 19r; scattered marginal notes, some quite long.

———, M 134, 15th cent. (1464 for *PN*), central European (Troppau, Austria), *accessus* begins on fol. 75r; *PN* on fols. 76r–160r. Commentary: very full, written around and between text, with interlinear glosses; quotes Dybinus's *thema*. Incipit of *accessus:* "Diuo <confitiendum> [confisiendum *MS*] presidio cuius absque nutu nihil in natura potest subsistere . . . "

Prague, Národní Knihovna České Republiky, III.G.22, 14th cent., central European, *PN* on fols. 1r–36r, *accessus* starts on flyleaf. Commentary: *accessus* and extensive marginal and interlinear glosses. Incipit: "PAPA STUPOR MUNDI sicut dicit quod iste liber prima <secundum diuisionem> [sui diuisione *MS*] diuiditur in duas partes quorum prima dicitur prohemium" (cf. Uppsala, Universitetsbiblioteket, C 40).

———, VIII.D.19, central European, 14th cent. (1376), *PN* on fols. 2r–38v; *accessus* starts on fol. 1r. Commentary: long *accessus,* extensive marginal notes throughout most of the text, and interlinear glosses through fol. 6. Primary incipit: "Sicut dicit Plato in *Timaeo,* nichil est ortum cuius causa legitima non precesserit." Incipit of secondary *accessus:* "PAPA STUPOR MUNDI SI DIXERO PAPA NOCENTI Accedendo ad formam tractatus istius libri cuius subiectum est modus persuadendi ex his que sunt communia arti poetice et rethorice. . . . "

———, VIII.H.22, 14th cent. (1389 for *PN*), central European (Prague?), fols. 27r–93r, *accessus* on 26r–v. Commentary by Dybinus of Prague (*scripta* version), incomplete; marginal glosses stop at 35v for most part, but there are short marginal notes on digression and description (e.g., 43r) and at the very end; interlinear glosses rare after fol. 49r. Primary incipit: "'Amice, ascende superius.' Hec uerba scripta sunt in ewangelio Luce quarto capitulo in quibus verbis rethorice generositas excellensque precelsitas potest commendari." Incipit of secondary *accessus:* "Tamen antequam liber diuidatur, dicendum est quod rethorica consideratur dupliciter." Some of its interlinear glosses also in Giessen, Universitätsbibliothek, 68. For MSS of another version see Prague, Národní Knihovna České Republiky, XII.B.12.

———, XII.B.12, 14th cent. (1375), central European (Prague), commentary only on fols. 1r–42r. Commentary by Dybinus of Prague, taken down via dictation (*dicta* format). Versions of this commentary also in Gdansk, Biblioteka Gdańska Polskiej Akademii Nauk, Mar. Q.9; Krakow, Biblioteka Jagiellońska, 2141; Vienna, Österreichische Nationalbibliothek, 3251; and Vienna, Schottenkloster, 399. Primary incipit: "'Amice, ascende superius' scribitur Luce capitulo quarto [*sic*]. Philosophicalis sciencia quemlibet secundum racionem viventem elevat." Incipit of secondary *accessus:* "Antequam habeatur diuisio littere prius videamus quid sit rethorica" (also in Munich, Bayerische Staatsbibliothek, Clm 18780; different secondary *accessus* in Vienna, Schottenkloster, 399).

Princeton, Princeton University Library, Robert Garrett Library Collection, MS 120, 14th–15th cent., Italian, pages 3–155. Commentary by Benedict of Aquilegia (unidentified), also in Naples, Biblioteca Nazionale "Vittorio Emanuele III," V.D.6, here without prologue and some introductory material. Primary incipit (very worn): "I*** est omnino non . . . " Incipit of secondary *accessus:* "PAPA etc. Liber iste diuiditur in partes tres."

———, Robert Garrett Library Collection MS 121, 13th cent.?, Italian, fols. 1r–61r. Commentary: some, very worn and much illegible.

———, Taylor MS 14, 13th cent.?, Italian, fols. 1r–30r. Commentary: some glosses, both marginal and interlinear, in two hands.

Reggio Emilia, Biblioteca Municipale, Var. f. 64, 15th cent. (1478), Italian?, fols. 1r–43r. Commentary: scattered notes.

Reims, Bibliothèque municipale, 1247, 15th cent., fols. 1r–67v. Commentary: extensive, to 2021; no *accessus*. Incipit: "Titulus huius libri talis est: Gaufredi Hibernii regis Anglie scriptoris

Novelle poetrie de artificio loquendi liber incipit."

Rome, Biblioteca Casanatense, 311, 15th cent., Italian, fols. 2r–70v, *accessus* on 1r. Commentary by Bartholomew of Pisa (also in New Haven, Beinecke Library, Osborn fa. 6) alternating with sections of text. Primary incipit: "<S>ecundum sententiam Tullii *De officiis* inter omnes scientias que hominem honorabilem reddunt rethorica obtinet principatum." Incipit of secondary *accessus:* "Iste liber diuiditur principaliter in tres partes."

Rome, Biblioteca Corsiniana, Rossi 22 (36 G 15), 15th cent. (first half [Petrucci, *Catalogo,* 12]), Italian, separate commentary on fols. 2ra–24va, *PN* on fols. 25r–56r. Commentary: separate commentary is shorter version of Pace of Ferrara; for other MSS see Seville, Biblioteca Capitular y Colombina, Col. 5–4–30. Primary incipit: "Consueuerunt namque maiores nostri cum aliquod operis noui p<ro>ponunt . . . " Incipit of secondary *accessus:* "Incepturos librum artis poetrie oportet duo considerare." A few interlinear glosses on beginning of text of *PN*.

Rome, Biblioteca Nazionale Centrale, Fondo Vittorio Emanuele 1057, 14th cent., Italian, fols. 1r–41v. Commentary: some marginal glossing in several hands throughout, sporadic interlinear glosses; no *accessus*. Incipit: "Hic papa Innocentius fuit qui composuit librum *De contemptu mundi*."

St. Florian (Enns), Stiftsbibliothek, XI 108, 15th cent., central European, *PN* on fols. 35r–99r; *accessus* begins on fol. 34r. Commentary: *accessus* and copious marginal and interlinear glossing to fol. 38v, sporadic marginal notes thereafter. Incipit: "Rhetorica a Quintiliano sic diffinitur . . . "

St. Gall, Stiftsbibliothek, 856, 15th cent., central European, pp. 283–534. Commentary: marginal comments throughout with much interlinear glossing and several diagrams; draws on version of *EC* in St. Gall 875. Primary incipit: "Item(?) quia *** de qua proprium intendimus liberalium disciplinarum. . . . " Incipit of secondary *accessus:* "PAPA STUPOR Liber iste diuiditur in septem partes principales."

————, 875, 14th cent., central European, pp. 3–87. Commentary: *EC;* for other MSS see Munich, Bayerische Staatsbibliothek, Clm 4603. Incipit: "PAPA STUPOR etc. Liber iste diuiditur in septem partes principaliter."

St. Petersburg, Biblioteka Rossiiskoi akademii nauk, Q. 433, 14th cent. (1345), Italian (northern? [Baswell, *Virgil in Medieval England,* 310]), *PN* on fols. 65r–96v, *accessus* on fol. 64v. Commentary: *accessus* and some marginal glossing. Incipit: "In huius libri principio attendenda sunt, uidelicet quis auctor . . . "

St. Petersburg, Rossiiskaia natsionalnaia biblioteka, Lat. O. XIV, no. 6, 14th–15th cent., central European?, fols. 2r–11r (incomplete; ends at line 156); *accessus* begins on fol. 1v. Commentary: full commentary and interlinear glossing (some pages with just commentary). Incipit: "Notandum dicit PAPA STUPOR nam hoc nomen dicitur ab interiectione amirantis 'pape' . . . "

Salamanca, Biblioteca Universitaria, 72, 15th cent., Italian, fols. 194r–229r (first folio of text missing), commentary from fol. 193v. Commentary: *accessus* and marginal glosses. Incipit (doubling of some letters): "In priincipio huius operis sicut in prrincipiis aliorum <tria> [terti *MS*] sunt per ordinem inquirenda." See also Venice, Biblioteca Nazionale Marciana, Marc. lat. XII.244 (10531). Information and digitized images from Óscar Lilao Franca.

Salzburg, Stiftsbibliothek St. Peter, a.V.13, 14th cent., fols. 38r–66v. With commentary. Information from *Iter ital.* 3.39.

Seville, Biblioteca Capitular y Colombina, Cap. 56–2–27 (82–1–19bis), 15th cent. (1448), Italian, fols. 3r–39v, *accessus* on fol. 2r–v. Commentary by Giovanni Travesi. Primary incipit: "Venerationis uirtute maxime . . . " Incipit of secondary *accessus:* "PAPA STUPOR etc. In principio huius libri sicut in principiis aliorum . . . "

———, Col. 5–4–30, 14th cent. (1395), Italian, separate commentary on fols. 2ra–102ra (5ra–105ra). Commentary by Pace of Ferrara (in at least two hands); also found in Assisi, Biblioteca Storico-Francescana della Chiesa Nuova, 309; Bergamo, Biblioteca Civica "Angelo Mai," MA 484; Cremona, Biblioteca Statale, Fondo Governativa 88; Klagenfurt, Bundesstaatliche Studienbibliothek, Pap. 109; London, BL Add. 10095; Rome, Biblioteca Corsiniana, Rossi 22 (36 G 15). Primary incipit: "<C>onsvevervnt antiquiores nostri cum aliquid noui proponunt . . . " Incipit of secondary *accessus:* "<I>ncepturos librum artis poetice oportet duo considerare."

———, Col. 7–1–27, 14th–15th cent., Italian?, fols. 1r–96r. Commentary: no *accessus;* interlinear glosses to fol. 32v, marginal glosses to 59v. Incipit: "Hic est figura que dicitur aufexis" (same incipit but different commentary in Vienna, Österreichische Nationalbibliothek, 2401).

Sibinik, [Franciscan Library] Šibenik Zeljko Lončar, OFM Šibenik, Sanòstan, Trg Tomasea MS 36, 15th cent., French, fasc. 3 (of "several"), 56 fols. Commentary: "with preface." Information from *Iter ital.* 5.445.

Siena, Biblioteca Comunale degli Intronati, K.V.4, 14th–15th cent.?, Italian, fols. 1r–44r. Commentary: none.

———, K.V.23, 14th–15th cent.?, Italian, fols. 1r–39v (misbound: first lines of *PN* on fol. 8r; explicit on fol. 7v). Commentary: some marginal glosses. Incipit: "PAPA etc. Opus istud diuiditur in sex partes, scilicet exordium, narrationem, diuisionem, <con>firmationem: confutationem, et conclusionem."

Stuttgart, Würtembergische Landesbibliothek, HB I 88 (formerly Kloster Weingarten K 93), 14th cent., central European, fols. 62r–103v. Commentary: none.

Turin, Biblioteca Nazionale Universitaria, F.IV.11, Italian, 15th cent. for *PN,* fols. 15r–41v. Commentary: a few marginal and some interlinear notes.

Udine, Archivio di Stato di Udine, 68, 13th cent., Italian, 8 folios (badly torn fragments from a single manuscript). Commentary: numerous interlinear and marginal glosses in at least two hands.

———, 196, 14th cent., Italian, fragment of 4 folios. Commentary: a few interlinear and marginal glosses.

———, 222, 13th–14th cent., Italian (northern [Scalon, *Libri,* 257]), one folio. Commentary: none.

Uppsala, Universitetsbiblioteket, C 40, 14th cent., central European, *PN* on fols. 20v–66v, commentary to 65v. Commentary in continuous columns outside text; some interlinear glossing. Incipit: "Iste liber cuius subjectum est sensus poeticus secundum quosdam vel ars poetica <principaliter secundum diuisionem> [principalis sui diuisione *MS*] diuiditur in duas partes, scilicet in prohemium et executionem" (cf. Prague, Národní Knihovna České Republiky, III.

G.22).

Valenciennes, Bibliothèque municipale, 14th cent., 242 (232bis), fols. 16r–44r. Commentary: none. Information from Nims, unpublished notebooks; *Cat. gen.* 25.297.

Vatican City, Biblioteca Apostolica Vaticana, Chig. I.IV.145, 14th cent., Italian, fols. 1r –49r. Commentary: later interlinear and some marginal glosses.

————, Chig. I.V.181, 14th cent., Italian, fols. 1r–34v. Commentary: none.

————, Chig. I.VI.229, 17th cent. (1662 and 1666), Italian, two copies of *PN* on fols. 1r–49r and fols. 51r–84r; evaluation etc. on fols. 85r–88v. Commentary: summary, evaluation, and table of contents by Athanasius Kircher.

————, Chig. I.VI.230, 17th cent., *PN* on fols. 5r–36v. Commentary: transcription of Pits's entry on Geoffrey of Vinsauf on fol. 2r–v.

————, Chig. L.IV.74, 15th cent., Italian, fols. 1r–55v. Commentary: extensive glosses to fol. 22. Incipit: "Auctor huius operis ut quidam dicunt clericus *** anglicus . . ." Similar short *accessus* and some interlinear glosses in Naples, Biblioteca Nazionale "Vittorio Emanuele III," Vind. lat. 53.

————, Ottob. lat. 1472 , 13th–14th cent., French, fols. 2r–28r. Commentary: marginal glosses but no *accessus*. Incipit: "In principio vtitur circumlocutione vbi dicit 'stupor mundi' captando benivolenciam pape." Similar incipit but different glosses in London, BL Harley 3775 and Berlin, Staatsbibliothek zu Berlin—Preussischer Kulturbesitz, lat. qu. 515.

————, Ottob. lat. 1961, 14th cent., Italian, fols. 32r–78v. Commentary: scattered marginal glosses on first half; some interlinear glosses to fol. 68.

————, Ottob. lat. 3291, 15th cent., Italian, separate commentary only on fols. 1r–17r. Commentary by Guizzardo of Bologna. Incipit: "<Q>voniam propter opinantes contrarium ueritati qui ob ornatum modum loquendi siue stilo dictaminis subiacentem suspicantes rhetoricam formaliter edocere, 'delfinum siluis appingit, fluctibus aprum' . . . "

[————, Reg. lat. 344, fols. 37–38 (Gallick, "Medieval Rhetorical Arts," 84). Probably an excerpt rather than a fragment; unable to verify.]

————, Reg. lat. 1615, 13th cent., fols. 1r–47r. Commentary: identification of techniques and examples only.

————, Reg. lat. 1982, 15th cent. (1440), Italian, fols. 49r–86v. Commentary: *accessus* and full commentary copied in margins on either side of text, with interlinear glosses; same commentary with alterations (some drastic) in Pistoia, Archivio del Duomo, C 143. Incipit: "PAPA STUPOR MUNDI Auctor in hoc opere intendit tractare de quinque partibus rethorice."

————, Ross. 513, 14th cent., Italian, fols. 1r–31v (incomplete; ends at 1842). Commentary: *accessus* and glosses (marginal and interlinear) that dwindle after a few folios. Incipit: "In principio huius libri tria sunt . . . " (very worn).

[————, Vat. lat. 2148, fol. 128v (Gallick, "Medieval Rhetorical Arts," 84); presumably an excerpt rather than a fragment because one folio side only; unable to verify.]

————, Vat. lat. 5344, 13th–14th cent., fols. 1r–31v. Commentary: no marginal glosses; some interlinear.

————, Vat. lat. 6890, 13th–14th cent., fols. 2r–40r. Commentary: *EC* without *accessus;* for other MSS see Munich, Bayerische Staatsbibliothek, Clm 4603.

Venice, Biblioteca Giustiniani Recanati, II 109 (477), 15th cent. Information from *Iter ital.* 6.285.

Venice, Biblioteca Nazionale Marciana, Marc. lat. XII.94 (4211), 15th cent. (1432), fols. 1r–44v. Commentary: mostly rubrics and identifications.

———, Marc. lat. XII.244 (10531), 14th cent., pp. 32–96. Commentary: later *accessus* and marginal glosses at beginning, interlinear glosses throughout. Incipit: "In principio huius libri sicut in principiis aliorum tria sunt per ordinem inquirenda." See also Salamanca, Biblioteca Universitaria, 72.

Vienna, Österreichische Nationalbibliothek, 312, 14th cent., central European, fols. 49v-82r, *accessus* on fol. 82v. Commentary: *accessus* only. Incipit: "Auctor premittit proemium . . . "

———, 526, 13th cent., central European, fols. 96vb-111vb; commentary from fol. 95vb. Commentary: *EC* written in margins and between sections of text. For other MSS see Munich, Bayerische Staatsbibliothek, Clm 4603. Incipit: "In principio huius libri uidendum est quid tractetur in hoc opere et quare et qualiter."

———, 1365, 13th-14th cent., central European, *PN* on fols. 70v–78r, commentary from fol. 69v, stops on 75v. Commentary: *EC;* for other MSS see Munich, Bayerische Staatsbibliothek, Clm 4603. Incipit: "In principio huius libri uidendum est quid tractetur in hoc opere et quare et qualiter."

———, 2340, 13th cent., central European, fols. 1r-11v. Commentary: none.

———, 2401, 15th cent., Italian, fols. 1r–44r. Commentary: no *accessus;* glosses on first folio, rapidly tapering off; new commenting hand begins on fol. 23r, concentrating on the figures; diagram of parts of rhetoric on fol. 44r. Incipit: "NOCENTI Hic est figura que dicitur auferexis . . . " Same incipit but different commentary in Seville, Biblioteca Capitular y Colombina, Col. 7–1–27.

———, 2490, 14th–15th cent., fols. 1r–38v (to 1973). Commentary: full on first few folios, sporadic marginal and intertextual glosses thereafter in more than one hand. Incipit: "Ait Tulius, 'Sapiencia sine eloquencia est . . . '"

———, 2513, 13th cent., central European, fols. 35v–61v (to 1955); *accessus* starts on fol. 34v. Commentary: *EC;* for other MSS see Munich, Bayerische Staatsbibliothek, Clm 4603. Incipit: "In principio huius libri primo videndum est quid tractetur in hoc opere et quare et qualiter."

———, 3251, 15th cent. (*PN* 1420), central European, *PN* fols. 1v–149v; commentary on fols. 1r–150r. Commentary: version of Dybinus written in margins and between sections of text; no interlinear glosses but room left for them. For other MSS see Prague, Národní Knihovna České Republiky, XII.B.12. Primary incipit: "'Amice, ascende superius' {Luke 14:10} phisicalis scienciam quemlibet secundum rationem viventem eleuat." Incipit of secondary *accessus:* "Antequam habeatur diuisio littere prius quid rethorica . . . "

———, 4959, 15th cent. (1424), central European, fols. 67r–178r. Commentary: *accessus,* extensive commentary in margins and between sections of text, and interlinear glosses. Incipit: "<P>APA STUPOR Iste est liber *Noue poetrie* summe subtilis rethorice . . . "

———, 5001, 15th cent., (1424 for *PN*), central European, fols. 3v–68v for *PN,* commentary from fol. 1v (preceded by a generic rhetorical *accessus*). Commentary: extensive; also interlinear glosses. Incipit: "PAPA STUPOR MUNDI SI DIXERO Ex quo presens liber est rethoricalis; ideo nota rethorica est sciencia . . . "

————, Ser. nov. 291, 13th cent., Italian, fragments bound together at fols. 1r–6v (lines 1–60, 431–618, 863–980). Commentary: no *accessus,* a few glosses. Incipit illegible.

Vienna, Schottenkloster, 399, 15th cent., central European, *PN* on fols. 3r–53v, *accessus* from fol. 1r (part of Dybinus's *accessus* to PN used to introduce another text at fol. 86v). Commentary: version of Dybinus's commentary with *accessus,* extensive marginal commentary, and interlinear glossing; see also MSS listed under Prague, Národní Knihovna České Republiky, XII.B.12. Primary incipit: "'Amice, ascende superius' [*in marg.* Luce 14] philozophicalis sciencia quemlibet racionem viventem eleuat." Incipit of secondary *accessus:* "PAPA STUPOR MUNDI Iste liber cuius subiectum est artificiosa eloquencia diuiditur in quinque tractatus speciales secundum quinque officia rethoris" (cf. Leipzig, Universitätsbibliothek, MS 1084).

Wolfenbüttel, Herzog August Bibliothek, Cod. Guelf. 37.34 Aug. 2°, 15th cent. (1480), central European, fols. 1r–35v. Commentary: very short *accessus* and marginal and interlinear glosses in several hands, drawing on Dybinus material; stops on fol. 33v. Incipit: "Iste liber cuius subiectum est ornatus modus loquendi procedendi persuadendi cuiuslibet persuasibilis prima sui disponi diuiditur in quinque tractatus secundum quod quinque sunt officia rethoris." See Giessen, Universitätsbibliothek, 68.

————, Cod. Guelf. 124 Gud. lat., 13th cent., central European, fols.1v–22r, *accessus* from fol. 1r. Commentary: *EC;* for other MSS see Munich, Bayerische Staatsbibliothek, Clm 4603. Incipit: "In principio huius libri uidendum est quid tractetur in hoc opere et quare et qualiter."

————, Cod. Guelf. 259 Gud. lat, 14th cent., fols. 1r–53v. Commentary: none.

————, Cod. Guelf. 286 Gud. lat., late 14th cent., German, fols. 1r–36v. Commentary by Reiner von Cappel; short *accessus* and marginal notes. Incipit: "Subiectum huius libri est modus persuadendi ex hiis que communia sunt arti poetice et rethorice."

————, Cod. Guelf. 289 Gud. lat., 15th cent., central European, fols. 1r–33v. Commentary: none.

Worcester, Cathedral and Chapter Library, Q. 79, 15th cent., English, fols. 1r–35v (first 57 lines missing); *PN* ends on fol. 34r, followed by verses from *De ornamentis verborum* of Marbode of Rennes copied as end of *PN.* Commentary: small amount of glossing; some rubrics.

Wrocław (Breslau), Biblioteka Uniwersytecka, IV Q 100, 15th cent. (1456), central European, fols. 218r–289v. Also with separate excerpt ("Scisne moram pigri," 1366 ff.) on fol. 216. Commentary: no real *accessus* (just short paragraph) but copious marginal and very full interlinear glosses, especially on first half. Incipit (difficult to read): "Subiectum istius libri est ornatus modus persuadendi cuiuslibet persuasibilis." Cf. Giessen, Universitätsbibliothek, 68.

York, Minster Library, XVI.Q.14, 13th cent. (early), English, fols. 106r–111v to 208r). Commentary: none.

[Zurich, Private Collection, Italian, 14th cent. (Gehl, *Moral Art,* 279, and "Latin Readers," 440). Now in Keio?]

Zwickau, Ratsschulbibliothek, LXVI, 17th cent., central European (Zwickau), *PN* on fols. 116r–153v; separate commentary on fols. 160r–179v. Commentary: *EC* copied from Wolfenbüttel, Herzog August Bibliothek, Guelf. 124 Gud. lat.; for other MSS see Munich, Bayerische Staatsbibliothek, Clm 4603.

LIST OF INCIPITS

Accedendo ad formam tractatus istius libri cuius subiectum est modus persuadendi
ex his que sunt communia arte poetice et rethorice . . .
> Prague, Národní Knihovna České Republiky, VIII.D.19

Ait Tulius, "Sapiencia sine eloquencia est . . . "
> Vienna, Österreichische Nationalbibliothek, 2490

"Amice, ascende superius et erit tibi gloria coram omnibus simul discumbentibus."
> Krakow, Biblioteka Jagiellońska, 2141

"Amice, ascende superius." Hec uerba scripta sunt in ewangelio Luce quarto capitulo in quibus verbis rethorice generositas excellensque precelsitas potest commendari.
> Prague, Národní Knihovna České Republiky, VIII.H.22

"Amice, ascende superius" que quidem verba licet Luce 14° capitulo sunt in parabola conscripta . . .
> Gdansk (Danzig), Biblioteka Gdańska Polskiej Akademii Nauk, Mar. Q.8

"Amice, ascende superius" scribitur Luce capitulo 4°. Philosophicalis sciencia
quemlibet secundum racionem viuentem eleuat.
> Gdansk (Danzig), Biblioteka Gdańska Polskiej Akademii Nauk, Mar. Q.9
> Prague, Národní Knihovna České Republiky, XII.B.12
> Vienna, Österreichische Nationalbibliothek, 3251
> Vienna, Schottenkloster, 399

Antequam Gualfredus accedat ad propositum principale premictit prologum . . .
>   Barcelona, Archivo de la Corona de Aragón, Ripoll 103

Antequam habeatur diuisio littere prius videamus quid sit rethorica.
>   Gdansk (Danzig), Biblioteka Gdańska Polskiej Akademii Nauk, Mar. Q.9
>   Munich, Bayerische Staatsbibliothek, Clm 18780 (abbreviated)
>   Prague, Národní Knihovna České Republiky, XII.B.12
>   Vienna, Österreichische Nationalbibliothek, 3251

Ars ista supponitur rethorice sciencie quia tendit ad suum finem per eundem methodum sicut rethorica . . .
>   Paris, Bibliothèque nationale de France, lat. 8173

Auctor huius operis secundum quosdam dicitur fuisse quidam clericus . . .
>   Naples, Biblioteca Nazionale "Vittorio Emanuele III," Vind. lat. 53

Auctor huius operis ut quidam dicunt clericus *** anglicus . . .
>   Vatican City, Biblioteca Apostolica Vaticana, Chig. L.IV.74

Auctor in hoc opere intendit tractare de quinque partibus rethorice.
>   Pistoia, Archivio Capitolare del Duomo, C. 143
>   Vatican City, Biblioteca Apostolica Vaticana, Reg. lat. 1982

Auctor premittit proemium . . .
>   Vienna, Österreichische Nationalbibliothek, 312

Causa efficiens huius operis fuit Gualfredus d'Anglia qui composuit ipsum ad decus domini pape Innocentii tercii a quo optinuit quoddam beneficium . . .
>   Florence, Biblioteca Nazionale Centrale, Conv. Soppr. I.VI.17

Causa materialis est ornatus modus persuadendi . . .
>   Munich, Bayerische Staatsbibliothek, Clm 237

Circa ea que in hoc libro dicenda sunt notandum primo quod secundum intencionem Aristotelis et Tullii triplex est rethorica . . .
>   Augsburg, Staats- und Stadtbibliothek, 2° 133

Circa inicium Ganfreydi siue *Poetrie noue* pro recommendacione rethorice sentencie est notanda illa proposicio, "Tota pulchra es amica mea."
>   Berlin, Staatsbibliothek zu Berlin–Preussischer Kulturbesitz, lat. qu. 17

Circa principium rethorice sciendum quod rethorica a Tulio sic describitur . . .
>   Krakow, Biblioteka Jagiellońska, 1891

Consueuerunt antiquiores nostri cum aliquid noui proponunt . . .

    Assisi, Biblioteca Storico-Francescana della Chiesa Nuova 309

    Bergamo, Biblioteca Civica "Angelo Mai," MA 484

    Cremona, Biblioteca Statale, Fondo Governativa 88

    Klagenfurt, Bundesstaatliche Studienbibliothek, Pap. 109 Columbina, Col. 5–4–30

    London, British Library, Add. 10095

    Rome, Biblioteca Corsiniana, Rossi 22 (36 G 15)

    Seville, Biblioteca Capitular y Colombina, Cap. 5–4–30

Cujusvis statuae cognitio a capite est.

    Copenhagen, Kongelige Bibliotek, Gl. kgl. Saml. 2037

Cum intentionis proposite sit quedam pauca de istius libri exposicione componere . . .

    Paris, Bibliothèque nationale de France, lat. 8173

Cum omnium creaturarum dignissima [= dignissima creatura] sit homo . . .

    Cambridge, Trinity College, R.3.29

Cum ornatus modus loquendi ***.

    Olomouc (Olmütz), Vědecká knihovna v Olomouci, C.O. 575

Cum ornatus modus loquendi non solum in prosa rerum eciam in metrica modulacione consistat.

    Prague, Knihovna Metropolitní Kapituli, L 97

Cum rerum noticiam precedat noticia causarum earum huius operis prius consideremus ut rei sequentis lucidius pateat cognicio.

    Cambridge, Trinity College, R.14.22

Diuo confitiendum presidio cuius absque nutu nihil in natura potest subsistere . . .

    Prague, Knihovna Metropolitní Kapituli, M 134

Ego tribuam tibi nomen acephalum.

    Florence, Biblioteca Medicea Laurenziana, Acquisti e doni 438

Et secundum illa officia presens liber cuius materia siue subiectum est ornatus modus persuadendi cuiuslibet persuasibilis diuiditur in quinque tractatus.

    Augsburg, Staats- und Stadtbibliothek, 2° 133

Ex quo liber iste supponitur rethorica videndum est quid sit rethorica et ex quibus rebus constituatur . . .

    Erfurt, Wissenschaftliche Allgemeinbibliothek der Stadt, Amplon. O.1

Ex quo presens liber est rethoricalis; ideo nota rethorica est sciencia . . .
  Vienna, Österreichische Nationalbibliothek, 5001

Exordium secundum Tullium in principio *Noue rethorice* . . .
  Fulda, Landesbibliothek, C 8 (Kloster Weingarten K 11)

Ganfredus vir eloquentissimus . . .
  Erfurt, Wissenschaftliche Allgemeinbibliothek der Stadt, Amplon. Q. 286

Hic autor utitur insinuacione exordio quod est prima pars prime partis rethorice.
  Munich, Universitätsbibliothek, 4° 814

Hic captat auctor beneuolenciam dicens "pape" ab ipsis rebus, idest ab ipsis uirtutibus . . .
  Ferrara, Biblioteca Comunale Ariostea, II. 175

Hic est figura que dicitur auferexis que . . .
  Vienna, Österreichische Nationalbibliothek, 2401

Hic est figura que dicitur aufexis.
  Seville, Biblioteca Capitular y Colombina, Col. 7–1–27

Hic in principio huius prohemii circumlocutione utitur auctor dicendo "stupor mundi."
  Berlin, Staatsbibliothek zu Berlin–Preussischer Kulturbesitz, lat. qu. 515

Hic in principio *Poetrie* utitur auctor circumlocutione . . .
  London, British Library, Harley 3775

Hic magister Gamfredus commendat papam . . .
  Melk, Stiftsbibliothek, 883.1

Hic papa Innocentius fuit qui composuit librum *De contemptu mundi.*
  Rome, Biblioteca Nazionale Centrale, Fondo Vittorio Emanuele 1057

*** hunc librum est docere quedam communia poetice et rethorice. . . .
  Erfurt, Wissenschaftliche Allgemeinbibliothek der Stadt, Amplon. O15

I*** est omnino non . . .
  Princeton, Princeton University Library, Robert Garrett Library Collection, MS 120

In hoc loco premittit actor prologum in quo tria facit . . .
  Erfurt, Wissenschaftliche Allgemeinbibliothek der Stadt, Amplon. O.17

In huius libri principio attendenda sunt, uidelicet quis auctor . . .
 St. Petersburg, Biblioteka Rossiiskoi akademii nauk, Q. 433

In nomine domini nostri Jesu Christi hic incipiunt diuisiones huius libri premissis primo causis operi cuilibet conuenientibus.
 Florence, Biblioteca Medicea Laurenziana, Strozzi 137

In principio huius libri dubitauerunt quidam an de materia sua rethorica diceretur.
 Naples, Biblioteca Nazionale "Vittorio Emanuele III," V.D.6

In principio huius libri hec sunt inquirenda, scilicet que materia, que utilitas . . .
 Engelberg, Stiftsbibliothek, 144

In principio huius libri isti sunt inquirendi: que causa suscepti operis, que materia, . . .
 Munich, Bayerische Staatsbibliothek, Clm 3220

In principio huius libri octo sunt uidenda: primo de vita auctoris . . .
 London, British Library, Add. 18153

In principio huius libri sicut in principiis aliorum ad ea . . .
 Seville, Biblioteca Capitular y Colombina, Cap. 56–2–27

In principio huius libri sicut in principiis aliorum tria sunt per ordinem inquirenda.
 Venice, Biblioteca Nazionale Marciana, Marc. lat. XII.244 (10531)

In principio huius libri sicut in quolibet opere sunt quattor inquirenda, scilicet que causa efficiens, que materialis, que formalis, et que finalis.
 Madrid, Biblioteca Nacional, 9589

In principio huius libri tria sunt . . .
 Vatican City, Biblioteca Apostolica Vaticana, Ross. 513

In principio huius libri videndum est de quattuor eius causis.
 Oxford, Corpus Christi College, 144

In principio huius libri videndum est quid tractetur in hoc opere . . .
 [Metz, Bibliothèque municipale, 516. Destroyed.]

In principio huius libri uidendum est quid tractetur in hoc opere et quare et qualiter.
 Munich, Bayerische Staatsbibliothek, Clm 4603
 Paris, Bibliothèque nationale de France, lat. 15135

Vienna, Österreichische Nationalbibliothek, 526
Vienna, Österreichische Nationalbibliothek, 1365
Vienna, Österreichische Nationalbibliothek, 2513
Wolfenbüttel, Herzog August Bibliothek, Cod. Guelf. 124 Gud. lat.

In principio huius operis sicut cuiuslibet artificis ista concurrunt inquisicioni, scilicet que causa
suscepti operis, que intencio, que vtilitas, cui parti philosophie supponatur, quis ordo, quis
titulus.
Paris, Bibliothèque nationale de France, lat. 8173

In principio huius operis sicut in principiis aliorum tria sunt per ordinem inquirenda.
Salamanca, Biblioteca Universitaria, 72

In principio istius auctoris sicut cuiuslibet alterius ista occiderunt inquisitioni, scilicet que causa
suscepti operis . . .
Cambridge, Trinity College, R.14.22

In principio istius libri sex sunt inquirenda . . .
Erfurt, Wissenschaftliche Allgemeinbibliothek der Stadt, Amplon. Q.75

In principio istius libri tria sunt precipue inquirenda, scilicet quid in hoc opere tractet, propter
quid, et qualiter.
London, British Library, Add. 18153

In principio videndum quid, qualiter, quare . . .
Erfurt, Wissenschaftliche Allgemeinbibliothek der Stadt, Amplon. O.17.

In principio vtitur circumlocutione vbi dicit "stupor mundi" captando benivolenciam pape.
Vatican City, Biblioteca Apostolica Vaticana, Ottob. lat. 1472

Incepturos librum artis poetice oportet duo considerare.
Bergamo, Biblioteca Civica "Angelo Mai," MA 484
Cremona, Biblioteca Statale, Fondo Governativa 88
Klagenfurt, Bundesstaatliche Studienbibliothek, Pap. 109 Columbina, Col. 5–4–30
London, British Library, Add. 10095
Rome, Biblioteca Corsiniana, Rossi 22 (36 G 15)
Seville, Biblioteca Capitular y Colombina, Cap. Col. 5–4–30

Incipit *Poetria noua* anglici poete Ganfredi Ysagogia . . .
Erlangen, Universitätsbibliothek, 635

Incipit *Poetria noua* magistri Gamfredi Anglici; in quinque tractatus diuisa est.
Brussels, Bibliothèque Royale Albert 1ᵉʳ, 9774

Incipit *Poetria noua* quam magister Ganfridus componit.
> Munich, Bayerische Staatsbibliothek, Clm 3220

Incipit prologus *Poetrie nouelle* in quo Gaufredus Anglicus hunc librum commendat pontifici . . .
> Paris, Bibliothèque nationale de France, lat. 8173

Iste est liber *Noue poetrie* summe subtilis rethorice . . .
> Vienna, Österreichische Nationalbibliothek, 4959

Iste liber cuius subiectum est artificiosa eloquencia diuiditur in quinque tractatus speciales secundum quinque officia rethoris.
> Vienna, Schottenkloster, 399

Iste liber cuius subiectum est ornatus modus loquendi procedendi persuadendi cuiuslibet persuasibilis prima sui disponi diuiditur in quinque tractatus secundum quod quinque sunt officia rethoris.
> Wolfenbüttel, Herzog August Bibliothek, Cod. Guelf. 37.34 Aug. 2°

Iste liber cuius subiectum est ornatus modus persuadendi cuiuslibet persuasibilis prima secundum diuisionem diuiditur in quinque tractatus secundum quod quinque sunt officia rethoris.
> Giessen, Universitätsbibliothek, 68

Iste liber cuius subiectum est ornatus modus persuadendi materiam cuiuslibet persuasibilis prima sui [*sic*] diuisione diuiditur in quinque tractatus.
> Berlin, Staatsbibliothek zu Berlin–Preussischer Kulturbesitz, lat. qu. 17
> Gdansk (Danzig), Biblioteka Gdańska Polskiej Akademii Nauk, Mar. Q.8

Iste liber cuius subjectum est sensus poeticus secundum quosdam vel ars poetica principaliter secundum diuisionem diuiditur in duas partes, scilicet in prohemium et executionem.
> Uppsala, Universitetsbiblioteket, C 40

Iste liber cuius subiectum videtur esse ornatus modus persvadendi de quocumque persvasibili diuiditur in quinque partes, siue tractatus speciales.
> Leipzig, Universitätsbibliothek, MS 1084

Iste liber diuiditur in partes principales in prohemium et in tractatum.
> Munich, Bayerisch Staatsbibliothek, Clm 594

Iste liber diuiditur principaliter in tres partes.
> New Haven, Yale University, Beinecke Rare Book Room and Manuscript Library, Osborn fa.6
> Rome, Biblioteca Casanatense, 311

Iste liber principaliter diuiditur in duas partes, scilicet prohemium et tractatum
>Milan, Biblioteca Trivulziana, 762

Iste liber principaliter in quinque partes.
>Erfurt, Wissenschaftliche Allgemeinbibliothek der Stadt, Amplon. O.17

Item(?) quia *** de qua proprium intendimus liberalium disciplinarum . . .
>St. Gall, Stiftsbibliothek, 856

Liber iste diuiditur in decem partes, quarum prima est de commendatione pape ibi, "Papa stupor mundi."
>Oxford, Bodleian Library, Digby 64, 15th cent.

Liber iste diuiditur in partes tres.
>Princeton, Princeton University Library, Robert Garrett Library Collection, MS 120

Liber iste diuiditur in prohemium et tractatum.
>London, British Library, Royal 12.E.XI

Liber iste diuiditur in septem partes principales.
>St. Gall, Stiftsbibliothek, 856

Liber iste diuiditur in septem partes principaliter.
>St. Gall, Stiftsbibliothek, 875

Liber iste per modum sciencie diuiditur in quinque partes . . .
>Erfurt, Wissenschaftliche Allgemeinbibliothek der Stadt, Amplon. O.17

Nota causa materialis est ars rethorica . . .
>Erfurt, Wissenschaftliche Allgemeinbibliothek der Stadt, Amplon. O.15

Nota prout ex Tullio colligi [sic] in Veteri et Nova Rhetorica sua rethorica sic describitur.
>Munich, Bayerische Staatsbibliothek, Clm 14529

Nota quod *** nomina queque(?) sint possunt poni.
>Besançon, Bibliothèque municipale, 534

Nota quod quinque sunt partes rethorice, scilicet inuentio, dispositio, elocutio, memoria, et pronuntiatio.
>Holkham Hall, Library of the Earl of Leicester, 423

Notandum dicit PAPA STUPOR nam hoc nomen dicitur ab interiectione amirantis "pape" . . .
>St. Petersburg, Rossiiskaia natsionałnaia biblioteka, Lat. O. XIV

"Omnia subiecisti sub pedibus eius oues et boues et universa pecora campi." Verba proposita scripta sunt per prophetam in Psalmo.

Erfurt, Wissenschaftliche Allgemeinbibliothek der Stadt, Amplon. F.50

O PAPA qui es STUPOR MUNDI quantum ad hoc quod te totus mundus admiratur, ego intendo . . .

London, British Library, Add. 37495

Opus istius potest diuidi secundum partem rethorice, et secundum sermonem rethoricum.

Brescia, Biblioteca Civica Queriniana. A.IV.10

Opus istud diuiditur in sex partes, scilicet exordium, narrationem, diuisionem, confirmationem, confutationem, et conclusionem.

Siena, Biblioteca Comunale degli Intronati, K.V. 23

Pro faciliori invitacione auditorum ad ea instituta que poete nostri. . . .

Krakow, Biblioteka Muzeum Narodowego w Krakowie, Oddzial Zbiory Czartorys kich, 1464

Quemadmodum wlt Aristotelis in libro *Predicamentorum,* "Omnis sciencia est in anima."

Erfurt, Wissenschaftliche Allgemeinbibliothek der Stadt, Amplon. Q.75

Quia iste liber retoricalis est . . .

London, British Library, Add. 15108

Quoniam circa elloquentiam quamplures dispersa uolumina condiderunt quorum alii mare alii riuulos emittentes . . .

Naples, Biblioteca Nazionale "Vittorio Emanuele III," V.D.6

Qvoniam propter opinantes contrarium ueritati qui ob ornatum modum loquendi siue stilo dictaminis subiacentem suspicantes rhetoricam formaliter edocere, "delfinum siluis appingit, fluctibus aprum" . . .

Vatican City, Biblioteca Apostolica Vaticana, Ottob. lat. 3291

Rhetorica a Quintiliano sic diffinitur . . .

St. Florian (Enns), Stiftsbibliothek, XI 108

Rhetorica superna gracia facundie red<dit> domina eloquencie et lepide oracionis urbanam fabri-catio ex superfund<en>cia sue benignitatis . . .

Krakow, Biblioteka Jagiellońska, 1934

Sciendum quod secundum Tulium . . .

Krakow, Biblioteka Jagiellońska, 2141

Secundum sententiam Tullii *De officiis* inter omnes scientias que hominem honorabilem reddunt
rethorica obtinet principatum.

> Rome, Biblioteca Casanatense, 311

SI QUIS HABET etc. Postquam autor posuit prohemium suum consequenter in hac parte aggreditur partem executiuam.

> Berlin, Staatsbibliothek zu Berlin–Preussischer Kulturbesitz, Hamilton 101

Sicut dicit Plato in *Timaeo,* nichil est ortum cuius causa legitima non precesserit.

> Prague, Národní Knihovna České Republiky, VIII.D.19

Sicut dicit quod iste liber prima secundum diuisionem diuiditur in duas partes quorum prima
dicitur prohemium

> Prague, Národní Knihovna České Republiky, III.G.22

STUPOR vno modo dicitur prout est asicnacio mentis . . .

> Angers, Bibliothèque municipale, 523

Subiectum huius libri est modus persuadendi ex hiis que communia sunt arti poetice et rethorice.

> Wolfenbüttel, Herzog August Bibliothek, Cod. Guelf. 286 Gud. lat.

Subiectum istius libri est ornatus modus persuadendi cuiuslibet persuasibilis.

> Wrocław (Breslau), Biblioteka Universytecka, IV Q 110

Tamen antequam liber diuidatur, dicendum est quod rethorica consideratur dupliciter.

> Prague, Národní Knihovna České Republiky, VIII.H.22

Titulus huius libri talis est: Gaufredi Hibernii regis Anglie scriptoris *Novelle poetrie de artificio
loquendi* liber incipit.

> Reims, Bibliothèque municipale, 1247

Tulius primo sue *Rethorice* describit rethoricam, dicens "Rethorica est sciencia docens de quocumque perswadibili . . . "

> Erfurt, Wissenschaftliche Allgemeinbibliothek der Stadt, Amplon. F.50

Ut huius auctoris intencio et principalis causa . . .

> Madrid, Biblioteca Nacional, 3699

Venerationis uirtute maxime . . .

> Seville, Biblioteca Capitular y Colombina, Cap. 56–2–27

BIBLIOGRAPHY

Agricola, Rudolf. *De inventione dialectica.* Cologne, 1539; rpt. Nieuwkoop, 1967.

Alan of Lille. *De planctu Nature.* Ed. N. Häring. *Studi medievali,* 3rd ser., 19 (1978): 797–879. English translation by James J. Sheridan. *The Plaint of Nature.* Toronto, 1980.

Aland, Kurt. *Die Handschriftenbestände der polnischen Bibliotheken, insbesondere an griechischen und lateinischen Handschriften von Autoren und Werken der klassischen bis zum Ende der patristischen Zeit.* . . . Berlin, 1956.

Alexander de Villa Dei. *Das Doctrinale des Alexander de Villa-Dei.* Ed. Dietrich Reichling. Berlin, 1893.

Allen, Judson Boyce. "Commentary as Criticism: Formal Cause, Discursive Form, and the Late Medieval Accessus." In *Acta Conventus Neo-Latini Louvaniensis.* Munich, 1973. 29–48.

———. *The Ethical Poetic of the Later Middle Ages: A Decorum of Convenient Distinction.* Toronto, 1982.

Allen, Percy Stafford. "The Young Erasmus." In *Gedenkschrift zum 400. Todestage des Erasmus von Rotterdam.* Basel, 1936. 25–33.

Allgemeine Deutsche Biographie. 56 volumes. Leipzig, 1875–1912.

Altamura, Antonio, ed. *Riccardo da Bury, Philobiblion.* Naples, 1954.

Anderson, Harald Jens. "Medieval *Accessus* to Statius." Ph.D. diss., The Ohio State University, 1997.

———. "Statius in the Middle Ages: A Source Guide." LMS thesis, Pontifical Institute of Mediaeval Studies, 1999. Forthcoming as *The Manuscripts of Statius.*

Andersson-Schmitt, Margarete, and Monica Hedlund. "Katalogisering av medeltida handskrifter vid Uppsala universitetsbiblioteket." *Nordisk tidskrift för obk-och biblioteks-väsen* 71 (1984): 113–117.

Andersson-Schmitt, Margarete, Hakan Hålberg, and Monica Hedlund. *Mittelalterliche Hand-schriften der Universitätsbibliothek Uppsala. Katalog über die C-Sammlung.* Vol. 1, Hand-schriften C I-IV, 1–50. Stockholm, 1988.

Aristoteles latinus: Codices. Ed. George Lacombe, Aleksander Ludwik Birkenmajer, Marthe Dulong, Ezlo Franceschini, and L. Minnio-Paluello. 2 vols. Rome, 1939–55.

Aschbach, Joseph. *Geschichte der Wiener Universität im ersten Jahrhunderte ihres Bestehens.* Vienna, 1865.

Ascheri, Mario. "The Formation of the Consilia Collection of Bartolus of Saxoferrato and Some of His Autographs." In *The Two Laws: Studies in Medieval Legal History Dedicated to Stephan Kuttner.* Ed. Laurent Mayali and Stephanie A. J. Tibbets. Washington, D.C., 1990. 188–201.

Ascoli, Albert Russell. "Access to Authority: Dante in the *Epistle to Cangrande.*" In *Seminario Dantesco Internzaionale / International Dante Seminar I. Atti del primo convegno tenutosi al Chauncey Conference Center, Princeton, 21–23 ottobre 1994.* Florence, 1995. 309–352.

Asztalos, Monika, and Claes Gejrot. *Symbolae Septentrionales. Latin Studies Presented to Jan Öberg.* Stockholm, 1995

Auct. Aris. See Abbreviations.

Augustijn, Cornelius. *Erasmus: His Life, Works, and Influence.* Trans. C. C. Grayson. Toronto, 1991.

Autenrieth, Johanne, and Virgil Ernst Fiala. *Die Handschriften der ehemaligen Hofbibliothek Stutt-gart.* Wiesbaden, 1968.

Avesani, Rino. "Il primo ritmo per la morte del grammatico Ambrogio e il cosiddetto 'Liber Catonianus.'" *Studi medievali,* 3rd ser., 6.2 (1965): 455–488.

Babcock, Robert G. *Reconstructing a Medieval Library: Fragments from Lambach.* New Haven, 1993.

Bainton, Roland Herbert. *Erasmus of Christendom.* New York, 1969.

Baker's Biographical Dictionary of Musicians. Ed. Nicolas Slonimsky. 8th ed. New York, 2001.

Baldwin, Thomas Whitfield. *William Shakspere's Small Latine & Lesse Greeke.* 2 vols. Urbana, 1944.

Baldzuhn, Michael. "*Quidquid placet:* Stellung und Gebrauchsformen der 'Fabulae Aviani' im Schulunterricht des 15. Jahrhunderts." In *Schule und Schüler im Mittelalter: Beiträge zur europäischen Bildungsgeschichte des 9. bis 15. Jahrhunderts.* Ed. Martin Kintzinger, Sönke Lorenz, and Michael Walter. Cologne, 1996. 327–383.

Bale, John. *Scriptoru(m) illustrium maioris Brytanni(a)e.* Basel, 1558.

Baron, Frank E. "The Beginnings of German Humanism: The Life and Work of the Wandering Humanist Peter Luder." Ph.D. diss., University of California at Berkeley, 1966.

Bartòla, A. "Alessandro VII e Athanasius Kircher S.J. Ricerche ed appunti sulla loro corrispon-denza erudita e sulla storia di alcuni codici chigiani." *Miscellanea Bibliothecae Apostolicae Vaticanae* 3 (1989): 7–105.

Baswell, Christopher. *Virgil in Medieval England: Figuring the* Aeneid *from the Twelfth Century to Chaucer.* Cambridge, 1995.

Battistella, Antonio. "Un inventario di libri e oggetti domestici d'un maestro friulano del quattrocento." *Memorie storiche forogiuliesi* 21 (1925): 137–159.

Baumgart, Peter, and Notker Hammerstein. *Beiträge zu Problemen deutscher Universitätsgründungen der frühen Zeit.* Nendeln, Liechtenstein, 1978.

Bedaux, J. C., et al. *Stads- of Athenaeumbibliotheek 1560–1985.* Deventer, 1985.

Bédier, Joseph. *Les fabliaux: Études de littérature populaire et d'histoire littéraire du moyen âge.* Paris, 1925.

Beer, Rudolf. *Los manuscrits del monestir de Santa María de Ripoll.* Trans. Pere Barnies y Giol. Barcelona, 1910. Trans. of *Die Handschriften des Klosters Santa Maria de Ripoll.* Vienna, 1908.

Bell, David N. *The Libraries of the Cistercians, Gilbertines, and Premonstralensians.* London, 1995.

Beltrami, Achilles. "Index codicum classicorum latinorum qui in bybliotheca Quiriniana Brixiensi adservantur." *Studi italiani di filologia classica* 14 (1906): 17–96.

Bénabou, Marcel. "Rule and Constraint." In *Oulipo: A Primer.* 40–47.

Bergh, Birger. "Galfridi de Vinso salvo *Poetria nova* critice inspecta." In Asztalos and Gejrot, *Symbolae Septentrionales.* 103–111.

———. See also Matthias of Linköping.

Bernardus Silvestris. *Cosmographia.* Ed. Peter Dronke. Leiden, 1978. *The Cosmographia of Bernardus Silvestris.* Trans. Winthrop Wetherbee. New York, 1973.

———. *Commentum quod dicitur Bernardi Silvestris super sex libros Eneidos Virgilii.* Ed. Julian Ward Jones and Elizabeth Frances Jones. Lincoln, 1977. *Commentary on the First Six Books of Virgil's Aeneid.* Trans. Earl G. Schreiber and Thomas E. Maresca. Lincoln, 1979.

Bernays, Anne, and Pamela Painter. *What If? Writing Exercises for Fiction Writers.* Rev. and exp. ed. New York, 1995.

Bernicoli, Silvio. "Maestri e scuole letterarie in Ravenna nel secolo XIV." *Felix Ravenna* 32 (1927): 61–69.

Bertini, Ferruccio, ed. *Commedie latine del XII e XIII secolo.* Vol. 3. Genoa, 1980.

Bertolucci Pizzorusso, Valeria. "Gli smeraldi di Beatrice." *Studi mediolatini e volgari* 17 (1969): 7–16.

Bertoni, Giulio, and Emilio P. Vicini. *Gli studi di grammatica e la rinascenza a Modena.* Modena, 1905.

La Biblioteca Colombina y Capitular. Seville, 1991.

Billanovich, Giuseppe. "Giovanni del Virgilio, Pietro da Moglio, Francesco da Fiano." *Italia medioevale e umanistica* 6 (1963): 203–234 and 7 (1964): 279–324.

———, and C. M. Monti. "Una nuova fonte per la storia della scuola de grammatica e retorica nell'Italia del Trecento." *Italia medioevale e umanistica* 22 (1979): 367–412.

Billanovich, Guido. "Il prehumanismo padovano." *Storia della cultura veneta.* Vol. 1, *Il trecento.* Vincenza, 1976. 19–110.

Binz, Gustav. *Die deutschen Handschriften der öffentlichen Bibliothek der Universität Basel.* Basel, 1907.

Birkenmeyer, Aleksander. "Andrzej Grzymała z Poznania astronom i lekarz z XV wiekŭ." *Kwartalnik Historii Nauki i Techniki* 1958 (3): 409–22.

———. "Grzymała, Andrzej z Poznania." *Polski Słownik biograficzny.* Krakow, 1935. 9.114–116.

Bischoff, Bernhard. "Studien zur Geschichte des Klosters St. Emmeram im Spätmittelalter (1324–1525). Mit vier Abbildungen (Tafel IV und V)." *Mittelalterliche Studien: Ausgewählte Aufsätze zur Schriftkunde und Literaturgeschichte.* Stuttgart, 1967. 2.115–155.

Bistřický, Jan, Miroslav Boháček, and František Čáda. *Seznam rukopisů metropolitní kapituly v Olomouci.* Vol. 3, *Státní archiv v Opavě. Průvodce po archivních fondech.* Prague, 1961.

Black, Robert, and Gabriella Pomaro. *Boethius's* Consolation of Philosophy *in Italian Medieval and Renaissance Education. Schoolbooks and their Glosses in Florentine Manuscripts.* Florence, 2000.

Black, Robert. "Cicero in the Curriculum of Italian Renaissance Grammar Schools." *Ciceroniana,* ns 9 (1996): 105–120.

———. "The Curriculum of Italian Elementary and Grammar Schools, 1350–1500." In *The Shapes of Knowledge from the Renaissance to Enlightenment.* Ed. Donald R. Kelley and Richard H. Popkin. Dordrecht, 1991. 137–163.

———. *Education and Society in Florentine Tuscany: Teachers' Pupils and Schools, c. 1250–1500.* Vol. 1. Leiden, 2007.

———. *Humanism.* See Abbreviations.

Blair, Ann M. "Lectures on Ovid's *Metamorphoses.* The Class Notes of a 16th-Century Paris Schoolboy." *Princeton University Library Chronicle* 50 (1989): 117–144.

———. "*Ovidius Methodizatus:* The *Metamorphoses* of Ovid in a Sixteenth-Century Paris College." *History of Universities* 9 (1990): 73–118.

———. "Reading Strategies for Coping with Information Overload ca. 1550–1700." *Journal of the History of Ideas* 64 (2003): 11–28.

Blos, Peter. *The Adolescent Passage: Developmental Issues.* New York, 1979.

Blume, Friedrich. *Bibliotheca librorum manuscriptorum Italica.* Göttingen, 1834.

Boas, M. "De librorum Catonianorum historia atque compositione." *Mnemosyne* 42 (1914): 27–46.

Bodemann, Ulrike. "Cedulae actuum: Zum Quellenwert studentischer Belegzettel des Spätmittelalters. Mid dem Abdruck von Belegzetteln aus dem 14. bis frühen 16. Jahrhundert." In Grubmüller, *Schulliteratur im späten Mittelalter.* 435–499.

———, and Hartmut Bleumer. "Die 'Flores grammaticae' Ludolfs de Luco. Materialien zur Überlieferungsgeschichte." In Grubmüller, *Schulliteratur im späten Mittelalter.* 281–301.

———, and Beate Kretzschmar. "Textüberlieferung und Handschriftengebrauch in der mittelalterlichen Schule. Eine Untersuchung am Beispiel des 'Speculum grammaticae' und seines Kommentars." In Grubmüller, *Schulliteratur im späten Mittelalter.* 243–280.

Boese, Helmut. *Die lateinischen Handschriften der Sammlung Hamilton zu Berlin.* Wiesbaden, 1966.

Boethius. *Anicii Manlii Severini Boethii Philosophiae consolatio.* Ed. Ludwig Bieler. Turnhout, 1984. *The Consolation of Philosophy.* Trans. S. J. Tester. Cambridge, MA, 1973.

[Pseudo-]Boethius. *Pseudo-Boèce. De disciplina scolarium.* Ed. Olga Weijers. Leiden, 1976.

Boháček, Miroslav. "Le opere delle scuole medievali di diritto nei manoscritti della Biblioteca del Capitolo di Olomouc." *Studia Gratiana* 8 (1962): 305–421.

Boort, Henricus. *Fasciculus Morum ex Approbatorum Poetarum Auctoritatibus Collectus.* Antwerp, [ca. 1503].

Bourdieu, Pierre. *Language and Symbolic Power.* Ed. John B. Thompson. Trans. Gino Raymond

and Matthew Adamson. Cambridge, 1991.

Bowers, John M. "Augustine as Addict: Sex and Texts in the *Confessions*." *Exemplaria* 2 (1990): 404–448.

Brandis, Tilo. *Die Handschriften der S. Petri-Kirche Hamburg*. Hamburg, 1967.

Brassel, Kate Meng. "The Composition of Medieval Love: Reading *Amor* and *Amicitia* in *Parce Continuis*." *The Columbia Journal of Literary Criticism* 3 (2005): 40–56.

Brown, Virginia. "Gasparino Barzizza and Virgil." In *Gasparino Barzizza e la rinascita degli studi classici: Fra continuità e rinnovamento. Atti del Seminario di Studi Napoli—Palazzo Sforza, 11 aprile 1997*. Ed. Lucia Gualdo Rosa. *A.I.O.N.* 21 (1999): 189–208.

Bulaeus. See Du Boulay.

Buonocore, Marco. *Codices Horatiani in Bibliotheca Apostolica Vaticana*. Vatican City, 1992.

Calboli Montefusco, Lucia, ed. *Papers on Rhetoric V. Atti del Convegno Internazionale "Dictamen, Poetria and Cicero: Coherence and Diversification," Bologna 10–11 Maggio 2002*. Rome, 2003.

Calvo Revilla, Ana María. *La* Poetria Nova *de Godofredo de Vinsauf. Traducción Estudio de la estructura textual comunicativa*. With introduction by Tomás Albaladejo Mayordomo. Madrid, 2007.

Camargo, Martin. *Ars Dictaminis, Ars Dictandi*. Turnhout, 1991.

———. "'Colores rethorici seriatim': An Unknown Work by Matthew of Vendôme?" Unpublished paper quoted with the author's permission.

———. "The English Manuscripts of Bernard of Meung's 'Flores dictaminum.'" *Viator* 12 (1981): 197–219.

———. "How the Anonymous *Tria sunt* Defined Rhetoric in Late-Medieval Oxford." Unpublished paper quoted with the author's permission.

———. "If You Can't Join Them, Beat Them: or, When Grammar Met Business Writing (in Fifteenth-Century Oxford)." In *Letter-Writing Manuals and Instruction from Antiquity to the Present*. Ed. Carol Poster and Linda C. Mitchell. Columbia SC, 2007. 67–87.

———. "Latin Composition Textbooks and *Ad Herennium* Glossing: the Missing Link?" In Cox and Ward, *The Rhetoric of Cicero*. 267–288.

———. "Medieval Rhetoric Delivers: or, Where Chaucer Learned How to Act." *New Medieval Literatures* 9 (2008, for 2007): 41–62.

———. *Medieval Rhetorics of Prose Composition: Five English Artes Dictandi and Their Tradition*. Binghamton, 1995.

———. "Models." See Abbreviations.

———. "The Pedagogy of the *Dictatores*." In Calboli Montefusco, *Papers on Rhetoric*. 65–94.

———. "Rhetoricians in Black: Benedictine Monks and Rhetorical Revival in Medieval Oxford." In *New Chapters in the History of Rhetoric*. Ed. Laurent Pernot. Leiden 2009. 375–384.

———. "'Si dictare velis': Versified *Artes dictandi* and Late Medieval Writing Pedagogy." *Rhetorica* 14 (1996): 265–288.

———. "Toward a Comprehensive Art of Written Discourse: Geoffrey of Vinsauf and the *Ars Dictaminis*." *Rhetorica* 6 (1988): 167–194.

———. Translation and annotation of excerpt from *Tria sunt*. In Copeland and Sluiter. *Medieval Grammar and Rhetoric*. Forthcoming.

———. "*Tria sunt*." See Abbreviations.

———. "A Twelfth-Century Treatise on 'Dictamen' and Metaphor." *Traditio* 47 (1992): 161–213.

———. "What's in a Name?: The Titles of Medieval Arts of Poetry and Prose as Indices of Reception." Unpublished paper quoted with the author's permission.

Campbell, James. "Gloucester College." In Wansbrough and Marett-Crosby. 37–47.

Carley, James P. "John Leland and the Contents of English Pre-Dissolution Libraries: Glastonbury Abbey." *Scriptorium* 40 (1986): 107–120.

Carlsmith, Christopher. "The Child in the Classroom: Teaching a Course on the History of Childhood in Medieval/Renaissance Europe." In Classen, *Childhood in the Middle Ages*. 415–427.

———. "Le *scholae* e la scuola: l'istruzione 'Amore dei' in Bergamo tra '500 e '600." *Atti dell'Ateneo di Scienze, Lettere ed Arti di Bergamo* 60 (1996–97): 235–56.

Carlson, Evelyn. "The *Laborintus* of Eberhard, Rendered into English with Introduction and Notes." PhD diss., Cornell University, 1930.

Carruthers, Mary J. *The Book of Memory: A Study of Memory in Medieval Culture.* 2nd ed. Cambridge, 2008.

Catalogo della Biblioteca di un amatore bibliofilo. [By G. B. Pittaluga?]. Genoa [1834–35].

Catalogue des manuscrits de la Bibliothèque Royale des Ducs de Bourgogne. Brussels, 1842.

Catalogue des manuscrits hagiographiques latins conservés à la Bibliothèque nationale de Paris. Paris, 1893.

Catalogue général des manuscrits des bibliothèques publiques des départements. Paris, 1849–1885.

Catalogue général des manuscrits des bibliothèques publiques de France. Départements Paris, 1885-.

Catalogue général. See also Paris, Bibliothèque nationale.

Catalogue of Additions to the Manuscripts in the British Museum, 1841–1845. London, 1850.

Catalogue of the Harleian Manuscripts . . . in the British Museum. . . . 4 vols. London, 1803–1912.

Catalogus Translationum et Commentariorum. See *CTC* in Abbreviations.

Catto, J. I., ed. *The Early Oxford Schools.* Vol. 1 of *The History of the University of Oxford.* Oxford, 1984.

Cenci, Cesare. *Bibliotheca Manuscripta ad Sacrum Conventum Assisiensem.* 2 vols. Assisi, 1981.

Ceresi, Maddalena. *Catalogo dei Manoscritti della Biblioteca Casanatense* 4. Rome, 1961.

Charland, Thomas Marie. *Artes praedicandi: Contribution à l'histoire de la rhétorique au moyen âge.* Paris and Ottawa, 1936.

Cheney, Christopher Robert. "The Eve of Magna Carta." *Bulletin of the John Rylands Library* 38 (1955): 313.

———, and Mary G. Cheney. *The Letters of Pope Innocent III (1198–1216) concerning England and Wales: A Calendar with an Appendix of Texts.* Oxford, 1967.

Chojnacki, Stanley. *Women and Men in Renaissance Venice: Twelve Essays on Patrician Society.* Baltimore, 2000.

Chomarat, Jacques. *Grammaire et rhétorique chez Erasme.* 2 vols. Paris, 1981.

Clark, James G. *A Monastic Renaissance at St Albans: Thomas Walsingham and his Circle c. 1350–1440.* Oxford, 2004.

Clarke, Peter D., ed. *The University and College Libraries of Cambridge.* London, 2002.

Classen, Albrecht, ed. *Childhood in the Middle Ages and the Renaissance: The Results of a Paradigm Shift in the History of Mentality.* Berlin, 2005.

Clemen, O. "Handschriften und Bücher aus dem Besitze Kaspar v. Barthes in der Zwickauer Ratsschulbibliothek." *Zentralblatt für Bibliothekswesen* 37 (1921): 267–289.

Clogan, Paul M., ed. *The Medieval Achilleid of Statius.* Leiden, 1968.

Cobban, Alan B. *English University Life in the Middle Ages.* Columbus, 1999.

———. *The Medieval English Universities: Oxford and Cambridge to c. 1500.* Berkeley and Los Angeles, 1988.

Cockcroft, Robert, and Susan Cockcroft. *Persuading People: An Introduction to Rhetoric.* 2nd ed. New York, 2005.

Cohen, Gustave, ed. *La "comédie" latine en France au xiie siècle.* 2 vols. Paris, 1931.

Cohen, Jeffrey J. *Medieval Identity Machines.* Minneapolis, 2003.

Colfi, Benedetto. *Di un antichissimo commento all'*Ecerinide *di Albertino Mussato.* Modena, 1891.

Colomb de Batines, Paul. *Bibliografia dantesca.* Prato, 1845–46.

Commedie latine del xii e xiii secolo. 6 vols. Genoa, 1976–1998.

Connell, Susan. "Books and Their Owners in Venice: 1345–1480." *Journal of the Warburg and Courtauld Institutes* 35 (1972): 163–186.

Connors, Robert J. "The Erasure of the Sentence." *College Composition and Communication* 52 (2000): 96–128.

———, Lisa S. Ede, and Andrea A. Lunsford, eds. *Essays on Classical Rhetoric and Modern Discourse.* Carbondale, 1984.

Copeland, Rita, ed. *Criticism and Dissent in the Middle Ages.* Cambridge, 1996.

———. *Pedagogy, Intellectuals, and Dissent in the Later Middle Ages: Lollardy and Ideas of Learning.* Cambridge, 2001.

———. *Rhetoric, Hermeneutics, and Translation in the Middle Ages: Academic Traditions and Vernacular Texts.* Cambridge, 1991.

Copeland, Rita, and Ineke Sluiter, eds. *Medieval Grammar and Rhetoric: The Language Arts and Literary Theory AD 300–1475.* Oxford, 2009.

Corbett, Edward P. J., and Robert J. Connors. *Classical Rhetoric for the Modern Student.* 4th ed. Oxford, 1998.

Coulson, Frank T. "Addenda and Corrigenda to *Incipitarium Ovidianum.*" *The Journal of Medieval Latin* 12 (2002): 154–180.

———. "Hitherto Unedited Medieval and Renaissance Lives of Ovid (I)." *Mediaeval Studies* 49 (1987): 152–207.

———. "Hitherto Unedited Medieval and Renaissance Lives of Ovid (II): Humanistic Lives." *Mediaeval Studies* 59 (1997) 111–153.

———, and Bruno Roy. *Incipitarium Ovidianum: A Finding Guide for Texts Related to the Study of Ovid in the Middle Ages and Renaissance.* Turnhout, 2000.

———. "Ovid's Transformations in Medieval France (ca. 1100-ca. 1350)." In *Metamorphosis: The Changing Face of Ovid in Medieval and Early Modern Europe.* Ed. Alison Keith and Stephen Rupp. Toronto, 2007. 33–60.

———. "The Vulgate Commentary on Ovid's *Metamorphoses.*" In "Ovid in Medieval Culture."

Ed. Marilynn Desmond. *Mediaevalia* (1987) [1989]: 29–61.

———, ed. *The "Vulgate" Commentary on Ovid's Metamorphoses: The Creation Myth and the Story of Orpheus, Edited from Sélestat, Bibliothèque humaniste, MS. 92.* Toronto, 1991.

Courtenay, William J. "Programs of Study and Genres of Scholastic Theological Production in the Fourteenth Century." In Hamesse, *Manuels.* 325–350.

———. *Schools & Scholars in Fourteenth-Century England.* Princeton, 1987.

———, and Jürgen Miethke, eds., with David B. Priest. *Universities and Schooling in Medieval Society.* Leiden, 2000.

Cox, Virginia, and John O. Ward., eds. *The Rhetoric of Cicero in Its Medieval and Early Renaissance Commentary Tradition.* Leiden, 2006.

Coxe, Henry E. *Catalogi codicum manuscriptorum Bibliothecae Bodleianae. Pars secunda. Codices Latinos et Miscellaneos Laudianos complectens.* Oxford, 1858.

———. *Catalogus codicum manuscriptorum qui in collegiis aulisque Oxoniensibus hodie adservantur.* 2 vols. Oxford, 1852.

Crane, Mary Thomas. *Framing Authority: Sayings, Self, and Society in Sixteenth-Century England.* Princeton, NJ, 1993.

Crowley, Sharon, and Debra Hawhee. *Ancient Rhetorics for Contemporary Students.* 3rd ed. Boston, 2003.

Curtius, Ernst Robert. *European Literature and the Latin Middle Ages.* Trans. Willard R. Trask. New York, 1953.

Cysarz, Herbert. *Deutsche Barockdichtung.* Leipzig, 1924.

Czerny, Albin. *Die Handschriften der Stiftsbibliothek St. Florian.* Linz, 1871.

———. *Die Bibliothek des Chorherrenstiftes St. Florian.* Linz, 1874.

Dain, Alphonse. "De mercatore." In Gustave Cohen, *Comédie latine.* 2.259–278.

D'Amato, Jean M. "A New Fragment of Eustasius of Matera's *Planctvs Italie.*" *Mediaeval Studies* 46 (1984): 487–501.

D'Angelo, Frank. *Composition in the Classical Tradition.* New York, 1999.

Davies, Jonathan. *Florence and Its University during the Early Renaissance.* Leiden, 1998.

D'Avray, D. L. "Portable *Vademecum* Books Containing Franciscan and Dominican Texts." In *Manuscripts at Oxford. An Exhibition in Memory of Richard William Hunt.* Ed. A. C. de la Mare and B. C. Barker-Benfield. Oxford, 1980. 60–64.

———. *The Preaching of the Friars: Sermons Diffused from Paris before 1300.* Paris, 1985.

De disciplina sc(h)olarium. See [Pseudo-]Boethius.

Dazzi, Manlio. *Il Mussato preumanista (1261–1329), l'ambiente e l'opera.* Vincenza, 1964.

Delisle, Léopold Victor. *Catalogue des manuscrits des fonds Libri et Barrois.* Paris, 1888.

———. Bibliothèque nationale. *Manuscrits latins et français ajoutés . . . 1875–1891.* Paris, 1981.

———. "Inventaire des manuscrits latins de Saint-Victor conservés à la Bibliothèque Impériale sous les nos. 15176–16718 du fonds latin." *Bibliothèque de l'École des chartes* 30 (1869): 1–79.

DeMolen, Richard L. "Erasmus as Adolescent: 'Shipwrecked am I, and Lost, 'Mid Waters Chill': Erasmus to Sister Elizabeth." *Bibliothèque d'humanisme et renaissance. Travaux et documents* 38 (1976): 7–25.

Denifle, P. Heinrich. *Die Entstehung der Universitäten des Mittelalters bis 1400.* Berlin, 1885.

Destrez, J. *La pecia dans les manuscrits universitaires du xiiie et du xive siècle.* Paris, 1935.

Deutscher Biographischer Index / German Biographical Index. 8 vols. 2nd ed. Munich, 1998.

Dictionary of Film Makers. By Georges Sadoul. Ed. and trans. Peter Morris. Berkeley and Los Angeles, 1972.

Dörrie, Heinrich. *Der heroische Brief. Bestandsaufnahme, Geschichte, Kritik einer humanistisch-barocken Literaturgattung.* Berlin, 1968.

Donahue, Patricia and Ellen Quandahl. "Freud and the Teaching of Interpretation." In *Reclaiming Pedagogy: The Rhetoric of the Classroom.* Ed. Patricia Donohue and Ellen Quandahl. Carbondale, 1989. 49–59.

Dorer-Gommermann, Silke. "Erasmus." *The Encyclopedia of Christianity.* Leiden, 1999—. 2.119–20.

Doskočil, Karel. *Mistr Dybin, rétor doby Karlovy.* Prague, 1948.

Doyle, A. I., ed. *The Libraries of the Carthusians.* See Gillespie, *Syon Abbey.*

Dronke, Peter. See Bernardus Silvestris.

Du Boulay, César-Egasse. *Historia Universitatis Parisiensis . . .* Vol. 2. Paris, 1665.

Ducci, Edda. *Un saggio di pedagogia medioevale. Il "De disciplina scholarium" dello Pseudo-Boezio.* Torino, 1967.

Eberhard of Béthune. *Grecismus.* See Wrobel.

Eberhard the German, *Laborintus.* Latin text in Far., pp. 337–77. English translation in Carlson.

Eck, Johannes Georgius. *Symbolae ad historiam litterariam Lipsiensem.* Vol. 3. Leipzig, 1796.

Eden, P. T. *Theobaldi "Physiologus."* Leiden: 1972.

Egger, Christoph. "Papst Innocenz III., De missarum mysteriis. Studien und Vorarbeiten zu einer kritischen Edition. Mit besonderer Berücksichtigung der schriftstellerischen Persönlichkeit des Papstes." Ph.D. diss., Universität Wien, 1996.

Einbinder, Susan L. *Beautiful Death: Jewish Poetry and Martyrdom in Medieval France.* Princeton, 2002.

———. "The Voice from the Fire: The Medieval Literature of Jewish Martyrdom." Unpublished paper quoted with the author's permission.

Eisenbichler, Konrad, ed. *The Premodern Teenager: Youth in Society 1150–1650.* Toronto, 2002.

Eitner, Robert. *Biographisch-bibliographisches Quellenlexikon der Musiker und Musikgelehrten der christlichen Zeitrechnung bis zur Mitte des 19. Jahrhunderts.* 10 vols. Leipzig, 1900–04.

Elliott, Alison Goddard. "*Accessus ad auctores:* Twelfth-Century Introductions to Ovid." *Allegorica* 5 (1980): 6–48.

———. "The *Facetus:* or, *The Art of Courtly Living.*" *Allegorica* 2 (1977): 27–57.

———. *Seven Medieval Latin Comedies.* New York, 1984.

Enciclopedia Italiana. 26 vols. Milan, 1929–1939.

Encyclopedia of Science Fiction. Ed. John Clute and Peter Nicholls. New York, 1993.

Enders, Jody. "Rhetoric, Coercion, and the Memory of Violence." In Copeland. *Criticism and Dissent.* 24–55.

Engelhardt, George J. "Mediaeval Vestiges in the Rhetoric of Erasmus." *PMLA* 63 (1948): 739–744.

Erasmus. *The Correspondence of Erasmus: Letters 1–141: 1484–1500.* Trans. R. A. B. Mynors and D.

F. S. Thomson. *CWE* 1. Toronto, 1974.

———. *Declamatio de pueris statim ac liberaliter instituendis.* Ed. and trans. Jean-Claude Margolin. Geneva, 1966.

———. *A Declamation on the Subject of Early Liberal Education for Children.* Trans. Beert C. Verstraete. In *Literary and Educational Writings,* vol. 4. *CWE* 26, 291–346. Ed. J. K. Sowards. Toronto, 1985.

———. *Opus epistolarum Des. Erasmi Roterodami.* Vol. 1, *1484–1514.* Ed. P. S. Allen. Oxford, 1906.

Fabricius, Johannes Albertus. *Bibliotheca latina mediae et infimae aetatis.* . . . 6 vols. Passau, 1754; rev. ed., Florence, 1858–59.

Far. See Abbreviations.

Faral, Edmond. "Le manuscrit 511 du 'Hunterian Museum' de Glasgow." *Studi medievali* n.s. 9 (1936): 18–119.

Faulhaber, Charles B. "The Date of Stanzas 553 and 1450 of the *Libro de Buen Amor* in MS 9589 of the Biblioteca Nacional, Madrid." *Romance Philology* 27 (1974): 31–34.

———. *Latin Rhetorical Theory in Thirteenth and Fourteenth Century Castille.* Berkeley and Los Angeles, 1972.

———. "Medieval Spanish Metrical Terminology and MS 9589 of the Biblioteca Nacional, Madrid." *Romance Philology* 33 (1979): 43–61.

———. "Retóricas clásicas y medievales en bibliotecas castellanas." *Abacó* 4 (1973): 151–300.

———. "Rhetoric in Medieval Catalonia: The Evidence of the Library Catalogs." *Studies in Honor of Gustavo Correa.* Ed. Charles B. Faulhaber, Richard P. Kinkade, and T. A. Perry. Potomac, MD, 1986.

Faye, C. U., and W. H. Bond. *Supplement to the Census of Medieval and Renaissance Manuscripts in the United States and Canada.* New York, 1962.

Federici Vescovini, Graziella. "Due commenti inediti del XIV secolo al *De consolatione Philosophiae* di Boezio." *Rivista critica di storia della filosofia* 13 (1958): 384–414.

Findlen, Paula, ed. *Athanasius Kircher: The Last Man Who Knew Everything.* New York, 2004.

Fischer, Hans. *Katalog der Handschriften der Universitätsbibliothek Erlangen.* Vol. 2, *Die lateinischen Papierhandschriften.* Erlangen, 1936.

Flacius, Matthias. *Varia doctorum piorum virorum de corrupta ecclesiae statu, poemata.* . . . Basel, 1557.

Fletcher, John, ed. *Athanasius Kircher und seine Beziehungen zum gelehrten Europa seiner Zeit.* Wiesbaden, 1988.

Fletcher, J. E. "A Brief Survey of the Unpublished Correspondence of Athanasius Kircher, S.J. (1602–1680)." *Manuscripta* 13 (1969): 150–160.

Fletcher, John Malcolm. "Some Problems of Collecting Terms Used in Medieval Academic Life as Illustrated by the Evidence for Certain Exercises in the Faculty of Arts at Oxford in the Later Middle Ages." In Weijers. *Terminologie.* 47–53.

Flüeler, Christoph. "Die verschiedenen literarischen Gattungen der Aristoteleskommentare: zur Terminologie der Überschriften und Kolophone." In Hamesse, *Manuels.* 75–116.

Foa, Simona. "Guizzardo da Bologna." *DBI* 61.555–556.

Förstemann, Joseph. "Vermischte Beiträge aus Handschriften und Urkunden der Leipziger Universitätsbibliothek. Meldungen von Baccalaureanden zum Examen bei der Leipziger Facultas artium aus dem Sommersemester 1464." *Neues Archiv für Sächsische Geschichte* 18 (1897): 126–147.

Frati, Carlo. *Indice dei codici latini conservati nella R. Biblioteca Universitaria di Bologna.* Florence, 1909.

Frati, Lodovico. *Pietro da Moglio e il suo commento a Boezio.* Modena, 1920.

Fredborg, Karin Margareta. "Ciceronian Rhetoric and the Schools." In *Learning Institutionalized: Teaching in the Medieval University.* Ed. John Van Engen. Notre Dame, 2000. 21–41.

———. "Rhetoric and Dialectic." In Cox and Ward, *The Rhetoric of Cicero.* 165–192.

Freud, Sigmund. "Transformations of Puberty." In *Three Essays on Sexuality and Other Works.* Trans. James Strachey. Standard Edition, Vol. 7. London, 1953. 207–230.

Friis-Jensen, Karsten. "The *Ars Poetica* in Twelfth-Century France: The Horace of Mathew of Vendôme and John of Garland." *CIMAGL* 60 (1990): 319–388.

———. "The *Ars Poetica* in Twelfth-Century France: Addenda and Corrigenda." *CIMAGL* 61 (1991): 184.

———. "Horace and the Early Writers of Arts of Poetry." In *Sprachtheorien in Spätantike und Mittelalter.* Ed. Sten Ebbesen. Tübingen, 1995. 360–401.

———, and James M. W. Willoughby. *Peterborough Abbey.* London, 2001.

Gallick, Susan. "Medieval Rhetorical Arts in England and the Manuscript Traditions." *Manuscripta* 18 (1974): 67–95.

Gallo, Ernest A. "The Grammarian's Rhetoric: The *Poetria nova* of Geoffrey of Vinsauf." In Murphy, *Medieval Eloquence.* 68–84.

———. *The Poetria nova and Its Sources in Early Rhetorical Doctrine.* The Hague, 1971.

Galyon, Aubrey E. See Matthew of Vendôme.

Gardner, John. *The Art of Fiction: Notes on Craft for Young Writers.* New York, 1991.

Gargan, Luciano. "Un maestro di grammatica a Padova e a Feltre nel secondo Trecento." *Quaderni per la storia dell'Università di Padova* 2 (1969): 71–77.

———. "Oliviero Forzetta e la diffusione dei testi classici nel Veneto al tempo del Petrarca." In *Classical Influences on European Culture, A.D. 500–1500. Proceedings of an International Conference Held at King's College, Cambridge, April 1969.* Ed. R. R. Bolgar. Cambridge, 1971. 73–80.

———. "Il preumanesimo a Vicenza, Treviso e Venezia." In *Storia della Cultura Veneta.* Vol. 2, *Il trecento.* Vicenza, 1976. 142–170.

Garin, Eugenio. "La cultura milanese nella prima metà del XV secolo." In *Storia di Milano* 6. Milan, 1955. 545–608.

Garland, John of. See John of Garland.

Gaskell, Philip. *From Writer to Reader: Studies in Editorial Method.* Oxford, 1978.

Gatti Perer, Maria Luisa. *Codici e incunaboli miniati della Biblioteca Civica di Bergamo.* Bergamo, 1989.

Gehl, Paul F. "Latin Readers in Fourteenth-Century Florence: Schoolkids and Their Books." *Scrittura e civiltà* 13 (1989): 387–440.

———. *A Moral Art: Grammar, Society, and Culture in Trecento Florence.* Ithaca, 1993.

————. "Preachers, Teachers, and Translators: The Social Meaning of Language Study in Trecento Tuscany." *Viator* 25 (1994): 289–323.

Geoffrey of Vinsauf. *Poetria nova.* Latin text in Far., pp. 197–262, and Gallo, *Poetria nova;* see also Polycarp Leyser. English translations by Nims, Gallo, and Kopp. Spanish translations in Ponce and in Calvo Revilla. Billingual Latin and German edition and translation by Manfred Kraus in progress.

Gerald of Wales. *Giraldi Cambrensis Opera.* Ed. J. S. Brewer. London, 1861.

Gervase of Melkley. *Ars poetica.* Ed. Hans Jurgen Gräbener. Münster, 1965. English translation by Catherine Yodice Giles. "Gervais of Melkley's Treatise on the Art of Versifying and the Method of Composing in Prose: Translation and Commentary." Ph.D. diss., Rutgers University, 1973.

Ghisalberti, Fausto, ed. *Integumenta Ovidii. Poemetto inedito del secolo xiii.* By John of Garland. Milan, 1933.

Gibson, Margaret T., Danuta R. Shanzer, and Nigel Palmer. "Manuscripts of Alan of Lille, 'Anticlaudianus' in the British Isles." *Studi medievali,* 3rd ser., 28 (1987): 905–1001.

Giles. See Gervase of Melkley.

Gillespie, Vincent. "From the Twelfth Century to *c.* 1450." In Minnis and Johnson, *Cambridge History.* 145–235.

————. "The Literary Form of the Middle English Pastoral Manual with Particular Reference to the *Speculum Christiani.*" Ph.D. diss., University of Oxford, 1981.

————, ed. *Syon Abbey.* [With] *The Libraries of the Carthusians.* Ed. A. I. Doyle. London, 2001.

Gillingham, John. *Richard the Lionheart.* London, 1978.

Glassner, Christine. *Inventar der Handschriften des Benediktinerstiftes Melk.* Vol. 1, *Von den Anfängen bis ca. 1400.* Vienna, 2000.

Glauche, Günther. *Katalog der lateinischen Handschriften der Bayerischen Staatsbibliothek München. Die Pergamenthandschriften aus Benediktbeuren, Clm 4501–4663.* Wiesbaden, 1994.

————. *Schullektüre in Mittelalter: Entstehung und Wandlungen des Lektürekanons bis 1200 nach den Quellen dargestellt.* Munich, 1970.

Glendinning, Robert. "Pyramus and Thisbe in the Medieval Classroom." *Speculum* 61 (1986): 51–78.

————. "Eros, Agape and Rhetoric around 1200: Gervase of Melkley's *Ars poetica* and Gottfried von Strassburg's *Tristan.*" *Speculum* 67 (1992): 892–925.

Glomski, Jacqueline. "The Italian Grammarians and Early Humanism at Cracow." *Studi Umanistici Piceni* 19 (1999): 47–53.

Gloria, Andrea. *Monumenti della Università di Padova (1222–1318).* Padua, 1884.

————. *Monumenti della Università di Padova (1318–1405).* 2 vols. Padua, 1888.

Glorieux, Palémon. *La Faculté des arts et ses maîtres au xiiiᵉ siècle.* Paris, 1971.

Godwin, Joscelyn. *Athanasius Kircher: A Renaissance Man and the Quest for Lost Knowledge.* London, 1979.

Gompf, Ludwig, ed. *Joseph Iscanus, Werke und Briefe.* Leiden, 1970.

Gottlieb, Theodor. *Mittelalterliche Bibliothekskataloge Österreichs.* Vienna, 1915.

Gräbener. See Gervase of Melkley.

Grafton, Anthony, and Lisa Jardine. *From Humanism to the Humanities: Education and the Liberal Arts in Fifteenth- and Sixteenth-Century Europe.* Cambridge, MA, 1986.

Grafton, Anthony. *Joseph Scaliger: A Study in the History of Classical Scholarship.* Vol. 1, *Textual Criticism and Exegesis.* Oxford, 1983.

Grendler, Paul F. *Schooling in Renaissance Italy: Literacy and Learning, 1300–1600.* Baltimore, 1989.

———. *The Universities of the Italian Renaissance.* Baltimore, 2002.

Grenzman, Ludger, and Karl Stackmann, eds. *Literatur und Laienbildung im Spätmittelalter und in der Reformationszeit: Symposion Wolfenbüttel 1981.* Stuttgart, 1984.

Gress-Wright, David Richard. "The 'Gesta Innocentii III': Text, Introduction and Commentary." PhD diss., Bryn Mawr College, 1981.

Grubmüller, Klaus, ed. *Schulliteratur im späten Mittelalter.* Munich, 2000.

Gueudet, Guy. *L'art de la lettre humaniste.* Ed. Francine Wild. Paris, 2004.

Guillén Torralba, Juan. "Las bibliotecas de la Catedral: La Colombina." In *La Biblioteca Colombina y Capitular.* 5–41.

Guizzardo of Bologna and Castellano of Bassano. *Commentum super tragoedia Ecerinidie.* In Padrin, *Ecerinde.* 69–247.

Günther, Otto. *Die Handschriften der Kirchenbibliothek von St. Marien in Danzig.* Gdansk, 1921.

Guthmüller, Bodo. "Bartolomeo da San Concordio." In *Die Literatur bis zur Renaissance.* Vol. 2 of *Die italienische Literatur im Zeitalter Dantes und am Übergang vom Mittelalter zur Renaissance.* Ed. August Buck. Heidelberg, 1989. 245–247.

Haenel, Gustavo. *Catalogus librorum manuscriptorum qui in bibliothecis Galliae, Helvetiae, Belgii, Britanniae, Hispaniae, Lusitaniae asservantur.* Leipzig, 1830.

Halm, C., G. Laubmann, et al., eds. *Catalogus codicum latinorum Bibliothecae Regiae Monacensis.* 4 vols. Munich, 1876–1894.

Hamesse, Jacqueline. "Approche terminologique de certaines méthodes d'enseignement et de recherche à la fin du moyen âge. *Declarare, Recitare, Conclusio.*" In Weijers, *Vocabulary of Teaching.* 8–28.

———. *Les auctoritates Aristotelis. Auct. Arist.* See Abbreviations.

———. "L'importance de l'étude d'Aristote dans les universités médiévales allemandes. Le témoinage des manuscrits conservés à la Bibliothèque d'Erfurt." In Speer, *Die Bibliotheca Amploniana.* 54–72.

———, ed. *Manuels, programmes de cours et techniques d'enseignement dans les universités médiévales. Actes du Colloque international de Louvain-la-Neuve (9–11 septembre 1993).* Louvain-la-Neuve, 1994.

———. *Les prologues médiévaux. Actes du Colloque international organisé par l'Academia Belgica et l'École française de Rome avec le concours de la F.I.D.E.M. (Rome, 26–28 mars 1998).* Turnhout, 2000.

———. "La technique de la reportation." In Weijers and Holz, *L'enseignement des disciplines.* 405–421.

———. "Le vocabulaire de la transmission orale des textes." In Weijers, *Vocabulaire du livre.* 168–194.

Hasebrink, Burkhard. "Latinität als Bildungsfundament." In Grubmüller, *Schulliteratur im späten*

Mittelalter. 49–76.

Harbert, Bruce. *A Thirteenth-Century Anthology of Rhetorical Poems: Glasgow MS Hunterian V.8.14.* Toronto, 1975.

Harper, Anthony J. "Leipzig Poetry after Paul Fleming. A Re-Assessment." *Daphnis* 5 (1976): 145–170.

Harrison, Robert, trans. *Gallic Salt: Eighteen Fabliaux Translated from the Old French.* Berkeley and Los Angeles, 1974.

Hautz, Johann F. *Geschichte der Universität Heidelberg.* Mannheim, 1884; rpt, Hildesheim and New York, 1980.

Haye, Thomas. *Das lateinische Lehrgedicht im Mittelalter: Analyse einer Gattung.* Leiden, 1997.

Heinemann, Otto von, et al. *Die Handschriften der Herzoglichen Bibliothek zu Wolfenbüttel.* Wolfenbüttel, 1884–1919. See also Köhler and Milchsack, *Die Gudischen Handschriften.*

Helk, Vello. "Dänische Romreisen von der Reformation bis zum Absolutismus (1536–1660)." *Analecta Romana* 6 (1971): 107–96.

Helssig, Rudolf. *Katalog der lateinischen und deutschen Handschriften der Universitäts-Bibliothek zu Leipzig.* Vol. 3, *Die juristischen Handschriften.* Leipzig, 1905.

Henderson, Judith Rice. "Epistles and *Copia* before Erasmus." *Studi Umanistici Piceni* 23 (2003): 169–178.

———. "Valla's *Elegantiae* and the Humanist Attack on the *Ars dictaminis.*" *Rhetorica* 19 (2001): 249–268.

Henkel, Nikolaus. *Deutsche Übersetzungen lateinischer Schultexte: Ihre Verbreitung und Funktion im Mittelalter und in der frühen Neuzeit.* Munich, 1988.

———. "Leipzig als Übersetzungszentrum am Ende des 15. und Anfang des 16. Jahrhunderts." In Grenzmann and Stackmann, *Literatur und Laienbildung.* 559–576.

Henry of Kirkestede. *Catalogus de libris autenticis et apocrifis.* Ed. Richard H. and Mary A. Rouse. London, 2004.

Hermann the German. "Translation of Averroes' 'Middle Commentary' on Aristotle's *Poetics:* Extracts." In Minnis and Scott, *Medieval Literary Theory.* 289–307.

Hermann, Julius. *Die Handschriften und Inkunabeln der italienischen Renaissance.* Vol. 1, *Oberitalien: Genua, Lombardei, Emilia Romagna.* Leipzig, 1930.

Hernad, Béatrice. *Die Graphiksammlung des Humanisten Hartmann Schedel.* Munich, 1990.

Hexter, Ralph J. *Ovid and Medieval Schooling: Studies in Medieval School Commentaries on Ovid's Ars amatoria, Epistulae ex Ponto, and Epistulae heroidum.* Munich, 1986.

Holtz, Louis. "La main de Franciscellus Mancinus et le fonds ancien de San Severino e Sossio de Naples." *Scriptorium* 44 (1990): 217–258 [and plates 26–30].

Horace. *Satires, Epistles, and Ars poetica.* Trans. H. Rushton Fairclough. Cambridge, MA, 1926; rpt. 1966.

Hübl, Albert. *Catalogus codicum manu scriptorum qui in Bibliotheca Monasterii Beate Marie Virginis ad Scotos Vindobonae servantur.* Vienna, 1899.

Hugh of Trimberg. *Das* Registrum multorum auctorum *des Hugo von Trimberg. Ein Quellenbuch zur lateinischen Literaturgeschichte des Mittelalters.* Ed. Johannes Huemer. Vienna, 1888.

Huglo, Michel. *The Theory of Music.* Vol. 3, *Manuscripts from the Carolingian Era up to c. 1500 in the Federal Republic of Germany.* Munich, 1986.

Humphreys, K. W. *The Friars' Libraries.* London, 1990.

Hunt, R. W. "The Introductions to the 'Artes' in the Twelfth Century." In *Studia Mediaevalia in honorem Raymundi Josephi Martin, Ordinis Praedicatorum S. Theologiae Magistri, LXX^{um} Natalem Diem Agentis.* Bruges, 1948. 85–112.

Hunt, Tony. *Teaching and Learning Latin in Thirteenth-Century England.* 3 vols. Rochester, NY, 1991.

Huygens, R. B. C., ed. *Accessus ad auctores. Bernard d'Utrecht. Conrad d'Hirsau, Dialogus super auctores.* Leiden, 1970.

Hyatte, Reginald. *The Arts of Friendship: The Idealization of Friendship in Medieval and Early Renaissance Literature.* Leiden, 1994.

Hyde, John Kenneth. *Padua in the Age of Dante.* New York, 1966.

Hyma, Albert. *The Brethren of the Common Life.* Grand Rapids, 1950.

———. *The Youth of Erasmus.* Ann Arbor, 1930.

IJsewijn, Jozef. *Companion to Neo-Latin Studies.* 2nd ed. Louvain, 1990.

Initia humanistica latina: Initienverzeichnis lateinischer Prosa und Poesie aus der Zeit des 14. bis 16. Jahrhunderts. Ed. Ludwig Bertalot and Ursula Jaitner-Hahner. 3 vols. Tübingen, 1985–2004.

Inventario general de manuscritos de la Biblioteca Nacional. Vol. 10 (3027 a 5699). Madrid, 1984. Vol. 14 (9501–10200). Madrid, 2000.

Inventario generale di tutti i codici manoscritti della Biblioteca Nazionale. 5 vols. Naples. Typescript.

Inventario Ceruti dei manoscritti della Biblioteca Ambrosiana. Comp. Antonio Ceruti. Ed. Angelo Paredi. 5 vols. Etimar, 1973–1979.

Iter ital. See Abbreviations.

Jacobus de Voragine. *Legenda aurea.* Ed. Th. Graesse. Breslau, 1890; rpt. Osnabrück, 1969.

———. *The Golden Legend.* Trans. Granger Ryan and Helmut Ripperger. New York, 1969.

Jaeger, C. Stephen. *The Envy of Angels: Cathedral Schools and Social Ideals in Medieval Europe, 950–1200.* Philadelphia, 1994.

Jaffe. *Declaracio.* See Abbreviations.

James, Montague Rhodes. *A Descriptive Catalogue of the Manuscripts in the Library of Corpus Christi College, Cambridge.* 2 vols. Cambridge, 1911.

———. *A Descriptive Catalogue of the Manuscripts in the Library of Gonville and Caius College.* 2 vols. Cambridge, 1907–1908.

———. *A Descriptive Catalogue of the Manuscripts in the Library of Sidney Sussex College, Cambridge.* Cambridge, 1895.

———. *Western Manuscripts in the Library of Trinity College.* 4 vols. Cambridge, 1900–1904.

Jenaro-MacLennan, L. "Autocomentario en Dante y comentarismo latino." *Vox Romanica* 19 (1960): 82–123.

Jensen, Kristian. "Text-books in the Universities: The Evidence from the Books." In *The Cambridge History of the Book in Britain.* Vol. 3, *1400–1557.* Ed. Lotte Hellinga and J. B. Trapp. Cambridge, 1999. 354–379.

Jensen, Minna Skafte. "Dänische Lateindichtung als Vermittlerin europäischer Kulturströmungen nach Dänemark 1550–1660." *Studia septemtrionalia* 2 (1994): 85–90.

———. "A Latin Poem by Zacharias Lund (1608–1667)." In *Erudition and Eloquence: The Use of Latin in the Countries of the Baltic Sea (1500–1800). Acts of a Colloquium Held in Tartu, 23–26 August, 1999.* Ed. Outi Merisalo and Raija Sarasti-Wilenius. Saarijärvii, 2003. 33–49.

———. "Latindigtern Zacharias Lund (1608–1667)." *Fund og Forskning* 33 (1994): 19–34.

———. "En ønskedrøm." In Asztalos and Gejrot, *Symbolae Septentrionales.* 317–31.

Jeudy, Colette, and Yves-François Riou. *Les manuscrits classiques latins des bibliothèques publiques de France.* Vol. 1, *Agen-Évreux.* Paris, 1989.

John of Garland. *The* Parisiana Poetria *of John of Garland.* Ed. [and trans.] Traugott Lawler. New Haven, 1974.

———. See also Ghisalberti.

John of Hautville. *Architrenius.* Ed. Paul Gerhard Schmidt. Munich, 1974. Edition and English translation by Winthrop Wetherbee. Cambridge, 1994.

John of Salisbury. *Metalogicon: A Twelfth-Century Defense of the Verbal and Logical Arts of the Trivium.* Trans. Daniel D. McGarry. Berkeley and Los Angeles, 1955; rpt. 1962.

Jordan, William Chester. "Adolescence and Conversion in the Middle Ages: A Research Agenda." In Signer and Van Engen*, Jews and Christians. 77–93.*

Jørgensen, Ellen. *Catalogus codicum latinorum medii aevi Bibliothecae Regiae Hafniensis.* Copenhagen, 1926.

Kadenbach, Johannes. "Die Bibliothek des Amplonius Rating de Bercka. Entstehung, Wachstum, Profil." In Speer, *Die Bibliotheca Amploniana.* 16–31.

Kaeppeli, Thomas. *Scriptores Ordinis Praedicatorum Medii Aevi.* 4 vols. Rome, 1970–1993.

Kallendorf, Craig. *Virgil and the Myth of Venice: Books and Readers in the Italian Renaissance.* Oxford, 1999.

Karras, Ruth Mazo. *From Boys to Men: Formations of Masculinity in Late Medieval Europe.* Philadelphia, 2003.

Keil, Heinrich, ed. *Grammatici latini.* 7 vols. Leipzig, 1855–1928.

Kelly, Douglas. "Accessus ad auctores." *Historisches Wörterbuch der Rhetorik,* 1. Tübingen, 1992. 27–36.

———. *Arts.* See Abbreviations.

———. "The Scope of the Treatment of Composition in the Twelfth- and Thirteenth-Century Arts of Poetry." *Speculum* 41 (1966): 261–278.

———. "Theory of Composition in Medieval Narrative Poetry and Geoffrey of Vinsauf's *Poetria nova.*" *Mediaeval Studies* 31 (1969): 117–148.

Kelly, H. A. "Aristotle-Averroes-Alemannus on Tragedy: The Influence of the 'Poetics' on the Latin Middle Ages." *Viator* 10 (1979): 161–209.

Ker, Neil R. *Medieval Libraries of Great Britain: A List of Surviving Books.* 2nd ed. London, 1964. *Supplement to the Second Edition.* Ed. Andrew G. Watson. London, 1987.

Kern, Anton. *Die Handschriften der Universitätsbibliothek Graz.* Vol. 2. Vienna, 1956.

Kern, Claudia. "Patterns in Arts Teaching at the Medieval University of Vienna." *Viator* 18 (1987): 321–327 and tables.

Killy, Walther, ed. *Literatur-Lexikon Autoren und Werke deutscher Sprache.* 12 vols. Munich, 1988–1992.

Kink, Rudolf. *Geschichte der kaiserlichen Universität zu Wien.* Vienna, 1854; 3 vols. rpt. in 2, Frankfurt, 1969.

Kiseleva, L. I. *Latinskie rukopisi Biblioteki AN SSR. Opisanie rukopisei latinskogo alfavita X-XV vv.* [Latin Manuscripts of the Library of the Academy of Sciences: A Catalog of 10th–15th-Century Latin-Alphabet Manuscripts]. Ed. A. D. Lyublinskaya. Leningrad, 1978. 123–25, 286.

Kline, Daniel T., ed. *Medieval Literature for Children.* New York, 2003.

Knox, Dilwyn. *Ironia: Medieval and Renaissance Ideas on Irony.* Leiden, 1989.

———. "Order, Reason and Oratory: Rhetoric in Protestant Latin Schools." In Mack, *Renaissance Rhetoric.* 63–80.

Knudsen, Christian. "Intentions and Impositions." In Kretzmann et al., *Cambridge History.* 479–495.

Koch, A. C. F. "De collecties van de Athenaeumbibliotheek in historisch perspectief." In Bedaux et al., *Stads- of Athenaeumbibliotheek.* 30–95.

Köhler, Franz, and Gustav Milchsack. *Die Gudischen Handschriften.* Section 4 of *Die Handschriften der Herzoglichen Bibliothek Wolfenbuttel.* See Heinemann.

Kopp, Jane Baltzell, trans. "Geoffrey of Vinsauf: *The New Poetics (Poetria nova).*" In Murphy, *Three Medieval Rhetorical Arts.* 27–108.

Kosegarten, Johann. *Geschichte der Universität Greifswald mid urkundlichen Beilagen.* Greifswald, 1857.

Kraus, Manfred. See Geoffrey of Vinsauf.

Kretzmann, Norman, Anthony Kenny, and Jan Pinborg, eds. *The Cambridge History of Later Medieval Philosophy: From the Rediscovery of Aristotle to the Disintegration of Scholasticism, 1100–1600.* Cambridge, 1982.

Kristeller, Paul Oskar. *Iter italicum.* See Abbreviations.

Krochalis, Jeanne Elizabeth. "Alain de Lille: *De planctu Nature:* Studies towards an Edition." Ph.D. diss., Harvard University, 1973.

Kutrzeba, Stanisław. *Catalogus codicum manu scriptorum Musei Principum Czartoryski Cracoviensis* 2. Krakow, 1908–1913.

Lafferty, Maura K. *Walter of Châtillon's* Alexandreis*: Epic and the Problem of Historical Understanding.* Turnhout, 1998.

Latham, Ronald Edward. *Dictionary of Medieval Latin from British Sources.* London, 1975–.

———. *Revised Medieval Latin Word-List from British and Irish Sources.* London, 1965.

Lawler, Traugott. See John of Garland.

Leader, Damian Riehl. *A History of the University of Cambridge.* Vol. 1, *The University to 1546.* Cambridge, 1988.

Lehmann, Paul, and Otto Glauning. *Mittelalterliche Handschriftenbruchstücke der Universitätsbibliothek und des Georgianum zu München.* Leipzig, 1940.

Lehmann, Paul. *Pseudo-Antike Literatur des Mittelalters.* Leipzig, 1927; rpt. Damrstadt, 1964.

Leitschuh, Friedrich, and Hans Fischer. *Katalog der Handschriften der Königlichen Bibliothek zu Bamberg.* Vol. 12. Bamberg, 1895.

Leland, John. *Commentarii de scriptoribus Britannicis.* Ed. Anthony Hall. Oxford, 1709.

LeMarchand, M. Albert. *Catalogue des manuscrits de la Bibliothèque d'Angers.* Angers, 1963.

Lemcke, Hugo. "Die Handschriften und alten Drucke der Bibliothek des Marienstifts-Gymnasiums." In *Königliches Marienstifts-Gymnasium zu Stettin. Michaelis Programm 1897*. Stettin, 1897. 1–44.

Léotaud, Alban, and Rupert G. M. McHardy. "The Benedictines at Oxford, 1283–1539." In Wansbrough and Marett-Crosby, *Benedictines in Oxford*. 20–36.

Leupin, Alexandre. "Absolute Reflexivity: Geoffrey of Vinsauf's *Poetria nova*." In *Barbarolexis: Medieval Writing and Sexuality*. Tr. Kate M. Cooper. Cambridge, MA: Harvard University Press, 1989. 17–39. Reprinted from *Medieval Texts & Contemporary Readers*. Ed. Laurie A. Finke and Martin B. Shichtman. Ithaca, 1987. 120–141.

Lexikon des Mittelalters. 10 vols. Munich, 1977–1999.

Lewry, P. Osmund. "Grammar, Logic and Rhetoric 1220–1320." In Catto, *The Early Oxford Schools*. 401–433.

Leyser, Polycarp, ed. *Historia poetarum et poematum medii aevi decem post annum a nato Christo CCCC, seculorum centum et amplius codicum mstorum [= manuscriptorum] ope carmina varia elegantia, ingeniosa, curiosa*. . . . Halle, 1721. Rpt. in 2 vols., Bologna, 1969.

———, ed. *Galfridi de Vinosalvo Ars Poetica ante quingentos annos conscripta. Ex quatuor codicibus manuscriptis et fragmentis impressis*. . . . Helmstadt, 1724.

Lhotsky, Alphons. *Die Wiener Artistenfakultät 1365–1497*. Vienna, 1965.

Liber decanorum facultatis philosophicae universitatis pragensis ab anno christi 1367, usque ad annum 1585. . . . Prague, 1830.

Licitra, Vincenzo. "La *Summa de arte dictandi* di Maestro Goffredo." *Studi medievali*, 3rd ser., 7 (1966): 865–913.

Lilao Franca, Óscar, and Carmen Castrillo González. *Catálogo de manuscritos de la Biblioteca Universitaria de Salamanca*. Vol. 1, *Manuscritos 1–1679 bis*. Salamanca, 1997.

Lipton, Emma, "Language on Trial: Performing the Law in the N-Town Trial Play." In *The Letter of the Law: Legal Practice and Literary Production in Medieval England*. Ed. Emily Steiner and Candace Barrington. Ithaca, NY, 2002. 115–135.

Livi, Giovanni. *Dante e Bologna: Nuovi studi e documenti*. Bologna, 1921.

Löffler, Karl. *Die Handschriften des Klosters Weingarten*. Leipzig, 1912.

Lohmeier, Dieter. "Lund, Zacharias, Dichter." *Neue Deutsche Biographie*. 15:520–21. Berlin, 1953.

Lord, Mary Louise. "Benvenuto da Imola's Literary Approach to Virgil's *Eclogues*." *Mediaeval Studies* 64 (2002): 287–362.

Lorenz, Sönke. "*Libri ordinarie legendi*. Eine Skizze zum Lehrplan der mitteleuropäischen Artistenfakultät um die Wende vom 14. zum 15. Jahrhundert." In *Argumente und Zeugnisse*. Ed. Wolfram Hogrebe. Frankfurt am Main, 1985. 204–258.

———. *Studium generale Erfordense zum Erfurter Schulleben im 13. und 14. Jahrhundert*. Stuttgart, 1989.

Mack, Peter. *Elizabethan Rhetoric: Theory and Practice*. Cambridge, 2002.

———. *Renaissance Argument: Valla and Agricola in the Traditions of Rhetoric and Dialectic*. Leiden, 1993.

———, ed. *Renaissance Rhetoric*. New York, 1994.

Macray, William D. *Catalogus Codicum Manuscriptorum Bibliothecae Bodleianae, Pars Nona*. Cat-

alogus Codicum Mss Kenelm Digby. Oxford, 1883.

Maier, Christoph T. *Preaching the Crusades: Mendicant Friars and the Cross in the Thirteenth Century.* Cambridge, 1994.

Manacorda, Giuseppe. "Fra Bartolomeo da S. Concordo grammatico e la fortuna di Gaufredo di Vinesauf in Italia." In *Raccolta di studi di storia e critica letteraria dedicata a Francesco Flamini da'suoi discepoli.* Pisa, 1918. 139–152.

———. *Storia della scuola in Italia.* Vol. 1, *Il medio evo.* Milan, 1913.

Manhardt, Hermann. *Handschriftenverzeichnis der Kärntner Bibliotheken.* Vol. 1, *Klagenfurt, Maria Saal, Friesach.* Vienna, 1927. Vol. 1 of Smital, *Handschriften.*

Manuscrits datés. See Samaran and Marichal.

Manuscrits datés conservés en Belgique. Vol. 3, *1441–1460.* Brussels, 1968.

Margolin. See Erasmus.

Marguin-Hamon, E. "Tradition manuscrite de l'oeuvre de Jean de Garlande." *Revue d'histoire des textes,* n.s. 1 (2006): 189–257.

Marti, Berthe M. *The Spanish College at Bologna in the Fourteenth Century.* Philadelphia, 1966.

Martini, E. "Sui codici Napoletani restituiti dall'Austria." *Atti della Reale Accademia di Archeologia Lettere e Belle Arti,* n.s. 9 (1926): 155–182.

Matsuda, Takami, ed. *Mostly British: Manuscripts and Early Printed Materials from Classical Rome to Renaissance England in the Collection of Keio University Library.* Keio, 2001.

Matthew of Vendôme. *Ars versificatoria. Opera* 3. Ed. Franco Munari. Rome, 1988. English translation by Aubrey E. Galyon, *The Art of Versification.* Ames, 1980.

Matthias of Linköping. *Magister Mathias Lincopensis: Testa nucis and Poetria.* Ed. and trans. Birger Bergh. Arlöv, 1996.

Mazal, Otto, Eva Irblich, and István Nemeth. *Wissenschaft im Mittelalter. Ausstellung von Handschriften und Inkunabeln der Österreichischen Nationalbibliothek. Prunksaal 22. Mai bis 18. Oktober 1975.* Vienna, 1975.

Mazal, Otto, and Franz Unterkircher. *Katalog der abendländischen Handschriften der Österreichischen Nationalbibliothek "Series Nova,"* vol. 1. Vienna, 1965.

Mazzatinti, G. *Gli archivi della storia d'Italia,* vol. 3. Rocca S. Casciano, 1900–1901.

———, A. Sorbelli, et al. *Inventari dei manoscritti delle biblioteche d'Italia.* Forli (later Florence), 1890–.

McConica, James. "The Rise of the Undergraduate College." In *The History of the University of Oxford.* Vol. 3, *The Collegiate University.* Ed. James McConica. Oxford, 1986. 1–68.

McCarver, Tim, with Danny Peary. *Tim McCarver's Baseball for Brain Surgeons and Other Fans: Understanding and Interpreting the Game So You Can Watch It Like a Pro.* New York, 1998.

McGuire, Brian Patrick. *Friendship & Community: The Monastic Experience, 350–1250.* Kalamazoo, 1988.

McKinley, Kathryn L. "The Medieval Homer: The *Ilias Latina.*" *Allegorica* 19 (1998): 3–61.

McLaughlin, Martin. *Literary Imitation in the Italian Renaissance.* Oxford, 1995.

Megas, Anastasios. *O Prooumanistikos kuklos tês Padouas (Lovato Lovati—Albertino Mussato) kai oi tragôdies tou L. A. Seneca* [The Pre-Humanist Circle of Padua (Lovato Lovati—Albertino Mussato) and the Tragedies of L.A. Seneca]. Thessaloniki, 1967.

Mercati, Giovanni. *Codici latini Pico Grimani Pio e di altra biblioteca ignota del secolo XVI esistenti nell'Ottoboniana e i codici greci Pio de Modena, con una digressione per la storia dei codici di S. Pietro in Vaticano.* Vatican City, 1938.

Mercer, R. G. G. *The Teaching of Gasparino Barzizza: With Special Reference to His Place in Paduan Humanism.* London, 1979.

Merrill, Brian L. *Athanasius Kircher (1602–1680), Jesuit Scholar: An Exhibition of His Works in the Harold B. Lee Library Collections at Brigham Young University.* Provo, 1989.

Meyer, Heinz. "*Intentio auctoris, utilitas libri.* Wirkungsabsicht und Nutzen literarischer Werke nach Accessus-Prologen des 11. bis 13. Jahrhunderts." *Frühmittelalterliche Studien* 31 (1997): 390–413.

Mezger, C. C. *Geschichte der vereinigten Kgl. Kreis- und Stadt-Bibliothek in Augsburg.* Augsburg, 1842.

Miani, Laura. "I manoscritti della Biblioteca del SS. Salvatore dall'età napoleonica alla restaurazione." In Maria Cristina Bacchi and Laura Miani, eds. *Vicendi del Patrimonio librario Bolognese. Manoscritti e incunaboli della Biblioteca Universitaria di Bologna. I libri prelevati dall'istituto delle scienze e dal convento del. SS. Salvatore 1796. Estratto di Pio VI Braschi e Pio VII Chiaramonti. Due Pontefici cesenati nel bicentenario della Campagna d'Italia, Atti del Convegno internazionale maggio 1997.* N.p., n.d.

Michels, Ulrich. *Die Musiktraktate des Johannes de Muris.* Wiesbaden, 1970.

Milde, Wolfgang. "Lateinische Handschriften der ehemaligen Preußischen Staatsbibliothek Berlin in der Biblioteka Jagiellońska Krakau." *Codices manuscripti* 12 (1986): 85–89.

Millett, Bella, and Jocelyn Wogan-Browne. *Medieval English Prose for Women: Selections from the Katherine Group and* Ancrene Wisse. Oxford, 1990.

Minnis, Alastair, and Ian Johnson, eds. *The Cambridge History of Literary Criticism.* Vol. 2, *The Middle Ages.* Cambridge, 2005.

Minnis, Alastair, and A. Brian Scott, eds, with the assistance of David Wallace. *Medieval Literary Theory and Criticism c. 1100–c.1375: The Commentary Tradition.* Rev. ed. Oxford, 1991.

Minnis, Alastair. *Medieval Theory of Authorship: Scholastic Literary Attitudes in the Later Middle Ages.* London, 1984.

Mittelalterliche Bibliothekskataloge Deutschlands und der Schweiz. See *MBDS* in Abbreviations.

Moerke, Ulrich. *Die Anfänge der weltlichen Barocklyrik in Schleswig-Holstein. Hudemann–Rist–Lund.* Neumünster, 1972.

Moller, Johannes. *Cimbria Literata.* Copenhagen, 1744.

Monfasani, John. *Language and Learning in Renaissance Italy. Selected Articles.* Aldershot, 1994.

Montaiglon, Anatole de. *Recueil géneral et complet des fabliaux des xiii*^e *et xiv*^e *siècles.* 6 vols. Paris, 1872–1890.

Montfaucon, Bernard de. *Biblioteca Bibliothecarum manuscriptorum nova . . .* Vols. 1–2. Paris, 1739.

Montor, François Artaud de. *Lives and Times of the Popes Including the Complete Gallery of the Portraits of the Pontiffs* [1867]. [no trans.] 10 volumes. New York, 1911.

Monumenta historica Universitatis Carolo-Ferdinandeae. See *Liber decanorum facultatis philosophicae.*

Moran, Jo Ann Hoeppner. *The Growth of English Schooling, 1340–1548: Learning, Literacy, and Laicization in Pre-Reformation York Diocese.* Princeton, 1984.

Moraw, Peter. "Die Universität Prag im Mittelalter. Grundzüge ihrer Geschichte im europäischen Zusammenhang." In *Die Universität zu Prag.* Ed. Richard Wenzler Eichler. Munich 1986. 9–134.

Morettus, Petrus. *Ritus dandi presbyterium papae, cardinalibus, et clericis nonnullarum ecclesiarum urbis.* Rome, 1741.

Moss, Ann. *Printed Commonplace-Books and the Structuring of Renaissance Thought.* Oxford, 1996.

Muczkowski, Joseph. *Statuta nec non liber promotionum philosophorum ordinis in universitate studiorum jagellonica ab anno 1402 ad annum 1849.* Krakow, 1849.

Müller, Winfried. "Die Anfänge der Humanismusrezeption im Kloster Tegernsee." *Studien und Mitteilungen zur Geschichte des Benediktinerordens* 92 (1981): 28–90.

Münster-Swendsen, Mia. "The Making of the Masters: Scholastic Self-Fashioning in High-Medieval France (1150–1280)." Masters thesis, University of Copenhagen, 1999.

———. "The Model of Scholastic Mastery, c. 1000–1200." Unpublished paper quoted with the author's permission,

———. "The Model of Scholastic Mastery in Northern Europe *c.* 970–1200." In *Teaching and Learning in Northern Europe, 1000–1200.* Ed. Sally N. Vaughn and Jay Rubenstein. Turnhout, 2006. 306–342.

Mulchahey, M. Michèle. *"First the Bow is Bent in Study . . . ": Dominican Education before 1350.* Toronto, 1998.

Munari. *Catalogue.* See Abbreviations.

———. *Catalogo.* See Abbreviations.

Munari, Franco. "Il 'Piramus et Tisbe' di Matteo di Vendôme." *Studi italiani di filologia classica* 31 (1959): 65–78.

Murano, Giovanna, Giancarlo Savino, Stefano Zamponi, et al. *I manoscritti medioevali della provincia di Pistoia.* Pistoia, 1998.

Murano, Giovanna. *Opere diffuse per exemplar e pecia.* Turnhout, 2005.

Murphy, James J. "The Arts of Poetry and Prose." In Minnis and Johnson, *Cambridge History.* 42–67.

———. "The Discourse of the Future: Toward an Understanding of Medieval Literary Theory." In *Conjunctures: Medieval Studies in Honor of Douglas Kelly.* Ed. Keith Busby and Norris J. Lacy. Amsterdam, 1994. 359–73.

———, ed. *Medieval Eloquence: Studies in the Theory and Practice of Medieval Rhetoric.* Berkeley and Los Angeles, 1978.

———. *Rhetoric in the Middle Ages.* Berkeley and Los Angeles, 1974.

———, ed. *A Short History of Writing Instruction: From Ancient Greece to Modern America.* 2nd ed. Mahwah, NJ, 2001.

———, ed. *Three Medieval Rhetorical Arts.* Berkeley and Los Angeles, 1971.

Mussato, Albertino. See Padrin.

Mynors, R. A. B. *Catalogue of the Manuscripts of Balliol College, Oxford.* Oxford, 1963.

Nardi, Bruno. "Osservazioni sul medievale '*Accessus ad Auctores*' in rapporto all'Epistola a Cangrande." In *Studi e problemi di critica testuale: Convegno di studi di filologi itialiana nel centenario della Commissioni per i testi di lingua, 7–9 aprile, 1960.* Bologna, 1961. 273–305.

Nardi, Paulo. "Relations with Authority." In Ridder-Symoens, *History of the University.* 77–107.

Nauta, Lodi, ed. *Guillelmi de Conchis: Glosae super Boetium.* Turnhout, 1999.

———. "'Magis sit Platonicus quam Aristotelicus': Interpretations of Boethius's Platonism in the *Consolatio Philosophiae* From the Twelfth to the Seventeenth Century." In *The Platonic Tradition in the Middle Ages: A Doxographic Approach.* Ed. Stephen Gersh and Maarten J. F. M. Hoenen. Berlin, 2002. 165–204.

———. "Some Aspects of Boethius' *Consolatio Philosophiae* in the Renaissance." In *Boèce ou la chaîne des savoirs. Actes du Colloque International de la Fondation Singer-Polignac.* . . . Ed. Alain Galonnier. Louvain, 2003. 767–778.

———. "The Study of Beothius's *Consolatio* in the Middle Ages and the Renaissance: Italy versus Western Europe." Unpublished paper quoted with the author's permission.

———. "William of Conches and the Tradition of Boethius' *Consolatio Philosophiae.* An Edition of his *Glosae super Boetium* and Studies of the Latin Commentary Tradition." PhD diss., Rijksuniversiteit Groningen, 1999. See also William of Conches.

Never Rub Bottoms with a Porcupine. And Other Gems from the New Statesman *Weekend Competitions 1968–1978.* Ed. Arthur Marshall. London, 1979.

New Statesman Competitions. London, 1946. See also *Salome Dear* and *Never Rub Bottoms.*

Nicholson, Helen J., trans. *Chronicle of the Third Crusade: A Translation of the "Itinerarium Peregrinorum et Gesta Regis Ricardi."* Brookfield, VT, 1997.

Niermeyer, J. F. *Mediae latinitatis lexicon minus.* Leiden, 1997.

Nims. See Abbreviations.

Nims, Margaret F. "*Translatio:* 'Difficult Statement' in Medieval Poetic Theory." *University of Toronto Quarterly* 43 (1973–74): 215–30.

———. Unpublished notebooks.

Olden-Jørgensen, Sebastian. *Poesi og politik. Lejlighedsdigtningen ved enevoeldens indførelse 1660.* Copenhagen, 1996.

———. "Zacharius Lunds sidste år 1657–67 eller Dichtung und Wahrheit i lyset af et regnskabsbilag." *Fund og Forskning* 35 (1996): 249–55.

Omont, Henri. "Nouvelles acquisitions du departement des manuscrits de la Bibliothèque nationale pendant les années 1896–1897." *Bibliothèque de l'École des chartes* 59 (1898): 81–135.

Orme, Nicholas. *English Schools in the Middle Ages.* London, 1973.

Osmond, Patricia J., and Robert W. Ulery, Jr. "Sallustius." *CTC* 8: 183–326.

Osternacher, Johannes. "Die Ueberlieferung der *Ecloga Theoduli.*" *Neues Archiv* 40 (1916): 331–376.

Oulipo: A Primer of Potential Literature. Ed. and trans. Warren F. Motte, Jr. Lincoln, 1986.

Oulipo Compendium. Ed. Harry Matthews and Alastair Brotchie. London, 1998.

Ovid. *Heroides.* Trans. Harold Isbell. London, 1990.

———. *Metamorphoses.* Trans. Charles Martin. New York, 2004.

Overfield, James H. *Humanism and Scholasticism in Late Medieval Germany.* Princeton, 1984.

Oxford Dictionary of Nursery Rhymes. Ed. Iona and Peter Opie. New ed. Oxford, 1997.

Pace of Ferrara. *Evidentia Ecerinidis.* In Megas, *O Prooumanistikos kuklos.* 203–05.

Padrin, Luigi, ed. *Ecerinide: Tragedia.* By Albertino Mussato. Bologna, 1900.

Palmer, Nigel. "Latin and Vernacular in the Northern European Tradition of the *De Consolatione Philosophiae.*" In *Boethius: His Life, Thought and Influence.* Ed. Margaret Gibson. Oxford, 1981. 362–409.

Paradisi, Bruno. "La diffusione europea del pensiero di Bartolo e le esigenze attuali della sua conoscenza." In *Bartolo da Sassoferrato: Studi e documenti per il VI centenario. Convegno commemorativo del VI centenario di Bartolo, Perugia, 1959.* Ed. Danilo Segoloni. 2 vols. Milan, 1962. 1.395–472.

Paravicini-Bagliani, Agostino. *The Pope's Body.* Trans. David S. Peterson. Chicago, 2000.

Paris, Bibliothèque nationale de France. Departement des manuscrits. *Catalogue général des manuscrits latins. . . .* Paris, 1939–. See also listings under *Catalogue général.*

Passalacqua, Marina, and Lesley Smith. *Codices Boethiani: A Conspectus of Manuscripts of the Works of Boethius.* Vol. 3, *Italy and the Vatican City.* London, 2001.

Pastor, Ludwig, Freiherr von. *The History of the Popes: From the Close of the Middle Ages, Drawn from the Secret Archives of the Vatican and Other Original Sources.* Trans. Dom Ernest Graf. 40 vols. London, 1938–1961.

Patera, Adolf, and Antonín Podlaha. *Soupis Rukopisů Knihovny Metropolitní Kapitoly Pražské.* Soupis Rukopisů Knihoven a Archivů Zemí Českých Jakož i Rukopisných Bohemik Mimočeskýc 1. Prague, 1910. See also Podlaha.

Pellegrin, Elisabeth. "Les *Remedia amoris* d'Ovide, texte scolaire médiéval." *Bibliothèque de l'Ecole des chartes* 115 (1957): 172–179.

———, Jeannine Fohlen, Colette Jeudy, et al. *Les manuscrits classiques latins de la Bibliothèque Vaticane.* Paris, 1975–.

Pepin, Ronald E. *An English Translation of* Auctores Octo*: A Medieval Reader.* Lewiston, 1999.

Perec, Georges. *Je me souviens: Les choses communes 1.* Paris, 1978.

Petersen, Erik. "Gudiani Haunienses Galteriani: Notes on the Bibliotheca Gudiana, J.A. Fabricius and Two Codices of the *Alexandreis.*" *Codices manuscripti. Zeitschrift für Handschriftenkunde* 11 (1985): 140–145.

Petrocchi, Massimo. "L'ultimo destino perugino di Innocenzo III." *Bollettino della storia patria per l'Umbria* 64 (1967): 201–207.

Petrucci, Armando. *Catalogo sommario dei manoscritti del Fondo Rossi, Sezione Corsiniana.* Rome, 1977.

Petrucciani, Alberto, and Dino Puncuh. *Giacomo Filippo Durazzo (1729–1812), Il bibliofilo e il suo "Cabinet de Livres."* Genoa, 1996.

Pigman, G. W., III. "Barzizza's Studies of Cicero." *Rinascimento* 21 (1981): 123–163.

Pinborg, Jan. "The 14th Century Schools of Erfurt: Repertorium Erfordiense." *CIMAGL* 41 (1982): 171–192.

———. "Speculative Grammar," In Kretzman et al., *Cambridge History.* 254–269.

Pits, John. *De illustribus Angliae scriptoribus.* Paris, 1619.

Podlaha, Antonín. *Soupis Rukopisů Knihovny Metropolitní Kapitoly Pražské.* Soupis Rukopisů

Knihoven a Archivů Zemí Českých Jakož i Rukopisných Bohemik Mimočeských 2. Prague, 1922. See also Patera and Podlaha.

Polak. *Eastern Europe*. See Abbreviations.

———. *Western Europe*. See Abbreviations.

Pollard, Graham. "The *Pecia* System in the Medieval Universities." In *Medieval Scribes, Manuscripts and Libraries: Essays Presented to N. R. Ker*. Ed. M. B. Parkes and Andrew G. Watson. London, 1978. 145–161.

Ponce, Carolina, trans. *La poética nueva*. Mexico City, 2000.

Porro, Giulio. *Catalogo dei codici manoscritti della Trivulziana*. Turin. 1884.

Powicke, Frederick Maurice. *The Medieval Books of Merton College*. Oxford, 1931.

Powicke and Emden. See Rashdall.

Puncuh, Dino. *I manoscritti della Raccolta Durazzo*. Genoa, 1979.

Purcell, William. *Ars Poetriae: Rhetorical and Grammatical Invention at the Margin of Literacy*. Columbia, SC, 1996.

———. "Transsumptio: A Rhetorical Doctrine of the Thirteenth Century." *Rhetorica* 5 (1978): 369–411.

Quadlbauer, Franz. *Die antike Theorie der Genera dicendi im lateinischen Mittelalter*. Vienna, 1962.

———. "Zur Theorie der Komposition in der mittelalterlichen Rhetorik und Poetik." In *Rhetoric Revalued: Papers from the International Society for the History of Rhetoric*. Ed. Brian Vickers. Binghamton, 1982. 115–131.

Quain, Edwin A. "The Medieval *Accessus ad auctores*." *Traditio* 3 (1945): 215–264.

Queneau, Raymond. *Exercices du style*. Paris, 1947.

———. "Potential Literature." In *Oulipo: A Primer*. 51–64.

Quinn, Betty Nye. "ps. Theodolus." *CTC* 2.383–408.

Quinque claves sapientiae. Incerti auctoris rudium doctrina. Bonvicini de Ripa, Vita scolastica. Ed. Anezka Vidmanová-Schmidtová. Leipzig, 1969.

Raby, Frederic James Edward "*Amor* and *Amicitia*: A Mediaeval Poem." *Speculum* 40 (1965): 599–610.

———. *A History of Secular Latin Poetry in the Middle Ages*. Oxford, 1934.

Radio France Culture. "Des papous dans la tête." 1 June 2003. http://www.radiofrance.fr/chaines/france-culture2/papous/

Raine, J., ed. *Catalogi veteres librorum Ecclesiae Cathedralis Dunelmensis*. London, 1838.

Rashdall, Hastings. *The Universities of Europe in the Middle Ages*. Ed. F. M. Powicke and A. B. Emden. 3 vols. Oxford, 1936.

Redlich, P. Virgil. *Tegernsee und die deutsche Geistesgeschichte im 15. Jahrhundert*. Munich, 1931.

Reichling. See Alexander de Villa Dei.

Reilly, P. Conor. *Athanasius Kircher, S.J., Master of a Hundred Arts 1602–1680*. Wiesbaden and Rome, 1974.

Rendel, Mats. "Athanasius Kircher on the Web." http://www.bahnhof.se/~rendel/kirlinx.html

Reuter, Marianne, Gerhard Schott, Natalia Daniel, and Peter Zahn. *Die lateinischen mittelalterlichen Handschriften der Universitätsbibliothek München: Die Handschriften aus der Quartreihe*.

Wiesbaden, 2000.

Reynolds, Leighton Durham, ed. *Texts and Transmission: A Survey of the Latin Classics.* Oxford, 1983.

Reynolds, Suzanne. "Inventing Authority: Glossing, Literacy and the Classical Text." In *Prestige, Authority and Power in Late Medieval Manuscripts and Texts.* Ed. Felicity Riddy. Woodbridge, 2000. 7–16.

———. *Medieval Reading: Grammar, Rhetoric, and the Classical Text.* Cambridge, 1996.

Ricci, Pier Giorgio. "La cronologia dell'ultimo 'certamen' Petrarchesco." *Studi Petrarcheschi* 4 (1951): 47–57.

Ricci, Seymour de. *Census of Medieval and Renaissance Manuscripts in the United States and Canada.* New York, 1935–40. See also Faye and Bond.

———. *English Collectors of Books & Manuscripts (1530–1930) and Their Marks of Ownership.* Cambridge, 1930.

Richardson, Henry Gerald. "The Schools of Northhampton in the Twelfth Century." *English Historical Review* 56 (1941): 595–605.

Richmond, Velma Bourgeois. *Laments for the Dead in Medieval Narrative.* Pittsburgh, 1966.

Riddehough, Geoffrey B. "Joseph of Exeter: The Cambridge Manuscript." *Speculum* 24 (1949): 389–96.

Ridder-Symoens, Hilde de, ed. *A History of the University in Europe.* Vol. 1, *Universities in the Middle Ages.* Cambridge, 1992.

Rigg, A. George. *A History of Anglo-Latin Literature, 1066–1422.* Cambridge, 1992; rpt. 1996.

———. "Medieval Latin Poetic Anthologies (IV)." *Mediaeval Studies* 43 (1981): 472–497.

Riley, Henry Thomas, ed. *Registrum Abbatiae Johannis Whethamstede, Abbatis Monasterii Sancti Albani.* 2 vols. London, 1872–1873.

Rix, H. D. "The Editions of Erasmus' *De copia.*" *Studies in Philology* 43 (1946): 595–618.

Robert of Basevorn. *Ars predicandi.* Latin text in Charland, *Artes praedicandi.* 233–323. English translation by Leopuld Krul. "Robert of Basevorn: *The Form of Preaching (Forma praedicandi).*" In Murphy, *Three Medieval Rhetorical Arts.* 109–215.

Roberts, Michael John. *The Jeweled Style: Poetry and Poetics in Late Antiquity.* Ithaca, NY, 1989.

Roest, Bert. *A History of Franciscan Education (c. 1210–1517).* Leiden, 2000.

Rolland, Joachim. *Les origines latines du théâtre comique en France. Essai bibliographique.* Paris, 1927; rpt. Geneva, 1972.

Rosa, Mario. "Alessandro VII." *DBI* 2.205–215.

Rose, Valentin. *Die Handschriftenverzeichnisse der Königlichen Bibliothek zu Berlin.* Berlin, 1905.

Rosenthal, Bernard M. *The Rosenthal Collection of Printed Books with Manuscript Annotations: A Catalog of 242 Editions Mostly before 1600 Annotated by Contemporary or Near-Contemporary Readers.* New Haven, 1997.

Rosłanowski, Tadeusz. "Universitäten und Hochschulen in Polen." In *Stadt und Universität im Mittelalter und in der früheren Neuzeit: Arbeitsgatung in Tübingen, 8–10.11. 1974.* Ed. Erich Maschke and Jürgen Sydow. Sigmaringen, Ger., 1977. 166–170.

Rossi, Vittorio. "Un grammatico cremonese a Pavia nella prima età del Rinascimento." *Bollettino della Società pavese di storia patria* 1 (1901): 16–46.

Rouse, Mary A., and Richard H. Rouse. *Authentic Witnesses: Approaches to Medieval Texts and Manuscripts.* Notre Dame, 1991.

———, eds. *Catalogus.* See Henry of Kirkestede.

———. *Preachers, Florilegia and Sermons: Studies on the* Manipulus florum *of Thomas of Ireland.* Toronto, 1979.

Rubió i Balaguer, Jordi. "Els llibres de l'abat Savarés a la Biblioteca de Ripoll." *Analecta Montserratensia* 9 (1962): 227–237.

Rüegg, Walter. "Themes." In Ridder-Symoens, *History of the University.* 3–34.

Rud, Thomas. *Codicum manuscriptorum ecclesiae cathedralis Dunelmensis Catalogus classicus.* Durham, 1825.

Ruf, Paul. *Säkularisation und Bayerische Staatsbibliothek.* Vol. 1, *Die Bibliotheken der Mendikanten und Theatiner (1799–1802).* Wiesbaden, 1962.

Sabbadini, Remigio. *Il metodo degli umanisti.* Florence, 1922.

———. *Le scoperte dei codici latini e greci ne' secoli XIV e XV.* 2 vols. Florence, 1905–1914.

Saenger, Paul. "Silent Reading: Its Impact on Late Medieval Script and Society." *Viator* 13 (1982): 367–414.

Salmon, Paul. "Über den Beitrag des grammatischen Unterrichts zur Poetik des Mittelalters." *Archiv für das Studium der neueren Sprachen und Literaturen* 199 (1963): 65–84.

Salome dear, NOT in the fridge! Parodies . . . misleading advice for foreigners, all from the New Statesman *competitions 1955–1967 chosen for their brilliance, hilarity, originality, elegance and wit.* Ed. Arthur Marshall. London, 1968.

Samaran, Charles, and Robert Marichal. *Catalogue des manuscrits en écriture latine portant des indications de date, de lieu ou de copiste.* Vols. 2–3. Ed. Marie-Thérèse D'Alverny. Paris, 1962 and 1974.

Sandkühler, Bruno. *Die frühen Dantekommentare und irh Verhältnis zue mittelalterlichen Kommentartradition.* Munich, 1967.

Sanford, Eva Matthews. "Some Literary Interests of Fifteenth Century German Students." *Transactions and Proceedings of the American Philological Association* 59 (1928): 72–98.

———. "The Use of Classical Latin Authors in the *Libri manuales.*" *Transactions and Proceedings of the American Philological Association* 55 (1924): 190–248.

Santoro, Caterina. *I codici medioevali della Biblioteca Trivulziana.* Milan, 1965.

Sarti-Fattorini. See Sarti, Maurus, and Maurus Fattorini.

Sarti, Maurus, and Maurus Fattorini. *De claris archigymnasii bononiensis professoribus a saeculo 11. usque ad saeculum 14.* Ed. C. Albicinio and C. Malagola. 2 vols. 2nd ed. Bologna, 1888–1896; rpt. Torino, 1962. (First published by Sarti in 1769–1772.)

Scalon, Cesare. *Libri, scuole e cultura nel Friuli medioevale: "membra disiecta" dell'Archivio di Stato di Udine.* Padua, 1987.

Schaller, Hans Martin, and Bernhard Vogel. *Handschriftenverzeichnis zur Briefsammlung des Petrus de Vinea.* Hannover, 2002.

Scherrer, Gustav. *Verzeichniss der Handschriften der Stiftsbibliothek von St. Gallen.* Halle, 1875; rpt. Hildesheim, 1975.

Schiavetto, Franco Lucio. "Giovanni da Aquileia (Giovanni Bondi o dei Pitacoli)." *DBI* 55.682–683.

Schimmelpfennig, Bernhard. "'Mitbestimmung' in der römischen Kirche unter Innocenz III." In *Proceedings of the 8th International Congress of Medieval Canon Law, San Diego 21–27 August 1988.* Ed. Stanley Chodorow. Vatican City, 1972.

Schipke, Renate. *Die Maugérard-Handschriften der Forschungsbibliothek Gotha.* Gotha, 1972.

Schmidt, *Architrenius.* See John of Hautville.

Schmitt, Charles B. "Auctoritates, Repertorium, Dicta, Sententiae, Flores, Thesaurus, and Axiomata: Latin Aristotelian Florilegia in the Renaissance." In *Aristoteles, Werk und Wirkung.* Vol. 2, *Kommentierung, Überlieferung, Nachleben.* Ed. Jürgen Wiesner. Berlin, 1987. 515–537.

Schoeck, R. J. *Erasmus of Europe: The Making of A Humanist, 1467–1500.* Edinburgh, 1990.

Schubert, Ernst. "Motive und Probleme deutscher Universitätsgründungen des 15. Jahrhunderts." In Baumgart and Hammerstein, *Beiträge zu Problemen.* 13–74.

Schum, Wilhelm. *Beschreibendes Verzeichniss der Amplonianischen Handschriften-Sammlung zu Erfurt.* Berlin, 1887.

Schwinges. Rainer C. "On Recruitment in German Universities in the Fourteenth to Sixteenth Centuries." In Courtenay and Miethke, *Universities and Schooling.* 32–48.

Segre, Cesare. "Bartolomeo da San Concordio (Bartolomeo Pisano)." *DBI* 6.768–70.

Selden, John. *Historiae Anglicanae Scriptores . . . ex vetustis manuscriptis nunc primùm in lucem editi.* London, 1652.

Seneca. *Tragedies.* Trans. John G. Fitch. 2 vols. Cambridge, MA, 2004.

Seymour, M. C., ed. *On the Properties of Things: John Trevisa's Translation of Bartholomaeus Anglicus De Proprietatibus Rerum.* Vol. 1. Oxford, 1975.

Shailor, Barbara A. *The Medieval Book:* New Haven, 1991; rpt. Toronto, 1994.

Sharpe, Richard, James P. Carley, Rodney M. Thomson, and Andrew G. Watson. *English Benedictine Libraries: The Shorter Catalogues.* London, 1996.

Shooner, Hugues V. *Codices manuscripti operum Thomae de Aquino.* Vol. 2, *Bibliothecae Gdansk–Münster.* Rome, 1973.

Signer, Michael A., and John Van Engen, eds. *Jews and Christians in Twelfth-Century Europe.* Notre Dame, 2001.

Singleton, Charles S. *An Essay on the* Vita nuova. 2nd ed. Baltimore, 1977.

Siraisi, Nancy G. *Arts and Sciences at Padua: The* Studium *of Padua before 1350.* Toronto, 1973.

Šmahel, František. "Scholae, Collegia et Bursae Universitatis Pragensis. Ein Beitrag zum Wortschatz der mittelalterlichen Universitäten." In Weijers. *Vocabulaire des collèges universitaires.* 115–130.

Smital, Ottokar. *Handschriftenverzeichnisse Österreichischer Bibliotheken.* Vienna, 1927.

Sommerlechner, Andrea. *Stupor mundi? Kaiser Friedrich II. und die mittelalterliche Geschichtsschreibung.* Vienna, 1999.

Sottili, Augostino. *I codici del Petrarca nella Germania occidentale.* Padua, 1971.

Sowards. See Erasmus. *A Declamation.*

Spector, Stephen, ed. *The N-Town Play: Cotton MS Vespasian D.8.* 2 vols. Oxford, 1991.

Speer, Andreas, ed. *Die Bibliotheca Amploniana: Ihre Bedeutung im Spannungsfeld von Aristotelismus, Nominalismus und Humanismus.* Berlin, 1995.

Spilling, Herrard. *Die Handschriften der Staats- und Stadtbibliothek Augsburg 2° Cod. 101–250.*

Wiesbaden, 1984.

Spunar, Pavel. "The Literary Legacy of Prague Dominicans and the University in Prague." In *Société et église: Textes et discussions dans les universités d'Europe centrale pendant le moyen âge tardif. Actes du Colloque international de Cracovie 14–16 juin 1993.* Ed. Sophie Włodek. Turnhout, 1995. 91–100.

———. "La Faculté des Arts dans les universités de l'Europe centrale." In Weijers and Holtz, *L'enseignement des disciplines.* 467–475.

Stadter, Philip A. "Planudes, Plutarch, and Pace of Ferrara." *Italia medioevale e umanistica* 16 (1973): 137–161.

Staphorst, N. *Historia ecclesiae Hamburgensis diplomatica.* Part I, vol. 3. Hamburg, 1727.

Statius. See Clogan.

Stock, Brian. "*Parce Continuius:* Some Textual and Interpretive Notes." *Mediaeval Studies* 31 (1969): 162–173.

Stoneman, William P., ed. *Dover Priory.* London, 1999.

Sturlese, Loris. "Der Söster Lektor Reiner von Cappel O.P. und zwei Wolfenbütteler Fragmente aus Kapitelsakten der Dominikanerprovinz Saxonia (1358, ca. 1370)." *Wolfenbütteler Beiträge* 16 (1983): 186–201.

Suerbaum, Almut. "*Accessus ad auctores:* Autorkonzeptionen in mittelalterlichen Kommentartexten." In *Autor und Autorschaft im Mittelalter. Kolloquium Meißen 1995.* Ed. Elizabeth Andersen, Jens Haustein, Anne Simon, and Peter Strohschneider. Tübigen, 1998. 29–37.

———. "*Litterae et mores.* Zur Textgeschichte der mittelalterlichen Avian-Kommentare." In Grubmüller, *Schulliteratur im späten Mittelalter.* 383–434.

Summit, Jennifer. *Lost Property: The Woman Writer and English Literary History, 1380–1589.* Chicago, 2000.

Sweeney, Robert Dale. *Prolegomena to an Edition of the Scolia to Statius.* Leiden, 1969.

Szklenar, Hans. "Hat Nicolaus de Dybin in Prag studiert und gelehrt?" *Blätter für deutsche Landesgeschichte* 114 (1978): 151–164.

———. *Magister Nicolaus.* See Abbreviations.

———. "Nikolaus von Dybin (Du-, Di-, Ty-, Tibinus)." *Verfasserlexikon* 8.1062–67.

Tabulae codicum manu scriptorum praeter graecos et orientales in Biblioteca Palatina Vindobonensi asservatorum. Vienna, 1864–1870; rpt. in 4 vols, Graz, 1965.

Tanner, Thomas. *Bibliotheca Britannico-Hibernica.* London, 1748.

Teeuwen, Mariken. *The Vocabulary of Intellectual Life in the Middle Ages.* Turnhout, 2003.

Thomas de Chobham. *Summa de arte praedicandi.* Ed. Franco Morenzoni. Turnhout, 1988.

Thomas, Paul. *Catalogue des manuscrits de classiques latins de la Bibliothèque Royale de Bruxelles.* Gand, 1896.

Thomson, David. *A Descriptive Catalogue of Middle English Grammatical Texts.* New York, 1979.

———. "The Oxford Grammar Masters Revisited." *Mediaeval Studies* 45 (1983): 298–310.

Thomson, Ian, and Louis Perraud, trans. *Ten Medieval Latin Schooltexts of the Later Middle Ages: Translated Selections.* Lewiston, NY, 1990.

Thomson, Rodney M., with Michael Gullick. *A Descriptive Catalogue of the Medieval Manuscripts in Worcester Cathedral Library.* Cambridge, 2001.

Thorndike, Lynn. *University Records and Life in the Middle Ages.* New York, 1944.

Thurot, Charles. *Notices et extraits de divers manuscrits latins pour servir à l'histoire des doctrines grammaticales au moyen âge.* Paris, 1868; rpt. Frankfurt, 1964.

Tilliette, Jean-Yves. *Des mots à la parole: Une lecture de la Poetria nova de Geoffroy de Vinsauf.* Geneva, 2000.

Tiner, Elza C. "Evidence for the Study of Rhetoric in the City of York to 1500." LMS thesis. Pontifical Institute of Mediaeval Studies, 1984.

Travis, Peter. "*The Nun's Priest's Tale* as Grammar School Primer." In *Reconstructing Chaucer.* Ed. Paul Strohm and Thomas J. Heffernan. Knoxville, 1985. 81–91.

Tříška, Josef. *Literární Činnost Předhusitské University.* Prague, 1967.

Trombelli, Giovanni Crisostomo. *Memorie istoriche concernente le due canoniche di S. Maria di Reno e di S. Salvatore.* Bologna, 1752.

Truhlář, Josepho. *Catalogus codicum manu scriptorum latinorum, qui in C. R. Bibliotheca Publica atque Universitatis Pragensis asservantur.* 2 vols. Prague, 1905–06.

Tsai, Eugenie. *Robert Smithson Unearthed: Drawings, Collages, Writings.* New York, 1991.

Tseng, Marie Shively. "Paolo da Perugia and His Influence on the Beginnings of Italian Humanism As Seen Through His Commentary on Horace's *Ars poetica.*" Ph.D. diss., University of Southern California, 1984.

Turner, Ralph V. *King John.* London, 1994.

Uebach, Heinz Peter. *Zwei mittellateinische Pyramus- und Thisbe-Dichtungen.* Bern, 1975.

Uiblein, Paul. *Acta Facultatis Artium Universitatis Vindobonensis 1385–1416.* Graz, 1968.

Unterkircher, Franz, ed. *Katalog der datierten Handschriften in lateinischer Schrift in Österreich.* Vol. 1, *Die datierten Handschriften der Österreichischen Nationalbibliothek bis zum Jahre 1400.* Vienna, 1969.

Valentinelli, Joseph. *Bibliotheca manuscripta ad S. Marci Venetiarum.* 6 vols. Venice, 1868–1873.

Verger, Jacques. "Patterns." In Ridder-Symoens, *History of the University.* 35–76.

Verstraete. See Erasmus.

Vickers, Brian. "Some Reflections on the Rhetoric Textbook." In Mack, *Renaissance Rhetoric.* 81–102.

Vinsauf, Geoffrey of. See Geoffrey of Vinsauf.

Vitalis of Blois. *Geta.* Latin text in Bertini, *Commedie* 3.139-242; and Gustave Cohen, *La comédie,* 1.1-57. English translation in Elliott, *Seven Medieval Latin Comedies,* 26–49.

Waddel, Helen. *Mediaeval Latin Lyrics.* 5th ed. New York, 1966.

Wagner, Klaus. "Hernando Colón: El hombre y su biblioteca." In *La Biblioteca Colombina y Capitular.* 43–67.

Walker, Jeffrey. *Rhetoric and Poetics in Antiquity.* Oxford, 2000.

Walther. See Abbreviations.

Wansbrough, Henry, and Anthony Marrett-Crosby, eds. *Benedictines in Oxford.* London, 1997.

Ward, John O. "The *Catena* Commentaries on the Rhetoric of Cicero and Their Implications for Development of a Teaching Tradition in Rhetoric." *Studies in Medieval and Renaissance Teaching* 6 (1998): 79–95.

———. *Ciceronian Rhetoric in Treatise, Scholion and Commentary.* Turnhout, 1995.

———. "From Marginal Gloss to *Catena* Commentary: The Eleventh-Century Origins of a Rhetorical Teaching Tradition in the Medieval West." *Parergon* (special issue on *Text, Scribe, Artefact*), ns 13.2 (1996): 109–120.

———. "Rhetoric and the art of dictamen." In Weijers, *Méthodes et instruments*. 20–61.

———. "Rhetoric in the Faculty of Arts at the Universities of Paris and Oxford in the Middle Ages: A Summary of the Evidence." *Archivum Latinitatis Medii Aevi* (Union Académique Internationale: *Bulletin Du Cange*) 54 (1996): 159–231.

Warner, George F., and Julius P. Gilson. *Catalogue of Western Manuscripts in the Old Royal and King's Collections.* 4 vols. London, 1921.

Watson, Andrew G. *Dated and Datable Manuscripts c. 700–1600 in the Department of Manuscripts, The British Library.* 2 vols. London, 1979.

———. See also Ker, *Medieval Libraries.*

Watson, Don. *Death Sentences: How Clichés, Weasel Words, and Management-Speak are Strangling Public Language.* New York, 2005.

Wattenbach, Wilhelm. "Peter Luder, der erste humanistische Lehrer in Heidelberg." *Zeitschrift für die Geschichte des Oberrheins* 22 (1869): 33–127.

Webber, Teresa, and Andrew G. Watson. *Libraries of the Augustinian Canons.* London, 1998.

Weber, Jaroslav, Josef Tříška, and Pavel Spunar. *Catalogus codicum manuscriptorum Trzebonae Crumloviique asservatorum.* Prague, 1958.

Weijers, Olga. *Dictionnaires et répertoires au moyen âge. Une étude du vocabulaire.* Turnhout, 1991.

———, ed. *De disciplina scolarium.* See [Pseudo-]Boethius.

———. *Le maniement du savoir. Pratiques intellectuelles à l'époque des premières universités (xiiie– xive siècles).* Turnhout: 1996.

———, ed. *Terminologie de la vie intellectuelle au moyen âge. Actes de colloque Leyde/La Haye 20–21 septembre 1985.* Turnhout, 1988.

———. *Le travail intellectuel à la Faculté des arts de Paris: textes et maîtres (ca. 1200–1500).* Vol. 1, *Répertoire des noms commençant par A-B.* Studia Artistarum 1. Turnhout, 1994.

———, ed. *Vocabulaire des collèges universitaires (xiiie-xvie siècles). Actes du colloque Leuven 9–11 avril 1992.* Turnhout, 1993.

———, ed. *Vocabulaire des écoles et des méthodes d'enseignement au moyen âge. Actes du colloque Rome 21–22 octobre 1989.* Turnhout, 1992.

———, ed. *Vocabulaire du livre et de l'écriture au moyen âge. Actes de la table ronde, Paris 24–26 septembre 1987.* Turnhout, 1989.

———, ed. *Vocabulary of Teaching and Research Between Middle Ages and Renaissance. Proceedings of the Colloquium, London, Warburg Institute, 11–12 March 1994.* Turnhout, 1995.

———, and Louis Holtz, eds. *L'enseignement des disciplines à la Faculté des arts (Paris et Oxford, xiiie-xve siècles).* Studia artistarum 4. Turnhout, 1977.

Weissenborn, J. C. Hermann. *Acten der Erfurter Universität,* vol. 2. Geschichtsquellen der Provinz Sachsen und angrenzender Gebiete 8.2. Halle, 1884; rpt. Nendeln, Liechtenstein, 1976.

Wenger, Etienne. *Communities of Practice: Learning, Meaning, and Identity.* Cambridge, 1998.

Wetherbee. See Bernardus Silvestris and John of Hautville.

Wheatley, Edward. *Mastering Aesop: Medieval Education, Chaucer, and His Followers.* Gainesville, 2000.

Wieland, Gernot Rudolf. "The Glossed Manuscript: Classbook or Library Book?" *Anglo-Saxon England* 14 (1986): 153–173.

———. "Interpreting the Interpretation: The Polysemy of the Latin Gloss." *The Journal of Medieval Latin* 8 (1998): 59–71.

———. *The Latin Glosses on Arator and Prudentius in Cambridge University Library MS Gg.5.35.* Toronto, 1983.

Wilkins, Ernest Hatch. *Petrarch's Later Years.* Cambridge, MA, 1959.

William of Conches. See Nauta, Lodi.

Wilmart, Dom André. "L'art poétique de Geoffroi de Vinsauf et les commentaires de Barthélemy de Pise." *Revue bénédictine* 41 (1929): 271–75.

Wisłocki, W. *Catalogus codicum manuscriptorum Bibliothecae Universitatis Jagellonicae Cracoviensis.* 2 vols. 1877–1881.

Witt, Ronald G. *Coluccio Salutati and his Public Letters.* Geneva, 1976.

———. *Footsteps.* See Abbreviations.

———. "The French Cultural Invasion." In Calboli Montefusco, *Papers on Rhetoric.* 229–259.

Woods, Marjorie Curry. "Boys Will Be Women: Musings on Classroom Nostalgia and the Chaucerian Audience(s)." In *Speaking Images: Essays in Honor of V. A. Kolve.* Ed. Robert F. Yeager and Charlotte C. Morse. Asheville, NC, 2001. 143–166.

———. "Chaucer the Rhetorician: Criseyde and Her Family." *The Chaucer Review* 20 (1985): 28–39.

———. "Classical Examples and References in Medieval Lectures on Poetic Composition." *Allegorica* 10 (1989): 3–12.

———, and Rita Copeland. "Classroom and Confession." In *The Cambridge History of Medieval English Literature.* Ed. David Wallace. Rev. ed. Cambridge, 2002. 376–406.

———. "The Classroom as Courtroom: Cicero's Attributes of Persons and the Interpretation of Classical Literacy Characters in the Renaissance." Forthcoming in *Colloquium Tullianum* 13.

———, ed. [and trans.] See *EC* in Abbreviations.

———. "In a Nutshell: *Verba* and *Sententia* and Matter and Form in Medieval Composition Theory." In *The Uses of Manuscripts in Literary Studies: Essays in Memory of Judson Boyce Allen.* Ed. Charlotte Cook Morse, Penelope Reed Doob, and Marjorie Curry Woods. Kalamazoo, 1992. 19–39.

———. "Innocent III As a Rhetorical Figure." In *Innocenzo III: Urbs et Orbis. Atti del Congresso Internazionale (Roma, 9–15 settembre 1998).* Ed. Andrea Sommerlechner. 2 vols. Rome, 2003. 2.1346–1362.

———. "A Medieval Rhetoric Goes to School—And to the University: The Commentaries on the *Poetria nova.*" *Rhetorica* 9 (1991): 55–65.

———. "A Medieval Rhetorical Manual in the 17th Century: The Case of Christian Daum and the *Poetria nova.*" *Classica et Beneventana: Essays Presented to Virginia Brown on the Occasion of Her 65th Birthday.* Ed. Frank T. Coulson and Anna A. Grotans. Turnhout, 2008. 201–209.

———. "Poetic Digression and the Interpretation of Medieval Literary Texts." In *Acta Conventus*

Neo-Latini Sanctandreani. Ed. I. D. McFarlane. Binghamton, NY, 1986. 617–624.

———. "Quintilian and Medieval Teaching." In *Quintiliano: Historia y Actualidad de la Retórica: Actas del Congresso Internacional "Quintiliano: historia y actualidad de la retórica: XIX Centenario de la 'Institutio Oratoria.'* Ed. Tomás Albaladejo, Emilio del Rio, and José Antonio Caballero. 3 vols. Logroño, 1998. 3.1531–1540.

———. "Rape and the Pedagogical Rhetoric of Sexual Violence." In Copeland, *Criticism and Dissent.* 56–86.

———. "La retórica latina en la España medieval: Los comentarios sobre la *Poetria nova* en las bibliotecas españolas." Trans. Rocío Garcilazo and María Ángeles Fernández. In *Ensayos solore la tradición retórica.* Ed. Helena Beristáin and Gerardo Ramírez Vidal. Bitácora de Retórica 15. Mexico City. 271–292.

———. "Shared Books: Primers, Psalters, and the Adult Acquisition of Literacy among Devout Laywomen and Women in Orders in Late Medieval England." *New Trends in Feminine Spirituality. The Holy Women of Liège and Their Impact.* Ed. Juliette Dor, Leslie Johnson, and Jocelyn Wogan-Browne. Turnhout, 1999. 179–193.

———. "Some Techniques of Teaching Rhetorical Poetics in the Schools of Medieval Europe." In *Learning from the Histories of Rhetoric: Essays in Honor of Winifred Bryan Horner.* Ed. Theresa Enos. Carbondale, 1993. 91–113.

———. "The Teaching of Poetic Composition in the Later Middle Ages." In *A Short History of Writing Instruction: Antecedents of American Composition Practices.* 2nd ed. Ed. James J. Murphy. Mahwah, NJ, 2001. 123–143.

———. "Teaching the Tropes in the Middle Ages: The Theory of Metaphoric Transference in Commentaries on the Poetria nova." In *Rhetoric and Pedagogy: Its History, Philosophy, and Practice: Essays in Honor of James J. Murphy.* Ed. Winifred Bryan Horner and Michael Leff. Mahwah, NJ, 1995. 73–82.

———. "An Unfashionable Rhetoric in the Fifteenth Century." *Quarterly Journal of Speech* 75 (1989): 312–320.

———. "Using the *Poetria nova* to Teach Dictamen in Italy and Central Europe." In Calboli Montefusco, *Papers on Rhetoric.* 261–279.

———. "Weeping for Dido: Epilogue on a Premodern Rhetorical Exercise in the Postmodern Classroom." *Latin Grammar and Rhetoric: From Classical Theory to Medieval Practice.* Ed. Carol Dana Lanham. London, 2002. 284–294.

Woolf, Rosemary. *The English Mystery Plays.* London, 1972.

Worstbrock, Franz Josef, Monika Klaes, and Jutta Lütten. *Repertorium der Artes dictandi des Mittelalters.* Munich, 1992.

———. "Hartmann Schedel." *Verfasserlexikon* 8.609–25.

———. "Otto von Lüneburg." *Verfasserlexikon* 7.226–28.

Wrobel, Johannes, ed. *Graecismus.* By Eberhard von Bethune. Hildesheim, 1987.

Young, Karl. "Chaucer and Geoffrey of Vinsauf." *Modern Philology* 41 (1944): 172–82.

Zabłocki, Stefan. "The Medieval Versified Treatises and the Eighteenth-Century Jesuit Teaching in Poland." Unpublished paper quoted with the author's permission.

Zarncke, Friedrich. *Die Statutenbücher der Universität Leipzig aus den ersten 150 Jahren ihres Beste-*

hens. Leipzig, 1861.

Zinner, Ernst. *Verzeichnis der astronomischen Handschriften des deutschen Kulturgebietes.* Munich, 1925.

Ziolkowski, Jan M., ed. and trans. *The Cambridge Songs (Carmina Cantabrigiensia).* Tempe, 1998.

———. "Twelfth-Century Understandings and Adaptations of Ancient Friendship." *Medieval Antiquity.* Ed. Andries Welkenhuysen, Herman Braet, and Werner Verbeke. Leuven, 1995. 59–81.

INDEX LOCORUM

INDEX OF MANUSCRIPTS CITED

GENERAL INDEX

A

abbreviation, 16, 18, 19, 66–67, 72–73, 156, 170, 175

Abraham and Isaac, as example in the *PN*, 144–45

accessus: Aristotelian, 31–33, 34; arrangement in, 28; of Bartholomew of Pisa, 104; of Benedict of Aquileia, 149; of Dybinus of Prague, 189–98; definition of, 17, 27; in BL Royal 12.E.XI, 229; of Franciscellus Mancinus, 153; of Johannes Tegernpeck, 224; of John Bamburgh, 230; method of proceeding in, 28; of Pace of Ferrara, 108, 112–18, 120–27; of Reiner von Cappel, 56–57; in St. Florian (Enns) Stiftsbibliothek XI 108, 221; as separate text, 27; shorter versions of, 35–36; structure of, 26–41; in student-owned manuscripts, 52; subject in, 28; titles in, 27–28; Type C, 27, 29–31, 32, 34; types of, 27; in Uppsala Universitetsbibliioteket, C 40, 173–75, 182; usefulness in, 28; in Vienna Österreichische Nationalbibliothek 4959, 213; in Wissenschaftliche Allgemein-

Bibliothek Amplon. Q.75, 217; of Zacharias Lund, 248

adolescents: as audience for the *PN*, 7–8, 60–63, 65; defined, 7; interests of, 60–63; teaching of, 8–12. *See also* school text; students

Alan of Lille, 5, 33, 48, 143, 144, 147, 179, 210, 223, 228, 231, 265, 266

Alexander de Villa Dei, 6, 7, 22, 183, 212, 223, 259, 260

Alexander VII, 240–41

al-Farabi, 113

Allen, J., 105n

allusivity, of G., 65

amplification, 16, 17, 18, 25, 67–70, 170, 175; Bartholomew of Pisa on, 103; and the female body, 67–70

analysis, in *PN* commentaries, 166. *See also* division; scholasticism

Androgeos, 58–59. *See also* Minos

antipophora, and poetic composition, 90

antiquarianism, and the *PN*, 246, 251, 253

apostrophe, 18, 46; Bartholomew of Pisa on, 102; to King Richard I, 23–26, 41, 50, 143, 144, 175, 242

Architrenius (satirical poem), 147

Aristotle, 1n, 14n, 22, 31–34, 99, 112–13, 114, 115, 118, 119, 121,

O

occupatio, definitions of, 78–79
Oracio de beata Dorothea (Dybinus of Prague), 179, 183, 220, 221. See also *Declaracio oracionis de beata Dorothea;* Dybinus of Prague
oral delivery, of exercises and lectures, 66, 215. *See also* lectures, recording of; memorization
order, of topics in the *PN,* 28, 30, 39, 256. See also *accessus;* division
ornament, 16, 36–37, 75
Otto of Lüneburg, 215
Oulipo school, 265
Overfield, J., 178, 211n, 217n, 218, 259n, 260n
Ovid, 6, 228

P

Pace of Ferrara, 12, 13, 16, 52, 54n, 96, 105, 106, 107–34, 138, 162, 166, 167, 172n, 173, 176, 177, 185, 209, 245, 261; *accessus* of, 108, 112–18, 120–27; on Albertino Mussato, 118–20; contrasted with Bartholomew of Pisa, 112, 117; contrasted with Guizzardo, 143–44; dedication by, 111–12; on G.'s plea to Innocent, 132–33; as intermediate commentator, 131; on metaphoric transference, 131; poetics of, 112–17, 139–40; as possible influence on Benedict of Aquileia, 150–51; rhetoric dismissed by, 117; as teacher, 109; as university commentator, 109; use of citation by, 112–14; use of myth by, 141
Painter, P., 264n, 265, 266n
Palmer, N., 167, 220n
Pandarus, in Chaucer, 40
paper, use of, 181, 283. *See also* economics; printing; writing technology
paraphrase, as introduction to commentary, 12, 204, 209
Paris, Matthew, 4n
Paris, University of, 164
parody, of the *PN* by Chaucer, 25–26

Perec, G., 265
Persius, 6
personification, 19
Peter of Spain, 223, 226
Petersen, E., 247n
Petrarch, 151
Petrocchi, M., 5n
Petrus Helias, 113
philosophy: focus of central European commentators on, 177–78; *PN*'s relation to, 118, 133–34; in rhetorical teaching, 28. *See also* Aristotle
Pietro da Muglio, 96
Pigman, G. W., 137n
Pits, John, 236–38, 241–42, 248, 251
Pizzorusso, B., 67n
poetics: humanistic emphasis on, 120; Pace of Ferrara's concern with, 112–17, 119, 139–40; and rhetoric, 13–14, 29, 48, 98, 139, 166, 248–49
Poetics (Aristotle), 14n, 99, 113, 115, 118, 119, 179. *See also* Aristotle
poetry: as medium for instruction, 22–23; status of, 47–49; teaching of, 14–16, 95. *See also* prose composition
Polak, E., 43n, 133n, 219
Pollard, G., 186n
Pomaro, G., 136n
Ponce, C., 267n
popes, responsibility of, 3–4, 43, 80, 82, 151, 241, 243, 244–45. *See also* Innocent III; Nicholas VII; Urban V
power, reversals of, 8, 9. *See also* boy made master
Powicke, F., 184n
praecisio, definitions of, 78–79
Prague, teaching of the *PN* at, 178–81
prestige: of teaching Aristotle, 178–79, 211–12; of teaching the *PN,* 178, 211–12
printing: invention of, 263; of the *PN,* 234, 238, 241–42, 254. *See also* economics, of book production and writing; writing technology
prologue. See *accessus*
prose composition, *PN*'s usefulness for, 14–16, 95, 171, 231, 249. *See also* poetry
prosopopeia, 80

TEXT AND CONTEXT SERIES

FRANK COULSON, SERIES EDITOR

- *Renaissance Postscripts: Responding to Ovid's* Heroides *in Sixteenth-Century France*
  PAUL WHITE